SERMONS AND REMAINS

OF

HUGH LATIMER.

[LATIMER, II.]

SERMONS AND REMAINS

OF

HUGH LATIMER,

SOMETIME BISHOP OF WORCESTER,

MARTYR, 1555.

EDITED FOR

The Parker Society,

BY THE

REV. GEORGE ELWES CORRIE, B.D.

FELLOW AND TUTOR OF CATHARINE HALL, CAMBRIDGE,
AND NORRISIAN PROFESSOR OF DIVINITY IN THAT UNIVERSITY.

WIPF & STOCK · Eugene, Oregon

Wipf and Stock Publishers
199 W 8th Ave, Suite 3
Eugene, OR 97401

Sermons and Remains of Hugh Latimer, Sometime Bishop of Worcester, Martyr, 1555
By Latimer, Hugh
ISBN 13: 978-1-60608-424-3
Publication date 3/27/2009
Previously published by Cambridge University Press, 1845

CONTENTS.

	PAGE
LIFE, Acts, and Doings of Latimer, from Foxe	ix
Ralph Morice's Account of his Conversion	xxvii

SERMONS preached in Lincolnshire, 1552.

The Sixth: On the Epistle for the First Sunday in Advent	1
The Seventh: On the Gospel for St Andrew's Day	23
The Eighth: On the Gospel for the Second Sunday in Advent	44
The Ninth: On the Gospel for the Third Sunday in Advent	65
Sermon preached at Bexterley on Christmas Day, 1552	84
Sermon preached at Grimsthorpe on St Stephen's Day, 1552	96
Sermon preached at Grimsthorpe on St John the Evangelist's Day, 1552	111
Sermon preached at Grimsthorpe on Twelfth Day, 1553	129
Sermon preached the First Sunday after the Epiphany, 1552[?]	143
Sermon preached the Second Sunday after the Epiphany	160
Sermon preached the Third Sunday after the Epiphany	167
Sermon preached the Fourth Sunday after the Epiphany	181
Sermon preached the Fifth Sunday after the Epiphany	188
Sermon preached on Septuagesima Sunday	198
Sermon preached on Sexagesima Sunday	209

MISCELLANEOUS REMAINS.

Articles to which Mr Latimer was required to subscribe, 1531	218
Articles devised by the Bishops for Mr Latimer to subscribe unto	219
Latimer's Communication with Mr Bainham in Newgate	221
Articles imputed to Latimer by Dr Powell	225
Bishop Latimer's Injunctions to the Prior and Convent of St Mary's House, Worcester, 1537	240
Injunctions to the Clergy, 1537	242
Arguments against Purgatory, with King Henry VIII.'s answers	245
Disputation at Oxford, 18th of April, 1554, with Mr Smith and others	250
Examination before the Commissioners, Sept. 30, 1555	278
Verses to be said in giving Holy Water and Holy Bread	294

CONTENTS.

LETTERS.

	PAGE
To Dr Greene	295
To Dr Redman	297
To King Henry VIII.	297
To Dr Sherwood	309
To Mr Hubbardine	317
To Sir Edward Baynton	322
To Ditto	334
To the Archbishop of Canterbury	351
To Mr Greenwood	356
To Mr Morice	357
To Secretary Cromwell	367—418
To a certain Gentleman	419
To one in prison for the profession of the Gospel	429
To the Lovers of God's Truth	435
To Mrs Wilkinson	444

APPENDIX ... 445

INDEX ... 495

THE Editor desires to acknowledge his obligations to Mr Lemon of the State Paper Office, for the valuable aid afforded by him in securing accurate transcripts of such of Bishop Latimer's Letters as are here printed from the Cromwell Correspondence, and for suggestions respecting the probable dates of several of the letters. The Editor's best thanks also are due to the Rev. Joseph Romilly for the ready kindness with which he supplied information from the Register of the University of Cambridge; to Mr J. Darling of the Clerical Library, Little Queen Street, London, for the obliging manner in which he obtained a copy of several MSS. in the British Museum, and of the Latin Sermon from a very rare printed copy in the Archiepiscopal Library at Lambeth; and to J. H. Clifton, Esq. of the Registrar's Office, Worcester, for the trouble he was kind enough to take in making some researches connected with Bishop Latimer's episcopate.

CAMBRIDGE,
May 30, 1845.

THE

LIFE, ACTS, AND DOINGS

OF

MASTER HUGH LATIMER,

THE FAMOUS PREACHER AND WORTHY MARTYR OF
CHRIST AND HIS GOSPEL[1].

[Foxe, Acts and Mon. p. 1297, &c. edit. 1563.]

Now after the life of the reverend father in God, D. M. Latimer. Nicolas Ridley, and also his conference with master Latimer, with other his letters written in prison, followeth likewise the life and doings of this worthy and old practised soldier of Christ, master Hugh Latimer, who was the son of one Hugh Latimer, of Thirkesson, in the county of Leicester, a husbandman of a good and wealthy estimation, where also he was born and brought up, until he was of the age of four years or thereabout. At which time his parents (having him as then left for their only son, with six other daughters), seeing his ready, prompt, and sharp wit, purposed to train him up in erudition and knowledge of good literature; wherein he so profited in his youth, at the common schools of his own country, that at the age of fourteen years he was sent to the university of Cambridge: where, after some continuance of exercises in other things, he gave himself to the study of such divinity as the ignorance of that age did suffer. Zealous he was then in the popish religion, and therewith so scrupulous, as himself confesseth, that being a priest and using to say mass, he was so servile an observer of the Romish decrees, that he had thought he had never sufficiently mingled his massing wine with water; and moreover, that he should never be damned, if he were once a professed friar,

[1 A general sketch of the life and martyrdom of Bishop Latimer has been given in the former volume, but it is thought desirable to prefix to the present (even at the expense of some repetition) the chief part of Foxe's graphic account of the venerable martyr, and also Ralph Morice's account of his conversion, which has been already printed by Strype from the Harleian MSS.]

with divers such superstitious fantasies. Whereupon in this blind zeal he was a very enemy to the professors of Christ's gospel, as his oration made, when he proceeded bachelor of divinity in the said university of Cambridge, against Philip Melancthon and his works, did plainly declare. But such was the goodness and merciful purpose of God, that where he thought by that his oration to have utterly defaced the professors of the gospel and true church of Christ, he was him-. self, by a member of the same, prettily, yet godly, catched in the blessed net of God's word. For master Thomas Bilney (of whom mention is made before), being at that time a trier out of Satan's subtleties, and a secret overthrower of antichrist's kingdom, and seeing master Latimer to have a zeal in his ways, although without knowledge, was stricken with a brotherly pity towards him, and bethought what means he might best win this his zealous, yet ignorant, brother to the true knowledge of Christ. And therefore, after a short time, he came to master Latimer's study, and desired him to hear him make his confession. Which thing he willingly granted: with the hearing whereof he was, by the good Spirit of God, so touched, that hereupon he forsook his former studying of the school doctors, and other such fooleries, and became a true scholar in the true divinity, as he himself confesseth, as well in his conference with master Ridley, as also in his first sermon made upon the *Pater noster*. So that, whereas before he was an enemy, and almost a persecutor of Christ, he was now an earnest seeker after him, changing his old manner of calumnying into a diligent kind of conferring, both with master Bilney and others, with whom he was often and greatly conversant. After this his winning to Christ, he was not satisfied with his own conversion only, but like a true disciple of the blessed Samaritan, pitied the misery of others; and therefore he became both a public preacher, and also a private instructor to the rest of his brethren within the university, by the space of two years; spending his time partly in the Latin tongue amongst the learned, and partly amongst the simple people in his natural and vulgar language. Howbeit, as Satan never sleepeth, when he seeth his kingdom begin to decay, so likewise now seeing that this worthy member of Christ would be a shrewd shaker thereof, he raised up his children to molest and trouble him. Amongst these there

Latimer converted by M. Bilney.

was an Augustine friar, who took occasion upon certain sermons that master Latimer made about Christenmas, 1529, as well in the church of St Edward, as also in St Augustine's, within the university of Cambridge, to inveigh against him, for that master Latimer, in the said sermons, alluding to the common usage of the season, gave the people certain cards out of the 5th, 6th, and 7th chapters of St Matthew, whereupon they might, not only then, but always else, occupy their time. For the chief, as their triumphing card, he limited the heart, as the principal thing that they should serve God withal: whereby he quite overthrew all hypocritical and external ceremonies, not tending to the necessary beautifying of God's holy word and sacraments. For the better attaining hereof he wished the scriptures to be in English, that the common people might thereby learn their duties, as well to God as to their neighbours.

The handling of this matter was so apt for the time, and so pleasantly applied of Latimer, that not only it declared a singular towardness of wit in him that preached, but also wrought in the hearers much fruit, to the overthrow of popish superstition and setting up of perfect religion. For on the Sunday before Christenmas-day, coming to the church, and causing the bell to be tolled to a sermon, entereth into the pulpit. Upon the text of the gospel read that day in the church, *Tu quis es?* &c. in delivering his cards as is above-said, he made the heart to be triumph, exhorting and inviting all men thereby to serve the Lord with inward heart and true affection, and not with outward ceremonies; adding moreover to the praise of that triumph, that though it were never so small, yet it would make up the best coat card beside in the bunch, yea, though it were the king of clubs, &c.; meaning thereby how the Lord would be worshipped and served in simplicity of the heart and verity, wherein consisteth true christian religion, and not in the outward deeds of the letter only, or in the glistering shew of man's traditions, of pardons, pilgrimages, ceremonies, vows, devotions, voluntary works, and works of erogation, foundations, oblations, the pope's supremacy, &c.; so that all these either be needless, where the other is present, or else be of small estimation in comparison thereof.

The difference betwixt trump and false religion.

The copy and effect of these his sermons, although they

were neither fully extracted, neither did they all come to our hands, yet so many as came to our hands, I thought here to set abroad, for that I would wish nothing of that man, which may be gotten, to be suppressed[1].

* * * * *

This preaching of master Latimer, as it was then fruitful and plausible to all honest and good natures, so again, it was as odious to the contrary part, such as were his adversaries, of whom was then in Cambridge a great number, that preached against him, as the bishop of Ely, who then in the King's college preached against him; D. Watson, Master of Christ's college; D. Notaris, Master of Clare hall; D. Philo, Master of Michael-house; D. Metcalfe, Master of St John's; D. Blith, of the King's hall; D. Bullock, Master of Queens' college; D. Cliffe, of Clement hostel; D. Donnes, of Jesus college; D. Palmes, Master of St Nicholas hostel; Bayne of St John's, bachelor of divinity, and after doctor. All these adversaries did master Latimer sustain: but especially a black friar, the prior of our Lady friars, called then *Domine Labia*, was a great doer against him; who about the same time of Christmas, when master Latimer brought forth his christian cards, to deface belike the doings of the said Latimer, he brought out his Christmas dice, casting there to his audience *cinque* and *quatre;* meaning by the *cinque* five places in the New Testament, and the four doctors by the *quatre;* by which his *cinque quatre* he would prove that it was not expedient the scripture to be in English, lest the ignorant and vulgar sort, through the occasion thereof, might happily be brought in danger to leave their vocation, or else to run into some inconvenience: as the ploughman, when he heareth this in the gospel, "No man that layeth his hand on the plough, and looketh back, is meet for the kingdom of God," might peradventure hearing this, cease from his plough. Likewise the baker, when he heareth that "a little leaven corrupteth a whole lump" of dough, may percase leave our bread unleavened, and so our bodies shall be unseasoned. And the simple man, when he heareth in the gospel, "If thine eye offend thee, pluck it out, and cast it from thee," may make himself blind, and so fill the world full of beggars. These, with other more, this clerkly friar brought out, to the number

D. Buck.

[1 See Vol. I. pp. 3—24.]

of five, to prove his purpose. To whom master Latimer answereth again briefly, requiring no more but this, that the scripture may be so long in English, until the people thus do as he hath said, and he would ask no more.

Notwithstanding the withstanding of this friar, and the malice of all his enemies, master Latimer, with master Bilney, continued yet in Cambridge a certain space, where he with the said Bilney used much to confer and company together, insomuch that the place where they most used to walk in the fields, was called long after the heretics' hill. *Bilney and Latimer joint companions.*

The society of these two, as it was much noted of many in that university, so it was full of many good examples to all such as would follow their doings, both in visiting the prisoners, in relieving the needy, in feeding the hungry; whereof somewhat is before-mentioned in the history of master Bilney. In a place of his sermons this master Latimer maketh mention of a certain history which happened about this time in Cambridge between them two, and a certain woman, then prisoner in the castle or tower of Cambridge, which I thought here not unworthy to be touched. The history is this: it so chanceth that after master Latimer had been acquainted with the foresaid master Bilney, he went with him to visit the prisoners in the tower in Cambridge; and being there, among other prisoners, there was a woman which was accused that she had killed her own child, which act she plainly and stedfastly denied. Whereby it gave them occasion to search for the matter; and at length they found that her husband loved her not, and therefore sought all means he could to make her away: the matter was thus. *A story of a certain woman condemned, who was saved by master Latimer.*

A child of hers had been sick a whole year, and at length died in harvest-time, as it were in a consumption: which when it was gone, she went to have her neighbours to help her to the burial, but all were in harvest abroad, whereby she was enforced with heaviness of heart alone to prepare the child to the burial: her husband coming home, and not loving her, accused her of murdering the child. This was the cause of her trouble; and master Latimer, by earnest inquisition, of conscience thought the woman not guilty. Then immediately after was he called to preach before king Henry the Eighth at Windsor; where, after his sermon, the king's majesty sent for him, and talked with him familiarly. At which time master Latimer finding opportunity, kneeled down, opened his whole matter to the king, and begged her pardon; which the king most graciously granted, and gave it him at his return homeward. The mean time the woman was delivered of a child in prison, whose godfather master Latimer was, and mistress Cheke godmother. But all that while he would not tell her of the pardon, but laboured to have her confess the truth of the matter. At length time came when she looked to suffer; and master Latimer came, as he was wont, to instruct her: unto whom she made great lamentation and moan to be purified before her suffering; for she thought to be damned, if she should suffer without purification. Then master Bilney being with master Latimer, both told her that that law was made to the Jews, and not to us, and how women be as well in the favour of God before they be purified as after; and rather it was appointed for a civil and politic law, for natural honesty sake, than that they should any thing the more be purified from sin thereby, &c. So thus they travailed with this woman till they had brought her to good trade, and then at length shewed her the king's pardon, and let her go.

Purification of women.

This good act, among many other at this time, happened in Cambridge by master Latimer and master Bilney: but this was not alone, for many more like matters were wrought by them, if all were known, whereof partly some are touched before, such especially as concern master Bilney, mention whereof is above expressed; but as it is commonly seen in the natural course of things, that as the fire beginneth more to kindle, so the more [smoke] ariseth withal, in much like condition it happened with master Latimer, whose towardness the more it began to spring, his virtues seen, and his doings to be known, the more his adversaries began to spurn and kindle against him.

* * * * *

Master Latimer called up to the cardinal.

After M. Latimer had thus travailed in preaching and teaching in the university of Cambridge, about the space of two years, at length he was called up to the cardinal for heresy, by the procurement of certain of the said university; where he was content to subscribe and grant to such articles and illations as then they propounded unto him, &c. After that he returned to the university again, where shortly after, by the means of D. Buttes, the king's physician, a singular good man, and a special favourer of good proceedings, he was in the number of them which laboured for the maintenance of the king's supremacy. Then went he to the court, where he remained a certain time in the said D. Buttes' chamber, preaching then in London very often. At last, being weary of the court, having a benefice offered by the king, at the suit of the lord Cromwell and D. Buttes, was glad thereof, seeking by that means to be rid out of the court, wherewith in no case he could agree: so having a grant of the benefice, he was glad thereof, and contrary to the mind of D. Buttes, would needs enjoy the same. *Dr Buttes.*

This benefice was in Wiltshire, under the diocese of Sarum, the name of which town was called West Kington. Where this good preacher did exercise himself with much diligence of teaching to instruct his flock; and not only them, his diligence extended also to all the country about. In fine, his diligence was so great, his preaching so mighty, the manner of his teaching so zealous, that there in like sort he could not escape without enemies. So true it is that St Paul doth forewarn us: "Whosoever will live virtuously shall suffer persecution." It so chanced, as he there preaching upon the virgin, Christ's mother, whom we call our lady, had thereupon declared his mind, referring and reducing all to Christ only our Saviour, certain popish priests being therewith offended, sought and wrought much trouble against him, drawing articles against him, both concerning the matter of our lady, as also of other points of doctrine, as of praying to saints, of purgatory, &c. Unto the which articles, thus conceived against him, he answereth again at large. *Latimer's benefice.*

*   *   *   *   *

Amongst many other impugners and adversaries, whereof there was no small sort, which did infest this good man in sermons, some also there were which attempted the pen against him. In the number of whom was one D. Sherwode, who upon the same occasion of preaching of the Virgin Mary (or, as they thought, against our lady) did invade him with his pen, writing against him[1].

*   *   *   *   *

[[1] For Latimer's reply to him, see p. 309, &c. of this volume.]

In this letter you hear mention is made of a citation, sent down to master Latimer, for him to appear at London before the bishop of London.

* * * * *

Upon this citation master Latimer, although he did appeal to his own ordinary, requiring by him to be ordered, yet all that notwithstanding he was had up to London before Warham the archbishop of Canterbury, and the bishop of London, where he was greatly molested and detained a long space from his cure at home. There he, being called thrice every week before the said bishops to make answer for his preaching, had certain articles or propositions drawn out and laid to him, whereunto they required him to subscribe. At length he, not only perceiving their practical proceedings, but also much grieved with their troublesome unquietness, which neither would preach themselves, nor yet suffer him to preach and to do his duty, writeth to some one prelate or other, partly excusing his infirmity, whereby he could not appear at their commandment, partly expostulating with them for so troubling and detaining him from his duty-doing, and that for no just cause, but only for preaching the truth against certain vain abuses crept into religion, much needful to be spoken against. Which all may appear by his epistle sent to a certain bishop or archbishop, whose name here is not expressed[1].

* * * * *

In this foresaid epistle, as ye hear, he maketh mention of certain articles or propositions, whereunto he was required by the bishops to subscribe[2].

* * * * *

Latimer subscribing.

To these articles whether he did subscribe or no, it is uncertain. It appeareth by his epistle above written to the bishop, that he durst not consent unto them, where he writeth in these words: *Hinc ego nudis sententiis subscribere non audeo, quia popularis superstitionis diutius duraturæ, quoad possum, auctorculus esse nolo,* &c. But yet, whether he was compelled afterward to agree, through the cruel handling of the bishops, it is in doubt. By the words and the title in Tonstal's register prefixed before the articles, it may seem that he subscribed: the words of the registers be these:

[1 See p. 351, &c.]   [2 See pp. 218—220.]

Hugo Latimerus in sacra Theologia Bacc. in universitate Cantab. coram Cant. Archiepiscopo, Johan. Lond. Episcopo, reliquaque concione apud Westmonast. vocatus, confessus est, et recognovit fidem suam, sic sentiendo ut sequitur, in his artic. 21. die Martii. Anno. 1531. If these words be true, it may be so thought that he subscribed. And whether he so did, no great matter nor marvel, the iniquity of the time being such, that either he must needs so do, or else abide the bishop's blessing, that is, cruel sentence of death, which he at that time (as himself confessed, preaching at Stamford) was loth to sustain, for such matters as these were, unless it were for articles necessary of his belief; by which his words I conjecture rather that he did subscribe at length, albeit it was long before he could be brought so to do. Yet this by the way, it is to be noted, concerning the crafty and deceitful handling of these bishops in his examinations, what subtle devices they used the same time to entrap him in their snares. The story he sheweth forth himself in a certain sermon preached at Stamford anno 1550, Octob. 9.[3]

The crafty handling of the bishops in examining master Latimer.

*   *   *   *   *

And thus hitherto you have heard declared the manifold troubles of this godly preacher, in the time not only of his being in the university, but especially at his benefice, as by his own sermons and letters here above expressed may appear. Here followeth another letter of his writing unto king Henry[4], where with most christian boldness he persuadeth the king, that the scriptures and other good wholesome books in the English tongue may be permitted to the people; which books the bishops at that time, wickedly conspiring together, went about by a public and authentic instrument to suppress.

The bishops in king Henry's time inhibited the scriptures and good books in English.

*   *   *   *   *

Thus have we discoursed and run over hitherto the laborious travails, the painful adventures, and dangerous hazards, and manifold plunges, which this true-hearted and holy servant of God suffered among the pope's friends, and God's enemies, for the gospel's sake. In the which so great and so many dangers it had been impossible for him to have escaped and to have continued so long, had not the almighty helping hand of the Highest, as he stirred him up, so preserved him

[3 See Vol. I. pp. 282, 294.]
[4 See pp. 297—309, of this vol.]

through the favour and power of his prince; who with much favour embraced him, and with his mere power sometime rescued and delivered him out of the crooked claws of his enemies; moreover at length also, through the procurement partly of Doctor Buttes, partly of good Cromwell, whom we mentioned before, avanced him to the degree and dignity of a bishop, making him the bishop of Worcester, which so continued a few years, instructing his diocese according to the duty of a diligent and vigilant pastor with wholesome doctrine, and example of perfect conversation, duly agreeing to the same. It were a long matter to stand particularly upon such parts as might here be brought in to the commendations of his pains, study, readiness, and continual carefulness in teaching, preaching, exhorting, visiting, correcting, and reforming, either as his ability could serve, or else the time would bear. But the days then were so dangerous and variable, that he could not in all things do that he would: yet what he might do, that he performed to the uttermost of his strength; so that although he could not utterly extinguish all the sparkling relics of old superstition, yet he so wrought, that though they could not be taken away, yet they should be used with as little hurt and with as much profit as might be. As, for example, in this thing as in divers other it did appear, that when it could not be avoided, but holy water and holy bread must needs be received, yet he so prepared and instructed them of his diocese with such informations and lessons, that in receiving thereof superstition should be excluded, and some remembrance taken thereby, teaching and charging the ministers of his diocese, in delivering the holy bread and holy water, to say these words following[1].

* * * * *

By this it may be considered, what the diligent care of this bishop was in doing the duty of a faithful pastor among his flock. And moreover it is to be thought that also he would have brought more things to pass, if the time then had answered to his desire: for he was not ignorant how the institution of holy water and holy bread not only had no ground in scripture, but also how full of profane exorcisms and conjurations they were, contrary to the rule and learning of the

[1 See p. 294.]

gospel. Thus this good man with much diligence behaved himself in his diocese; but as before, both in the university and at his benefice, he was tossed and turmoiled by wicked and evil-disposed persons, so in his bishopric also he was not all clear and void of some that sought his trouble. As among many other evil-willers, one especially there was, and that no small person, which accused him then to the king for his sermons. The story, because he sheweth himself in a sermon of his before King Edward, I thought therefore to use his own words, which be these[2].

* * * * *

Besides this, divers other conflicts and combats this godly bishop sustained in his own country and diocese, in taking the cause of right and equity against oppression and wrong. As, for another example, there was at that time not far from the diocese of Worcester a certain justice of peace, whom here I will not name, being a good man afterward, and now deceased. This justice, in purchasing of certain land for his brother, or for himself, went about to injure or damnify a poor man, who maketh his complaint to master Latimer: he first hearing, then tendering his rightful cause, writeth to the said gentleman, exhorting him in private letters to remember himself, to consider the cause, and to abstain from injury. The justice of peace, not content withal, as the fashion of men is grieved to be told of their fault, sendeth word again, in great displeasure, that he will not so take it at his hands, with such threatening words, &c. Master Latimer, hearing this, answered again by writing; the copy of which his letter I thought not unworthy here of setting out, either that the virtue of that gracious man may appear more at large, or that other bishops may take by him example of like stomach in like causes, or that injurious oppressors may thereby take some fruit of his wholesome admonition. The tenour of his letter written to the gentleman is this[3].

* * * * *

It were a large and a long process to story all the doings, travails, and writings of this christian bishop, neither have we expressed all that came to our hands; but this I thought sufficient to testify of the goodness of this man. Thus he continued in this laborious function of a bishop the

[2 See Vol. I. pp. 134, 5.]   [3 See p. 419.]

space of certain years, till the coming in of the six articles, and altering of religion. Then being distressed through the straitness of time, so that either he must lose the quiet of a good conscience, or else must forsake his bishopric, he did of his own free accord resign and renounce his pastorship. At which time also Shaxton, bishop of Salisbury, resigned also with him his bishopric. And so these two remained a great space unbishopped, keeping silence till the time of king Edward of blessed memory. And yet neither did Latimer all this while escape without danger and molestation, as there was no part or portion of his life, in what state soever he stood, clearly free and void of all perturbations. For a little after he had renounced his bishopric, first, he was almost slain, but sore bruised with the fall of a tree. Then coming up to London for remedy, he was molested and troubled of the bishops; whereby he was again in no little danger, and at length was cast into the Tower, where he continually remained prisoner till the time that blessed king Edward entered his crown, by means whereof the golden mouth of this preacher, long shut up before, was now opened again. And so he beginning afresh to set forth his plough again, continued all the time of the said king labouring in the Lord's harvest most fruitfully, discharging his talent, as well in divers other places of this realm, as in Stamford, and before the duchess of Suffolk, whose sermons be extant and set forth in print, as also at London in the convocation-house; and especially before the king at the court, in the same place of the inward garden, which was before applied to lascivious and courtly pastimes, there he dispensed the fruitful word of the glorious gospel of Jesus Christ, preaching there before the king and his whole court, to the edification of many.

Master Latimer cast into the Tower.

In this his painful travail he occupied himself all king Edward's days, preaching for the most part every Sunday twice, to no small shame of all other loitering and unpreaching prelates, which occupy great rooms, and do little good: and that so much more to their shame, because he being a sore bruised man by the fall of the tree, mentioned a little before, and above sixty-seven years of age, took so little ease and care of sparing himself, to do the people good. Not to speak of here his indefatigable travail and diligence in his own private studies, who, notwithstanding both his years and other

The diligent travailing of master Latimer in king Edward's time.

pains in preaching, every morning ordinarily, winter and summer, about two of the clock in the morning was at his book most diligently. So careful was his heart of the preservation of the church, and the good success of the gospel, his letters can testify, wherewith he continually admonished such as then were in authority of their duty, and assisted them with his godly counsel. As the diligence of this man of God never ceased, all the time of king Edward, to profit the church both publicly and privately; so among other doings in him to be noted, this is not lightly to be over-passed, but worthily to be observed, that God not only gave unto him his Spirit plenteously and comfortably to preach his word unto his church, but also by the same Spirit he did most evidently prophesy of all those kinds of plagues which afterward ensued, so plainly, that if England ever had a prophet, he might seem to be one. And as touching himself, he ever affirmed that the preaching of the gospel would cost him his life, to the which he no less cheerfully prepared himself, than certainly he was persuaded that Winchester was kept in the tower for the same purpose, as the event did too truly prove the same. For after the death of the said blessed king Edward, not long after queen Mary was proclaimed, a pursuivant was sent down, by the doing, no doubt, of Winchester, into the country, to call him up: of whose coming although master Latimer lacked no forewarning, being premonished about six hours before by one John Carless, (whose story hereafter followeth,) yet so far was it that he thought to escape, that he prepared himself towards his journey before the said pursuivant came to his house. At the which thing when the pursuivant marvelled, seeing him so prepared towards his journey, he said unto him: "My friend, you be a welcome messenger to me; and be it known unto you, and to the whole world, that I go as willingly to London at this present, being called by my prince to render a reckoning of my doctrine, as ever I was to any place in the world. And I doubt not, but that God, as he hath made me worthy to preach his word before two excellent princes, so he will able me to witness the same unto the third, either to her comfort or discomfort eternally," &c. At the which time the pursuivant, when he had delivered his letters, departed, affirming that he had commandment not to tarry for him. By whose

Latimer prophesieth what plagues are to come in queen Mary's time.

Latimer called up to London.

sudden departure it was manifest that they would not have him to appear, but rather to have fled out of the realm. They knew that his constancy should deface them in their popery, and confirm the godly in the truth.

Thus master Latimer being sent for, and coming up to London through Smithfield, where merely he said that Smithfield had long groaned for him, was brought before the council; where he patiently bearing all the mocks and taunts given him by the scornful papists, was cast again into the Tower; where being assisted with the heavenly grace of Christ, sustained most patient imprisonment a long time, notwithstanding the cruel and unmerciful handling of the lordly papists, which thought then their kingdom would never fall: yet he shewed himself not only patient, but also cheerful, in and above all that which they could or would work against him; yea, such a valiant spirit the Lord gave him, that he was able not only to despise the terribleness of prisons and torments, but also to deride and laugh to scorn the doings of his enemies. It is not unknown to the ears of many what he answered to the lieutenant, being then in the Tower. For when the lieutenant's man upon a time came to him, the aged father, kept without fire in the frosty winter, and well nigh starved for cold, merely bade the man tell his master, that if he did not look the better to him, perchance he would deceive him.

Latimer cheerful in imprisonment.

The lieutenant, hearing this, bethought himself of these words, and fearing lest that indeed he thought to make some escape, began to look more straitly to his prisoner. And so coming to him, beginneth to charge him with his words, reciting the same unto him which his man had told him before; how that if he were not better looked unto, perchance he would deceive them, &c. "Yea, master lieutenant, so I said," quod he, "for you look, I think, that I should burn: but except you let me have some fire, I am like to deceive your expectation; for I am like here to starve for cold."

Many such-like answers and reasons, merry, but savoury, proceeding not from a vain mind, but from a constant and quiet reason, proceeded from that man, declaring a firm and stable heart, little passing for all this great blustering of such termagants, but rather deluding the same. Neither is it easy to say whether the doings and proceedings of the papists were more to be lamented for their detestable absurdity of grave persons, or else more to be scorned and derided for their so trifling and extreme folly. What Democritus or Calphurnius could abstain from laughter, beholding only the fashion of their mass from the beginning to the latter end, with such turning, returning, half turning and whole turning, such kissing, blissing, crouching, becking, crossing, knocking, ducking, washing, rinsing, lifting, touching, fingering, whispering, stopping, dipping, bowing, licking, wiping, sleeping, shifting, with an hundred things more? What wise man, I say, seeing such toyish gauds, can keep from laughter? And what be all the pope's doings, with the whole circumstance of his religion and manner of his popelings, but matters almost to be laughed at, &c.? But to return again where as we left. Thus master Latimer passing a long time in the Tower with as much patience as a man in his case could do, from thence he was transported to Oxford, with doctor Cranmer archbishop of Canterbury, and master Ridley bishop of London, there to dispute upon articles sent down from Gardiner bishop of Winchester, as is before touched; the manner and order of which disputations between them and the university doctors is also before sufficiently expressed. Where also it is declared, how and by whom the said Latimer, with his other fellow-prisoners, were condemned after the disputations, and so committed again to the prison, where they continued from the month of April above-mentioned to this present month of October: where they were most godly occupied, either with brotherly conference, or with fervent prayer, or with fruitful writing. Albeit master Latimer, by reason of the feebleness of his age, wrote least of them all in this latter time of his imprisonment. But in prayer he was fervently occupied, wherein oftentimes so long he continued kneeling, that he was not able to rise without help; and amongst other things, these were three principal matters he prayed for. First, that as God had appointed him to be a preacher of his word, so also he would give him grace to stand to his doctrine until his death, that he might give his heart-blood for the same. Secondly, that God of his mercy would restore his gospel to England once again; and these words, 'once again,' 'once again,' he did so inculcate and beat into the ears of the Lord God, as though he had seen God before him, and spoken to him face to face. The third

Whether the papists' doings are more to be lamented, or to be derided.

Three requests of master Latimer's prayer.

Once again, once again.

matter was, to pray for the preservation of the queen's majesty that now is; whom in his prayer he was wont accustomably to name, and even with tears desired God to make her a comfort to his comfortless realm of England. These were the matters he prayed for so earnestly; neither were these things of him desired in vain, as the good success thereof after following did declare. For the Lord most graciously did grant all these his requests.

First, concerning profession, even in the most extremity the Lord graciously assisted him. For when he stood at the stake without Bocardo-gate at Oxford, and the tormentors about to set the fire upon him, and upon the learned and godly bishop master Ridley, he lifted up his eyes towards heaven with an amiable and comfortable countenance, saying these words: *Fidelis est Deus, qui non sinit nos tentari supra id quod possumus;* "God is faithful, which doth not suffer us to be tempted above our strength." And so afterwards by and by shed his blood in the cause of Christ; the which blood ran out of his heart in such abundance, that all those that were present, being godly, did marvel to see the most part of the blood in his body so to be gathered to his heart, and with such violence to gush out, his body being opened by the force of the fire: by the which thing God most graciously granted his request, which was that he might shed his heart-blood in the defence of the gospel.

How mercifully the Lord heard his second request, in restoring his gospel once again to this realm, these present days can bear record. And what then shall England say now for her defence, which, so mercifully visited and refreshed with the word of God, so unthankfully considereth either her own misery past, or the great benefit of God now present? The Lord be merciful unto us!

Again, concerning his third request, it seemeth likewise most effectuously granted, to the great praise of God, the furtherance of his gospel, and to the unspeakable comfort of this realm. For whether at the request of his prayer, or of other God's holy saints, or whether God was moved with the cry of his whole church, the truth is, that when all was deplorate and in a desperate case, and so desperate that the enemies mightily flourished and triumphed, God's word banished, Spaniards received, no place left for Christ's servants to cover their heads,—suddenly the Lord called to remembrance his mercy, and forgetting our former iniquity, made an end of all these miseries, and wrought a marvellous change of things, at the change whereof she was appointed and anointed, for whom this grey-headed father Latimer so earnestly prayed in his imprisonment; through whose true, natural, and imperial crown the brightness of God's word was set up again to confound the dark and false-visored kingdom of antichrist, the true temple of Christ re-edified, the captivity of sorrowful Christians released, which so long was wished for in the prayers of so many good men, specially of this faithful and true servant of the Lord, master Latimer. The same God, which at the request of his holy and faithful saints hath poured upon us such benefits of his mercy, peace, and tranquillity, assist our most virtuous and christian prince and her subjects, that every one in his state and calling we may so serve his glory, and walk in their wholesome example, that we lose not that which they have obtained, but may proceed in all faithfulness to build and keep up the house and temple of the Lord, to the advancing of his glory, and our everlasting comfort in him! And thus much concerning the prayers of master Latimer, to the which prayers only he gave himself, as I said, in this his latter imprisonment: for else we read but little that he did write at Oxford, save only a few lines to one mistress Wilkinson of London, a godly matron, an exile also for the gospel sake, and by whom divers of God's saints and learned bishops, as master Hooper the bishop of Hereford, master Coverdale, master Latimer, master Cranmer, with many more, were graciously supported and relieved, the copy and effect of which letter here followeth[1].

Mistress Wilkinson.

* * * * *

And thus hast thou, gentle reader, the whole life both of master Ridley and of master Latimer, two worthy doers in the church of Christ, severally and by themselves set forth and described to thee, with all their doings, writings, disputations, sufferings, their painful travails, faithful preachings, studious service in Christ's church, their patient imprisonment, and constant fortitude in that which they had taught, with all other their proceedings from time to time, since their first institution to this present year and month of queen

[1 See p. 444.]

Mary, being the month of October, anno 1555. In the which month they were both brought forth together to their final examination and execution. Wherefore, as we have heretofore declared both their lives severally and distinctly one from the other, so now joining them both together, as they both joined together in one cause and kind of suffering, so will we by the grace of Christ prosecute the rest that remaineth concerning their latter examination, disgrading, and constant martyrdom, with the order and manner also of the commissioners, to wit, master White, bishop of Lincoln, master Brockes, bishop of Gloucester, with others, and what were their words, their objections, their orations set out as it was, and what again were the answers of these men to the same, as in process here followeth to be seen[1].
(∴)

[1 See pp. 278—293 of this volume, and also the volume of Bishop Ridley's works, pp. 255—299.]

LATIMER'S FIRST CONVERSION AT CAMBRIDGE.

[Printed by Strype[2], Eccl. Mem. III. i. 368, Oxf. Harl. MS. No. 422, Art. 12.]

WHEN as it pleased Almighty God to call Mr Hugh Latimer unto the knowledge of the truth of God's holy word by the godly lecture of divinity, read by Mr Geo. Stafford[3] in the university school at Cambridge, and of a Saul had, as it were, made him a very Paul; for otherwise, all the days of his life he had bestowed his time in the labyrinth study of the school-doctors, as in Dunce[4], Dorbell[5], Tho. of Aquine[6], Hugo de Victore[7], with such like; insomuch that, being mightily affected that way, he of purpose (perceiving the youth of the university inclined to the reading of the scriptures, leaving off those tedious authors and kinds of study, being a bachelor of divinity, and for his gravity and years preferred to the keeping of the University Cross, which no man had to do withal but such an one as in sanctimony of life excelled other) came into the Sophany[8] school among the youth, there gathered together of daily custom to keep their sophanis and disputations; and there most eloquently made to them an oration, dissuading them from this new-fangled kind of study of the scriptures, and vehemently persuaded them to the study of the school-authors, which he did, not long before that he was so mercifully called to the contrary. And as he felt, by this his divine vocation, that all his other study little profited him, but was rather a stumbling-block

[2] Strype observes, "I do now but transcribe from a writing of Ralph Morice, bishop Cranmer's secretary."]

[3] Foxe, Acts and Mon. Vol. III. p. 375. Edit. 1684.]

[4] Duns Scotus.]

[5] Nicholas Dorbell, a French Minorite, and a strenuous disciple of Scotus. Cave, Hist. Liter. Append. p. 174. Oxon. 1743.]

[6] Thomas Aquinas.]

[7] See Cave, Tom. II. pp. 207 et seq.]

[8] Or *Sophister*, now abbreviated into *Soph*. This term designated, at that time, a student who, having completed his studies in logic, was authorised to take part in the disputations in the public schools of the university.]

unto him then intending to preach to the world the sincere doctrine of the gospel; so he mightily, tracting no time, preached daily in the university of Cambridge, both in English and *ad clerum*, to the great admiration of all men that aforetime had known him of a contrary severe opinion. Insomuch that bishop West[1], then bishop of Ely, hearing of this Mr Latimer's conversion[2], determined with himself to come to hear him preach; but that should be sudden, and withouten any intelligence to be given to Latimer. And so it came to pass, that on a time when Mr Latimer had prepared to preach in the university church a sermon *ad clerum*, in Latin, the bishop, hearing thereof, came secretly and suddenly from Ely, and entered into the university church, accompanied with certain men of worship (Latimer being then well entered into his sermon); whose approach being honourable, Latimer gave place, and surceased from farther speaking until the bishop and his retinue were quietly placed. That done, after a good pause, Latimer beginneth to speak to his auditory after this sort: "It is of congruence meet" (quoth he) "that a new auditory, namely being[3] more honourable, requireth a new theme, being a new argument to entreat of. Therefore it behoveth me now to divert from mine intended purpose, and somewhat to entreat of the honorable estate of a bishop. Therefore let this be the theme, (quoth he) *Christus existens pontifex futurorum bonorum, &c.*" This text he so fruitfully[4] handled, expounding every word, and setting forth the office of Christ so sincerely, as the true and perfect pattern unto all other bishops that should succeed him in his church, that the bishop then present might well think of himself that he, nor none of his fellows, were of that race of bishops which Christ meant to have succeed in his church, but rather of the fellowship of Caiaphas and Annas.

This notwithstanding, the bishop, being a very wise and politique worldly man, after the sermon finished called to him Mr Latimer, and said, "Mr Latimer, I heartily thank you for

[1 Nicholas West, bishop of Ely, 1515—1533. Godwin, De Præsul. pp. 271, et seq. Edit. Richardson.]
[2 new conversion. Harl. MS.]
[3 audience being namely. Harl. MS.]
[4 so fruitfully he. Harl. MS.]

your good sermon; assuring you that, if you will do one thing at my request, I will kneel down and kiss your foot[5] for the good admonition that I have received of your sermon; assuring you that I never heard mine office so well and so substantially declared before this time." "What is your lordship's pleasure that I should do for you?" quoth Mr Latimer. "Marry," quoth the bishop, "that you will preach me, in this place, one sermon against Martin Luther and his doctrine." Said then Mr Latimer again, "My lord, I am not acquainted with the doctrine of Luther; nor are we permitted[6] here to read his works; and therefore it were but a vain thing for me to refute his doctrine, not understanding what he hath written, nor what opinion he holdeth. Sure I am," quoth Latimer, "that I have preached before you this day no man's doctrine, but only the doctrine of God out of the scriptures. And if Luther do none otherwise than I have done, there needeth no confutation of his doctrine. Otherwise, when I understand that he doth teach against the scripture, I will be ready with all my heart to confound his doctrine, as much as lieth in me." "Well, well, Mr Latimer, I perceive that you somewhat smell of the pan; you will repent this gear one day." And so the bishop, never a whit amended by the sermon, practised with Mr Latimer from that day forwards to put him to silence; insomuch that grievous complaint was made of him by divers papists of the university, as by Mr Tirrell [fellow of the king's hall] and others, unto cardinal Wolsey, that he preached very seditious doctrine, infecting the youth of the university with Luther's opinions. Whereupon the cardinal sent for him to York place; and there attending upon the cardinal's pleasure he was called before him into his inner chamber by the sound of a little bell, which the cardinal used to ring when any person should come or approach unto him. When Mr Latimer was before him, he well advised him, and said, "Is your name Latimer?" "Yea, forsooth," quoth Latimer. "You seem," quoth the cardinal, "that you are of good years nor no babe, but one that should wisely and soberly use yourself in all your doings; and yet it is reported to me of you, that you are much infected with this new fan-

[5 feet, Harl. MS.]
[6 nor we are not permitted, Harl. MS.]

tastical doctrine of Luther and such like heretics; that you do very much harm among the youth, and other light heads, with your doctrine." Said Mr Latimer again, "Your grace is misinformed; for I ought to have some more knowledge than to be so simply reported of, by reason that I have studied in my time both of the ancient doctors of the church and also of the school-doctors." "Marry, that is well said," quoth the cardinal; "I am glad to hear that of you; and therefore," quoth the cardinal, " Mr doctor Capon[1], and you Mr doctor Marshal, (both[2] being there present,) say you somewhat to Mr Latimer touching some question in Dunce." Whereupon Dr Capon propounded a question to Mr Latimer. Mr Latimer, being fresh then of memory, and not discontinued from study as those two doctors had been[3], answered very roundly; somewhat helping them to cite their own allegations rightly, where they had not truly nor perfectly alleged them. The cardinal, perceiving the ripe and ready answering of Latimer, said, "What mean you, my masters, to bring such a man before me into accusation? I had thought that he had been some light-headed fellow that never studied such kind of doctrine as the school-doctors are. I pray thee, Latimer, tell me the cause why the bishop of Ely and other doth mislike thy preachings: tell me the truth, and I will bear with thee upon amendment." Quoth Latimer, "Your grace must understand that the bishop of Ely cannot favour me, for that not long ago I preached before him in Cambridge a sermon of this text, *Christus existens pontifex*, etc., wherein I described the office[4] of a bishop so uprightly as I might, according to the text, that never after he could abide me; but hath not only forbidden me to preach in his diocese, but also found the means to inhibit me from preaching in the university." "I pray you tell me," quoth the cardinal, "what thou didst preach before him upon that text?" Mr Latimer plainly and simply (committing his cause unto Almighty God, who is director of princes' hearts) declared unto the cardinal the whole effect of his sermon

[1 Caponer, Harl. MS.]
[2 as I suppose, both being, Harl. MS.]
[3 Dr Capon seems to have proceeded to his doctor's degree in 1517; Dr Marshall in 1533.]
[4 estate, Harl. MS.]

preached before the bishop of Ely. The cardinal, nothing at all misliking the doctrine of the word of God that Latimer had preached, said unto him, "Did you not preach any other doctrine than you have rehearsed?" "No, surely," said Latimer. And, examining thoroughly with the doctors what else could be objected against him, the cardinal said unto Mr Latimer, "If the bishop of Ely cannot abide such doctrine as you have here repeated, you shall have my licence, and shall preach it unto his beard, let him say what he will." And thereupon, after a gentle monition given unto Mr Latimer, the cardinal discharged him with his licence home to preach throughout England.

Now, when Latimer came to Cambridge, every man thought there that he had been utterly put to silence. Notwithstanding, the next holiday after, he entered into the pulpit, and shewed his licence, contrary to all men's[5] expectation. Not long after, it chanced the cardinal to fall into the king's displeasure; whereupon divers report that Mr Latimer's licence was extincted. Mr Latimer, answering thereunto in the pulpit, said, "Where ye think that my licence decayeth with my lord cardinal's temporal fall, I take it nothing so. For he being, I trust, reconciled to God from his pomp and vanities, I now set more by his licence than ever I did before, when he was in his most felicity."

[[5] all expectation, Harl. MS.]

CORRIGENDA.

Some facts, which the Editor overlooked at the time, lead him to believe that the examination of Lambert, mentioned Vol. I. p. x. should have been placed at least a year earlier in the history of Bishop Latimer.

p. 312, line 6 from the bottom, *for* "derogating to" *read* "derogating from".

THE SIXTH SERMON, PREACHED ON THE FIRST SUNDAY IN ADVENT, 1552, BY MASTER HUGH LATIMER.

ROMANS XIII. [8, 9.]

Owe nothing to any man but this, that ye love one another: for he that loveth another fulfilleth the law. For this commandment, Thou shalt not commit adultery: Thou shalt not kill: Thou shalt not steal: Thou shalt not bear false witness: Thou shalt not lust, and so forth; if there be any other commandment, it is all comprehended in this saying. *This Epistle is read in the church the first Sunday in Advent.*

As for the first part of this epistle, we have[1] spoken of it before. For St Paul entreateth of love; and I told you how[2] that love is a thing which we owe[3] one to another; and we are never quit[4] of this debt, we can never discharge ourselves of it: for as long as we live we are in that debt. I will not tarry now to entreat of it; for I told you, since I came into this country, certain special properties of this love. Therefore, I will only desire you to consider, that this love is the livery of Christ; they that have this livery be his servants. Again, they that have it not, be the servants of the devil; for Christ saith, "By this they shall know that ye be my disciples, if ye love one another." They that bear ill will, hatred, and malice, to their neighbours be the devil's servants. And whatsoever such men do that hate their neighbours, pleaseth not God; God abhorreth it; they and all their doings stink before him. For if we would go about to sacrifice and offer unto God a great part of our substance, if we lack love, it is all to no purpose; he abhorreth all our doings: therefore our Saviour giveth us warning, that we shall know that our doings please not God when we are out of charity with our neighbour, have grieved, or injured him. These be his words: "Therefore if thou offerest thy gift at the altar, and there rememberest that thy brother hath ought *A debt that never can be all paid. Love is Christ's livery. John xiii. 1 Cor. xiii. Matt. v.*

[1 elsewhere spoken, 1607.]   [2 plainly how, 1607.]
[3 every one of us in duty oweth, 1607.]
[4 freely quit, 1607.]

against thee, leave[1] thy offering before the altar, and go thy way first, and be reconciled to thy brother, and then come and offer thy gift." For certain it is, that when we be without love and charity, we please not God at all, neither in sacrifices or any manner of things. Therefore I desire you, call to remembrance what I said at the same time when I entreated of love; for I tell you God will not be mocked: *We must love with the whole heart.* it is not enough to pretend a love and charity with our mouth, and to speak fair, and in our hearts to hate our neighbour; this is naught. We should not only speak well by our neighbour, but also we should love him indeed; we should help him in his need; should forgive him with all our hearts, when he hath done any thing against us: for if he needeth help, and I help him not, being able, then my love *Love must be shewed by our works. James ii.* is not perfect. For the right love sheweth herself by the outward works: like as St James saith, "Shew me thy faith by thy works;" so I say unto you, shew your love by your works. Now to the other matters.

"This also, we know the season, how that it is time that we should now awake out of sleep; for now is our salvation nearer than when we believed. The night is passed, the day is come nigh: let us therefore cast away the deeds of darkness, and let us put on the armour of light; let us walk honestly, as it were in the day-light; not in eating and drinking, neither in chambering and wantonness, neither in strife and envying; but put ye on the Lord Jesus Christ, and make not provision for the flesh, to fulfil the lusts of it."

Here St Paul requireth a great thing of us, namely, that we should awake from sleep. He argueth of the circumstances *Two manner of sleeps forbidden.* of the time. But that sleep of which he speaketh is specially a spiritual sleep, the sleep of the soul: yet we may learn by this text, that too much sluggishness of the body is naught and wicked; to spend that good time which God hath given us to do good in, to spend it, I say, in sleeping. For we ought to keep a measure, as well in sleeping as in eating and drinking; and we please God as well in sleeping our natural sleep, as in eating and drinking; but we must see that we *Measure must be had in all things.* keep a measure, that we give ourselves not to much sluggishness. For like as we may not abuse meat and drink, so we may not abuse sleeping, to turn our natural sleep into slug-

[[1] leave there, 1562.]

gishness. But St Paul speaketh here specially of the sleep of the soul; that is, of sin and wickedness, which is called in scripture sleep or darkness, from which sleep St Paul would have us to rise. "For our salvation is come nearer." How chanceth it that St Paul saith, that our salvation is come nearer? Do we not believe now as the prophets and patriarchs did? and how is then our salvation come nearer? You must understand that there be two times from the beginning: the first time was from the beginning of the world till Christ's coming; the other time is since he came. For when he came, he wrought the work of our salvation, and taught us the way to heaven; suffered that pain for us which we should have suffered in hell world without end, and rose again from the death, declaring his resurrection unto his disciples; and so ascended into heaven, where he sitteth at the right hand of God his Father, where he with his intercession applieth unto us which believe in him his passion and all his merits; so that all that believe in him shall be quit from their sins. For his passion is profitable only unto them that believe: notwithstanding that his death might be sufficient for all the whole world, yet for all that no man shall enjoy that same benefit, but only they that believe in him; that put their hope, trust, and confidence in him. Now therefore St Paul saith, "Our salvation is come nearer," because Christ is come already, and maketh intercession for us. All they that were before his coming, as the patriarchs and prophets, and all other faithful, they believed that he should come, but so do not we: we believe that he is come already, and hath fulfilled all things. The Jews, which are at our time, believe that he shall come: but they tarry in vain; their faith is a deceitful faith, because it is against God's word; for Christ is not to be looked for to come again and suffer. No, not so; but he will come again to judge both the quick and the dead.

Our salvation is now nearer than it was at the first.

Christ's death profiteth none that believe not.

    Our Saviour Christ was revealed long before he came to suffer. First in Paradise, when God spake of the woman's seed; and said, *Conteret caput serpentis*, "The seed of the woman shall break the serpent's head." And this was a gospel, a glad tidings: for the serpent had deceived Adam and Eve, and brought them from their felicity, to which they were created: so that Adam and Eve could not help themselves,

Christ was revealed long before he came.

The gospel was preached in Paradise.

nor amend the matter. Now then cometh God with his gospel, and promiseth that there shall be one born of a woman, which shall quash the serpent's head; and this was a gospel. And no doubt as many as did believe these words, and did put their hope in the seed of the woman, and believed to be delivered from their sins through that seed,—as many, I say, as believed so, were saved; as Seth, Enoch, and other good and godly men, which were at that time: but there was not a great number of those; for the most part ever was the worst.

<small>The most part are ever the worse.</small>

Further, this gospel was revealed unto Abraham, when God did promise him, saying, *In semine tuo benedicentur omnes gentes;* "In thy seed all nations shall be blessed:" so that it appeared, that without Christ we are under the curse of God; and again, by Christ we have the benediction of God. Likewise, this gospel was opened unto David, and all the holy prophets. They spake of this gospel, and taught the people to look for their Saviour; but their sayings and prophecies were somewhat dark and obscure. Now when he came and dwelt amongst us, and shewed us the way to heaven, with his own mouth he taught us this gospel, and suffered his painful passion for us: this was a more clearer revelation than the prophets had. Therefore Christ our Saviour saith to his disciples, "Happy are the eyes which see those things which ye see: for I tell you, that many prophets and kings have desired to see those things which ye see, and have not seen them, and to hear those things which ye hear, and have not heard them." But wherefore were they called blessed? That they saw him? Then, if the blessedness stand in the outward seeing, then Adam and Eve, and all the prophets were not blessed, but cursed. If the blessedness standeth in the bodily sight, then the brute beasts were blessed which saw him; the ass whereupon he rode was blessed; yea, his very enemies, Annas and Caiaphas, and Pilate, and other that consented unto his death, were blessed. But it is not so: ye must understand that our Saviour in that manner of speaking putteth only a difference between the times. For at that time when he was here on earth, he was more clear revealed than afore, when he was only promised to come. When he did miracles, cast out devils, healed the sick, it was a more clearer revelation than when God said,

<small>The prophets' sayings were dark and obscure.</small>

<small>Luke x. Matt. xiii.</small>

<small>To see Christ maketh blessed.</small>

Semen mulieris conteret caput serpentis; "The seed of the woman shall break the head of the serpent." When John Baptist pointed and shewed him with his finger, it could be better understood than the prophecies which were spoken of him. Therefore, this blessedness whereof Christ speaketh, and St Paul, when he saith that "our salvation is come nearer," must be understood of the diversity of the time: for Christ was clearer revealed in the end of the world than before. But as touching the blessedness which we have by Christ, it was alike at all times; for it stood Adam in good stead to believe the first promise which God made unto him, and he was as well saved by it, in believing that Christ should come, as we be which believe that he is come, and hath suffered for us. So, likewise, the prophets were saved in believing that he should come and suffer, and deliver mankind by his most painful death. But now, since he is come indeed, and hath overcome the devil, and redeemed our sins, suffered the pains, not for his own sake, but for our sakes; (for he himself had no sin at all, he suffered to deliver us from everlasting damnation; he took our sins, and gave us his righteousness;) now, since that all these things are done and fulfilled, therefore saith Paul, *Propius nos est salus nunc, quam tunc cum credebatur;* " Our salvation is come nearer now, than when we believed:" taking occasion of the time, to move us to rise from our sleep; as who say, "Christ is come now, he hath fulfilled all things, of which things the prophets have spoken; now therefore arise from your sins." The same sleep of which St Paul speaketh here, is the sleep of sin, a spiritual sleep, not a natural sleep of the body: as for the natural sleep, it is lawful for us to sleep and to take our rest, when we do it measurably; not too much setting aside our business, whereunto God hath called us, and do nothing but play the sluggards: when we do so, then we do naught, and sin against God. Therefore we must awake from the sinful sleep, we must set aside slothfulness, with all other vices and sins.

But I pray you, what is sin? I think there be many which can commit sin, and do wickedly; but I think there be but few of those which know what is sin. Therefore I will tell you what is sin: all that that is done against the laws of God, contrary to his will and pleasure, that is sin and wickedness.

Two manner of laws, general and special.

Now there be two manner of laws. There be general laws, pertaining to every man and woman, and there be special laws. The general laws are comprehended in the ten commandments, which ten commandments are comprehended in the law of love, "Thou shalt love God with all thy heart, &c. And thy neighbour as thyself." These be general laws. Now then there be special laws, which teach us how every man and woman shall live in their calling, whereunto God hath called them. These laws teach how magistrates shall do their duty; execute justice, punish the wicked, defend the good; to see that the commonwealth be well ordered, and governed; that the people live godly, every man in his calling. So likewise married folk have their special calling and laws. There is appointed in scripture how the man shall nourish his wife, rule her with all lenity and friendliness: the woman, likewise, shall obey her husband, be loving and kind towards him. So masters ought to do according unto their calling; that is, to rule their house well and godly; to see that their servants be well occupied, and to let them have their meat, and drink, and wages. So servants have their laws; that is, to obey their masters; to do diligently all business whatsoever their masters command unto them, so far *No obedience against God.* as it is not against God: for when a master will command unto his servants to do such things, which are against God, then the servant ought not to obey, to do those things.

Now whosoever transgresseth these laws, either the general or the special laws, he sinneth: and that which is done *Learn to find sin enough.* contrary to these laws, is sin. When ye will know now, whether ye have sinned or not, see and consider these laws, and then go into thy heart and consider thy living, how thou hast spent all thy days: if[1] thou dost so, no doubt thou shalt *The law is a looking-glass.* find innumerable sins done against these laws. For the law of God is a glass, wherein a man may see his spots and filthiness: therefore, when we see them, let us abhor them and leave them; let us be sorry for that which is passed, and let us take a good purpose to leave all sins from henceforward.

And this is it that St Paul saith, "Let us arise from the sleep of sin and wickedness, for our salvation is come nearer; our Saviour he is clearly opened unto us; he hath suffered

[1 when, 1562.]

for us already, and fulfilled the law to the uttermost, and so by his fulfilling taken away the curse of the law."

But there be two manner of sins: there is a deadly sin, and a venial sin; that is, sins that be pardonable, and sins that be not pardonable. Now how shall we know which be venial sins, or which be not? for it is good to know them, and so to keep us from them. When ye will know which be deadly sins or not, you must first understand, that there be two manner of men: when I say men, I understand also women, that is, all mankind: and so doth scripture understand women[2] by this word men; for else we should not find in scripture that we should baptize women, for the scripture saith, *Baptizate eos*, "Baptize them." He speaketh in the masculine gender only. Also[3], *Nisi quis renatus fuerit ex spiritu et aqua*, "Except a man be born again through spirit and water." Here is made no mention of women, yet they be understood in it: for the salvation and everlasting life pertaineth as well unto faithful women as it doth unto faithful men; for he suffered as well for the women, as he did for the men. God would have them both to be saved, the men and the women: so ye see that this word men signifieth or containeth both kinds[4], the men and the women, at some times, though not always. But I say there be two manner of men: some there be that be not justified, not regenerate, nor yet in the state of salvation; that is to say, not God's servants: they lack the renovation or regeneration; they be not come yet to Christ. Now these persons that be not come yet to Christ, or if they were come to Christ, be fallen again from him, and so lost their justification, (as there be many of us, which when we fall willingly into sin against conscience, we lose the favour of God, our salvation, and finally the Holy Ghost;) all they now that be out of the favour of God, and are not sorry for it, sin grieveth them not, they purpose to go forward in it; all those that intend not to leave their sins, are out of the favour of God, and so all their works, whatsoever they do, be deadly sins: for as long as they be in purpose to sin, they sin deadly in all their doings. Therefore, when we will speak of the diversity of sins, we must speak of those that be faith-

margin notes: Two manner of sins. Under the name of men women are expressed. The word signifieth both man and woman. Who be they that sin deadly.

[2 scripture too, understanding the women, 1562.]
[3 Item, 1562.]   [4 the sexes, 1562.]

ful, that be regenerated and made new, and clean from their sins through Christ.

All sins are pardonable to them that believe the gospel.

Now this I say: I have venial sins, and deadly sins. Which be venial sins? Every sin that is committed against God not wittingly, nor willingly; not consenting unto it: those be venial sins. As for an ensample: I see a fair woman, I am moved in my heart to sin with her, to commit the act of lechery with her: such thoughts rise out of my heart, but I consent not unto them; I withstand these ill motions, I follow the ensample of that godly young man, Joseph; I consider in what estate I am, namely, a temple of God, and that I should lose the Holy Ghost; on such wise I withstand my ill lusts and appetites, yet this motion in my heart is sin; this ill lust which riseth up; but it is a venial sin, it is not a mortal sin, because I consent not unto it, I withstand it; and such venial sins the just man

Prov. xiv.

committeth daily. For scripture saith, *Septies cadit justus,* "The righteous man falleth seven times;" that is, oftentimes: for his works are not so perfect as they ought to be. For I pray you, who is he that loveth his neighbour so perfectly and vehemently as he ought to do? Now this imperfection is sin, but it is a venial sin, not a mortal: therefore he that feeleth his imperfections, feeleth the ill[1] motions in his heart, but followeth them not, consenteth not unto the wickedness

Which are venial sins, and which are deadly.

to do them; these be venial sins, which shall not be imputed unto us to our damnation. So all the ill thoughts that rise up in our hearts are venial, as long as we consent not unto them, to fulfil them with the deed. I put the case, Joseph had not resisted the temptations of his master's wife, but had followed her, and fulfilled the act of lechery with her; had weighed the matter after a worldly fashion, thinking, "I have my mistress's favour already, and so by that mean I shall have my master's favour too; nobody knowing of it." Now if[2] he had done so, this act had been a deadly sin; for any act that is done against the law of God willingly and

If sin have once the victory over us, then are we nothing.

wittingly, is a deadly sin. And that man or woman that committeth such an act, loseth the Holy Ghost and the remission of sins; and so becometh the child of the devil, being before the child of God. For a regenerate man or woman, that believeth, ought to have dominion over sin; but as soon

[1 evil, 1584, 1607.]   [2 when, 1562.]

as sin hath rule over him, he is gone: for she leadeth him to delectation of it, and from delectation to consenting, and so from consenting to the act itself. Now he that is led so with sin, he is in the state of damnation, and sinneth damnably.

And so ye may perceive which be they that sin deadly, and what is the deadly sin; namely, that he sinneth deadly that wittingly falleth in sin: therefore it is a perilous thing to be in such an estate, to be in the state[3] of damnation and everlasting perdition. Let us follow, therefore, this good warning which St Paul giveth us here; let us rise from the sleep of sin; let us take a hearty purpose to leave all wickedness. But may we do so? May we rise from sin? Yes, that we may: for God hath provided a remedy for us. What is that? Forsooth[4], penance; we must have the staff of penance, and rise up withal. And this penance is such a salve, that it healeth all sores: if a man have done all the world's sin, yet when he taketh this staff of penance in his hand, that is to say, when he is sorry for it, and intendeth to leave them, no doubt he may recover; and God is that same physician which useth but one manner of salve to all manner of sores. *Penance and repentance is a salve to heal all sin.*

We read in the gospel of Luke, that when Pilate had done a notable murder, and had mingled the blood of certain Jews with their own sacrifices, now some came and told Christ what Pilate had done: our Saviour maketh them answer, saying, "I tell you, except ye repent, ye shall all likewise so perish." As who say, "Whatsoever Pilate hath done, see you that ye do penance, and amend your naughty livings, or else ye shall all be destroyed." This was a good quip that he giveth[5] unto the Jews, which were ready to speak of other men's faults, but of their own faults they made no mention; as it is our nature, to be more readier to reprove other men's faults than our own; but our Saviour he commandeth them to look home, to see to themselves. And this penance is the chiefest thing in all the scripture. John Baptist when he began to preach, his sermon was, *Pœnitentiam agite*, "Do penance:" so likewise Christ saith, *Pœnitentiam agite, et credite evangelio*, "Do penance, and believe the gospel." But wherein standeth the right penance, and what is penance? Answer: Penance is a turning from sin *Luke xiii. All must repent. Our nature is to see other men's faults, but not our own. What repentance is.*

[3 estate, 1571.]　　[4 marry, 1562.]　　[5 gave, 1584, 1607.]

unto God, a waking up from this sleep of which St Paul speaketh here. But wherein consisteth this penance? The right penance consisteth in three points: the first is contrition; that is, I must acknowledge myself that I have transgressed God's most holy laws and commandments. I must confess myself to be faulty and guilty; I must be sorry for it, abhor myself and my wickedness. When I am now in that case, then I shall see nothing but hell and everlasting damnation before me, as long as I look upon myself and upon the law of God. For the law of God, when it is preached, bringeth us to the knowledge of our sins: for it is like as a glass which sheweth us the spots in our faces, that is, the sins in our hearts. But we may not tarry here only in the law and ourselves; for if we do, we shall come to desperation. Therefore, the first point is to acknowledge our sins, and to be sorry for the same; but, as I said before, we must not tarry here: for Judas was come so far, he had this point; he was, no doubt, a sorrowful man as any can be in the world: but it was to no purpose; he was lost for all his sorrowfulness: therefore we must have another point.

Repentance consisteth of three parts.

The law of God is a looking-glass.

What is that? Marry, faith, belief: we must believe Christ, we must know that our Saviour is come into this world to save sinners: therefore he is called Jesus, because "he shall save his people from their sins;" as the angel of God himself witnesseth. And this faith must not be only a general faith, but it must be a special faith. For the devil himself hath a general faith: he believeth that Christ is come into this world, and hath made a reconciliation between God and man; he knoweth that there shall be remission of our sins, but he believeth not that he shall have part of it; that his wickedness shall be forgiven unto him, this he believeth not; he hath but a general faith. But I say that every one of us must have a special faith: I must believe for myself, that his blood was shed for me. I must believe that when Christ saith, "Come to me, all ye that labour and are heavy laden, and I will ease you;" here I must believe that Christ calleth me unto him, that I should come and receive everlasting life at his hands. With such a special faith I do apply his passion unto me. In that prayer that our Saviour made when he was going to his death, "I pray not for them alone," saith he, "but for them also which shall believe in

Faith must be joined with our repentance.
Matt. i.

The devil doth believe that Christ came into this world.

Every man that will be saved must have a stedfast faith.

me through their preaching, that they all may be one, as thou, Father, art in me, and I in thee; and that they also may be one in us:" so that Christ prayeth for us as well as for his apostles, if we believe in him; and so Christ's prayer and our belief bringeth the salve unto our souls. Therefore I ought to believe, and so through faith apply Christ's merits unto me: for God requireth a special faith of every one of us, as well as he did of David, when the prophet Nathan came unto him and said, *Abstulit Dominus peccatum tuum,* "The Lord hath taken away thy wickedness;" which words of the prophet David believed[1], and so according unto his belief it happened unto him. For David had not such a contrition or penance as Judas had: for Judas indeed had a contrition, he was sorry for his sins, but without faith. David was sorry for his sins, but he joined faith unto it; he believed stedfastly, without all doubting, that God would be merciful unto him. *Abstulit Dominus,* "The Lord hath taken away thy sins;" and God required of him that he should believe those words. Now, like as he required of David to believe his words, so also he requireth of us too, that we should believe him: for like as David was remedied through his faith in God, so shall we be remedied also, if we believe as he did: and God will be as glad of us when we repent and leave our sins, as he was of David; and will also that we should be partakers of the merits of Christ.

{{marginal: Christ prayed for us.}}
{{marginal: David and Judas did both repent.}}

So ye have heard now these two points which pertain to the right penance: the first is contrition; when we acknowledge our sins, be sorry for them, and that they grieve us very sore. The second point is faith; when we believe that God will be merciful unto us, and through his Son forgive us our wickedness, and not impute the same to our eternal destruction. But yet there is another point left behind, which is this, that I must have an earnest purpose to leave sin, and to avoid all wickedness as far forth as I am able to do. I must wrestle with sin. I must not suffer the devil to have the victory over me: though he be very subtil and crafty, yet I must withstand him; I must disallow his instinctions and suggestions. I must not suffer sin to bear rule over me: for no doubt, if we will fight and strive, we may have the victory over this serpent;

{{marginal: The first point of penance.}}
{{marginal: The second point of penance.}}
{{marginal: We must play the part of a warrior and fight with sin.}}

[[1] prophet Nathan he believed, 1571, 1584.]

for Christ our Saviour hath promised unto us his help and comfort: therefore St James saith, *Resistite diabolo, et fugiet a vobis;* "Withstand the devil, and he shall fly from you." For at his first coming he is very weak; so that we are able, if we will take heed and fight, to overcome him: but if we suffer him to enter once, to possess our hearts, then he is very strong, so that he with great labour can scant be brought out again. For he entereth first by ill thoughts: then when he hath cast us in ill thoughts, if we withstand not, by and bye followeth delectation: if we suffer that, then cometh consenting; and so from consenting to the very act: and afterward from one mischief unto another. Therefore it is a common saying, *Principiis obsta,* " Resist the beginnings:" for when we suffer him once to enter, no doubt it is a perilous thing, we are then in jeopardy of everlasting death.

marginal notes: We may if we have faith overcome the devil. Resist the devil at the first.

So ye have heard now wherein standeth right penance. First we must know and acknowledge our sins, be sorry for them, and lament them in our hearts. Then the second point is faith: we must believe that Christ will be merciful unto us, and forgive us our sins, and not impute them unto us. Thirdly, we must have an earnest purpose to leave all sins and wickedness, and no more commit the same. And then ever be persuaded in thy heart, that they that have a good-will and an earnest mind to leave sin, that God will strengthen them, and he will help them. But and if we by and bye, at the first clap, give place unto the devil, and follow his mischievous suggestions, then we may be sure that we highly displease God our heavenly Father, if[1] we forsake him so soon. Therefore St Paul saith, *Ne regnet igitur peccatum in vestro mortali corpore;* " Let not sin bear rule in your mortal bodies:" be not led with sin, but fight against it. When we do so, it is impossible but we shall have help at God's hand.

marginal notes: Right penance wherein it standeth. Rom. vi.

As touching confession I tell you, that they that can be content with the general absolution which every minister of God's word giveth in his sermons, when he pronounceth that all that be sorry for their sins, and believe in Christ, seek help and remedy by him, and afterward intend to amend their lives, and avoid sin and wickedness, all these that be

[1 when, 1562.]

so minded shall have remission of their sins; now, I say, they that can be content with this general absolution, it is well: but they that are not satisfied with it, they may go to some godly learned minister, which is able to instruct and comfort them with the word of God, to minister that same unto them to their contentation and quieting of their consciences. As for satisfaction, or absolution for our sins, there is none but in Christ: we cannot make amends for our sins but only by believing in him which suffered for us. For he hath made the mends for all our sins by his painful passion and blood-shedding. And herein standeth our absolution or remission of our sins, namely, when we believe in him, and look to be saved through his death; none other satisfaction we are able to make. But I tell you, that if any man or woman hath stolen[2] or purloined away somewhat from his neighbour, that man or woman is bound[3] to make restitution and amends. And this restitution is so necessary, that we shall not look for forgiveness of our sins at Christ's hand, except this restitution be made first; else the satisfaction of Christ will not serve us: for God will have us to restore or make amends unto our neighbour, whom we have hurt, deceived, or have in any manner of ways taken from him wrongfully his goods, whatsoever it be.

The use of auricular confession.

The true satisfaction for sins.

Restitution of goods taken away must be made. This must be understood conditionally, that is, as we are able.

By this now that I have said ye may perceive, what manner of sleeping is this of which St Paul speaketh here, namely, the sleep of sin. When we live and spend our time in wickedness, then we sleep that deadly sleep which bringeth eternal damnation with him. And again, ye have heard how you shall rise up from that sleep, how ye shall fight and wrestle with sin, not suffer her to be the ruler over you. Let us therefore begin even now, while God giveth us so good and convenient a time; let us tarry no longer; let us awake from this deadly sleep of sin, which bringeth[4] eternal death and everlasting pains and sorrows: let us therefore rise to a godly life, and continue in the same till to the end.

These things St Paul speaketh generally to all men, and against all manner of sins; but now he cometh to specialties. And first he sheweth what we shall not do, then afterward

[2 man hath stolen, 1562.]   [3 ought, 1562.]
[4 sleep of sin: it may well be called a deadly sleep, for this sleep of sin bringeth, 1562.]

Rom. xiii.

A fault in the English translation.

Man's diet before the flood.

The cause why man had liberty to feed on flesh.

Hedges that we may not leap over.

he telleth us what we shall do: "Not in eating and drinking, neither in chambering and wantonness, neither in strife and envying." I marvel that the English is so translated, "In eating and drinking:" the Latin exemplar hath, "*Non in comessationibus*," that is to say, "Not in too much eating and drinking;" for no doubt God alloweth eating and drinking, so that it be done measurably and thankfully. In the beginning of the world, before God punished the world with the flood, when he destroyed all mankind and beasts, save only Noah, that good father; in the beginning, I say, mankind ate nothing but herbs, and roots, and sallads, and such gear as they could get: but after the flood God gave unto mankind liberty to eat all manner of clean beasts, all that had life, be it fish or flesh. And this was done for this cause, that the earth was not so fruitful, nor brought not forth so wholesome herbs after the flood, as she did before the flood: therefore God allowed unto man all manner of meat, be it fish or flesh; yet it must be done measurably. But seeing I have occasion to speak of eating, I will entreat somewhat of it, and tell you what liberties we have by God's word.

Truly we be allowed by God's word to eat all manner of meat, be it fish or flesh, that be wholesome for to eat[1]. But ye must understand that there be certain hedges, over which we ought not to leap; but rather keep ourselves within those same hedges. Now the first hedge is this, *Carnem cum sanguine ne comederitis*, "Ye shall not eat the flesh with the blood;" that is to say, we shall not eat raw flesh: for if we should be allowed to eat raw flesh, it should engender in us a certain cruelness, so that at the length one should eat another. And so all the writers expound this place: so that God forbiddeth here that mankind, or man's flesh, may not be eaten. We read in the books of the Kings, and so likewise in Josephus[2], that certain women had eaten their own children, at the time when Jerusalem was besieged: which thing no doubt displeased God, and they did naughtily in so doing. For mankind may not be eaten: therefore the first hedge is, that we must abstain from raw flesh, and so likewise from man's flesh; one may not eat another. Neither yet we may not

[1 be eatable, 1562.] [2 Bell. Judaic. vi. 3. §. 4.]

shed blood of private authority: a man may not kill another; but the magistrate he hath the sword committed unto him from God; he may shed blood when he seeth cause why; he may take away the wicked from amongst the people, and punish him according unto his doing or deserving. *The magistrates may shed blood.*

Now will ye say, "I perceive, when I eat not raw flesh or man's flesh, then I may eat all manner of flesh, or fish, howsoever I can get it." But I tell thee, my friend, not so: you may not eat your neighbour's sheep, nor steal his fishes out of his pool and eat them: ye may not do so, for there is a hedge made, for that God saith, *Non facies furtum,* "Thou shalt do no theft:" here am I hedged in, so that I may not eat my neighbour's meat, but it must be my own meat. I must have gotten it uprightly, or else by buying, or else by inheritance, or else that it be given unto me: I may not steal it from my neighbour; when I leap over this hedge, then I sin damnably. *Another hedge for eating.* *Exod. xx.*

Now then ye will say, "So it be my own, then I may eat of it[3] as much as I will." No, not so; there is another hedge. I may not commit gluttony with my own meat; for so it is written, *Attendite vobis a crapula et ebrietate,* "Take heed of gluttony and drunkenness." Here is a hedge; we may not eat too much; for when we do, we displease God highly. So ye see that we may not eat of our own meat as much as we would, but rather we must keep a measure; for it is a great sin to abuse or waste the gifts of God, and to play the glutton with it. When one man consumeth as much as would serve three or four, that is an abominable thing before God; for God giveth us his creatures, not to abuse them, but to use them to our necessity and need. Let every one, therefore, have a measure, and let no man abuse the gifts of God. One man sometimes eateth more than another; we are not all alike: but for all that we ought[4] to keep us within this hedge; that is, to take no more than sufficeth our nature; for they that abuse the gifts of God, no doubt they greatly displease God by so doing. For it is an ill-favoured thing, when a man eateth or drinketh too much at a time. Sometimes, indeed, it happeneth that a man drinketh too much; but every good and *A third hedge for eating.* *All men's eating is not like.* *A good man will refrain from evil.*

[3 this, 1584, 1607.]
[4 ought all to keep, 1571, 1572.]

godly man will take heed to himself; when he once hath taken too much he will beware afterward. We read in scripture of Noah, that good man, which was the first that planted vineyards after the flood; he was once drunken, before he knew the strength and the nature of wine, and so lay in the tent uncovered. Now one of his sons, whose name was Cham, seeing his father lying naked, went and told his brethren of it, and so made a mocking-stock of his father. Therefore Noah, when he arose and had digested his wine, and knowing what his son had done unto him, cursed him: but we read not that Noah was drunken afterward at any time more. Therefore if ye have been drunken at any time, take heed henceforward, and leave off; abuse not the good creatures of God.

_{Gen. ix.}

_{A fourth hedge for eating.} Now then ye will say, "If I take them measurably, then I may eat all manner of meat at all times and everywhere." No, not so; there is another hedge behind: ye must have a respect to your own conscience, and to your neighbour's. For I may eat no manner of meat against my conscience, neither may I eat my meat in presence of my neighbour, whereby he might be offended; for I ought to have respect unto him, as St Paul plainly sheweth, saying, "I know and am assured by the Lord Jesus, that there is nothing unclean of itself, but unto him that judgeth it to be common, to him it is common: if thy brother be grieved with thy meat, now walkest thou not charitably; destroy not him with thy meat, for whom Christ died." As for an ensample: when I should come into the north country, where they be not taught[1], and there I should call for my eggs on a Friday or for flesh, then I should do naughtily; for I should destroy him for whom Christ did suffer. Therefore I must beware that I offend no man's conscience, but rather travail with him first, and shew him the truth: when my neighbour is taught, and knoweth the truth, and will not believe it, but will abide by his old *Mumpsimus*[2], then I may eat, not regarding him:

_{Rom. xiv.}

_{Obstinate blind are not to be passed upon.}

[1 How slowly teaching reached the "north country," even at a later period than is here referred to, may be gathered from Archbishop Grindal's "Injunctions." Grindal, Remains, pp. 123, et seq. Park. Soc. Edit. Gilpin, Life of Bern. Gilpin, pp. 85, 93, 188, &c.]

[2 The allusion here is to a story, related by Pace in his book *De fructu qui ex doctrina percipitur* (p. 80), respecting an unlearned

for he is an obstinate fellow, he will not believe God's word. And though he be offended with me, yet it is but a pharisaical offence, like as the Pharisees were offended with Christ our Saviour: the fault was not in Christ, but in themselves. So, I say, I must have a respect to my neighbour's conscience, and then to my own conscience.

But yet there is another hedge behind; that is, civil laws, the king's statutes and ordinances, which are God's laws; forasmuch as we ought to obey them as well as God's laws and commandments. St Paul saith, "Let every soul submit himself unto the authority of the higher power; for there is no power but it is of God: the powers that be are ordained of God. Whosoever therefore resisteth the power, resisteth the ordinance of God: but they that resist shall receive to themselves damnation." Now, therefore, we dwell in a realm, where it hath pleased the king's majesty to make an Act[3], that all his subjects shall abstain from flesh upon Fridays and Saturdays, and other days which are expressed in the[4] Act: unto which law we ought to obey, and that for conscience' sake, except we have a privilege, or be excepted by the same law. And although scripture commandeth me not to abstain from flesh upon Fridays and Saturdays, yet for all that, seeing there is civil law and ordinance made by the king's majesty, and his most honourable council, we ought to obey all their ordinances, except they be against God. *The fifth hedge for eating. Rom. xiii.* *Necessity has no law in these points.*

These be the hedges wherein we must keep ourselves. Therefore I desire you, in God's behalf, consider what I have said unto you, how ye shall order yourselves, how ye shall not eat raw flesh: that is, ye shall not be cruel towards your neighbour: also[5], you shall not steal your meat from your neighbour, but let it be your own meat, and then ye shall take of it measurably: also, ye shall not offend your

English priest who for thirty years had been accustomed, in repeating the prayer, *Quod ore sumpsimus*, to say *mumpsimus;* and who, on being told of his mistake, refused to be corrected, alleging "that he would not give up his old *mumpsimus* for his corrector's new *sumpsimus.*" This passed into so common a proverb, to indicate a person obstinate in religious matters, that we find Henry VIII. using the expression in his speech to his Parliament, Nov. 25, 1545.]

[3 2 and 3 Edw. VI. c. 19.]
[4 that, 1584, 1607.] [5 item, 1562.]

[LATIMER, II.]

neighbour's conscience: also, ye shall keep you within the laws of the realm.

Now to the matter again. St Paul saith, we shall take heed of too much eating and drinking; and I have shewed you, how ye shall keep you within the hedges which are appointed in God's laws. Let us, therefore, take heed now, and let us rise up from the sleep of sin: whatsoever we have done before, let us rise up now, while we have time; every man go into his own heart, and there when he findeth any thing amiss, let him rise up from that sleep, and tarry not in it: if thou remain lying, thou shalt repent it everlastingly.

<small>*He that will not rise from sin shall repent it everlastingly.*</small>

"Neither in chambering and wantonness." Beware of St Paul's *nots* and *nons*. For when he saith *non*, we cannot make it yea: if we do contrary to his sayings, we shall repent it. Beware therefore of "chambering." What is this? Marry, he understandeth by this word "chambering" all manner of wantonness. I will not tarry long in rehearsing them; let every man and woman go into his own conscience, and let them consider that God requireth honesty in all things. St Paul useth this word "chambering;" for when folks will be wanton, they get themselves in corners: but for all that God he seeth them, he will find them out one day, they cannot hide themselves from his face. I will speak no farther of it, for with honesty no man can speak of such vile vices; and St Paul commandeth us that we shall not speak any vile words: therefore by this word "chambering" understand the circumstances of whoredom and lechery and filthy living, which St Paul forbiddeth here, and would have that nobody should give occasion unto the other to such filthiness.

<small>*What chambering is.*</small>

"Neither in strife, nor envying." Envy is a foul and abominable vice, which vice doth more harm unto him that envieth another than unto him which is envied. King Saul he had this spirit of envy; therefore he had never rest day nor night, he could not abide when any man spake well of David. And this spirit of envying is more directly against charity than any other sin is: for St Paul saith, *Caritas non invidet*, "Charity envieth not:" therefore take it so, that he that envieth another is no child of God; all his works, whatsoever he doeth, are the devil's service; he

<small>*Envy hurteth the envious most.*
1 Kings xviii.</small>

<small>*No envious man is the child of God.*</small>

pleaseth God with nothing as long as he is an envious person. Who would be so mad now, as to be in such an estate, that he would[1] suffer the devil to bear so much rule over him? No wise nor godly man will be in this estate: for it is an ill estate to be out of the favour of God, to be without remission of sin. Therefore, whosoever is an envious man, let him rise up from that sleep, lest he be taken suddenly, and so be damned everlastingly.

Now ye have heard what we shall not do: we shall not too much eat and drink, and so abuse the gifts of God; we shall not have pleasure in chambering, that is, in wantonness; neither shall we be envious persons; for if we be, we be out of charity, and so be out of the favour of God[2]. *What we should not do.*

Now followeth what we should do. "But put ye on the Lord Jesus Christ." Every man and woman ought to put on Christ: and all they that have that apparel on their backs, they are well; nothing can hurt them, neither heat nor cold, nor wind nor rain. Here I might have occasion to speak against this excess of apparel, which is used now every where, which thing is disallowed in scripture. There be some that will be conformable unto others, they will do as others do; but they consider not with themselves, whether others do well or not. There be laws made and certain statutes, how every one in his estate shall be apparelled; but, God knoweth, the statutes are not put in execution. St Paul he commandeth us to put on Christ, to leave these gorgeous apparels: he that is decked with Christ is well[3]. And first we be decked with Christ in our baptism, where we promise to forsake the devil with all his works. Now when we keep this promise, and leave wickedness, and do that which Christ our Saviour requireth of us, then we be decked with him; then we have the wedding-garment; and though we be very poor, and have but a russet coat, yet we are well, when we are decked with him. There be a great many which go very gay in velvet and satin; but for all that, I fear they have not Christ upon them, for all their gorgeous apparel. I say not this to condemn rich men or their riches; for no *What all men should do.* *We should conform ourselves to them that do well.*

[1 should, 1584, 1596.]

[2 for if we be out of charity, we be out of the favour of God, 1584, 1596, 1607.]

[3 he is well, 1562.]

doubt poor and rich may have Christ upon them, if they will follow him and live as he commandeth them to live. For if we have Christ upon us, we will not make provision for the flesh; we will not set our hearts upon these worldly trifles, to get riches to cherish this body withal. As we read of the rich man in the gospel, which thought he had enough for many years; he had pulled down his old barns, and had set up new ones which were greater and larger[1] than the other; and when all things were ready after his mind and pleasure, then he said to himself, "Soul, thou hast much goods laid up for many years; take thine ease, eat, drink, and be merry." But what saith God unto him? "Thou fool," saith God, "this night they will fetch away thy soul again from thee; then whose shall these things be which thou hast provided? So it is with him that gathereth riches to himself, and is not rich toward God." I will not say otherwise but a man may make provision for his house, and ought to make the same: but to make such provision to set aside God's word and serving of him, that[2] is naught; to set the heart so upon the riches, as though there were no heaven nor hell. How can we be so foolish to set so much by this world, knowing that it shall endure but a little while? For we know by scripture, and all learned men affirm the same, that the world was made to endure six thousand years. Now, of these six thousand be passed already five thousand five hundred and fifty-two, and yet this time which is left shall be shortened for the elect's sake, as Christ himself witnesseth.

Therefore let us remember that the time is very short, let us study to amend our lives: let us not be so careful for this world, for the end of it no doubt is at hand; and though the general day come not by and bye, yet our end will not be far off; death will come one day and strip us out of our coat, he will take his pleasure of us. It is a marvellous thing to see, there be some which have lived in this world forty or fifty years, and yet they lack time: when death cometh, they be not ready. But I will require you for God's sake, rise up from your sleep of sin and wickedness; make yourselves ready; set all things in an order, so that ye may be ready whensoever death shall come and fetch you: for die we must,

[[1] were bigger than, 1562.]   [[2] this, 1562.]

there is no remedy; we must leave one day this world; for we are not created of God to the end that we should abide here always. Therefore let us repent betime of our wicked life; for God will not the death of a sinner, but rather that he shall turn from his wickedness and live. *Vivo ego, nolo* Ezek. xviii. *mortem peccatoris, sed ut convertatur, et vivat;* "As truly as I live, saith God, I will not the death of a sinner, but rather that he shall turn from his wickedness and live." These are most comfortable words; for now we may be sure that when we will leave our sins and wickedness, and turn unto him with all our hearts earnestly, then he will turn himself unto us, and will shew himself a loving father. And to the intent that we should believe this, he sweareth an oath: we ought to believe God without an oath, yet he sweareth to make us more surer. What will he have us to do? Surely[3], to rise up from this sleep of sin, to leave wickedness, to forsake all hatred and malice, that we have had towards our neighbours; to turn from envying, from stealing, and make restitution; from slothfulness to diligence and painfulness, from gluttony and drunkenness to soberness and abstinence, from chambering and filthy living to an honest and pure life; and so, finally, from all kinds of vices to virtue and godliness; and whatsoever hath been in times past, be sorry for it; cry God mercy, and believe in Christ, and rise up from sleep; do no more wickedly, but live as God would have thee to live.

Now I will bring in here a notable sentence, and a comfortable saying, and then I will make an end: *Justitia justi* Ezek. xxxiii. *non liberabit ipsum in quacunque die peccaverit; et impietas impii non nocebit ei in quacunque die conversus fuerit ab impietate sua;* "The righteousness of the righteous shall not save him, whensoever he turneth away unfaithfully:" again, "the wickedness of the wicked shall not hurt him, Sin not in whensoever he turneth from his ungodliness. And the right- hope of mercy. eousness of the righteous shall not save him whensoever he sinneth. If I say unto the righteous that he shall surely live; and so he trusteth to his own righteousness, and doth sin, then shall his righteousness be no more thought upon, but in the wickedness that he hath done he shall die. Again,

[3 Marry, 1562.]

Despair not of mercy. if I say unto the wicked, Thou shalt surely die, and so he turn from his sins, and doth the thing that is lawful and right: then he shall surely live;" that is to say, all his sins which he hath done before shall not hurt him. Here ye hear what promises God hath made us, when we will rise from the sleep of our sins, and leave the affections of the flesh, and do such things as he hath appointed unto us in his laws; if we do so, then we shall surely live and not die:—that is to say, we shall attain after this corporal life to everlasting life; which grant us God the Father, Son, and Holy Ghost! *Amen.*

THE SERMON PREACHED UPON SAINT ANDREW'S DAY, 1552,
BY MASTER HUGH LATIMER.

MATTHEW IV. [18, 19, 20.]

As Jesus walked by the sea of Galilee, he saw two brethren, Simon which was called Peter, and Andrew his brother, casting a net into the sea; for they were fishers: and he said unto them, Follow me, and I will make you fishers of men: and they straightway left their nets and followed him. *This gospel is read in the church on St Andrew's day.*

THIS is the gospel which is read in the church this day: and it sheweth unto us how our Saviour called four persons to his company; namely, Peter and Andrew, James and John, which were all fishers by their occupation. This was their general vocation; but now Christ our Saviour called them to a more special vocation. They were fishers still, but they fished no more for fish in the water, but they must fish now[1] for men, with the net which was prepared to the same[2] purpose, namely, with the gospel; for the gospel is the net wherewith the apostles fished after they came to Christ, but specially after his departing out of this world: then they went and fished throughout the whole world. And of these fishers was spoken a great while ago by the prophet: for so it is written, *Ecce ego mittam piscatores multos, dicit Dominus, et piscabuntur eos; et post hæc mittam eis venatores multos, et venabuntur eos de omni monte et de omni colle et de cavernis petrarum;* "Behold, saith the Lord, I will send out many fishers to take them; and after that will I send hunters to hunt them out from all mountains and hills, and out of the caves of stone." By these words God signified by his prophets, how those fishers, that is, the apostles, should preach the gospel, and take the people therewith, (that is, all they that should believe,) and so bring them to God. It is commonly seen that fishers and hunters be very painful people both; they spare no labour to catch their game, because they be so desirous and so greedy over their game, that they care not for pains. Therefore our Saviour *The apostles fished after men.* *Jer. xvi.*

[1 must fish for, 1562.]   [2 this purpose, 1562.]

<small>Why Christ called fishers to be apostles.</small> chose fishers, because of these properties, that they should be painful and spare no labour; and then that they should be greedy to catch men, and to take them with the net of God's word, to turn the people from wickedness to God. Ye see by daily experience, what pain fishers and hunters take; how the fisher watcheth day and night at his net, and is ever ready to take all such fishes that he can get, and come in his way. So, likewise, the hunter runneth hither and thither after his game; leapeth over hedges, and creepeth through rough bushes; and all this labour he esteemeth for nothing, because he is so desirous to obtain his prey, and catch his <small>The office of prelates.</small> venison. So all our prelates, bishops, and curates, parsons and vicars, should be as painful and greedy[1] in casting their nets; that is to say, in preaching God's word; in shewing unto the people the way to everlasting life; in exhorting them to leave their sins and wickedness. This ought to be done of them, for thereunto they be called of God; such a <small>The doings of prelates.</small> charge they have. But the most part of them set, now-a-days, aside this fishing; they put away this net; they take other business in hand: they will rather be surveyors or receivers, or clerks in the kitchen, than to cast out this net: they have the living of fishers, but they fish not, they are otherways occupied[2]. But it should not be so: God will plague and most heinously punish them for so doing. They shall be called to make account one day, where they shall not be able to make answer for their misbehaviours, for not casting out this net of God's word, for suffering the people to go to the devil, and they call them not again, they admonish them not. Their perishing grieveth them not; but the day will come when they shall repent from the bottom of <small>The reward of negligent prelates.</small> their hearts; but then it will be too late: then they shall receive their well deserved punishment for their negligence and slothfulness, for taking their living of the people, and not teaching them.

The evangelists speak diversely of the calling of these four men, Peter, Andrew, James, and John. Matthew saith, <small>Matt. iv.</small> that "Jesus called them, and they immediately left their nets,

[1 so painful, so greedy, 1562.]
[2 See Strype, Eccles. Mem. II. ii. p. 141. Oxf. Edit. Bern. Gilpin, Sermon before K. Edw. VI. p. 21, et seq. at the end of Gilpin, Life of Bern. Gilpin.]

and followed him." Luke saith, that our Saviour "stood by the lake of Genezareth, and there he saw two ships standing by the lake side, and he entered in one of these ships, which was Peter's, and desired him that he would thrust it a little from the land: and so he taught the people; and after that, when he had made an end of speaking, he said to Simon Peter, Cast out thy net in the deep: and Simon answered, We have laboured all night and have taken nothing; nevertheless at thy commandment I will loose forth the net. And when they had cast it out, they inclosed a great multitude of fishes. Now Peter, seeing such a multitude of fishes, was beyond himself, and fell down at Jesus's knees, saying, Lord, go from me, for I am a sinful man: for he was astonished, and all that were with him, at the draught of the fishes which they had taken. And there were also James and John the sons of Zebedee. And Jesus said unto Peter, Fear not, from henceforth thou shalt catch men: and they brought the ships to land, and forsook all, and followed him." So ye hear how Luke describeth this story, in what manner of ways Christ called them; and though he make no mention of Andrew, yet it was like that he was amongst them too, with Peter, John, and James. The evangelist John, in the first chapter, describeth this matter of another manner of ways, but it pertaineth all to one end and to one effect: for it was most like, that they were called first to come in acquaintance with Christ, and afterwards to be his disciples; and so in the end to be his apostles, which should teach and instruct the whole world. John the evangelist saith, that Andrew was a disciple of John Baptist: and when he had seen his master point to Christ with his finger, saying, *Ecce Agnus Dei, qui tollit peccata mundi,* "Lo the Lamb of God, that taketh away the sins of the world;"—(they used in the law to offer lambs for the pacifying of God: now John called Christ the right Lamb which should take away indeed all the sins of the world:) now when Andrew heard whereunto Christ was come, he forsook his master John, and came to Christ; and fell in acquaintance with him, asked him where he dwelled; and finding his brother Simon Peter, he told him of Christ, and brought him to him. He brought him not to John, but to Christ: and so should we do too; we should bring to Christ as many as we could, with good exhortations and admonitions. Now

[side notes: The miraculous doing of our Saviour Christ. John the evangelist was a disciple of John Baptist.]

Christ seeing Peter, said unto him, "Thou art Simon the son of Jonas; thou shalt be called Cephas, which is by interpretation, a stone:" signifying that Peter should be a stedfast fellow; not wavering hither and thither.

The apostles were divers times called. So ye see how diversely the evangelists speak of the calling of these four apostles, Peter, Andrew, James, and John: therefore it is like they were called more than one time: they were called first to come to acquaintance with him, then afterward to be his disciples; and so at the last to be his apostles, *Luke vi.* and teachers of the whole world. For we read in the gospel of St Luke, that our Saviour, when he would choose apostles which should teach others, he continued a whole night in prayer, desiring God to give him worthy men which he might send. *Mark this, ye that choose officers.* Where we have a good monition, how careful they should be that ought to choose men and set them in offices; how they should call upon God, that they might have worthy men. For it appeared by our Saviour, that he was very loth to have unworthy men; insomuch that he ceased not all night to cry unto God, that he might have worthy men, which he might send; and such men as might be able to tell the truth, and when they had done, to stand unto it. For when a preacher preacheth the truth, but afterward is fearful, and dare not stand unto it, is afraid of men, this preacher shall do but little good: or when he preacheth the truth, and is a wicked liver, after that he hath done, this man shall do but little good: he shall not edify, but rather destroy, when his words are good, and his living contrary unto the same. Therefore *A good wish and profitable.* I would wish of God, that all they that should choose officers, would give themselves most earnestly to prayer; desiring God, that they may choose such men as may do good in the commonwealth, amongst the flock of God! And I would wish, that there should be none other officers, but such as be called thereunto lawfully; for no man ought to seek for promotions, to bear rule, to be an officer; but we should tarry our vocation till God call us; we should have a calling of God. *A lamentable thing.* But it is to be lamented how inordinately all things be done. For I fear me, that there hath been but very few offices in England but they have been either bought or sold: for I have heard say many times, that some paid great sums of money for their offices. No man can persuade me that these men intend to do good in the commonwealth, which buy their offices: for they intend to get that money again which they have laid out, and afterward to scrape for purchasing. But such ambitious men that offer themselves, they should be refused, they should not be suffered to live in a commonwealth; for they be ambitious and covetous. We read that Jethro, Moses's father-in-law, gave unto Moses counsel to choose men to offices, and that same counsel that Jethro gave was God's counsel; God spake by the mouth of Jethro. Now what saith Jethro, or God by Jethro, what manner of men would he choose to offices, to serve the commonwealth? "Thou shalt seek out," saith Jethro, "amongst all the people, men of activity, and such as fear God; true men, hating covetousness; and make them heads over the people, &c." Jethro would not have him to take those which offer themselves, or which buy their offices with money and fair speaking: no, no; he would none of that gear, he would not have such fellows. But I pray you, how many officers are sought out now-a-days? I think but very few; the most part offer themselves before they be called: but it should not be so; justices of peace, sheriffs, and other officers, they should be sought out, they should be called thereunto; they should not come before they be sent for. Now when they be sought out, what manner of men should they be? Men of wisdom and "of activity[1];" that is to say, men of knowledge and understanding, which be able to execute that office: and "such as fear God;" for no doubt he must have the fear of God in his heart that shall be an officer; or else he shall never well execute his office; he shall soon be corrupted with gifts or rewards. Further, he must be "a true man;" such a one whom a man may trust by his words: he must be his word's master; he may not be a dissembler, a liar, or a false dealer. And last of all, he must be a "hater of covetousness[2]." A man of activity and knowledge; a man that feareth God, a true man, and a man which hateth covetousness: he must not only not be covetous, but he must be a "hater of covetousness." Now, when he must hate covetousness, then he must needs be far off from that foul vice of covetousness and immoderate desire to have goods. This is the duty of every

Ambitious men should not live in a commonwealth.

Exod. xviii.

Officers should be sought.

An officer must hate covetousness.

[1 Marry, "men of activity," 1562.]
[2 "a hater of covetousness:" he must first be a man of activity, &c., 1562.]

officer; so he shall be disposed before he be admitted thereunto. But whether they be so or not, let others judge: it is seen by daily experience what they be, a great part of them. I fear me, that if Jethro should see them, their doings would mislike him; he would say, "These are not such men as I have appointed." But it is no matter: though Jethro see them not, God he seeth them, which will reward them according to their deserts.

Jethro would not allow our officers.

And so likewise they that be of the spiritualty, the clergymen, they must not run themselves, they must tarry till they be called. They must not flatter for benefices; and therefore the king and his most honourable council must take heed, and not set up those which call themselves: for no doubt they that call themselves intend not to do good, nor to profit the people; but only they seek to feed themselves, and to fill their coffers. And so likewise all patrons that have to give benefices, they should take heed and beware of such fellows, which seek for benefices, which come before[1] they be called. For such fellows intend not to feed the people with the wholesome doctrine of the word of God; but rather they seek to be fed of the people; to have their ease, for that they look for. If they were minded to do good unto the people of God, they would tarry till God did[2] call them, and then, when they be called, do their duties: but to run without the calling of God, is a manifest token that they have another respect; that they are worldly-minded; and therefore God complaineth by the prophet, saying, *Multi currebant quos ego non mittebam;* "There were many of those that ran before I sent them, which were not sent by me." Therefore I will desire patrons to take heed upon what manner of men they bestow their benefices; for it is a great charge, a great burthen before God to be a patron. For every patron, when he doth not diligently endeavour himself to place a good and godly man in his benefice, which is in his hands, but is slothful, and careth not what manner of man he taketh; or else is covetous, and will have it himself, and hire a Sir John Lack-Latin, which shall say service so that the people shall be nothing edified; no doubt that patron shall make answer before God, for not doing of his duty.

Clergymen must not flatter for benefices.

Jer. xxiii.

Mark this, ye that be patrons.

It is a great thing to be a patron.

Mark this, ye that buy patronage.

[1 come themselves before, 1562.]
[2 should, 1562.]

And look, how many soever perish in that same parish because of lack of teaching, the patron is guilty of them; and he must make answer for them before God. Therefore it appeareth most manifestly, that patrons may not follow friendships, or other affections: but they must see that God's honour be promoted, that they place such men as may be able to teach and instruct the people[3].

Now to the matter. These men, Peter, Andrew, James, and John, they were called from catching of fishes to the catching of men: they had a calling, they ran not before they were called: but we do not so; we order the matter as though God saw us not: and no doubt there be some that think in their hearts, "What, shall I tarry till God call me? Then peradventure I shall never be called, and so I shall never get any thing." But these be unfaithful men; they consider not that God seeth us every where: in what corner soever we be, God seeth us, and can fetch us if it please him[4] that we should be officers, or be curates, or such-like things. Therefore, thou runner, tarry till thou art called; run not before the time. John Baptist, that holy man, he would not take upon to come before he was bidden. Where was he? Verily[5], in the wilderness; he made no suit, I warrant you, for any office; he tarried till God called him: for Luke saith, "The word of the Lord came unto John, being in the wilderness." It is no marvel that God fetched him out of the wilderness; for there is no corner in the whole world where any man can hide himself from his presence. Therefore when he will have a man, he can call him, though he be hid in corners; for the prophet saith, *Deus in altis habitat, sed humilia respicit;* "God dwelleth aloft, but yet he seeth those things which be here in the lowest parts of the earth: he dwelleth in heaven, but for all that he overseeth all the whole earth, and what therein is." For though we were

The apostles came not before they were called.

John Baptist sued for no benefice.

Psal. cxiii.

[3 Thus Gilpin in his sermon before the court of Edw. VI. complained: "You should find a small number of patrons that bestow rightly their livings, seeking God's glory, and that his work and business may be rightly applied, without gaining, or seeking their own profit...A great number...keep them [the livings] as their own lands, and give some three-halfpenny priest a curate's wages, nine or ten pounds."]

[4 when it pleaseth, 1562.]   [5 Marry, 1562.]

God looketh upon low things.

cast down in a deep pit, or dungeon, as Jeremie the prophet was, yet for all that he can see us, he will not forget us; for he looketh down upon those things that be below. Therefore let no man think in his heart, I must put myself forward, I must seek to bring myself aloft. No, no: consider rather that God seeketh thee, that he can bring thee aloft when it pleaseth him; when it is to the furtherance of his glory, and to the salvation of thy soul. John Baptist made no suit for that office, namely, to be a preacher, and to baptize the people; yet for all that God sought him out, God called him thereunto: God would have him in this office of preaching.

Gen. xxxix.

So likewise Joseph, when he was in Egypt, sold of his own brethren, where he served with a great man, a great officer he was, Putiphar was his name: now when he had been a while with him, his mistress, perceiving his beauty, cast her love upon him, and so would have him to be naught with her: but Joseph, being a man that feared God, would not follow her, but rather withstood her beastly lusts, ran his ways, and left his cloke behind him; and so afterward, through false accusations, he was cast into prison. Think ye now that God saw him not? Yes, yes, he saw him; though he was in the dark prison, yet he saw him. For when it seemed him good, he brought him out again of the prison, and made him lord and ruler over all Egypt: though he lay in a dungeon, though he could make no suit for his office, yet God, when it pleased him, could call him thereunto. Therefore, let us learn here, by the ensample of this good Joseph, let us learn, I say, that when we be meet, and that God will have us to bear offices, he will call us thereunto by lawful means, by his magistrates; he will not forget us, for he seeth us in every corner; he can pick us out, when it is his will and pleasure.

God saw Joseph in the prison.

Moses was a shepherd.

Moses, that great friend of God, what was his occupation? Verily[1], he was a shepherd, he kept his father-in-law's sheep; and though he was in a great wilderness, where there was no body about him, yet it pleased God to call him, and to make him a captain over his people Israel. And this Moses was very loth to go, to take such a great charge[2] upon him; yet at the length he went, because it was the

[[1] Marry, 1562.]   [[2] such a charge, 1584, 1596.]

calling of God. Therefore let us follow this ensample of Moses; let us not take in hand any office, except we be called thereunto of God; except we have a lawful calling. Our Saviour commandeth his disciples, and also us, that we shall "pray unto God, that he will send labourers into his harvest;" that is to say, that he will send preachers. Whereby it appeareth, that our Saviour would that no person should take upon him that office, except he be sent of God, except God call him thereunto. *Luke x.*

King Saul, though he was a wicked man in his end, yet he was made a great king of God; for what was his father? No very great man, I tell you: and Saul, his son, went to seek his father's asses, and so by chance, because he could not find the asses, he came to the prophet Samuel, which by and bye, before he departed from him, anointed him to be king over Israel, God commanding him so to do. Now this Saul, the son of Cis, did not seek[3] for it; it came never in his heart to think that he should be king; insomuch that he hideth himself when Samuel would proclaim him king before the whole congregation: yet for all that, he could not hide himself so but God spieth him out; and so finally brought him to the kingdom. Here ye see most manifestly, that when God will have a thing to be done, he can find such means, whereby it must needs be done; yea, contrary to our expectation. Wherefore should now any of us go about to thrust ourselves into offices without the calling of God? And no doubt they that do so, shew themselves to have no faith in God at all; they trust not God; they think they shall bring all matters to pass by their own power and wits: but it is seen that such fellows speed ever ill, that will take in hand to exalt themselves, without any lawful calling. *Saul sought not to be made king.* *Mark the end.*

David, that godly man and holy prophet of God, what was he? Marry, a keeper of sheep: he thought not that he should be king, till he was called thereunto of God. But, I pray you, what was Jonas the prophet? Was he not in the bottom of the great sea, in the belly of a great and horrible whale? What happened unto him? Saw not God him? Yes, yes, he saw him; he had not forgotten him, he called him out again, and so sendeth him to Nineveh, to preach unto them, and teach them penance, to leave their *David was a shepherd.* *Jonas was found out.*

[3 he seeketh not, 1562.]

sinful life. Now God would have him to that office, therefore he called him; and was able to do it, though he lay even in the horrible fish's belly.

Now therefore let us well consider this, that when God will have a man to bear an office, he can and is able to fetch him, wheresoever he be: and that man that is so called[1] of God to any office, no doubt God will work with him; he will prosper all his doings; he will defend him from all his ene-

God will punish the ambitious.

mies; he will not let him perish. But and if any man take in hand an office whereunto he is not called, no doubt, that man shall have no good luck; God will not prosper him. And not only that, but he will extremely punish that man that will take in hand an office whereunto he is not called of God; which seeketh promotions, or goeth about to promote

Num. xvi.

himself: as we have an example in the book of Numbers, that when Corath, Dathan, and Abiram, would not be content with their vocation, whereunto they were called of God, but would climb higher and promote themselves, what hap-

An horrible example.

pened? The ground clave asunder, and swallowed them up, with wife and children, and all that they had; this was their end, this reward they had for their ambition. Whereby it appeareth, that God will that every man shall keep himself in his vocation, till he be further called of God. We read

1 Kings vi.

further in the books of the kings, that when David would bring in the ark of God into his city, as they were going with it, there was one, Oza by name, he fearing lest the ark should fall, because the oxen stumbled, went and held it up with his hands, which was against his vocation; for he was not appointed thereunto, for it was the office of the Levites to keep the ark, nobody else should come near unto it. Now what happened? God struck him by and bye to death, because he took upon him an office unto which he was not called. Yet, after man's reason, this Oza had done a good work in keeping the ark from falling; but what then? God will that his order shall be kept, which he hath appointed in

2 Chron. xxvi.

his word. Further, we read in the bible of a king who was called Uzia, which would take upon him the office of a priest, to offer incense unto the Lord, whereunto he was not called of God, but would do it of his own voluntary will; would promote himself to the office of the high priest, being not

[[1] that is called, 1584, 1596.]

called of God thereunto. But what followed? How sped he? What reward had he for so doing? Whilst he was yet about it, the Lord smote him by and bye with leprosy; and so this great king endured a leper all the days of his life.

These be ensamples now, which should make us afraid, if we had any fear of God in our hearts, to promote ourselves. And we should learn here to beware of that pestilent poison of ambition, which poison (ambition, I say,) hath been the cause of the perishing of many a man: for this ambition is the most perilous thing that can be in the world. For an ambitious man is able to subvert and disturb a whole commonwealth: as it most plainly appeared by the Rhodians; which Rhodians at our time were very mighty, and of great estimation through all the world. Now what was their destruction? Truly[2], ambition; through ambition this mighty island of the Rhodes was lost, and came into the hands of the Turks. For the Chronicle[3] sheweth, that before their destruction, when all things were well yet, the grand Master of Rhodes died. Now there was one called Andrew Admirall, a Portingall, he desired to be grand Master: he was an ambitious man, he went about to promote himself, before he was called of God: but for all that, he missed his purpose, so that he was not chosen; for there was one chosen whom they call Philippe de Vyllers. But what doth this Andrew? Because he could not bring his purpose to pass, he sendeth letters to the great Turk, signifying, that if[4] he would come, he would help him to get the island; which afterwards he did: but yet it cost him his life; for his treason was espied, and so he received a reward according unto his doings[5].

So ye may perceive by this ensample, which was done in our time, how ungracious a thing this ambition is: for no doubt where there is ambition, there is division; where there is division, there followeth desolation; and so finally de-

The hurt that cometh of ambition.

Ambition lost the Rhodes.

[2 Marry, 1562.]
[3 Hall, Chronicle, pp. 653. et seq. edit. 1809.]
[4 when, 1562.]
[5 The Island of Rhodes was not taken possession of by the Turk till Christmas-day 1522, but Andrew d'Amaral was beheaded on the 30th October in that year.]

Matt. xii.

struction: even according unto our Saviour's saying, "Every kingdom divided against itself shall be brought to nought; and every city or house divided against itself shall not stand, &c."

God defendeth them that be called to office.

Well, Andrew, Peter, James, and John, were not ambitious, they tarried their calling: so I would wish that every man would follow their ensamples, and tarry for their[1] vocation, and not thrust themselves in till they be called of God. For, no doubt, vocation hath no fellow; for he that cometh by the calling of God to an office, he may be sure that his adversaries shall not prevail against him, as long as he doth the office of his calling. An ensample we have in our Saviour: he was sent from God into this world, to teach us the way to heaven. Now in what peril and danger

Luke iv.

was he, as long as he was here! When he began to preach at Nazareth amongst his kinsfolks, he displeased them so that they went and took him, and were minded to cast him headlong from the rock, whereupon their city was builded: but when it came to the point, he went away from amongst them, because his hour was not come yet; he had not yet fulfilled or executed that office whereunto God had sent him.

John x.

So likewise we read by the evangelist John, that the Jews many a time took up stones to stone him, but they could not. And how many times sent they their men to take him! yet for all that they could not prevail against him. And these things are not written for Christ's sake, but for our sake; that we should learn thereby, that when we do diligently our office whereunto God hath called us, then no doubt our enemies shall as little prevail against us, as they prevailed against Christ; for God will be as careful for us as he was for Christ. And this appeareth most manifestly in the apostle Paul: I pray you, in what danger and peril was he! How mighty and strong enemies had he, which took in hand to rid him out of the way! Yet for all that

The cause why Paul was so often delivered.

God delivered him. Wherefore? Because[2] Paul was called and ordained of God to that office: and therefore God ever delivered him out of all troubles, because Paul did according unto his calling.

Peter, when Herod that tyrant had killed James with the sword, and cast him into prison, so that he thought

[1 tarry their, 1584, 1596.]   [2 Marry, because, 1562.]

he should die by and bye, yet God delivered him wonderfully. And no doubt this is not written for Peter's sake, but also to our comfort; so that we shall be sure, that when we follow our vocation, being lawfully called unto[3] it, God will aid and assist us in all our troubles; whatsoever shall happen unto us, he will be present and help us. Therefore take this for a certain rule, that no man with following of his vocation, and doing his duty, shall shorten his life; for it is not the following of our vocation that shall shorten our life.

No man can shorten his life by doing his duty.

We read in the gospel, that when Christ saith unto his disciples, "Let us go up into Jewry again;" his disciples made answer unto him, saying, "Master, the Jews sought lately to stone thee, and wilt thou go thither again? Jesus answered, Are there not twelve hours of the day? If a man walketh in the day, he stumbleth not: but if a man walketh in the night, he stumbleth, because there is no light in him." With these words our Saviour signifieth, that he that walketh in the day, that is to say, he that walketh truly and uprightly in his vocation whereunto God hath called him, that man shall not stumble; he shall not shorten his life, till the twelfth hour cometh; that is to say, till it pleaseth God to take him out of this world. He shall be sure that he shall not shorten his life, in doing that thing which God hath appointed him to do.

John xi.

I pray God give unto us such hearts, that we may be content to live in our calling, and not to gape further! And first, we must walk in the general vocation; and after that, when God calleth us, leave the general calling, and follow the special: if we would walk so, we should be sure that our enemy should not prevail against us: and though we die, yet our death shall be nothing else but an entrance into everlasting life. Again, we shall be sure, that if we will follow our vocations, we shall lack nothing, we shall have all things necessary to our bodily sustenance. And this appeareth by many ensamples. When our Saviour sendeth out those seventy men before him to preach the gospel, having no money in their purses, nor any thing whereupon to live; when they came home again, he asked them, "Whether they had lacked any thing?" They said, "No." For

The commodities that we shall have by walking in our calling.

[3 come by, 1562.]

they did as Christ had commanded unto them; therefore they lacked nothing: and so it followeth, that they that will follow their vocations shall lack nothing.

Jacob followed his vocation in flying from Esau.

Jacob, that holy patriarch, had a vocation to go into Mesopotamia; for his father and mother commanded him to do so, because they feared lest Esau his brother should have killed him. Now when he went thither, he confessed that he had nothing but a staff upon his back; but following his calling, God brought him again with great droves of all manner of cattle. These things are written for our sake, to make us lusty to follow our vocation, and to do as we are appointed of God to do.

Further, when the people of Israel were in the wilderness, they had a vocation; for God commanded Moses to bring them out of Egypt: now he brought them in the wilderness, where there was no corn, nor any thing to live upon. What doth God? He sendeth them bread from heaven, rather than they should lack, and water out of the rock. And this is written to our instruction. Therefore God saith, *Non solo pane, &c.,* "Man shall not live by bread only, but by every word that proceedeth out of the mouth of God." For whensoever a man applieth that vocation which God hath appointed for him, no doubt he shall not be disappointed of living, he shall have enough. Therefore our Saviour Christ saith, *Quærite primo regnum Dei, et justitiam ejus, et cetera omnia adjicientur vobis;* "Seek first the kingdom of God, and his righteousness, and all other things shall be ministered unto you." That is to say, let us live godly, as he hath appointed unto us: as for other things, *Jacta super Dominum curam, et ipse faciet;* "Cast thy care upon the Lord, and he will make it;" he will finish all things, for he is able to make a good end of all matters: therefore saith the prophet, *Timete Dominum, omnes sancti ejus,* "Fear the Lord, all ye his saints:" *Non est inopia timentibus eum,* "They that fear the Lord, they shall not come to any poverty." Alack, what a pitiful thing is it, that we will not believe these fatherly promises which God hath made unto us in his word! What a great sin is it to mistrust God's promises! For to mistrust his promises is as much as to make him a liar; when we will not believe him.

Matt. iv. Deut. viii.

Matt. vi.

1 Pet. v.

Psal. xxxiv.

To distrust the promise of God is to make him a liar.

Every man hath his vocation: as these men here were fishers, so every man hath his faculty wherein he was brought up: but and if there come a special vocation, then we must leave that vocation which we have had before, and apply that whereunto we be called specially, as these apostles did. They were fishers, but as soon as they were called to another vocation, they left their fishings. But ever remember, that when we have a vocation, we regard most above all the special points in the same, and see that we do them rather than the accidents. As for an ensample: unto great men God alloweth hunting and hawking at some times; but it is not their chiefest duty whereunto God hath called them: for he would not that they should give themselves only to hawking and hunting, and to do nothing else. No, not so; but rather they ought to consider the chiefest point than the accidents. Hawking and hunting is but an accessary thing; but the chiefest thing to which God hath ordained them is to execute justice, to see that the honour and glory of God be set abroad: this is the chiefest point in their calling, and not hawking and hunting, which is but an accident. So, likewise, a serving man may use shooting, or other pastimes; but if a serving man would do nothing else but shoot, setting aside his master's business, this man no doubt should not do well: for a serving man's duty is to wait upon his master; and though he may shoot sometimes, yet his special and chiefest duty is to serve his master in his business.

Hunting and hawking is not the chief point of great men's calling.

The chief point of a serving man's office.

Our Saviour went once abroad, and by the way as he went, he said to one, "Follow me:" the fellow made answer, saying, "Let me first bury my father." Our Saviour said unto him again, "Let the dead bury their dead, and come thou and follow me." Where our Saviour teacheth us, that when we have a special vocation, we shall forsake the general: for to bury father and mother is a godly deed, for God commanded to honour father and mother; yet when we have such a special calling as this man had, we must leave all other vocations. For our Saviour would rather have the dead to bury the dead, than that this man should forsake or set aside his vocation. But our spiritualty, what do they? Forsooth[1], some be occupied with worldly businesses, some

Matt. viii.

Our special vocation must be followed.

A note for the spiritualty.

[1 Marry, 1562.]

be clerks of the kitchen, surveyors, or receivers; which no doubt is wicked, and they must make a heavy account for it. For their special calling is to fish, to preach the word of God, and to bring the people from ignorance unto the knowledge of God's word: this they ought to do.

Abraham did follow his calling.

Abraham, the patriarch, had a vocation, when God called him out of his country; this was a vocation. So likewise, when God commanded him to offer his son, he was ready and willing to do it: for because God had commanded him, he made no excuses, but went and followed his vocation most diligently and earnestly. But this I would have you to note well; that they that have but general vocations, may not follow those which have special vocations. As if[1] we would follow the ensample of Abraham, we may not. Abraham had a special vocation of God to offer his son: therefore they that afterward followed the ensample of Abraham, and burned their children, they did naughtily; for they had no commandment of God to do so.

The man that hath but a general calling may not follow his example that had a special vocation.

Num. xxv.

Phinees, that godly man, seeing one of the great men of Israel do wickedly with a naughty woman, went thither and killed them both, whilst they were yet doing the act of lechery. Now in so doing he pleased God, and is highly commended of God for it: shall we now follow the ensample of Phinees? Shall we kill a man by and bye when he doth wickedly? No, not so; we have no such commandment of God as Phinees had; for he had a special calling, a secret inspiration of God to do such a thing: we, which have no such calling, may not follow him, for we ought to kill nobody; the magistrates shall redress all matters. So to preach God's word it is a good thing, and God will have that there shall be some which do it: but for all that a man may not take upon him to preach God's word, except he be called unto it. When he doth it, he doth not well, though he have learning and wisdom to be a preacher; yet for all that he ought not to come himself without any lawful calling: for it was no doubt a good thing to keep the ark from falling; yet for all that Oza was stricken to death because he took in hand to meddle with it without any commission.

No man may preach except he be called.

We have a general vocation, which is this, *In sudore vultus tui vesceris pane tuo;* "In the sweat of thy face thou

Gen. iii.

[1 when, 1562.]

shalt eat thy bread, till thou be turned again into the ground, out of which thou wast taken." This text doth charge all us to labour, rich and poor, no man excepted; but he must labour that labour which God hath appointed for him to do: for God loveth not slothfulness, he will have us to labour, to do our business: and upon the holy-day he will have us to cease from bodily labour; but for all that he will not have us to be idle, but to hear his word, to visit sick folks and prisoners. These are holy-days' work, which God requireth of us; therefore we may not be let of those works with bodily labour: we must set aside bodily² labour, and feed our souls upon Sundays in hearing of God's most holy word, and in receiving his holy sacraments. So, I say, labour is commanded unto us, unto every one, no man excepted. All Adam's children are bound to labour; for that which was said unto Adam, is said likewise unto us: and our Saviour himself teacheth us to labour, when he saith to Peter, *Duc in altum,* "Lead thy boat into the deep;" and, *Relaxate ad capturam,* "spread out thy net to catch." Here Christ commanded Peter to do his duty, to follow his occupation. Now he that commanded Peter, saying, "Cast out thy net," he commandeth also us, every one in his estate, to do the business of his calling. He will have the farmer to follow his trade, to till the ground, to sow, &c., and yet it is God that giveth the increase of the labour. For we may not think, as though we by our labour may get somewhat; no, not so: we must labour indeed, but we must pray him to send the increase; for except he bless our labour, no doubt we shall labour all in vain. The ordinary way, whereby God sendeth us our food is labour; yet for all that we must not set our hearts upon our labour, nor trust therein, but only hang upon God.

The right holy-day's work.

All Adam's children must labour.

Luke v.

Labour is the ordinary mean whereby we live.

It is written, *Egestatem operatur manus remissa;* "A hand that will not labour," saith scripture, "shall come to poverty:" that is to say, that man or that woman that will not labour, will not do the work of his vocation, shall not prosper in this world: but a diligent hand, a man that will labour, Almighty God will send him increase, he shall have enough. So that certain it is, that we must labour; for

Prov. x.

God will increase our labour.

[² all bodily, 1607.]

St Paul saith, *Qui non laborat non manducet;* "He that laboureth not, let him not eat." I would wish that this commandment of St Paul were kept in England, that these idle lubbers that will not labour, that they should not eat neither: for no doubt, if they were served so, it would make them to apply their bodies to a better use than they do.

St Paul, in the second epistle to the Thessalonians, the last chapter, saith: "We have heard say, that there are some which walk amongst you inordinately, working not at all, but being busy-bodies. Them that are such we command and exhort, by our Lord Jesu Christ, that they work with quietness, and eat their own bread." In these words we may note two things: first, that every one of us ought to labour, and do the office of his calling: secondarily, we may note here, that a preacher may speak by hearsay, as St Paul doth here. I spake unto you since I came into this country by hearsay: for I heard say, that there were some homely thieves, some pickers in this worshipful house; which no doubt is a miserable thing, that in such a house things should be so purloined away: therefore I exhorted you at the same time to beware of it, and to make restitution. Now since, there were some of you which were offended with me, because I spake by hearsay: they said I slandered the house in speaking so. But I tell you, that I slandered nobody at that time; I spake but only to the amendment of the guilty; and therefore the guiltless must give leave unto the preacher to reprove sin and wickedness. For the preacher when he reproveth sin, he slandereth not the guiltless, but he seeketh only the amendment of the guilty. Therefore God saith by the prophet, *Annuncia populo scelera illorum;* "Shew unto the people their sins." Therefore, when such a thing is spoken, they that be guiltless should be content when sin and wickedness is reproved.

There is a common saying, that when a horse is rubbed on the gall, he will kick: when a man casteth a stone among dogs, he that is hit will cry: so it is with such fellows too; belike they be guilty, because they cannot suffer to be againsaid. I remember the prophet Isaiah, in what manner of wise he reproved the sins of the people, saying, *Argentum tuum versum est in scoriam;* "Thy silver is turned into dross." So no doubt the fall of the money[1] hath been here in England the undoing of men. *Et vinum tuum mixtum est aqua;* "And thy wine is mingled with water." Here the prophet speaketh generally: and he goeth forth, saying, *Principes tui, &c.* "Thy princes are wicked, and companions of thieves, they love rewards altogether: as for the fatherless, they help them not to right; neither will they let the widow's cause come before them." These be sore words, spoken generally against all the princes, where I doubt not but there were some good amongst them; yet for all that the prophet slandereth them not, for he speaketh not against the good, but against the wicked, he meaneth not the guiltless. For such a manner of speaking is used in the scripture, to speak by the universal, meaning a great number, but yet not all, only those that be guilty; therefore such manner of speaking is no slander. Therefore I said at the same time, as St Paul saith to the Thessalonians, "I hear say, that there be some amongst you that will not labour:" so I said, I hear say, that there be some amongst you, which are given to picking and stealing; and so I shewed you the danger of it, and told you how you should make restitution secretly, without any open shame: for it is no shame to forsake sin, and to come to[2] godliness. For no doubt restitution must be made either in effect, or affect: that is to say, when thou art able, then thou must make it in effect; when thou art not able, then thou must be sorry for it in thy heart, and ask God forgiveness. This I told you at the same time, where I slandered nobody: therefore I would wish that ye would expound my words now forwards better than ye have hitherto.

Now to the matter again. If[3] a man should ask this question, saying, "We are all bound to work for our livings, but I pray you by whom cometh the gain of our works? Who giveth the increase of it?" There be some kind of people which think, that they bring all things to pass by their[4] labour; they think they get their livings with their own hand-work. Some again there be, which think that

A terrible saying to all princes.

A great number is meant when we speak by the universal.

Restitution of two sorts.

[1 It will have been observed that Bishop Latimer frequently alludes to the practice of debasing the coinage, which was so common in the reign of Hen. VIII., and was not unknown in that of Edw. VI.]

[2 to such godliness, 1504, 1596.]

[3 when, 1562.]   [4 their own, 1607.]

Some think their increase cometh of the devil.

the increase of their labour cometh by the devil; that he increaseth and blesseth their labours. But think ye that any body will say so, that his increase cometh by the devil? No, I warrant you, they will not say so with their mouth; yet, for all that, their conversation and living sheweth it to be so indeed[1]. For all they that live of usury, they have their gains by the devil. So likewise all they that sell false wares, or sell by false weight, or use any manner of falsehood, they be in the devil's service, they have his livery; therefore they seek all their gains at his hands, through false and deceitful dealing; and so it appeareth that the devil is the increase of their gains. And, no doubt, the devil taketh upon him to be lord over all things in earth, as it plainly appeareth by the gospel of Matthew, where he took in hand to tempt Christ our Saviour, and brought him upon a high hill, where he shewed unto him all the kingdoms of the world, saying, *Hæc*

Matt. iv.

omnia dabo tibi, si prostratus adoraveris me; " All these things I will give thee, if thou wilt fall down and worship me." By these words it appeareth, that the devil beareth himself in hand to be lord and ruler over the whole world:

The devil is not worth a goose feather.

but in very deed, he hath not so much as a goose feather by right. And yet for all that, he hath many children here upon earth, which hang upon him, and seek their increase by him, through falsehood and deceit. Therefore such worldlings have a common saying amongst them; they say, "When a man will be rich, he must set his soul behind the door:" that is to say, he must use falsehood and deceit. And there-

Many set their souls behind the door.

fore, I fear me, there be many thousands in the world which set their souls behind the doors. The merchant commonly in every city doth teach his prentice to sell false wares: so that a man may say to all cities, as Isaiah saith to Jerusalem, *Argentum tuum versum est in scoriam;* "Thy silver is turned into dross;" thy ware is false; thou hast a delight in falsehood and deceit; thou gettest thy goods *per fas et nefas*, "by lawful and unlawful means." But the increase that the godly man hath, cometh of God; as the scripture saith,

Prov. x.

Benedictio Dei facit divitem, "The blessing of God maketh rich."

Now there be some that will say, "If the blessing or the increase come not of my labour, then I will not labour

[1 indeed with them, 1562.]

at all; I will tarry till God sendeth me my food, for he is able to feed me without my labour or travail." No, we must labour, for so are we commanded to do; but we must look for the increase at God's hands: like as Peter did; he laboured the whole night, yet he took nothing at all, till Christ came. And yet this is not a certain rule, he that much laboureth, shall have much. For though a man labour much, yet for all that he shall have no more than God hath appointed him to have; for even as it pleaseth God, so he shall have. *Nam Domini est terra et plenitudo ejus;* "For the earth is the Lord's, and all that is therein;" and when we have much, then we are accountable for much. For no doubt we must make a reckoning for that which we receive at God's hands. Psal. xxiv.

He that hath much, must account for much.

Now to make an end: I desire you, let us consider our general vocation, that is to say, let us labour every one in that estate wherein God hath set him: and as for the increase, let us look for it at God's hands, and let us be content with that which God shall send us; for he knoweth what is best for us. If we have *victum et vestitum,* "meat, and drink, and clothing, let us be content withal;" for we cannot tell when death[2] will come, and make an end of all together. For happy shall he be whom the Lord, when he cometh, shall find well occupied in his vocation! 1 Tim. vi.

And if we have special vocations, let us set aside the general, and apply the special points of our vocation, rather than the accidents; and let us labour in our calling, and yet not think to get any thing by it, but rather trust in God, and seek the increase at his hands. Let us look for his benediction; then it shall go well with us: but, above all things, beware of falsehood, for with falsehood we serve the devil. But, as I told you before, I fear me the devil hath a great number of servants in England.

The almighty God grant us grace to live so here in this world, and to apply our business in such wise, that he may be glorified amongst us; so that we may finally come to that felicity which he hath prepared for us! *Amen.*

[2 good-man death, 1572.]

THE EIGHTH SERMON OF MASTER DOCTOR LATIMER.
THE SECOND SUNDAY IN ADVENT, 1552.

LUKE XXI. [25—28.]

This gospel is read in the church the second Sunday in Advent.

And there shall be signs in the sun and in the moon, and in the stars, and in the earth: the people shall be at their wit's end through despair; the sea and the water shall roar, and men's hearts shall fail them for fear, and for looking after those things which shall come on the earth. For the powers of heaven shall move: and then shall they see the Son of man come in a cloud with power and great glory. When these things begin to come to pass, then look up and lift up your heads, for your redemption draweth near.

THIS gospel is read this day in the church, and it shall be for our lesson. It is taken out of the twenty-first chapter of Luke, and it maketh mention of the glorious coming of our Saviour Christ, how and in what manner of form he shall come: for, as the scripture witnesseth, we shall all come before the judgment of Christ, and there receive every one according unto his deserts; after his works he shall be rewarded of Christ, which shall be at that time their judge: and there shall be signs and tokens before his glorious and fearful coming; for then he shall come to judgment. His first coming into this world was to suffer his painful passion, and to deliver mankind out of the bondage and dominion of the devil. But when he cometh again he will come of[1] another manner of wise than he did the first time: for he will come with great power and might, with the host of heaven, with all the angels of God, and so sit at the audit and judge all men. *It is certain that Christ shall come.* And this is most certain, that he will come; but we cannot tell when, or at what time his coming shall be. For the day of his coming is hidden from us, to that end that we should be ready at all times. Therefore, I desire you, for God's sake, make you ready; put not off your preparation. For seeing that we be certain that danger and peril shall come upon us, all they that be wise and godly will prepare themselves, lest they be taken suddenly

2 Cor. v

[1 after, 1607.]

unawares, or unready. And therefore, I say, this day is hidden from us, to the intent that we ever should be ready. For if we should know the day or the hour, at what time he would come, no doubt we would be careless, we would take our pleasure as long as we might, till at such time as we should depart. And therefore, lest we should be made careless, this day is hidden from us: for the angels of God themselves know not the hour or moment of this great and fearful day. Neither did Christ himself know it as he was man; but as he is God he knoweth all things; nothing can be hid from him, as he saith himself: *Pater commonstrat mihi omnia;* "The Father sheweth me all things." Therefore his knowledge is infinite, else he were not very God. But as concerning his manhood, he knew not that time; for he was a very natural man, sin excepted: therefore like as he was content to suffer heat and cold, to be weary and hungry; like as he was content to suffer such things, so he was content, as concerning his manhood, to be ignorant of that day. He had perfect knowledge to do his Father's commission, to instruct us, and teach us the way to heaven; but it was not his commission to tell us the hour of this day. Therefore he knew not this day, to tell us of it any thing, as concerning when it should be. For as far forth as ignorance is a painful thing unto man, so far forth he was content to be ignorant; like as he did suffer other things.

The cause why the day of judgment is hid from us.

The angels know not that day.

John v.

Christ knew his commission.

I will rather spend the time in exhorting you to make ready against that day, to prepare yourselves, than curiously to recite or expound the signs thereof, which shall go before this fearful day.

"And there shall be signs in the sun and moon, &c." There be some learned men which expound those tokens of the destruction of Jerusalem, but that is not the matter: if they have gone before the destruction of Jerusalem, then they have gone before the end of the world, and so admonish us to make ready, to leave sin, lest we be taken with it. As touching the Jews, our Saviour Christ wept over them, and threatened them what should come upon them, because they despised him, and would not receive God's holy word, and leave their sins; like as we do, which take our own pleasure[2], care little for him or his word: we cannot suffer

The cause of the destruction of Jerusalem.

[2 our pleasure, 1562.]

when our faults are told us; we repine and grudge at it, like as the Jews did. Therefore our Saviour, knowing what should come upon them, wept over the city, prophesying that it should so be destroyed; that one stone should not be left upon another: and so it came to pass according unto his word. For Titus, the son of Vespasian, which was emperor at that time, destroyed that same city Jerusalem utterly, like a forty years after the death of our Saviour Christ. But wherefore were they so destroyed? Because they would not believe the sayings of our Saviour Christ: they would take their pleasures; they would follow their forefathers, as our papists are wont to say. When they cannot defend themselves with scripture, then they will defend themselves with the ignorance of their forefathers; much like unto the Jews, which could not away with the doctrine of our Saviour, because it was disagreeing from the customs and traditions of their forefathers. But what happened? Their destruction fell upon them before they perceived it, and destroyed the most part of them full miserably, God knoweth: and not only that, but, as the story doth shew, they that were left, and not brought to destruction, were so vilely handled, and so despised amongst all men, that thirty were sold for a penny; and so by that means they were scattered throughout all the world; and in every country where they came, they were made slaves and tributaries, and shall be so till to the end of the world. For scripture saith, *Hierusalem calcabitur a gentibus, donec implebuntur tempora gentium;* "Jerusalem shall be trodden under the feet, till the times of the gentiles be fulfilled." By this prophecy is signified that the Jews never shall come together again, to inhabit Jerusalem and Jewry, and to bear rule there, as they have done: for by this word *calcabitur* is signified as much as, it shall be inhabited, it shall be under the dominion of the gentiles.

Now which are gentiles? Answer; all the people in the whole world are gentiles, be it whatsoever they will, except the Jews: all other are gentiles. We Englishmen are gentiles; so are likewise the Frenchmen, Dutchmen, and other nations; all are gentiles. Now the prophet saith, that Jerusalem shall not be inhabited, *donec implebuntur tempora gentium,* "till the times of the gentiles be fulfilled;" that is to say, till all they are come into the world which are appointed of God to come; that is to say, they shall never come together again till to the end of the world. Wherefore? Because they were stiff-necked[1], that they would not be ruled by God's most holy word, but despised it, and lived according unto their own phantasies and vanities: like as we do now-a-days the most part of us. Therefore we may reckon that it shall go with us one day as it went with them, which are made now outcasts of the whole world; every man despiseth them, and regardeth them for nothing, for they have no dominion more; no king, nor ruler, no cities, nor policy. And though Jerusalem be builded again, yet the Jews shall have it no more, they shall never have dominion over it; but the gentiles, they shall have it, it shall be in their hands. And this is the meaning of this prophecy against the Jews, and this God hath performed hitherto; for the Jews have many times attempted to build it again, yet for all that they were not able to bring it to pass: for God's word will not nor cannot be falsified; for the wrath of God hangeth upon their heads, because of their wickedness, wherewith they have provoked God. Further, you must understand, that not only Jews[2] were at Jerusalem, but they were scattered throughout all the world; in every country were some; and therefore they were not all destroyed when Jerusalem was destroyed: but for all that they were cursed in the sight of God, so that they should not inhabit any more that city.

Like sin, like punishment.

The cause why the Jews cannot have Jerusalem.

We read in stories[3], that in the days of the emperor Adrian the Jews gathered themselves together out of all cities, a wonderful number of men, all the Jews which could be gotten, to the intent that they might get Jerusalem again; which Jerusalem was at that time in the emperor's hands, and therefore they made great preparations to have it again: but what doth the emperor? He gathered together a great and strong host, and made against them, and in the end scattered them; so that they were without any hope afterward to recover that city again. After which things the emperor made a proclamation, that not one Jew should come into the city, neither to buy or to sell; yea, and furthermore,

The Jews' vain enterprise.

[1 so stiff-necked, 1607.]   [2 the Jews, 1596.]
[3 See Euseb. Eccl. Hist. IV. 6, and the Notes of Valesius.]

to the intent that they should be without any hope of recovery, he changed the name of the city, and called it Ælia. So that by this story it most manifestly appeareth, that the word of God cannot be falsified by any man's power or cunning; for though they had a strong and mighty host, yet, for all that, God, which is the ruler of things, confounded them, so that they could bring nothing to pass after their minds, as they would have it, but rather were banished further from the city. For they were in worse case after this fighting, than they had been before; for they had an access unto the city before, which liberty afterward they lost.

Julianus an apostate and persecutor.

After that in Julianus the emperor's time, which emperor was an apostata, for he had been a Christian, and after he came to be emperor, he forsook the christian faith, and all goodness and godliness; and not only that, but he did all that he could to vanquish and pull down Christ's true religion, and therefore he went about to set up the Jews again, and gave them liberties to gather themselves together, and to return again to Jerusalem; and not only gave them this liberty, but also he helped them with all manner of things, that they might bring to pass their purpose; and so upon that the Jews gathered themselves together with[1] an infinite number of people, and went to Jerusalem, and so began to make preparations for the building of the temple, and so finally laid the foundation. The story saith, that this host of the Jews was a wonderful rich host; for their mattocks and spades, and the other instruments which they occupied to[2] the building of the temple were made of fine silver. So these Jews had the emperor's favour, his aid and help: they were rich, and able to set up their kingdom again, and so falsify the word of God, after man's reason; for they lacked no worldly things.

God can blow when he will.

But what doth God? When he saw that no man would withstand them; to verify his word, he sendeth a wind, a strong hurling wind, which blew away all their provisions which were made by them for the building of the temple; all the sand and mortar, and such like things, which men use in such buildings; and after that there came such an earthquake, that they were almost out of their wits. And this was not enough, but there came also fire, and burned up all

[1 in, 1562.]   [2 about, 1607.]

their works; and so finally they were scattered again one from another[3].

So by these stories it manifestly appeareth, that no man's power is able to stand against God, or to disappoint him of his purposes: for Christ our Saviour had told them, that they should never come to their rule again. And so his words are verified till this day, and shall be still to the world's end: for he saith, *Cœlum et terra peribunt, verbum autem meum non peribit;* "Heaven and earth shall perish, but my word shall endure for ever." A man would think, that there were nothing so durable as heaven and earth is; yet for all that they shall rather perish than that the word of God should be falsified. And this appeared in the Jews, which though they had the aid and help of this great emperor, and the mighty power of this world, yet for all that they brought nothing to pass at all, for God was able to confound them; and so, no doubt, he will confound all his[4] enemies till the end of the world: for he is as able to verify his words now, as he was then. I would have you to consider well the causes wherefore they were cast away from God, and were made a mocking-stock unto the whole world. Wherefore, I say? Verily[5], for their wicked and sinful lives. Seeing then that they were cast out of their land, it shall be meet for us to take heed; for no doubt this is written for our instruction, to give us warning, as the epistle which is read of this day exhorteth us.

Matt. v.

God is still Almighty.

Now God hath fulfilled his word as touching the destruction of Jerusalem: he hath made true his word of wrath; think ye not that he will fulfil his word of mercy too? Yes, no doubt; ye may be sure of it, that he which promised that if we believe in Christ we shall be saved, he will as well execute and bring to pass that word, as he hath brought to pass the word of his wrath and indignation over the Jews. The temple which was at Jerusalem, was called the temple of God; the people was God's people: but when they would not come unto him, and live according as he would have them to live, he cast them away, and utterly destroyed their domi-

God will perform his promise.

[3 Theodorit. Hist. Eccl. iii. 20. Paris, 1673. See also, Warburton's Julian, and Fabricius, *Lux Evangelii, &c.* pp. 124 et seq. where all the testimonies bearing on this event are collected.]

[4 confound our, 1596.]   [5 Marry, 1562.]

nions and kingdoms, and made them slaves and bondmen for ever. And, no doubt, this is written for our instruction and warning: for no doubt, when we follow them in their wickedness, despise God's word, regard it as nothing, but live rather according unto our phantasies and appetites, than after his word, no doubt we shall receive like reward with them. And though God tarry long, yet it shall be to our greater destruction: for his longanimity and long tarrying for our amendment shall increase, augment, and make greater our punishment and damnation. But if we will leave sin and wickedness, and study to live according unto his will and commandments, no doubt he will fulfil his promises which he hath made unto us of everlasting life; for we have his warrant in scripture, therefore we ought not to doubt of it: for so he saith, *Sic Deus dilexit mundum,* " So entirely hath God loved the world, that he sent his only-begotten Son, to that end that all that believe in him should not perish, but have life everlasting." This is now a[1] comfortable thing, and a great promise, which God maketh unto the whole world. And, no doubt, he is as able to fulfil that promise of grace, as he was able to fulfil his wrathful word against the Jews. So likewise he saith, *Vivo ego, dicit Dominus, nolo mortem peccatoris, sed ut convertatur et vivat;* " As truly as I live, saith the Lord God, I will not the death of a sinner, but rather that he shall turn and live." It is not his pleasure when we be damned, therefore he sweareth an oath: we ought to believe him without an oath; yet to satisfy our minds, and to the intent that we should believe him, and be the better assured of his good will towards us, he sweareth an oath[2]. Now therefore, if we will follow him and leave our wicked living, convert and turn ourselves unto him, be[3] sorry for that which is past, and intend to amend our life now forward; if we do so, no doubt we shall live with him everlastingly, world without end. Therefore let every one of us go[4] into his own heart, and where[5] he findeth that he hath been a wicked man, an ireful man, a covetous or slothful man, let him repent and be sorry for it, and take a good purpose to leave that same sin wherein he hath lain before. Let us not do as the Jews did, which were stiff-necked: they

Deferring of punishment maketh it greater.

John iii.

Ezech. xviii.

The cause why God sware.

[1 a very, 1607.] [2 this oath, 1562.] [3 be heartily, 1607.]
[4 enter, 1607.] [5 when, 1562.]

would not leave their sins, they had a pleasure in the same, they would follow their old traditions, refusing the word of God: therefore their destruction came worthily upon them. And therefore, I say, let us not follow them, lest we receive such a reward as they had; lest everlasting destruction come upon us, and so we be cast out of the favour of God, and finally lost world without end. *The reward of the stiffnecked.*

"And there shall be signs in the sun, and in the moon, and in the stars, and in the earth." There be some which think that there shall be great eclipses, against the course of nature; and ye know that there hath been strange[6] things seen in the element divers times. Sometimes men have seen a ring about the sun; sometimes there hath been seen three suns at once; and such like things hath been seen in times past: which no doubt signifies that this fearful day is not far off, in which Christ will come with his heavenly host, to judge and reward every one of us according unto his deserts. *Suns that have been seen.*

"And the people shall be at their wits' end through despair:" men shall be wonderous[7] fearful; they shall pine away for fear: and no doubt they[8] shall be good men, which shall be thus troubled, with such a fear of this day: for you know the worldlings care not for that day; yea, they will scant believe that there shall be such a day, that there shall be another world, or at the least way they would not wish that there should be another world. Therefore they shall be godly men which shall be so used, to be tokens unto the world. And no doubt there hath been here in England many already, which have been so vexed and turmoiled with such fear. That same Master Bilney, which was burnt here in England for God's word sake, was induced and persuaded by his friends to bear a fagot, at the time when the cardinal was aloft and bore the swing. Now when that same Bilney came to Cambridge again, a whole year after, he was in such an anguish and agony, so that nothing did him good, neither eating nor drinking, nor any other communication of God's *Good men shall by mourning foreshew the end.* *Bilney bare a fagot.*

[6 great, 1562.—Many accounts of "strange things seen in the element divers times" are given by Wolff, in his *Lectiones Memorabiles, &c.* See also a treatise, "Of the end of this world," translated from the Latin of Scheltco à Jueren, of Emden, by Thomas Rogers, pp. 9, et seq. London, 1589.]

[7 wonderful, 1562.]   [8 these, 1562.]

word; for he thought that all the whole scriptures were against him, and sounded to his condemnation. So that I many a time communed with him, (for I was familiarly acquainted with him;) but all things whatsoever any man could allege to his comfort, seemed unto him to make against him. Yet for all that, afterwards he came again: God endued him with such strength and perfectness of faith, that he not only confessed his faith, the gospel of our Saviour Jesus Christ, but also suffered his body to be burnt for that same gospel's sake, which we now preach in England. Martin Luther, that wonderful instrument of God, through whom God hath opened the light of his holy word unto the world, which was a long time hid in corners and neglected, he writeth of himself[1], that he hath been sometimes in such an agony of the spirit, that he felt nothing but trembling and fearfulness. And I myself know two or three at this present hour which be in this case.

<small>Martin Luther felt the horror of the end.</small>

But as concerning the ungodly, they say, *Pax et tuta omnia*, all things are well with them; they care for no more but for this world: like as in the flood time, they were careless at all, they thought all things were cock-sure, till at such time when the flood fell upon their heads. And so it is at this time with the ungodly too: they care not for this day of judgment, it grieveth them not, till it fall upon their heads one day. It is said in scripture that God "leadeth into hell, and bringeth up again:" and so it is with such fearful men; for God doth cast them into hell, he hideth himself from them; but at the length he bringeth them out again, and stablisheth them with a constant faith, so that they may be sure of their salvation and everlasting life. I knew once a woman that was seventeen years in such an exercise and fear, but at the length she recovered again; and God endued her with a strong and stedfast faith in the end. Therefore, no doubt, these be warnings wherewith the Almighty God warneth us to make ready against that horrible and fearful day; which day, no doubt, is not far off. For the world was ordained of God to endure, as scripture and all learned men agree, six thousand years: now of this number are gone five thousand five hundred fifty-two, so that there

<small>Before the flood men were careless.</small>

<small>1 Sam. ii.</small>

<small>A woman afflicted in conscience.</small>

<small>The time of the world.</small>

[1 See Melchior Adam, Vitæ German. Theologorum, p. 134. Francof. 1653.]

is left only four hundred and fifty lacking two: and this is but a little time; and yet this time shall be shortened, as scripture plainly witnesseth, for the elect's sake: so that peradventure it may come in my days, as old as I am; or in our children's days. Therefore let us begin to strive and fight betimes with sin: let us not set all our hearts and minds upon this world; for, no doubt, this day, whensoever it shall come, will be wonderous[2] fearful unto all mankind, and specially unto the wicked. There will be great alterations at that day; there will be hurly burly, like as ye see in a man when he dieth. What deformity appeareth; how he stretcheth out all his members; what a winding is there, so that all his body cometh out of frame! So will it be at this fearful, horrible day: there will be such alterations of the earth, and the element; they will lose their former nature, and be endued with another nature. *(The end compared to a man's death.)*

"And then shall they see the Son of man come in a cloud with power and great glory." Certain it is, that he shall come to judge, but we cannot tell the time when he will come: therefore, seeing that he will come, let us make ready, lest he find us unprepared. And take this for a rule, that as he findeth us, so he shall judge us. St Paul to the Thessalonians, when he speaketh of the resurrection of the good, saith, "That at the same day the trumpet shall blow, and all shall rise which died since the world began; then they that shall be found alive upon the earth shall be changed suddenly, and shall be rapt up into the air, and so meet Christ our Saviour." All those, I say, that be content to strive and fight with sin, that will not be ruled by sin, these shall in such wise be taken up in the air and meet with Christ, and so shall come down with him again. But as for the other sort, which be wicked, and have a delight in wickedness, and will not leave it, but rather go forwards in all mischief, they shall be left upon the earth with the devils, until they be judged. And after that they have received their sentence, they shall go to hell with the devil and all his angels, and there be punished for their sins in hellish fire, world without end: for so it is written, *Vermis eorum non moritur;* "Their worm dieth not." *(1 Thess. iv. The manner of our resurrection. The just shall come with Christ to judge the unjust.)*

"The sun shall be darkened, and the moon shall not give

[2 wonderful, 1562.]

her light." Ye shall not take these words so, as though the sun and moon should be obscured or darkened, their light being taken from them. But it is to be understood, that through the brightness of his glory they shall be obscured and darkened. The sun, no doubt, will shine, but her light shall not be seen, because of the brightness of his glory; like as when ye set a burning candle in the sun, the candle burneth indeed, but her light is not seen, because of the brightness of the sun. So it will be at that time with the sun: for though she be the brightest and clearest creature above all others, yet for all that, Christ with his glory and majesty will obscure her; for his light, that he shall bring with him, shall be so bright that the other shall not be seen. And this his coming shall be wonderful comfortable and joyful unto them which are prepared, or chosen to everlasting life: unto them, I say, that be content to leave their sins and wickedness here in this world, and live conformable to God and his holy word; which are not proud or stout; not covetous, or whoremongers; or if they have been so, they will leave it, and do no more so; they are sorry for it from the bottom of their hearts. Also[1], they that forsake all manner of falsehood, or slothfulness, and all manner of vices, as gluttony, lechery, swearing; and all[2] that be content to wrestle with sin; they, I say[3], shall rejoice at that time and be merry beyond all measure. And this is the thing wherefore all godly and faithful people pray in this petition, *Adveniat regnum tuum;* "Thy kingdom come:" they desire of God the Almighty, that his kingdom, that is to say, the last day may come; that they may be once delivered from their sins, and live with him everlastingly world without end.

This interpretation is true, but not the meaning of the place.

The end shall be fearful.

As for the other part, this shall be a heavy and fearful coming unto them that intend not to leave their sins and wickedness, but rather will take their pleasures here, in this world: it shall be a heinous sentence unto them, when he shall say unto them, *Ite maledicti in ignem æternum;* "Go, ye cursed, into everlasting fire, which is prepared for the devil and all his angels. Get you hence from me; for ye might have been saved, but ye would not; ye despised my words and commandments; ye regarded more your own pleasure than

Matt. xxv.

[1 Item, they, 1562.]   [2 they, I say, 1562.]
[3 they shall, 1562.]

that which I had commanded you. Hence, therefore, get
you hence to the devil and all his angels, after whose will
and commandments ye have lived; his reward therefore ye
shall have." Of such manner Christ our Saviour will talk
with the ungodly, and in the end send them to everlasting
damnation. And this shall be an heavy burthen for them:
and though they can cloke and hide their sins in this world, *At the end all shall be open.*
yet for all that God will open their wickedness and filthy
living at that day, where all the world shall know it, and
where they shall not be able to hide themselves or their sins.

This day will be like unto a parliament. Ye know, when
things are amiss in a realm, or out of order, all they that be
good-hearted, that love godliness, they wish for a parliament:
these would fain have that all the rulers of the realm should
come together, and bring all things in good order again.
For ye know that parliaments are kept only for this purpose, that things which be amiss may be amended. And
so it will be at this last day, at this general parliament,
where God himself with all his heavenly power will be
present, and oversee all things, and hear all causes, so that
nothing shall escape him: for then all these things which
the devil hath brought out of order, they shall be amended;
and the devil shall not be able afterward to corrupt them
any further; but all things shall be well for ever. Let us,
therefore, ever have in fresh remembrance this day, that it
will be a heavy day unto them that be wicked; and again,
a joyful, pleasant day unto them that have no delight in *The end shall be gainful to the godly.*
wickedness. Therefore Christ saith, *Erigite capita vestra,*
"When ye see these things, then hold up your heads;" that *Luke xxi.*
is to say, "Be merry and rejoice:" for ye know, when we
be merrily disposed, we hold up our heads, and laugh. So
Christ biddeth us to hold up our heads, that is to say, to be
merry; "for our redemption is come near." So Christ comforteth us, and maketh us to hold up our heads, for our redemption is come nearer than it was before.

What! Hath he not redeemed us before by his death
and passion? How chanceth it then, that our redemption is
come nearer? Truly[4], Christ redeemed us before, indeed,
by his death and passion: yet it appeareth not unto us who
it is that shall be saved or damned; for we see the good and

[4 Marry, 1562.]

the bad bear both the name of Christians. Good and bad, faithful and unfaithful, are baptized in the name of Christ; so likewise they go to the communion; so that there is no great difference here in this world between the elect and reprobate: for the very unfaithful give alms, and do such outward acts which seem unto us to be good, and to be done with a good heart, when it is nothing less. So that, I say, we cannot tell, as long as we be here in this world, which be elect, and which not. But at the last day, then it shall appear who is he that shall be saved; and again, who shall be damned. And therefore Christ saith, "our redemption draweth near;" that is to say, it shall appear unto the whole world that we be the children of God. Therefore his coming will be a glad and joyful coming unto the faithful, for they shall be the children of God; they shall be delivered and rid out of all miseries and calamities. But the unfaithful shall fall to desperation at that day: they that take their pleasures here, they that remember not this day, they shall be condemned with the irrevocable[1] and unchangeable judgment of God. And they shall not need any men of law, to go about to defend or discern their causes. No, no; the men of law shall not be troubled at that day in defending of other men's causes; but rather they themselves shall be called to make an account for their doings, and there they shall be judged; so that they shall not be able to speak any thing against it, for their own hearts and consciences shall and will condemn them.

The meaning of Christ's words.

Men of law shall not be troubled with other men's matters at the end.

And though this great and general day come not in our time, yet let us consider that we shall die, and that we have but a short time to live here in this world. And as we die, so we shall rise again. If we die in the state of damnation, we shall rise in that same estate: again, if we die in the state of salvation, we shall rise again in that same estate, and come to everlasting felicity, both soul and body. For if we die now in the state of salvation, then at the last general day of judgment we shall hear this joyful sentence, proceeding out of the mouth of our Saviour Christ, when he shall[2] say, *Venite, benedicti Patris mei, possidete regnum paratum vobis ab exordio mundi;* "Come, ye blessed of my Father, possess that kingdom which is prepared for you from the beginning of the world." And though we have much

There is no purgatory.

Matt. xxv.

[¹ irrefragable, 1562.]   [² will, 1562.]

misery here in this world, though it goeth hard with us, though we must bite on the bridle, yet for all that we must be content; for we shall be sure of our deliverance, we shall be sure that our salvation is not far off. And, no doubt, they that will wrestle with sin, and strive and fight with it, they shall have the assistance of God; he will help them, he will not forsake them; he will strengthen them, so that they shall be able to live uprightly: and though they shall not be able to fulfil the laws of God to the uttermost, yet for all that God will take their doings in good part for Christ his Son's sake, in whose name all faithful people do their good works; and so for his sake they be acceptable unto God, and in the end they shall be delivered out of all miseries and troubles, and come to the bliss of everlasting joy and felicity. *He that will fight shall have help.*

I pray God, that we may be of the number of those, which shall hear this joyful and most comfortable voice of Christ our Saviour when he will say, *Venite, benedicti Patris,* "Come, ye blessed of my Father, possess the kingdom which is prepared for you before the foundation of the world was laid!" There be a great number amongst the christian people, which in the Lord's prayer, when they pray, "Thy kingdom come," pray that this day may come; but yet, for all that, they are drowned in the world: they say the words with their lips, but they cannot tell what is the meaning of it; they speak it only with their tongue: which saying indeed is to no purpose. But that man or woman that saith these words, "Thy kingdom come," with a faithful heart, no doubt he desireth in very deed that God will come to judgment, and amend all things in this world, and to pull down Satan, that old serpent, under our feet. But there be a great number of us which be not ready. Some have lived in this world fifty years, some sixty; yet for all that they be nothing prepared towards his coming; they think ever he will not come yet. But I tell you that though his general coming be not yet, yet for all that he will come one day, and take us out of this world. And, no doubt, as he findeth us, so we shall have: if he find us ready, and in the state of salvation, no doubt we shall be saved for ever, world without end. Again, if he find us in the state of damnation, we shall be damned world without end: there is no remedy, after we be *Some do not know what they ask in prayer.* *He will come to us by death.*

once past this world; no penance will help then, nor nothing that man is able to do for us. Therefore it is meet for every one of us to take heed betimes. Let us not tarry too long with our amendment, lest peradventure we shall come too short; for no doubt we shall be rewarded according unto our deserts.

But there be some, and hath been a great number of us, which have trusted in masses and pilgrimages, in setting up candles, and such like foolishness; but I tell you, all this gear will not help, it is to no purpose: for if all the masses which were said in all Christendom since the mass began, if all these masses, I say, were bestowed upon one man to bring him out of the state of damnation, it were all to no purpose and to no effect. Therefore let us not put our hope and trust in such fooleries; for if we do, no doubt we shall deceive ourselves. Again, there be some people which defer and delay their amendments of life, till such time as they shall die; then they take in hand to leave sin, when they are not able to do any more: they will take their pleasure as long as they be able to have it; they think it be time enough to repent at the last hour, when they shall depart, and forsake this world. Such people do very naughtily; and no doubt they be in a dangerous state: for they are not sure whether they shall have at that same last time grace, or not, to repent and be sorry for their sins. Peradventure their hearts shall be so hardened in sin and wickedness, that they shall not be able to repent or be sorry for their faults. Therefore, the best and surest way is to repent betimes, while we have time; and to be sorry for our wickedness, and to take an earnest mind and purpose to leave sin. If[1] we do so, then no doubt we shall be taken up with Christ, and dwell with him in heaven everlastingly, in great honour and glory, where we shall have such joy, which no tongue can express, no eyes hath seen, nor ears hath heard the inestimable felicities and treasures which God hath laid up for his faithful. And like as our pleasure and joy shall be inestimable, if we repent betimes and leave sin; so likewise the pains of them that will not leave sin, but ever go forward in the same, shall be inestimable and intolerable[2]; their pains shall be intolerable, and yet they shall bear them. There-

The mass is but a foolery.

The surest way.

1 Cor. ii.

[1 when, 1562.]   [2 intolerable too, 1562.]

fore let every man take heed how he spendeth his time, how he taketh his pleasure in this world; for like as the general great day shall be uncertain, so also our particular day, when we shall depart this world, shall be uncertain. Peradventure some of us shall die to-morrow or the next day: therefore it shall be meet and necessary for us to make ready, lest we be taken suddenly unawares. Our end shall be uncertain.

"And then shall they see the Son of man come in a cloud with power and great glory." St Paul to the Thessalonians setteth out the coming of Christ and our resurrection; but he speaketh in the same place only of the rising of the good and faithful that shall be saved. But the holy scripture in other places witnesseth, that the wicked shall rise too, and shall receive their sentence of Christ, and so go to hell, where they shall be punished world without end. Now St Paul's words be these: "This say we unto you in the word of the Lord, that we which shall live and shall remain in the coming of the Lord, shall not prevent[3] them which sleep. For the Lord himself shall descend from heaven with a shout, and the voice of the archangel and trump of God, and the dead in Christ shall arise first: then we which shall live, even we which shall remain, shall be caught up with them also in the clouds to meet the Lord in the air; and so shall we ever be with the Lord. Wherefore comfort yourselves one another with these words." By these words of St Paul it appeareth, that they which died in the beginning of the world shall be as soon by Christ[4] as they which shall be alive here at the time of his coming. I would have you to note well the manner of speaking which St Paul useth: he speaketh like as if the last day should have been come in his time. Now, when St Paul thought that this day should have been come in his time, how much more shall we think that it shall be in our time! For no doubt he will come, and it is not long thereunto; as it appeareth by all scriptures which make mention of this day. It will come, but it shall come suddenly, unawares, "as a thief in the night." For a thief, when he intendeth a robbery, to rob a man's house, to break up his chests, and take away his goods, he giveth him not warning; he letteth not the good man of the 1 Thess. iv. St Paul thought the last days might come in his days. The last day compared to a thief.

[3 come before, 1562.]
[4 shall as soon be saved by Christ, 1607.]

house know at what time he intendeth to come; but rather he intendeth to spy such a time that no man shall be ware of him. So, no doubt, this last day will come one day suddenly upon our heads, before we be ware of it; like as the fire fell down from heaven upon the Sodomites unlooked for: they thought that all things were well, therefore they took their pleasures, till at such time when the fire fell down from heaven and burned them up all, with all their substance and goods. So likewise as it happened unto the first world, which would not amend their lives, but followed their carnal lusts and appetites; God sent the flood upon their heads, and so destroyed them all together. Therefore let us take heed lest this great day do fall upon us, like as the flood and fire fell upon the world, and upon the Sodomites. St Jerome, that holy man, writeth in a place, that he thought ever he heard this trumpet of God and the archangel blow. I would wish that we would follow the ensample of Jerome in that point; that we would be so fearful lest this day come upon us unawares!

St Jerome looked for the end.

" And he shewed them a similitude: Behold the fig-tree, and all the trees; when they shoot forth their buds, ye see and know of your ownselves that summer is then near at hand." So when ye see the tokens which shall go before this fearful day, it is time to make ready. But here a man might ask a question, saying, " I pray you, wherein standeth this preparation? How shall I make me ready?" About this matter hath been great strife; for there hath been an infinite number, and there be some yet at this time, which think that this readiness standeth in masses, in setting up candles, in going of pilgrimage; and in such like gear[1] they thought to be made ready towards that day, and so to be made worthy to stand before the Son of man, that is, before our Saviour Christ. But I tell you, this was not the right way to make ready. Christ our Saviour he sheweth us how we shall make ready ourselves, saying: "Take heed to yourselves, lest at any time your hearts be overcome with surfeiting, and drunkenness, and cares of this world, and so this day come upon you unawares: for as a snare shall it come upon all them that dwell upon the face of the whole world. Watch ye therefore continually, and pray, that ye may escape

A good doctrine to teach us to be ready against that day of judgment.

[1 things, 1607.]

all those things that shall come; and that you may stand before the Son of man." Here Christ sheweth wherein this preparation standeth; namely, in keeping ourselves from superfluous eating and drinking, and in watching and praying. For how cometh it to pass that the whole world is so deceitful and false? Because every man would fain fare well; every one loveth to have good meat and drink, and to go gaily. And when they have not wherewith to get such things, then they fall to picking and stealing, and to falsehood, and so deceive their neighbours. But our Saviour he giveth us warning that we shall eat and drink measurably and soberly, every one according to his estate and measure[2]. Further, we ought not to be careful for this life: we should labour and do our business diligently, every one in that estate in which God hath set him; and let us trust in God, which no doubt will send us increase of our labour.

The right way to make ready for the last day.

Therefore Christ addeth, saying, *Vigilate et orate*, "Watch and pray:" as who say, "Be ever in a readiness, lest ye be taken unawares." But those sluggards, which spend their time vainly in eating and drinking and sleeping, they please not God; for he commandeth us to watch, to be mindful, to take heed to ourselves, lest the devil, or the world, or our own flesh, get the victory over us. We are allowed to take our natural sleep; for it is as necessary for us as meat and drink, and we please God as well in that same as we please him when we take our food. But we must take heed that we do it according as he hath appointed us: for like as he hath not ordained meat and drink to the end that we should play the glutton with it, so likewise the sleep is not ordained, that we should give ourselves to sluggishness or over-much sleeping; for no doubt, when we do so, we shall displease God most highly. For Christ saith not in vain, "Watch and pray." He would have us to be watchers, to have at all times in remembrance his coming, and to give ourselves to prayer, to that end that we may be able to stand before him at this great and fearful day: meaning, that we should not trust in ourselves, but call upon[3] God, saying, "Lord God Almighty, thou hast promised to come and judge the quick and the dead! We beseech thee give us thy grace and Holy Ghost, that we may live so according unto thy

Our allowance at God's hands.

A form of prayer.

[[2] degree, 1607.]   [[3] unto, 1562.]

holy commandments, that when thou comest, thou havest not cause to bestow thy fearful anger, but rather thy loving kindness and mercy upon us!" So likewise, when we go to bed, we should desire God that we sleep not in the sleep of sin and wickedness; but rather that we may leave them, and follow his will and pleasure, that we be not led with the desires of this wicked world. Such an earnest mind we should have towards him, so watchful we should be. For I tell you, it is not a trifling matter; it is not a money matter: for our eternal salvation and our damnation hangeth upon it. Our nature is to do all things that is possible for us, to get silver and gold: how much more then should we endeavour ourselves to make ready towards this day, when it shall not be a money matter, but a soul matter! For at that day it will appear most manifestly who they are that shall enjoy everlasting life, and who shall be thrust into hell. Now as long as we be in this world, we have all one baptism; we go all to the Lord's supper; we bear all the name of Christians: but then it will appear who are the right Christians; and, again, who are the hypocrites or dissemblers.

Our corrupt nature is to covet all things in this world, but we covet not heavenly things.

Hypocrites cannot be well espied in this world.

Well, I pray God grant us such hearts, that we may look diligently about us, and make ready against his fearful and joyful coming;—fearful to them that delight in sin and wickedness, and will not leave them; and joyful unto them that repent, forsake their sins, and believe in him: which, no doubt, will come in great honour and glory, and will make all his faithful like unto him, and will say unto them that be chosen to everlasting life, *Venite, benedicti Patris mei;* "Come, ye blessed of my Father, possess that kingdom which is prepared for you from the beginning of the world!" Again, to the wicked, which will not live according unto his will and pleasure, but follow their own appetites, he will say, *Ite, maledicti, in ignem æternum;* "Go, ye cursed, into everlasting fire." O, what a horrible thing will this be, to depart from him which is the fountain of all goodness and mercy, without whom is no consolation, comfort nor rest, but eternal sorrow and everlasting death! For God's sake, I require you let us consider this, that we may be amongst them which shall hear *Venite,* "Come to me;" that we may be amongst them which shall enjoy eternal life! And no doubt we shall be amongst them, if we will be content to leave sin and

The commodity that cometh of leaving sin.

wickedness, and strive with it, and let it not have the rule and governance over us. When we have done any man wrong, or have taken away his good from him wrongfully, if we be content to restore it again; (for no doubt restitution must be made, as I told you many a time before: *Restitutiones famæ et rerum sunt opera debita*, " Restitution of a man's goods, or his name, must needs be made :" for in that point agree all the writers new and old[1] : they say that restitutions must needs be made, either in effect or affect. For this is a sure probation, that this man or woman is not right sorry for his sins and wickedness, that is[2] not content to make restitution when he hath taken away things unlawfully, against conscience, from his neighbour :) therefore he that is content to leave his sins, and to make restitution of such things which he hath taken away wrongfully from his neighbour, sheweth himself to be a very penitent man: so likewise they that live in soberness, abuse not the gifts of God, but use them with thanksgiving. Item[3], he that liveth chastely, keepeth himself from filthiness, and, when he feeleth that he hath not the gift of chastity, marrieth in the fear of God, according unto his ordinance, maketh ready for that day. And as concerning young folks, all the writers agree that, with a mean diligence, young folk may live chaste: when they be well governed and ruled, and kept from idleness, then it is no great matter for them to live chaste, as long as they be in growing. But such young persons must beware, above all things, of foul and filthy talk; for it is as St Paul saith, *Corrumpunt bonos mores colloquia prava*, "Foul and filthy talks destroy good manners and good bringing up." And then, again, young folks must beware of overmuch eating and drinking; for St Jerome saith[4], "He that is a great drinker of wine, I will never believe that he is a chaste man." Therefore let young unmarried folk

Sobriety, the commendation thereof.

[1 See Vol. I. p. 414, note: also Gregory Sayer, Clavis Regia, pp. 688 et seq. Antverp. 1619, by whom very many of the "new writers" are referred to.]

[2 those men or women are...their...are, in the old editions after 1562.]

[3 Also, 1607.]

[4 The preacher seems to have had in mind Jerome's Epist. ad Eustochium, Oper. Tom. IV. par. 2. col. 30. edit. Bened. Paris. 1706.]

Idleness is a door for the devil to come in at.

beware of drinking: and then, again, of idleness; for when the devil findeth them idle, he entereth with them, and[1] they are soon overcome. Therefore let them ever be well occupied till they come to age, and then let them be married in the Lord; for the scripture most highly praiseth marriage. St Paul saith, *Honorabile conjugium inter omnes;* "Marriage is honourable amongst all men."

Swearing is both lawful and unlawful.
None must be sworn but by God only.
Swearing and lying go together.

Further, let us take heed of swearing: for we may not swear at all, and we may swear by nothing but by God; by whom we may not swear, except it be a great urgent cause; except I be called thereunto by a magistrate; and when I am called so, then I must swear by nobody else, save only by God. Therefore they that are so used to swearing do very naught, and no doubt God's vengeance hangeth over their heads. For certain it is, that he which is a great swearer is also a great liar. But, as I said before, they that will leave such wickedness, and will live conformable unto God's word, and then believe in Christ our Saviour, trust and believe to be cleansed from their sins through his death and passion, no doubt they shall hear this joyful sentence of Christ our Saviour, "Come to me, ye blessed of my Father, possess the kingdom which is prepared for you from the beginning of the world." We esteem it to be a great thing to have a kingdom in this world, to be a ruler, to be aloft, and bear the swing: how much more then should we regard this kingdom, which Christ our Saviour offereth unto us, which kingdom will be an everlasting kingdom, where there shall be no end of joy and felicity! Therefore all they that will be content to follow our Saviour's steps, to suffer with him here in this world, and bear the cross after him, they shall reign with him in everlasting glory and honour. Which grant us God the Father, Son, and Holy Ghost! *Amen.*

[[1] it is done with them, they, 1562.]

THE SERMON OF MASTER DOCTOR LATIMER, PREACHED
ON THE THIRD SUNDAY IN ADVENT, 1552.

MATTHEW XI. LUKE VII.

When John being in prison heard the works of Christ, he sent two of his disciples, and said unto him, Art thou he that shall come, or do we look for another? Jesus answered and said unto him, Go and shew John again what ye have heard and seen, &c. *This gospel is read in the church the third Sunday in Advent.*

THIS is read in the church this day, and it shall serve us this day for our lesson. It beginneth thus: "When John being in prison heard the works of Christ." And here is to be had in consideration, of whom he had heard these wonderful works, which our Saviour did, for he could not hear it without a teller; somebody told him of it. The evangelist Saint Luke in the seventh chapter doth shew, how and by whom John Baptist heard such things which our Saviour Christ did; namely, by his own disciples. For when our Saviour had raised up the widow's son, which was dead at Nain, the disciples of John came by and bye unto John their master, and told him all things; namely how Christ raised up that same young man which had been dead already. And this is a thing to be marvelled at, that John had so much liberty, that his disciples could come to[2] him, and speak with him; Herod, the king, being a cruel man, a heathen king, a miscreant, a man of unbelief. No doubt it is a great matter, that his disciples could have liberty to speak with him; for a man would think that no man should have been permitted to come near him. For I know that in christian realms some being cast into prison for the truth's sake, for God's word sake, have not been suffered that their friends should have come near unto them. And here it appeareth most manifestly, that christian princes have sometimes more cruelly and extremely used God's preachers than the gentiles used their preachers, sent unto them from God *Luke vii. John's disciples told him of the works of Christ.* *The heathen rulers more merciful than christian.*

[2 at, 1562.]

[LATIMER, II.]

to teach them: they were more straitly holden, and more extremely handled than John was. So we read, likewise, of St Paul, which was cast into prison at Rome by that wicked and cruel tyrant, the emperor Nero; which emperor, though he was a cruel tyrant, a wicked man, and a venomous persecutor of God's church and his holy word, yet, for all that, Paul had liberty to speak with every one that would come unto him, and commune with him: so that there came unto him who would; and they might speak with him what they would. For St Luke saith, in the last chapter of the Acts, these words: "And Paul dwelt two years full in his lodging, and received all that came in unto him; preaching the kingdom of God, and teaching those things which concern the Lord Jesus with all confidence, no man forbidding him." Here by these words we may perceive, that Paul had liberty to say his mind, and to commune with his friends; he was not so straitly kept. But we see, and have had experience, that preachers which profess the[1] same word, which Paul taught, are more straitly handled in christian realms, than in times past they were, when the rulers and princes were not Christians. Christian princes be more earnest to extinguish God's word and his true religion, than the heathen were which knew not, or would not know God.

Acts xxviii.

A note for christian rulers.

But here ye may ask[2], what manner of works were these which our Saviour had done in the presence of John's disciples, which, by and bye, afterward went and told their master of it; what special things had our Saviour wrought? Answer: Luke, the evangelist, sheweth a great and marvellous act, which Christ our Saviour had done immediately as John's disciples came unto him. The story is this: "When Christ went into a city which is called Nain, and many of his disciples following him, and much people, when he was come nigh to the gate of the city, behold, there was a dead man carried out, which was the only son of his mother, and she was a widow; and much people of the city went with her." And here you may note, by the way, that these citizens had their burying-place without the city, which no doubt is a laudable thing: and I do marvel[3] that London, being so rich a city, hath not a burying-place without; for

Luke vii.

Burial without cities.

[1 that, 1562.]   [2 But now ye might, 1562.]
[3 much marvel, 1562.]

no doubt it is an unwholesome thing to bury within the city, specially at such a time when there be great sicknesses, so that many die together. I think, verily, that many a man taketh his death in Paul's church-yard: and this I speak of experience; for I myself, when I have been there in some mornings to hear the sermons, have felt such an ill-favoured, unwholesome savour, that I was the worse for it a great while after. And I think no less but it be the occasion of much sickness and diseases: therefore the citizens of Nain had a good and laudable custom, to bury the corses without the city, which ensample we may follow. *Many take their death in Paul's church-yard.*

Now when our Saviour saw this corse, and the widow, which was now a miserable and sorrowful woman, for she had lost first her husband, and afterward her son in whom she had all her hope and comfort in this world; him she had lost now, therefore she was sorrowful, and not without cause. But what doth our Saviour? Verily[4], he comforted her, saying, "Weep not." Here may all widows, which are destitute of comfort in this world, here, I say, they may learn to trust in Christ, and to seek aid and help by him. For no doubt, like as he hath comforted this miserable widow, so he will comfort and help all them that call upon him in their need and necessity. For his hand is not abbreviated, or his power diminished; he is as strong, as rich, and as mighty as ever he was: therefore let widows learn here to seek aid and help by him. Now, when he had comforted her with his words, he came nigh, and touched the coffin; and they that bare the coffin stood still. "And he said, *Adolescens, tibi dico, surge;* 'Young man, I say unto thee, arise.' And he that was dead sat up, and began to speak." Now upon this there went such a rumour throughout all the countries, so that every man marvelled at it. And John's disciples went to their master, and told him of it, what wonderful things he did. Note here, that when we hear that our Saviour is a doer of such wonderful supernatural works, it shall be a wondrous great comfort unto us. For by this his deed it appeared manifestly, that he is a master over death, and hath power to command him; so that death is in his dominion. For to raise a man up, whom death hath devoured already, is as much as to command death. But I tell you, *A comfort for all widows.* *Christ is Lord over death.*

[4 Marry, 1562.]

Death is such an arrogant fellow and proud, yea, and of so great might and strength, that he will give no man place, nor submit himself to any man, save only unto God: unto him he must obey, and humble himself before his divine majesty. And therefore it appeareth here, that our Saviour is very God, because Death, that stout fellow, must obey him; he is not able to withstand or disobey his commandments: which is a most comfortable thing unto us that[1] believe in such a Saviour, which hath power over death. And therefore, if he hath power over death, then we shall be sure that death shall, or cannot[2] hurt us which believe in him: for when we believe in him, he is able to defend us from death, hell, and the devil; so that they shall not be able, with all their might or power, to hurt us, or do us any mischief; but we shall have life everlasting. For he saith, *Qui credit in me, etsi mortuus fuerit, vivet;* "He that believeth in me, and though he die, yet he shall live." That is to say, "Though he depart out of this natural bodily life, yet for all that, he shall live everlastingly with me, world without end." This is now an exceeding comfort to all christian people; for they may be assured that when they believe in Christ, and Christ taketh their parts, there shall be nothing neither in heaven nor in earth, that shall be able to hurt them, or let them of their salvation: and so we learn by this wonderful miracle which our Saviour did before all the multitude, that he proved himself to be very God, and one that hath power over death.

John xi.

An objection.

But peradventure ye will say, "No: it followeth not, he raised up the dead, therefore[3] he is very God; for we read in the Old Testament, that Elias and Elisa, these holy prophets of God, did such works too: they raised up the dead as well as he; and yet for all that they were not gods, but sinful men as we be: though they had such a special gift of God, yet they were not gods, nor yet took upon them to be gods.

Answer by another question.

To this question or objection I will answer hereafter, and if I forget it not. In the mean season I will move another question, which is this: What should move John's disciples to come and tell him the miracles which Christ our Saviour did? Think ye, came they with a good will to set

[¹ which, 1562.] [² neither shall nor can, 1607.] [³ *ergo*, 1562.]

out Christ, and to magnify his doings; or came they with an ill will, with envious heart, which they bare towards Christ? Answer: They came with an ill will and envious heart which they bare against Christ; as it appeareth most manifestly by the circumstances being well considered. For ye must understand, that John had very much ado to bring his disciples to Christ: they thought that Christ and his doings, his conversation, were nothing in comparison of John. For John's strait life which he led in the wilderness, made such a shew and outward glistering, that our Saviour was regarded for nothing[4] in comparison of him. For our Saviour led not so hard and strait a life as John did: he ate and drank, and would come to men's tables when he was bidden; he would keep company with every-body, rich and poor, whosoever received him, and would believe in him: but John was ever in the wilderness, out of the company of all men. Therefore the disciples of John, they much more regarded John their master, than Christ their Saviour. And therefore they ever lay upon John, in exhorting him, that he would take upon him to be Christ and the Saviour of the world. And when they had heard of any miracles that Christ had done, they by and bye came unto their master, and told him of it disdainfully; as who say, "Thus and thus, we have heard that Christ hath done, wherefore shewest not thou thyself too? Wherefore workest thou not as well miracles as Christ doth? Every man speaketh of him; do thou somewhat too, that the people may know thee to be a great man, as well as Christ." We read in the gospel of Matthew, that John's disciples came once to Christ, and quarrelled with him; saying, *Cur nos et Pharisæi jeju-* *namus frequenter, discipuli autem tui non jejunant?* "Wherefore fast we and the Pharisees so many times, but thy disciples fast not at all?" They thought in their own opinions, that John's life was a great deal more to be esteemed than Christ's, because John's life was more painful in the outward shew of the world; therefore it grieved them, that Christ should be more esteemed than John. So that we may perceive by John's disciples, that they had a good zeal, *sed non secundum scientiam,* "but not according unto knowledge." For it is a good thing for a servant to love his master; but John's

John's disciples would have had him Christ.

Matt. ix.

[4 was very little regarded, 1607.]

disciples did naught, in that they envied Christ, and went about to stir up their master to take upon him to be Christ.

John's disciples did naught.

Now John, intending to correct and amend their false opinion, which they had in Christ and in him; (for they regarded him too much, and Christ, which was to be most regarded, him esteemed they for nothing in comparison of John;) therefore John, that good and faithful man, seeing the ignorance of his disciples, playeth a wise part: for hearing them talk of the wonderful works which Christ our Saviour did, he sendeth them to Christ with this question, "Art thou he that shall come, or shall we look for another?"

John playeth a wise part.

If[1] we look only upon the outward shew of these words, a man might think that John himself was doubtful whether Christ were the Saviour of the world or not, because he sendeth his disciples to ask such a question of him. But ye must understand, that it was not done for John's sake, to ask such a question, but rather for his disciples' sake. For John thought that this should be the way to bring them to a good trade, namely, to send them to Christ. For as for John himself, he doubted not; he knew that Christ was the Saviour of the world; he knew it, I say, whilst he was yet in his mother's womb. For we read in the gospel of Luke, that after the angel came unto Mary and brought her such tidings, she arose, and went through the mountains, and came to Jerusalem[2] to Elizabeth her cousin; and as she saluted her, the evangelist saith, *Saliit infans in utero suo*, "The infant, which was John, leapt in his mother's belly." So that John, being in his mother's belly, yet knew Christ, which should be born out of the virgin Mary. After that, we read in the third chapter of Matthew, when John should baptize Christ, he said unto Christ, *Ego potius*, &c. "I have more need to be baptized of thee, than thou of me." So that it manifestly appeareth that John doubted not of Christ, but knew most certainly that he was the eternal Son of God, and the Redeemer which was promised unto the fathers to come into the world. For it was told him from above, that upon whomsoever he should see the Holy Ghost coming down from heaven visibly, that same was he; which afterward

John knew Christ in his mother's womb.

Matt. iii.

[1 When, 1562.]
[2 So all the old editions: it should most probably be *Hebron*. See Luke i. 39.]

happened: for John, after he had baptized him, saw the Holy Ghost come down in a form of a dove. Further, John pointed him with his finger, saying, *Ecce Agnus Dei qui tollit peccata mundi;* "See the Lamb of God, which taketh away the sins of the world." So, I say, it is most evident, that John himself doubted not, for he knew it assuredly that Christ was the Saviour; but he did it only to remedy the doubts of his disciples. Now when John's disciples came to Christ, they did their message, saying, *Es tu ille, qui venturus est, an alium expectamus?* "Art thou he that shall come, or shall we look for another?" What doth Christ? He made not answer with words, but with deeds. He made not much ado in setting out himself with great words, but he shewed himself to be Christ indeed: for he did such miracles which no man else could do but only he which was both very God and man. I would wish of God that we would do so too; that when we be asked a question, whether we be Christians, whether we have the gospel, the true word of God, or not? I would wish, I say, that we could shew our faith by our works and godly conversation, like as he shewed himself to be Christ by his acts and deeds. But, I tell you, we be far otherwise; our acts and deeds disagree far from our profession. For we are wicked; we care not for God's laws, nor his words; we profess with our mouth that we be the haters of sins, but our conversation sheweth that we love sin, that we follow the same, that we have a delight in it. So it appeareth, that our words and deeds agree not: we have God's holy word in our mouth, but we follow the will and pleasure of the devil in our outward conversation and living. But Christ he did not so; for he shewed himself by his outward works and conversation, that he was very Christ the Saviour of the world. So we should do too: we should live so uprightly, so godly, that every one might know us by our outward conversation to be very Christians. We should so hate and abhor sins, that no man justly might or could disallow our doings.

But what manner of works doth Christ, whereby he sheweth himself to be the very Messias and Saviour of the world? Answer: He healeth all manner of diseased folks, the blind, the lame, the lepers, and all other which would come unto him, and desire help at his hands. And finally, he preached the gospel, this joyful tidings, unto the poor; unto them Christ preached the gospel. But, I pray you, how chanced it, that he saith, *Pauperes evangelizantur,* "The poor receive the gospel?" Answer: Because the most part of the rich men in this world despise and contemn the gospel; they esteem it for nothing. Why, wherefore despise they the gospel? Because they put their hope, trust, and confidence in their riches. For the most part of the rich men in this world (I will not say all) do either put their hope in their riches; or else they come naughtily by their riches; or else they keep it[1] ill: they heap them up together, or else they spend them ill. So that it is a very rare thing to find a godly rich man: for commonly they are given to gather and to make heaps, and to[2] forget the poor in the mean season, whom they ought to relieve; or else, when they spend them, they spend them naughtily, not as God hath appointed unto them, namely, to help their poor and needy neighbour; but rather to use them to excess, wantonness and pleasure. Therefore Christ saith, "The poor receive the gospel;" for they are most meet thereunto; they are all comfortless in this world, and so most meet to receive the gospel.

The prophets, long afore hand, had prophesied of these works, which Christ, when he should come, should do: for so it is written, "God cometh his own self, and will deliver you: then shall the eyes of the blind be lightened, and the ears of the deaf opened; then shall the lame man leap as an hart, and the dumb man's tongue shall give thanks: in the wilderness also there shall be well-springs." This text of the prophet witnesseth, that Christ is very God; for he hath done such tokens and miracles of which the prophet speaketh. Now, in the same prophet it is further written, how that Christ should preach the gospel unto the poor comfortless people; for so he saith, "The Spirit of the Lord God is upon me, for the Lord hath anointed me to preach good things unto the poor; that I might bind up the wounded hearts; that I might preach deliverance to the captive, and open the prison to them that are bound; that I might declare the acceptable year of the Lord." Here the prophet prophesied that when Christ should come, he should be a worker

[1 them, 1607.]   [2 so, 1562.]

Marginal notes:
- The cause why rich men contemn the gospel.
- The poor are most meet to receive the gospel.
- Isai. xxxv.
- Isai. lxi.

of such acts, and a preacher which should preach the gospel unto the poor: and therefore now, when the disciples of John came unto him, demanding of him whether he were Christ or not, he answered by his works. Like as he saith in another place in the gospel, to the Pharisees: "The works which I do bear witness of me." As who say, "I prove myself what I am by my works." Again he saith, "If I do not the works of my Father, believe me not." So that most manifestly he proveth himself to be that prophet, which was spoken of before by the prophets, and other holy men of God. John the evangelist, in his gospel, saith: "And many other signs truly did Jesus in the presence of his disciples, which are not written in this book. These are written that ye might believe that Jesus is Christ the Son of the living God, and that in believing ye might have life through his name." This is a very notable saying, and most comfortable to all troubled consciences. Jesus hath done many things which are not written, but these are written that we should believe him to be Christ; that that Jesus, Mary's son, that was born at Bethlehem, and nourished at Nazareth, that he is the[3] Saviour of mankind; and so in believing in him we shall have life everlasting. So that there was never none that believed in Christ, which was lost, but all believers were saved: therefore it is not to be doubted, but that if we will believe, we shall be saved too.

Christ's works make answer for him.

John xx.

A comfortable saying.

We read in a book which is entitled *Vitæ Patrum*, "The Lives of the Fathers,"—in that same book[4] we read that there was once a great holy man (as he seemed to all the world), worthy to be taken up into heaven: now that man had many disciples, and at a time he fell sick; and in his sickness he fell in a great agony of his conscience, insomuch that he could not tell in the world what to do. Now his disciples standing about him, and seeing him in this case, they said unto him: "How chanceth it that ye are so troubled, father? For certainly, there was nobody so good a liver, so holy as ye have been: therefore you have not need to fear; for no doubt but you shall come to heaven[5]." The old father made them answer again, saying: "Though I have lived

An history.

[3 the very, 1607.]
[4 pp. 524, 621. Antverp. 1615.]
[5 or more holy than....you need not fear, for no doubt ye, 1607.]

uprightly, yet for all that it will not help me: I lack something yet." And so he did indeed; for certainly, if he had followed the counsel of his disciples, and had put his trust in his godly conversation, no doubt he should have been gone to the devil. For though we are commanded to do good works, and we ought to do them, yet for all that we must beware how we do them: when we do them to the end to be saved by them, then we do them not as we ought to do; then we thrust Christ out of his seat and majesty. For indeed the kingdom of God is merited, but not by us. Christ, he merited the kingdom of heaven for us through his most painful death and passion. There hath been many perfect men among the heathen, which lived very well and uprightly, as concerning their outward conversation; but for all that they went to the devil in the end, because they knew not Christ: for so saith scripture, "Whosoever believeth not in the Son he is judged already." Therefore let us learn to know Christ, and to believe in him; for knowledge must go before the belief. We must first hear the word of God and know it; and afterward we must believe the same; and then we must wrestle and strive with sin and wickedness, as much as it is possible for us, and so live well and godly, and do all manner of good works which God hath commanded us in his holy laws; and then we shall be rewarded in everlasting life, but not with everlasting life; for that everlasting life is a gift of God, a free gift given freely unto men through Christ.

We must not put trust in our works.

John iii.

Everlasting life is the gift of God.

Now, when the disciples of John were come to Christ, and had done their errand, had asked him whether he were Christ or not, our Saviour said unto them, "Go and shew John again what ye have heard and seen." And here we may learn by the way, what a patient man our Saviour Christ was, which could so well bear with the grossness of John's disciples: for they had heard before many times, of John their master, that Christ was the Saviour of the world, yet they could not believe it; and so with their unbelief they came to Christ, which refused them not, nor yet reviled them, but entreating them most lovingly and gently, beareth with their weakness, leaving us an ensample to do so too. For we may learn here by his ensample, not to be hasty, but to bear with our neighbours. Though they be not by and bye as we would have them to be, yet we should not by and bye

An example of bearing in Christ.

revile them, or banish them out of our company, as obstinate fellows; but rather bear with their weakness, like as Christ beareth with the disciples of John.

Now to my question which I moved before. How could the works which our Saviour did in raising up the dead, how could they prove him to be the Saviour of the world, which was promised of God by his holy prophets, when other holy men did the same works as well as he? And this must be answered too; we may have no doubts in that matter. For when we doubt whether he be the very Saviour or not, then we cast down the foundation of our faith, and so bring ourselves to the very pit of hell. Therefore this shall be my answer: Elias and Elisa raised up dead bodies, to prove by such miracles, that they were the right ministers of the living God, and that their doctrine was the true doctrine and the very word of God: to that end did they their miracles; but they never said, "We be Christs," or, "We be the sons of God, yea, and very Gods." No, no; they never took upon them such things. But our Saviour, when he did the same works, he took upon him to be Christ, to be the Saviour of the world, to be the natural Son of God; and so to the confirmation of such his sayings he did such works. Therefore he saith, "I am the bread of life." Also[1], *Ego sum resurrectio et vita;* "I am the resurrection and the life." Also[1], *Ego sum via, veritas, et vita;* "I am the way, the truth, and the life." Yea, and when he talked with the woman at the well, she said unto him, "When the Messias cometh, he shall teach us all things." Then he saith unto her, "I am he that speaketh unto thee: I am that same Messias which was to come, and promised of God; I am he." Further, he saith, *Venite ad me, omnes qui laboratis;* "Come to me, all ye that labour and are laden, and I will ease you." So it appeareth that Christ is the very Saviour of the world, because he did the deeds of our Saviour: and then again, he took upon him to be he indeed, and openly confessed it.

Further, the time giveth it that Christ should come: for so it was prophesied of the good holy father and patriarch Jacob. When he blessed his sons, he said: "The sceptre shall not depart from Juda, and a law-giver from between his feet, until Schilo come: and unto him shall the gather-

The answer promised before.

John vi.
John xi.
John xiv.

John iv.

Matt. xi.

Gen. xlix. Shilo signifieth the author of felicity.

[¹ Item, 1562.]

ings of the people be." Now at that time, when our Saviour was come, the sceptre was taken from Juda: for all Jewry was under the dominion of the Romans; therefore Schilo must needs come. So it appeareth, that by the reason of the time Christ must needs come at the same season. So likewise Daniel in his vision shewed, that after sixty-two weeks should Christ be slain, and they shall have no pleasure in him. So ye see that, by the reason of the time, he must needs be the right Saviour of all mankind.

<small>Dan. ix.</small>

<small>Christ is proved Messiah by sundry reasons.</small>
Again, Christ raised up the dead, and healed the sick in his own name, by his own authority: so did not the prophets, or the apostles; for they did it not in their own strength, but by the help of God. St Peter[1] raised up Dorcas, that good godly woman, but not by her own power: but Christ our Saviour he did all things, *tanquam auctoritatem habens,* "as he that had authority." *Adolescens, tibi dico, surge;* "Young man, I say unto thee, arise." So his works which he did by his own divine power proved[2] him to be very God, and the same Saviour which was promised unto the world.

<small>John's disciples are rubbed on the gall.</small>
Now when our Saviour had told the disciples of John his works and miracles which he did, he addeth a pretty clause, and giveth them a goodly privy nip, saying, *Et beatus qui non fuerit offensus in me;* "And blessed is he that is not offended by me." Here he toucheth them, he rubbeth them at the gall. He did not mean John, for John was not offended; but he did mean them themselves, for they were offended because of his familiar and mean conversation. But ye will say, how can a man be hurt by him from whom cometh no hurt at all? I tell[3] you, John's disciples were hurt of Christ; and yet the fault was not in Christ, but in them. Christ lived a common life; he was a good familiar man; he ate and drank as others did; he came to men's tables when he was called, insomuch that some called him a glosser: therefore the disciples of John, seeing his simple life, were offended with him. But, I pray you, should Christ have forsaken his manner of living and follow the life of John, because some were offended with him? No, not so. It was *Scandalum acceptum et non datum;* "They took offences

[1 So St Peter, 1584, 1607.]   [2 prove, 1562.]
[3 Marry, I tell, 1562.]

themselves, he gave them none." He did according unto his calling, as he was appointed of his Father. *An offence taken and not given.*

Here I have occasion to speak of offences. *Scandalum* is slander[4]; but it hath another signification with us, it is taken for an offence or hurt. Ye may define it so: an offence is when I say or do any thing great or small, or speak any word, whereby my neighbour is made the worse. But this offence is of[5] two manner of ways: first, when I do well, and another man is offended with my well-doings. This is *Scandalum acceptum:* he taketh offence, I give him none. Again, *Scandalum datum* is, when I do wickedly, and with my ill ensample hurt my neighbour: this is offence given. There were many at[6] our Saviour's time which were offended with him, because he preached the word of God and rebuked sins; but Christ saith, *Sinite illos,* "Let them alone." Care not for them, let them be offended as long as they will; we may not leave the preaching of the truth for offences' sake, because my neighbour cannot away with it. No, not so: let us say the truth, having a calling, as indeed every man hath a calling, and most specially preachers. We read in the gospel of John, when our Saviour saith unto his disciples and to the other people, *Nisi comederitis,* "Except ye eat the flesh of the Son of man, ye shall have no life in you:" by these sayings of Christ were many offended with him, insomuch that the greatest number went from him, and forsook him; they could not abide him. Now, was Christ to be blamed for that, because he said so? No, no; for he said nothing but the truth. So likewise the preacher, when he saith the truth, is not to be blamed though some be offended with him. When Moses came into Egypt, what inconveniences happened because of his coming; insomuch that almost the whole land perished! Was he faulty? No; for he did nothing but that which God commanded him. But the Egyptians, they were obstinate, they would not obey the voice of God; therefore Moses hurt them not, but they hurt themselves with their infidelity and obstinate heart. *Offence is of two sorts.* *Matt. xv.* *John vi.*

So ye see, that we may not leave the truth to be unspoken, or an honest deed to be undone, because some will be offended with it. As for an ensample, here is a priest which perceiveth by himself that he hath not the gift of chastity, and *A good thing must not be left undone.*

[4 a slander, 1607.]   [5 after, 1607.]   [6 in, 1596, 1607.]

therefore would fain marry; but he is afraid that some of his parishioners should be offended with his marriage[1]. Now, shall he leave his marriage because some will be offended with him? No, that he shall not: let the priest instruct his parishioners, tell them out of the word of God, that it is as lawful for him to marry, as well as for another man. After that he hath taught them, if they will not believe him, or refuse his doctrine, let him marry, and care not for their offences. I told you before, that there be two manner of offences, "*Scandalum datum*" and "*Scandalum acceptum.*" "*Scandalum datum*" is, when I offend my neighbour by my wickedness, by my outrageousness[2] and inordinate living: "*Scandalum acceptum,*" when he is offended with me, when I do a good deed. But for all that, we ought not to leave an honest act, because of another man's offences. But I tell you, it is a perilous thing, and a heinous sin to do such a thing, whereby my neighbour shall be made the worse by my wicked ensample. As we have an ensample of Jeroboam, which offended all Israel: for he went and set up two golden calves, by which act he gave occasion to the whole people to commit idolatry against God; and this was a heinous horrible sin; for of it came wonderful mischief after. So likewise we read of a great man in scripture, which is called Zamri, which gave an ill ensample in committing lechery openly with a whore; whom Phinees that godly man killed: for his act of lechery was a stumbling-block to all the people of Israel. So ye see that "*scandalum datum*" is a wicked act, which I do, whereby my neighbour is made the worse. Therefore I pray you, for God's sake, beware of such offences: for so it is written in the gospel of Matthew, *Væ homini per quem scandala veniunt;* "Wo be unto that man or woman by whom offences come!" Therefore I say, let us beware; let us keep ourselves within the hedges of God's holy word, so that all our doings may be agreeable unto the same; and then, if when we agree with God's word, the world will needs be offended with us, let us not care for that, for they hurt not us, but themselves. Let us, therefore, take good heed to ourselves, lest we do any thing whereby our neighbour might be offended: for our Saviour saith, "Whosoever

Jeroboam offended all Israel.

Matt. xviii.
Agree with God's word and pass not for offence.

[¹ with it, with his marriage, 1562.]
[² outrageous, 1562.]

doth offend one of these little ones, which believe in me, it were better for him that a mill-stone were hanged about his neck, and that he were drowned in the deep of the sea[3]."

Therefore let parents take heed how they speak in the presence of their[4] children; and masters ought to take heed how they give ensamples unto their servants: for there be some masters and parents, that will speak so lecherously and filthy before their children and servants, that it is out of measure: and not only that, but they will also swear in the presence of their children; yea, they will teach them to swear. But note our Saviour, how earnestly he commanded us to beware of swearing: therefore parents ought to take heed, and specially such as be rulers over houses, or be officers: if they do swear, all the household will swear too, for it is commonly seen that the servant followeth the behaviours of his master, when they be ill; but the servants are not so hasty to follow their masters in goodness. And this swearing is so come in an use, that we can say nothing at all, but we must swear thereunto, by God, or by my faith, or such like gear. But there be some which, when they be reprehended because of their swearing, they will say, "Men will not believe me except I swear;" which is a token that they have been great liars. For every true man is to be believed without swearing: and therefore take this for a certain rule;—that when a man is not ashamed, or hath not a conscience to break this law of God, that is, to swear, he will not be ashamed, neither have any conscience to lie, to do against the commandment. For because swearing is as well forbidden as lying, and lying as swearing; therefore he that maketh no conscience in the one, will make less conscience in the other. I myself have had sometimes in use to say in my earnest matters, "Yea, by St Mary," and such like things; which indeed is naught: for we are commanded not to swear at all. Therefore woe be unto them that swear, that offend their neighbours or their children by swearing, or other wickedness! For it were better that a mill-stone were hanged about our neck than to offend any body: that is to say, he were better to be killed bodily, to suffer extreme punishment bodily: for they that offend, they be killers of their neighbours. But we are faulty, the most

The servants are not hasty to follow good ensamples.

Swearing and lying go together.

[3 cast into the sea, 1607.]   [4 their little, 1571, 1572.]

part of us, two manner of ways: first, we will be offended when there is no offence given; and, again, we will be bold to do that thing whereby our neighbour may be justly offended. But he that is a charitable man, will not be lightly offended; for certainly it is a great fault to be rashly offended, and to judge our neighbour's doings to be naught and wicked, afore we know the truth of the matter: for we cannot see the hearts of men. Therefore, as long as the thing is not openly wicked, let us not be offended. Again, if the thing be necessary and good, let us not fear offences; yet we must take heed that we walk charitably. We have a liberty in the gospel, yet we must take heed that we use that same liberty aright, according unto the rule of charity; for St Paul saith, *Omnia mihi licent, sed non omnia conducunt;* "All things are allowed unto me, but not all things are expedient[1]." I must bear with him that is weak in faith. As for an ensample, we may eat flesh upon Fridays by God's word, if there were not a law made by the king and his most honourable council[2]: if there were no law, I say, then I might eat flesh upon Friday; yet for all that we must use our liberty so that the use of it may edify our neighbour, or intermit it when it may do harm. So like as my liberty must be subject to charity, so my charity must be agreeable to the sincerity of the faith; for we may by no means leave the truth, leave God's word, which we must most stedfastly keep. We have a law that saith, *Ab omni specie mala abstinete;* "Abstain from all shew of evil." So that it is not a small matter to be a Christian. We read a story, that one Attalus and Blandina[3] were cast into prison for God's religion's sake; in which prison there were some which would not eat flesh, nor drink wine. Now the same Attalus was instructed of God, that he should monish those prisoners of their rigorousness; which Attalus did, and so at the length brought them to leave their foolishness. But we cannot do so here in England; for our indifferency is taken away by a law. If there were no such law, then we might eat as well flesh upon Fridays as upon holidays. And this law is

A great fault to be soon offended.

1 Cor. vi.

1 Thess. v.
The history of Attalus.

[1 profit, 1562.]   [2 2 and 3 Edw. VI. c. 19.]

[3 The old editions read "Baldwine:" see Eusebius, Hist. Eccles. v. 1, 3: also, "The martyrloge after the use of the chirche of Salysbury," &c. fol. xi. lxi. edit. 1526.]

but a matter of policy, not of religion or holiness; and we ought to live according unto the laws of the realm, made by the king's majesty: for in all manner of things we ought to keep ourselves within the hedges[4] of the laws; in eating and drinking, in apparel, in pastimes. Finally[5], our whole conversation should be agreeable unto the laws. For scripture saith, that we should be obedient to all manner of ordinances, made by the lawful magistrate: therefore we must spend our life, and take our pastime so that it may stand with the order of the realm. Oh that we would have in consideration these offences, to take heed of giving offences! And again, to beware of hastiness, or rashness to judge or condemn our brother; for to be offended hastily is against charity[6]! But the world is so full of offences, and so ready to be offended, that I think if our Saviour were here upon earth again, as he hath been bodily, and should talk with a woman at the well as he did once, I think that there would some be found amongst us, which would be offended with him; they would think that he had been naught with her: but I pray you, beware of rash offences and rash judgments. If my neighbour doth somewhat whereby I am offended, let me go unto him and speak with him; but to judge him by and bye without knowledge, that same is naught. And further, we must follow this rule, *Nemo quod suum est quærat, sed quod alterius;* "No man shall seek his own profit, but his neighbour's." I must use my liberty so that my neighbour be not hurt by it, but rather edified. So did St Paul when he circumcised Timothy; and at another time, when he perceived that the people were stout in defending the ceremonies of the law, he would not circumcise Titus.

Now, when the disciples of John were gone, then he beginneth to speak to the people of John Baptist: for our Saviour had a respect to John, to his estimation, lest the people should think that John were in doubt of him, whether he were Christ or not. "What went ye out into the wilderness to see? a reed that is shaken of the wind?" There was once an old man which counselled a young man, that he should be like as a reed, he should be ruled as the world

Restraining of flesh is but a matter of policy.

1 Pet. ii.

Rash offences must be avoided.

1 Cor. x.

Wicked counsel given by an old man.

[4 compass, 1607.]   [5 In summa, 1562.]

[6 to beware of hasty or rash judgment against our brother; for it is a sign of small charity, 1607.]

[LATIMER, II.]

goeth; for a reed never breaketh, but it followeth the wind which way soever it bloweth, and the oak-tree sometimes breaketh because she will not bend. But Christ speaketh these words to the great commendation of John, because of his stedfastness. There be many reeds now-a-days in the world, many men will go with the world: but religion ought not to be subject unto policy, but rather policy unto religion. I fear me there shall be a great number of us reeds, when there shall come a persecution, that we must suffer for God's word sake: I fear me there will be a great many that will change, which will not be constant as John was. When a man is in the wrong or erroneous way, then he may and should change: but *"persistite,"* saith St Paul; we must endure and stand stedfast in that which is good and right: in God's word we should stand fast, but not in popery. So that first we must see that we be right, and afterward we must stand. This is a great praise wherewith our Saviour praised John; for it is no small matter to be praised of him which knoweth the least thoughts of all men.

Many reeds in the world now.

God giveth no small praise.

"Or what went ye out to see? a man clothed in soft raiment? Behold, they that wear soft raiment are in kings' houses." Here in these words our Saviour condemned not fine gear, as silk, satin, or velvet: for there is nothing so costly but it may be worn; but not of every body. Kings and great men are allowed to wear such fine gear; but John he was a clergyman, it behoved not him to wear such gear. Peradventure if he had been a flatterer, as some be now-a-days, then he might have gotten such gear; but John, knowing his office, knew well enough that it behoved not him to wear such fine gear. But how our clergymen wear them, and with what conscience, I cannot tell: but I can tell it behoveth not unto them to wear such delicate things. St Peter doth disallow gorgeousness in women: how much more then in men! For a man would think that women should have more liberty in such trifles: but holy scripture disalloweth it; and not only in women, but also in men. For he nameth women, because they are more given to that vanity than men be. For scripture useth some times by this word women to understand men too. And again, by the word men it understandeth women too: for else we should not find in all scripture that women should be baptized.

Clergymen ought not to wear fine gear.

Men understood by the word woman, and contra.

Here were a good[1] place to speak against our clergymen which go so gallantly now-a-days. I hear say that some of them wear velvet shoes and velvet slippers. Such fellows are more meet to dance the morrice-dance than to be admitted to preach. I pray God amend such worldly fellows; for else they be not meet to be preachers!

Now I will make an end as concerning offences. Peradventure ye will say, "How chanceth it that God suffereth such offences in the world?" Answer: *Inscrutabilia sunt judicia altissimi;* "The judgments of the most Highest are inscrutable:" God can use them to good purposes; therefore he saith, *Necesse est ut scandala veniant,* "It is necessary that there be offence." Then ye will say, "Why should we then be damned for offences, when offences are needful?" Answer: When we do ill, we shall receive our reward for our illness; for it is no thanks to us, when God can use them to good purposes: we ought to be punished when we do naught. Therefore the best is to beware and take heed of offences, and all other ungodliness; and live uprightly in the fear of God: so that we may inherit the life everlasting, which he hath prepared for us from the beginning of the world. Which grant us God the Father, God the Son, and God the Holy Ghost, one God and three persons, now and ever, world without end! *Amen.*

Rom. xi.

[1 goodly, 1584, 1596.]

A SERMON MADE ON CHRISTMAS-DAY, BY MASTER HUGH LATIMER, AT BEXTERLY[1], 25 DECEMBER 1552.

LUKE II. [7].

Factum est autem in diebus illis: exiit decretum a Cæsare Augusto, &c.

THIS gospel maketh special mention of the nativity of our Saviour Jesus Christ; declaring how Mary, with her husband Joseph, came, after the commandment of the emperor, from Nazareth unto Bethlehem, the city of David, of whose lineage and tribe she was; what miseries and calamities she suffered by the way; and how poor and miserable she was, having nothing that pertained to a woman being in her case, you may right well consider: and as touching his nativity, his poverty; how he was born in a stable among beasts, lacking all manner of necessary things which appertained to young children; insomuch that he had neither cradle nor clouts. Wherefore Mary, his mother, wrapped him, as it is most like, in her own apparel, and laid him in a manger; where he was shewed, not to the rulers of this world, neither to kings, potentates, or bishops, but rather to simple shepherds, and poor servants keeping their sheep in the field. To these poor wretches the angel of God was sent, which proclaimed these great things unto them, saying: "Be not afraid, for behold, I bring you tidings of great gladness, that shall come to all people: for unto you is born this day in the city of David a Saviour, which is Christ the Lord," &c.

The birth of Christ.
The poverty of Christ.
Christ openeth himself to the poor.
Angels witness the birth of Christ.
Christ our Saviour.

This is the greatest comfort in the world, to know that our Saviour is born, that he is abroad, and at hand unto

[1 Bexterly-Hall, co. of Warwick was the residence of John Glover, brother to the Robert Glover who suffered martyrdom at Coventry in the reign of queen Mary. Dugdale, Warwickshire, p. 1054, 2nd Edit.

It is to be observed also, that, as it is intimated in the Sermons which follow that they were preached to the same audience to whom this Sermon was addressed, it must be concluded either that the Title should have been, "preached at Bexterly and afterwards at Grimsthorpe," or that "Bexterly" is a mistake.]

every one that calleth upon him. What greater gladness can be unto a man that feeleth his sin, and seeth his damnation before his eyes? Unto such a man nothing is more acceptable than to hear that there is a Saviour, which will help him and heal his sores. Therefore this message of the angel was very joyful tidings.

The angel bade them go unto Bethlehem, and to search for the child: and forthwith a great many of angels came together rejoicing, singing, and praising God for our sakes, that the Redeemer of mankind was born into the world. For without him nothing availeth in the sight of God the Father. Without him no man can praise God; because it hath pleased God for his Son's sake only, to shew himself favourable and loving unto mankind, and to receive only that prayer which is made unto him in the name of Christ, our Saviour. Therefore all those which come without him before God, shall be rejected as persons rebellious against God and his constitutions. For the will, pleasure, and counsel of God is, to receive only those which come to him in the name of his Son, our Saviour; which know themselves, lament their own sins, and confess their own naughtiness and wickedness, and put their whole trust and confidence only in the Son of God, the Redeemer of mankind, as the angels themselves testify. *Christ is our only mediator.*

Here in this gospel note, that here was singing and rejoicing for the great and unspeakable goodness and mercy of Almighty God the Father, whom it pleased to redeem mankind through the death of his only, natural, and most dearly beloved Son, our Saviour and Redeemer, Jesus Christ; very God and very man; the Son of God, after his Godhead; the Son of Mary after his manhood, which he hath taken upon him for man's sake; to redeem and deliver the same from all misery, and to set him at unity with God, the Father; and, finally, to bring him to everlasting life. *Christ the son of God and man.*

Now it followeth in the text, "As soon as the angels were gone from them," &c. Mark here, that the angels, as soon as they had done their business, they returned unto their master which had sent them. By the which all good and godly servants may learn, that whensoever their masters send them on their business, they ought to do the same diligently, and quickly to return again to their masters; not *A good lesson for servants.*

spending the time in loitering and lewdness, as the common sort of servants do in these days, clean contrary to the example of these angels of God, which returned to God immediately after their message was done. And would to God that all servants would consider this, and keep in remembrance these angels of God! For if this were well considered, there would not be so great complaints of the lewd service of servants, as there is every where. God amend it!

<small>Angels are appointed of God to defend us.</small>

We read here that the angels appeared visibly and in sight: by the which we shall consider, that whensoever or wheresoever the word of God is preached, there are the angels present, which keep in safe custody all those which receive the word of God, and study to live after it: for St <small>Heb. i.</small> Paul calleth them *Administratores Spiritus*, "The administrators and servants of the Spirit." Therefore seeing the angels are present, it is meet for us to come with great reverence to the word of God, where himself with his angels are present.

"The angels return to heaven," &c. Here I will not dispute before you, where heaven is, nor how many heavens there be. Such obscure questions appertain not to you that <small>Heaven, where it is.</small> are ignorant and unlearned. For this is sufficient for you to know, that wheresoever God doth exhibit and shew himself, there is heaven. God is every where, as he saith, <small>Jer. xxiii.</small> *Cœlum et terram impleo.* But wheresoever most apparently he exhibiteth himself to his saints and angels, the same properly is called heaven: and thither went these angels, after they had done their message, to wait upon the Lord; ready to go and do all that which he would command them. <small>The great love of Almighty God to mankind.</small> Wherein you may learn the great love and kindness of God, the heavenly Father, which hath made and created them for our sakes, to this end, that they should defend and keep us from our strong and mighty enemy, the prince of this world, the devil, whose power passeth all man's power; insomuch that, except God did preserve us from him by the ministration of his obedient angels, we should all perish both soul and body. But thanks be unto God, which never ceaseth to provide for us, to preserve both <small>Angels are not to be prayed unto.</small> our souls and bodies! But mark here, that we are not bound to call upon the angels, when we hear that they serve us; but rather to give God thanks in them, that he hath vouchsafed to set such watchmen about us. Therefore learn only to hope and trust in the Lord, and give laud and thanks unto him, like as the angels themselves do, singing with great pleasant voice, as Luke saith. This is enough of the angels. Now let us come to the shepherds.

"The shepherds said one to another, Let us go unto Bethlehem, and see these things which we hear say is happened, that the Lord hath shewed unto us." Here note the faith of these poor shepherds, which believed the saying of the angels so stedfastly, that they were ready to go and do after the commandment of the said angels. They did not as many of us do, which are so slothful that we will not scant abide one hour to hear the word of God: and when we have heard the same, we believe it not, we regard it not; it goeth in at one ear and out at the other. Wherefore it is not to be marvelled that God is angry with us; seeing we are so forgetful and unthankful for his great and exceeding benefits shewed unto us in these latter days of the world. This is a comfortable place for servants, which should be more diligent in their business than they be; considering that God regardeth them so much, that he is content to open his great and high mysteries unto servants first, setting aside all kings and rulers in this world, which are only esteemed in the sight of men. Here therefore learn, O ye servants, and consider that God no less regardeth you than the greatest lords in the world, if you live after his commandments; which is, that you shall serve your masters truly and uprightly, and not with a feigned heart.

The great faith of shepherds.

Another good lesson for servants.

"Let us go to Bethlehem," saith the shepherds. Here is to be noted in these shepherds a great charity among themselves, in that one exhorteth another to go to follow the word of God. Many folks now-a-days agree and exhort themselves to do wickedly, to steal, to pick, and to do all lewdness: but to exhort their neighbours to any goodness[1], as those shepherds did, they will not agree. Therefore let us not be ashamed to learn of these poor shepherds; to follow their examples. When we hear the word of God, let one exhort another to follow the same: and let us agree in

A great charity of the shepherds.

A good lesson taught us by the shepherds.

[1 to do any good, 1596.]

goodness; to seek Christ and to follow him according to his word; and then we shall find him. Let the curate exhort his parishioners to follow the commandments of God: let the householder exhort his wife, children, servants, and family to the seeking of Christ: let every neighbour exhort another to goodness; yea, let every one consider that no one person is born into the world for his own sake, but for the commonwealth sake. Let us, therefore, walk charitably; not seeking our own commodities, but the honour and glory of God, and the wealth of our even Christian[1]; with exhortations, admonitions, and prayers one for another, that the name of God may be magnified among us, and his will known and fulfilled. Of these poor shepherds we may learn much goodness; yea, the best doctor of divinity need not be ashamed to learn of them, and to follow their ensamples, which are now saints in heaven, and the inheritors of everlasting life. But yet we must beware that we go not too far. For we may not make gods of them, nor call upon them, as we have been taught in times past; because God will be called upon, honoured, and worshipped alone: he may not suffer any to be fellow with him; as he himself saith, "I give mine honour to none." Therefore we must call upon him only, and seek all manner of comfort at his hand, which is the fountain of all goodness; and not at the saints. But if thou wilt needs worship them, will you hear how you shall worship them? Live godly and uprightly after their ensample; follow their charitable life and stedfast faith; then you worship them as they ought to be worshipped. But to call upon them is not a worship, but a detestable idolatry; because, as I said before, we must call upon God only, and not saints. For when we call upon them, we make them gods; and then we put God out of his seat, and place them in it: which manner of doing God cannot suffer unpunished; and therefore beware.

Further, we learn in this gospel the nature of very true and unfeigned faith. These shepherds, as soon as the angels were gone from them, they laid their heads together and consulted what was to be done: and at the length with one consent concluded to forsake and set aside all their flocks of sheep and cattle, and to go unto Bethlehem to seek the

[1 of all christians, 1607.]

Saviour. Here appeareth their excellent, marvellous, and great faith; for they were in peril of body and goods. To leave a flock of sheep a whole night without a shepherd, could not be done without great danger; for that the same country, as is said before, brought forth many wild and harmful beasts, ready to devour the whole flock of sheep in one night: as we read of a lion that killed a prophet, but not without the sufferance of God: also of the lion which Samson killed, when he went to see his new married wife: also, we read in the scripture, of two bears that killed at one instant forty-two young children, that mocked the prophet Eliseus. So that it appeareth, partly by the holy scripture, and partly by other writers[2] (as Josephus), that the same country is full of such manner of devouring beasts. Therefore to leave a flock of sheep without a shepherd was a great matter for them to do, which were but servants, and were bound to make amends for all that should happen to be lost; as we read of Jacob, which ever made good out of his own flock unto Laban, his father-in-law, when any thing had been lost. So it appeareth that these shepherds were in peril of body and goods; for if they had not been able to make amends, then they themselves should have been sold to perpetual slavery and bondage, like horses or brute beasts. But faith, when it is not feigned, feareth no peril nor danger: a faithful man knoweth that God is able to defend him, and to help him in all tribulation. And here[3] is verified the saying of our Saviour Christ, that "whosoever shall lose his life, shall find it." These shepherds put their lives in adventure, yea, they put themselves in the greatest peril that might be; but at the length they found the Saviour, which restored to them their souls, and bodies, and everlasting life.

    Here we may learn to be hearty, and to do manfully for the gospel's sake; believing undoubtedly that God is able, and will preserve us in the midst of all our tribulations, so that we do that which is our duty to do: that is, to live and die in God's quarrel, and so to forsake ourselves, that we may find him which will give us life everlasting. Further, here may all those be ashamed which set so much by this world,

marginal notes: 1 Kings xiii. / Judg. xiv. / 2 Kings ii. / Gen. xxx. / Faith unfeigned feareth no peril. / Matt. xvi. / God's quarrel we ought to live and die in.

[2 For much that has been written on this subject see Bochart, Hierozoicon, Part I. Lib. III. Lond. 1663.]

[3 herein, 1571.]

that they cannot find in their hearts to forego one farthing for God's sake. Such shall receive their judgment of these shepherds, that were so hearty in God's cause, and not without peril of their lives. Therefore return, O thou covetous heart, return to God, amend thy life: consider the momentary and short time that thou hast here to live; and that when thou shalt depart hence, thou must be judged after thine own wickedness. And the more careful thou art to keep thy money and substance, the sooner shalt thou lose both that and thy soul also, which is the greatest treasure above all other.

"They came with haste unto Bethlehem," &c. Here let every man learn quickly to go about his business to the which God hath appointed him; and especially servants may learn here to do their business truly and speedily; not spending the time in vain going up and down, when their masters are absent; but rather to be diligent, knowing that they serve not only their bodily master, but Christ himself, as St Paul saith. Therefore consider this, O ye servants, and know that God will reward you for your well doing; and, again, punish you for your slothfulness and deceitful doings.

"They found Mary and Joseph, and the babe laid in a manger, according to the saying of the angel," &c. Here let every man follow the ensample of the angel, which told the shepherds no lies: so let every man be upright in his talk, and talk nothing abroad, except he be sure that it be so. For when you do otherwise, you follow not this angel. Make no manner of promise, neither great nor small, except you be able to keep it. Above all things, beware of perjury and lies, which are abominable in the sight of God; as the prophet saith, *Odisti qui loquuntur mendacium linguis suis;* that is to say, "Thou hatest those, O God, that speak lies with their tongue." But God knoweth that many things are now promised, and nothing performed. Every man is more liberal in speech than in deed; whereas it should be contrary. Likewise, servants are not angels when they deal deceitfully with their masters, and when they are slothful in their doings, not regarding their promise made unto their masters. For they promise to serve diligently in all manner of business; which, God knoweth, is not kept by a great many of servants: yea, there is none serve as they ought for to do; therefore all such are not angels.

"The same Mary, Joseph, and the babe," &c. Here we may not take heed of the order of this speech or writing; as, Mary is set before her child: *ergo*, she hath more authority than her child hath. As the bishop of Rome maketh an argument, saying: Peter is ever first named before the apostles; *ergo*, he is the principal and chief apostle, and all the other are subjects unto him. Which manner of reasoning is false. For after that reasoning, Mary should be more esteemed than our Saviour; which were abominable and clean against the verity of the scripture: and therefore the setting and placing of names in scripture is not to be observed, nor no arguments may be made after that manner, which be set first or last. *[margin: A popish argument.]*

"They find Mary and Joseph, and the child lying in a manger." Here is the faith of the shepherds proved. They had heard a voice from heaven which promised unto them a Saviour; and now when they come, they find nothing but a poor infant lying in a manger. This was a great matter to them: for they thought they should have found him keeping a state after his name, that is, like a Saviour; but they found a poor child, which, after man's reason, was not able to help himself. Notwithstanding, they had conceived such a strong and hearty faith, which faith preserved them from all such outward storms and offences. By the which we may learn of these shepherds, not to be offended with the poor kingdom that our Saviour kept in this world: for we see, most commonly, that the rich and wealthy of this world despise and contemn the word of God. Let us therefore be despised in this world with Christ, our King, that we may have afterward with him everlasting life, when the proud and sturdy fellows shall be thrust into everlasting fire. For these shepherds were not offended with the poverty of our Saviour, and did therefore stay and meddle no further; but they went forth and preached and talked of it to other folks; which thing they could not do without peril of their lives. For the Pharisees and spiritualty were so stubborn, that they would suffer none other doctrine to be taught than their own phantasies; as it appeared afterward, when they killed Christ himself, and after him a great number of the *[margin: The kingdom of Christ in this world is poor.]*

apostles: yet for all that these poor shepherds were content to lose their lives in God's quarrel. Therefore they go and teach their neighbours and others, how the Messias and Saviour of the world was born of a virgin; and how the angel of God had opened it unto them. But what followed of their teaching, or what became of it? It begot a wondering and a gazing: every body marvelled at it, and was desirous to talk of it, because it was a new matter; as we see in this our time, a great number of people pretend the gospel, and bear the name of gospellers, because it is a new thing, and therefore it is the more pleasant unto them. So was it at that same time: every body would talk of it in all places, but there were few or none that believed. For we read not that any of them went forth to seek the child, and so to confirm his or their faith; no, there was none. It was but a talk, and so they used it. Wherein you may note the unfaithfulness and unthankfulness of this world, which will not receive the great benefits of God offered unto us. The shepherds told them how the angel of God had opened the matter to them, but the foolish people would not believe it. And even so at this time: the preachers go abroad, and shew unto the people what God hath done for them; how he hath delivered them from sin, death, and hell; but the people are so blinded with unthankfulness, that they will not believe the benefits of God, nor receive them, but make a gazing and a wondering at the matter.

Faithful and good shepherds.

Talkers and not walkers are no true gospellers.

People are unthankful.

But what did Mary the mother of Christ? What did she? The evangelist saith, "she pondered it in her heart;" she weighed the matter with herself. She did not as our well-spoken dames do; she took not in hand to preach: she knew that silence in a woman is a great virtue; therefore she made nothing of the matter. She boasted not of her stock, to be of the lineage of noble king David; neither did she praise her own child, but would rather hear him to be praised of another. She tarried until the Lord himself had opened the matter: neither would she be too hasty in promoting herself to honour. Here may all women learn to follow the ensample of Mary; to leave their talk and vain speaking, and to keep silence. For what was the cause of the fall of mankind, but the unmeasurable talk of Eve, which took in hand to reason the matter with the serpent?

Silence in a woman is a great virtue.

She thought herself very learned, and able to convince him. So are there too many now which take too much upon them. Such women may learn here of Mary to keep their tongues in better order. All women commonly make much of the mother of Christ; yea, some call upon her: but for all that they will not follow her ensample and goodness.

Further, here is to be noted the temptation and trial wherewith Mary was tempted and tried. She heard of the angel that she should bring forth a Saviour, whose kingdom should last for ever. And now that he is born, there cometh nobody to visit him but poor shepherds: which seemed strange unto her, and such as might make her much to marvel at the matter, and to overthrow her faith. But Mary comforted herself with the word and promise of God, which was, that her son should reign for ever. This she believed, and therefore took no harm of the said temptation or trial, but rather much good; for this visitation of the shepherds was an establishment of her faith, and a great increase of the same. And here is verified the saying of St Paul: *Bonis* [Rom. viii.] *omnia cooperantur in bonum;* that is, "All things work for the best to them that love God."

Further, by these shepherds we learn, that God is not partial: he hath not respect to any person, neither to the rich, wise, nor mighty; but he delighteth in those which are meek and lowly in spirit: unto such God openeth himself, as Christ saith, *Ago tibi gratias, Pater;* "I thank thee, heavenly Father, that thou hast hidden these things from the wise men of this world, and hast opened them unto the simple." Which saying of Christ is verified now upon us; for God hath hidden the divine mysteries of his word from the pope, cardinals, bishops, and the great learned[1] of this world, and hath opened it unto us. Therefore let us be thankful for his innumerable benefits poured upon us so richly and abundantly. Let us follow therefore the ensample of these shepherds. Let us come to Bethlehem, that is, to Christ, with an earnest mind and hearty zeal to hear the word of God, and then follow it indeed; for not the hearer shall be saved, but the doer and follower thereof, as he saith: "Not those that call me, Lord, Lord, shall enter into the kingdom of God, but those which do the will of my Father

[God respecteth no persons.]

[Matt. xi.]

[God ought to be thanked and praised for his great mercies poured upon us.]

[James i.]

[Matt. vii.]

[1 learned men, 1607.]

which is in heaven." Wherefore let us follow the word of God; let us glorify and magnify his holy name in all our works and conversations, wherein consisteth the very thankfulness and true service which we owe unto him.

"And the shepherds returned lauding and praising God for all the things that they had heard and seen," &c. They were not made religious men, nor monks; but returned again to their business and to their occupation. Where we learn every man to follow his occupation and vocation, and not to leave the same, except God call him from it to another: for God would have every man to live in that order that he hath ordained for him. And no doubt, the man that plieth his occupation truly, without any fraud or deceit, the same is acceptable to God, and he shall have everlasting life.

Every man ought to walk in his calling.

We read a pretty story of St Anthony[1], which, being in the wilderness, led there a very hard and strait life, insomuch that none at that time did the like: to whom came a voice from heaven, saying, "Anthony, thou art not so perfect as is a cobbler that dwelleth at Alexandria." Anthony, hearing this, rose up forthwith, and took his staff, and went till he came to Alexandria, where he found the cobbler. The cobbler was astonished to see so reverend a father come to his house. Then Anthony said unto him, "Come and tell me thy whole conversation, and how thou spendest thy time?" "Sir," said the cobbler, "as for me, good works have I none, for my life is but simple and slender; I am but a poor cobbler. In the morning when I rise, I pray for the whole city wherein I dwell, specially for all such neighbours and poor friends as I have: after, I set me at my labour, where I spend the whole day in getting my living; and I keep me from all falsehood, for I hate nothing so much as I do deceitfulness: wherefore, when I make to any man a promise, I keep it and do[2] it truly. And so I spend my time poorly, with my wife and children, whom I teach and instruct, as far as my wit will serve me, to fear and dread God. And this is the sum of my simple life." In this story, you see how God loveth those that follow their vocation and live uprightly, without any falsehood in their dealing. This Anthony was a great holy man; yet this cobbler was as much esteemed before God as he.

A story of St Anthony.

[1 See Vol. I. p. 392.]   [2 perform, 1607.]

Here I might take occasion to speak of all estates, and what pertaineth to every one of them; but the time is past. I will make[3] an end, without any rehearsal or recital of that which is already said. The Lord of heaven and earth make us diligent and ready to do his will, and live after his commandment; and so to come finally to everlasting life, through Christ our Lord; to whom, with God the Father and the Holy Ghost, be all honour and glory, for ever and ever, world without end! *Amen, Amen.*

The conclusion and end.

[[3] will therefore make, 1607.]

A SERMON, PREACHED ON SAINT STEPHEN'S DAY, BY
MASTER HUGH LATIMER, AT GRIMSTHORPE, AN. 1552.

LUKE II. 6, 7.

And it fortuned that while they were there, her time was come that she should be delivered: and she brought forth her first-begotten son, and wrapped him in swaddling clothes, and laid him in a manger, because there was no room for them in the inn.

I SHEWED you yesterday, right worshipful audience, what was the occasion that Mary, the mother of Christ our Saviour and Redeemer, came to Bethlehem, where as it was prophesied that he should be born. The occasion was this: Octavius, being emperor over that great empire of Rome, at that time when Christ should be born, (as it was prophesied he should be born while the second temple stood;) now this Octavius sent out a general proclamation, that all countries underneath his dominion should be taxed, and to give him a certain money. Now God intended another thing. Octavius with this proclamation sought nothing but to fill his purse, and to make money; but God sought occasion that way to fulfil his prophecy: for it was prophesied a long time, that Christ should be born before at Bethlehem. Now she could not come thither except by some occasion; and therefore this was the occasion, namely, that she should come and be taxed, and pay a certain money to the officers. And here we shall consider and weigh the obedience that Mary, the mother of Christ, and her husband shewed toward the magistrates; that she was content to take such a great journey in hand with her husband Joseph, to shew herself obedient unto the magistrates. And here I took occasion the last time to speak somewhat of obedience, how we ought to shew ourselves obedient in all things which be not against God. I think of this matter we cannot speak too much; for it is a thing most necessary to be known. For if the parents of our Saviour were content to be obedient unto a heathen king, how much more should we shew ourselves obedient unto our natural king, which feedeth us with the holy word of

The occasion why Mary the mother of Christ went to Bethlehem.

Note here the purpose of God, and the purpose of man.

Note here the obedience of magistrates.

Note here wholesome and necessary doctrine of obedience.

God, and seeketh not alone our bodily health and wealth, but also the health of the soul! How much more ought we to reverence him and honour him, which not tyrannously ruleth over us, as Octavius did over the Jews, but most lovingly governeth and ruleth us, seeking not his own commodities, but our good estate!

Now by this occasion, as I told you, namely, to shew themselves obedient, came Joseph and Mary unto Bethlehem; a long journey, and poor folks, and peradventure on foot: for we read of no great horses that she had, as our great ladies have now-a-days; for truly she had no such jolly gear. Now he that would shew the good behaviour that was between them two, he must surely have much time. We read of no falling out between them, or any ill behaviour that was between them[1]. Wherefore all husbands may learn by Joseph to do their duties toward their wives; and again, all wives may learn by her. *The modest and sober quiet life between Mary and Joseph is meet to be considered.*

Well, she was great with child, and was now come to Bethlehem. A wonderful thing to consider the works of God! The emperor Octavius served God's purpose, and yet knew nothing of him; for he knew not what manner of man was born at that time when his proclamation was sent out. But John Baptist, that went before our Saviour Christ, he shewed what manner of man Christ was, when he said, *Ecce Agnus Dei, qui tollit peccata mundi;* "Lo[2]! the Lamb of God, that taketh away the sins of the world." By these words is shewed to what end Christ was sent into the world, namely, to take away sins. And before this, Zachary, the father of John Baptist, fell out[3] in praising of God, saying, *Benedictus Deus Israel,* "Blessed be the Lord God of Israel, for he hath visited and redeemed his people, and hath raised up a horn of salvation." Now if Zachary because of the birth of John rejoiced in God, how much more should we laud and praise God, that Christ our Saviour himself is born! for John Baptist was the precursor. He was but a servant of God; yet Zachary his father so much rejoiced in him. How much, I say, shall we praise God, that the Lord above all lords hath taken upon him our humanity, and is made man, for this great benefit! that he would vouchsafe to *John i. The cause of Christ's coming into this world was to take away our sins.*

[1 behaviour on either side, 1607.]
[2 Behold, 1607.]   [3 brake forth, 1607.]

humble himself so much, as to take our nature upon him, for this cause, to deliver us out of the hands of the old serpent, the devil, in whose kingdom and dominion all mankind should have been, if this Saviour had not come into the world! And thus his first coming is but very poorly, without any jollity or pomp; but his second coming (as I have told you many a time before) shall be a glorious coming, a beautiful coming: for he shall come accompanied with all his angels; he shall come with such clearness, that the sun and the moon shall be darkened at his coming. Not that the sun itself of her[1] substance shall be darkened: no, not so; for she shall give her light[2], but it shall not be seen for this great light and clearness wherein our Saviour shall appear. Now at the first he is come, not with glory or majesty, but with great poverty and misery, which he hath sustained for our sakes.

By Christ we are delivered from the power of the devil.
Christ's first coming was poor, but his latter coming shall be glorious.

We have here to consider the great benefits of God, the almighty Father, that it hath pleased him, through his great goodness and love which he bare towards us which were his enemies, that it hath pleased him, I say, to give unto us for our sakes his only Son into these miseries and calamities, and to suffer him to take our nature upon him, and to deliver us with[3] his most painful and grievous passion. We cannot express the worthiness of it; but though we are not able to express it, yet we must do as much as we can.

Now for to come to the knowledge of this benefit, you must consider, first, what he was before he was incarnate and made man: for when we know what he was before he was made man, then we shall know what he hath done for us. Now, therefore, you must know, that he was the natural Son of God, yea, God himself, the Lord and King over heaven and earth; through whom all things were made and created, and by whom all things are kept and sustained, ruled, and governed. That same God, that same Son of God, refused not to humble himself far beyond all measure, to take upon him such a vile nature; for he was made very man. You must not think as the Arians[4] did, which said that he

What Christ was before he was made man.

The Arians' opinion of Christ.

[[1] his, 1607.]   [[2] it shall give his, 1607.]   [[3] by, 1607.]
[[4] The Marcionites. Tertullian, adv. Marcion, IV. 40: Mosheim, Comment. on the affairs of the Christians before Constant. Vol. II. p. 330, by Vidal. A kind of Arianism, however, did exist in England at that time. Strype, Eccl. Mem. II. i. 334. Oxf.]

was not a very man, nor suffered very pains upon the cross, but had a fantastical body. And I know where there was one of such an erroneous opinion, not many years ago; he belonged to a great man at that time. Therefore, I say, we must beware of this opinion, and believe stedfastly that he was a very natural man, sin excepted. Again, we must believe that he was God's Son, not by adoption, as we be; for we all be adopted and taken for the children of God. But he was before the world began with God, the very natural Son of God, and God himself; very God's Son without a mother, like as he was very man without a father. I will prove him to be very God, because we are commanded to call upon him. Now ye know that to call upon God is to honour God. And God saith in his word that he will give his honour unto nobody; but Christ hath the honour of God, therefore he must needs be very God. And here we have occasion to be sorry that we have called upon the saints; and so deprived God of his honour and dignity, and made them *Deos tutelares*, tutelary gods. But Christ is he on whom we must call, and put our confidence in: for it is written, *Adorabunt eum omnes reges terræ;* "All the kings of the world shall honour him, and call upon his name." And therefore here it appeareth most manifestly that he is very God, coequal unto the Father after his divinity.

Christ was the very Son of God, not adopted as we be, but the true Son of God, without a mother, as he was the son of Mary without a father.

Christ is very God, and therefore is only to be called upon.

You have heard this day, in the service of St Stephen, how he called upon Christ, saying, *Domine Jesu, suscipe spiritum meum;* "Lord Jesus, take thou my spirit." The Jews stoned him, but he made his prayer, saying, *Domine Jesu, suscipe spiritum meum;* "Lord Jesu, take my spirit[5];" lifting up his eyes unto heaven, signifying that Christ is very God; which thing, no doubt, St Stephen would not have done, if Christ had not been very God. Now, this day is St Stephen's day, which was put to death because he rebuked the stubbornness of the wicked priests and bishops; which bishops stirred up false witnesses against him, and so stoned him: but well is he that ever he was born. Now, therefore, if you will worship St Stephen, I will tell you how ye shall worship him. Consider his faith and heartiness which he had in God's cause, and pray unto God

Acts vii.

The death of St Stephen.

A right worshipping of St Stephen.

[5 The Jews stoned...my spirit, not in 1607.]

that thou mayest have such a strong faith too[1], that thou mayest be ready to forsake the world, and suffer for the word of God, like as he hath[2]. And, further, pray unto God that thou mayest have such a strong faith to pray unto him, as St Stephen had. This is the right worshipping of St Stephen, to follow his ensample, and[3] not to call upon him.

A fond custom without reason. But I marvel much how it chanced[4] that upon this day we were wont to let our horses blood[5]: it is like as though St Stephen had some great government over the horses, which thing no doubt is a vain invention of man. We ought to commit ourselves, and all that we have, under the governance of God, and not to be so foolish as to commit them unto saints. God grant us that we may say with a good faith, from the bottom of our hearts, *Domine Jesu, suscipe spiritum nostrum*, "Lord Jesu, receive our spirits!"

Christ hath witnesses what he was. Further, Christ himself shewed most manifestly what he was, for he hath witnesses enough; the Father, the Holy Ghost, John Baptist, and the works which he did: and finally he himself witnesseth what he is; for he saith, *Qui credit in me habet vitam æternam;* "He that believeth in me hath everlasting life." Here is evidently[6] shewed by his own words what he was, namely, the Redeemer of mankind, and very God; for nobody can give everlasting life save only God. But Christ giveth everlasting life; *ergo*, he is very natural God. Item[7], in another place he saith, Christ is very God. *Quemadmodum Pater mortuos suscitat, sic et Filius;* "Like as the Father raised up the dead, so doth the Son too." Where it most manifestly appeareth that he is equal unto the Father; they work their works together unseparably. This I say unto[8] you to the intent that you should consider with yourselves what Christ hath been[9] before he took our

---

[1 as he had, 1607.]   [2 hath done, 1607.]
[3 but, 1607.]   [4 came to pass, 1607.]
[5 "On St Stephen's day we must let all our horses blood with a knife, because St Stephen was killed with stones." Sir T. More, Dialogue concerning Heresies, Book II. chap. 10. See also Brand, Observations on Popular Antiq. by Ellis, Vol. I. pp. 416, et seq. Hampson, Medii Ævi Kalendarium, &c. pp. 118 et seq.]
[6 plainly, 1607.]   [7 And, 1607.]
[8 tell, 1607.]   [9 was, 1607.]

nature upon him: and again, to consider what he hath done for us, and how exceedingly he hath humbled himself.

Now I will shew you what man is of his own nature, left unto himself; but I will not speak of that singular Son of man, which was Christ, for he had two natures in unity of persons: he was very God and very man; he was a privileged man from all other men; that man never sinned, therefore I speak not of him: I speak of the nature which mankind hath inherited of Adam after he had sinned; for as he was, that is, a sinful wicked man, disobedient unto the word of God, such he brought into the world. Now what is man, what is the nature of the son of Adam? I speak not of Christ, for he was not born of the seed of Adam. When we know what man is, then we shall perceive what great benefit we have received of God, the Father Almighty, in that he hath sent his only Son to be a sacrifice for us, and to help us out of the estate of damnation, and to remedy this impureness of our nature. Now this our nature David, the holy king and prophet, describeth with few words, saying, *Ecce iniquitatibus natus sum et in peccatis concepit;* " Lo, in iniquity am I born, and in sin hath my mother conceived me." Which words are not so to be understood as though the act of generation, and the lawful use of matrimony, be defiled and unclean before God. He speaketh not here of the lawful bed-company that is between married folks: for this hath his warrant in scripture, in God's book; therefore he speaketh not here of the company that is between man and wife: but he will[10] signify by his words what he had inherited of his parents, of Adam, namely, sin and wickedness: and he speaketh not of himself only, but of all mankind. He painteth us out in our own colour; shewing that all we be contaminate, from our birth, with sin, and so should justly be firebrands in hell world without end. This the holy prophet shewed in these words, to put us in remembrance of our own wretchedness; to teach us to despair of our own holiness and righteousness; and to seek our help and comfort by that Messias whom God hath promised our forefathers, and now hath fulfilled the same promise.

Another scripture signifieth unto us further, what we be of ourselves, of our own nature: for it is written, *Omnis*

Christ had two natures in one person, that is, very God, and very man.

The nature of man is sinful and wicked.

Psal. li.

We have by our parents sin and wickedness.

[[10] doth, 1607.]

All men are liars.

homo mendax, "All men are liars;" therefore man is not clean, but full of falsehood and deceit, and all manner of sin and wickedness: yet we may learn what we be of our own nature, namely, poisoned and corrupt with all manner of uncleanness. Another scripture we have, which sheweth us in the same thing[1]: *Dominus de cœlo despexit, et omnes declinaverunt, simul inutiles facti sunt;* "The Lord looked down from heaven, to see whether any man be[2] that did well; but they are[3] all declined, they were all naught together." God looked down to consider whether there were some that had understanding of him, or not. What brought he to pass? What found he when he made inquisition? Marry this, *Omnes declinaverunt*, "All men have declined from God; there was not one that did good, no not one." Here we may perceive what we be of ourselves, of our own nature. And, again, here we may see what Christ, the Son of God, hath done for us; what inestimable benefits we have received at his hands, namely, to suffer for us and to cleanse us from all our sins and wickedness; to make us just before the face of God; to purge us from all iniquity, as well from original sin as actual: for if he had not done so, we should never have been able to escape the wrath of God. For, *Quicquid natus ex carne caro est*, "Whatsoever is born of flesh is flesh;" that is to say, is sinful, wicked, and so destitute of the glory of God, and the child of the devil. If Christ had not been come and cleansed our filthiness, if he had not suffered death for us, we had perished. Now afore[4] he suffered, he was born and lived a great while in the[5] miserable world; or else he could not have suffered if he had not been born, for no man can suffer before he be alive. Further, it is written in God's book, *Conclusit Deus omnes sub peccato, ut omnium misereatur;* "God hath concluded all mankind under sin;" so that all mankind was sinful, and destitute of the favour of God, save only Christ.

Wherefore, I pray you, have I rehearsed all these scriptures? Marry, to this intent I have rehearsed them, to bring you to knowledge how great need we have had of Christ: for no doubt if we had not had him, all mankind should

[1 saith to this purpose, 1607.]
[2 if there were any man that, 1607.]   [3 were, 1607.]
[4 before, 1607.]   [5 this, 1607.]

have been damned, yea, the best of us, world without end. But that we have deliverance, that the kingdom of heaven is opened unto us, that same brought he to pass with his passion; for he took upon him our nature, and so deserved for us everlasting life: for by him we have it, and therefore we must thank him for it, we must to him give all honour and praise.

It is a great unity between the two natures in Christ, between the manhood and Godhead: for the body and the soul make a man, but the manhood and the Godhead are joined so together, they make but one Christ, and yet they are not confounded; so that the Godhead is not turned into the manhood, neither the manhood into the Godhead. And thus Christ, which was very God and very man, died not for himself nor of necessity, for death had no right unto him, because he was without sin; but he died for our sakes, willingly, without any compulsion, moved by the great love that he bare unto man: and therefore he saith, *Nemo tollit animam meam a me, sed ego repono illam;* "No man taketh away my life, but I myself put it away; but I will receive it again. I am willing to die, for with my dying[6] I will destroy the kingdom of the devil; and by my death all mankind shall be saved." And here he shewed himself what he was, namely, very God; for he had power over death, and not death over him: and so he died not by compulsion nor necessity, but willingly; for it was his will and pleasure to help us, and deliver us from our wretchedness; for nothing could help us else but the death of the eternal Son of God.

Sidenotes: A great unity in Christ of the manhood and Godhead. John x. Christ's death was of necessity for us.

And here you may note, by the way, what a heinous thing sin is before the face of God; how he abhorreth sin, that he would be with nothing reconciled, save only with the death of his Son, our Saviour Jesus Christ. And this shall make us to hate sin, and avoid all occasions of sin, and not to fall willingly and wittingly into all kinds[7] of sin again; but rather to live uprightly and godly, according unto his will and commandment: seeing that he beareth such a loving and fatherly heart towards us, that he spared not his only Son, but gave him even to the most vile and painfullest death for our sakes, for our sins and wickedness' sake.

Sidenote: Sin is a hateful thing in the sight God.

David, that holy man, when he considered this great

[6 by my death, 1607.]   [7 any kind, 1607.]

Psal. cxvi. benefit, what saith he? He fell out into these words, *Quid retribuam Domino pro omnibus quæ tribuit mihi?* "What shall I give unto the Lord for all those things which he hath given unto me?" Then he made himself answer, and saith, *Nomen Domini invocabo,* "I will call upon the name of the
Psal. cxvi. Lord:" *Calicem salutaris accipiam,* "I will take up the cup of health;" that is to say, "I will bear his[1] cross, that he shall lay upon me, willingly, without any grudge and murmuring." Now, therefore, let us say so too: "O Lord, what shall we give unto thee again? What amends shall we make thee, seeing thou hast given us thine only natural Son, which took upon him a[2] vile nature, and suffered most painful death?" For that we have a brother in heaven, what shall we now do? How shall we shew ourselves thankful? Marry, *Nomen Do-*
We must call upon the name of the Lord, and be thankful. *mini invocabimus,* "We will call upon the name of the Lord:" we will praise him for all his goodness; we will shew ourselves thankful with a godly, upright conversation. *Calicem salutaris accipiemus,* "We will take the cup of health; we will bear all calamities and crosses, that thou shalt lay upon us, willingly, without any grudging." This is all that we can do; and when the devil cometh and tempteth us, as
By Christ we are made able to defy the devil and all his power. no doubt he will not sleep, we shall defy him, knowing that we have a brother in heaven which hath overcome him and all his power: therefore we shall not need to fear him, or care for him, though he be busy with us, and tempt us in all manner of things, to bring us to destruction. Let us defy him, and give God thanks which so mercifully hath dealt with us, and delivered us from all our sins. Let us take the
Christian men do rejoice in the cross of Christ. cross meekly, whatsoever it be; though it be in misery or poverty, or other calamities. Let us be content withal; for they be but examinations and proofs, to provoke us to call upon God, when we feel the burden: and, no doubt, we
If we call upon Christ in faith, we shall be heard. shall be heard when we call as we ought to do, that is to say, with a faithful heart; then, no doubt, he will take them away, so that we shall be no more troubled with them; or else he will mitigate and assuage them in such sort, that we shall be able to bear the burden of them.

"And she brought forth her first-begotten Son." These words, after the outward appearance, sound as though Mary the mother of Christ had more sons than Christ. And there

[1 the, 1607.]   [2 our, 1607.]

was an heretic[3] which steadfastly said, that Mary had more *A great and horrible heresy.*
sons after she had brought forth Christ: and here he took
his arguments, saying, "We read in scripture that Christ
had brethren, which argueth that Mary had more sons besides Christ." Which, indeed, is a foolish argument against
all learning: for we must consider the phrases of the Hebrew *The phrases of scripture are specially to be marked.*
tongue. The Jews in their tongue call all those which are
kinsmen brethren; and so the kinsmen of our Saviour were
called his brethren, after the manner of their language; not
that they had one mother, or that Mary had more sons but
Christ: therefore these heretics go far wide to prove that
Mary had more sons besides Christ, because we read that he
had brethren. Let them consider the propriety of the
Hebrew tongue; then they shall soon perceive how fond and
foolish their arguments be.

The second argument which these fond fellows make is
this: the Evangelist saith, "And she brought forth her first- *A false argument well confuted.*
begotten son." By these words they will prove, *ergo*, she
had more than one son: Christ was the first-begotten, but
she had more beside him. Here I would have them to consider this word *primogenitum*, which signifieth him *qui primo* *A goodly note.*
aperuit vulvam, "him that first opened the womb:" but
she had no more, neither before nor after, but was a clear
virgin before she brought forth, and after she brought forth
him she remained a virgin. And therefore these heretics
do wrongfully violate, toss, and turmoil the scriptures of God,
according to their own fantasies and foolish minds.

Another argument they make, taken out of the first
chapter of Matthew, where the Evangelist saith, *Et non cog-* *Matt. i.*
novit illam donec peperisset filium suum primogenitum;
"And Joseph took his wife, and knew her not till she had
brought forth her first-begotten son." Hereupon they make
this argument: "Joseph knew her not till she had brought
forth her first son; *ergo*," they say, "he knew her after:"
which no doubt is a foolish argument. For the mind of the
Evangelist, when he declared Christ to be the first son of
Mary, was to prove that he was the son of a virgin, according to the prophecy that was of him, and not to declare that
Mary had more children after him, as some do fantasy. For

[3 Helvidius, against whom St Jerome wrote a treatise. Oper. Tom. IV. par. 2, coll. 129 et seq. Edit. Bened. Paris. 1706.]

Christ was the only Son of the Virgin Mary.

we, in our English tongue, have such a manner of speaking, when we say, "I will never forgive him so long as I live:" or when we be ill-entreated in a city, we say, "I will no more come thither so long as I live." By which manner of speaking we do not signify that we will come thither after our death, or forgive after our death. No. And so likewise it is here; when he saith, "He knew her not until she had brought forth her first-begotten son." It followeth not, *ergo*, that he knew her after. Like as it followeth not when I say, I will do this thing no more so long as I live, *ergo*, I will do it after I am dead. And here you may perceive how foolishly and fondly these heretics have handled the scripture.

Now let us go forward, and consider his great extreme poverty. They came to Bethlehem, where they could get never a lodging in no inn, and so were compelled to lie in a stable; and there Mary the mother of Christ brought forth *In Christ all nations are blessed.* that blessed child, through whom, and in whom, all the nations of the earth are and shall be blessed: and there "she wrapped him in swaddling-clothes, and laid him in a manger, because there was no room for them in the inn." Here began *The poverty of Christ and his parents was great.* the misery of the Lord above all lords, even at his first coming into this world, when he was laid in a manger; as soon as he was born, to taste poverty and miseries; to make amends for our sins and wickedness, and so to take away from us the wrath of God, the[1] heavenly Father, which lay upon all mankind so heavy, that we should all have been condemned world without end, if this child had not been born into this world.

And here we may learn by this poverty to comfort ourselves, when God sendeth poverty unto us; and not to think, because we are poor, *ergo*, God hateth us, or will condemn us; but rather consider with ourselves, and call to remembrance the poverty of Christ, our Saviour. He was the beloved Son of God, and God himself; and yet he was content to be born in misery, and to sustain most vile poverty, and penury of all manner of those things which are required *A christian man must bear the cross that God layeth upon him patiently.* necessarily to the sustentation of this life. There be some which when they be in trouble say, "Oh, if God loved me, he would not punish me so; he would not suffer me to be vexed so grievously with poverty and lack of necessaries!"

[1 our, 1607.]

Which indeed is not so; for those whom God loveth he punisheth. Ensamples we have in David, what troubles, calamities, and miseries he had; and yet God loved him, insomuch that he called him a man after his heart's desire. But though he was well-beloved of God, yet he must taste of miseries and calamities, of which he had not a little: but he ever sticked unto God, who delivered him out of all his trouble. Hebr. xii.

Now some will say, when they hear what poverty our Saviour suffered, and how Mary his mother was compelled to take a stable for lack of a better lodging; some will say now[2], "O what a wicked city was this! What a cruel people was this[3]!" But when we consider all things well, we shall find that we be even as wicked as they were. For are not we given now-a-days to covetousness, so that we regard not the poor and[4] miserable people? Seek we not our own commodities, and despise and neglect the poor? Therefore if thou wilt cry out upon the Bethlehemites, then cry out on thyself; for thou art as wicked, yea, more wicked than they were. For the most part of all Bethlehem knew nothing of our Saviour Christ that he was born; but we know it, therefore we are inexcusable. God hath sent unto us his preachers, which teach us the way to heaven; they shew us wherein standeth our redemption; they exhort us to godliness, to do good works, to be pitiful, and liberal unto the poor, to help them, and comfort them: but what do we? Marry, we despise the preachers, we abhor their doctrine, and so consequently refuse Christ himself: for he saith, *Qui vos suscipit, me suscipit;* "He that receiveth you, receiveth me[5]." This Christ speaketh by his preachers: therefore, as I said before, we need not to cry out against Bethlehem, but let us cry out on ourselves; for we are as ill, in all points, as they were. Covetousness and uncharitableness reign as well among us as they did among the Jews.

Matt. x.

But I warrant you, there was many a jolly damsel at that time in Bethlehem, yet amongst them all there was not one found that would humble herself so much as once to go see poor Mary in the stable, and to comfort her. No, no; Fine damsels travail not much to visit the poor.

[2 better lodging, "O what," 1607.]
[3 what a company of cruel people were these! 1607.]
[4 poor, needy and, 1607.]
[5 "receiveth me. He that refuseth you, refuseth me:" 1571, 1572.]

they were too fine to take so much pains. I warrant you, they had¹ bracelets and vardingals; and were trimmed with all manner of fine² raiment; like as there be many now-a-days amongst us, which study nothing else but how they may devise fine raiment: and in the mean season they suffer poor Mary to lie in the stable; that is to say, the poor people of God they suffer to perish for lack of necessaries. But what was her swaddling-clothes wherein she laid the King of heaven and earth? No doubt it was poor gear; peradventure it was her kercher which she took from her head, or such like gear; for I think Mary had not much fine linen; she was not trimmed up as our women be now-a-days. I think indeed Mary had never a vardingal; for she used no such superfluities as our fine damsels do now-a-days: for in the old time women were content with honest and single garments. Now they have found out these round-abouts; they were not invented then; the devil was not so cunning to make such gear, he found it out afterward. Therefore Mary had it not. I will say this, and yet not judge other bodies'³ hearts, but only speak after daily appearance and experience: no doubt it is nothing but a token of fair pride to wear such vardingals; and I therefore think that every godly woman should set them aside. It was not for nought that St Paul advertised all women to give a good ensample of sadness, soberness, and godliness, in setting aside all wantonness and pride. And he speaketh of such instruments⁴ of pride as was used in his time: *Non tortis crinibus,* "Not with laying out the hair artificially;" *Non plicatura capillorum,* "Not with laying out the tussocks." I doubt not but if vardingals had been used in that time, St Paul would have spoken against them too, like as he spake against other things which women used at that time, to shew their wantonness and foolishness. Therefore, as I said before, seeing that God abhorreth all pride, and vardingals are nothing else but an instrument of pride; I would wish that women would follow the counsel of St Paul, and set aside such gorgeous apparel, and rather study to please God, than to set their mind upon pride: or else, when they will not follow the counsel of St Paul, let them scrape out those words wherewith he forbiddeth them their proud-

Side notes: The poor state of Mary the virgin. — The excess of pride in apparel is odious. — Vardingals are learned from players that decked giants after that manner. — 1 Tim. ii.

[¹ their bracelets, 1607.]   [² fine, and costly, 1607.]
[³ folks, 1607.]   [⁴ manner, 1607.]

ness; else[5] the words of St Paul will condemn them at the last day. I say no more; wise folks will do wisely; the words of St Paul are not written for nothing: if they will do after his mind, they must set aside their foolish vardingals: but if[6] they will go forward in their foolishness and pride, the reward which they shall have at the end shall not be taken from them.

Pride in trimming and setting forth ourselves to the shew of the world is abominable.

Here is a question to be moved. Who fetched water to wash the child after it was born into the world, and who made a fire? It is like that Joseph himself did such things; for, as I told you before, those fine damsels thought it[7] scorn to do any such thing unto Mary; notwithstanding that she had brought into the world the Lord over heaven and earth.

Poverty joined with simplicity is laudable.

Alack! shall we murmur and grudge against God when we be in distress or poverty? Shall we cry out against him, seeing that Christ the Saviour of the world himself was handled so extremely? Therefore let us learn to be patient in all our troubles; let us be content with all that God shall send us: if we do so, he will plenteously reward us in everlasting life.

Learn of Christ to be patient in poverty.

This day, on which our Saviour was come into the world, we were made one flesh with the Son of God. Oh, what a great honour is this unto us! Which honour exceedeth the dignity of the angels. For though the angels are better in substance, yet we are better in the benefit: for "Christ took not upon him the nature of angels, but he took our nature upon him," man's nature, I say. Oh, what an exceeding thing is this! Oh, how much are we bound to give him thanks for these his profound and inestimable benefits! We read a story[8], (take it as you will, though it be not a true story:) The devil came once into the church whilst the priest was saying mass; and when he was at these words, *Et homo factus est*, the devil looked about him, and seeing no man kneel down, or bow his knees, he strake one of them in the face, saying, "What! will you not reverence him for this great benefit which he hath done unto you? I tell you, if he had taken

As many of us as believe in Christ are made one flesh with the Son of God.

A merry tale worthy to be noted.

[5 otherwise, 1607.]
[6 when, in the editions, except 1607.]
[7 great, 1607.]
[8 The story is read, among other places, in Ludolph Saxo, de Vita Christi, par. I. c. xviii. h. Lugdun. 1510.]

upon him our nature, as he hath taken upon him yours, we would more reverence him than ye do." This story is prettily devised; for we should reverence him; we should honour him, and shew ourselves thankful for his inestimable benefits that he hath shewed upon us miserable wretched sinners, in taking upon him our nature.

<small>Christ was born very man without sin.</small>

Now the same Christ was born, as this day, of the virgin Mary, very man except sin; for sin hath not defiled his flesh: for he was not begotten of the seed of man, after the manner of other men, but by the power of the Holy Ghost. Mary[1] was his very natural mother, and he was born to that end that he might deliver us from our sins and wickedness. To whom, with God the Father, and the Holy Ghost, be praise and honour everlastingly, world without end! *Amen.*

[[1] And Mary, 1571.]

A SERMON PREACHED BY MASTER HUGH LATIMER, ON
SAINT JOHN EVANGELIST'S DAY, AT GRIMSTHORPE,
ANNO 1552.

LUKE II. [8—12.]

And there were in the same region shepherds abiding in the field, and watching their flock by night. And, lo, the angel of the Lord stood hard by them, and the brightness of the Lord shone round about them, and they were sore afraid. But the angel said unto them, Be not afraid; for, behold, I bring you tidings of great joy, that shall come unto all the people; for unto you is born this day in the city of David a Saviour, which is Christ the Lord. And take this for a sign, you shall find the child swaddled and laid in a manger, &c.

The birth of Christ.

YESTERDAY I entreated somewhat of the nativity of Christ our Saviour. And you have heard by what occasion Mary, his mother, came to Bethlehem with her husband Joseph, namely, to shew obedience, as all subjects ought to do, to their governors. You hear what good chance she had in that she was obedient; and so all those that be obedient to their rulers and governors, according to the ordinance of God, they shall have good speed. Now what happened unto Mary? She brought forth the Saviour of the world. Oh, what good chance was this! And here we learn, that it is a good thing for every one to keep him in that order as God hath appointed him. Mary with her husband Joseph were subjects, and therefore, in doing their duties, in obeying the magistrate, they pleased God: which ensample of Mary and Joseph should occasion all us to follow them in their doing; and if we do so, we shall please God. There is one thing I did forget, the last time when I spake of obedience, which is, an objection that some do make, when they are required to do their duties to the magistrates. I told you at that time, that we must bear willingly those burthens which are laid upon us, considering that God commanded us so to do: and then, again, that he hath delivered us from that great burthen of our sins, which should have thrust us into everlasting damnation; willing and commanding us to

Obedience is acceptable before God.

What true obedience is.

bear, with a good will, such little burthens as the magistrates shall lay upon us. Again, I told you, at the same time, that whosoever beareth with a good will the common burthen of this realm, they shall be blessed in all things: it shall not be a diminishing of their stocks, but it shall be rather an increase than a diminishing.

All such as bear willingly the burthen of the realm shall be happy in their need.

Now cometh the objection that some make: they say, "To bear the common burthen is not an increase, but a diminishing and hurt; for there hath been many burthens in England, as the burthens of the fall of money: therefore that is not so as you say; for I know that some have lost so much, that they cannot recover the same again so long as they live." And, indeed, I know myself a man that lost eight score pounds by the fall of money; yet as for that man, he took it well, and I doubt not but God will work with him, so that it shall be nothing to his hurt. But to answer this carnal man, which maketh such a carnal objection against the promise of God: I deny not but that there be some, which indeed shall never recover that which they have lost. But I tell you what is the cause: the cause is not in God, or in his promises or fidelity, but the fault is in themselves. As thus: you must understand that where God requireth a thing to be done, he will have it done with a good-will, with a merry heart, with a loving countenance. Now there be many of us which do it indeed, but with cursing and banning; so that, though they be no rebels outwardly, yet they rebel in their hearts. Unto such fellows God is not bound to keep his promise, for he made them no promise; but unto them that do it with a willing heart, and loving countenance, he hath promised increase. And they that do it with an ill will, they rather provoke God to anger, than that they should receive any benefit of him. For St. Paul commandeth us to obey the magistrates, *Non propter iram, sed propter conscientiam,* "Not for fear of their punishment, but rather for conscience sake, for God's sake, in respect of God, of whom we have all things, who willeth us to do so." So that they that do it with an ill will, and afterward having no increase, are not able to recover again, the fault is in themselves, and not in God; for they obey not for conscience sake, as St Paul would have them do, but rather for fear of punishment.

A carnal and worldly objection.

God suffereth not the obedient person to perish.

Rom. xiii.

Yesterday, also, I shewed you the commodities which we receive by the coming of Christ; and, again, the discommodities if he should not have come; namely, that we should have been lost for ever, world without end. To this end I spake of such things, to give you occasion to consider his goodness and wonderful benefits, and to shew yourselves thankful towards him. Further, I shewed you what he was before he took our vile nature upon him; namely, the eternal Son of God the Father; begotten before the world began; equal to his Father in power and dignity: he took our vile nature upon him, was made very man, to the end that he might deliver man from the curse of God and eternal damnation. Then, I shewed you what we be without God, without this Saviour; namely, cursed and banished out from everlasting life to everlasting damnation. This we are, without him, of our own nature; for we can do nothing but commit sin, and are not able to make amends for the least sin that we commit: but he, our Saviour, I say, hath made satisfaction upon the cross for the sins of all mankind. Then, again, I told you how we should follow the ensample of David, which when he considered the great benefits of God, burst out in these words, saying, *Quid retribuam Domino pro omnibus quæ tribuit mihi?* "What shall I give unto the Lord for all that which he hath given unto me?" Then he concludeth and saith, *Accipiam calicem salutaris*, "I will take the chalice of health;" that is, I will bear all the crosses which the Lord shall lay upon me. And so we must do when we consider the great benefits which God hath done unto us: then we must be content with all our hearts to bear such crosses as he shall lay upon us, and to shew ourselves thankful with a godly and honest life, for that he suffered for us; which passion he suffered, not compelled thereunto, but willingly he suffered it, moved by that great love which he bare towards us. Therefore, let us shew ourselves thankful: let us take all calamities and miseries that he shall lay upon us willingly: and in all these crosses let us call upon him, and take in good worth whatsoever it shall please him to lay upon us. This is the chiefest honour that we can do unto him.

Now let us a little better consider his poverty, which he suffered as soon as he was born. We read not that Mary his mother had any midwife when she was delivered of him. And here we have occasion to speak of midwives. The same office of a midwife is a necessary office; but I would wish the bishops[1] would see better unto them, that they might be better instructed in God's word: for no doubt these midwives are the occasion of much superstition and dishonouring of God. The fault is, because they are not instructed in the word of God; and therefore, when the women be in travailing, and so in peril of their lives, they cause them to call upon our Lady: which no doubt is very idolatry, and dishonouring of God; for we ought not to call upon any creature; we must call only upon God alone; unto him only pertaineth that honour.

Midwives are superstitious.

Further, I told you that our Saviour Christ was formed and framed of the most poorest flesh; and he became the natural son of Mary, and she also was his natural mother. I told you, the last time, of one Joan of Kent[2], which was in this foolish opinion, that she should say our Saviour was not very man, and had not received flesh of his mother Mary: and yet she could shew no reason why she should believe so. Her opinion was this, as I told you before. The Son of God, said she, penetrated through her, as through a glass, taking no substance of her. But our creed teacheth us contrariwise; for we say, *Natus ex Maria Virgine*, "Born of the Virgin Mary:" so this foolish woman denied the common creed, and said that our Saviour had a phantastical body; which is most untrue, as it appeareth evidently in the epistle to the Hebrews, where St Paul plainly saith, that Christ was made of the woman, that he took his flesh from the woman. And though Mary had a prerogative, as she had indeed, namely, that she knew no man, that she was a virgin; yet her prerogative took not away the very humanity of Christ. She alone, above all other women, had this prerogative, to be a

Mary was the natural mother of Christ.
Joan Butcher of Kent was an heretic.

Christ took flesh of the virgin Mary.

[1 Midwives used to be licensed by the archbishop, or bishop of the diocese; and the terms of the oath administered at the time of granting a licence to the parties who exercised the "necessary office" alluded to by the preacher, would indicate that they required to be looked after. Strype, Ann. of Reformat. II. ii. pp. 242, et seq. Oxf. Edit.; Book of Oaths, pp. 191, et seq. Lond. 1689.]

[2 Full particulars are given of this person and of her opinions, in Hutchinson's Works, pp. 2, et seq., 145, et seq. Park. Soc. Edit.]

virgin, and yet to bring forth a child: the Holy Ghost did supply the office of a father; she was filled with the Holy Ghost: but he was her natural son in all other points; but yet this his humanity was preserved from all sin and wickedness. In all other things he was very man, and she his very natural mother. And no doubt she had a great belly, as it appeared in the first chapter of Matthew, where the evangelist saith, *Inventa est gravida,* "She was found with child;" Matt. i. and so Joseph seeing it, could not but suspect her, and therefore was minded to go away from her, if he had not been admonished by the angel: but being in this perplexity, the angel came unto him, saying, *Ne timeas,* "Fear not, Joseph, for that which is conceived in her is of the Holy Ghost. She shall bring forth a son, and thou shalt call his name Jesus." So here appeared plainly that Mary was big with child, after the manner of all other women: for we may not make him a phantastical body, but a very body, having flesh, blood, and bones, as our bodies have; and I think that Mary travailed after the manner of other women. I doubt not but she had pains as other women have; for I think she was obedient unto that law, which was made by God himself, *In dolore paries filios tuos,* "In sorrow and pain thou shalt Gen. iii. bring forth thy children." For she kept other laws too, to which she was not bound, to which she had no need; as of purification; and he of circumcision: so that it is to be pre-supposed, seeing she obeyed other laws, she obeyed this law too, to shew and to signify unto the whole world her obedience. Therefore they that will go about and say that she brought him forth without pain, not after the manner of other women, they seem to do more hurt than good: for so we might come in doubt whether he had a very body or not.

Now the evangelist saith there was no place in the inn, they had no room to refresh themselves: for the innkeepers took only those which were able to pay for their good cheer; they would not meddle with such beggarly folk as Joseph and Mary his wife were. And here we may learn, by the ensample of Joseph and Mary, to take all things in good part, We must bearpatiently and to be content with poverty and miseries. Let us follow all adversity. their ensample. We read not that they grudged or murmured against God; but they were content to take all things in good worth, though they could get never a lodging in the whole city; so that they were fain to take a stable there, to repose themselves. And, as some writers say, it was a common stable in the market-set[1], as some towns have common stables for the folk that come to the market; for they are not able to spend money in the inn, and therefore they set their cattle there[2]. But this is no certainty, whether it was such a common stable or not; but this is certain that they were in great poverty and misery; no doubt of that. Therefore, you poor folk, comfort yourselves with this ensample, though you have no houses after your mind: consider that Mary, the mother of Christ, lacked a lodging, and that in her greatest need. But I tell you where you may have houses enough, and that good cheap; for little money you may have them. *In domo Patris mei sunt multæ habitationes;* "In the house of my Father be many dwelling-places." There you may have them, they are offered you in Christ, and through Christ; ye need not to give money for them. Therefore, I would not have you in any wise to grudge or murmur because ye lack houses; for no doubt, if we will be content with that that God sendeth unto us, and be thankful unto him, houses or no houses in this world, we shall be sure that we shall lack no houses in the other world.

John xiv.

If we trust in God and be thankful, we shall lack nothing.

Now you hear how Mary, the mother of Christ, brought forth her son into this world in a stable. But here I would not have you to think that Mary was saved because she brought forth Christ; no, not so. She was saved because she believed in him; because she set her hope and confidence in him. She doubted not but that he should take away her sins, and all the world's sins; so that she was not only his mother after the flesh, but she was his spiritual mother: she believed in him; she seeketh neither salvation by her own works.

Mary was saved by believing in Christ.

There was once a woman, when she heard our Saviour make a sermon, she thought him to be a wonderful man: she could no longer hold her tongue, but burst out into these words, saying, *Beatus venter qui te portavit, et ubera quæ suxisti;* "Blessed is that womb that hath borne thee, and

Luke xi.

[1 Market-sted or place.]

[2 This gloss was current among the later interpreters, being probably borrowed from Peter Comestor's Historia Evangelica.]

happy are the teats that gave thee suck:" that is to say, Happy is that woman that hath such a son. But what answer made our Saviour unto her? *Quin imo beati qui audiunt verbum Dei, et custodiunt illud;* "But blessed are those that hear the word of God and keep the same." For Mary was not justified nor saved because she was his natural mother; for if she had not believed in him, she should never have obtained the felicity of heaven: though she was a singular woman, yet if she had only staid at that, all had been to no purpose. But she was otherwise his mother with believing him to be the Son of the eternal God, and the Saviour of the world, according to the promise made of God the Father himself in Paradise; namely, that "the Seed of the woman should break the serpent's head." And in such wise all we may be the mother, sister, and brethren of Christ. *[margin: Mary the virgin believed in Christ.]*

Furthermore, we read in the gospel of St Matthew, that once she was pricked with vain-glory; for when he was preaching, she came and would needs speak with him, for she would have been known to be his mother: which doing of hers no doubt had a smell of ambition[3]. And it is good for us to know such things, for so we may comfort ourselves; when we hear that the very mother of Christ had sins, and yet was saved, we shall be saved too. God is as merciful as ever he was: so we shall comfort and keep ourselves from despair. But, I pray you, what answer made he unto her, when she interrupted his sermon? "Who is my mother? And who are my brethren? And he stretched forth his hands over his disciples, and said, Behold my mother, and my brethren: for whosoever doth my Father's will that is in heaven, the same is my brother, sister, and mother." Here you see, that he would not be led by the affections of his mother, and set aside his calling. This ensample all we ought to follow, and specially preachers: they may not preach after affection; they shall not rule the word of God, but they must be ruled by the same. Likewise we read in the gospel of John, that when he was at the marriage in Cana of Galilee, and his mother too, and there was wine lacking, she would take upon her to appoint him what he should do[4], saying, *Vinum non habent;* "They have no wine, thou must needs help." But what answer made he unto her? *[margin: Mark iii. Luke viii. Mary sinned and was saved, and so shall we be. He that doth the will of God, is mother and brother to Christ. John ii.]*

[3 See Vol. I. p. 383, note.]　　[4 See Vol. I. p. 515.]

Mulier, quid mihi est tecum? "Woman, what have I to do with thee? Shall I be at your commandment?" Here you see that Christ would not bear with his mother in her folly. Which ensample we ought to follow: we shall not bear or comfort any man in his sins and wickedness, but admonish him; nor[1] flatter him against our conscience, as some do, which will not displease, but rather allow things against their own conscience. But our Saviour did not so; he would not bear with his own mother: therefore, as I told you before, she was not only his carnal mother, but by faith she believed in him. And so ought we to do, if we will be saved: for when we believe in him, undoubtedly then we conceive Christ; then we be his mother; then we shall reign with him world without end.

Now followeth in the text, "And there were shepherds in the same region," &c. You know there is a common saying, *Ignoti nulla cupido;* "When a body knoweth not a thing, he desireth it not greatly:" so it had been with us, if this birth of our Saviour should have been hid from us; we should not have desired the same, and he had done unto us no good at all. Therefore it must needs be known; it must needs be opened. Now here the evangelist beginneth to shew to whom this birth was opened at the first, and through whom it was first published; who were the first preachers; which were the angels of God, they were the first preachers. And here you may perceive what is the office of the angels of God, namely, to serve, to keep us; and therefore St Paul calleth them, *administratorios spiritus,* "serving spirits." But now you will say, how chanced it that the angels teach not us as well as they did the shepherds? Sirs, you must understand, that God hath appointed another office, other officers, which shall teach us the way to heaven; which way to heaven was opened first by the angel. He told the shepherds that Christ the Saviour was born: but now God sheweth unto us the self-same sermon of the angel by and through his ministers, which teach us the same. But, I pray you, to whom was the nativity of Christ first opened? To the bishops, or great lords which were at that time at Bethlehem? or to those jolly damsels with their vardingals, with their roundabouts, or with their bracelets? No, no:

[1 not, 1571, 1572.]

Preachers must rebuke sin openly.

By faith we are made the mother and brethren of Christ.

they had so many lets to trim and dress themselves, that they could have no time to hear of the nativity of Christ: their minds were so occupied otherwise, that they were not allowed to hear of them. But his nativity was revealed first to the shepherds: and it was revealed unto them in the night-time, when every-body was at rest; then they heard the joyful tidings of the Saviour of the world. For these shepherds were keeping their sheep in the night-season from the wolf or other beasts, and from the fox: for the sheep in that country do lamb two times in the year[2], and therefore it was needful for the sheep to have a shepherd to keep them. And here note the diligence of these shepherds: for whether the sheep were their own, or whether they were servants, I cannot tell, for it is not expressed in the book; but it is most like they were servants, and their masters had put them in trust to keep their sheep. Now if these shepherds had been deceitful fellows, that when their masters had put them in trust to keep their sheep, they had been drinking in the alehouse all night, as some of our servants do now-a-days, surely the angels had not appeared unto them, to have told them this great joy and good tidings. And here all servants may learn by these shepherds to serve truly and diligently unto their masters: in what business soever they are set to do, let them be painful and diligent, like as Jacob was unto his master Laban. Oh, what a painful, faithful, and trusty man was he! He was day and night at his work, keeping his sheep truly, as he was put in trust to do: and when any chance happened that any thing was lost, he made it good, and restored it again of his own. So likewise was Eleazarus a painful man, a faithful and trusty servant. Such a servant was Joseph in Egypt to his master Putiphar. So likewise was Daniel unto his master, the king. But, I pray you, where are these servants now-a-days? Indeed I fear me, there be but very few of such faithful servants.

The vanities of this world are lets that keep us from Christ.

Servants ought to be diligent in their master's service.

Now these shepherds, I say, they watch the whole night, they attend upon their vocation; they do according to their

[[2] Bis pariebant in anno. Augustin. Quæst. in Genesim Quæst. 95. Oper. Tom. III. col. 300. Edit. Bened. Antwerp. 1700. See also Jerome, Quæst. Hebraic. in Genes. Oper. Tom. II. col. 535, Edit. Bened. Paris, 1699, Bochart, Hierozoic. Lib. II. c. 46.]

calling; they keep their sheep: they run not hither and thither, spending the time in vain, and neglecting their office and calling. No, they did not so. Here, by these shepherds, all men may learn to attend upon their offices and callings. I would wish that clergymen,—the curates, parsons, and vicars, the bishops, and all other spiritual persons, would learn this lesson by these poor shepherds; which is this, to abide by their flocks and by their sheep, to tarry amongst them, to be careful over them; not to run hither and thither after their own pleasure, but to tarry by their benefices and feed their sheep with the food of God's word; and to keep hospitality, and so to feed them both soul and body. For I tell you these poor unlearned shepherds shall condemn many a stout and great learned clerk: for these shepherds had but the care and charge over brute beasts, and yet were diligent to keep them, and to feed them; and the other have the cure over God's lambs, which he bought with the death of his Son, and yet they are so careless, so negligent, so slothful over them: yea, and the most part intendeth not to feed the sheep, but they long to be fed of the sheep. They seek only their own pleasures, their own pastimes, they care for no more. But what said Christ to Peter? What said he? *Peter, amas me?* "Peter, lovest thou me?" Peter made answer, "Yes:" "Then feed my sheep." And so the third time he commanded Peter to feed his sheep. But our clergymen do declare plainly that they love not Christ, because they feed not his flock. If they had an earnest love to Christ, no doubt they would shew their love; they would feed his sheep. But it is a thing to be lamented, that the prelates and other spiritual persons will not attend upon their offices: they will not be amongst their flocks, but rather will run hither and thither, here and there, where they are not called; and, in the mean season, leave them at adventure of whom they take their living. Yea, and furthermore, some will rather be clerks of kitchens, or take other offices upon them besides that which they have already: but with what conscience these same do so, I cannot tell. I fear they shall not be able to make answer at the last day for their follies, as concerning that matter: for this office is such a heavy and weighty office that it requireth a whole man. Yea, and let every curate or parson keep his cure to which God hath appointed him, and let him do the best that he can; yet, I tell you, he cannot choose but the devil will have some: for the devil sleepeth not; he goeth about day and night to seek whom he may devour. Therefore it is need for every godly minister to abide by his sheep, seeing that the wolf is so near; and to keep them, and withstand the wolf. Indeed, there be some ministers here in England which do no good at all; and, therefore, it were better for them to leave their benefices, and give room unto others.

Again, I will not be so precise, but I say a man may be away from his benefice for a little while, having urgent and lawful causes; yet I would not allow him to tarry long: for a curate or whatsoever[1] he be, having a cure committed unto him of God to feed, cannot be from them with a safe conscience. He may not run hither and thither after his own pleasure, but must wait upon his office: for, no doubt, the devil will be wonderful busy when the preacher or curate is long absent from his cure. Moses, that worthy man and faithful minister of God, was away from his people, which was to him committed, but two days; but what came of it? Marry, they committed idolatry in his absence: this came of it; which, no doubt, they would not have done, if he had been present: yet he was not faulty, for he was called by God himself. I would wish all curates and parsons would tarry at their cures, till they be called from it as Moses was called: for certain it is, that as many as perish in his absence, he must make answer for them before God. *Si non locutus fueris;* "If thou dost not reprove them, if thou dost not teach them, they shall die, but I will require their blood[2] at thy hand," saith God. Again, if thy parish be stout and hard-necked, and will not hear the word of God, nor pass of it, yet the curate doing that which pertaineth unto him to do, he is discharged before God; and their blood shall be upon their own heads. But it is required of a curate to be with them, to exhort and admonish them. Therefore St Peter saith, *Pascite quantum in vobis est gregem Christi,* "Feed as much as in you lieth the flock of Christ." Then they may not be from their flock, for they cannot feed them being absent: and therefore those fellows[3] that neglect or set

How and in what manner spiritual men may be from their benefices.

Preachers may not be long absent from their flocks.

Ezek. xxxiii.

1 Pet. v.

[1 whosoever, 1607.]   [2 their blood will I require, 1607.]
[3 ministers, 1607.]

aside their own cures, and run here and there before they be called, are no doubt in great danger; and they do against the ordinance of God. Therefore let them not be ashamed to learn of these shepherds here, to abide by their flock, till such time as God shall call them, like as he called these shepherds. I will not say, but they may be from it, but no longer than these shepherds; that is to say, no longer than they have lawful business. And here God doth consecrate every man's vocation; that he that feareth God, loveth his word, and liveth according unto the same, he shall be acceptable unto God; though he be a poor shepherd, or cobbler, that is not the matter.

<small>All that fear God are accepted of God though they be poor.</small>

The evangelist saith, "And there were in that same region shepherds abiding in the field." Oh, what fidelity was in these men! They would not deceive their masters, or put their sheep in jeopardy, but they were content to watch all the whole night. And, lo! the angel of the Lord stood hard by them. The angel of God was a preacher at that time; the people and audience were the shepherds: but they were greatly astonied; they knew not what God intended to do. But the angel said unto them, *Nolite timere,* "Fear not." As who say, "Ye have no cause to be afraid, when you know how the matter goeth; for I come to bring you word that the light is come into the world." For Christ is the light, the life, the resurrection, the way to heaven; when we believe in him, the gates of hell shall not prevail against us. The sermon of the angel was this, *Ecce,* "Lo!" When this word, *Ecce,* "Lo," is set in scripture, then ever followeth a great and weighty matter after it. And therefore he required audience and silence. He would have them to bear it away and note it well, what he would say unto them: *Annuncio vobis gaudium magnum;* "I bring you tidings of great joy, that shall come to all people." I bring you good news, which pertaineth unto all the world, if they will receive it: but they that will not, if they refuse the offer of God, then they themselves are the cause of their own damnation. The let is not in God, but in themselves.

<small>Christ is the life and light of the world.</small>

<small>The gospel is glad and joyful tidings.</small>

Quia vobis natus est hodie, "Unto you is born this day in the city of David a Saviour." This was a good angel, and he was already in the state of salvation. Therefore he saith, "Unto you is born a Saviour." He saith not, Unto us;

<small>The birth of Christ.</small>

for the good angels of God are in the state of salvation already. Therefore Christ suffered not for them, nor saved them, but us. As for the other angels, the angels of darkness, the devil I say, they are without hope of salvation: and therefore Christ suffered not for them, but only for mankind, which was lost by the craft of the old serpent the devil.

Christ suffered only to redeem mankind.

The fall of the devil was this. When Lucifer, which was at the same season the greatest angel in heaven, when he perceived that the Son of God would become man, he fell into such an enviousness against man, and in such a hatred and proudness against God, because the Son of God would not take his nature upon him; he fell therefore into such a pride, that he would set his seat above God, or like God, saying, *Similis ero Altissimo*, "I will be like unto the Highest." But what was his end? He was cast down from heaven, he and all his fellows with all their whole company. And here they be amongst us, to let us of our salvation, and to occasion us to sin and to do wickedly before the face of the Lord. And no doubt this is a great matter, if we had grace to consider it, and to beware of his instinctions; for he knoweth that it is the will of God that we should be saved, and this grieveth him: but the good angels they rejoice when we do well, when we receive the word of God and follow it; but the devil waxeth sorry, he cannot abide that, in no wise; for he knoweth that if we should receive God's word, it should be to the destruction and hinderance of his kingdom. After that when Christ was born into the world, he did what he could to rid him out of the way; therefore he stirred up all the Jews against him: but after that he perceived that his death should be our deliverance from our everlasting death, he did what he could to let his death; and therefore he stirred up Mistress Pilate, which took a nap in the morning, as such fine damsels[1] are wont to do, that she should not suffer her husband to give sentence against Christ. For, as I told you, when he perceived that it was to his destruction, he would let it, and did what he could with hand and foot to stop it. But yet he was not able to disannul the counsel and purpose of God.

The manner of the fall of Lucifer.

Isai. xiv.

The angels in heaven rejoice for our salvation. The devil is a great enemy to our salvation.

Further, it is not enough to believe Christ to be a

[1 dames, 1607.]

Saviour, but you must know what manner of Saviour he is; how far forth he saveth: and therefore you must understand that he was not such a Saviour as Moses was, which saved the people of Israel from hunger and thirst in the wilderness, but could not deliver them from everlasting death. Christ therefore, our Saviour, is such a Saviour which saved us from eternal damnation, from the power of the devil, and all our enemies. The angel of God himself shewed[1] us what manner of Saviour Christ is, in the first of Matthew, saying, *Quia salvum faciet populum suum a peccatis suis;* "For he shall save his people from their sins." So we must believe him to be such a Saviour which released us from our[2] sins; as well our original as actual wickedness. But the papists, as is most manifest, make him but half a Saviour: for they think that they with their good works must help him to save them half. So they blaspheme him, and take away his dignity; for he only hath merited with his painful passion to be a Saviour of the whole world, that is, to deliver all them that believe in him from their sins and wickedness. This we must believe undoubtedly, that he was born into this world to save mankind from their sins. Again, we must not only believe that he is a Saviour of mankind, but also that he is my Saviour, and thy Saviour. I must have such a trust and hope in him, that he will save me from all my sin and wickedness: so every man must have a special faith. We must apply his passion unto us, every one to himself. For when it is not applied unto us with a special faith, it is to no purpose: for what commodity have I, when I believe Christ saved St Peter, and St Paul, and other good men, and go no further? Therefore I must have a special faith; I must believe that he saved them, and also will save me, and forgive me my sins.

Christ saveth us from sin and hell.

Christ is a whole and only Saviour.

The Jews, that same obstinate people, think that the Messias, the Saviour, for whom they long, shall be a great ruler in this world, shall have the swing in this world; no man shall be able to withstand him: so they believe that their Saviour shall be a great king in the[3] world; which is contrary to the most holy, infallible word of God. Again, the papists, as I told you before, make him but a half Saviour: for they think and believe that Christ is a Saviour;

The Jews look for another manner of Saviour than poor Christ.

The papists' opinion of Christ.

[¹ sheweth, 1607.]   [² all our, 1571, 1572.]   [³ this, 1607.]

but how? Marry, thus: they say that all they that have lived well in this world, have deserved heaven with their good works; with almsgiving, and other such works merited everlasting life: and therefore, when they die, they shall be received of Christ, and he shall give them everlasting life, which they in their life-time have deserved with their own deeds: so that our Saviour shall be, after their sayings, only a judge. He shall judge which be those which have deserved heaven, and them he shall receive into everlasting life; and so he shall give unto every one according to his merits. Such a Saviour the papists make him.

But, I pray you, if it should be so as they say, which of us should be saved? Whose works are so perfect that they should be able to deserve heaven? For, I tell you, heaven and everlasting life is a more precious thing than can be deserved with our doings, with our outward works. And therefore the papists deprave Christ, and spoil him of his honour and dignity: for he is another manner of Saviour than they fantasy him to be; for he reputeth all them for just, holy, and acceptable before God, which believe in him, which put their trust, hope, and confidence in him: for by his passion, which he hath suffered, he[4] merited that as many as believe in him shall be as well justified by him, as though they themselves had never done any sin, and as though they themselves had fulfilled the law to the uttermost. For we, without him, are under the curse of the law; the law condemneth us; the law is not able to help us; and yet the imperfection is not in the law, but in us: for the law itself is holy and good, but we are not able to keep it, and so the law condemneth us; but Christ with his death hath delivered us from the curse of the law. He hath set us at liberty, and promiseth that when we believe in him, we shall not perish; the law shall not condemn us. Therefore let us study to believe in Christ. Let us put all our hope, trust, and confidence only in him; let us patch him with nothing: for, as I told you before, our merits are not able to deserve everlasting life: it is too precious a thing to be merited by man. It is his doing only. God hath given him unto us to be our[5] deliverer, and to give us everlasting life. O what a

Christ hath delivered us from the curse of the law.

[4 he hath, 1571, 1572.]   [5 a deliverer, 1607.]

joyful thing was[1] this! What a comfortable thing is it, that we know now that neither the devil, hell, or any thing in heaven or earth, shall be able to condemn us when we believe in Christ!

Now to our matter. The angel, after he had told them these good tidings, how the King of all kings was born, he gave them a sign or token whereby they should know him; and saith, *Reperietis infantem jacentem in præsepe,* "Ye shall find the babe lying in a manger." This was a goodly sign. Indeed, if we consider the matter well, it was enough to make them astonished, and to cast down their belief, to tell them first of a great Saviour, and then to say, that they should find him in a stable, lying in a manger. But the wisdom of God is not according to the wisdom of this world. He went not about to please the foolish of this world, but his counsel was to deliver the world by his Son; which should not come in riches and great pomp, but in poverty and in rags. His kingdom in this world should be a weak kingdom. And so his disciples afterward were taken out of the lowest sort of men. They were poor fishers, and the most vilest men in this world; as St Paul saith, *Excrementa mundi,* "Outcasts of the world." And so shall all his disciples be, all they that will be saved by him; and specially the preachers of his holy word shall be *excrementa,* they shall be outcasts. When they will go about to reprove sin, as a preacher should do, as their office requireth, *arguere mundum de peccato,* "to rebuke the world of sin;" I warrant you that man shall have little favour in this world. So, I say, God hath no respect of persons: though they be vile before this world, and counted for nothing, yet he is content to work his will with them and through them, as here in these shepherds appeared: though they were poor, yet the angel opened unto them such things which were hidden from these glorious prelates and stubborn bishops, which in all time do but little good, for they disdain to preach *Jesum crucifixum.*

Now, like as he was born in rags, so the converting of the whole world is by rags, by things which are most vile in this world. For to go to the matter: what is so common as

[[1] is, 1571, 1572.]

water? Every foul ditch is full of it: yet we wash our remission of our sins by baptism: for like as he was found in rags, so we must find him by baptism. There we begin; we are washed with water; and then the words are added: for we are baptized in the name of the Father, the Son, and Holy Ghost, whereby the baptism receiveth his strength. Now this sacrament of baptism is a thing of great weight; for it ascertaineth and assureth us, that like as the water washeth the body and cleanseth it, so the blood of Christ our Saviour cleanseth and washeth it from all filth and uncleanness of sins. So likewise go to the Lord's supper: when the bread is consecrated, when the words are spoken over it, then it is such an office that it beareth the name of the body and blood of Christ. Like as the magistrates because of their office are called *Dii*, " Gods;" so the bread presenteth[2] his body, so that we go unto it worthily, and receive it with a good faith. Then we be assured that we feed upon him spiritually. And like as the bread nourisheth the body, so the soul feedeth upon the very body and blood of Christ by faith, by believing him to be a Saviour which delivered man from his sin.

He that receiveth the sacrament in faith spiritually, receiveth the very body and blood of Christ.

And so it appeareth that we may not seek Christ in the glistering of this world: for what is so common as water? what is so common as bread and wine? Yet he promised to be found there, when he is sought with a faithful heart. So will you have Christ? Where shall you find him? Not in the jollities of this world, but in rags, in the poor people. Have you any poor people amongst you in your town or city? Seek him there amongst the rags, there shall you find him. And I will prove it on this wise. He saith himself with his own mouth, " Whatsoever ye do to these little ones, *minimis*, that do ye unto me." By these words appeareth manifestly, that whatsoever ye do unto the poor people which are despised in this world, ye do it to himself. Therefore I say yet again, when ye will seek Christ, seek him in the rags, seek him in the manger amongst the poor folk: there[3] you shall find him. But you must understand that when I speak of poverty, I speak not of this wilful poverty of the monks and friars; for that same was an hypocritical poverty;

Seek Christ among the poor, and then you shall find him.

[2 representeth, 1571, 1572; presented, 1584, 1596.]
[3 where, 1607.]

that same poverty was full of all manner of delicate things. *Nihil habeant, et tamen omnia habeant;* "They had nothing, and yet they had all." They were wise enough; they could make shift for themselves, I warrant you: therefore I speak not of that poverty; for it was a wicked, abominable, and hypocritical poverty. But I speak of the very poor and needy flock of Christ, which have not wherewith to live in this world. Those I would have you to refresh, to cherish, to help them with your superfluity. Amongst that poor company seek Christ, and no doubt you shall find him.

<small>The conclusion of this Sermon.</small> Now to make an end: consider what I have said, how Christ was born, in what poverty, and in what misery. Remember what manner of Saviour he is; namely, a perfect Saviour, which saveth and healeth all our sorrows, when we believe in him. I told you where you should seek him, namely, amongst the poor; there he will be found.

The Almighty God give us grace to live and believe so, that we may attain to that felicity which he hath promised by his Son, our Saviour! To whom, with God the Father and the Holy Ghost, be honour world without end! *Amen.*

A SERMON PREACHED BY MASTER HUGH LATIMER ON TWELFTH DAY, AT GRIMSTHORPE, ANNO 1553.

MATTHEW II. [1, 2.]

When Jesus was born in Bethlehem in Jewry, in the time of Herod the king; Behold, there came wise men from the east to Jerusalem, saying, Where is he that is born king of the Jews? We have seen his star in the east, and are come to worship him.

RIGHT worshipful, you heard the gospel read before you, which gospel is the beginning of the second chapter of Matthew, and it comprehendeth good matters. It speaketh of the Epiphany of Christ; how our Saviour was opened, by the providence of God, to the gentiles. Notwithstanding, I intend not to tarry long in that gospel, or to entreat of it; for, if ye remember, I promised you the last Sunday[1] three things: first, I promised you, that I would speak generally of the circumcision, what it is, and what it signifieth: secondly, I promised you to speak of the circumcision of our Saviour Christ, and how it chanced that he would be circumcised: thirdly, I promised you to speak of his manhood. Now you know, at the same time, I did not perform my promise, because I had no time; therefore I intend now, by the help of God, to perform that which I then promised. But yet, because the gospel containeth so good matter, I cannot go over it, but shew you certain specialties which are contained in it[2]. *Circumcision, what it is. Circumcision of Christ.*

The evangelist Matthew in this gospel goeth about to prove, that Jesus was this[3] Messias which was spoken of so much beforetimes by the prophets: and this he doth, by the place where he was born, namely, at Bethlehem; and also by the time, namely, when Herod was king over the Jews. But here be no Jews; therefore it needeth not to entreat of this matter. *Jesus Christ is the true Messias.*

[1 The Sunday alluded to was the Feast of the Circumcision: but the sermon preached on that occasion does not seem to have been reported.]

[2 in the same, 1607.]   [3 the, 1607.]

Furthermore, here we shall note the simplicity and heartiness of these men, which came a great way out of their countries, where the prophet Daniel had been beforetimes; for no doubt but they had learned of Daniel, that there should a Messias come. Therefore now, when they perceived by the star that he is[1] born, they are ready to forsake their countries, and come into Jewry, such[2] a great way, to make inquisition for him; and there go very simply to work, casting no peril. They ask openly at Jerusalem for him, saying, *Ubi est Rex?* "Where is he that is born king of the Jews?" Here you must understand, that after Pompey the Great had subdued the Jews, in process of time Herod had gotten the rule over them, by the means and appointment of the emperor: which Herod was not a Jew, but an Idumean; a cruel, wicked, and forecasting man; for he trusted not constantly upon the Jews. He was ever afraid he should be deprived of his kingdom. Now at that time, when this wicked man had the rule, these wise men came into the city, and inquired for the king of the Jews; and openly protested their faith which they had in Christ. They were nothing afraid of Herod; for they had such a trust and confidence in God, that they knew he was able to[3] deliver them from his hands.

Matt. ii.

Herod feared the loss of his kingdom by Christ.

But worldly-wise men will say, they were but fools to put themselves in danger[4] without need: they might have asked for him secretly, so that the king might not have heard of it. Such is the wisdom of these[5] which have no faith nor confidence in God: they will not abide any peril for God's sake; they seek rather[6] all corners to hide themselves in, rather than they will profess God's word openly. I pray you note and mark well their words: they say, "We are come to worship him; to do homage to him, to acknowledge him to be our Lord." Then, again, note the words of Herod: he saith unto them, "Go and search diligently for the child, and when you have found him, bring me word, that I may come and worship him also." Lo here, what a fox was this Herod! Who can judge of man's words, except God which knoweth the hearts of men?

Herod was a false fox.

[1 was, 1607.]   [2 being, 1607.]
[3 they were sure he would.]   [4 such danger, 1607.]
[5 those, 1607.]   [6 they seek all, 1607.]

Note another thing, which is this: as soon as this was published, that these strangers were come, asking for the king of the Jews, "Herod was troubled," saith the text, "and all Jerusalem with him." This was a strange thing, that Jerusalem should be troubled, which longed so long time for that king, for that Messias, for that Saviour. But they were even as we are: they cared not for God's word; they sought nothing but their ease, and to be at rest; they cared not greatly for religion; they thought, if we receive him, we shall have trouble with him, therefore it is better for us to leave him, and to let him alone, rather than to disquiet ourselves: they were even right merchantmen; they sought nothing but to save their substance in this world; this was all that they looked for: therefore they were troubled when they heard that Christ was born. *The lovers of this world care not for religion.*

Now what doth Herod? Forsooth, he calleth all the bishops and learned men, and inquireth of them the time at the which Christ should be born. They were well seen in the law and the prophets, after the letter, and therefore by and bye made answer unto him, saying, "At Bethlehem Judah he shall be born;" for so it is written in the fifth chapter of Micah, *Et tu, Bethlehem Juda,* "And thou, Bethlehem Judah, thou art not the least concerning the princes of Judah; for out of thee shall come the captain that shall govern my people Israel." After that Herod had heard this, he called the wise men, and bade them that they should "go and search out the child, and when they had found him, they should bring him word again, that he might come and worship him also." O what a fox is this! There hath been many such foxes in England, specially in the time of persecution; which pretended great holiness and zeal to God-ward with their will[7], but their hearts are poisoned with the cruelty of Herod. *Micah v.*

Now as soon as they were out of the city, the star appeared unto them again, and went before them till it came to the place, where it stood still. But yet you must understand, that our Saviour was born in a stable, but Joseph had gotten a house in process of time, so that they found him not in the stable. There be some learned men that think,

[7 mouth, 1607.]

that these wise men came a year or two after his birth[1], for they came a great way: and when they had found him, they did homage unto him, and acknowledged him to be the Lord; and declared their faith that they had in him, and brought[2] him gold, frankincense and myrrh. And here is to be noted the provision of God: there was nobody, that we read of, which gave any thing unto him; yet God could stir up the hearts of those strangers to shew their liberality towards him. They bring gold, which signified him to be the right king above all kings; and like as gold exceedeth all other metals, so gold signified him to be the king above all kings, and that the doctrine of him is the very true doctrine. Frankincense signified the prayer of the faithful, which maketh a good savour before God, for he greatly delighteth therein: myrrh, which they offered, signified [the] afflictions of those which confess Christ.

How the wise men honoured Christ.

Gold, frankincense, myrrh.

But here, as I told you before, you must note God's provision; for now Mary and Joseph must be gone to Egypt, see what provision God made for them: he sent them gold and other treasures out of a far country. Again, how God so wonderfully preserved those wise men, which were going again to Herod, if they had not been admonished by the angel of God. Therefore learn here, that they that believe in God, and put their hope and trust in him, shall be provided for: God will not forget them. But how these men came to Coleyne, in Germany, I marvel greatly[3]. I think it be but the fantasies and illusions of the devil, which stirred men up to worship stone and wood.

The three wise men came not to Coleyne.

But I will now leave that place of scripture, and return again to my promise, and to speak somewhat of circumcision, and so make an end.

God Almighty made this promise unto Abraham, saying,

[1 This opinion was maintained by Epiphanius, among the older writers, and was made to rest on Matt. ii. 16.]

[2 giving him, 1607.]

[3 The story of "these men" may be seen both in the *Legenda Sanctorum*, and in the *Sermones Aurei de Sanctor. Festis*, of Jacobus de Voragine, or in the *Liber Festivalis*. For a specimen of the devotion offered to them in this country anterior to the Reformation, reference may be had to "Reflections upon the devotions of the Roman Church," pp. 17, et seq. London, 1674.]

Ego ero Deus tuus, et seminis tui post te; "I will be thy God, and the God of[4] thy seed after thee." This was the promise of God, which promise was confirmed by that sign and outward token of circumcision. Now the covenant or promise of God abideth; but the circumcision, which was the sign of it, is gone and taken away by the coming of Christ, and instead thereof is ordained baptism. This you have heard the last time, when I told you that circumcision was not only a mark or naked token, whereby men might know a Jew from a gentile, but it had a further signification; namely, that like as the privy member was circumcised, the foreskin cut off, so the heart of every man must be circumcised, and the foreskin of all wickedness cut off, or pulled away: like as our baptism is not only ordained for that cause, to know a Christian from a Turk or heathen, but it hath a further signification; it signifieth that we must wash away the old Adam, forsake and set aside all carnal lusts and desires, and put on Christ; receive him with a pure heart, and study to live and go forward in all goodness, according unto his will and commandment. So, I say, at that time circumcision was not only an outward bare token, but had an inward signification; namely, that the heart of man should be circumcised from all sin, and cleansed from all wickedness.

Gen. xvii.

The signification of circumcision.

Now come to the point: circumcision at that time was a certain, sure, infallible, and effectual token of God's good-will towards them to whom it was given: for as many as did believe the covenant of God, it did ascertain them of the good-will of God towards them, that they should be delivered out of all their troubles and adversities, and that they should be sure of the help of God. An example we have in that good young man Jonathan: he comforted himself with his circumcision, saying to his weapon-bearer, *Veni, transeamus ad incircumcisos;* "Come, let us go to these uncircumcised." As though he had said, "Come, let us go, we have circumcision; God hath promised to be our God to aid and help us, and deliver us out of all our troubles and calamities." And so went on he and his weapon[5]-bearer only, and set upon them, and killed a great number of them that same day: which victory happened by the occasion of this faithful Jonathan, the king's son. So likewise did David, when he

Circumcision was to the Jews a sure and certain token of God's favour.

1 Sam. xiv.

God giveth victory to the faithful.

[4 the God of, 1607 only.]   [5 armour, 1607.]

should fight against Goliath the Philistine, he saith, *Quis est ille incircumcisus?* "What is this uncircumcised Philistine, that he should revile the host of the living God?" So they exhorted themselves, and confirmed their faith with this circumcision. So[1] let us ever consider, in what trouble and calamity soever we be, let us remember that we be baptized; that God hath promised to help us, to deliver us from all our sins and wickedness, to be our God[2]. And again, let us consider our promise which we have made unto him; namely, that we will forsake sin, the devil, and all his crafts and illusions, and cleave unto God only: and so by the remembrance of this, we shall be more ready and earnest to strive and fight against the devil.

Now let us come to the circumcision of our Saviour Christ. A man might marvel how it came to pass that our Saviour would be circumcised, being, as he was indeed, *Ipsissima justitia,* "The righteousness itself." What needeth him[3] to be circumcised? For he was no sinner, nor had need that his faith should be confirmed by circumcision; being very God, and the material Son of God. Again, to do a thing that needeth not, it is but lost labour and the time ill-spent. And St Paul saith, *Si circumcidamini, Christus vobis nihil proderit;* "If[4] you be circumcised, Christ doth you no good; you need not look[5] to be saved by him." To make answer to these questions: first, I would not have you to think that Christ, being but eight days old, knew not whereabouts his parents went; what they did when they circumcised him. Yes, yes; he knew it well enough: for though he was but a child, yet he was such a child that had no fellow; for, as St Paul witnesseth, *Plenitudo divinitatis habitabat in illo corporaliter;* "The abundancy of the Godhead dwelt in him corporally." God dwelleth in all them that be faithful, spiritually; for we be the temples of God: but in Christ he dwelleth corporally; that is to say, he with the plenteousness of his Godhead dwelleth in Christ. You must understand that Christ hath a soul and body, and united with his divinity; therefore it is said that he dwelleth in Christ corporally. Now he, being very God, would not have

[1 wherefore, 1607.]   [2 God and Comforter, 1607.]
[3 needed he, 1607.]   [4 when, 1571 and others.]
[5 to look, 1584.]

been circumcised against his will, but he did it voluntarily. As for the saying of St Paul, *Si circumcidamini, Christus nihil vobis proderit*, it hath his understanding: for St Paul in that place speaketh not of the outward work of circumcision, but against that wicked opinion which the gentiles had; for they thought that circumcision was a work meriting remission of sins; which opinion took away the office of Christ. Now St Paul warneth them of it, and sheweth that this was a wicked opinion, to think to be saved by the circumcision.

The causes wherefore Christ our Saviour would be cir-cumcised are these: first, because he would be a testimony that the old law was God's law; and for that time they were the very laws of God, and therefore he suffered himself to be circumcised, notwithstanding that he had no need of it: but this is but a secondary cause. Another cause is, to be obedient unto common orders: therefore he would suffer rather to be circumcised, than to give an occasion of hurly-burly or uproar: for the will of the Father was, that subjects should obey magistrates, and keep orders. *Subjecti estote cuivis humanæ potestati;* "Be obedient unto them." Look, what laws and ordinances are made by the magistrates, we ought to obey them. Therefore we must consider ever, in all our doings, what be the laws of the realm, and according unto the same we must live. And this is to be understood as well in spiritual matters as temporal matters; so far forth as their laws be not against God and his word. When they will move us to do any thing against God, then we may say, *Oportet magis obedire Domino quam hominibus;* "We must more be obedient unto God than unto man:" yet we may not withstand them with stoutness, or rise up against them, but suffer whatsoever they shall do unto us; for we may for nothing in the world rebel against the office of God, that is to say, against the magistrate. *The causes why Christ was circumcised.* *1 Pet. ii.* *Acts v. God is more to be obeyed than man.*

Now, Christ himself giveth an ensample of this obedience; and no doubt it was a painful thing to be circumcised, as it appeared by a notable act in the first book of Moses. When Jacob, that holy man, was coming home again, out of Mesopotamia, with his wives and children and all his substance, as he came by the way, he pitched his tents about the Sechemites. Now he had a daughter called Dina, which gazing damsel went about to see the countries, and so came into the *Gen. xxxiv.*

town among the strangers. Now the governor's son of the city, seeing her to be a fair maiden, cast his love upon her; and went and took her and ravished her, and afterward made suit unto Jacob, her father, and got her to[1] his wife. At the length, after much ado, they agreed upon that, that he, his father, and all his people should be circumcised: which was done; for upon a day all their males were circumcised. And here was a religion of policy: they were circumcised, not for God's sake, to acknowledge him to be their God, but only to satisfy the request of a foolish, wanton young man; as we read in Chronicles of such religion of policy. Now what happened? The third day, when their sores were very great, two of Jacob's sons went into the city, and slew all together, men, women, and children; and took their sister away again. Here by this appeared what pain it was, that[2] they were not able to withstand or defend themselves. But our Saviour he was well content to suffer that great pain.

Circumcision was painful.

But these causes are not the chiefest; but there hangeth more of it. St Paul shewed the chiefest cause in the epistle to the Galatians, saying: *Postquam venit plenitudo temporis, misit Deus Filium suum factum ex muliere;* "After that the fulness of the time came[3], God sent[4] his Son made of a woman." This is the principal cause; for "when the fulness of time was come,"—as God will have all things done in a convenient time, and the same time must be appointed by him, and not by us,—when the time was full come, then God sendeth his Son made of a woman. "Made of a woman," he saith; which signifieth that Christ took the substance of his body of the woman. In all things he was like unto other children, except that he had no carnal father, and was without sin; else he was very man: for we may make[5] him so spiritual, that we should deny his humanity. No, not so; he was very man, and was bound to the law. To what end? *Ut eos qui legi erant obnoxii liberaret;* "That he might deliver us from the law, to the which we were bound;" and that we might receive the right of the children of God by adoption, through God's goodness, by his deserving; that we might have, through his fulfilling of the law, remission of

Gal iv.

Christ took very flesh of Mary the virgin.

Gal. iv.

[1 that he might have her to, 1607.] [2 seeing, 1607.]
[3 of time was come, 1607.] [4 sent forth, 1607.]
[5 may not make, 1571.]

sins and eternal life. These are his gifts, which he hath deserved with his keeping of the law.

Thus you see to what end he was circumcised, and wherefore he kept the law; namely, to deliver us from the condemnation of it. For if he had not kept the law, the law had such power, that it should[6] have condemned us all: for so it is written, *Maledictus qui non manserit in omnibus;* "Cursed be he that abideth not by all that which is written in this[7] law." So that the least cogitation that we have against that[7] law of God, bringeth this curse upon our heads: so that there was never man, nor shall be one, that could remedy himself by this law; for it is spiritual; it may not be fulfilled but by the Spirit. It requireth us to be clean from all spot of sin, from all ill thoughts, words, and deeds: but we be carnal, and as St Paul saith, *venditi sub peccato,* "sold under sin and wickedness." Therefore he concludeth thus: *Ex operibus legis nemo justificabitur;* "And by the works of the law no man can be justified." For you must consider the works of the law, how they ought to be done; and again, how we do them. As Christ did them, they merit; for he did them perfectly, as they ought to be done: but as we do them, they condemn; and yet the lack is not in the law, but in us. The law for[8] itself is holy and good, but we are not able to keep it; and therefore we must seek our righteousness, not in the law, but in Christ, which hath fulfilled that[9] same, and given us freely his fulfilling.

Christ is the fulfilling of the law.

Gal. iii.

Christ's deeds were perfect, our deeds are imperfect.

And this is the chiefest cause wherefore Christ would fulfil the law. But all the papists think themselves to be saved by the law: and I myself have been of that dangerous, perilous, and damnable opinion, till I was thirty years of age. So long I had walked in darkness, and in the shadow of death! And, no doubt, he that departeth from[10] this world in this opinion, he shall never come to heaven. For when we well consider the works of the law, which the law requireth, and again, how we do them, we shall find that we may not be justified by our doings: for the flesh reigneth in us; it beareth rule and letteth[11] the Spirit, and so we never fulfil the law. Certain it is that they that believe in Christ have the Holy Ghost, which ruleth and governeth

None can, nor hath fulfilled the law, but Christ only.

[6 would, 1607.]   [7 the, 1607.]   [8 of, 1607.]
[9 the, 1607.]   [10 out of, 1607.]   [11 hindereth, 1607.]

them: yet for all that there be a great many lacks in them; so that if they would go about to be saved by their works, they should come too short; for their works are not able to answer the requests of the law. And so Christ should be but a judge, which should give[1] every one according to his merits, and should not deserve for us. If we had no other help but that, then we should go all to the devil. But God, the everlasting, be praised, we have a remedy and a sure helper! Christ, the Son of the living God, hath fulfilled the law for us, to deliver us from sin. Such is the office of Christ, to deliver us from the law and the wrath of it. The law required[2] a perfect righteousness and holiness: now all they that believe in Christ, they are holy and righteous, for he hath fulfilled the law for us which believe in him: we be reputed just through faith in Christ. What required[2] the law of us? Marry, righteousness and holiness. This we have, we are righteous; but how? Not by our works, for our works are not able to make us just, and deliver us from our sins; but we are just by this, that our sins are pardoned unto us through faith[3] which we have in Christ our Saviour: for he, through his fulfilling of the law, took away the curse of the law from our heads. *Qui de peccato condemnavit peccatum,* "He took away the power of the sin." Sin is made no sin.

Christ hath overthrown the power of sin.

I desire you in the reverence of God to bear away this one sentence, which I will tell you now[4]; for it shall be a good stay[5] against the temptations of the devil. The sentence is this: *Quod lex præstare non potuerat,* "That the law could not do, for it was letted by the flesh:" what can the law do when it hath no let? Marry, it can justify. *Sed infirmabatur per carnem;* that is to say, "by the infirmity of our flesh" man was not able to do it; the lack was in us: for we are wicked, and the law is holy and good. Now that which we lacked, that same hath God fulfilled and supplied, *misso Filio suo;* in that he hath sent his Son to supply that which man's works could not do: and with his fulfilling of the law and painful death he merited, that as many as believe in him, though they had done all the sins of the world, yet shall they not be damned, but are righteous before the

Rom. viii.

Christ's merits are our merits.

[1 give to, 1607.] [2 requireth, 1596, 1607.] [3 the faith, 1607.]
[4 I will now speak unto you, 1607.] [5 stay for you, 1607.]

face of God, believing in Christ; so that remission of sins and everlasting life may be sought no where else but only in Christ. *Qui proprio Filio non pepercit, sed dedit illum pro nobis,* "He that spared not his only Son, but gave him for us, why should he not have given us all things with him[6]?" Rom. iii.

By this text it appeareth, that he which hath Christ hath all things. He hath Christ's fulfilling of the law; he hath remission of his sins; and so, consequently, everlasting life. Is not this a comfort? What greater consolation, comfort, and heart's-ease can there be in heaven and earth, than that; namely, to be sure of the remission of thy sins, and that Christ bound himself unto the law, to that end that he might fulfil it to the uttermost? This, I say, is the greatest comfort; specially when the devil goeth in hand with us, and casteth[7] our sins in our teeth: as, no doubt, he forgetteth them not, but hath them (as they say) at his finger's-end; when he will so go to work with us, saying, "Sir[8], thou art damned; thou art a sinful wicked man[9], thou hast not kept God's most holy commandments: God must needs judge thee according unto his law."

Now then, when I have the grace to have in remembrance the circumcision of Christ; when I remember that Christ hath fulfilled the law for me; that he was circumcised; that he will stand between me and my damnation; when I look not upon my works, to be saved by them, but only by Christ; when I stick unto him; when I believe that my soul is washed and made clean through his blood;—then I have all his goodness, for God hath given him unto me: and when I believe in him, I apply all his benefits unto me. I pray God, the Almighty, to give us[10] such a heart that we may believe in him, for he is *finis legis,* "the end of the law;" *perfunctio legis,* "the fulfilling of the same, to the salvation of all that believe on him!" What can be more comfortable? Therefore let us believe in him and be thankful.

There is no salvation for us without Christ.

How we may apply all the benefits of Christ, and make them our benefits.

Now I must needs speak a word or two of good works, lest, peradventure, some of you be offended with me. I told you before wherein standeth our righteousness; namely in

[6 with him give us all things also, 1607.]
[7 goeth about to cast, 1607.]   [8 Sirra, 1607.]
[9 fellow, 1607.]   [10 every one of us, 1607.]

this, that our unrighteousness is forgiven us: for we must needs confess, that the best works that we do have need of remission of sins, and so not meritorious; for they be not perfect as they ought to be; and therefore we live of borrowing. We have no proper righteousness of our own; but we borrow, that is to say, we take the righteousness of Christ, which he offered freely to as many as believe in him. And this treasure of his righteousness is not wasted or spent; he hath enough for all the world, yea, if this were a thousand worlds. Therefore, when we have been wicked, let us be sorry for our wickedness, and come to Christ, and call for forgiveness; and then take a good earnest purpose to leave sin.

Every thing as it is, and not as it is taken.

There is a common saying amongst us here in England, "Every thing is, say they, as it is taken;" which indeed is not so: for every thing is as it is, howsoever it be taken. But in some manner of ways[1] it is true, as in this matter: we of ourselves are unjust, our works are unperfect, and so disagreeable unto God's laws; yet for Christ's sake we be taken for just, and our works are allowable before God: not that they be so indeed for themselves, but they be taken well for his sake. God hath a pleasure in our works;

God will reward our good works, not for the worthiness of them, but for his pleasure' sake.

though they be not so perfectly done as they ought to be, yet they please him, and he delighteth in them, and he will reward them in everlasting life. We have them not by our merits, but by Christ. And yet this sentence is true, *Reddit*

Rom. ii.

unicuique juxta opera; "He will reward every one according to his deserving:" he will reward our good works in everlasting life, but not with everlasting life: for our works are not so much worth, nor ought not so to be esteemed as to get heaven; for it is written, *Cœli gloria donum Dei,* "The kingdom of heaven is the gift of God." So likewise St Paul saith, *Gratis enim estis salvati per fidem absque operi-*

Ephes. ii.

bus, "Ye are saved freely without works." Therefore, when ye

We are freely saved.

ask, "Are they saved?" Say, "yes." How? Marry, *gratis,* freely: and here is all our comfort to stay our consciences.

You will say now, "Here is all faith, faith; but we hear nothing of good works;" as some carnal people make such carnal reasons like themselves. But, I tell you, we are bound to walk in good works; for to that end we

[1 things, 1607.]

are come to Christ, to leave sin, to live uprightly, and so to be saved by him: but you must be sure to what end you must work; you must know how to esteem your good works. As if I fast and give alms, and think to be saved by it, I thrust Christ out of his seat: what am I the better when I do so? But I[2] tell you how ye shall do them. First, consider with yourselves how God hath delivered you out of the hands of the devil. Now to shew yourselves thankful, and in consideration that he commandeth you to do good works, ye must do them; and therefore we wrestle with sin. When the devil tempteth me, or in any wise moveth me to wickedness, then I must withstand, disallow and reprove it; and when he hath gotten at any time the victory, we must rise again, and beware[3] afterward. And when I feel myself feeble and weak, what shall I do? Marry[4], call upon God; for he hath promised that he will help: there was never man yet, nor never shall be, but he either hath or shall find ease and comfort at God's hand, if he call unto[5] him with a faithful heart. For, as St Paul saith, *Benedictus est Deus qui non sinet vos temptari, supra quod ferre potestis:* "God is true," saith he, "he will not suffer us to be tempted further than we may bear." If therefore we would once enter into a practice to overcome the devil, it were but an easy thing for us to do, if every one in his calling would direct his ways to Godward, and to do good works: as the parents in their calling, to live quietly and godly together, and to bring up their youth in godliness: so likewise masters should shew good ensamples, to keep their servants in good order, to keep them from idleness and wickedness[6]. These are good works, when every one doth his calling, as God hath appointed him to do: but they must be done to that end, to shew ourselves thankful; and therefore they are called in scripture sacrifices of thanksgiving: not to win heaven withal; for if I should do so, I should deny Christ my Saviour, despise and tread him under my feet. For to what purpose suffered he, when I shall with my good works get[7]

How and wherefore good works are to be done.

We must do good works because God commandeth us to do them.

1 Cor. x.

The pathway of good works.

[2 I will tell, 1607.]   [3 be more wary, 1607.]
[4 when thou feelest thyself feeble and weak, then call, 1607.]
[5 upon, 1607.]
[6 masters should shew good ensamples, to keep their servants from idleness, 1607.]   [7 merit, 1607.]

heaven?—as the papists do, which deny him indeed; for they think to get heaven with their pilgrimages, and with running hither and thither. I pray you, note this; we must first be made good, before we can do good: we must first be made just, before our works please God: for when we are justified by faith in Christ, and are made good by him, then cometh our duty; that is, to do good works, to make a declaration of our thankfulness.

Good works follow faith.

I have troubled you a good while, and somewhat the longer, because I had much pleasure to comfort myself in it. In times past we were wont to run hither and thither, to this saint and to that saint; but it is all but fig-leaves what man can do. Therefore let us stick to Christ, which is the right, perfect, and absolute Saviour, and able to deliver us from all our sins; and not only able to do it, but also willing. He offereth himself unto us: therefore, I say, let us believe in him, and afterward shew our thankfulness through an honest, godly conversation and living; so that his holy name may be praised amongst us, and that they that know him not as yet, may be[1] brought to the knowledge of him through our godly conversation. The Almighty God, whose kingdom is everlasting, give us his grace[2]! To whom, with God the Son, and the Holy Ghost, be all honour and glory now and ever, world without end. *Amen.*

[1 may more willingly be brought, 1607.]
[2 grace to do well, 1607.]

A SERMON PREACHED BY MASTER HUGH LATIMER, THE FIRST SUNDAY AFTER THE EPIPHANY, ANNO 1552.

[LUKE II. 42.]

The father and mother of Jesus went to Jerusalem, after the custom, &c.

HERE in this gospel is to be noted, how Mary the mother of Christ[3] went to Jerusalem, having her husband, and the child Jesus, which was twelve years of age, in her company, &c. But before I come to this gospel, I will rehearse unto you something which I took in hand last holy-day[4], where I, taking occasion of the gospel that was read the same day, made mention how Jesus the Son of God, and Saviour of the world, was born in Bethlehem; and how God opened his birth unto the gentiles; which were the three wise men, commonly called the three kings of Collen: but they were not kings, as the fond opinion of the common people is, but they were religious men, and men that feared God; yea, and as some great learned men gather, they were of the remnant of those which Daniel the prophet had taught, and instructed in the knowledge of God and of his will. For Daniel, being in captivity, bare great rule among the gentiles, as it appeareth in his book of prophecy; and therefore was able to set forth and promote the true religion of God, which was known at that time only among the Jews: which knowledge these wise men had; and had also a special understanding of astronomy. And now they, seeing the star, perceived that it was not a common thing, but a token that the greatest king was born, of whom they had heard their forefathers talk; and therefore they came to Jerusalem, and inquired for this king, &c.

Matt. ii.

Christ shewed himself to the gentiles.

[3 our Saviour Christ, 1607.]
[4 If the date of 1552, prefixed to this Sermon, be correct, it seems probable, from the allusion here so expressly made to the preceding Sermon, that this Sermon at least (and perhaps some of those which follow) was preached again in 1553. The Sermons therefore are left in the arrangement of the old editions, and thus follow the order which the Church observes in commemorating the great events of the Gospel history.]

The last holy-day I had no time to entreat of this matter fully, and therefore I intend to speak somewhat of it at this time. And first of this word, "Jesus," what it is.

Jesus, what it is.

The evangelist saith here, "When Jesus was born." What is "Jesus?" Jesus is an Hebrew word, and signifieth, in our English tongue, a Saviour and Redeemer of all mankind, born into this world. This title and name, "to save," pertaineth properly and principally unto him: for he saveth us, else we had been lost for ever. Notwithstanding, the name of saviour is used in common speech; as the king is called a saviour, for he saveth his subjects from all danger and harm that may ensue of the enemies. Likewise, the physician is accounted a saviour; for he saveth the sick man from the danger of his disease with good and wholesome medicines. So fathers and mothers are saviours; for they save their children from bodily harm, that may happen unto them. So bridges, leading over the waters, are saviours; for they save us from the water. Likewise ships and boats, great and small vessels upon the seas, are saviours; for they save us from the fury, rage, and tempest of the sea. So judges are saviours; for they save, or at least should save, the people from wrong and oppression. But all this is not a perfect saving: for what availeth it to be saved from sickness, calamities, and oppression, when we shall be condemned after our death both body and soul for ever to remain with the devil and his angels? We must therefore come to Jesus, which is the right and true Saviour: "And he it is that hath saved us from sin." Whom hath he saved? His people. Who are his people? All that believe in him, and put their whole trust in him; and those that seek help and salvation at his hands: all such are his people. How saved he them? First, by magistrates, he saved the poor from oppression and wrong: the children he saved through the tuition of the parents, from danger and peril: by physicians he saveth from sickness and diseases: but from sin he saveth only through his passion and blood-shedding. Therefore he may be called, and is, the very right Saviour; for it is he that saveth from all infelicity all his faithful people: and his salvation is sufficient to satisfy for all the world as concerning itself; but as concerning us, he saved no more than such as put their trust in him. And as many as believe in him

A saviour is used in sundry speeches.

Jesus Christ is our only Saviour.

How many ways Christ saveth us.

Christ's death is our only salvation.

shall be saved; the other shall be cast out as infidels into everlasting damnation; not for lack of salvation, but for infidelity and lack of faith, which is the only cause of their damnation.

He saved us, from what? Even from sin. Now when he saved us from sin, then he saved us from the wrath of God, from affliction and calamities, from hell and death, and from damnation and everlasting pain: for sin is the cause and fountain of all mischief. Take away sin, then all other calamities wherein mankind is wrapped, are taken away, and clean gone and dispersed: therefore he, saving us from sin, saved us from all affliction. But how doth he save us from sin? In this manner: that sin shall not condemn us, sin shall not have the victory over us. He saved us not so, that we should be without sin, that no sin should be left in our hearts. No, he saved us not so; for all manner of imperfections remain in us, yea, in the best of us; so that if God should enter into judgment with us, we should all be damned. For there are none[1], nor ever was any man born into this world, which could say, "I am clean from sin," except Jesus Christ. Therefore he saved us not so from sin, in taking clean away the same[2], that we should not[3] be inclined to it; but rather, the power and strength of the same sin he hath so vanquished, that it shall not be able to condemn those which believe in him: for sin is remitted, and not imputed unto the believers.

Sin is the only cause of damnation.

How we be saved from sin.

Christ only is void of sin.

So likewise he saved us from sin, not taking it clean away, but rather the strength and force of the same: so he saved us from other calamities, not taking the same clean away, but rather the power of the same; so that no calamity nor misery should be able to hurt us that are in Christ Jesu. And likewise he saved us from death; not that we should not die, but that death should have no victory over us, nor condemn us; but rather to be a way and entrance into salvation and everlasting life: for death is a gate to enter into everlasting life. No man can come to everlasting life, but he must first die bodily; but this death cannot hurt the faithful, for they are exempted from all danger through the death and passion of Jesus Christ, our Saviour, which with his death hath overcome our death.

The power and force of sin is taken away by Christ.

[1 neither is, 1607.] [2 same from us, 1607.] [3 no more, 1607.]

The error of the Jews.

Here is to be noted the error of the Jews, which believed that this Saviour should be a temporal king and ruler, and deliver them out of the hands of the Romans: for the Jews at that time were under the governance of the Romans; subdued by Pompeius, the great and valiant captain, as Josephus[1], a great and learned man amongst the Jews, and Titus Livius[2], do witness. Therefore they believed that this Saviour should not only set them at liberty, but should subdue all nations; so that the Jews only, with their Saviour, should be the rulers of all the whole world, and that the whole world should serve them. This was at the same time, and is yet still, the opinion of the Jews; which will not learn nor understand, that Jesus saved them and us, not from the power of the Romans, but from sin, death, the devil and hell; and set us at liberty, and made us *filii Dei,* the children of God, and the inheritors of life everlasting.

The papists' opinion of Christ's death.

The papists, which are the very enemies of Christ, make him to be a Saviour after their own fantasy, and not after the word of God; wherein he declareth himself, and set out and opened his mind unto us. They follow, I say, not the scripture, which is the very leader to God, but regard more their own inventions; and therefore they make him a Saviour after this fashion. They consider how there shall be, after the general resurrection, a general judgment, where all mankind shall be gathered together to receive their judgment: then shall Christ, say the papists, sit as a judge, having

The doctrine of papists.

power over heaven and earth: and all those that have done well in this world, and have stedfastly prayed upon their beads, and have gone a pilgrimage, &c., and so with their good works have deserved heaven and everlasting life,—those, say they, that have merited with their own good works, shall be received of Christ, and admitted to everlasting salvation. As for the other, that have not merited everlasting life, [they] shall be cast into everlasting darkness: for Christ will not suffer wicked sinners to be taken into heaven, but rather

The papists' opinion of Christ.

receive those which deserve. And so it appeareth, that they esteem our Saviour not to be a Redeemer, but only a judge; which shall give sentence over the wicked to go into everlasting fire, and the good he will call to everlasting felicity. And this is the opinion of the papists, as concerning our

[1 Antiq. xiv. 4.]   [2 Epitom. 102]

Saviour; which opinion is most detestable, abominable, and filthy in the sight of God. For it diminisheth the passion of Christ; it taketh away the power and strength of the same passion; it defileth the honour and glory of Christ; it forsaketh and denieth Christ, and all his benefits. For if we shall be judged after our own deservings, we shall be damned everlastingly. Therefore, learn here, every good Christian, to abhor this most detestable and dangerous poison of the papists, which go about to thrust Christ out of his seat: learn here, I say, to leave all papistry, and to stick only to the word of God, which teacheth thee that Christ is not only a judge, but a justifier; a giver of salvation, and a taker away of sin; for he purchased our salvation through his painful death, and we receive the same through believing in him; as St Paul teacheth us, saying, *Gratis estis justificati per fidem,* "Freely ye are justified through faith." In these words of St Paul, all merits and estimation of works are excluded and clean taken away. For if it were for our works' sake, then it were not freely: but St Paul saith, "freely." Whether will you now believe St Paul, or the papists? It is better for you to believe St Paul, rather than those most wicked and covetous papists; which seek nothing but their own wealth, and not your salvation. *[margin: A detestable opinion of the papists. Faith only justifieth. Rom. iii.]*

But if any of you will ask now, How shall I come by my salvation? How shall I get everlasting life? I answer: If you believe with an unfeigned heart that Jesus Christ, the Son of God, came into the world, and took upon him our flesh of the virgin Mary; and suffered under Pontius Pilate, in the city of Jerusalem, most[3] painful death and passion upon the cross; and was hanged between two thieves, for our sins' sake: for in him was no sin, "neither," as the prophet Isaiah saith, "was there found in his mouth any guile or deceit." For he was a Lamb undefiled, and therefore suffered not for his own sake, but for our sake; and with his suffering hath taken away all our sins and wickedness, and hath made us, which were the children of the devil, the children of God; fulfilling the law for us to the uttermost; giving us freely as a gift his fulfilling to be ours, so that we are now fulfillers of the law by his fulfilling: so that the law may not condemn us, for he hath fulfilled it, that we, be- *[margin: The bye way and right path to salvation. Isai. liii. By Christ we are fulfillers of the law.]*

[3 the most, 1607.]

lieving in him, are fulfillers of the law, and just before the face of God. For Christ with his passion hath deserved, that all that believe in him shall be saved, not through their own good works, but through his passion.

To obtain salvation is to believe in Christ.

Here thou seest whereupon hangeth thy salvation; namely, believing in the Son of God, which hath prepared and gotten heaven for all those that believe in him, and live uprightly according to his word. For we must do good works, and God requireth them of us: but yet we may not put our trust in them, nor think to get heaven with the same; for our works are wicked and evil, and the best of them be imperfect. As for those which are evil, no man is so foolish to think to get heaven with evil doing. And as concerning our good works, they are unperfect, and not so agreeable to the law of God, who requireth most perfect works: by the which appeareth, that the best works which are done by man are hateful before God, and therefore not able to get or deserve salvation. Wherefore we must be justified, not through our good works, but through the passion of Christ; and so live by a free justification and righteousness in Christ Jesu. Whosoever thus believeth, mistrusting himself and his own doings, and trusting in the merits of Christ, he shall get the victory over death, the devil, and hell; so that they shall not hurt him, neither all their powers [be] able to stand against any of those which are in Christ Jesu. Therefore, when thou art in sickness, and feelest that the end of thy bodily life approacheth, and that the devil with his assaults cometh[1] to tempt thee, and have thy soul, and so to bring thee to everlasting confusion; then withstand him strongly in faith; namely, when he bringeth thee low: for he is an old doctor, and very well learned in the scripture, as it appeareth in the fourth chapter of Matthew, where he reasoned with Christ. So will he reason with thee, saying: "Sir, it is written in the law, that all those which have not fulfilled the law to the uttermost, shall be condemned. Now thou hast not fulfilled it, but hast been wicked, and a transgressor of it; thou[2] art mine; and therefore thou shalt go to hell, and there to be punished world without end." Against such temptations and assaults of the devil, we must fight on this wise, and answer:

Good works are to be done.

The works of man are unperfect.

Christ's death apprehended by faith is our justification.

A godly counsel to be used in sickness.

[1 coming, 1584; is coming, 1607.]
[2 *ergo*, thou art, 1571, 1572.]

"I acknowledge myself to be a sinner most miserable, and filthy in the sight of God, and therefore, as of myself, I should be damned, according to thy saying: but there is yet one thing behind, that is this, I know and believe without all doubt, that God hath sent his Son into the world, which suffered a most painful and shameful death for me; and fulfilled the law wherewith thou wouldest condemn me: yea, he hath given me, as a gift, his fulfilling, so that I am now reckoned a fulfiller of the law before God. Therefore avoid, thou most cruel enemy, avoid; for I know that my Redeemer liveth, which hath taken away all my sin and wickedness, and set me at unity with God his heavenly Father, and made me a lawful inheritor of everlasting life." *Christ's fulfilling of the law is made, by faith, our fulfilling of the law.*

Whoso in such wise fighteth with the devil, shall have the victory, for he is not able to stand against Christ; and it appeareth throughout all the scripture most plainly and manifestly, that the power of the devil is vanquished, when the word of God is used against him: and not alonely in the scripture, both new and old Testament, but also in other writings. For Eusebius Pamphilius[3] hath many stories, wherein is mentioned the impotency of the devil. And at this time we have a story, written by a Spaniard in the Latin tongue, and affirmed by many godly and well learned men: which story happened in a town of Germany[4]; where a poor husbandman, lying sore sick and ready to die, they that kept him company in the chamber where he lay, saw a man of great stature, and very horrible to look upon, his eyes being all fiery, coming into the chamber. This terrible devil, turning himself unto the sick body, said, "Sir, thou must die this day, and I am come hither to fetch thy soul; for that pertaineth unto me." The sick man answered with a good countenance, saying, "I am ready to depart whensoever I shall be called of my Lord, which gave unto me my *The devil cannot withstand the scripture.* *A strange tale of the devil.*

[3 The preacher, it may be presumed, had in view those "stories" in the Ecclesiastical History, which relate the constancy of the primitive martyrs when assailed by the violent persecutions which the devil stirred up against the church:—παντὶ γὰρ σθένει ἐνέσκηψεν ὁ ἀντικείμενος. Euseb. Histor. Eccles. v. 1; VIII.]

[4 A similar story is given by Wolff, who cites his authorities, and states that the circumstances he relates occurred at Fribourg in the year 1533. Lectiones Memorab. Tom. II. p. 412. Francof. ad Mœn. 1671.]

soul, and put the same into my body: therefore unto him only will I deliver it, and not unto thee; for he hath delivered my soul from thy power with the precious blood of his only Son." Then said the devil, "Thou art laden with many sins, and I am come hither to write them together." And forth he draweth out of his bosom pen, ink, and paper, setting himself at the table, that stood there, ready to write. The sick man hearing his mind, and perceiving his intent, said: "I know myself laden with many sins; but yet I believe that the same are taken away through the passion and suffering of Christ, through whom I stedfastly believe that the heavenly Father is pleased with me: but yet, if thou wilt write my sins, thou mayest do it, and then write thus, that all my righteousness is as cloth stained with the flowers of a woman. Therefore I cannot stand in the judgment of God." The devil, sitting at the table, wrote this with a good will; and desired the sick man to go forward in confessing and numbering his sins. Then the sick man, alleging the scriptures, saith, "That the eternal and living God promised, saying, 'For mine own sake only I take away your iniquities.' Further, Thou, O God, hast promised, that 'though our sins be as red as the scarlet, thou wilt make them as white as snow.'" But these words he wrote not; but instantly desired him to go forward as he had begun. The sick man, with great sorrow and heaviness, cried out, saying, "The Son of God appeared to that end, that he might destroy the works of the devil." And after these words the devil vanished out of sight; and shortly after the sick man departed unto the living God. Here you see how the devil will go to work with us, when we are sick: therefore let us learn now when we are in health to know God and his word, that we may withstand this horrible enemy; knowing that we shall have the victory through Christ our Saviour, in whom and by whom God is pleased with us, and taketh in good part all our doings.

Isai. lxiv.

Isai. xliii.

We have a common saying amongst us, "Every thing is as it is taken." We read of king Henry the seventh, at a time as he was served with a cup of drink, a gentleman that brought the cup, in making obeisance, the cover fell to the ground: the king, seeing his folly, saith, "Sir, is this well done?" "Yea, Sir," said he, "if your majesty take it well."

A pretty example of king Henry the seventh.

With this pretty answer the king was pacified. So it is with us, as touching our salvation. Our works are unperfect, but God taketh the same well for Christ's sake: he will not impute unto us the imperfectness of our works, for all our imperfections and sins are drowned in the blood of our Saviour, Jesus Christ; and whosoever believeth the same stedfastly, shall not perish. But we must be sure of it: we may not doubt, but be certain that Christ hath destroyed the works of Satan; that is, he hath taken his power from him, so that he can do us no more harm. And we must certainly believe his promises, which are, that we shall have life everlasting in believing in him; and being sure of his promises, then are we sure of our salvation. Here you see, that we must seek our salvation, not in our works, but in Christ. For if we look upon our works, we shall never be sure: as I said before, they be evil and imperfect; and evil works deserve anger, and imperfect works are punishable, and not acceptable; and therefore they deserve no heaven, but rather punishment.

A comfortable doctrine.

Our salvation consisteth in faith and not in works.

But you will say, "Seeing we can get nothing with good works, we will do nothing at all; or else do such works as shall best please us; seeing we shall have no rewards for our well-doings." I answer: we are commanded, by God's word, to apply ourselves to goodness, every one in his calling; but we must not do it to the end to deserve heaven thereby: we must do good works to shew ourselves thankful for all his benefits, which he hath poured upon us, and in respect of God's commandment; considering that God willeth us to do well, not to make a merit of it; for this were a denying of Christ, to say, "I will live well and deserve heaven." This is a damnable opinion: let us rather think thus, "I will live well to shew myself thankful towards my loving God, and Christ my Redeemer."

How good works ought to be done.

Further, in this gospel is to be noted the earnestness of these three men which were but gentiles, as you have heard before. These men were not double-hearted, speaking one thing with their tongues, and thinking another thing in their hearts. No; they are none such: but they openly profess wherefore they come, and say, "Where is this new-born king of the Jews? for we have seen his star, and are come to worship him." This is a great matter for them to do. For the Jews at that time had a king whose name was Herod, not a Jew born, but an Idumean, which was not their lawful nor natural king, but somewhat with craft and subtilty, and somewhat with power, had gotten the crown and the kingdom. Now the men came inquiring for the lawful king, which was newly born; which thing they could not do without danger of their lives. But here appeareth, that faith feareth no danger. They had seen the star, and they were sure and certain in their hearts, that the King of kings was born: and they believed that this king was able to deliver them out of trouble; and this confidence and faith in God made them hearty to go and inquire without any dissembling for this new king, not fearing the old, &c.

<small>Faith feareth no danger.</small>

Herod, hearing these news, was much troubled; for he was afraid the matter would go against him, and that he should be thrust out of his seat: which had been a great displeasure unto him; for he was not minded to give place to any other king, with his good will. And all[1] the citizens were sore dismayed; for they would rather have rest and quietness, and serve the old, than to receive the new, with peril of their goods and bodies. So we see at this day, where this gospel is preached, and this new king proclaimed, there are more which had rather be in quietness and serve the devil, than to stand in jeopardy of their lives and serve God; and so they esteem this world more than God, his word, and their own salvation.

<small>Herod feared the birth of Christ.</small>

The said Herod, as soon as he heard these tidings, sent for the bishops and learned, and inquired of them where Christ should be born. The bishops were well seen in the prophets and the law, and made answer forthwith, that Christ should be born at Bethlehem. Herod, hearing that, sent for the wise men, to examine them better of the matter; asking them what time they had seen the star? And after he had reasoned enough with them, he sent them to Bethlehem, saying, "Go and search for the child; and when you have found him, bring me word again, that I may come and worship him also." See what a crafty fox this Herod was, as our Saviour called him! He made a pretence like as if he were willing to give over his kingdom, and to give place unto the new king. Such was his pretence outwardly; but his

<small>Herod a crafty fox.</small>

[¹ also, 1571, 1572.]

heart was poisoned with the poison of cruelness and ambition, *Herod a cruel and ambitious tyrant.* so that he was minded to have killed this child as soon as he might get him: which his intent appeared afterward. For he, hearing that the wise men were returned another way into their country, sent by and bye his guard, and killed all the children that were two years of age and under at Bethlehem, and in the country. But for all his cruelty, God was able to preserve Christ, that he should not be slain amongst these children. Therefore the angel giveth Joseph warning that he should go into Egypt. Here learn to trust in God; for *adversus altissimum non est consilium*, that is, "Against *Prov. xxi.* the Almighty prevaileth no counsel." This Herod thought himself wiser than God and the whole world; yet for all that he was much deceived: for he could neither destroy the wise men, nor Christ, with all his wit and counsel: "the Lord *Psal. ii.* that sitteth above laughed him to scorn;" he brought his counsel to nought, and he delivered them out of his hands. So undoubtedly he will do with us. He will deliver us out *God will be our defender, if we put our trust in him.* of all our troubles, and from all our enemies whensoever they shall oppress us, if we do put our trust in him.

Now after they were departed from Herod, they go their ways seeking the child. And as soon as they came out of the city, they see the star, which guided them until they came unto the house where Jesus was, with his mother, and Joseph his father in the law. And when these men came thither, what did they? They worshipped him. Note here, they *Matt. ii.* worshipped him, saith the evangelist. Here is confounded and overthrown the foolish opinion and doctrine of the papists, which would have us to worship a creature before the Creator; Mary before her Son. These wise men do not so; they worship not Mary; and wherefore? Because God only is to *God only to be worshipped.* be worshipped: but Mary is not God; therefore they worship not her, but him, which is the very natural Son of God, yea, God himself, and yet very man. And therefore, if it had been allowed or commanded that Mary the mother of Christ should have been called upon and worshipped, surely then had these wise men been greatly to blame: but they knew that Mary was a blessed woman, above all women[2], and yet not such a one as should be called upon and worshipped. Let all those learn here, that are so foolish, that they will call

[[2] above all women, only in 1571, 1572.]

rather upon Mary, on whom they have no commandment to call, than upon God who hath commanded us to call upon him; as he saith every where in the Psalms, *Invoca me in die tribulationis,* "Call upon me in the time of thy trouble, and I will hear thee."

<small>Gifts given to Christ, what they signified.</small>

They gave him gifts, gold, myrrh, and frankincense. Gold they gave him to signify his kingdom; myrrh, to signify his mortality; frankincense, to signify his priesthood. And afterward they departed another way into their countries, by the admonition of the angel. After their departure Joseph, with Mary and the child, fled into Egypt, for fear of Herod, which was minded to destroy the child. Where you learn to know the wonderful provision that God ever maketh for those that put their trust in him; for to the intent they might have wherewith to bear their costs for such a journey, God moved their hearts, that they should give

<small>He that putteth his trust in God shall not lack.</small>

him gold. Learn, I say, here to put your trust in God, and to have a good confidence in him; for he is such a loving father to those that trust in him, that he will not suffer them to have lack or need of any thing in this world, of food and necessary things; for he careth for us that believe in him, as well as for Mary and her Son. Therefore he will not suffer us to have lack of that is needful to soul or body; for the king and prophet David saith, *Nunquam vidi justum*

<small>Psal. xxxvii.</small>

derelictum; that is, "I have never seen the just man forsaken or rejected of God, nor cast away." No, saith he, I have never seen the just man perish for lack of necessary things.

<small>Who they be that are just men.</small>

But what is a just man? He is just that believeth in our Saviour: for, as you have heard before, those who believe in Christ are justified before God; they are clean delivered from all sins, and therefore may be called just, for so they are in the sight of God: such, saith the prophet, he hath never seen forsaken of God.

But for all this, we may not tempt God; we must labour and do our business, every one in his vocation and order wherein God hath called him. Labour thou, and God will bless thee, and increase thy labours; so that thou shalt have no lack of necessary things, so long as thou walkest uprightly in thy vocation; like as he provided for Mary and her child. But yet thou must labour and do thy business, as it is written: *Labores manuum tuarum edes, et bene tibi erit;*

"Be content to work for thy living, and it shall go well with thee, and thou shalt have enough, for I will make thee a living:" which promise of God is surely a comfortable thing, but little regarded of the people; for they do like as there were no God, and deceive and oppress one another. Every man scrapeth for himself; ever in fear that he shall lack, nothing regarding that promise of God. But God is yet alive; and surely he will most grievously punish such wicked unthankfulness and mistrust of his word and promise. What might be more comfortable unto us, if we had grace to believe it, than his loving promises, wherein he sheweth himself a loving Father? David saith, *Juvenis fui, et senui;* "I have been young, and now am old; but yet I never saw the righteous lack bread." Here learn, O man, to have respect to God-ward: esteem the word of God and his promises as they are, that is, most certain and true: believe them; hang upon them; labour and do thy business truly, *et bene tibi erit,* "and it shall be well with thee." Thou shalt have enough; thou shalt have a store-house that never shall be empty, that is, thy labour: for the poor man's treasure-house is his labour and travail; and he is more sure of his living than the rich: for God's promises cannot be stolen by any thief. God promiseth him a living, that truly laboureth, and putteth his trust in him. But the rich man is not sure of his riches, for a thief may come and steal them; or else the same may perish by fire, or one way or other: therefore the poor faithful man is more sure of his living, than if he had the same in his chest; for God's promises are not vain; they are most certain. And happy are those which believe the same; they shall have not only in this world enough, but afterward everlasting life, without all sorrow and misery!

Thus much I was minded to tell you of this gospel: now let us return to the gospel of this day, wherein I will note two or three short notes; for I will not trouble you much longer, because the time is much spent.

"And when he was twelve years old," &c. God Almighty had commanded in his law, Deuteronomy, the sixteenth chapter, that all the males should come together three times in the year, for these three causes:—the first was, that they should learn to trust in God, and not in their

Psal. cxxviii. 2.

The covetous man trusteth not in God.

Psal. xxxvii.

Luke ii.

Deut. xvi.

The causes why the Jews resorted to Jerusalem.

own strength: and it was a great matter unto them to leave the land void. As if we Englishmen had commandment to come all to London, and leave our country, were it not to be feared that the country should be hurt either by the Scots or Frenchmen in our absence? Surely, I think it were very dangerous. So at that time the Jews had great and mortal enemies round about them, yet God commanded them to leave the land void: as who would say, "Come you together after my commandment, and let me alone with your enemies; I will keep them from you that they shall not hurt you." And this was the first cause why he would have them come together.

The second cause was, that they should learn the law and commandments of God: for there was the chief temple of the Jews; and all the spiritualty of the whole land were there gathered together, and taught the people the law, and how they should walk before God: and this was the second cause.

The third cause of their coming together was for acquaintance sake; for God would have them knit together in earnest love and charity. And therefore he willed them to come together, that they that dwelled on the one side of the land might be acquainted with them that dwelled on the other side; so that there might be a perfect love between them: for God hateth nothing more than discord. And these are the causes why they were commanded to come together every year three times.

Now at this time Mary went with her husband Joseph. Belike she was desirous to hear the word of God, which made her to take so great a journey in hand; for she was not commanded by the law to be there, for women were at their liberty to go or tarry. Here note the painfulness of Mary, that she was content to go so great a journey for God's sake. I fear, this journey of hers will condemn a great many of us, which will not go out of the door to hear God's word. Therefore learn here, first, to love and embrace God's word: secondly, to follow all good orders: thirdly, to be content to go with thy neighbours every holy-day to the church; for it is a good and godly order, and God will have it so. But peradventure you will say unto me, "How chance you go not to the service upon the

<small>The travail of the virgin Mary to hear God's word taught.</small>

holy-days?" I have none other excuse but this, namely, that I shall go thither in vain. Mary went thither to hear the word of God; and if I might hear the word of God there, I would go thither with a good will. But first, the parson of the church is ignorant and unable to teach the word of God, neither beareth he any good will to the word of God; therefore it were better for me to teach my family at home, than to go thither and spend my time in vain, and so lose my labour. This I have to allege for myself, that if the curate were as he ought to be, I would not be from the church upon the holy-day.

Jesus and Mary, with all their neighbours, were at Jerusalem: and after they had done their business, they came home again; Mary in the company of other women, and Joseph her husband in the company of men: but Jesus the child was left behind; for Mary thought he was with his father, and Joseph thought he was with his mother. At night, when they were met together, she asked him, and he asked her, for the child; for before they were not aware that they had lost him. O, what sorrow and tribulation rose then in their hearts! I think no tongue can shew what pain and sorrow this mother felt in her heart for the loss of her child: for she thought thus, "God hath rejected me, and therefore hath taken my son from me: I shall no more find him. Alas, that ever I was born, that I should lose my son, whom I heard say should be the Saviour of the world! This Saviour is lost now through my negligence and slothfulness. What shall I do? Where shall I seek him?" In this great heaviness she turned back again to Jerusalem, inquiring for him by the way amongst their friends and acquaintance; but he could neither be heard of nor found, until they came to Jerusalem, where they found him amongst the doctors and learned men, arguing with them, and posing them. *Jesus disputed with the doctors.*

Here is to be noted a negligence in Mary and Joseph: therefore they which go about to make Mary to be without sin are much deceived; for here it appeareth plainly that Mary was in fault. Here, also, all parents may learn to be diligent and careful about their children. The common sort of parents are either too careful for their children, or else too negligent. But the right carefulness that you should *Mary the virgin was not without sin.*

have over your children, is, first to consider that God hath appointed his angels to keep and save your children from all peril and danger that may happen unto them, as it plainly appeareth daily; for surely a child is in many dangers of his life daily, but the angel of God keepeth them. And therefore the parents should not be too careful, neither yet too negligent; for they should consider, that it is the will, pleasure, and commandment of Almighty God, that they should keep their children in safe custody, and to preserve them, as much as in them lieth, from all danger and harm. Further, here is to be noted, that this fault and sin of Mary was not set out to bolden us to sin, but rather to keep us from desperation when we have sinned; making this reckoning, Hath God pardoned his saints and forgiven their faults? Then he will be merciful unto me, and forgive my sin. So by their ensample we may strengthen our faith, and not to take boldness of them to sin.

<small>*Parents may not be careless of their children, nor yet too careful.*</small>

<small>*A goodly lesson.*</small>

After that they found him, Mary beginneth to quarrel with him, saying, "Son, why hast thou done this unto us?" Here she speaketh like a mother, and is very quick with him. But he made her as quick an answer, saying, "Know ye not that I must do the business of my Father?" &c. We learn here, how far forth children are bound to obey their parents; namely, so far as the same may stand with godliness. If they will have us go further, and pluck us from true religion and the serving of God, make them this answer, *Oportet magis obedire Deo quam hominibus;* that is, "We ought rather to obey God than men; for otherwise we are not bound to obey our parents," &c. Here not only children may learn, but subjects and servants, to obey their king and masters, so far as it may stand with God's pleasure; and further to go we ought not.

<small>*Children, what obedience they owe to their parents.*</small>

<small>Acts v.</small>

<small>*True obedience, what it is.*</small>

The child went home with them, and was obedient to them. Although partly he had signified unto them wherefore he was sent into the world, namely, to teach men the way to heaven; yet he remained with them in his obedience from this time, being of the age of twelve years, unto the age of thirty years. And in this mean time (as it is to be thought) he exercised his father's occupation, which was a carpenter. This is a wonderful thing, that the Saviour of the world, and the King above all kings, was not ashamed

<small>*Labour is allowed by Christ.*</small>

to labour; yea, and to use so simple an occupation. Here he did sanctify all manner of occupations, exhorting and teaching us with this ensample every man to follow and keep the state whereunto[1] God hath called him; and then we shall have living enough in this world, doing well and after his pleasure; and in the world to come life everlasting, which Christ by his death and passion hath deserved for us. To whom, with God the Father and the Holy Ghost, be all honour and glory, both now and for ever! *Amen.*

[1 wherever, 1571.]

A SERMON PREACHED BY MASTER HUGH LATIMER, THE
SECOND SUNDAY AFTER THE EPIPHANY, THE 17TH
DAY OF JANUARY, ANNO 1552.

JOHN II. [1.]

And upon the third day there was a marriage in Cana, a city of Galilee, and Mary the mother of Jesus was there.

"THE third day," that was the third day after he came into Galilee; for before he was in Jewry, and now was come into Galilee. And there was a marriage the third day after his coming, and Mary his mother was present, and, as it was most like, she was there as an helper; for she was no bidden guest; but Christ was called unto it, with his disciples, being thirty years of age: at which time he began to preach the kingdom of God; but as yet he had done no miracles, except that which he did when he was twelve years of age; that was, he disputed in the temple with the doctors; which certainly was a miracle: but this now was the first that he did after his preaching. And now, being a preacher, he beginneth to confirm all his doctrine with miracles, to get himself authority, and to allure his audience to believe; and therefore he set forth his power by miracles.

Christ being thirty years old began to preach.

And here, peradventure, some will say, How happeneth it that there are no miracles done in these days by such as are preachers of the word of God? I answer: The word of God is already confirmed by miracles; partly by Christ himself, and partly by the apostles and saints. Therefore they which now preach the same word need no miracles for the confirmation thereof; for the same is sufficiently confirmed already. Now to the gospel.

The word of God is confirmed by miracles.

Preachers in these days need no miracles.

"There was a marriage," saith the evangelist. This is a comfortable place for all married folks: for it here appeareth that marriage is a most honourable and acceptable thing in the sight of God; yea, God Almighty himself is the author of it, as the scripture saith, "Those that God hath joined together man shall not separate;" meaning that all those

A marriage in Cana, a city in Galilee.

Matt. xix.

that come together by the appointment of God and his holy institution, such shall not man separate, nor put asunder. Here all those which go about marriage, may learn to examine their consciences; and to be sure that it is the pleasure and will of God that man and wife should marry and dwell together. And they which are married already may comfort themselves in all afflictions, adversities, and miseries that come by marriage; namely, that they are in the favour of God, and that God hath joined them together in that estate; which estate although it bring with it great affliction and tribulation, (as we may see by Adam and Eve when they were in Paradise, where God grievously punished their sins: for before the fall the wife had like power with her husband Adam, and was in like dignity with him; but after the fall came the commandment of God to the man, saying, "In the sweat of thy face thou shalt eat thy bread;" which is a great bondage unto man; for in this compaction is contained the whole burthen and charge laid upon the man's back; that is to say, that he hath the charge over his household, to provide for their livings and sustenance with his labour and occupation: and unto the woman he said, "In sorrow and pain thou shalt bring forth thy children, and thou shalt be in obedience to thy husband; he shall govern thee, and thou shalt not have thine own will nor liberty:" which is a great matter, for women have many and great sorrows and pains in travail with children, and other calamities; and being before at liberty, must now be obedient to their husbands; which also seemeth a great pain and burthen unto them: but for all this) they may comfort themselves with the word of God, and think in their hearts, and say: "O God, thou hast brought us together in the estate of matrimony; it was thy ordinance and pleasure that we should join together: now therefore be merciful unto us; forsake us not, which live in thy ordinance and after thy commandments: pour thy Spirit into our hearts, that we may bear and suffer all these miseries which thou layest upon our necks." And in this manner married folks may comfort themselves with the word of God in all their adversities, because they are sure that marriage is a thing that pleaseth God.

Here learn to abhor the abominable opinion of the papists,

The opinion of the papists against marriage.

which hold that marriage is not an holy thing; and that the ministers of the word of God be defiled through marriage, if they enter into the same: which is an abominable doctrine, and clean against God and his word. Therefore St Paul

[1 Tim. iv.] A devilish doctrine of the papists.

seeing beforehand in the Spirit[1], "In the latter times there shall come deceivers, and false teachers, which should teach *doctrinam dæmoniorum*, that is, the doctrine of devils, forbidding marriage:" which prophecy of St Paul is verified now, in this our time, in the papists; for they say and teach, that marriage is not lawful to every man; despising also the ordinance of God. Therefore their doctrine may be called, as it is indeed, the doctrine of the devil: against which doctrine St Paul made a proclamation, saying, *Hono-*

Heb. xiii.

rabile conjugium inter omnes; "Marriage is lawful, honourable, and most godly among all men; and as for adulterers and fornicators, God shall judge them." This St Paul speaketh by occasion, seeing in spirit that there would come such papists as would pervert the ordinance of God, and say that marriage was unholy; and that a man may not marry in Lent, for it is a holy time; as though marriage were

Marriage is honourable.

unholy and filthy. But here ye may see it is the very ordinance of God, and is commended by Christ himself; for he cometh unto it, and with his presence he sanctifieth it. And not only that, but he did a miracle at this marriage; whereby he confirmed marriage to be good, holy, and acceptable before God. Therefore all those that go about marriage ought to know that it is good, holy, and lawful before God. Only thus I admonish you, have a respect to God-ward; that is to say, endeavour yourself so that God may be with you at your marriage, and that Christ be one of the guests; for if he be there, you shall have no lack of any thing. And to signify that he would help them that lacked, he did a miracle at this marriage: he remedied what lacked; wine lacked, and forthwith he turned water into wine.

Christ turned water into wine.

Here note, that it is lawful for poor men sometimes to be merry, specially at a marriage: for these were but poor men, yet they had wine at the marriage; where their common drink was but water, but now at the wedding they had wine, because they might be merry at the solemnity of God's

[1 in the Spirit that, 1571.]

ordinance. Which as it is lawful, so let it be done honestly and godly, as becometh christian men.

Wine moderately and well used is commendable.

Further, we learn here that the saints in heaven have been sinners: for after St Augustine's mind[2], Mary was here moved with vain-glory, and went about to provoke Christ to do some new thing; not seeking the honour of God, but her own glory, that it might be said she had a son that could do this and that. But here we must take heed, that we use well their ensample, not thinking after this manner, The saints of God have sinned, and yet have been saved; and therefore I will sin, and nevertheless I shall be saved: for so to think were very detestable, and a great abuse. But we must rather comfort ourselves by their sins, saying, when the devil tempteth us, and goeth about to bring us to confusion, then let us call to remembrance, that the saints of God have been sinners, and yet are saved; and that God will be likewise as merciful to us, and will forgive us our sins. And therefore let us not despair, but put our trust in him, and hope and believe in him, and in no wise to shrink from him: for he is as merciful as ever he was, and he will pardon and remit our sins: he is as mighty as ever he was, and therefore may do it: wherefore I will seek unto him, like as Mary Magdalene and other his saints have done, and therefore are saved. In this manner let us use ensamples of the saints to our comfort, and not to embolden us to sin.

Saints in heaven have been sinners.

Beware of comparisons and presumption.

A wholesome and good doctrine.

Whosoever trusteth in God by Christ shall be saved.

Further, let us here learn by the mother of Christ, whither we shall run for help, when we are in necessity and distress. Mary perceived that there was lack of wine, and had therefore pity over her poor friends: now in this distress, whither runneth she for her help? even to Christ himself. Then let us follow her ensample. Art thou poor? Run to Christ, and call upon God in the name of Christ: ask forgiveness of thy sins in his name, and God will hear thee, and grant thy petition; for he hath promised, that all that come to him in the name of Christ, shall lack nothing, neither shall they be rejected of him.

In all our necessities let us come to Christ for succour.

Here also note, further, the great charity that was in Mary the mother of Christ, which prayed for her friends, namely in the time of their lack and necessity, saying, οἶνον οὐκ ἔχουσι, *Vinum non habent;* that is, "They have

[2 See vol. I. p. 383.]

no wine." As who should say, "They are poor honest folks, and have here an honest company at their marriage; now they lack wine, I pray you help." She was not long in bibble-babble, with saying she wist not what, but saith at one word, "Help, for it is need." She doth not, as our papists do, which prittle-prattle a whole day upon their beads, saying our lady's psalter; but she only saith, "They have no wine; help," &c.

Much babbling prayer in papistry.

Christ answered, "Woman, what have I to do with thee?" Here appeareth the great faith that Mary had in our Saviour Jesu Christ her son: for notwithstanding she had received of him this hard and sharp answer, yet she despaired not, but commanded the serving-men to do all that he should command them. Here let us learn not to despair in the help of God, though we be not heard and obtain our petition at the first; as many do, which call upon God a day or two, and obtain not, then they despair and give over. But we may not so do; we must tarry for the Lord, as the prophet David saith, and not give over: we must call upon him with a strong faith in Christ Jesu our Mediator, without intermission; not doubting but that he will help us. Therefore tarry for the Lord, as the prophet David saith, and give not over in haste; but continue and abide his godly will and pleasure, and doubt not but he will hear thee.

The great faith of Mary the virgin.

A good lesson against desperation.

Our duty is to call upon God without ceasing.

"Woman?" What a thing was this, to call his mother "Woman!" These words might not only sound to the dishonesty of his mother, but also to his own rebuke: for it might be judged, that he was one that neither loved nor reverenced his mother, in calling her, "Woman." To this objection this answer may be made: Christ, as long as he was under the government of his mother, did all his duty as appertained unto him; but now being a preacher and a common person, serving in the common ministry, he is not bound to be ruled by his mother; neither did it appertain to his mother, either to appoint him what he should do, or when he should do it: and therefore this seemed a great presumption in her, and therefore he answered her so sharply. St Augustine saith, that Mary was moved with vain-glory, to get some praise of the miracle of her son. Here is to be noted, how far we are bound to obey father and mother; which is, so far as the same may stand with godliness. If

A strange speech of our Saviour Christ.

An objection well answered.

St Augustine's opinion of Mary the virgin.

THE SECOND SUNDAY AFTER THE EPIPHANY.

they require of us any thing that is against God, we shall answer them as our Saviour Christ answered his mother, "Woman, what have I to do with thee?" For here our Saviour in a certain manner sheweth, that he would not be led with affection. As at another time when he was making a sermon, there came one interrupting him, and said, "Thy mother and thy brethren would speak with thee;" then Christ stretched out his hands and said, "Whosoever doth the will of my Father which is in heaven, the same is my mother and brethren:" and at another time another woman hearing him cried out, saying, "Blessed is the womb that bare thee, and the paps that gave thee suck: he answered and said, Blessed are those which hear the word of God, and follow the same:" so at this time he made such an answer unto his mother, signifying that he would not be led by her affections; and also would shew, that he was not only her son, but he was "the Son of God."

The obedience due to father and mother.

Matt. xii.

"Six waterpots of stone," &c. The six pots were filled with water to wash withal: for the Jews occupy much washing; as when they went to market, coming home they washed themselves, lest they should be defiled; so this water was set there, partly for washing, and partly to drink. And here we may learn, that when Christ is bidden to our marriage, there shall lack nothing; for he will turn the sour water into sweet wine. For water signifieth all such anguishes, calamities and miseries as happen by marriages: and all such kind of water, that is, all such calamities and miseries, he turned into wine; that is, he sendeth comfort, he sendeth his Spirit, that maketh those miseries, that were before very bitter, most sweet and pleasant: the same Spirit of God comforteth the heart, and keepeth it from desperation. Also, we may learn here by this marriage, to keep a good order in our business: here, as one appointed had the oversight of all, so we may not let every body be rulers; but to keep good order in all our business, let some rule, and some be ruled.

It is good to bid Christ to a marriage.

Water, what it signifieth.

God by Christ maketh our sour and unpleasant life most acceptable.

Note here an order to be kept in all our affairs.

"They filled them up to the brim," &c. This was all done that the miracle might be known; not seeking his own honour and glory, but rather the honour and glory of God his Father, and our wealth and salvation; and to allure and bring us to have faith in him; and to teach us to put our trust in him; and, also, to bring us from carefulness of this

A notable miracle wrought by Christ for our doctrine and comfort.

life, unto the consideration of the life to come. This is a comfortable story: this miracle of our Saviour, whereby he sheweth that whosoever believeth and trusteth him, shall not lack any thing. For, as a very learned man saith, If a labouring man should see all that he gathereth and spendeth in a year in a chest, it would not find him half a year: yet it findeth him; God multiplieth it day by day, and so he will do unto all them that believe and trust in him.

<small>The epilogue or summary of the sermon.</small>
Now you have heard in this gospel, beside other good matters, of marriage, how holy a thing it is, how it is the ordinance of God himself: also, how we shall take marriage in hand, namely, call Christ unto it, and let him be one of the guests, and then all things will be well; for without him nothing will be aught. Marriage is like a school-house, where you shall have occasion of patience, and occasion of love. Now except Christ be in this school-house of marriage, you cannot be patient in trouble; neither can you truly love; neither can you do any thing acceptable unto him[1]. Wherefore, whosoever will take in hand marriage, let him take it so in hand that it may redound to the honour and glory of God: then will he be there, and turn the water into wine; that is to say, he will mitigate and assuage all calamities and miseries with his Spirit and grace; so that no adversity shall hurt us in this world, and in the world to come we shall have life everlasting. Which grant us God the Father, through Jesus Christ our Lord and Saviour; to whom, with God and the Holy Ghost, be honour and glory, world without end! *Amen.*

[1 God, 1607.]

A SERMON PREACHED BY MASTER HUGH LATIMER, THE
THIRD SUNDAY AFTER THE EPIPHANY, THE 24TH
DAY OF JANUARY, ANNO 1552.

MATTHEW VIII. [1, 2, 3.]

Cum descendisset autem de monte, ecce leprosus.

[When he was come down from the mountain, much people followed him. And behold, there came a leper and worshipped him, saying, Lord, if thou wilt, thou canst make me clean. And Jesus put forth his hand and touched him, saying, I will, be thou clean. And instantly his leprosy was cleansed.]

THIS is a notable miracle, and a most comfortable history: which though it were done upon a lazar man only, yet the doctrine of the same appertaineth to us and to all men; and so shall it do unto the end of the world. For St Paul saith, *Quæcunque scripta sunt, ad nostram eruditionem scripta sunt;* "Whatsoever is written, is written for our instruction." Therefore if we will consider and ponder this story well, we shall find much matter in it to our great comfort and edifying. Rom. xv.

"When he was come down," &c. He had been upon the mountain making a sermon, the which is contained in the fifth, sixth, and seventh chapters of this Evangelist; which sermon is very notable, and containeth the sum of a christian man's life: at the which sermon the people were greatly astonied, and much marvelled. Whereby you may note the strength and efficacy of the word of God; which word, if it light upon good ground, that is, upon a good heart that will receive it, it turneth with his strength the same, and bringeth a marvelling; like as it happened unto this people which had received the word, and marvelled at it. Also, you may note here the inconstancy of the people; which now greatly esteemed and regarded our Saviour and his word, and shortly after consented to his death, by persuasion of the bishops: which was a great and heinous wickedness in the face of God. Therefore let us not follow The word of God is of great efficacy.

People are inconstant.

their ensample, neither let us be persuaded by any man living to forsake God and his word; but rather let us suffer death for it. Howbeit, I fear me, that if there should come a persecution, there would be a great number of those which now speak fair of the gospel, like unto this people; for I fear me, they would soon be persuaded by the papistical priests to do and say against Christ, to forsake his word, and deny the gospel: like as these people did; forgetting clean, and setting aside all that which they had heard of our Saviour upon the mountain. Let us therefore, I say, beware; and let us knowledge the great love of God our heavenly Father, shewed unto us[1] in these latter days, in opening his blessed word unto us so plainly, that none, except he be wilful and obstinate, but he may understand the same: the which is as great a benefit as may be. And happy are we if we consider this great goodness of God, and shew ourselves thankful unto him by godly living, and honest conversation, according to his commandment! And in this gospel is specially to be noted the great love and kindness of Christ our Saviour toward mankind, which first preached unto the people, and taught them the way unto everlasting life, and then came down and healed the diseased man: that is, he first succoured our souls, and afterward comforted our bodies.

There cometh a leper unto him, saying, "Lord, if thou wilt, thou canst help me." This lazar, or leper, took Christ to be a Saviour, and therefore he cometh to him for help. So let us come unto him, for he is the Saviour of mankind; and he is the only helper that succoureth both our bodies and souls. He saveth our souls by his word, if when we hear the same we believe it. The salvation of our bodies shall appear at the last day, where soul and body shall come together, and there shall be rewarded: so that if the soul be saved, the body is saved; for soul and body shall go together; and so he saveth both our bodies and souls. Note here, also, the behaviour of this lazar-man; for by his ensample the best doctor in divinity need not be ashamed to learn: for in him appeareth a marvellous strong faith and confidence that he had in Christ; for he doubted not but that Christ was able to help him: neither mistrusted

[1 so plainly in these latter days, 1584, 1596.]

he his goodness and mercy. Therefore faith hath moved him to come to Christ, and to desire help of him. And note here, also, the love and great charity of our Saviour Christ, which first he shewed to the whole multitude, in teaching of them so earnestly and diligently the way to everlasting life; and then he extended his great compassion and mercy unto this leper, whom all men abhorred, because of his filthiness and uncleanness: but Christ abhorred him not; yea, he is content not only to hear his request, and to talk with him, but also laid his hands upon his filthy body. O how great a kindness was this! O what a wonderful thing is this, that the King of all kings talketh here most familiarly with a poor wretch and filthy leper! O what profound and incomprehensible love beareth he unto us! It is esteemed a great thing, when a king vouchsafeth to talk with a poor man, being one of his subjects: what a great thing then is this, when that the King of all kings, yea, the Ruler of heaven and earth, talketh with a poor man, heareth his request, and mercifully granteth the same! This evangelist saith, "Behold, there came a leper, and worshipped him;" but another evangelist saith, "he fell upon his knees before him." These are gestures and behaviours, which signify a reverence done unto him, or a subjection, or submission.

Note the great love and charity that was in Christ.

For although our Saviour went like a poor man, yet this leper had conceived such a faith and trust in him, that he had no respect of his outward appearance, but followed his faith; which faith told him, that this was the Saviour. Therefore he set aside all outward shew, and came with great reverence unto him, desiring his help. And here you may learn good manners: for it is a good sight, and very commendable, and is also the commandment of God, that we should give honour to those to whom honour belongeth; specially preachers ought to be reverenced, and that for their office' sake, for they are the officers of God, and God's treasurers. And such as are proud persons may be ashamed by this leper: for this is certain and true, that a proud heart prayeth never well, and therefore is hated before God. Wherefore, amongst other vices, beware of pride and stoutness. For what was the cause that Lucifer, being the fairest angel in heaven, was made the most horrible devil, and cast

Give honour unto them to whom honour belongeth.

Lucifer thrust into hell for pride.

down from heaven into hell? Pride only was the cause thereof. Therefore St Augustine hath a pretty saying: *Quemcunque superbum esse videris, diaboli filium esse ne dubites;* that is to say, "Whensoever thou seest a proud man, doubt not but he is the son of the devil." Let us learn here therefore by this leper, to have a humble and meek spirit.

Moreover, this man was a leper and a miserable man, one despised of all men, and an outcast. For it was commanded in the law of God, that no man should keep company with a leper: therefore it appeareth that he was in great misery. But what doth he? Whither runneth he for help or succour? Even to Christ, for to him only he runneth; not to witchcraft or sorcery[1], as ungodly men[2] do; but he seeketh for comfort of our Saviour. Now, when thou art in distress, in misery, in sickness, in poverty, or any other calamity, follow the ensample of this leper; run to Christ; seek help and comfort only at his hands; and then thou shalt be delivered and made safe, like as he was delivered after he came to Christ.

<small>Seek for Christ in all necessities, and he will help.</small>

But what brought he with him? Even his faith. He believed that Christ was able to help him, and therefore according to his faith it happened unto him. Then it shall be necessary for thee to bring faith with thee; for without faith thou canst get nothing at his hands: bring therefore, I say, faith with thee; believe that he is able to help thee, and that he is merciful, and will help thee. And when thou comest furnished with such a faith, surely thou shalt be heard: thou shalt find him a loving Father, and a faithful friend, and a Redeemer of thee out of all tribulation. For faith is like a hand wherewith we receive the benefits of God; and except we take his benefits with the hand of faith, we shall never have them.

<small>Faith apprehendeth all the benefits of Christ.</small>

Here, in this gospel, you may learn the right use of scripture: for when you shall hear and read such stories as this is, you may not think that such stories and acts done by our Saviour are but temporal; but you must consider that they are done for our sake, and for our instruction and teaching. Therefore, when you hear such stories, you must consider eternal things which are set before your eyes

<small>A right use for the understanding of the stories contained in the scripture.</small>

[1 witches and sorcerers, 1607.]   [2 men are wont to, 1571, 1572.]

by such stories; and so we must apply them to ourselves. As for ensample; here is a lazar, and he calleth upon Christ with a good faith, and was healed. You will say, "What is that unto us?" Even as he was a leper of his body, so are we lepers of[3] our souls. He was unclean in his body, and we are unclean in our souls. He was healed by believing in Christ; so we must be healed by him, or else perish eternally. Therefore, if thou wilt not perish, then call upon him as this lazar did, and thou shalt be holpen and cleansed of thy leprosy, that is, from all thy sin. So, I say, we must apply the scriptures unto us, and take out some good thing to strengthen our faith withal, and to edify ourselves with the word of God. *A profitable and wholesome doctrine.*

Another ensample we read in the scripture, that God destroyed with fire Sodome and Gomorra. Wherefore? For sin's sake. What manner of sin? Whoredom, lechery, and other uncleanness: also, for despising and abusing of poor men and strangers. What is this to us now? We learn in this story, how that God will not suffer sin, nor wilful sinners; but he will punish the same either here, or else in the world to come, or else in both: he will not let them go unpunished. Therefore, when we hear this story, we may learn to avoid sin and all wickedness, and to live uprightly and godly: and this we learn by that story, which is an ensample of God's wrath and indignation[4] against sin. *Gen. xix.* *God will not suffer sin unpunished.*

Take another ensample of faith. We read in the scripture, that Abraham believed God, and his faith justified him. Now when I hear this, I must apply it to myself in this manner. Abraham believed God, and his faith justified him; I will believe in God and follow his word, then shall I also be justified: for St Paul saith, that the same believing of Abraham is not written for Abraham's sake, but for our sakes; to teach us that God will justify us if we believe in him, and punish us when we are unfaithful, &c. *Rom. iv.* *Faith justifieth.*

Now note here how this [man] came; see how humbly and meekly he cometh, and what a good and strong faith he had in Christ: which faith appeared by his coming; for if he had been without faith, he would not have come unto him, because our Saviour kept but a mean estate, not a

[3 in, 1571.]   [4 anger, 1607.]

king's court; he was poor, and therefore the more despised of the misbelievers. But this man believed, and therefore he came unto him. Learn therefore by his ensample, to go to Christ in what affliction soever we be. Let us run to him, and pray unto God for his sake. Allege him; put him before thee; and beware that thou call not upon any creature or saint: for that is a great wickedness before God, in praying to saints; for with the saints we have nothing to do, but to keep in memory and follow their godly life and righteous living. But our prayer must be made unto Christ only, like as this man doth here in this gospel.

But peradventure you will say, he was upon the earth when this man called upon him, and therefore he was so soon heard. I answer: He promised to his disciples after his resurrection, that he would be with us to the end of the whole world[1]: his words be true, for he cannot be made a liar; therefore we must believe him, and no doubt but he will be present with us whensoever we call upon him. Call upon him therefore, and not upon saints; for if we call upon saints, we make them gods. For if I call upon St Paul here, and another man that is a thousand miles off calleth upon him also, then we make him like unto God, to be everywhere, to hear and see all things; which is against all scripture: for God only is omnipotent, that is, he only is almighty, and he is everywhere, and seeth all things, and so doth no creature else. Therefore those which do attribute such things as appertain to God only, that is our Creator, to any creature, they do naughtily and wickedly, and shall be punished for it in hell-fire, except they amend and be sorry for their faults.

But what was this man's prayer? Did he pray upon his beads, and say our lady's psalter? No, no; he was never brought up in any such popish schools. What said he? *Domine, si vis, potes me sanare;* "If thou wilt, O Lord, thou canst make me clean, and put away my disease." This is but a short prayer, but it containeth much: for first it teacheth how we should pray unto God; namely, conditionally in our outward and bodily things, that is to say, when it pleaseth him: and so did our Saviour himself pray unto his heavenly Father, saying, *Si vis, Pater, transeat a me calix iste;* "If thou wilt, Father, let this cup pass from me." So

[1 the world, 1571.]

XL.] THE THIRD SUNDAY AFTER THE EPIPHANY. 173

we should do, when we are in any manner of tribulation or sickness, that is, pray unto God conditionally, saying, "O Lord God, if it please thee, and if it may stand with thy honour and glory, and the salvation of my soul, help and deliver me." We must put the matter to him, for he knoweth best what is good for us. Peradventure he seeth, that if we should be without affliction, we would be wanton, wicked, and proud; and so sin against him, and damn our souls; and then it were better for us to be in sickness than in health. Therefore we must desire help, if it please him; that is to say, when it appertaineth to our salvation: or else it were a thousand times better to be sick still, than to be out of sickness, and fall from God and all goodness: he therefore knoweth best what is good for us. Trust him; be content to be ruled by him; he shall and will order the matter so, that thou shalt find him a loving Father unto thee, like as this man did here. *God only knoweth what is meet for us.*

Secondarily, this prayer expresseth the faith that this poor man had in Christ: for he saith, "Lord, if thou wilt, thou canst help me." "If thou wilt," saith he, noting him to be omnipotent and almighty. And in these words he expresseth the divinity of Christ our Saviour, "If thou wilt." He believeth him to be able to help him: so we should do in our prayers. We must believe that he may and will help us; as it appeareth by this man, which was whole straightway. Also it appeareth, partly by the confession and faith of this man, and partly by the end of the matter, that he was made perfectly whole. So we shall be healed from our diseases, when we come unto him with such a faith as this man did; and specially if we call so earnestly upon him. But, O Lord, what slothfulness is in our hearts! How slender a faith have we! How unperfect and cold is our prayer! so that it is no marvel that it is not heard of God. But we must always consider that God is able to save us, and believe undoubtedly that he will save us. So that when I am sick, as is said before, I may doubt whether God will deliver me from my sickness, or no; but I may not doubt of everlasting life. Therefore, if I be sick, I must pray as this man, *Domine, si vis*, "Lord, if thou wilt;" conditionally. For peradventure[2], when I come out of my sickness, I shall become *God only is Almighty. Call on Christ with a faith unfeigned, and he will hear thee. Call upon Christ both in sickness and health.*

[2 it may be, 1607.]

more wicked and ungodly; which God knowing, keepeth me still in sickness: and so it is better for me to be in sickness still, than whole. So we may learn here to call upon God conditionally. As for our general salvation, which is the salvation of our souls, we may not doubt in that, nor call for it conditionally; but apprehend God by his promise, saying, "Lord, thou hast promised that all that believe in thee shall be saved: Lord, for thy mercy and promise' sake, and for thy death and passion' sake, take away my sin; wash me with the blood which thou hast shed upon the cross, and hast promised that all that believe shall be saved through thee. Now, Lord, for thy promise' sake, help me. I believe, O Lord, help my infirmity and increase my faith." As touching thy bodily health, put it to his good-will, and offer thyself unto him, saying, "Lord, I am thy creature, thou hast given unto me soul and body: my body is sick now, when it pleaseth thee help me; if not, give me grace to bear patiently this thy visitation: for in like manner didst thou visit thy holy martyrs which suffered great calamity[1]; and they desired to be delivered, but thou deliveredst them not bodily, but yet thou savedst them after their death. So I trust thou wilt with me."

Now, how came it to pass that this leper had such a great faith and confidence in our Saviour? Truly, by hearing the word of God; for he had heard our Saviour say, "Come unto me, all ye that are laden and oppressed with miseries, and I will refresh you." This he had heard and believed; therefore he came boldly unto him, desiring him of help: and so here is verified the saying of St Paul, *Fides ex auditu,* "Faith cometh by hearing." The ordinary way to get faith is through the hearing the word of God: for the word of God is of such a power, that it entereth and pierceth the heart of man that heareth it earnestly; as it doth well appear in this leper.

We read in the Acts of the Apostles, that when St Paul had made a long sermon at Antioch, there believed, saith the Evangelist, " as many as were ordained to life everlasting:" with the which saying a great number of people have been offended, and have said, "We perceive, that only those shall come to believe, and so to everlasting life, which are chosen

[1 calamities, 1571.]

of God unto it: therefore it is no matter whatsoever we do; for if we be chosen to everlasting life, we shall have it." And so they have opened a door unto themselves of all wickedness and carnal liberty, against the true meaning of the scripture. For if the most part be damned, the fault is not in God, but in themselves: for it is written, *Deus vult omnes homines salvos fieri;* "God would that all men should be saved:" but they themselves procure their own damnation, and despise the passion of Christ by their own wicked and inordinate living. Here we may learn to keep us from all curious and dangerous questions: when we hear that some be chosen and some be damned, let us have good hope that we shall be amongst the chosen, and live after this hope; that is, uprightly and godly; then thou shalt not be deceived. Think that God hath chosen those that believe in Christ, and that Christ is the book of life. If thou believest in him, then thou art written in the book of life, and shalt be saved. So we need not go about to trouble ourselves with curious questions of the predestination of God. But let us rather endeavour ourselves that we may be in Christ; for when we be in him, then are we well, and then we may be sure that we are ordained to everlasting life.

_{A lewd opinion of predestination.}

_{1 Tim. ii.}

_{We ourselves procure our own damnation.}

_{Curious questions are to be avoided.}

But you will say, How shall I know that I am in the book of life? How shall I try myself to be elect of God to everlasting life? I answer: First we may know, that we may one time be in the book, and another time come out again; as it appeareth by David, which was written in the book of life: but when he sinned, he at that same time was out of the book of the favour of God, until he had repented and was sorry for his faults. So we may be in the book one time, and afterward, when we forget God and his word and do wickedly, we come out of the book; that is, out of Christ, which is the book. And in that book are written all believers. But I will tell you how you shall know when you are in the book; and there are three special notes whereby ye may know the same. The first note is, if you know your sin, and feel your own wretchedness and filthiness, which is a great matter; for the most part of people are so drowned in sin, that they no more feel the same; for sin grieveth them no more, according to the saying of Salomon, *Impius cum in medium peccatorum venit, contem-*

_{How we may know when we are in the state of salvation, and when not.}

_{The special points to be marked which de-}

clare when we are in the state of salvation. Eccles. vii.

nit; that is, "The ungodly man, when he entereth into the midst of all sin and mischief, despiseth the same; he regardeth sin nothing at all, neither is he sorry for it." But, as I said, the first note is, when you know your sins, and feel the same; then are they heavy unto you and grieve you. Then follows the second point, which is faith in Christ; that is, when you believe most stedfastly and undoubtedly, that God our heavenly Father through his Son will deliver you from your sins: when you believe, I say, that the blood of our Saviour is shed for you, for the cleansing and putting away of your sins; and believing this most stedfastly with an unfeigned heart, then you have the second point. The third point is, when you have an earnest desire to amendment and hatred against sin; study to live after God's will and commandments, as much as is possible for you to do, then have

A worthy note to know when you are in the true state of salvation.

you the third point. And when you find these three points to be in you; namely, first, when you know your sin and be sorry for the same; and afterward believe to be saved through the passion of Jesus Christ; and thirdly, have an earnest desire to leave sin, and to fly the same; when you find these three things in your hearts, then you may be sure that your names are written in the book: and you may be sure also, that you are elect and predestinate to everlasting

An evident and plain doctrine that sheweth when you are out of the favour of God.

life. And, again, when you see not your wickedness, and that sin grieveth you not, neither have you faith or hope in our Saviour; and therefore are careless and study not for amendment of life; then you are in a heavy case, and then you have cause to be sorry, and to lament your wretchedness: for truly you are not in the book of life; but the devil hath power over you as long as ye are in such a state. Here you see now, how you shall try yourselves whether you be in the book of life or no, &c.

True prayer consisteth not in many words.

"Lord, if [1] thou wilt," &c. I learn here, that a few words spoken with faith is better than a long bibble-babble. For right prayer standeth not in many words, or long babbling. Right prayer requireth the whole heart; for there is no greater thing in the world than right prayer.

Prayer joined with faith is heard of God.

For prayer, joined with faith, is the instrument wherewith we receive the benefits of God. Now, when faith and prayer are joined together, it is impossible but God heareth it; for

[1 when, all the old editions.]

they must needs go together; for else it availeth nothing, except faith be joined with it; as Christ said unto the centurion, *Juxta fidem tuam fiat tibi;* "According to thy faith be it unto thee." Luke vii.

Here I might take occasion to entreat of prayer, if the time would serve. But to be short: three things may move us to pray. First, the commandment of God, which biddeth us to call upon him in the day of our trouble: which commandment hath no less authority than this, "Thou shalt not kill:" the selfsame God that saith, "Thou shalt not kill," the selfsame saith, "Thou shalt pray;" that is, "Thou shalt call upon me." Whereby it appeareth, that we seem damnable when we intermit prayers. The second cause that should move us is the promise of God; for he promiseth us every where in the scripture, that he will hear us when we call upon him: which promise is not to be despised, for he saith, *Petite, et dabitur vobis,* "Ask, and it shall be given you;" *Quicquid petieritis Patrem in nomine meo dabitur vobis;* that is, "Whatsoever you shall desire of my Father in my name, it shall be given unto you." Such promises ought to allure us to pray without intermission. The third cause is the ensample of all the prophets, the saints of God, that move us thereunto. For Moses, leading the people out of Egypt, after that he came at the Red sea, Pharao with his power followed at his back; and on both sides there were great hills, and before him the great sea. Then Moses, being in such danger, cried unto God, not speaking many words, but lifting up his heart unto God. Then God said unto him, "Why criest thou?" Here you see that Moses fighteth only with his prayer against his enemies: so should we fight against our enemies, the devil, the world, and the flesh, with earnest and fervent prayer. Likewise Joshua being in great distress, (for his people had lost the victory, and his enemies had gotten the upper hand of him,) what doth he? He crieth unto God. So doth David the king: as it appeareth throughout all the psalms, how fervent is he in prayer, giving us an ensample to follow him.

Thus much I thought good to speak of prayer, and to move you thereunto; for I fear there are many of you that little regard the same. All such may learn here to be more diligent and earnest in prayer than they have been; especially considering that it is the commandment of God that we shall pray. Also, we have great store of the promises of God, that we shall be heard: also, the ensample of good and godly men may move us thereunto: for if they[1] found ease with their prayers, we shall find the like.

Prayer is commanded by God.

But now to return to the text: *Tetigit eum,* "Christ touched him." Here appeareth the friendliness and kindness of our Saviour Christ: he is not so proud as the common sort of lords be, that none may speak with them. No, no; he is friendly[2]. The poor man came to speak with him, and he forthwith came to him and spake with him: wherefore all lords and men in authority need not be ashamed to learn here of our Saviour Christ, to be gentle and meek of spirit to the poor people. It is also to be considered, that our Saviour did against the law outwardly; for there was a law that no man should touch a leper man, yet Christ touched this man. Where you must consider, that civil laws and statutes must be ordered by charity: for this act of Christ was against the words of the law, but not against the law itself. This law was made to that end, that no man should be hurt or defiled by a leper; but Christ touched this man, and was not hurt himself, but cleansed him that was hurt already. And here we learn rather to follow the mind of the law, than the rigour of the words; and to bring charity with us, which is an interpreter of the law; for else we may miss by extremity. Further, what meant it that Christ touched him with his hand? And how chanced it that his word and hand went together? Because he would shew and declare unto us the profitableness of his flesh, how it was a flesh by the which all we should be saved; so that no salvation may be looked for, except by him, and except he be eaten and drunken. Again, sometimes he healed by his word and divine power only, as it appeareth by the servant of the centurion; to signify unto us, that it were not necessary for us to have him here bodily always: and to assure us of his help without his bodily presence, he said, *Expedit vobis ut abeam;* "It is good for you that I go from you." And so, to signify his power, he used the authority of his word, both in his presence and absence. Therefore

The kindness of our Saviour Christ.

Lords and men in authority should be gentle to the poor.

The mind of laws is to be followed, and not the rigour of words.

John xvi.

[1 they have, 1571.]
[2 more friendly, 1607.]

we may be certain and sure, that he can and will help us with power[3] divine when we call upon him, as well absent as present; for he is every where, and will be with us unto the end of the world, as he promised unto his apostles after his resurrection, saying, "Lo, I will be with you until the end of the world:" which is the greatest comfort that may be unto a christian heart; for it is a stay to all trouble. *Matt. xxviii.*

We read further, that he sent him to the priest, and commandeth him that he should tell no man. What meant he by this? He would have him not to be his own judge. There was a law that the leprosy should be examined by the priest, and that the priest should give the sentence whether the leper were clean or unclean. Now Christ would not have this man to be his own judge, and to pronounce himself clean; but biddeth him to go to the ordinary. And this he did for two considerations: the first was, to convince the Jews with their own wickedness, in that they would not believe in him, but despised and maliced him. Therefore he sent this man unto them, which had been infected with leprosy, so that when they pronounced him clean, they might perceive their own wickedness and obstinacy, which would not believe. The second cause was, for the observation of the law, and for that he would give none occasion to carnal liberty. He would have every man in his order, as well the magistrates as the subjects: where we may learn to follow his ensample, to keep all good laws and orders, and the rather, for that Christ himself kept them. *The law for leprosy. The causes that moved Christ to send the leper to the priests. Good laws are to be observed.*

Here our papists make ado with their auricular confession, proving the same by this place. For they say Christ sent this man unto the priest to fetch there his absolution; and therefore we must go also unto the priest, and, after confession, receive of him absolution of all our sins. But yet we must take heed, say they, that we forget nothing: for all those sins that are forgotten, may not be forgiven. And so they bind the consciences of men, persuading them that when their sins were all numbered and confessed, it was well. And hereby they took clean away the passion of Christ. For they made this numbering of sins to be a merit; and so they came to all the secrets that were in men's hearts: so that emperor nor king could say or do, nor think any *The doctrine of the papists for auricular confession. A subtle practice of papists.*

[3 his power, 1607.]

thing in his heart, but they knew it; and so applied all the purposes and intents of princes to their own commodities. And this was the fruit of their auricular confession. But to speak of right and true confession, I would to God it were kept in England; for it is a good thing. And those which find themselves grieved in conscience might go to a learned man, and there fetch of him comfort of the word of God, and so to come to a quiet conscience: which is better and more to be regarded than all the riches of the world. And surely it grieveth me much that such confessions are not kept in England, &c.

<small>True and meet confession is very necessary.</small>

<small>The conclusion and short rehearsal of this sermon.</small>

Now to make an end. You have heard in this gospel of divers things which I will not rehearse; but I would have you to keep in remembrance the great faith that this man had in our Saviour, which faith restored him to his health again; and learn by him to believe as he did, that our Saviour will restore unto us the health of soul and body. Also, note here the great love that our Saviour bare unto this man; stedfastly believing that he will be like loving unto thee, when thou callest upon him with earnest prayer. For prayer, as I have told you, is all together: for prayer with faith goeth through the clouds. But it is a great matter to pray; it is *ars artium*, that is, an art above all arts. Let us therefore give ourselves to prayer and godly living, so that his name may be glorified in us both now and ever! *Amen.*

A SERMON PREACHED BY MASTER HUGH LATIMER, THE FOURTH SUNDAY AFTER THE EPIPHANY, AND THE LAST DAY OF JANUARY, ANNO 1552.

MATTHEW VIII. [23, 24, 25, 26.]

Et cum esset ingressus navem, sequuti sunt eum discipuli sui: ecce, motus magnus ortus est in mari, &c.

And he entered into a ship, his disciples followed him. And behold there arose a great tempest in the sea, insomuch that the ship was covered with waves; and he was asleep. And his disciples came to him, and awoke him, saying, Lord, save us, we perish. And he saith unto them, Why are ye fearful, O ye of little faith? Then he arose, and rebuked the wind and the sea: and there followed a great calm.

HERE in this gospel we have a notable story, and a wonderful miracle which our Saviour did, being with his disciples upon the sea; which story is written for our doctrine and instruction, that we may comfort ourselves withal, when we are in like trouble in the tempests of this world. For we may learn here many good things, if we consider the story itself, and the circumstance thereof. The evangelist saith, that our Saviour, accompanied with his disciples, went into a ship, where he laid himself upon a pillow and slept; which sleep signified his very manhood, as you shall hear afterward. Now whilst he lay thus asleep, lo, there arose suddenly so great and horrible a tempest, that they thought they should all have perished out of hand; such a fearful weather lighted upon them. The disciples, being sore astonished at this horrible weather, wist not what to do. At the last they remembering themselves ran to our Saviour, which lay there asleep, crying, "Lord, we perish:" or else the evangelist Matt. viii. Mark saith, "Lord, carest thou not that we perish?" He, Mark iv. being awaked, first rebuked them because of their unbelief: after that he rebuked the wind, and commanded the tempest to leave off and cease. The disciples, seeing before the horrible tempest, and now the sudden calmness made through his word, marvelled much; for they never had seen before such things. They had never heard that at any time any man might, or had power to rule the sea and the wind before this time; and therefore they were astonished at it; and every one of them said, "O, what a man is this, which ruleth with his word the sea and the wind!" This is the sum of this gospel, which containeth many good things for our instruction, learning, and comfort.

Here appeared in Christ the almighty power of God.

First, we may learn here, that the ship signified the congregation of Christ and his church. The disciples being in the ship are preserved through Christ: so all those which are in the church of Christ shall be saved and preserved by him. The others, which are without this church, shall be damned and perish.

Note the signification of the ship.

Learn here also, by the ensample of the disciples of Christ, two things: the first, not to presume too much; that is to say, not to stand in thine own conceit, thinking thyself to be perfect in faith: secondly, not to despair because of thy imperfections. The disciples thought themselves perfect and strong in faith, before they came into this tempest; but what doth our Saviour? Perceiving their presumptions, he sendeth a tempest to bring them to the knowledge of themselves; and then they, feeling the weakness of their faith, ran to our Saviour crying for help. Whereby every man may learn, not to think too much of himself: and when he feeleth himself very weak, he may not despair, but run to Christ, like as these disciples did; which, although their heart was weak and feeble, yet were they preserved.

Two profitable lessons.

A comfortable doctrine against desperation.

Moreover, we learn here that our Saviour Christ is both very God and very man. His Godhead appeared in that the wind and waters obeyed him, and reformed themselves according to his word. For what king or emperor is in the whole world, that can or may command the wind or seas? None at all: yea, if the whole world should be set together with all their power and wits, they should not be able to do any such thing. Therefore learn here to know the majesty of Christ, his power and stay, and to believe him to be very God. Secondly, learn here to know his manhood: for the evangelist saith, "He slept;" which signifieth his very manhood; and that all things were in him that are in us, except sin; and that he can have compassion with us, for that he

Christ is both God and man.

Christ was endued with all our infirmities.

himself hath been in all miseries and troubles as well as we, as St Paul testifieth to the Hebrews. He slept here for weariness; he eateth, he drinketh, he wept; and in him are all these infirmities, and chiefly for two causes: first, to signify unto us his very manhood; secondarily, to comfort us with the ensample. When we are in trouble and miseries, we shall think and know that our Saviour Christ will have compassion over us; for he himself hath tasted of all trouble, and therefore he will be the more inclined to help and assist us with his holy Spirit.

Also, we may note here, that the disciples of our Saviour have passed many a time before upon the water, and yet they were never so troubled, nor in such danger. What meaneth this, that they are in trouble now, when our Saviour is with them, and never before when they were not with him? For it was no dangerous water, it was but a little pond. What meaneth it then, that this marvellous tempest so suddenly arose? It signifieth that all those that believe in Christ, and take his part, and study to live after his will and commandment, and forsake the world and all wickedness, all such, I say, must have much trouble and affliction. For it is the will of God, that those which seek to be saved, shall be proved and tried through the fire of tribulation: as it appeareth here by the disciples, who were never before in such trouble and danger; for they had ever good luck, as the most part of these worldlings commonly have, for all things go well with them, and after their mind: but as soon as they receive Christ into their ship, that is, as soon as they believe in him, and receive his word, they shall have trouble and affliction. Whereof we have a great number of ensamples in the scriptures, that plainly teach us not to seek good cheer by the gospel in this world, but rather misery and adversity. But the most part of gospellers are contrary-minded; for they seek good cheer and promotions through the gospel: which is an horrible abuse of God's most holy word. Moses, that excellent prophet of God, as long as he was in Pharaoh's house, he was well; he had all things after his mind: but as soon as God called him to be his minister, and to do him service, all things were turned: that is, all sweet things were made sour; all the great cheer was gone; so that he was compelled by necessity to keep sheep, where before he was

All that shall be saved must suffer adversities.

The professing of the gospel bringeth trouble.

Example of Moses.

a prince, and an inheritor of the crown of Egypt. Here you see how God doth exercise his which appertain to everlasting life. Also St Paul, as long as he was without Christ, was in great authority and estimation among the Jews; insomuch as he had letters of authority to afflict and put in prison all those which held of Christ: but after that he once came to Christ, what had he? Afflictions and miseries plenty; as it appeareth through all the Acts of the Apostles, and his Epistles; where also it appeareth, that he had a most irksome and painful life; namely, as soon as he came to the knowledge of Christ and his gospel. Also the Israelites, as long as they were in Egypt, serving for the most part false gods, they had no lack of meat[1] or drink: but as soon as they came again to the knowledge of God, they were in great misery, lacking all manner of necessaries; insomuch that they say, as Jeremy the prophet reporteth, "We will turn again to the queen of heaven," &c. Now come to our time: we see daily that they that take part with Christ and his gospel, are most commonly nothing regarded in this world. The world and they cannot agree together, for they love godliness, and the other love wickedness[2]; which two can never be set together. But there are very few, God knoweth, that take part with Christ; for every man will rather apply himself after the world, and have quietness and a merry life, than to forsake the same, and to have trouble with Christ and his flock: but what reward they shall have, it will appear in the end.

A man may marvel how God can suffer his to be so punished and afflicted in this world; and again, the wicked to have ever the upper hand, and to be merry in this world: because God and the devil are two Lords, most repugnant in conditions. For God is good, just, merciful and liberal, and kind towards his; offering unto them which live after his will life everlasting: but the devil is a most wicked minister, unmerciful and cruel; rewarding his servants with everlasting pain and damnation. Now these two Lords have their servants. God suffereth his to be much afflicted and plagued, for these two causes. The first is, though they be justified before God through the passion of our Saviour, yet remaineth a great many of sins and imperfections within

[1 wanted neither meat, 1607.]   [2 evil, 1607.]

them. Now, to put in remembrance how abominable a thing sin is in the face of God, he sendeth unto them calamities and miseries, to teach them to beware of sin, and to live uprightly and holily[3]. Secondarily, to teach them to pray and call upon God. And thirdly, to teach us to know ourselves. For when we be in prosperity and wealth, we think we have faith, and that all things are safe; but when there cometh affliction, then our imperfection appeareth: therefore God sendeth affliction, to verify the saying of St Peter, *Judicium Dei a domo Dei incipit;* "The judgment of God beginneth at the house of God." As for the wicked, for the most part, he letteth them alone until they come to their death-bed; and then they shall find all their wickedness together, and suffer punishment world without end. By the afflictions of the household of God appeareth most plainly the power and strength of God. For Christ confoundeth the devil with his weak members; as it appeareth daily, how God giveth unto such as have his Spirit power to suffer death for his word's sake: and so he confoundeth the devil and all his members, as it appeareth in John Baptist, and Christ himself. For the devil thought that Christ, after he hanged upon the cross, had been destroyed and clean overcome; but it was clean contrary.

A faithful man is tried by afflictions.

1 Pet. iv.

Christ confoundeth the devil.

Thus you see the causes wherefore God suffereth his to be in tribulation and affliction. Now, when we have affliction, we must pray unto him to take away the same from us; but this prayer must be but conditionally,—when it shall please him: as we have ensample of David the king, which when he was driven out of his kingdom by Absalom his son, he said, *Si Dominus volet, reducet me.* Therefore then, being in sickness, follow the ensample of David: call upon him for deliverance conditionally. But, above all things, beware of murmuring and rebelling against God; for he will have us obedient to his will and pleasure. The best service that thou canst do, is to take the[4] cross patiently, which God hath laid upon thee. Some men, when they be sick, say, "It grieveth my heart that I do spend my time so idly; for if I were whole, I might do much good." These are much deceived; for they cannot spend their time better than

In all our afflictions we must call upon God for help, but yet conditionally.

2 Sam. xv.

A christian man must patiently bear the cross of Christ.

[3 upright and holy, 1607.]   [4 thy, 1571.]

when they suffer the cross that God hath laid upon them, and bear the same willingly and obediently. For, as I said before, it is the best service that we can do to God, when we bear our afflictions and troubles well and godly: yet we may pray that he will be merciful unto us, and not lay more upon us than we are able to bear, according to his promises.

Also note here, in necessity whither went the disciples? Even to Christ, being asleep. We think that he is asleep, if he hear us not so soon as we call upon him; but for all that he sleepeth not: *Non dormitabit, neque dormiet, qui custodit Israel.* He is called a helper in due time. But here learn, by the ensample of the disciples, whither thou shalt run in thy distress; namely, to Christ, (for he is the right helper,) and not to his saints: for when I call upon any creature, I commit most abominable idolatry. For this is one apparent and great argument to make Christ God, if we call upon him as St Stephen did; who said, *Domine Jesu, suscipe spiritum meum;* that is, "Lord Jesus, receive my spirit:" for invocation declareth an omnipotency: so that when I call upon saints, I make them omnipotent, and so I make them gods: for omnipotency pertaineth properly and principally only to God. And therefore beware that you call upon no creature, but upon God only: for if you do the contrary, you do against God most wickedly.

Here is also to be noted, that the very saints of God have but little faith: they have little, but yet they have some. They are not altogether without faith, for they that are altogether without faith are in an evil case; for they are, and remain in the kingdom and dominion[1] of the devil. The disciples had but a little faith; yet they go and waken Christ, and desire his help. And here note also, that he is not angry for wakening of him, but he blamed them for their unbelief: which is a very comfortable doctrine for us, that when we feel ourselves weak in faith, we shall not despair, but rather run to him, for he will increase our faith. Some think themselves to have very much faith, when they have none at all: and, again, some think themselves to have none, when they have some: therefore it is needful

[1 domination, 1607.]

for us to pray without intermission, *Domine, adauge nobis fidem,* "Lord, increase our faith;" *adjuva incredulitatem meam,* " O Lord[2], help my unbelief." Luke xvii.

Here learn, by the ensample of our Saviour, not to flatter with any body when they do naughtily and wickedly: for Christ, perceiving his disciples to be unbelievers, flattered them not, but told them plainly, and rebuked them for their faults. Also, we may here learn not to be too hasty with our neighbours when they do fall; but to bear with them, like as our Saviour did bear with his disciples. He thrusteth them not away because of their unbelief: so we may not give over our neighbour when he is fallen, for he may rise again. *Flattery is not to be used. One of us ought to bear another's infirmity.*

Now to make an end. Here learn, by the ensample of these disciples, to run to Christ when thou art in tribulation. Seek help at his hand: and if thou have not a perfect faith, yet despair not; for he is merciful, loving, and kind unto all that call upon him: to whom, with the Father and the Holy Ghost, be all honour and glory, both now and ever, world without end! *Amen.* *The conclusion of this sermon.*

[2 Help, O Lord, 1571.]

A SERMON PREACHED BY MASTER HUGH LATIMER, THE FIFTH SUNDAY AFTER THE EPIPHANY, THE 7TH DAY OF FEBRUARY, ANNO 1552.

MATTHEW XIII. [24—30.]

Simile factum est regnum cœlorum homini qui seminat bonum semen in agro suo; cum autem dormirent homines, venit inimicus ejus, et superseminavit, &c.

[The kingdom of heaven is likened unto a man which sowed good seed in his field: but while men slept, his enemy came and sowed tares among the wheat, and went his way, &c.]

A parable, what it is.

THIS is a parable, or similitude, wherein our Saviour compared the kingdom of God, that is, the preaching of his word, wherein consisteth the salvation of mankind, unto an husbandman that soweth good seed in his field. But before we come unto the matter, you shall first learn to understand what is this word "parable," which is a Greek word, and used in the Latin and English tongue. *Parabola est rerum dissimilium comparatio;* that is to say, "A parable is a comparison of two things that are unlike outwardly." But, in effect, they signify but one thing, for they do appertain to one end; as in this place Christ compared the word of God unto a sower: which two things are unlike, but yet they teach one thing; for like as the seed is sown in the earth, so is the word of God sown in our hearts. And thus much of this word "parable."

The sum of this gospel is: first, he speaketh of a husbandman that soweth good seed; after that he maketh mention of an enemy that soweth evil seed. And these two manner of seeds, that is, the husbandman's seed that was good, and the enemy's seed which was naught, came up both together: so that the enemy was as busy as the other in sowing his evil seed. And while he was busy in sowing it, it was unknown. And at the first springing up it seemeth all to be good seed: but at the length the servant of this husbandman perceived the evil seed sown amongst the good; therefore he came and told his master, shewing him all the matter, and required leave to gather the evil seed from amongst the other. The husbandman himself said, *Inimicus homo hoc fecit;* "Our enemy hath done this; but for all that, let it alone until the harvest, and then will I separate the good from the evil." This is the sum of this gospel.

First, note that he saith, *Dormientibus hominibus,* "When every body was asleep, then he came and sowed his seed." Who are these sleepers? The bishops and prelates, the slothful and careless curates and ministers: they with their negligence give the devil leave to sow his, for they sow not their seed; that is, they preach not the word of God; they instruct not the people with wholesome doctrine; and so they give place to the devil to sow his seed. For when the devil cometh, and findeth the heart of man not weaponed nor garnished with the word of God, he forthwith possesseth the same, and so getteth victory through the slothfulness of the spiritualty; which they shall one day grievously repent. For the whole scripture, that is to say, both the old and new Testament, is full of threatenings of such negligent and slothful pastors; and they shall make an heavy and grievous account one day, when no excuse shall serve, but extreme punishment shall follow for a reward of their slothfulness. *Bishops and ministers must be watchers, that the devil sow not evil seed in the field of God.*

This gospel giveth occasion to speak of many things: for our Saviour himself expoundeth this parable unto his disciples after the people were gone from him, and that he was come into the house. For the disciples were not so bold as to ask him of the understanding of this parable in the presence of the people: whereby we may learn good manner, to use in every thing a good and convenient time. *Here is good manner to be learned.* Also, we may here learn to search and inquire earnestly, and with great diligence, for the true understanding of God's word. And when you hear a sermon, and are in doubt of something, inquire for it, and be desirous to learn; for it is written, *Omni habenti dabitur,* "Whosoever hath, unto him shall be given;" *et abundabit,* "and he shall have abundance." What meaneth this saying? When we hear the word of God, and have tasted somewhat thereof, and are afterwards desirous to go forward more and more, then shall we have further knowledge; for God will give us of *We ought to be diligent to search for the understanding of the word of God.*

his grace, to come to further understanding. And so the saying of our Saviour shall be fulfilled in us.

Now when our Saviour had heard the request of his disciples, he performeth their desire, and beginneth to expound unto them the parable, saying: "I am he that soweth the good seed," *Inimicus homo*, that is, "the adversary, the devil, soweth[1] evil seed." Here our Saviour, good people, maketh known that he goeth about to do us good; but the devil doth the clean contrary, and he seeketh to spoil and destroy us with his filthy and naughty seed of false doctrine. The field here is the whole world. The harvest is the end of the world. The reapers are the angels of God, which are his servants: for like as every lord or master hath his servants to wait upon him, and to do his commandments, so the angels of God wait upon him to do his commandments. The angels at the time of the harvest shall gather first *offendicula*; that is, all such as have been evil and given occasion of wickedness, and go forward in the same without repentance or amendment of their lives. All such, I say, shall be gathered together and cast *in caminum ignis*, "into the chimney of fire, where shall be weeping and gnashing of teeth." For in the end of this wicked world all such as have lived in the delectations and pleasures of the same, and have not foughten with the lusts and pleasures of their flesh, but are proud and stubborn; or bear hatred and malice unto their neighbour; or be covetous persons; also, all naughty servants that do not their duties; and all those that use falsehood in buying and selling, and care not for their neighbours, but sell unto them false wares, or otherwise deceive them; all these are called *offendicula mundi*, "the offenders[2] of this world:" and all such shall be cast into the "chimney[3], where shall be weeping, and wailing, and gnashing of teeth."

In like manner, all idle persons that will not work for their living, but go about loitering and be chargeable unto others; and also drunken persons, that abuse the benefits of God in dishonesting themselves, so that they lose the use of reason, and their natural wits wherewith God hath endued them, and make themselves like swine and beasts;

[1 is he who soweth, 1607.] [2 offences, 1571.]
[3 burning chimney, 1571.]

also those which break wedlock, and despise matrimony, that is instituted of God himself; hereunto add all swearers, all usurers, all liars, and deceivers: all these are called the seed of the devil; and so they are the devil's creatures through their own wickedness. But yet it is true that wicked men have their souls and bodies of God, for he is their Creator and Maker: but they themselves, in forsaking God and his laws, and following the devil and his instructions, make themselves members of the devil, and become his seed; therefore they shall be cast out in the last day into everlasting fire, when the trumpet shall blow, and the angels shall come and gather all *offendicula* from amongst the elect of God.

The form of judgment shall be in this wise: Christ our Saviour at the day of judgment, being appointed of God, shall come down with great triumph and honour; accompanied with all his angels, and saints, that departed in faith out of this world beforetimes: they shall come with him now, and all the elect shall be gathered to him, and there they shall see the judgment; but they themselves shall not be judged, but shall be like as judges with him. After that the elect are separated from the wicked, he shall give a most horrible and dreadful sentence unto the wicked; commanding his angels to cast them into everlasting fire, where they shall have such torments as no tongue can express. Therefore our Saviour, desirous to set out the pains of hell unto us, and to make us afraid thereof, calleth it fire, yea, a burning and unquenchable fire. For like as there is no pain so grievous to a man as is fire, so the pains of hell passeth all the pains that may be imagined of any man. There shall be sobbing and sighing, weeping, and wailing, and gnashing of teeth; which are the tokens of unspeakable pains and griefs, that shall come upon those that die in the state of damnation. For you must understand that there are but two places appointed of Almighty God for all mankind; that is, heaven and hell. And in what state soever a man dieth in, in the same he shall arise again; for there shall be no alteration or change. Those which die repentantly and are sorry for their sins, cry God mercy, be ashamed of their own wickedness, and believe with all their hearts that God will be merciful unto them through the passion of our Saviour Christ,—

those which die in such a faith shall come into everlasting life and felicity; and shall also rise in the last day in the state of salvation. For look, as you die, so shall you arise. Whosoever departeth out of this world without a repentant heart, and hath been a malicious and envious man, and a hater of the word of God, and so continueth and will not repent, and be sorry, and call upon God with a good faith, or hath no faith at all,—that man shall come to everlasting damnation; and so he shall arise again at the last day: for there is nothing that can help him out of his damnation, or hinder him of his salvation. For when a man dieth without faith in Christ, all the masses in the world are not able to relieve him: and, to conclude, all the travails that we have had in time past by seeking of remedy by purgatory, and all the great costs and expenses that may be bestowed upon any soul lying in the state of damnation, it can avail nothing, neither can it do any good. For, as I said before, the judgments of God are immutable; that is, as you die, so shall you rise. If thou die in the state of salvation, thou shalt rise so again, and receive thy body, and remain in salvation. Again, if thou die in damnation, thou shalt rise in the same estate, and receive thy body, and return again to the same estate, and be punished world without end with unspeakable pains and torments. For our natural fire, in comparison to hell-fire, is like a fire painted on a wall; for that shall be so extreme, that no man is able to express the terrible horror and grief thereof.

O what a pitiful thing is it, that man will not consider this, and leave the sin and pleasure of this world, and live godly; but is so blind and mad, that he will rather have a momentary, and a very short and small pleasure, than hearken to the will and pleasure of Almighty God! That might avoid everlasting pain and wo, and give unto him everlasting felicity. For that a great many of us are damned, the fault is not in God; for *Deus vult omnes homines salvos fieri,* "God would have all men be saved:" but the fault is in ourselves, and in our own madness, that had rather have damnation than salvation. Therefore, good people, consider these terrible pains in your minds, which are prepared for the wicked and ungodly: avoid all wickedness and sin; set before your eyes the wonderful joy and felicity, and the innumerable treasures which God hath laid up for you that fear and love him, and live after his will and commandments: for no tongue can express, no eye hath seen, no heart can comprehend nor conceive the great felicity that God hath prepared for his elect and chosen, as St Paul witnesseth. Consider therefore, I say, these most excellent treasures, and endeavour yourselves to obtain the fruition of the same. Continue not, neither abide or wallow too long in your sins, like as a swine lieth in the mire: make no delay to repent your sin, and to amend your life; for you are not so sure[1] to have repentance in the end. It is a common saying, *Pœnitentia sera raro vera:* therefore consider this thing with yourself betimes, and study to amend your life; for what availeth it to have all the pleasures of the world for awhile, and after that to have everlasting pain and infelicity?

Therefore let every one go into his own consience, when he findeth himself unready: for all such as, through the goodness of God, have received faith, and then wrestle with sin, consent not unto it, but are sorry for it when they fall, and do not abide nor dwell in the same, but rise up again forthwith, and call for forgiveness thereof through the merits of our Saviour Jesus Christ,—all such are called just: that is to say, all that die with a repentant heart, and are sorry that they have sinned, and are minded, if God give them longer time to live, that they will amend all faults, and lead a new life; then are they just, but not through their own merits or good works. For if God should enter into judgment with us, none are able to stand before his face; neither any of his saints may be found just, neither St John Baptist, St Peter, nor St Paul, no, nor the mother of our Saviour Christ herself is not just, if she should be judged after the rigour of the law. For all are, and must be, justified by the justification of our Saviour Christ; and so we must be justified, and not through our own well-doings, but our justice standeth in this, that our unrighteousness is forgiven us through the righteousness of Christ; for if we believe in him, then are we made righteous. For he fulfilled the law, and afterward granted the same to be ours, if we believe that his fulfilling is our fulfilling: for St Paul[2]

Our justification cometh only of God through faith in Christ our Saviour.

Wherein our justice standeth.

[1 not sure, 1571.]   [2 the apostle St Paul, 1607.]

saith, *Qui proprio Filio non pepercit;* "He hath not spared his own Son, but hath given him for us; and how then may it be, but we should have all things with him?" Therefore it must needs follow, that when he gave us his only Son, he gave us also his righteousness, and his fulfilling of the law. So it appeareth that we are justified by the free gift of God, and not of ourselves, nor by our merits: but the righteousness of Christ is accounted to be our righteousness, and through the same we obtain everlasting life, and not through our own doings: for, as I said before, if God should enter into judgment with us, we should be damned.

Rom. viii.
Christ is given unto us and all his righteousness.

Therefore take heed and be not proud, and be humble and low, and trust not too much in yourselves; but put your only trust in Christ our Saviour. And yet you may not utterly set aside the doing of good works: but specially look that you have always oil in readiness for your lamps; or else you may not come to the wedding, but shall be shut out, and thrust into everlasting darkness. This oil is faith in Christ, which if you lack, then all things are unsavoury before the face of God. But a great many of people are much deceived; for they think themselves to have faith when indeed they have it not. Some peradventure will say, "How shall I know whether I have faith or not?" Truly, thou shalt find this in thee, if thou have no mind to leave sin, then sin grieveth thee not, but art content to go forward in the same, and thou delightest in it, and hatest it not, neither feelest thou what sin is; when thou art in such a case, then thou hast no faith, and therefore like to perish everlastingly. For that man that is sore sick, and yet feeleth not his sickness, he is in great danger, for he hath lost all his senses: so that man which hath gone so far in sin, that he feeleth his sin no more, is like to be damned, for he is without faith. Again, that man is in good case, that can be content to fight and strive with sin, and to withstand the devil and his temptations; and calleth for the help of God, and believeth that God will help him, and make him strong to fight. That man shall not be overcome by the devil. And whosoever feeleth this in his heart, and so wrestleth with sin, may be sure that he hath faith, and is in the favour of God.

Good works are to be done, but not to be saved by.

A doctrine to teach us to know when we have faith.

But if thou wilt have a trial of thy faith, then do this:

examine thyself toward thine enemy: he doth thee harm, he slandereth thee, or taketh away thy living from thee; how shalt thou now use thyself towards such a man? If thou canst find in thy heart to pray for him, to love him with all thine heart, and forgive him with a good will all that he hath sinned against thee; if thou canst find this readiness in thy heart, then thou art one of those which have faith, if thou wouldest him to be saved as well as thyself. And if thou canst do this, thou mayest argue that thy sin is forgiven thee, and that thou art none of those that shall be cast out, but shall be received and placed among the number of the godly, and shall enjoy with them everlasting life. For St Paul saith[1] that "Those that are just," that is, those that are justified by faith, and exercise faith in their living and conversation, *fulgebunt tanquam sol*, "they shall shine like unto the sun in the kingdom of God;" that is to say, they shall be in exceeding great honour and glory. For like as the sun exceedeth in brightness all other creatures of God, and is beautiful in the eyes of every man; so shall all the faithful be beautiful and endued with honour and glory, although in this world they be but outcasts, and accounted as *expurgamenta mundi*; but in the other world, when the angels shall gather together the wicked, and cast them into the fire, then shall the elect shine as the sun in the kingdom of God. For no man can express the honour and glory that they shall have, which will be content to suffer all things for God's sake, and to reform themselves after his will; or are content to be told of their faults, and glad to amend the same, and humble themselves under the mighty hand of God.

Matt. xiii. 43.

The faithful which are counted vile in this world, shall be made glorious before God.

Also, the householder said unto his servants, "Let them alone until harvest." Here we may learn, that the preachers and ministers of the word of God have not authority to compel the people with violence to goodness, though they be wicked: but only with the word of God they shall admonish them, not to pull the wicked out by the throat; for that is not their duty. All things must be done according as God hath appointed. God hath appointed the magistrates to punish the wicked: for so he saith, *Auferes malum e medio populi;* "Thou shalt take away the evil from amongst the people;" *Non misereris ejus,* "Thou shalt have no pity of

The bishops and ministers of God may use no violence.

The office of the magistrates is to punish.

[1 So the old editions read.]

Wicked persons must be punished.

him." If he be a thief, an adulterer, or an whoremonger, away with him. But when our Saviour saith, "Let them grow," he speaketh not of the civil magistrates, for it is their duty to pull them out; but he signifieth, that there will be such wickedness for all the magistrates; and teacheth, that the ecclesiastical power is ordained, not to pull out the wicked with the sword, but only to admonish them with the word of God, which is called *gladius Spiritus*, that is, "the sword of the Spirit." So did John Baptist, saying, *Quis vobis subministravit ut fugeretis a ventura ira?* that is, "Who hath taught you to fly from the wrath of God that is at hand?" So did Peter in the Acts: *Quem vos crucifixistis*, "Whom you have crucified," he said unto the Jews. What followeth? They were *compuncti corde*. Contrition and repentance followed by and bye, as soon as the word was preached unto them. Therefore they said, *Viri fratres*, &c., "Brethren, what shall we do? How shall we be made clean from our sins, that we may be saved?" Then he *Preachers have not to do with any other sword than the word of God.* sendeth them to Christ. So that it appeareth in this gospel, and by these ensamples, that the preacher hath none other sword, but the sword of the word of God: with that sword he may strike them. He may rebuke their wicked living; and further he ought not to go. But kings and magistrates, they have power to punish with the sword the obstinate and vicious livers, and to put them to due punishment.

Now to make an end with this one lesson, which is: if thou dwellest in a town where are some wicked men, that will not be reformed, nor in any wise will amend their lives, *We may not run away from the place where evil persons dwell.* as there are commonly in every town some; run not thou therefore out of the town, but tarry there still, and exercise thy patience amongst them; exhorting them, whensoever occasion serveth, to amendment. And do not, as the fondness of the monkery first did: for they at the first made so great account of the holiness of their good life, that they could not be content to live and abide in cities and towns, where *Monkish foolishness.* sinners and wicked doers were, but thought to amend the matter, and therefore ran out into the wilderness; where they fell into great inconveniences. For some despised the communion of the body and blood of our Saviour Christ; and some fell into other errors[1]. So God punished them

[1 Hospinian, de Origine, &c., Monachatus, pp. 39, et seq.; 188, et seq. Genev. 1669.]

for their foolishness and uncharitableness. We are born into this world, not for our own sakes only, but for our even Christians' sake. They, forgetting this commandment of love and charity, ran away from their neighbours, like beasts and wild horses, that cannot abide the company of men. So the anabaptists in our time, following their ensample, segregated themselves from the company of other men; and therefore God gave them *reprobum sensum*, that is a pervert judgment. Therefore, when thou dwellest in an evil town or parish, follow not the ensample of the monks or anabaptists; but remember that Lot, dwelling in the midst of the Sodomites, was nevertheless preserved from the wrath of God; and such will preserve them[2] in the midst of the wicked. But for all that, thou must not flatter them in their evil doings and naughty livings; but rebuke their sins and wickedness, and in no wise consent unto them. Then it will be well with thee here in this world, and in the world to come thou shalt have life everlasting[3]: which grant, both to you and me, God the Father, the Son, and God the Holy Ghost! Amen.

marginal note: Anabaptists are a vile sect of lewd people.

[2 such surely will God preserve in, 1607.]
[3 through Jesus Christ our Lord. Which God the Father grant both to you and me for his mercy's sake: to whom, with the Son and the Holy Ghost, be all praise, honour and glory, both now and ever. *Amen:*—1607.]

A SERMON PREACHED BY MASTER HUGH LATIMER, ON THE SUNDAY CALLED SEPTUAGESIMA, THE 14TH DAY OF FEBRUARY, ANNO 1552.

MATTHEW XX. [14.]

Simile est regnum cœlorum patrifamilias, qui exiit primo diluculo ad conducendum operarios in vineam suam, &c.

[The kingdom of heaven is like unto a man that was an householder, which went out early in the morning to hire labourers into his vineyard, &c.]

THIS parable is written by the evangelist Matthew in the twentieth chapter, and is very dark and hard to be understand; yea, there is no harder piece of scripture written by any evangelist. Therefore it may well be called hard meat: not meat for mowers, nor ignorant people, which be not exercised in the word of God. And yet there is none other diversity in this scripture, than is in any other. For though many scriptures have diverse expositions (as is well to be allowed of, so long as they keep them in the tenor of the catholic faith), yet they pertain all to one end and effect, and they be all alike. Therefore, although this parable be harder to understand than the other, at the first hearing or reading, yet when we shall well advise and consider the same, we shall find it agreeable unto all the other.

Some apply this parable to the ages of a man.

Now to come to the matter. There are some learned men which apply this parable unto the ages of man[1]. For a man-child, when he is born, first he is a child; afterward he becometh a lad; then a young man; and after that a perfect man; and in process of time he becometh an old man; and at length a cripple and impotent.

Some apply it to the ages of the world.

Some there be that apply it to the ages of the world: as from Adam to Noah was the first hour; from Noah to Abraham; from Abraham to David; from David to Christ; from Christ to the end of the world.

Some make of this

Some there are which would have an allegory of it. But

[1 One or other of the following interpretations of the parable is recited in most of the commentaries and sermons on this portion of scripture, from St Jerome's time down to the Reformation.]

all agree in this point, namely, that it is not requisite in a parable to expound every word of the same. For every parable hath *certum statum,* "a certain scope," to the which we must have a respect; and not go about to set all words together, or to make a gloss for the same: for it is enough for us when we have the meaning of the principal scope; and more needeth not.

Parable an allegory.

Now to the principal cause and end to the which our Saviour hath had a respect in this parable, is that he will teach us hereby, that all christian people are equal in all things appertaining to the kingdom of Christ. So that we have one Christ, one Redeemer, one baptism, and one gospel, one supper of the Lord, and one kingdom of heaven. So that the poorest man, and most miserable that is in the world, may call God his Father, and Christ his Redeemer, as well as the greatest king or emperor in the world. And this is the scope of this parable, wherein Christ teacheth us this equality. And if this now were considered, the whole parable will be easily and soon understand.

All that profess Christ are equal in all things that came by Christ.

The poorest hath as much in Christ as the richest hath.

Here is declared unto us, that some laboured the whole day, which were hired for a penny; that is, of our money ten pence: for like as we have a piece of money which we call a shilling, and is in value twelve pence, so the Jews had a piece that they called *denarium,* and that was in value ten of our pence. The first company wrought twelve hours; and the other wrought, some nine hours, some six hours, and some three hours, and some but one hour. Now when evening was come, and the time of payment drew on, the householder said to his steward, "Go, and give every man alike, and begin at those that came last." And when the other, that came early in the morning, perceived that they should have no more than those that had wrought but one hour, they murmured against the householder, saying, "Shall they[2] which have laboured but one hour, have as much as we that have wrought the whole day?" The householder, perceiving their malicious mind, said to one of them, "Friend, wherefore grudgest thou? Is it not lawful for me to do with mine own what pleaseth me? Have I not given thee that I promised thee? Content thyself therefore, and go thy way; for it hath pleased me to give unto this man which

The sum of the parable.

[2 those, 1571.]

hath wrought but one hour as much as unto thee." This is the sum of this parable, which he concludeth with this sentence, *Primi erunt novissimi et novissimi primi;* "The first shall be the last, and the last first."

Merit-mongers are murmurers against Christ's poor flock.

First consider, Who are these murmurers? The merit-mongers, which esteem their own works so much, that they think heaven scant sufficient to recompense their good deeds; namely, for putting themselves to pain with saying of our lady's psalter, and gadding on pilgrimage, and such-like trifles. These are the murmurers; for they think themselves holier than all the world, and therefore worthy to receive a greater reward than other men. But such men are much deceived, and are in a false opinion; and, if they abide and continue therein, it shall[1] bring them to the fire of hell. For man's salvation cannot be gotten by any work; because the scripture saith, *Vita æterna donum Dei;* "Life everlasting is the gift of God." True it is, that God requireth good works of us, and commandeth us to avoid all wickedness. But for all that, we may not do our good works to the end to get heaven withal; but rather to shew ourselves thankful for that which Christ hath done for us, who with his passion hath opened heaven unto all believers; that is, to all those that put their hope and trust not in their deeds, but in his death and passion, and study to live well and godly; and yet not to make merits of their own works, as though they should have everlasting life for them; as our monks and friars, and all our religious persons were wont to do, and therefore may rightly be called murmurers: for they had so great store of merits, that they sold some of them unto other men. And many men spent a great part of their substance to buy their merits, and to be a brother of their houses; or to obtain one of their coats or cowls to be buried in[2]. But there is a great difference between the judgment of God and the judgment of this world. They in this world were accounted most holy above all men, and so most worthy to be *primi;* but before God they shall be *novissimi,* when their hypocrisy and wickedness shall be opened. And thus much I thought to say of murmurers.

Rom. vi.
Good works are to be done, but not to merit our salvation by them.

Monks and friars were merit-mongers.
Monks and friars had such store of merits that they made sale of them.
The judgments of God and the world differ greatly.

[1 will, 1571.]
[2 See Vol. I. p. 50, note 4; Reflexions upon the devotions of the Roman Church, pp. 258, et seq.]

Now I will go about to apply all the parts of this parable: for, as I said before, it is enough for us if we know the chief point and scope of the parable, which is, that there shall be one equality in all the things that appertain to Christ: inso- much that the rulers of this realm hath no better a God, no better sacraments, and no better a gospel, than the poorest in this world; yea, the poorest man hath as good right to Christ and his benefits, as the greatest man in the world. This is comfortable to every one; and specially to such as are in miseries, poverty, or other calamities: which if it were well considered, we would not be so desirous to come aloft, and to get riches, honour and dignities in this world, as we now are; nor yet so malicious one against another as we be. For we would ever make this reckoning with our- selves, each man in his vocation: the servant would think thus with himself: "I am a servant, poor and miserable, and must live after the pleasure of my master, I may not have my free-will; but what then? I am sure that I have as good a God as my master hath; and I am sure that my service and business pleaseth God as much (when I do it with a good faith) as the preacher's or curate's, in preaching or saying of [3] service." For we must understand, that God esteemeth not the diversity of the works, but he hath respect unto the faith: for a poor man which doth his business in faith, is as acceptable unto God, and hath as good right to the death and merits of Christ, as the greatest man in the world. So go through all estates: whosoever applieth his business with faith, considering that God willeth him so to do, surely the same is most beloved of God. If this were well considered and printed in our hearts, all ambition and desire of promo- tions, all covetousness, and other vices, would depart out of our hearts. For it is the greatest comfort that may be unto poor people, (specially such as are nothing regarded in this world,) if they consider that God loveth them, as well as the richest in the world, it must needs be a great comfort unto them.

God and his mercies are indifferent to poor and rich.

A godly lesson.

God respect- eth not the diversity of works.

God regard- eth and loveth the poor as well as the rich.

But there be some that say, that this sentence *primi et novissimi*, "the first shall be last," is the very substance of the parable. And here you shall understand, that our Saviour Christ took occasion to put forth this parable, when

[3 of the service, 1571.]

there came a young man demanding of him, in the nineteenth chapter of this evangelist, saying, "What shall I do to come to everlasting life?" Our Saviour, after he had taught him the commandments of God, bade him "go, and sell all that he had, and give to the poor; and come and follow him." He, hearing this, went away heavily, for his heart was cold. And then our Saviour spake very terribly against rich men, saying, "It is more easy for a camel to go through the eye of a needle, than for a rich man to enter into the kingdom of heaven." A camel *est funis nauticus*, that is, a great cable of a ship; which is more likelier than a beast that is called a camel. The disciples hearing this, said, "Who then can be saved?" He made them answer, saying, *Omnia possibilia sunt Deo;* "God is almighty, and that which is impossible to men, is possible with God:" signifying, that he condemneth not all rich men, but only those that set their hearts upon riches; that care not how they get them; and when they have them, they abuse them to the satisfying of their own carnal appetites and fleshly delights and pleasures, and not to the honour of God. And again, such riches as are justly, rightly, and godly gotten, those are the good creatures of God; being rightly used to the glory of God, and comfort of their neighbours; not hoarding nor heaping them up, to make treasures of them. For riches are indifferent, and are not evil of themselves; but they are made evil, when our heart is set upon them, and that we put hope in them; for that is an abominable thing before the face of God. Now, after these words spoken by our Saviour Christ, Peter cometh forth, saying, "Lo, we have forsaken all that we had; what shall be our reward?" Peter had forsaken all that he had; which was but little in substance, but yet it was a great matter to him, for he had no more but that little: like to the widow which cast into the treasury two mites, yet our Saviour praised her gift above all that gave before her. Here thou learnest, that when thou hast but little, yet give of the same little; as Tobias teacheth his son; for it is as acceptable unto God, as though it were a greater thing. So Peter, in forsaking his old boat and net, was allowed as much before God, as if he had forsaken all the riches in the world: therefore he shall have a great reward for his old boat; for Christ saith, that he shall be one of them that shall sit and judge the twelve tribes of Israel: and to signify them to be more than the others, he giveth them the name of judges; meaning, that they shall condemn the world: like as Almighty God speaketh of the queen of Sheba, that in the last day she shall arise and condemn the Jews that would not hear Christ, and she came so great a journey to hear the wisdom of Solomon. Then he answered and said, "Whosoever leaveth father, or mother, or brethren, for my sake, shall receive an hundred-fold, and shall inherit everlasting life." Now what is this, to leave father and mother? When my father or mother will hinder or let me in any goodness, or would persuade me from the honouring of God and faith in Christ; then I must forsake, and rather lose the favour and good-will of my father and mother, than to forsake God and his holy word. *We must forsake father and mother to go to Christ.*

And now Christ addeth and saith, "The first shall be the last, and the last shall be the first;" alluding to St Peter's saying, that soundeth as though Peter looked for a reward for his deeds: and that is it which is the let of all together. If a man come to the gospel, and heareth the same, and after hath a respect to reward, such a man shall be *ultimus*, that is, "the last." If these sayings were well considered of us, surely we would not have such a number of vain gospellers, as we now have; that seek nothing but their own commodities, under the name and colour of the gospel. Moreover, he teacheth us to be meek and lowly, and not think much of ourselves; for those that are greatly esteemed in their own eyes, they are the least before God. "For he that humbleth himself, shall be exalted;" according to the scripture, which saith, *Deus superbis resistit, humilibus autem dat gratiam;* "God resisteth the proud, and advanceth the humble and meek." And this is it that he saith, "the first shall be the last;" teaching us to be careful, and not to stand in our own conceit, but ever to mistrust ourselves: as St Paul teacheth, saying, *Qui stat, videat ne cadat,* "Whosoever standeth, let him take heed he fall not:" and therefore we may not put trust in ourselves, but rather in God. Further, in this saying of our Saviour is comprehended a great comfort: for those that are accounted of the world to be the most vilest slaves and *We must do good works without respect of reward. God despiseth the proud. 1 Cor. x.*

abject, may by this saying have a hope to be made the first and the principallest: for although they be never so low, yet they may arise again, and become the highest. And so this is to us a comfortable sentence, which strengtheneth our faith, and keepeth us from desperation and falling from God. And at the end he saith, *Multi sunt vocati, pauci vero electi;* that is, "Many are called, and few are chosen." These words of our Saviour are very hard to understand, and therefore it is not good to be too curious in them, as some vain fellows do[1]; who, seeking carnal liberty, pervert, toss, and turn the word of God, after their own mind and purpose. Such, I say, when they read these words, make their reckoning thus, saying: "What need I to mortify my body with abstaining from all sin and wickedness? I perceive God hath chosen some, and some are rejected. Now if I be in the number of the chosen, I cannot be damned: but if I be accounted among the condemned number, then I cannot be saved: for God's judgments are immutable." Such foolish and wicked reasons some have; which bringeth them either to desperation, or else to carnal liberty. Therefore it is as needful to beware of such reasons or expositions of the scripture, as it is to beware of the devil himself.

Curious interpretations of the scriptures are odious and wicked.

But if thou art desirous to know whether thou art chosen to everlasting life, thou mayest not begin with God: for God is too high, thou canst not comprehend him. The judgments of God are unknown to man; therefore thou mayest not begin there: but begin with Christ, and learn to know Christ, and wherefore he came; namely, that he came to save sinners, and made himself a subject to the law, and a fulfiller of the same, to deliver us from the wrath and danger thereof; and therefore was crucified for our sins, and rose again to shew and teach us the way to heaven, and by his resurrection to teach us to arise from sin: so also his resurrection teacheth and admonisheth us of the general resurrection. He sitteth at the right hand of God, and maketh intercession for us; and giveth us the Holy Ghost, that comforteth and strengtheneth our faith, and daily assureth us of our salvation. Consider, I say, Christ and his coming; and then begin to try thyself, whether thou art in the book of life or not. If

Enter not into the inscrutable mysteries of God.

Enter into Christ, and there seek thy salvation.

[1 be, 1607.]

thou findest thyself in Christ, then thou art sure of everlasting life. If thou be without him, then thou art in an evil case. For it is written, *Nemo venit ad Patrem nisi per me;* that is, "No man cometh unto the Father but through me." Therefore if thou knowest Christ, then thou mayest know further of thy election. But when we are about this matter, and are troubled within ourselves, whether we be elect or no, we must ever have this maxim or principal rule before our eyes; namely, that God beareth a goodwill towards us. God loveth us; God beareth a fatherly heart towards us. But you will say, "How shall I know that? Or how shall I believe that?" We may know God's will towards us through Christ: God hath opened himself unto us by his Son Christ: for so saith John, the evangelist, *Filius, qui est in sinu Patris, ipse revelavit;* that is, "The Son which is in the bosom of the Father, he hath revealed." Therefore we may perceive his good-will and love towards us: he hath sent the same his Son into this world, which hath suffered most painful death for us. Shall I now think that God hateth me? Or shall I doubt of his love towards me? Here you see how you shall avoid the scrupulous and most dangerous question of the predestination of God. For if thou wilt inquire his counsels, and enter into his consistory, thy wit will deceive thee; for thou shalt not[2] be able to search the counsels of God. But if thou begin with Christ, and consider his coming into the world, and dost believe that God hath sent him for thy sake, to suffer for thee, and deliver thee from sin, death, the devil and hell; then, when thou art so armed with the knowledge of Christ, then, I say, this simple question cannot hurt thee; for thou art in the book of life, which is Christ himself.

Also we learn by this sentence, *Multi sunt vocati,* that "many are called," that the preaching of the gospel is universal; that it pertaineth to all mankind; that it is written, *In omnem terram exivit sonus eorum,* "Through the whole earth their sound is heard." Now seeing that the gospel is universal, it appeareth that he would have all mankind saved; and that the fault is not in him, if we be damned. For it is written thus, *Deus vult omnes homines salvos fieri;* "God would have all men to be saved:" his

Margin notes: Christ is the book of life, wherein our names are written, if we believe in him. John i. God hath given his only Son to redeem sinners that repent and believe. How you shall know when you are in the book of life. Rom. x. God would that all should be saved.

[2 never, 1607.]

salvation is sufficient to save all mankind; but we are so wicked of ourselves that we refuse the same, and we will not take it, when it is offered unto us: and therefore he saith, *Pauci vero electi,* "Few are chosen;" that is, few have pleasure and delight in it: for the most part are weary of it, they cannot abide it. And there are some that hear it, but they will abide no danger for it: they love more their riches and possessions than the word of God. And therefore, *pauci sunt electi;* there are but a few that stick heartily unto it, and can find in their hearts to forego this world for God's sake and his holy word. There are some now-a-days that will not be reprehended by the gospel; they think themselves better than it. Some, again, are so stubborn, that they will rather forswear themselves, than confess their sins and wickedness. Such men are [the] cause of their own damnation; for God would have them saved, but they refuse it: like as did Judas, the traitor, whom Christ would have had to be saved, but he refused his salvation; he refused to follow the doctrine of his master Christ. And so, whosoever heareth the word of God, and followeth it, the same is elect by him: and again, whosoever refuseth to hear the word of God, and follow the same, is damned. So that our election is sure if we follow the word of God.

Here is now taught you, how to try out your election, namely, in Christ; for Christ is the accounting book and register of God: even in the same book, that is, Christ, are written all the names of the elect. Therefore we cannot find our election in ourselves, neither yet in the high counsel of God: for *inscrutabilia sunt judicia Altissimi.* Where shall I then find my election? In the counting book of God, which is Christ: for thus it is written, *Sic Deus dilexit mundum,* that is, "God hath so entirely loved the world, that he gave his only-begotten Son, to that end, that all that believe in him should not perish, but have life everlasting." Whereby appeareth most plainly, that Christ is the book of life; and that all that believe in him are in the same book, and so are chosen to everlasting life: for only those are ordained which believe. Therefore, when thou hast faith in Christ, then thou art in the book of life, and so art thou sure of thine election. And again, if thou be without Christ, and have no faith in him, neither art sorry for thy wickedness, nor have a mind and purpose to leave and forsake sin, but rather exercise and use the same; then thou art not in the book of life, as long as thou art in such a case: and therefore shalt thou go into everlasting fire, namely, if thou die in thy wickedness and sin, without repentance. *The unfaithful are not in the book of life.*

But there are none so wicked, but he may have a remedy. What is that? Enter into thine own heart, and search the secrets of the same. Consider thine own life, and how thou hast spent thy days. And if thou find in thyself all manner of uncleanness and abominable sins, and so seest thy damnation before thine eyes, what shalt thou then do? Confess the same unto thy Lord God. Be sorry that thou hast offended so loving a Father, and ask mercy of him in the name of Christ; and believe stedfastly that he will be merciful unto thee, in respect of his only Son which suffered death for thee; and then have a good purpose to leave all sin and wickedness, and to withstand and resist the affections of thine own flesh, which ever fight against the Spirit, and to live uprightly and godly, after the will and commandment of thy heavenly Father. If thou go thus to work, surely thou shalt be heard. Thy sins shall be forgiven thee. God will shew himself true in his promise; for to that end he hath sent his only Son into this world, that he might save sinners. Consider therefore, I say, wherefore Christ came into this world: consider also the great hatred and wrath that God beareth against sin; and again, consider his great love shewed unto thee, in that he sent his only Son to suffer most cruel death, rather than that thou shouldst be damned everlastingly. Consider therefore this great love of God the Father; amend thy life; fly all occasions of sin and wickedness, and be loath to displease him. And in this doing, thou mayst be assured that though thou hadst done all the sins of the world, they shall neither hurt nor condemn thee; for the mercy of God is greater than all the sins of the world. But we sometimes are in such a case, that we think we have no faith at all; or if we have any, it is very feeble and weak. And therefore these are two things; to have faith, and to have the feeling of faith. For some men would fain have the feeling of faith, but they cannot attain unto it; and yet they may not despair, but go forward in *The right way how thou mayest be assured of everlasting life.* *Faith is one, and the feeling of faith is another.*

calling upon God, and it will come at the length: God will open their hearts, and let them feel his goodness.

<small>Who are in the book of life, and who are not.</small> And thus may you see who are in the book of life, and who are not. For all those that are obstinate sinners, are without Christ; and so not elect to everlasting life, if they remain in their wickedness. There are none of us all but we may be saved by Christ; and therefore let us stick hard unto it, and be content to forego all the pleasures and riches of this world for his sake, who for our sake forsook all the heavenly pleasures, and came down into this miserable and wretched world; and here suffered all manner of afflictions for our sake. And therefore it is meet that we should do somewhat for his sake, to shew ourselves thankful unto him.

<small>The conclusion of this sermon.</small> And so we may assuredly be found among the first, and not among the last; that is to say, among the elect and chosen of God, that are written in the counting book of God; that are those who believe in Christ Jesu: to whom with God the Father, and the Holy Ghost, be all honour and glory, world without end! *Amen.*

A SERMON PREACHED BY MASTER HUGH LATIMER, ON THE SUNDAY CALLED SEXAGESIMA, BEING THE 21st DAY OF FEBRUARY, ANNO 1552.

MARK IV. [3.]

Exiit seminator ad seminandum semen suum.

[Behold, there went out a sower to sow.]

THIS parable needeth not to be expounded, for Christ our Saviour himself expounded the same unto his disciples. Therefore let us only consider and learn his exposition. He is the sower; the seed is his word; the people which hear the same is the ground wherein the seed is sown. Christ our Saviour is the chief preacher, and the chief sower. All that preach his word are sowers. And as it now chanced unto Christ, so happened it to all his preachers after him. For they labour, they sow, they till the ground, and they preach much; but it bringeth forth but little fruit: like as here, in the gospel, it appeareth that there was much ground; for there was hard trodden ground, also thorny ground, and stony ground, and good ground; so that only the fourth part was good ground, and bare fruit, notwithstanding that Christ himself preached, and sowed the seed. *[margin: All preachers are, or ought to be, sowers of the seed of God's holy word.]*

Here are matters to confound the Anabaptists, that affirm that they only have the true word of God and the right understanding of the same, because it beareth fruit. As for our preaching, they say it is naught, for it beareth no fruit; or if it do, it is very little: which opinion is most false and erroneous. For Christ, which was very God and very man, confesseth himself that the word of God, though it be most sincerely and purely preached, yet it taketh little fruit; yea, scant the fourth part doth prosper and increase. And this is to be noted throughout all the scripture, that is to say, both in the new and old Testament, that ever the great[1] number were those that refused the word of God, and the less number were they that received the same, and followed it. Therefore it appeareth, that this opinion of the Anabap- *[margin: It is much if the fourth part of the people love God and his word truly and faithfully. A devilish opinion of the Anabaptists.]*

[1 greater, 1596, 1607.]

The devilish opinion of the Anabaptists clean confuted.

tists is most wicked and erroneous, and clean against the truth of the scriptures. For the devil is not asleep; he resteth not whensoever the word of God is preached; there he is, fearing he shall suffer some wrong or sustain some loss.

What moved our Saviour Christ to use this parable, and to take a similitude of husbandry to teach the people withal? It is requisite in a preacher to apply himself after his audience; that is to say, when his audience is learned, or when he preacheth before learned men, then it is meet for a preacher to set out his matters learnedly: and again, when he is amongst the ignorant and unlearned people, to use himself so that they may perceive both him and his doctrine: for a good and godly preacher must endeavour himself to do good, and not to set out his learning, whereby to gain the praise of the world, and to be noted a learned man. Therefore our Saviour kept this rule; he, having a respect to his audience, used a common manner of teaching. For at that time some used to teach the people in apologues[1], bringing in how one beast talketh with another: which manner of teaching the heathen much used. And at this time, when Christ

The manner of the Jews' doctrine was to teach by parables.

preached, the Jews' manner was to teach commonly by similitudes. Therefore our Saviour, not intending to bring any new manner of teaching in amongst them, did therefore use their common manner of teaching, which was by similitudes. For as the coming of our Saviour Christ into this world was

The doctrine of Christ was simple and plain.

low and humble, so his preaching was simple and plain; and here he used this familiar and plain similitude of husbandry, giving therewith an ensample to all preachers of his word to beware of vain-glory, and only to seek to edify and to profit their audience: like as he himself did, which was not ashamed, after his coming down from heaven, to teach his audience by husbandry, and thereby to exhort them to goodness. So let not the preachers now, in this time, be ashamed to apply their matter after the capacity of their audience, that they may do them good.

Christ's exposition of the parable.

Now the seed is the word of God: the ground is the people. Like as the husbandman getteth much corn, when the ground is well tilled and dunged; so the word of God bringeth forth much fruit when it lighteth upon a good ground; that is, upon a heart that gladly receiveth the same.

[1 Old editions, *apologies.*]

But if it light in the highway, which is a trodden ground; that is, upon those that have been brought up in old customs and usages, by reason whereof they are made so hard that they cannot receive the good seed, &c. But before I come to entreat further of this matter, you must understand, that Christ speaketh here, in the beginning, of those that heard the word of God gladly, and willingly came to it. Now there are a great many that not only refuse to follow the gospel, but also utterly refuse the hearing of it. In what a miserable case are they that will not hear it, when so great number is lost and do perish that hear! For, first, there are Turks which refuse the gospel: the Jews also cannot abide it: yea, there are also a great many that bear the name of Christians, that cannot abide the name of the gospel, although it be the doctrine of Christ. Some be so obstinate in their old *mumpsimus*, that they cannot abide the true doctrine of God. Some also have this consideration; and if they come to hear sermons, peradventure they themselves are false and naughty people; as bribers, stealers, whoremongers and adulterers, and such like. For these, when they come to the sermon, hear all manner of vices rebuked: they hear the preacher say, *Non dimittitur peccatum, nisi restituatur ablatum;* "Sin cannot be forgiven, without that which was taken away be restored again." Now when a thief or a briber heareth this, it rubbeth him on the gall, he cannot away with it; therefore he maketh this reckoning with himself: "I know that *Servus qui non facit voluntatem domini,* &c., that is, 'The servant that knoweth the will of his master, and doth it not, he shall be beaten with many stripes;' therefore I will keep me from it, I will not meddle with it: for to follow it I cannot, nor will not, because it is against my profit; and I know I shall be the better if I meddle not with it at all, because then I am sure I shall have the lesser punishment." And such considerations keepeth some from the hearing of God's word. Such men shall have double punishment; first, for their wickedness, and then, for their wilful ignorance. For wilful ignorance is a great and grievous sin; and it is a despising of God and his word, in that I may come to the knowledge of God and his will, and yet I will not, but turn my heart from it. God in his holy scripture saith, "He that turneth from the hearing of me

Wo be to them that refuse the learning and doctrine of the gospel, when it is offered unto them.

The wicked hate and abhor to hear the word of God, because they shall hear their wickedness reproved.

The wicked and evil are more in fear of punishment than they are repentant of their wickedness.

14—2

and my word, his prayer is abominable in my sight." Now when his prayer is cursed and hated in the sight of God, then may he be well assured that he shall receive no favour at God's hands; and so all his doings are hateful, accursed and abominable. And here you may see, how great and abominable a sin wilful ignorance is in the face of God; in which state all they are, that when they may hear the word of God, and wilfully refuse the hearing thereof. But these are not those of which Christ speaketh in this gospel, and therefore we will return and speak of them.

Wilful ignorance is an abominable sin before God.

Those which our Saviour Christ speaketh of in this parable or similitude, saying, "Some falleth on the highway," which is the hard trodden ground, are those hearts that are blinded with old custom. And some are stony, and some are thorny, and set their hearts upon worldly riches; insomuch that all their mind is given to the pleasure and delight of this world, and utterly to forget God, and his holy word. Which are those that are the high-way, or hard trodden ground? Those are they that have been brought up in evil customs, and have had evil bringing up; have been swearers, and will abide so; have been thieves, and will be so still; have been backbiters and slanderers, wrathful and revengeable, and so continue, without amendment; and set more by their old customs, than they do by the word of God; and love better their wickedness than good living, and are in mind so to continue still. Wherefore the devil hath them in possession as long as they abide in such hardness of heart, and continue in such wickedness: for the devil fetcheth away the seed, that is, the word of God that is[1] sown in their hearts; like as a bird gathereth up the seeds that lie in the high-way. And there are many such kind of people, which, if they continue in that state, they shall be damned world without end. Yet they do well when they hear the word of God; for they are much better than those that will neither hear it nor follow it. And what shall they do that be in such a case? First, let them know themselves, and their own wickedness and sinful life; let them be sorry for it, and cry God mercy, and beware they fall not into further inconvenience: for if they go forward in their sinful life, they shall be

The seed that falleth in the high-way.

Those that have been brought up in evil customs, are those that are likened to the seed sown in the high-way.

The devil is diligent to take us negligent and forgetful of God.

Better is the hearer of the word of God, though he followeth not, than he that despiseth both hearing and following.

[1 was, 1571, 1572.]

damned world without end. Therefore, whosoever among you hath the nature of this high-way or trodden ground, and is hardened with old customs, let him be mollified with the sweet and pleasant water of the word of God.

The sweet water of God's word will mollify hard hearts.

"Some seed falleth upon the stony ground;" that is, such manner of men as, at the first, are very earnest to hear the word of God, and so continue still till some persecution or trouble shall arise for the same; and then they are gone, they will no longer tarry by it. For if he be asked a question of holy water, or holy bread, of mass or pilgrimages, or of any such trumpery, he yieldeth straight and granteth it; he will not stand against it, but will follow and go forward with the great number. But those that are godly do not so; they abide by it: they are content to lose their riches, wife, children, yea, and their lives also, for God's sake, and his holy word. But the others, that began so hot at the first, are quite gone. And truly, I fear me, that a great many of those are as the seed sown upon stones, which speak now fair, and make a goodly shew of the gospel; but if there come persecution or affliction, then they are gone. But peradventure some will say to me, "What shall I do? for I cannot abide persecution; I am so weak and so fearful, and my faith is so slender; therefore tell me what I may do, or what remedy I may have?" The[2] only remedy is to call upon God to strengthen thy faith, and to endue thee with the Holy Ghost, which is the Comforter; which will strengthen thee in all thy tribulation and affliction. Call, I say, upon Almighty God for this Ghost; and then, undoubtedly, thou shalt be made able to abide whatsoever tribulation or affliction cometh.

Persecution is the trial of a faithful man.

The godly do gladly embrace persecution.

Hot gospellers are no sufferers of persecution.

Call upon God in all tribulations in faith, and he will deliver thee.

There is another sort of seed, that falleth among the thorns and bushes; which signifieth those that are let and hindered by this world, and seek nothing but the world and riches. These men, when they hear that the word of God condemneth their greedy covetousness and heaping of riches, their ambition and desire of worldly honours, they will not hear it; they will not meddle with it; but go forward in their wicked studies. And thus it may appear, that riches are as thorns, that choke and kill the good seed, that it cannot come up and bring forth fruit. For like as

The covetous man will not hear any thing against covetousness.

[2 Thy, 1571.]

Worldly persons cannot abide to hear nor talk of the word of God.

you see how thorns letteth a man by the way; so that he cannot go speedily, but they hang upon him, and sometime tear his hose or his coat: so is riches a like let or impediment to us in our going to God; they are burthens that press us downward from God, which is above. Like as when a man going up a great hill, and hath a heavy bag upon his neck, that man cannot speedily go, neither can he *Covetousness of riches, hindereth men from coming to God.* make any great haste; so all they that are laden with riches and honours of this world cannot speedily go to God, for they are heavy laden; for this riches draweth them backward.

And here, peradventure, you will say, that it is not lawful for a christian man to have riches nor to have honours, neither *A christian man may well be both rich and honourable.* to bear high dignities. But I answer, We are not bounden by the commandment of God to cast away our substance and riches that God sendeth us, neither to refuse such honours as we shall be lawfully called unto. But we may not do, as many do, that greedily and covetously seek for it day and night: for some there are that have no rest, but still study and muse how they may get riches and honours. We must not do so; neither may seek for it after that sort. But if God call thee to honours, if our vocation requireth us so to do, then follow thy vocation with all humbleness and gentle-*Riches nor honours may not be sought greedily nor covetously.* ness. Seek not for it; for it is the greatest madness that may be, to seek for honours or riches. If God sendeth them, refuse them not; as the scripture teacheth us, saying, *Divi-* *Psal. lxii.* *tiæ si affluant, nolite cor opponere,* " If riches come unto you, set not your hearts upon them; neither put your trust in them." So St Paul commandeth the rich men, saying, " Ye rich men, be not proud-hearted, nor trust in your uncer-*The riches of this world is an uncertain riches.* tain riches." Surely St Paul giveth them a very apt name: for there is nothing so uncertain in this world as riches is, as we see daily by experience; but specially in these our days, where we daily see that men of great riches and honour *Have faith in God for Christ's sake, and we shall have riches that will not perish.* are by the mighty hand of God made humble and of base estate. Therefore let us lift up our hearts unto Almighty God, and trust in him, and leave all ambition and covetousness.

We subjects think in this manner, and say, " Oh, if I were a great man, or a rich man, as some men be, I would do much good; I would relieve the poor, and minister justice to them that have wrong." So the sick man thinketh, " If

I had my health and might go abroad, I would live after the will of God, and keep me from all sin and wickedness," &c. Such foolish reasoning some have with themselves, not considering that the best service that any man can do unto God, is to apply his business in such state and order, as God hath appointed and ordered them. For thou canst do God no better service, being a poor man, than to live uprightly in thine estate. And so the sick man pleaseth God as well in his sickness, if he bear the same patiently and willingly, as another doth in his health. Therefore these studies to come aloft, and such other vain desires, are naught and foolish: and every good Christian must beware of them, and study to live in his order, as God hath appointed him.

The fond minds of worldly men.

The best service that may be done to God is for every man to walk in his vocation.

Now to make an end. You have heard here in this gospel, that there are four manner of seeds. The first is sown in the way; the second upon the stones; the third among thorns; and the fourth in good ground. Now, let every man examine his own heart, and let him consider with himself whether he be amongst these or not? If he perceive himself to be like those seeds that fall upon the hard way, let him amend. And if he be like to those that lighted upon stones, let him amend. If he be like the seed fallen among thorns, let him not lie there, but get him out; or else he shall be stopped and choked up of them, to the danger of his eternal damnation. Also, you have heard that the last three manner of seeds have all one property, which is, *audire* and *suscipere*. They can be content to hear the word of God, and bear it away with them; but they forget it. But the good seed only hath a property beside that, which is, *audire et retinere*, "to hear it, and keep it." *Retinere* is the property of the good seed. Therefore if thou canst find this *retinere*, that is, the keeping of God's most holy word in thy heart, then thou art in the good ground, and shall bring forth much fruit. *Cum patientia*, saith Luke; that is, "Thou shalt keep the word of God with patience." For God hath ever a church; and those that be of the same church will keep his word with patience. For he that suffereth for God's sake is neither the high-way and hard trodden ground, neither a thorny nor stony ground; but is the very good ground that bringeth forth much fruit. For if he were a thorny ground, he would not suffer his riches to be taken

The conclusion of this sermon.

The true hearer of the word of God doth keep and observe it.

from him. This patience is not known in wealth, nor in prosperity, but only in adversity and tribulation. For when I am in tribulation or affliction for God's word's sake; when I am persecuted for it; lose my goods and substance, and my wife and children: when I am thus vexed *ex omni parte*, and suffer all these with patience, without any murmuring or grudging against God; then I am one of those that are sown in the good ground, and shall bring forth much fruit. But I fear me there are but few of such as can find in their hearts to do so; for every man is given so much unto this world, that they can scant find in their hearts to give any thing, for God's sake, unto the poor. How much less would they forego their treasures and their lives, if they should be driven unto it! I fear me, they would rather forsake God and his word, than their goods and lives. I beseech God Almighty, that he will turn our hearts unto him, and give us grace to rise from the evil ground, and that we may be sown in the good ground, and bring forth fruit manifold[1] to his honour and glory; to whom with the Son and the Holy Ghost be all honour and glory for ever! *Amen.*

[1 plenty of fruit, 1607.]

MISCELLANEOUS REMAINS

AND

LETTERS.

[ARTICLES TO WHICH MR LATIMER WAS REQUIRED
TO SUBSCRIBE, MARCH 11, 1531.]

[Harl. MS. 435, Art. 7.]

THE eleventh day of March, 1531, Master Hugh Latimer, Bachelor of Divinity, of Cambridge, noted and suspected of his faith and erroneous preachings, was called before the archbishop of Canterbury, the bishop of London, and other prelates and clerks of the province of Canterbury, in their Convocation holden at Westminster, did confess as followeth:

1. Inprimis, that there is a place of purgation for souls after this life.

2. That souls in purgatory are holpen by masses, prayer, and alms-deed.

3. That the holy apostles and martyrs of Christ, being dead, are in heaven.

4. That the same saints, as mediators, pray for us in heaven.

5. That the said saints are to be honoured in heaven.

That pilgrimages and oblations are meritorious for the sepulchres and relics of saints.

6. That whosoever hath vowed chastity may not marry, nor break their vow, without dispensation of the high bishop.

7. That the keys of binding and loosing, given unto Peter, doth remain to his successors bishops, although they live evil; and they were never given for any cause to laymen.

[8.] That it is profitable for christian men to invocate saints, that they, as mediators, may pray unto God for us.

[9.] That men by alms-deed, prayer, and other good works, may merit at God's hands.

[10.] That men forbidden of the bishops, by reason of suspicion, ought not to preach till such time as they had purged themselves to them or their superiors, and be lawfully restored.

[11.] That the Lent, and their fasting-days, commanded by the canons, and used with the Christians, are to be kept, except necessity require otherwise.

[12.] That God, by the merits of Christ's passion, doth

give his grace in all the whole seven sacraments to the lawful receiver.

[13.] That the consecrations, sanctifications, and benedictions, received in the christian church, are laudable and profitable.

[14.] That [it] is laudable and profitable, that the images of the crucifix and saints are to be had in the church, in memory, honour, and worship of Jesus Christ and his saints.

[15.] That it is laudable and profitable for the saints to be decked and trimmed; and to set candles burning before them, in the honour of the said saints.

ARTICLES DEVISED BY THE BISHOPS, FOR MASTER LATIMER TO SUBSCRIBE UNTO[1].

[Printed by Foxe, Acts and Mon. Vol. III. p. 383, edit. 1684; and in Latin, p. 1334, edit. 1563.]

I BELIEVE that there is a purgatory, to purge the souls of the dead after this life.

[[1] It will be recollected (Vol. I. p. vii.) that Latimer was summoned to appear before the bishop of London, in the cathedral church of St Paul, on the 29th of January 1531—2, to answer for certain ecclesiastical offences, alleged to have been committed within the jurisdiction of that prelate. Latimer, however, complains in a letter to the primate, that instead of being questioned by the bishop of London alone, the whole of the proceedings against him were carried on before the archbishop of Canterbury and other prelates. In confirmation of this complaint, we find that Latimer was called to appear before Convocation on the 11th of March 1531—2, and that he was there required to subscribe to certain articles. It may be concluded that the articles referred to were those printed above.

Foxe gives a copy of certain "Articles devised by the bishops for Master Latimer to subscribe to," but he gives no date. There seems no reason, however, to doubt but that the Articles printed by Foxe and those given above have reference to the same occasion: but as there are many points of difference in the wording and arrangement of the two drafts, and as neither agree in all respects with the Latin, the English Articles as printed by Foxe are subjoined, and the Latin given in the Appendix.—It is not improbable that the variations found in the several drafts of these Articles may have arisen from the desire on the part of the Convocation to meet the scruples of Latimer.]

That the souls in purgatory are holpen with the masses, prayers, and alms of the living.

That the saints do pray as mediators now for us in heaven.

That they are to be honoured of us in heaven.

That it is profitable for Christians to call upon the saints, that they may pray as mediators for us unto God.

That pilgrimages and oblations done to the sepulchres and relics of saints are meritorious.

That they which have vowed perpetual chastity may not marry, nor break their vow, without the dispensation of the pope.

That the keys of binding and loosing, delivered to Peter, do still remain with the bishops of Rome, his successors, although they live wickedly; and are by no means nor at any time committed to laymen.

That men may merit and deserve at God's hand by fasting, prayer, and other good works of piety.

That they which are forbidden of the bishop to preach, as suspect persons, ought to cease until they have purged themselves before the said bishop, or their superiors, and be restored again.

That the fast which is used in Lent, and other fasts prescribed by the canons, and by custom received of the Christians (except necessity otherwise require) are to be observed and kept.

That God in every one of the seven sacraments giveth grace to a man, rightly receiving the same.

That consecrations, sanctifyings, and blessings by use and custom received in the church, are laudable and profitable.

That it is laudable and profitable, that the venerable images of the crucifix and other saints should be had in the churches as a remembrance, and to the honour and worship of Jesus Christ, and his saints.

That it is laudable and profitable to deck and to clothe those images, and set up burning lights before them to the honour of the saints.

CONCERNING MR LATIMER'S COMMUNICATION WITH MR BAINHAM IN THE DUNGEON OF NEWGATE.

[Printed by Strype, Eccl. Mem. III. i. 372, Oxf. edit.]

[1] AFTER Mr Bainham[2] had been condemned between More the lord chancellor and the bishops[3], and committed unto the secular power to be brent; and so, immediately after his condemnation, lodged up in the deep dungeon in Newgate, ready to be sent to the fire, Edward Isaac[4], of the parish of Well, in the county of Kent, and William

[1 It is to be noted that, Harl. MS. 422, Art. 15.]

[2 James Bainham, the person referred to in the following account of Mr Latimer's "communication," was the son of a Gloucestershire knight, and bred to the law; but having fallen under the suspicion of heresy, was accused to Sir Thomas More, then chancellor of England. He was accordingly arrested and carried prisoner to Sir Thomas's house at Chelsea. With a view to extort from him the names of his associates in the Temple, Bainham was treated with great severity by the chancellor; and was ultimately induced to recant certain doctrines, with the holding of which he had been charged. He was made, also, to do penance at St Paul's Cross, during the sermon there. He very shortly, however, was struck with remorse of conscience, and openly bewailed the abjuration which had been extorted from him. This relapse (as it was termed) having been notified to the bishop of London, Bainham was again apprehended, and again cruelly treated in order to make him revoke his opinions; but as he now remained firm in his determination to maintain several doctrines that impugned the faith of the Roman church, he was condemned to the flames, and was in Newgate awaiting his death, when Mr Latimer visited him. It would seem from the account which follows, that the reasons why Bainham was a second time apprehended, were not generally known. Foxe, Acts and Mon. II. 245, et seq. Strype, Eccl. Mem. I. i. 315, 372—374.]

[3 was by the bishops condemned and, Harl. MS.]

[4 Edward Isaac, of Well-Court in the parish of Ickham, near Littleborne. His family seems to have been possessed of good estates in the county of Kent, and himself to have been a sufficiently marked favourer of the Reformation, to make it necessary for him to become an exile for religion in the reign of queen Mary. He appears to have lived chiefly at Frankfort during his absence from his native country; and his name occurs among those who were strongly opposed to John Knoxe. Hasted, History of Kent, III. 666, 722; Strype, Eccl. Mem. III. i. 231, 406; Ann. I. i. 153, Oxf. edit.]

Morice[1] of Chipping Ongar in the county of Essex, esquires, and Ralph Morice[2], brother unto the said William, being together in one company, met with Mr Latimer in London: and for that they were desirous to understand the cause of the said Bainham's condemnation, being to many men obscure and unknown, they entreated Mr Latimer to go with them to Newgate, to the intent to understand by him the very occasion of his said condemnation; and otherwise to comfort him to take his death quietly and patiently. When Mr Latimer and the other before-named, the next day before he was brent, were come down into the[3] dungeon where all things[4] seemed utterly dark, there they found Bainham, sitting upon a couch of straw, with a book and a wax candle in his hand, praying and reading thereupon. And after salutation made, Mr Latimer began to commune with him in[5] this sort:

"Mr Bainham, we hear say[6] that you are condemned for heresy to be brent, and many men are in doubt wherefore you should suffer; and I, for my part, am desirous to understand the cause of your death; assuring you that I do not allow that any man should consent to his own death, unless he had a right cause to die in. Let not vain-glory overcome you in a matter that men deserve not to die for; for therein you shall neither please God, do good to yourself, nor your neighbour: and better it were for you to submit

[[1] William Morice was the son of James Morice, a gentleman attached to the household of the Lady Margaret, countess of Richmond, and employed by her in the building of her colleges in Cambridge. This William was himself afterwards imprisoned on suspicion of heresy, and only escaped an end similar to that of Bainham, in consequence of the death of king Henry VIII. A curious display of the estimation in which Mr Morice was held by the Romanists of Chipping Ongar, may be seen in the preamble to an act (1 Mary, Sess. 3, c. 10), for "The repeal of a statute made Anno 2 Edw. VI. touching the consolidation and union of the parish churches of Ongar and Grensted in the county of Essex." Strype, Eccl. Mem. I. i. 596; III. i. 181, Oxf. edit.; Newcourt, Repertorium, II. 449, 450; Statutes of the Realm, Vol. IV. Part I. p. 234.]

[[2] Ralph Morice was secretary to archbishop Cranmer. A full account of him is given by Strype, Mem. of Cranmer, p. 611, Oxford edition.]

[[3] deep dungell, Harl. MS.]   [[4] things therein, Harl. MS.]
[[5] after, Harl. MS.]   [[6] hear that, Harl. MS.]

yourself to the ordinances of men, than so rashly to finish your life without good ground. And, therefore, we pray you to let us to understand the[7] articles that you are condemned for."

"I am content," quoth Bainham, "to tell you altogether. The first article that they condemn me for is this:—that I reported that Thomas Becket, sometime archbishop of Canterbury, was a traitor, and was damned in hell if he repented not: for that he was in arms against his prince, as a rebel; provoking other foreign princes to invade the realm, to the utter subversion of the same."

Then said Mr Latimer, "Where read you this?"

Quoth Mr Bainham, "I read it in an old history."

"Well," said Mr Latimer, "this is no cause at all worthy[8] for a man to take his death upon; for it may be a lie, as well as a true tale, and in such a doubtful matter it were mere madness for a man to jeopard his life. But what else is laid to your charge?"

"The truth is," said Bainham, "I spake against purgatory, that there was no such thing; but that it picked men's purses; and against satisfactory masses: which [assertions of mine] I defended[9] by the authority of the scriptures."

"Marry," said Mr Latimer, "in these articles your conscience may be so stayed, that you may seem rather to die in the defence thereof, than to recant both against your conscience, and the scriptures also. But yet beware of vain-glory; for the devil will be ready now to infect you therewith, when you shall come into the multitude of the people." And then Mr Latimer did animate him to take his death quietly and patiently.

Bainham thanked him heartily therefore. "And I likewise," said Bainham, "do exhort you to stand to the defence of the truth; for you that shall be left behind had need of comfort also, the world being so dangerous as it is." And so spake many comfortable words to Mr Latimer.

At the length Mr Latimer demanded of him, Whether he had a wife or no? With that question Bainham fell a weeping. "What," quoth Latimer, "is this your constancy to God-wards? What mean you, thus to weep?"

[7 those, Harl. MS.]   [8 at all for, Harl. MS.]
[9 which I defended, Harl MS.]

"O sir," said Bainham to Mr Latimer, "you have now touched me very nigh. I have a wife, as good a woman as ever man was joined[1] unto; and I shall leave her now, not only without substance, or any thing to live by, but also for my sake she shall be an opprobrie unto the world, and be pointed at of every man on this sort, 'Yonder goeth the heretic's wife.' And therefore she shall be defamed for my sake; which is no small grief unto me."

"Marry, sir," quoth Latimer, "I perceive that you are a very weak champion, that will be overthrown with such a vanity. Where are become all those comfortable words, that so late you alleged unto us that should tarry here behind you? I marvel what you mean! Is not Almighty God able to be husband to your wife, and a father unto your children, if you commit them to him as a strong father? I am sorry to see [you] in this taking; as though God had no care of his; when he numbereth the hairs of a man's head. If he do not provide for them, the fault is in us that mistrusteth him; it is our infidelity that causeth him to do nothing for ours: and therefore repent, repent, Mr Bainham, for this mistrusting of Almighty God's goodness. And be you sure, and I do most firmly believe it, that if you do commit your wife with a strong faith to the government of Almighty God, and so die therein, that within these two years—peradventure in one year—she shall be better provided for, as touching the felicity of this world, than you with all your policy could for yourself, if you were presently here." And so with such like words, expostulating with him for his feeble faith, he made an end.

Mr Bainham, calling his spirits to himself, most heartily thanked Mr Latimer for his good comfort and counsel, saying plainly, that he would not for much good but he had come thither to him; for nothing in the world so much troubled him as the care of his wife and family. And so they departed. And the next day[2] Bainham was burnt.

[1 yoked, Harl. MS.]   [2 30th April, 1532.]

ARTICLES[1] UNTRULY, UNJUSTLY, FALSELY, UNCHARITABLY IMPUTED TO ME, [HUGH LATIMER,] BY DR POWELL[2] OF SALISBURY.

[Printed in Foxe, ed. 1563, p. 1309.]

First, that " our lady was a sinner."
Occasioned of some, not only laymen, but also priests and beneficed men, which gave so much to our lady of devotion without judgment, as though she had not needed Christ to save her: to prove Christ her Saviour, to make Christ a whole Saviour of all that be or shall be saved, I reasoned after this manner: that either she was a sinner, or

[1 The following " Articles" were occasioned by the preaching of Mr Latimer at Bristol, in 1533. The report of certain commissioners, whom Cromwell appointed to inquire into the religious disputes which had arisen in that city, set forth, " That Latimer came [by invitation of some of the priests] to Bristol, and preached two sermons there on the second Sunday in Lent [March 9], one in St Nicholas' church in the forenoon, and another at the Black Friars in the afternoon; and on the Monday next following, he preached a third sermon in St Thomas's church; in the which sermons he preached divers schismatic and erroneous opinions: as in hell to be no fire sensible; the souls that be in purgatory to have no need of our prayers, but rather to pray for us; no saints to be honoured; no pilgrimages to be used; our blessed lady to be a sinner:—as it was reported and taken by the hearers." "Whereupon the worshipful men, doctor Powell, master Goodryche, master Haberdyne, master Prior of St James," and doctor John Hilsey, prior of the Dominicans in Bristol, preached against Mr Latimer; "approving purgatory, pilgrimages, the worshipping of the saints and images; also approving, that faith without good works is but dead; and that our lady, being full of grace, is, and was, without the spot of sin." Letters, relating to the Suppression of the Monasteries, &c., pp. 8, 12. See also, Latimer's letter to Morice.]

[2 Edward Powell was a native of Wales, and probably fellow of Oriel college, Oxford. He was afterwards prebendary of Salisbury and of Lincoln. He seems to have been a person of learning and a determined opponent of the divorce of king Henry VIII., and also of the many ecclesiastical changes which occurred during the reign of that monarch. For his denial of the royal supremacy, and for refusing to take the oath of succession, he was committed to prison, and after trial was executed as a traitor, in Smithfield, on the 30th of July, 1540. Wood, Athenæ Oxon. edit. by Bliss, Vol. I. pp. 117, et seq.]

no sinner: there is no mean. If she were a sinner, then she was redeemed or delivered from sin by Christ, as other sinners be: if she were no sinner, then she was preserved from sin by Christ; so that Christ saved her, and was her necessary Saviour, whether she sinned or no. Now certain authors (said I), as Chrysostom, Theophylact, and others, writeth[1] as though she had been something faulty in her time. Also I said that certain scriptures standeth something to the same, unless they be the more warily understood and taken; as in [Rom.] iii. 10, 19, "All have declined, that every mouth be stopped, and all the world be bounden or in danger to God." And after in the same chapter, "All have sinned, and need the glory of God." And in the fifth, "And so death passed through into all men and women, forasmuch as all have sinned." But to these scriptures, I said, it might be answered, that the privilege of one, or of a few, doth not derogate or minish the verity of a universal exposition in scriptures.

And as to the doctors, I said, that other more say otherwise[2]: and forasmuch as now it is universally and constantly received and applied that she was no sinner, it becometh every man to stand and agree to the same; "and so will I," quoth I, "nor any man that wise is will the contrary. But to my purpose, it is neither to nor from, to prove neither this nor that; for I will have her saved, and Christ her Saviour, whether ever she was," &c.

And to that, "What need you to speak of this?" I answered, "Great need: when men cannot be content that she was a creature saved, but as it were a Saviouress, not needing salvation, it is necessary to set her in her degree to the glory of Christ, Creator and Saviour of all that be or shall be saved." Good authors have[3] written that she was not a sinner; but good authors never wrote that she was not saved: for though she never sinned, yet she was not so im-

[1 See Vol. I. pp. 383, 384; Theophylact and Euthymius Zigabenus on John ii. 3, 4.]

[2 See Lombard. III. dist. 3; Thom. Aquinas, Sum. Theol. III. q. 27, a. 3, 4; Melchior Canus, Loci Theolog. VII. num. 9. Oper. pp. 356, &c. Colon. Agrip. 1605; Chemnitz. Examen Concil. Trident. Append. Decret. 5 Sess.]

[3 hath, 1563.]

peccable, but[4] she might have sinned, if she had not been preserved: it was of the goodness of God that she never sinned; it had come of her own illness if she had sinned: there was difference betwixt her and Christ: and I will give as little to her as I can (doing her no wrong), rather than Christ her Son and Saviour shall lack any parcel of his glory: and I am sure that our lady will not be displeased with me for so doing; for our lady sought his glory here upon earth; she would not defraud him now in heaven. But some[5] are so superstitiously religious, or so religiously superstitious, so preposterously devout toward our lady, as though there could not too much be given to her. Such are zeals without knowledge and judgment, to our lady's displeasure.

Our lady is not displeased to have God honoured.

No doubt our lady was, through the goodness of God, a good and a gracious creature, a devout handmaid of the Lord, endued with singular gifts and graces from above, which, through the help of God, she used to God's pleasure, according to her duty; so giving us ensample to do likewise: so that all the goodness that she had, she had it not of herself, but of God the author of all goodness. The Lord was with her favourably, and poured graces unto her plenteously, as it is in the *Ave Maria*. The Son of God, when he would become man, to save both man and woman, did choose her to his mother, which love he shewed to her alone, and to none other, of his benign goodness, by the which she was the natural mother of Christ: and through faith in Christ she was the spiritual sister of Christ, saved by Christ, blessed by hearing Christ's word, and keeping the same. It should not availed her to salvation to have been his natural mother, if she had not done the will of his heavenly Father. By him she was his mother: by him she did the will of his Father: she the handmaiden, he the Lord. The handmaiden did magnify her Lord, the handmaiden would that all should magnify the Lord, to whom be honour and glory. *Amen, &c.*

To honour him worthily is not to dishonour our lady:

[4 but that, 1563.]

[5 Sufficient proof of the truth of this assertion may be found in any old Roman breviary, (more especially in the breviary of the Franciscans,) in the services prescribed for such days as Aug. 15, Sept. 8, Dec. 8.]

he is as able to preserve from sin, as to deliver from sin. He was then subject to Joseph, his father-in-law, his mother's husband; Joseph is now subject to him. He never dishonoured Joachim and Anna, his grandfather and grandmother; and yet I have not read that he preserved them from all sin.

To say that Peter and Paul, David and Mary Magdalene, were sinners, is not to dishonour them: for then scripture doth dishonour them. It had not been for our profit to have preserved all that he could have preserved. For remembrance of that fall and uprising keepeth us in our fall from despairing: both is of God, to have not sinned, and to have forsaken and left sin. And as sure is this of heaven, as that; and this more common than that, and to us that have been sinners more comfortable.

It hath been said in times past, without sin, that our lady was a sinner; but it was never said, without sin, that our lady was not saved, but a Saviour. I go not about to make our lady a sinner, but to have Christ her Saviour. When mine adversaries cannot reprove the thing that I say, then they will belie me, to say the thing that they can reprove. They will sin to make our lady no sinner, to prove that that no man denieth: so hot[1] provers and so cold probations saw you never. It were better unproved, than so weakly proved. But they be devout towards honouring of our lady, as though there was no other honouring of our lady but to sin to have[2] our lady no sinner. I would be as loth to dishonour our lady as they: I pray God we may honour her as she would be honoured; for verily she is worthy to be honoured. To make a pernicious and a damnable lie, to have our lady no sinner, is neither honour nor yet pleasure to our lady; but great sin, to the dishonour and displeasure both of God and our lady. They should both please and honour our lady much better, to leave their sinful living, and keep themselves from sinfulness, as our lady did, than so sinfully to lie, to make our lady no sinner; which if they do not, they shall go to the devil certainly, though they believe that our lady was no sinner never so surely.

The "Ave Maria" a greeting, and not a prayer. As[3] for the *Ave Maria*, they lie falsely; I never denied it. I know it was a heavenly saluting or greeting of our

[1 such, 1684.]   [2 in having, 1563.]   [3 and, 1684.]

lady, spoken by the angel Gabriel, and written in holy scripture of St Luke: but yet it is not properly a prayer, as the *Pater noster* is. Saluting or greeting, lauding or praising, is not properly praying. The angel was sent to greet our lady, and to annunciate and shew the good will of God towards her; and therefore it is called the Annunciation of our lady; and not to pray her, or to pray to her properly. Shall the Father of heaven pray to our lady? When the angel spake it, it was not properly a prayer; and is it not the same thing now that it was then? Nor yet he that denieth the *Ave Maria* to be properly a prayer, denieth the *Ave Maria;* so that we may salute our lady with *Ave Maria*, as the angel did, though we be not sent of God so to do, as the angel was. So though we may so do, yet we have no plain bidding of God so to do, as the angel had: so that the angel had been more to blame peradventure to have left it unsaid, than we be; forasmuch as he was appointed of God to say it, and not we. But as I deny not but as we may say the *Pater noster* and the *Ave Maria* together, that to God, this to our lady, so we may say them sunderly, the *Pater noster* by itself, and the *Ave* by itself; and the *Pater noster* is a whole and a perfect prayer, without the *Ave Maria;* so that it is but a superstition to think that a *Pater noster* cannot be well said without an *Ave Maria* at its heel. For Christ was no fool; and when he taught the people to say a *Pater noster* to God, he taught them not to say neither *Pater noster* neither *Ave Maria* to our lady, nor yet *Pater noster* to St Peter, as master Hubberdin[4] doth: therefore to teach

[4 "Master Hubbardin," or Hyberden, was a divine of Exeter College, Oxford; of no great pretensions to learning, but of abundant zeal for the old superstitions. From the rather bitter manner in which Foxe speaks of him, it may be concluded that he was somewhat intemperate in his opposition to the Reformers. If the accounts given of him be literally accurate, he must have been a singular character: for he is described as "making long prayers, and fastings; riding in a gown of unusual length; preaching sermons stuffed full of tales and fables, dialogues and dreams. He would dance and hop and leap and use histrionical gestures in the pulpit: at which he was once so violent that the pulpit brake and he fell down and brake his leg, whereof he died." Strype, Eccl. Mem. I. i. 247, Oxf.; Foxe, Acts and Mon. III. 392. edit. 1684; Wood, Fasti Oxon. Vol. I. p. 64. edit. Bliss.]

On the superstitious numbering of "Ave Marias."

to say twenty *Ave Marias* for one *Pater noster*, is not to speak *sermones Dei ut sermones Dei*, "the word of God as the word of God." And one *Ave Maria* well said, and devoutly, with affection, sense, and understanding, is better than twenty-five said superstitiously. And it is not unlike but our lady said many times the *Pater noster*, forasmuch as her Son Christ, whom she loved and honoured over all, did make it, and taught it to be said. Whether she made an *Ave Maria* with all, or ten or twenty *Ave Marias* for one *Pater noster*, I will leave[1] that to great clerks, as Hubberdin and Powell, to discuss and determine. She was not saved by often saying of the *Ave Maria*, but by consenting to the will of him that sent the angel to salute her with *Ave Maria*. Wherefore, if the praying of them which decline[2] their ear from hearing the law of God is execrable in the sight of God, yea, though they say the *Pater noster*, I doubt not but the salutation of the same be unpleasant to our lady in her sight: for whatsoever pleaseth not her Son, pleaseth not her; for she hath delight and pleasure in nothing but in him, and in that that delighteth and pleaseth him. Now we will be traitors to her Son by customable sinful living; and yet we shall think great perfection and holiness in numbering every day many *Ave Marias* to our lady. And so we think to make her our friend and patroness, and then we care not for God: for, having our lady of our side, we may be bold to take our pleasure. For we fantasy as though the very work and labour of flummering the *Ave Maria* is very acceptable to our lady; and the more, the more acceptable: not passing how they be said, but that they be said. If the *Pater noster*, which Christ both made and bade us say it, may be said to Christ's displeasure, much more the *Ave Maria*, which neither Christ nor our lady bade to be said, may be said to our lady's displeasure; and better never once said, than often so said. So that I would have a difference betwixt well saying, and often saying; and betwixt that that Christ bid[3] us say, and that that he bid[3] not say. And whether *Ave Maria* be said in heaven or no, who can tell but Dr Powell? And if it be said alway there without a *Pater*

[1 I leave, 1563.] [2 declineth, 1563.] [3 bade, 1563.]

noster, why may not *Pater noster* be said here without *Ave Maria?* And whether doth our lady say it in heaven or no? Which thing I speak, not to withdraw you from saying of it, but to withdraw you from superstitious and unfruitful saying of it; so that by occasion of false faith and trust that ye have in the daily saying of it, you set not aside imitation and following of holy living; which will serve at length, when superstitious greeting will neither serve nor stand in strength. It is meet that every thing be taken, esteemed, and valued as it is.

We salute also and greet well the holy cross, or the image of the holy cross, saying, "All hail, holy cross, which hath deserved to bear the precious talent of the world[4]:" and yet who will say that we pray properly to the holy cross? Whereby it may appear that greeting is one thing, praying another thing. The cross can neither hear nor speak again, no more than this pulpit: therefore we do salute it, not properly pray to it.

Greeting the holy cross.

The angel spake also to Zachary, before he spake to our lady, *Ne timeas, Zacharia, &c.,* "Be not afraid, Zachary; for thy prayer is heard, and thy wife Elizabeth shall bring thee forth a child, which shall be called John, and great joy and gladness shall be at his birth, and he shall be great, and full of the Holy Ghost from the womb of his mother," &c. What if a man should[5] say these words every day, betwixt the *Pater noster* and the *Ave Maria*, in the worship of St Zachary, which I think is a saint in heaven, and was or ever our lady came there, and therefore to be honoured? I think he might please and honour St Zachary as well some other way, and better too, though they be words sent from God, spoken of an angel, and written in holy scripture of the evangelist Luke. And yet if[6] it were once begun and accustomed, I warrant[7] some men would make it more than sacrilege to leave it off, though the devil should sow never so much superstition by process of time unto it.

Christ made the *Pater noster* for a prayer, and bid his people say it to his heavenly Father; one God in Trinity of Persons, one Father and Comforter, one worker and doer of all things here in this world; saying unto us, *Vos autem sic*

[4 See the Roman Breviary, Festa Maii, die 3; Septem. die 12.]
[5 would, 1563.]   [6 and, 1563.]   [7 ween, 1563.]

orabitis; "So, or after such manner, shall ye pray, *Pater noster*," &c. God sent his Son amongst other things to teach his people to pray: God sent his angel to greet our lady, not to teach his people to pray. For neither Christ nor the angel said to the people, This shall ye pray, *Ave Maria.* When the apostles said to Christ, *Doce nos orare,* "Teach us to pray;" Christ said, *Cum oratis, dicite, Pater noster;* "When you pray, say *Pater noster:*" he said not, "When you pray, say *Ave Maria.*" I ween Christ could teach to pray, as well as Dr Powell and master Hubberdin. I say that the *Ave Maria* was before the *Pater noster:* Dr Powell saith, it shall endure after the *Pater noster.* I can prove my saying by scripture; so cannot he his. Yet as it is no good argument, The *Ave Maria* was before the *Pater noster;* ergo, it is properly a prayer: so it is no good argument, The *Ave Maria* shall last after the *Pater noster;* ergo, it is properly a prayer,—without the antecedent be impossible, which is not credible to come out of such a fantastical brain.

Who was ever so mad as to think that words of holy scripture could not be well said? And yet we may not be so peevish as to allow the superstitious saying of holy scripture. The devil is crafty, and we frail and prone to superstition and idolatry. God give me grace to worship him and his, not after our own curiosity, but according to his ordinance, with all humility!

St Zachary is to be honoured, and in no wise to be dishonoured: so that we may leave unsaid that that the angel said, without dishonouring him. It is not necessary to our salvation to make an ordinance of honouring him with saying as the angel did. It is better for a mortal man to do the office of a man, which God biddeth him do, than to leave that undone, and do the office of an angel which God biddeth us not do. If the other be presumption, I had rather[1] presume to pray to God, which is God's bidding and man's office, than to presume into the office of an angel without God's bidding. It is a godly presumption to presume to do the bidding of God.

Here I neither say, that our lady was a sinner, nor yet I deny the *Ave Maria.*

[[1] lieffer, 1563.]

"*Saints are not to be honoured.*"

I said this word "saints" is diversely taken of the vulgar people: images of saints are called saints, and inhabiters of heaven are called saints. Now, by honouring of saints is meant praying to saints. Take honouring so, and images for saints, so saints are not to be honoured; that is to say, dead images are not to be prayed unto; for they have neither ears to hear withal, nor tongue to speak withal, nor heart to think withal, &c.

They can neither help me nor mine ox; neither my head nor my tooth; nor work any miracle for me, one no more than another: and yet I shewed the good use of them to be laymen's books, as they be called; reverently to look upon them, to remember the things that are signified by them, &c. And yet I would not have them so costly and curiously gilded and decked, that the quick image of God (for whom Christ shed his blood, and to whom whatsoever is done, Christ reputeth it done to himself) lack necessaries, and be unprovided for, by that occasion; for then the layman doth abuse his book. A man may read upon his book, though it be not very curiously gilded; and in the day-time a man may behold it without many candles, if he be not blind. Now I say, there be two manner of mediators, one by way of redemption, another by way of intercession; and I said, that these saints, that is to say, images called saints, be mediators neither[2] way.

As touching pilgrimages, I said, that all idolatry, superstition, error, false faith, and hope in the images, must be pared away, before they can be well done; household looked upon, poor christian people provided for, restitutions made, all ordinance of God discharged, or ever they can be well done: and when they be at best, before they be vowed, they need not to be done. They shall never be required of us, though they be never done; and yet we shall be blamed when they be all done: wives must counsel with their husbands, and husbands with their wives, both with curates, ere ever they may be vowed to be done[3]. And yet idolatry may be committed in doing of them; as it appeareth by St Paul, in 1 Cor. x., where he biddeth the Corinthians this, to beware of idolatry, and that after[4] they had received the true faith

On pilgrimages and hope in images.

[2 nere nother, 1563.]   [3 See Vol. I. p. 54.]
[4 after that, 1563.]

in Christ; which had been vain, if they could not have done idolatry: and expositors add, to beware not only[1] of the act of idolatry, but also of all occasion of that act: which is plain against master Hubberdin, and the parson of Christ's church, which went about to prove, that now there could be no idolatry.

Efficacy of the blood of Christ.

As touching the saints in heaven, I said, they be not our mediators by way of redemption; for so Christ alone[1] is our mediator and theirs both: so that the blood of martyrs hath nothing to do by way of redemption; the blood of Christ is enough for a thousand worlds, &c. But by way of intercession, so saints in heaven may be mediators, and pray for us: as I think they do when we call not upon them; for they be charitable, and need no spurs; and we have no open bidding of God in scripture to call upon them, as we have to call upon God, nor yet we may call upon them without any diffidence or mistrust in God; for God is more charitable, more merciful, more able, more ready to help than them all. So that, though we may desire the saints in heaven to pray God for us, yet it is not so necessary to be done, but that we may pray to God ourselves, without making suit first to them, and obtain of him whatsoever we need, if we continue in prayer; so that, whatsoever we ask the Father in the name of Christ his Son, the Father will give it us. For saints can give nothing without him, but he can without them, as he did give to them. Scripture doth set saints that be departed before our eyes for ensamples; so that the chiefest and most principal worship and honouring of them is to know their holy living, and to follow them, as they followed Christ, &c.

God biddeth us come to him with prayer; and to do his bidding is no presuming, it is rather presuming to leave it undone, to do that that he biddeth us not do, &c. We must have saints in reverent memory; and learn at God's goodness towards them to trust in God; and mark well their faith toward God and his word, their charity toward their neighbour, their patience in all adversity; and pray to God which gave them grace so to do, that we may do likewise, for which like doings we shall have like speedings: they be well honoured when God is well pleased. The saints were not

[1 alonely, 1563.]

saints by praying to saints, but by believing in him that
made them saints; and as they were saints, so may we be
saints: yea, there be many saints that never prayed to saints.
And yet I deny not but we may pray to saints; but rather
to him, which can make us saints, which calleth us to him,
biddeth us call upon him, promiseth help, cannot deceive us
and break his promise. When we pray faithfully to him, we
honour him, not after our own fantastical imagination, but
even after his own most wisest ordination, whom to honour
is not to dishonour saints: therefore they lie, that say that
I would not have saints to be honoured, &c.

"*There is no fire in hell.*"

I never knew man that ever said so. I spake of divers
opinions[2] that have[3] been written of the nature of that fire;
some that it is a spiritual fire, or at leastway a spiritual pain
in the corporal fire; for as it is called a fire, so it is called
a worm. Now, because they think not that it is a corporal
worm, but a spiritual and metaphorical worm, so they think
of the fire: some, that it is a corporal and natural fire: some
have thought diversely, before the resurrection without body,
and after with body: some, that the soul without body suffereth in the fire, but not of the fire: some, both in and of the
fire. The scholastical authors[4] think, that the souls before
the resurrection, because they be spiritual substance, do not
receive the heat of the fire into them, which is a sensible and
a corporal quality; so that Athanasius[5], a Greek author, calleth their pain *tristitiam*, a heaviness or an anguish: and
this opinion is probable enough. Some think[6] that, though

[2 See Thom. Aquinat. Sum. Theolog. Supplem. par. 3, qu. 97, art. 2, 5. In IV. Dist. 44, qu. 2, art. 23, Dist. 50, qu. 2, art. 3; also, Dom. Soto in IV. Sent. Dist. 50, qu. unic. art. 1, 2; for the "divers opinions" respecting the torments of lost souls.]

[3 hath, 1563.]

[4 See Aquinat. Sum. Theolog. Supplem. p. 3, qu. 70, art. 3.]

[5 ἡ λύπη ἣν οἱ ἁμαρτωλοὶ ἔχουσι....Quæst. xx. ad Antiochum (attributed to Athanasius,) Oper. Tom. III. p. 272, edit. Bened. Paris. 1698.]

[6 The opinions entertained by divines in the middle ages, on this
awful subject, are no where more vividly expressed than in Dionysius
Carthusianus' once popular treatise, "De quatuor hominis novissimis,"
art. 40, "De diversitate et varietate tormentorum inferni," pp. 183,
et seq. Lovan. 1578.]

they be alway in pain, yet they be not always in fire, but go from waters of snow to exceeding heat; but it is when their bodies be there: but whether in cold or in heat, in water or in fire, in air or in earth, they lack no pain, their torment goeth with them; for they think that the devils that tempt us, though they have pain with them, yet they have not fire with them: for then they should be known by heat of the fire.

I am certain, saith St Augustine[1], that there is a fire in hell; but what manner of fire, or in what part of the world, no man can tell, but he that is of God's privy council. I would advise every man to be more careful to keep out of hell, than trust he shall find no fire in hell. Chrysostom[2] saith, that to be deprived of the fruition of the Godhead is greater pain than the being in hell. There is fire burning, there is the worm gnawing, there is heat, there is cold, there is pain without pleasure, torment without easement, anguish, heaviness, sorrow, and pensiveness, which tarrieth and abideth for all liars and hinderers of the truth.

Purgatory.   *" There is no purgatory after this life."*

Not for such liars that will bear me in hand to say that I said not. I shewed the state and condition of them that be in purgatory; then I denied it not: that they have charity in such sure tie that they cannot lose it, so that they cannot murmur nor grudge against God; cannot dishonour God; can neither displease God, nor be displeased with God; cannot be dissevered from God; cannot die, nor be in peril of death; cannot be damned, nor be in peril of damnation; cannot be but in surety of salvation. They be members of the mystical body of Christ as we be, and in more surety than we be. They love us charitably. Charity is not idle: if it be, it worketh and sheweth itself: and therefore I say, they wish us well, and pray for us. They need not cry loud to God: they be in Christ, and Christ in them: they be with Christ,

[1 Qui ignis cujusmodi, et in qua mundi vel rerum parte futurus sit, hominem scire arbitror neminem, nisi forte cui Spiritus divinus ostendit. De Civit. Dei, xix. 16. Oper. Tom. vii. col. 449, Edit. Bened. Antwerp, 1700.]

[2 In Epistol. ad Ephes. Hom. iii.: In Epist. ad Phil. Hom. xii. Oper. Tom. xi. pp. 21, 302. Edit. Bened. Paris. 1734.]

and Christ with them. They joy in their Lord Christ alway, taking thankfully whatsoever God doth with them; ever giving thanks to their Lord God; ever lauding and praising him in all things that he doth; discontent with nothing that he doth, &c.

And forasmuch as they be always in charity, and when they pray for us, they pray always in charity, and be always God's friends, God's children, brethren and sisters to our Saviour Christ, even in God's favour, even have Christ with them, to offer their prayer to the Father of heaven, to whom they pray in the name of the Son; and we many times for lack of charity, having malice and envy, rancour, hatred, one toward another, be the children of the devil, inheritors of hell, adversaries to Christ, hated of God, his angels, and all his saints; they in their state may do us more good with their prayers, than we in this state. And they do us alway good, unless the lack and impediment be in us: for prayer said in charity is more fruitful to him that it is said for, and more acceptable to God, than said out of charity; for God looketh not to the work of praying, but to the heart of the prayer. We may well pray for them, and they much better for us: which they will do of their charity, though we desire them not.

I had rather[3] be in purgatory, than in the bishop of London's prison; for in this I might die bodily for lack of meat; in that I could not: in this I might die ghostly for fear of pain, or lack of good counsel; in that I could not: in this I might be in extreme necessity; in that I could not, if extreme necessity be *periculum pereundi,* "peril of perishing." And then you know what followeth: if we be not bounden, *per præceptum,* to help but them that be in extreme necessity, we see not who needeth in purgatory; but we see who needeth in this world. And John saith, "If thou see thy brother, and help him not, how is the charity of God in thee?" Here either we be, or we may be in extreme necessity, both in body and soul: in purgatory neither one nor other[4]. Here we be bound to help one another, as we would be holpen ourselves, under pain of damnation. Here, for lack of help, we may murmur and grudge against God, dishonour God, foredote ourselves: which inconveniences shall

[3 lever, 1563.]   [4 one nere nother, 1563.]

not follow, if we do our duty one to another. I am sure the souls in purgatory be so charitable, and of charity so loth to have God dishonoured, that they would have nothing withdrawn from the poor here in this world, to be bestowed upon them, which might occasion the dishonour of God, &c.

Therefore, howsoever we do for purgatory, let us provide to keep out of hell. And had I[1] a thousand pounds to bestow, as long as I saw necessary occasion offered to me of God to dispense it upon my needy brother here in this world, according to God's commandment, I would not withdraw my duty from him for any provision of purgatory; as long as I saw dangerous ways unrepaired[2], poor men's daughters unmarried, men beg for lack of work, sick and sore for lack of succour. I would have difference betwixt that that may be done, and that that ought to be done; and this to go before that, and that to come after this. If God command one way, mine own devotion moveth me another way, whether way should I go? I may, by no trentals, no masses, no ladders of heaven, make no foundations for myself with other men's goods. Goods wrongfully gotten must needs home again; must needs be restored to the owners, if they can be known; if not, they be poor men's goods. Debts must needs be paid; creditors satisfied and content; God's ordinance toward my neighbour here in this world discharged; all affections and lusts moving to the contrary purged. Or else, though our soul-priests sing till they be blear-eyed, say till they have worn their tongues to the stumps, neither their singings nor their sayings shall bring us out of hell; whither we shall go for contemning of God's forbiddings. He that purgeth all errors of false opinions, all unlustiness to do God's ordinance, provideth not for hell and purgatory. Purgatory's iniquity hath set aside restitutions, and brought poor Christians to extreme beggary, replenished hell, and left heaven almost empty.

"*In purgatory there is no pain:*"

That can break their charity: that can break their patience: that can dissever them from Christ, that can dissever Christ from them.

That can cause them to dishonour God: that can cause

[[1] And I had, 1563.]   [[2] unprepared, 1563.]

them to displease God: that can cause them to be displeased with God: that can bring them to peril of death.

That can bring them to peril of damnation: that can bring them to extreme necessity: that can cause them to be discontent with God: that can bring them from surety of salvation.

And yet it followeth not that there is no pain.

Howbeit, if the bishop's two fingers can shake away a good part; if a friar's cowl, or the pope's pardon, or *scala cœli* of a groat, can dispatch for altogether, it is not so greatly to be cared for. I have not leisure to write at large; and I wrote before such things, which in this haste cometh now to mind.

They that can reclaim at this, that the souls in purgatory do pray for us; if they could get as much money for the prayer as the souls in purgatory sayeth for us, as they have done for that that they have said for them, they would not reclaim. You know the wasp that doth sting them, and maketh them so[3] swell. They that reclaim at that do not reclaim at this. Nor at this: Christ's blood is not sufficient without blood of martyrs.

Nor at this: Magdalene did not know Christ to be God before his resurrection.

Nor at this: There can be no idolatry.

Nor at this: Rome cannot be destroyed.

Nor at this: The pope is lord of the world.

Nor at this: Whatsoever he doeth is well done.

Nor at this: *Pater noster* is to be said to St Peter.

Nor at this: *Pater noster* is but a beggarly prayer.

Nor at this: *Ave Maria* is infinitely better.

Nor at this: Twenty *Ave Marias* for one *Pater noster*.

Nor at this: It was not necessary scripture be written.

Nor at this: He that leaveth father or mother maketh for our pilgrimage.

With many more[4].

[3 to, 1563.]

[4 The opinions then commonly held by such persons as Dr Powell, on several of the points discussed in the foregoing articles, may be seen in Sir Thomas More's Dialogue concerning Heresies, Book II. ch. viii. et seq.; The supplication of Souls, Book II.]

INJUNCTIONS BY HUGH LATIMER, BISHOP OF WORCESTER, TO THE PRIOR AND CONVENT OF ST MARY HOUSE IN WORCESTER, 1537.

[Printed in Wilkins' Concilia III. p. 832, Burnet, Hist. of Reform. Vol. II. Part II. pp. 404, et seq. Oxford, 1816.]

HUGH, by the goodness of God, bishop of Worcester, wisheth to his brethren the Prior and Convent aforesaid grace, mercy, peace, and true knowledge of God's word, from God our Father, and our Lord Jesus Christ.

Forasmuch as in this my visitation I evidently perceive the ignorance and negligence of divers religious persons in this Monastery to be intolerable and not to be suffered; for that thereby do reign idolatry, and many kinds of superstitions, and other enormities: and considering withal, that our sovereign lord the king, for some part of remedy of the same, hath granted, by his most gracious licence[1], that the scripture of God may be read in English of all his obedient subjects: I therefore, willing your reformation in most favourable manner, to your least displeasure, do heartily require you all and every one of you, and also in God's behalf command the same, according as your duty is, to obey me as God's minister, and the king's, in all my lawful and honest commandments; that you observe and keep inviolably all these injunctions following, under pain of the law.

First, Forasmuch as I perceive that some of you neither have observed the king's Injunctions[2], nor yet have them with you, as willing to observe them: therefore ye shall from henceforth both have and observe diligently and faith-

[1 This licence seems to have been obtained, by means of Cromwell, sometime in 1537; yet the scriptures could not be said to be within the reach of "all the king's obedient subjects," until the following year, when the Bible was ordered to be set up in some convenient place within every parish church. Strype, Mem. of Cranm. pp. 81, et seq. Oxf. 1812. Remains of Cranmer, edit. by Jenkyns, Vol. I. pp. 199, et seq.]

[2 "General Injunctions 1535, to be given on the king's highness' behalf in all monasteries, and other houses, of whatsoever order or religion they be." Wilkins' Concilia, III. p. 789. Burnet, Hist. of Reform. Vol. I. Part 2. pp. 215, et seq. Oxford, 1816.]

fully, as well special commandments of preaching, as other injunctions given in his grace's visitation.

Item, That the prior shall provide, of the monasteries' charge, a whole Bible in English, to be laid fast chained in some open place, either in their church or cloister.

Item, That every religious person have, at the least, a new Testament in English, by the Feast of the Nativity of our Lord next ensuing.

Item, Whensoever there shall be any preaching in your monastery, that all manner of singing, and other ceremonies, be utterly laid aside in his preaching time; and all other service shortened, as need shall be ; and all religious persons quietly to hearken to the preaching.

Item, That ye have a lecture of scripture read every day in English amongst you, save holy-days.

Item, That every religious person be at every lecture, from the beginning to the ending, except they have a necessary let allowed them by the prior.

Item, That every religious house have a layman to their steward, for all former businesses.

Item, That you have a continual schoolmaster, sufficiently learned to teach your grammar.

Item, That no religious person discourage any manner of layman, or woman, or any other, from the reading of any good book, either in Latin or English.

Item, That the prior have at his dinner or supper, every day, a chapter read, from the beginning of the scripture to the end, and that in English, wheresoever he be in any of his own places, and to have edifying communication of the same.

Item, That the convent sit together, four to one mess, and to eat together in common, and to have scripture read in like wise, and have communication thereof; and after their dinner, or supper, their reliques and fragments to be distributed to the poor people.

Item, That the convent and prior provide distributions to be ministered in every parish, where as ye be parsons and proprietaries, and according to the king's injunctions in that behalf.

Item, That all these my injunctions be read every month once in the chapter-house before all the brethren.

[LATIMER, II.]

INJUNCTIONS[1] GIVEN BY THE BISHOP OF WORCESTER
IN HIS VISITATION TO ALL PARSONS, VICARS AND
OTHER CURATES OF HIS DIOCESE, THE YEAR
OF OUR LORD GOD MDXXXVII. ANNO
REGIS HENRICI OCTAVI XXIX.

[Printed in Abingdon, Antiquities of the Cathedral Church of Worcester, pp. 157, et seq.]

HUGH, by the goodness of GOD bishop of Worcester, wisheth to all his brethren Curates grace, mercy, peace, and true knowledge of GOD's word, from GOD our Father, and our Lord Jesu Christ.

Forasmuch as in this my visitation I evidently perceive, that the ignorance and negligence of divers curates in this deanery to be intolerable and not to be suffered, for that thereby doth reign idolatry and many kinds of superstitions, and other enormities: and considering withal that our sovereign lord the king, for some part of remedy of the same, hath granted by his most gracious licence that the scripture of GOD may be read in English of all his obedient subjects: I therefore willing your reformation in most favourable manner, to your least displeasure, do heartily require you all and every one of you, and also in GOD's behalf command the same, according as your duty is to obey me as GOD's minister, and the king's, in all my lawful and honest commandments, that you observe and keep inviolably all these Injunctions following, under pain of the law.

First, Forasmuch as I perceive that ye neither have observed the king's Injunctions, nor yet have them with you, as willing to observe them: therefore ye shall from henceforth both have and observe diligently and faithfully, as well special commandments of preachings, as other Injunctions given in his grace's visitation.

[[1] The Injunctions given to the clergy of the diocese of Hereford by archbishop Cranmer are in several clauses almost verbally the same with these injunctions. See, also, Injunctions given by Edmund Bonner, bishop of London, to his clergy. Wilkins, Concilia, III. pp. 843, 864.]

Item, That ye, and every one of you, provide to have of your own a whole bible, if ye can conveniently, or at the least a new Testament, both in Latin and English, before the feast of the nativity of our Lord next ensuing.

Item, That ye, and every one of you, do read over and study every day one chapter at the least, conferring the Latin and the English together, proceeding from the chapter from the beginning of the book to the end, having no necessary let to the contrary.

Item, That you, and every one of you, provide to have of your own a book called *The Institution of a Christian Man,* lately set out of the king's grace's prelates by his grace's commandment.

Item, That in secret confession and making of testaments excite and stir your parishioners from will-works to the necessary works of GOD, works of mercy and charity.

Item, That ye, and every one of you, do at all times the best that you can to occasion your parishioners to peace, love and charity, so that none of ye suffer the sun to set upon their wrath.

Item, That ye, and every one of you, provide to have a copy of these mine injunctions within thirteen days at the uttermost.

Item, That you, and every one of you, shall from henceforth suffer no religious persons, friar, or other, to have any services in your churches, either trental, quarter-service, or other.

Item, That preaching be not set aside for any manner of observance in the church, as procession, and other ceremonies.

Item, That ye, and every one of you, do not admit any young man or woman to receive the sacrament of the altar, until that he or she openly in the church, after mass or evensong, upon the holiday, do recite in English the *Pater.*

Item, That ye, and every one of you, from henceforth bid beads[2] no otherwise than according to the king's grace's ordinance, lest long bead-telling let fruitful preaching of GOD's word.

Item, That ye, and every one of you, as often as there is any marriage within your parish, exhort and charge your

[2 See Wilkins, Concilia, III. 807, 808.]

parishioners openly in the pulpit, amongst other things in your sermons, that they neither make nor suffer to be made any privy contract of matrimony, as they will avoid the extreme pain of the law certainly to be executed upon them.

Item, That ye, and every one of you, that be chantry priests, do instruct and teach the children of your parish, such as will come to you at the least, to read English, so that thereby they may the better learn how to believe, how to pray, and how to live to God's pleasure.

Item, That no parson, vicar, curate, nor chantry priest, from henceforth do discourage any lay person from the reading of any good books either in Latin or English, but rather animate and encourage them unto such things.

Item, That ye, and every one of you, not only in preaching and open communication, but also in secret, say the *Pater noster,* the *Creed,* and the *Ten Commandments.*

Item, That in praise-time[1] no...body be brought into the church, but be brought into the church-yard, that the peril of infection thereby may the better be avoided.

Item, That no curate command the even to be fasted of an abrogate holiday.

[1 plague time.]

BISHOP LATIMER'S ARGUMENTS AGAINST PURGATORY, WITH KING HENRY VIII's ANSWERS[2].

[Printed by Strype, Eccl. Mem. I. ii. p. 388. Oxf. Edit. Cotton MSS. Cleopatra, E. v. 130.]

Modicum plora super mortuum, quoniam requievit[3].
Ecclus. cap. xxii. As who say, Thy brother is dead. If natural passion[4] move thee to weep, yet weep but little. For if he died in the faith of Christ repentantly, he is at rest; ergo[a], in no pain of purgatory. For where such pain is, there is no rest. For they that affirm purgatory, affirm the pain to pass all the pain in the world. Hugo de Vienna upon the same place, *Potius gaudendum est, inquit, quam flendum, quia quisquis sic moritur de labore*[b] *ad requiem, de luctu ad gaudium transivit.* What rest hath he gotten, that is removed from the stocks in Newgate to the rack in the Tower?

    [a] [K. Hen.] Ergo, yet in a place. For of pain we dispute not.
    [b] This Hugo speaketh, remembering no quietness in[5] this world, nor yet till we come to heaven, and not condemning of purgatory.

Eccles. xi. *Ubicunque lignum ceciderit, ibi erit.* In what state a man dies, in that he shall continue without end: *sive ad austrum, sive ad aquilonem;* either to heaven or to,

[2 In the Cottonian MS. the arguments and answers are in the hand-writing of the respective disputants. The remarks of the king are written in the margin of the MS. and are here distinguished by the smaller type.

The "Act of Parliament" alluded to at the close of these arguments is doubtless that of the 27. Hen. VIII. which dissolved the lesser monasteries; for Latimer was not in circumstances to hold an argument with the monarch subsequent to the act for the dissolution of the larger monasteries.]

[3 requiescunt, Cott. MS.]   [4 compassion, Cott. MS.]
[5 in this world .... purgatory, not in Cott. MS.]

hell. Non est medium, si Hieronymo credimus: et operæ pretium fuerit legere[1] Pellicanum.

Aug. super Psal. xxxi.[2] *Beati[3] quorum tecta sunt peccata. Si[c] texit peccata Deus, noluit advertere; si noluit advertere, noluit animadvertere; si noluit animadvertere, noluit punire, &c.* Ergo peccata in hoc seculo obtecta[4] et remissa non sunt in futuro punita[d]. Ergo frustraneum est... purgatorium[5].

[c] Mark well the very text of this.
[d] This argument is well and plying[6] more to carnal wits' way than to plainness of the text.

[The following additional remarks on these two texts are in King Henry's own hand-writing, and occur at the end of the MS., and are also printed by Strype.]

Ubicunque lignum ceciderit, ibi erit. This text itself[7], speaking of but one stick, doth not deny purgatory; nor the example of a dead stick can well, without great forcing of[8], be attribute to a soul repentant, not yet having his full judgment. And if you will turn it to a lively stick, then it seemeth me, that it will make much against your purpose. For a lively stick may chance with falling to grow, though not suddenly, and so come to some perfection of his fruits. So may the soul of man by this example, departing hence to purgatory in right faith, grow toward his perfection, abiding the day of judgment.

Beati quorum, &c. Jesus! How do you descant on this Psalm, and also on S. Augustine, when you would make folk believe that this was meant against purgatory, when the very text declareth nothing but the beatitude and hopefulness of them that hath their sins hid and forgiven! Herein do you shew your carnal wit, which in preaching you dispraise so much.

Id.[9] in De Ebrietate. *Nemo se decipiat, fratres; duo enim loca sunt, et tertius non est visus. Qui cum Christo regnare non meruit, cum diabolo absque ulla dubitatione*

[1 operæ pretium legere, Cott. MS.]
[2 Oper. Tom. IV. prim. par. col. 132. Antw. 1700.]
[3 Beati, not in Cott. MS.]   [4 obtacta sunt, Cott. MS.]
[5 frustraneum est .... purgatorium. K. Henry writing on this passage makes that of Latimer's illegible between "est" and "purgatorium."]
[6 well and wise yet plying.]
[7 in itself, Cott. MS.]   [8 of, not in Cott. MS.]
[9 August., Cott. MS. Oper. Tom. v. Append. col. 351, among the treatises ascribed to Augustine.]

peribit. Here he had occasion to make[10] mention of purgatory, if he had then known it[e].

> [e] Is this a sufficient confusion of purgatory, because he here, speaking of drunkenness, doth not mention of purgatory?

Aug. De Vanitate Seculi[11]. *Scitote vero quod cum anima a corpore avellitur, statim aut in paradiso, pro*[f] *meritis bonis collocatur; aut certe pro peccatis in inferni tartara præcipitatur.* Ecce! quam manifeste, quasi ex industria, absorpsit purgatorium!

> [f] Note[12] this text to make against you in another of your opinions; and also, that he rather putteth a mean place between heaven and hell, which he calleth paradise, [which] is a place of comfort toward salvation.

Hieronym. in Eccles. xi[13]. *Ubicunque ubi locum præparaveris futuramque sedem, sive ad austrum sive ad boream, ibi cum mortuus fueris permanebis.* If S. Hierome had regarded purgatory, there had been occasion to have made mention of it[g].

> [g] Must the saints take occasion to write where[14] you think place is for them, or where[15] they think it meetest?

Hilary[16] in Psal. ii. *Judicii dies vel beatitudinis retributio est æterna, vel pœnæ*[h]. *Tempus vero mortis habet interim unumquemque suis legibus, dum ad judicium unumquemque aut Abraam reservat, aut pœna.* Quis hic non videt purgatorium fore nullum?

> [h] Who ever held opinion, that in or after the day of judgment there was a purgation? This text maketh not against that opinion. Therefore nothing to your purpose.

Cyprian[17], Sermone 4to. *De Mortalitate. Amplectamur diem mortis, qui assignat singulos domicilio suo; qui nos hinc ereptos paradiso restituit et regno cælesti.* Cyprianus

[10 to have made, MS.]
[11 Oper. Tom. VI. Append. col. 754, 772. (spurious.)]
[12 Note, not in Cott. MS.]
[13 Oper. Tom. II. p. 778. Paris, 1699. Edit. Bened.]
[14 write how and where, Cott. MS.]
[15 or as and where, Cott. MS.]
[16 Oper. col. 52. Paris, 1693. Edit. Bened.]
[17 Oper. p. 166. Edit. Fell. Oxon. 1682.]

non abstinuisset hic a mentione purgatorii, si tale quid vel cogitasset[i].

[i] This your interpretation sheweth plainly men's affections. For it is evident in learning, that a copulative—not *eundem locum*. Wherefore the contrary is rather to be gathered on[1] this text.

Chrysost. in Jo. cap. undec. Homilia lxi.[2] pag. 9. et b. *Justus moriens cum angelis evolabit, etiamsi nemo exequiis interveniat: perditus autem, etsi in funere universam habuerit civitatem, nihil lucrabitur.* Quid aptius dici possit in condemnationem purgatorii, quam quod eruditissimus hic dicit[k]?

[k] To this authority answereth this text of scripture, *Justo non est posita lex. Perdito nulla redemptio.* So neither[3] of these, whereof this text speaketh, belong to a sinner repentant. Wherefore purgatory may yet stand for all this[4].

Breviter multa sunt multorum auctorum testimonia, quæ demoliuntur purgatorium; multa etiam in ejusdem auctoribus, quæ sonant esse purgatorium. Incertum est negotium, neque tutum quicquam determinare, ne incerta pro veris statuantur. Tametsi certissimum fuerit, ejusmodi purgatorium, quale trecentos jam annos creditum fuerit, non possit stabiliri. At quod ad auctoritatem scriptorum attinet, sic Lyranus audet pronuntiare: *Non debet aliquem movere, quod ego recedo in hoc a dictis Hieronymi; quia dicta sanctorum non sunt tantæ auctoritatis quin liceat sentire contrarium in his quæ non sunt per sacram scripturam determinata*[1]. *Unde dicit Aug. in Ep. ad Vincentium de Scripturis sanctorum doctorum: Hoc genus scripturarum a canonicis scripturis distinguendum est. Non enim ex eis sic testimonia perferuntur, ut contrarium sentire non liceat.* Hactenus Lyranus.

[1] Non solum suo sensu, adhærente tamen.

[1 from this, Cott. MS.]

[2 Ἐκεῖνος μὲν γὰρ ἀπελθὼν μετ' ἀγγέλων ἀπελεύσεται, κἂν μηδεὶς παρατύχῃ τῷ λειψάνῳ· ὁ δὲ διεφθαρμένος, κἂν τὴν πόλιν ἔχῃ προπέμπουσαν, οὐδὲν καρπώσεται. Chrysos. Oper. Tom. VIII. p. 374. Paris, 1728. Bened.]

[3 nother, Cott. MS.]   [4 all them, Cott. MS.]

Et hoc est apud Hieronym. et reliquos auctores vulgatissimos, quod quicquid citra scripturas asseritur, eadem facilitate rejicitur qua admittitur[m].

> [m] Hoc ergo sic intelligi debet, quod quicquid ecclesia receperit, id rejicere potuit; sed non quisquis sua sponte prædicando.

As touching purgatory, I might, by way of disputation, reason this against it: God is more inclined to mercy than to justice. He executeth justice upon those that be damned, mercy upon those that be saved. But they that be damned, as soon as the soul is separate from the body, goeth straight to hell. Ergo, if God be more inclined to mercy, them that be saved, as soon as the soul is out of the body, goeth by and bye to heaven. Of these there is no purgatory[n].

> [n] This is a false argument, and also a wrong example. For God is as merciful and indifferent in this world to him that may be damned as to him that may be saved; yet the obstinacy of the man lets not: whereby one may perceive that his justice and mercy dependeth on the will of the creature, and as you, in a text before, allege the merits of the person.

The founding of monasteries argued purgatory to be; so the putting of them down argueth it not to be. What uncharitableness and cruelness seemeth it to be to destroy monasteries, if purgatory be! Now it seemeth not convenient the Act of Parliament to preach one thing, and the pulpit another clean contrary[g].

> [g] Why then do you? Turpe enim est doctori, cum culpa redarguit[5] ipsum.

[[5] redarguit eum, Cott. MS.]

THE DISPUTATION HAD AT OXFORD, THE 18TH DAY OF APRIL, 1554, BETWEEN MR HUGH LATIMER, ANSWERER, AND MR SMITH AND OTHERS, OPPOSERS.

[Printed by Foxe, Acts and Mon. pp. 978, et seq. edit. 1563. Vol. III. pp. 65, et seq. edit. 1684.]

WEDNESDAY the 18th day of April began the disputation[1], at eight of the clock, in such form as before: but it was most English; for master Latimer, the answerer, alleged that he was out of the use with Latin, and unfit for that place. There replied unto him master Smith[2], of Oriel College; doctor Cartwright, master Harpsfield, and divers others had snatches at him, and gave him bitter taunts. He did not escape hissings and scornful laughing, no more than they that went before him. He was very faint, and desired that he might not long tarry. He durst not drink for fear of vomiting. The disputation ended before eleven of the clock. Master Latimer was not suffered to read that he had (as he said) painfully written: but it was exhibited up, and the prolocutor read part thereof, and so proceeded to the disputation.

The preface of Weston unto the disputation following:

Weston's preface.

"Men and brethren, we are come together this day, by the help of God, to vanquish the strength of the arguments and dispersed opinions of adversaries against the truth of the real presence of the Lord's body in the sacrament. And

---

[1 After these disputations of Bishop Ridley ended, next was brought out Mr Hugh Latimer to dispute, upon Wednesday, which was the 18th day of April. Which disputation began at eight of the clock...1684.]

[2 The name of this person occurs as one of the proctors of the University of Oxford, for the year 1546.

Nicholas Cartwright, M.A. and B.D., was once a great admirer of Peter Martyr, and the only assistant of that eminent person in his disputation at Oxford, with Tresham and Chedsey, in the reign of King Edward VI. He was Master of the Hospital of St John, near Banbury, and had preferment also in the Diocese of Lichfield. Wood, Fasti. Vol. I. pp. 103, 123. edit. Bliss.

A notice of the other persons, whose names occur in this disputation, is prefixed to the "Examination, &c." of Philpot. P. Soc. Edit.]

therefore you, father, if you have any thing to answer, I do admonish that you answer in short and few words."

Latimer :—" I pray you, good master Prolocutor, do not exact that of me which is not in me. I have not these twenty years much used the Latin tongue." *M. Latimer requireth to dispute in the English tongue.*

Weston :—" Take your ease, father."

Latimer :—" I thank you, sir, I am well. Let me here protest my faith, for I am not able to dispute; and afterwards do your pleasure with me."

THE PROTESTATION OF MASTER LATIMER, GIVEN UP IN WRITING TO DOCTOR WESTON[3], AND THE REST OF THE QUEEN'S COMMISSIONERS WITH HIM, AT OXFORD, CONCERNING CERTAIN QUESTIONS TO HIM PROPOSED.

[Strype, Eccles. Memor. Vol. i. ii. pp. 388, et seq. Oxf. Edit.]

The conclusions whereunto I must answer are these[4]:

1. The first is, That in the sacrament of the altar, by the virtue of God's word pronounced by the priest, there is really and naturally the very body[5] of Christ present, as it was conceived of the virgin Mary, under the kinds[6] of bread and wine. And, in like manner, his blood [in the cup.] *The three conclusions.*

2. The second is, That after the consecration[7] there remaineth no substance of bread and wine, nor none other substance but the substance of God and man.

3. The third is, That in the mass there is the lively sacrifice of the church, which is propitiatory as well for the[8] quick, as the dead.

[3 and the rest of the ...... to him proposed is not in, 1684.]

[4 The Protestation which follows is reprinted from Strype, as being fuller than that printed by Foxe. It is stated to have been "faithfully translated out of Latin into English;" and is given as from the "Foxe MSS." The various readings found in two MSS., one belonging to Caius College, the other to Emmanuel College, Cambridge, are designated by C and E, respectively; and those portions which, in the main, are peculiar to the protestation given in the text, are inclosed in brackets.]

[5 present the natural body of Christ, conceived of, 1684, very body, C.]   [6 the appearances of bread, 1684.]

[7 after consecration, 1684.]

[8 profitable as well for the sins of the, 1684.]

To these I answer:

1. Concerning the first conclusion, methinketh it is set forth with certain new[1] terms, lately found, that be obscure, and do not sound according to the scripture[2]. Nevertheless, however[3] I understand it, thus do I answer[4], although not without peril [of my life.] I say[5], That there is none other presence of Christ required than a spiritual presence; and this presence is sufficient for a christian man, as the presence[6] by the which we both abide[7] in Christ, and Christ in[8] us, to the obtaining of eternal life, if we persevere [in his true gospel.] And the same[9] presence may be called[10] a real presence[11], [because to the faithful believer there is the real, or spiritual body of Christ:] which thing I here rehearse[12], lest some sycophant or scorner should suppose me, with the anabaptist, to make nothing else of the sacrament but a bare and naked[13] sign. As for that which is feigned of many[14], I, for my part, take it[15] for a papistical invention. And therefore I think it utterly to be rejected [from among God's children, that seek their Saviour in faith; and be taught among the fleshly papists, that will be again under the yoke of antichrist.]

2. Concerning the second conclusion, I dare be bold to say, that it hath no stay nor ground of[16] God's [holy] word; but is a thing invented and found out by man, and therefore to be reputed and had as false[17]; and, I had almost said, as the mother and nurse of all[18] other errors. It were good for

[1 new found terms, 1684. C.]
[2 speech of the scripture, 1684, C.]
[3 Howbeit, howsoever, 1684, C.]
[4 thus I do answer plainly, 1684.]
[5 I answer, I say, 1684.]   [6 as a presence, 1684.]
[7 we abide, 1684.]   [8 Christ abideth in us, 1684.]
[9 this same, 1684, C.]   [10 called most fitly, 1684, C.]
[11 real presence, that is, a presence not feigned, but a true and a faithful presence, 1684.]
[12 I rehearse, C.]
[13 a naked and a bare, 1684, bare and naked, C.]
[14 many, concerning their corporal presence, 1684.]
[15 it but for, 1684, C.]   [16 in God's, 1684, C.]
[17 to be taken as fond and false, 1684; had and reputed, C; to be rejected, had and reputed as false, E.]
[18 of the other, 1684, C.]

my masters and lords, the transubstantiators[19], to take [better] heed [to their doctrine,] lest they conspire with the Nestorians. For [the Nestorians deny that Christ had a natural body: and] I cannot see how the papists can[20] avoid it: [for they would contain the natural body which Christ had, (sin excepted,) against all truth, into a wafer cake.]

3. The third conclusion, as I understand it, seemeth[21] subtilly to sow sedition against the offering which Christ himself offered for us in his own person[22], [and for all, and never again to be done;] according to [the scriptures written in God's book. In which book read] the pithy place of St Paul[23] [to the Hebrews, the 9th and 10th,] where he saith that Christ his own self hath made a perfect sacrifice[24] for our sins[25], [and never again to be done; and then ascended into heaven, and there sitteth a merciful intercessor between God's justice and our sins; and there shall tarry till these transubstantiators, and all other his foes, be made his footstool: and this offering did he freely of himself, as it is written in the 10th of John, and needed not that any man should do it for him.] I will speak nothing of the wonderful presumptions[26] of man, that dare[27] attempt this thing without any manifest calling: specially that which intrudeth to the overthrowing and fruitless-making (if not wholly, yet

Heb. ix. x.

John x.

[19 lords and masters of the transubstantions, 1684; lords and masters transubstantiators, C.]

[20 I do not see how they can, 1684. I cannot see how they can avoid it. The Nestorians deny that Christ had a true natural body, C.]

[21 as I understand, seemeth, C.]

[22 own proper person, 1684, own person, C.]

[23 that pithy place of St Paul to the Hebrews where, 1684, C.]

[24 purgation of, 1684,—for, C.]

[25 And afterward, "That he might," saith he, "be a merciful and faithful bishop, concerning those things which are to be done with God, for the taking away of our sins." So that the expiation, or taking away of our sins, may be thought rather to depend on this, that Christ was an offering bishop, than[a] that he was offered, were it not that he was offered of himself; and therefore it is needless that he should be offered of any other, 1684.]

[26 nothing of the presumptiousness, C.]

[27 to dare to, 1684.]

[a rather than, C.]

partly) of the cross of Christ[1]. And therefore worthily a man may say to my lords and masters offerers[2], By what authority do you this? And who gave you this authority? When, and where[3]? "A man cannot," saith St John[4], "take any thing except it be given him from above:" much less, then, may any man presume to usurp any honour, before he be called thereunto[5].

Again: "If any man sin," saith (St John), "we have," saith he, not a masser, nor an offerer[6] upon earth, which can sacrifice for us at mass; but "we have," saith he, "an Advocate [with God the Father,] Jesus Christ [the righteous" one;] which once offered himself [for us] long ago. Of which offering the efficacy and effect is perdurable for ever. So that it is needless to have such offerers. [But if they had a nail driven through one of their ears every time they offer, as Christ had four driven through his hands and feet, they would soon leave offering. Yet, if their offering did not bring gains withal, it should not be so often done. For they say, No penny, no *pater noster*.] What meaneth St Paul, when he saith[7], "They that preach the gospel shall live of the gospel?" Whereas he should [rather] have said, The Lord hath ordained, that they that sacrifice at mass, should live of the sacrificing[8]. [But although the Holy Ghost appointed them no living for their mass-saying in God's book, yet have they appointed themselves a living in

---

[1 derogation of the cross of Christ; for it is no base nor, E; a manifest vocation, specially in that it tendeth, making fruitless, 1684; specially that which intrudeth to the overthrowing and fruitless making, C; cross of Christ, for truly it is no base or mean thing to offer Christ, 1684.]

[2 masters the offerers, 1684; masters offerers, C.]

[3 Where? When? 1684. When and where? C.]

[4 the Baptist, 1684, C.]

[5 be thereunto called, 1684; called thereunto, C.]

[6 masser or offerer at home, 1684; an offerer at home, C.]

[7 he saith, "They that serve at the altar are partakers of the altar?" And so addeth, "So the Lord hath ordained that they that preach...1684, C.]

[8 their sacrificing, that there might be a living assigned to our sacrificers now, as was before Christ's coming to the Jewish priests, 1684; our sacrificers, for now they have nothing to allege for their living, as they that be preachers have, C.]

antichrist's decrees. For I am sure, if God would have had a new kind of sacrificing priest at mass, then he or some of his apostles would have made some mention thereof in their master Christ's will. But belike the secretaries were not the masser's friends; or else they saw it was a charge without profit. It must needs else have been remembered and provided for, as there was a living provided for the sacrificing priests before Christ's coming, in the Jews' times.] For now they have nothing to allege for [themselves, that is to say, for their sacrificing, nor for] their living; as those that preach the gospel have[9]. [For Christ himself, after he had suffered, and made a perfect sacrifice for our sins, and also when he rose again to justify us, commanded his disciples to go preach all the world over, saying, "Whosoever believeth, and is baptized, shall be saved." But he spake never a word of sacrificing, or saying of mass; nor promised the hearers any reward, but among the idolaters, with the devil and his angels, except speedy repentance with tears. Therefore, sacrificing priests should now cease for ever: for now all men ought to offer their own bodies a quick sacrifice, holy and acceptable before God.] The supper of the Lord was instituted to provoke us to thanksgiving[10], [and to stir us up

Matt. xxviii.

Rom. xii.

[9 as they that be preachers have. So that it appeareth, that the sacrificing priesthood is changed, by God's ordinance, into a preaching priesthood; and the sacrificing priesthood should cease utterly, saving inasmuch as all christian men are sacrificing priests, 1684; sacrificing priesthood should now cease for ever, forasmuch as, C, E.]

[10 thanksgiving, for the offering which the Lord himself did offer for us, much rather than that our offerers should do there as they do[a]. "Feed," saith Peter, "as much as ye may the flock of Christ;" nay rather, Let us sacrifice as much as we may for the flock of Christ. If so be as the matter be[b] as men now make, I can never wonder enough that Peter would or could forget this office of sacrificing, which at this day is in such price and estimation, that[c] to feed is almost nothing with many. If thou cease from feeding the flock, how shalt thou be taken? Truly, catholic enough. But if thou cease from sacrificing and massing, how will that be taken[d]? At the least, I warrant thee, thou shalt be called an heretic. And whence, I pray

[a much more than our offerers should do there as such do, E.]
[b If the mass be as now men make it, E.]
[c estimation, to feed, E.]
[d be taken? I warrant thee, thou shalt be called an heretic. And whence come these popish judgments, C.]

Rev. i. by preaching of the gospel to remember his death till he cometh again, according to his commandment. For Christ bade Peter feed the flock, and not sacrifice for the flock.] I can never wonder enough, that Peter [and all the apostles] would forget [thus negligently] the office of sacrificing, if they had thought it necessary; seeing that, at these days, it is had in such price and estimation, to feed the flock is almost nothing with many : for if you cease of feeding, you shall be taken for a good catholic; but if you cease from sacrificing and massing, you will be taken, I trow, for an heretic, [and come to such place as I and many of my brethren be in shortly.]

Thus, lo¹! [I have written an answer to your conclusions, even as I will answer before the majesty of our Lord and Saviour Jesus Christ; by whose only sacrifice I hope to possess heaven. Therefore I beseech your good masterships to take it in good part,] as I have done it with great pains, having no man to help me, as I never was before denied² to have. O sir, you may chance to come to this age and weakness, that I am of; [and then you would be loth to be used as I am at your hands; that no man may come to me, to help me for any need; no, not so much as to mend my hose or my coat. And you know, that he that hath but one pair of hose, had need sometime to have them mended.] I have spoken in my time before two kings, more than one³, two, or three hours together without interruption: but now, when⁴ [I should have spoken the truth out

you, come these papistical[a] judgments? Except perchance they think a man feedeth the flock in sacrificing for them; and then what needeth there any learned pastors? For no man is so foolish but soon he may learn to sacrifice and mass it, 1684.]

[¹ Thus lo! I have taken the more pains to write, because I refused to dispute, in consideration of my debility[b] thereunto; that all men may know how that I have so done, not without great pains, 1684; of debility thereunto, that all men may know that I have so done, not without a just cause. I beseech your good, C.]

[² as I never before have been debarred to have, C. E.]

[³ once, 1684; more than two or, C.]

[⁴ but now that I may speak the truth (by your leave) I could not be suffered to declare my mind before you, no not by the space, 1684, C.]

[a perverse, E.]   [b unability, Harl. MS.]

of God's book, (for that I ever took for my warrant,)] I could (by your leave) not be suffered to declare my faith before you, [for the which, God willing, I intend to give my life,] not by the space of a quarter of an hour, without snatches, [rages,] revilings, checks, rebukes, and taunts, such as I never heard the like[5], in such an audience, all my life long. Sure[6] it cannot be, but I have made some heinous

[[5] as I have not felt the like in such, C; heard nor felt, E.]
[[6] Surely it cannot be but an heinous offence that I have given. But what was it[a]? Forsooth, I had[b] spoken of the four marrow-bones of the mass. The which kind of speaking I never read[c] to be a sin against the Holy Ghost: I could not be allowed[d] to shew what I meant by my metaphor. But, sir, now, by your favour, I will shew your[e] mastership what I mean.

The first is the popish consecration; which hath been called[f] a God's-body-making, 1684. C. E.

The second is, transubstantiation.
The third is, missal oblation.
The fourth, adoration.

[g]The chief and principal portions, parts, and points belonging, or incident to the Mass, and most esteemed and had in price in the same, I call "the marrow-bones of the mass;" which, indeed, you by force[h], might, and violence intrude[i] in sound of words, in some of the scripture, with racking and cramping[k], injuring and wronging the same; but else, indeed, plain out of the scripture, as I am thoroughly[l] persuaded[m]; although in disputation I could now nothing do to persuade the same to others[n]; being both unapt to study, and also to make a shew of my former study, in such readiness as should be requisite to the same.

I have heard much talk of master doctor Weston, to and fro in my time; but I never knew your person, to my knowledge, till I came before you, as the queen's majesty's commissioner. I pray God send you so right judgment, as I perceive you have a great[o] wit, great learning, with many other qualities! God[p] give you grace ever to use them, and ever to have in remembrance, that he that dwelleth on high looketh on the low things on the earth; and that also there is no counsel against the Lord; and also that this world hath been, and yet is, a tottering world! and yet again, that though we must obey the princes, yet that hath this limitation, namely, in the Lord. For whoso

[[a] What a one is, C.]   [[b] I have freely, E.]   [[c] read yet, E; found yet, C.]
[[d] I could not then be, E; be suffered, C.]   [[e] I will tell you what, C.]
[[f] called of late, E.]   [[g] Meaning by marrow-bones the chief, &c. C.]
[[h] indeed may by force, C; same, which by force, E.]
[[i] violence trace and intrude, C.]   [[k] varking and vamping, E.]   [[l] truly.]
[[m] persuaded to the same, E.]   [[n] persuade to others, E.]   [[o] good, E.]
[[p] and, E; qualities; and ever to have in remembrance, C.]

offence. Forsooth, [I think it be this; I have spoken against the mass, and did ask, if their god of the altar had any marrow-bones. For I said I had read the testament over seven times, since I was in the prison, with great deliberation; and yet I could never find, as I said before, in the sacrament of the body and blood of Christ (which the papists call the sacrament of the altar) neither flesh, blood, nor bones, nor this word 'transubstantiation.' And because, peradventure, my masters (that can so soon make Christ's body of bread, which was not made, but conceived by the Holy Ghost in the virgin's womb, as God's invaluable word doth testify, and also all the ancient fathers) might say, that I doted for age, and my wits were gone, so that my words were not to be credited; yet, behold! the providence of God, which will have this truth known, (yea, if all men held their tongues, the stones should speak,) did bring this to pass that where these famous men, viz. Mr Cranmer, archbishop of Canterbury, Mr Ridley, bishop of London, that holy man, Mr Bradford, and I, old Hugh Latimer, were imprisoned in the Tower of London for Christ's gospel preaching, and for because we would not go a massing, every one in close

doth obey them against the Lord, they[a] be most pernicious to them, and the greatest adversaries that they have[b]. For so they procure God's vengeance upon them, if God only be the ruler of things[c].

There be some so corrupt[d] in mind, the truth being taken from them, that they think gains to be godliness: great learned men, and yet men of no learning, but of railing and raging[e] about questions and strife of words. I call them men of no learning, because they know not Christ, how much else so ever they know. And on this sort we are wont[f] to call great learned clerks, being ignorant of Christ, unlearned men: for it is nothing but plain ignorance to know any thing[g] without Christ; whereas whoso knoweth[h] Christ, the same hath knowledge enough, although in other knowledge he be to seek. The apostle St Paul confesseth of himself to the Corinthians[i], that he did know nothing but Jesus Christ crucified. Many men babble many things of Christ, which yet know[k] not Christ: but pretending Christ, do craftily colour and darken his glory. "Depart from such men," saith the apostle St Paul to Timothy. 1684.]

[a the same, E.] [b have, and affirm otherwise, C.]
[c if so be that God be the captain of the commonweal, E.]
[d corrupted, E; corrupt of, C.] [e raving, E.]
[f it is a wont to call great clerks, E.] [g many things, E.]
[h if a man know, E; if one know, C.] [i truth, E.]
[k babble much of Christ which know not, C.]

prison from other; the same tower being so full of other prisoners, that we four were thrust into one chamber, as men not to be accounted of, (but, God be thanked! to our great joy and comfort,) there did we together read over the new testament with great deliberation and painful study: and I assure you, as I will answer [at] the tribunal throne of God's majesty, we could find in the testament of Christ's body and blood no other presence, but a spiritual presence; nor that the mass was any sacrifice for sins: but in that heavenly book it appeared that the sacrifice, which Christ Jesus our Redeemer did upon the cross, was perfect, holy, and good; that God, the heavenly Father, did require none other, nor that never again to be done; but was pacified with that only omnisufficient and most painful sacrifice of that sweet slain Lamb, Christ our Lord, for our sins. Wherefore stand from the altar, you sacrileging (I should have said, you sacrificing) priests: for you have no authority in God's book to offer up our Redeemer; neither will he any more come in the hands of sacrificing priests, for the good cheer you made him when he was among your sworn generation. And I say, you lay people, as you are called, come away from forged sacrifices, which the papists do feign only, to be lords over you, and to get money; lest your bodies, which are, or should be Christ's temples, be false-witness bearers against the blood of our redemption. For the Holy Ghost had promised to St John in the 18th of the Revelation, that if you come from them, Rev. xviii. you get none of their plagues; but if you tarry with them, you have spun a fair thread; for you shall drink of the same cup of God's wrath that they shall. And thereby your playing at main chance, you bring all the righteous blood that wicked Cain hath shed, even upon your own heads. Choose you now whether you will ride to the devil with idolaters, or go to heaven with Christ and his members, by bearing the cross.

Now I am sure this speech hath offended my lords and masters; and I have marvel at it, for I ask none other question, in requiring to know if their bread-god had flesh, marrow and bones, or not, as our dear Redeemer had, and as they affirm and set forth with fire and fagot, good doctors, I warrant you, that their white idol (I should have said their altar-god) hath. Therefore, methinketh they are angry with me without a cause. But one thing this trouble hath brought me unto; that is, to be acquainted with Mr Doctor Weston, whom I never saw before; and I had not thought he had been so great a clerk. For in all king Edward's time he was a curate, besides Bishopsgate; and held him well content to feed his parishioners with the doctrine that he now calleth heresy, and is sent from the queen to judge us of the same. But I pray God send him a more merciful judgment at the hand of Christ, than we receive of him! And I would ever have him, and all those that be in Rome,] to remember, that he that dwelleth on high looketh on the things upon earth; and also that there is no counsel against the Lord, [as St Paul saith;] and that the world has and ever hath been a tottering world; and yet again, that though we must obey the princes, yet [are we limited, how far; that is, so long as they do not command things against the manifest truth. But now they do; therefore we must say with Peter and John, "We must obey God before man." I mean none other resistance, but to offer our lives to the death, rather than to commit any evil against the majesty of God, and his most holy and true word. But this I say unto you, if the queen have any pernicious enemy within her realm, those they be that do cause her to maintain idolatry, and to wet her sword of justice in the blood of her people, that are set to defend the gospel: for this hath been always the destructions both of kings, queens, and whole commonwealths; as I am afraid it will make this commonwealth of England to quake shortly, if speedy repentance be not had among the inhabitants thereof. But you cannot say but that you have had warning; and therefore take heed betimes, and be warned by a number of other countries that have forsaken God's known truth, and followed the lies of men. If not, other lands shall be warned by you. You that be here sent to judge our faith be not learned in deed, I mean not a right; be not right because you know not Christ and his pure word.] For it is nothing but plain ignorance to know many things without Christ and his gospel. St Paul saith, "that he did know nothing but Jesu Christ crucified." Many men babble much of Christ, which yet know not Christ; but, pretending Christ, do craftily cover and darken his glory. [And, indeed, these are meetest men to dishonour a man, that seem to be his friend.] Depart from such men, saith the apostle Timothy.

It is not out of the way to remember what St Augustine saith[1] against the Epistle of Petilianus: "Whosoever," saith he, "teacheth any thing necessary[2] to be believed, which is not contained in the old and new Testament, the same is accursed[3]." O! beware of that curse[4], [you that so stoutly set forth men's doctrines, yea, wicked blasphemy against the truth]. I am much deceived, if Basilius[5] have not such like words: "Whatsoever," saith he, "is besides the holy scripture, if the same be taught as necessary[6] to be believed, the same is sin." O! therefore, take [good] heed of this sin! There be some that speak false things, more[7] [profitable to the purse,] and more like the truth, than the truth itself. Therefore St Paul giveth a watch-word: "Let no man deceive you," saith he, "with probability and persuasions of words[8]." O good Lord! [what a damnable act you have done!] You have changed the most holy communion into a [wicked and horrible sacrifice of idolatry;] and you deny to the lay people the cup, which is directly against God's institution, [which saith, "Drink ye all of this." And where you should preach the benefit of Christ's

Lib. iii. c. 6. contra lit. Petilian.

[1 saith. The place where, I now well remember not, except it be against the epistle of Petilianus, 1684.]

[2 necessarily, 1684.]

[3 Sive de Christo, sive de ejus ecclesia, sive de quacunque alia re quæ pertinet ad fidem vitamque nostram . . . . *si angelus de cœlo vobis annunciaverit præterquam quod* in scripturis legalibus et evangelicis *accepistis, anathema sit.* Con. Literas Petil. III. 6.]

[4 that curse, if you be wise! 1684.]

[5 The martyr probably had in mind Basil's Sermon περὶ πίστεως. Oper. Tom. II. p. 24. Paris. 1722. Edit. Bened.]

[6 necessarily, 1684.] [7 more probable, and more like, 1684.]

[8 "But what mean you," saith one, "by this talk so far from the matter?" Well, I hope, good masters, you will suffer an old man a little to play the child, and to speak one thing twice. O Lord God! you have changed the most holy communion into a private action, and you deny to the laity the Lord's cup, contrary to Christ's commandment; and ye do blemish the annunciation of the Lord's death till he come. For you have changed the Common Prayer called, "The divine Service, with the Administration of the Sacraments," from the vulgar and known language, into a strange tongue, contrary to the will of the Lord revealed in his word. God open the door of your heart, to see the things you should see herein! I would as fain obey my sovereign as any in this realm; but in these things I can never do it with an upright conscience. God be merciful unto us! Amen. 1684.]

death to the people, you speak to the wall in a foreign tongue. God open the door of your heart, that you may once have a more care to enlarge the kingdom of God than your own, if it be his will!

Thus have I answered your conclusions, as I will stand unto, with God's help, to the fire. And after this I am able to declare to the majesty of God, by his invaluable word, that I die for the truth : for I assure you, if I could grant to the queen's proceedings, and endure by the word of God, I would rather live than die; but seeing they be directly against God's word, I will obey God more than man, and so embrace the stake.

By H. L.

Weston :—" Then you refuse to dispute ? Will you here then subscribe ?"

Latimer :—" No, good master; I pray you be good to an old man. You may, if it please God, be once old, as I am : ye may come to this age, and to this debility."

Weston :—" Ye said, upon Saturday last, that ye could not find the mass, nor the marrow-bones thereof, in your books ; but we will find a mass in that book."

Latimer :—" No, good master doctor, ye cannot."

Weston :—" What find you then there ?"

Latimer :—" Forsooth, a communion I find there."

Weston :—" Which communion, the first or the last[1] ?"

Latimer :—" I find no great diversity in them : they are one supper of the Lord ; but I like the last very well."

Weston :—" Then the first was naught, belike ?"

Latimer :—" I do not well remember wherein they differ."

<small>Dr Weston cavilleth against the name of the Lord's supper.</small>

Weston :—" Then cake-bread and loaf-bread are all one with you. Ye call it the supper of the Lord ; but you are deceived in that, for they had done the[2] supper before ; and therefore the scripture saith, *postquam cœnatum est,* that is, "After they had supped." For ye know, that St Paul findeth fault with the Corinthians, for that some of them were drunken at this supper ; and ye know no man can be drunken at your communion."

[[1] " By this first and second communion," observes Foxe, " the doctor meaneth the two books of public order set forth in king Edward's days; the one in the beginning, the other in the latter end of his reign."]   [[2] their, 1563.]

Latimer:—"The first was called *Cœna Judaica*, that is, the Jewish supper, when they did eat the paschal lamb together: the other was called *Cœna Dominica*, that is, the Lord's supper."

Weston:—"That is false, for Chrysostom denieth that; and St Ambrose[3], in cap. x. *prioris ad Corinthios*, saith, *Mysterium eucharistiæ inter cœnandum datum non est cœna Dominica;* that is, 'That the mystery of the sacrament, given as they were at supper, is not the supper of the Lord.' And Gregory Nazianzen saith the same: *Rursus Paschæ sacra cum discipulis in cœnaculo ac post cœnam dieque unica ante passionem celebrat: nos vero ea in orationis domibus et ante cœnam et post resurrectionem peragimus*[4]; that is, 'Again he kept the holy feast of passover with his disciples, in the dining chamber after supper, and one day before his passion: but we keep it both in the churches and houses of prayer, both before the supper, and also after the resurrection.' And that first supper was called ἀγάπη. Can you tell what that is?"

Latimer:—"I understand no Greek. Yet I think it meaneth charity."

Weston:—"Will you have all things done that Christ did then? Why, then must the priest be hanged on the morrow. And where find you, I pray you, that a woman should receive the sacrament?"

Latimer:—"Will you give me leave to turn my book? I find it in the eleventh chapter to the Corinthians. I trow these be the words: *Probet autem seipsum homo*, &c. I pray you, good master, what gender is *homo?*"

Weston:—"Marry, the common gender."

Cole:—"It is in the Greek ὁ ἄνθρωπος[5]."

Harpsfield:—"It is ἀνήρ[5], that is, *vir*."

Latimer:—"It is in my book of Erasmus' translation, *Probet seipsum homo*, &c."

Feckenham:—"It is *Probet seipsum*, indeed, and therefore it importeth the masculine gender."

[3 Ostendit illis mysterium eucharistiæ inter cœnandum celebratum non cœnam esse. Ambros. Oper. Tom. II. Append. col. 149. c.]

[4 Πάλιν μυσταγωγεῖ τὸ πάσχα τοῖς μαθηταῖς ἐν ὑπερώῳ καὶ μετὰ δεῖπνον, καὶ πρὸ μιᾶς τοῦ παθεῖν ἡμέρας· ἡμεῖς ἐν προσευχῆς οἴκοις καὶ πρὸ τοῦ δείπνου καὶ μετὰ τὴν ἀνάστασιν. Oper. Tom. I. p. 659. Paris. 1630.]

[5 Both these statements are erroneous. The reading in 1 Cor. xi. 28, is ἄνθρωπος.]

Latimer :—" What then? I trow when the woman touched Christ, he[1] said, *Quis tetigit me? Scio quod aliquis me tetigit;* that is, ' Who touched me? I know that some man touched me.' "

Weston :—" I will be at host with you anon. When Christ was at his supper, none were with him but his apostles only. *Ergo,* he meant no woman, if you will have his[2] institution kept."

Latimer :—" In the twelve apostles was represented the whole church; in which you will grant both men and women to be."

Weston :—" So through the whole heretical translated bible ye never make mention of priest, till ye come to the putting of Christ to death. Where find you then that a priest or minister (a minstrel I may call him well enough) should do it of necessity?"

Latimer :—" A minister is a more fit name for that office; for the name of a priest importeth a sacrifice."

Weston :—" Well, remember that ye cannot find that a woman may receive by scripture.—Master opponent, fall to it."

Smith :—" Because I perceive that this charge is laid upon my neck to dispute with you, to the end that the same may go forward after a right manner and order, I will propose three questions, so as they are put forth unto me. And first, I ask this question of you, although the same indeed ought not to be called in question: but such is the condition of the church, that it is always vexed of the wicked sort. I ask, I say, whether Christ's body be really in the sacrament?"

Latimer :—" I trust I have obtained of Mr Prolocutor[3], that no man shall exact that thing of me which is not in me. And I am sorry that this worshipful audience should be deceived of their expectation for my sake. I have given up my mind in writing to Mr Prolocutor."

Smith :—" Whatsoever ye have given up, it shall be registered among the acts."

Latimer :—" Disputation requireth a good memory. *Ast abolita est mihi memoria.* My memory is gone clean, and marvellously weakened, and never the better, I wis, for the prison."

[[1] Christ said, 1563.]   [[2] this, 1563.]   [[3] my good master, 1563.]

Weston:—" How long have ye been in prison ?"

Latimer:—" These three quarters of this year."

Weston:—" And I was[4] in prison six years."

Latimer:—" The more pity, sir[5]."

Weston:—" How long have you been of this opinion ?"

Latimer:—" It is not long[6], sir, that I have been of this opinion."

Weston:—" The time hath been when you said mass full devoutly[7]."

Latimer:—" Yea, I cry God mercy heartily for it."

Weston:—" Where learned you this newfangleness[8] ?"

Latimer:—" I have long sought for the truth in this matter of the sacrament, and have not been of this mind past seven years: and my lord of Canterbury's book[9] hath especially confirmed my judgment herein. If I could remember all therein contained, I would not fear to answer any man in this matter." *Master Latimer confirmed by Dr Cranmer's book.*

Tresham:—" There are in that book six hundred errors."

Weston:—" You were once a Lutheran."

Latimer:—" No. I was a papist: for I never could perceive how Luther could defend his opinion without transubstantiation. The Tigurines once did write a book against Luther[10], and I oft desired God that he might live so long to make them answer." *The zeal of Master Latimer sometimes in popery against the Tigurines.*

Weston:—" Luther, in his book *De Privata Missa*, said, that the devil reasoned with him, and persuaded him that the mass was not good, fol. 14. *Contigit me,* &c. Whereof it may appear, that Luther said mass, and the devil dissuaded him from it." *In that book the devil doth not dissuade him so much from saying mass, as he laboureth to bring him to desperation for mass.*

Latimer:—" I do not take in hand here to defend Luther's sayings or doings. If he were here, he would defend himself well enough, I trow[11]. I told you before, that* *Such temptations many times happen to good men.*

[4 have been, 1563.] [5 good master, 1563.] [6 It is long, 1563.]

[7 Ye have said mass at Greenwich full devoutly, 1563, Harl. MS.]

[8 Then they hissed and clapped their hands at him. Foxe.]

[9 Answer to a Crafty and Sophistical Cavillation devised by Stephen Gardiner. See below, p. 272.]

[10 See Hospinian, Historiæ Sacramentariæ, &c. Par. 2. pp. 221, et seq. Genev. 1681.]

[11 defend himself, I trow, 1563.]

I am not meet for disputations. I pray you, read mine answer, wherein I have declared my faith."

Weston:—" Do you believe this, as you have written?"

Latimer:—" Yea, sir."

Weston:—" Then have you no faith."

Latimer:—" Then would I be sorry, sir."

Tresham:—" It is written, (John vi.) 'Except ye shall eat the flesh of the Son of man, and drink his blood, ye shall have no life in you:' which[1] when the Capernaites and many of Christ's disciples heard, they said, 'This is a hard saying,' &c. Now, that the truth may the better appear, here I ask of you, whether Christ, speaking these words, did mean of his flesh to be eaten with the mouth, or of the spiritual eating of the same?"

Latimer:—" I answer, (as Augustine understandeth,) that Christ meant of the spiritual eating of his flesh."

Tresham:—" Of what flesh meant Christ? His true flesh, or no?"

Latimer:—" Of his true flesh, spiritually to be eaten, in the supper, by faith, and not corporally[2]."

Tresham:—" Of what flesh mean the Capernaites?"

Latimer:—" Of his true flesh also; but to be eaten with the mouth."

Tresham:—" They, as ye confess, did mean his true flesh to be eaten[3] with the mouth. And Christ also, as I shall prove, did speak of the receiving of his flesh with the mouth. *Ergo,* they both did understand it of the eating of one thing, which is done by the mouth of the body."

Dr Tresham's argument without form or mood concluding affirmatively in the second figure.

Latimer:—" I say, Christ understood it not of the bodily mouth, but of the mouth of the spirit, mind, and heart."

Tresham:—" I prove the contrary, that Christ understandeth it of the eating with the bodily mouth. For whereas custom is a right good mistress and interpreter of things, and whereas the acts put in practice by Christ do certainly declare those things which he first spake; Christ's deeds[4] in his supper, where he gave his body to be taken with the mouth, together with the custom, which hath been ever since[5]

Dr Tresham flieth to custom.

[1 Here Tresham began to dispute in Latin. Foxe.]
[2 sacramentally, 1563.] [3 taken, 1563.]
[4 his deed, 1563.] [5 used from, 1563.]

that time, of that⁶ eating which is done with the mouth, doth evidently infer that Christ did understand his words, here cited of me out of John vi., of the eating with the mouth."

Latimer :—" He gave not his body to be received with the mouth, but he gave the sacrament of his body to be received with⁷ the mouth: he gave the sacrament to the mouth, his body to the mind." *{The sacrament given to the mouth, the body to faith.}*

Tresham :—" But my reason doth conclude, that Christ spake concerning his flesh to be received with the corporal mouth: for otherwise (which God forbid!) he had been a deceiver, and had not been offensive to the Capernaites and his disciples, if he had not meant in this point as they thought he meant: for if he had thought as you do feign, it had been an easy matter for him to have said, 'You shall not eat my flesh with your mouth, but the sacrament of my flesh;' that is to say, ye shall receive with your mouth not the thing itself, but the figure of the thing; and thus he might have satisfied them: but so he said not, but continued in the truth of his words, as he was wont. Therefore Christ meant the self-same thing that the Capernaites did, I mean concerning the thing itself to be received with the mouth; *videlicet*, that his true flesh is truly to be eaten with the mouth. Moreover, forasmuch as you do expound for *corpus Christi*, 'the body of Christ,' *sacramentum corporis Christi*, 'the sacrament of the body of Christ,' and hereby do suppose that we obtain but a spiritual union, or union of the mind, between us and Christ; plain it is, that you are deceived in this thing, and do err from the mind of the fathers: for they affirm by plain and express words, that we are corporally and carnally joined together. And these be the words of Hilary: *Si vere igitur carnem corporis nostri Christus assumpsit, et vere homo ille qui ex Maria natus fuit Christus est, nos quoque vere sub mysterio carnem corporis sui sumimus, et per hæc unum erimus, quia Pater in eo est, et ille in nobis: quomodo voluntatis unitas asseritur, cum naturalis per sacramentum proprietas perfecte sacramentum sit unitatis*⁸. 'Therefore, if Christ did truly take the flesh of *{And what doth Christ else mean by those words, where he saith: "My words be Spirit and life, the flesh profiteth nothing"?}*

[⁶ the, 1563.] [⁷ of, 1563.]
[⁸ De Trinitate, Lib. VIII. 13. Oper. col. 955. Paris. 1693. Edit. Bened. See Cranmer, Park. Soc. Ed. pp. 413, 4.]

our body upon him, and the same man be Christ indeed, which was born of Mary; then we also do receive under a mystery the flesh of his body indeed, and thereby shall become one; because the Father is in him, and he in us. How is the unity of will affirmed, when a natural propriety by the sacrament is a perfect sacrament of unity[1]?" Thus far hath Hilary. Lo! here you see how manifestly these words confounded your assertion. *Master Latimer charged to preach the contrary doctrine before the king at Greenwich.* To be short, I myself have heard you preaching at Greenwich before King Henry the Eighth, where you did openly affirm, that no christian man ought to doubt of the true and real presence of Christ's body in the sacrament, forasmuch as he had the word of scripture on his side; *videlicet, Hoc est corpus meum,* 'This is my body:' whereby he might be confirmed. But now there is the same truth; the word of scripture hath the self-same thing, which it then had. Therefore why do you deny at this present that, whereof it was not lawful once to doubt before when you taught it?"

Latimer:—" Will you give me leave to speak?"

Tresham:—" Speak Latin, I pray you, for ye can do it, if ye list, promptly enough."

Latimer:—" I cannot speak Latin so long and so largely[2]. Mr[3] Prolocutor hath given me leave to speak English. And as for the words of Hilary, I think they matter not so much for you. But he that shall answer the doctors, had not need to be in my case, but should have them in a readiness, and know their purpose. *Melancthon's judgment of the old doctors.* Melancthon saith, " If the doctors had foreseen that they should have been so taken in this controversy, they would have written more plainly[4]."

Argument. *Smith:*—" I will reduce the words of Hilary into the form of a syllogism.

Da-[5]   'Such as is the unity of our flesh with Christ's flesh, such, yea greater, is the unity of Christ with the Father.

ti-[5]   'But the unity of Christ's flesh with ours is true and substantial.

si[5].   'Ergo, The unity of Christ with the Father is true and substantial.'"

[1 Propriety is a sacrament of unity perfectly by the sacrament, 1563.]
[2 large, 1563.]   [3 my good master, 1563.]   [4 plainer, 1563.]
[5 Not in 1563. See Ridley's Works, p. 197, note 1. Park. Soc. Ed.]

Latimer :—" I understand you not."

Seaton :—" I know your learning well enough, and how subtle ye be: I will use a few words with you, and that out of Cyprian, *De cœna Domini:* 'The old Testament doth forbid the drinking of blood: the new Testament doth command the drinking and tasting of blood[6].' But where doth it command the drinking of blood?" <small>Dr Seaton reasoneth against Mr Latimer out of Cyprian.</small>

Latimer :—" In these words, *Bibite ex hoc omnes;* i.e. 'Drink ye all of this.'"

Seaton :—" Then we taste true blood."

Latimer :—" We do taste true blood, but spiritually; and this is enough."

Seaton :—" Nay, the old and new Testament in this do differ[7]: for the one doth command, and the other doth forbid, to drink blood."

Latimer :—" It is true as touching the matter; but not as touching the manner of the thing."

Seaton :—" Then there is no difference between the drinking of blood in the new Testament, and that of the old: for they also drank spiritually."

Latimer :—" And we drink spiritually also; but a more precious blood."

Weston :—" Augustine[8], upon the 45th Psalm, saith: 'Drink boldly the blood which ye have poured out.' Ergo, it is blood."

Latimer :—" I never denied it, nor ever[9] will I go from it, but that we drink the very blood of Christ indeed, but spiritually; for the same St Augustine[10] saith, *Crede, et manducasti,* 'Believe, and thou hast eaten.'"

Weston:—"Nay, *Credere non est bibere nec edere;* 'To believe is not to drink or eat.' You will not say, 'I pledge you,' when I say, 'I believe in God.' Is not *manducare,* 'to eat,' in your learning, put for *credere,* 'to believe?'"

[6 Lex quippe esum sanguinis prohibet, evangelium præcipit ut bibatur. But the treatise is spurious.]

[7 By that reason the old and new Testament should not differ, but should be contrary one from the other, which cannot be true in natural or moral precepts. Foxe.]

[8 Opera, Tom. IV. prim. par. col. 300. Antwerp, 1700. Edit. Bened.]   [9 never will go, 1563.]

[10 In Evang. Johan. Tract. xxv. Opera, Tom. III. col. 354. Antwerp, 1700.]

Latimer:—" Yes, sir[1]."

Weston:—" I remember my Lord Chancellor[2] demanded master Hooper of these questions, Whether *edere*[3], 'to eat,' were *credere*, 'to believe;' and *altare*, 'an altar,' were Christ, in all the scripture, &c.: and he answered, 'Yea.' Then said my Lord Chancellor, 'Why then, *Habemus altare de quo non licet edere*[4]; i.e. We have an altar of which it is not lawful to eat, is as much to say, as *Habemus Christum, in quo non licet credere*; i.e. We have a Christ, in whom we may not believe.'"

Tresham:—" 'Believe, and thou hast eaten,' is spoken of the spiritual eating."

Latimer:—" It is true, I do allow your saying; I take it so also."

Weston:—" We are commanded to drink blood in the new law. Ergo, it is very blood."

Latimer:—" We drink blood, so as appertaineth to us to drink to our comfort, in sacramental wine. We drink blood sacramentally: he gave us his blood to drink spiritually: he went about to shew, that as certain as we drink wine, so certainly we drink his blood spiritually."

Weston:—" Do not you seem to be a papist, which do bring in new words, not found in scripture? Where find you that *sacramentaliter*, 'sacramentally,' in God's book?"

[1 The edition of 1684, and other editions of Foxe, erroneously read as follows:

Weston. "Nay, *credere non est bibere nec edere*, 'to believe is not to drink or eat.' You will not say 'I pledge you,' when I say, 'I believe in God'."

Latimer. "Is not *manducare*, 'to eat,' in your learning, put for *credere*, 'to believe'?"

Weston. "I remember, my lord chancellor, &c."

The reading given in the text is that of the edition of 1563, and of the Harleian MS. 422, Art. 16.]

[2 Stephen Gardiner, Bishop of Winchester.]

[3 *edere* in some places is taken for *credere*; but that in all places it is so taken, it followeth not. Foxe.]

[4 This place of the Hebrews alludeth to the old sacrifice of the Jews, who, in the feast of the propitiation, the tenth day, used to carry the flesh of the sacrifice out of the tents to be burnt upon the altar without, because none of them which served in the tabernacle should eat thereof: only the blood was carried by the high priest into the holy place. Foxe.]

Latimer:—" It is necessarily gathered upon scripture."
[I was in a thing, and have forgotten it[5].]

Weston:—" The old Testament doth forbid the tasting of blood, but the new doth command it."

Latimer:—" It is true, not as touching the thing, but as touching the manner thereof."

Weston:—" Hear, ye people, this is the argument:—

" That which was forbidden in the old Testament, is commanded in the new.

" To drink blood was forbidden in the old Testament, and commanded in the new.

" *Ergo*, it is very blood that we drink in the new[6]."

Latimer:—" It is commanded spiritually to be drunk. I grant it is blood drunk in the new Testament, but we receive it spiritually."

Pie:—" It was not forbidden spiritually in the old law."

Latimer:—" The substance of blood is drunk; but not in one manner."

Pie:—" It doth not require the same manner of drinking."

Latimer:—" It is the same thing, not the same manner. I have no more to say."

☞ Here Weston cited the place of Chrysostom, of Judas's treason: *O Judæ dementia! Ille cum Judæis triginta denariis paciscebatur, ut Christum venderet, et Christus ei sanguinem, quem vendidit, offerebat;* that is, " O the madness of Judas! He made bargain with the Jews for thirty pence to sell Christ, and Christ offered him his blood, which he sold[7]."

[5 Supplied from the edition 1563, and Harl. MS.]

[6 ¶ *This argument, because the major thereof is not universal, is not formal, and may well be retorted against* Weston, *thus:*
Ce-   "No natural or moral thing, forbidden materially in the old Testament, is commanded in the new.
la-   "To drink man's natural blood is forbidden materially in the old Testament.
rent. "*Ergo*, To drink man's natural blood materially is not commanded in the new."]

[7 Ὦ τῆς τοῦ Χριστοῦ φιλανθρωπίας, ὦ τῆς τοῦ Ἰούδα παραπληξίας, ὦ τῆς μανίας· ὁ μὲν γὰρ ἐπώλησεν αὐτὸν τριάκοντα δηναρίων· ὁ Χριστὸς δὲ

Latimer :—" I grant he offered Judas his blood, which he sold, but in a sacrament."

Weston :—" Because ye can defend your doctors no better, ye shall see how worshipful men ye hang upon; and one that hath been of your mind shall dispute with you. M. Cartwright, I pray you, dispute."

Cartwright :—" Reverend father, because it is given me in commandment to dispute with you, I will do it gladly. But first understand, ere we go any further, that I was in the same error that you are in; but I am sorry for it, and do confess myself to have erred. I acknowledge mine offence, and wish and desire God that you also may repent with me."

Latimer :—" Will you give me leave to tell what hath caused Mr Doctor to recant here[1]? It is *pœna legis*, the pain of the law, which hath brought you back[2], and converted you and many more: the which letteth many to confess God. And this is a great argument, there are few here can dissolve it."

Cartwright :—" This is not my case: but I will make you this short argument, by which I was converted[3] from mine errors:—

" If the true body of Christ be not really in the sacrament, all the whole church hath erred from the apostles' time:

" But Christ would not suffer his church to err:

" Ergo, it is the true body of Christ."

Latimer :—" The popish church hath erred, and doth err. I think, for the space of six or seven hundred years there was no mention made of any eating but spiritually: for before these five hundred years, the church did ever confess a spiritual manducation. But the Romish church begat the error of transubstantiation. My lord of Canterbury's book handleth that very well, and by him I could answer you if I had him[4]."

καὶ μετὰ τοῦτο οὐ παρῃτήσατο αὐτὸ τὸ αἷμα τὸ πραθὲν δοῦναι εἰς ἄφεσιν ἁμαρτιῶν τῷ πεπρακότι, εἴγε ἠθέλησε. Oper. Tom. II. p. 383. Paris. 1718. Edit. Bened.]

[1 persuaded Mr doctor to recant here, 1563.]

[2 brought you and converted you back, 1563.]

[3 See Dr Wordsworth's note, Eccles. Biogr. II. p. 600, 3rd Edit.]

[4 See Cranmer, Answer to Gardiner, pp. 91, et seq. Park. Soc Edit.]

Cartwright:—" Linus and all the rest do confess the body of Christ to be in the sacrament: and St Augustine also, upon the 98th psalm[5], upon this place, *Adorate scabellum pedum, &c.*, granteth it is to be worshipped."

Latimer:—"[I do not say that the doctors did err[6].] We do worship Christ in the heavens, and we do worship him in the sacrament; but the massing worship is not to be used."

Smith:—" Do you think that Cyril was of the ancient church?"

Latimer:—" I do think so."

Smith:—" He saith, 'That Christ dwelleth in us corporally.' These be Cyril's[7] words of the mystical benediction." Cyril. in Joh. Lib. x. c. 13.

Latimer:—" That 'corporally' hath another understanding than you do grossly take it."

¶ Cyril saith, that Christ dwelleth corporally in us, but he saith not that Christ dwelleth corporally in the bread. Which dwelling of Christ in us is, as our dwelling is also in Christ, not local or corporal, but spiritual and heavenly. " Corporally," therefore, is to be taken here in the same sense as St Paul saith, the fulness of divinity to dwell in Christ corporally; that is, not lightly nor accidentally, but perfectly and substantially, with all his virtue and power, &c., and so dwelleth corporally in us also.

[Here Smith repeateth these words of Cyril: *per communionem corporis Christi habitat in nobis Christus corporaliter;* that is, " by the communicating of the body of Christ Christ dwelleth in us corporally."]

[[5] Invenio quomodo sine impietate adoretur terra, sine impietate adoretur scabellum pedum ejus. Suscepit enim de terra terram, quia caro de terra est, et de carne Mariæ carnem accepit. Et quia in ipsa carne hic ambulavit, et ipsam carnem nobis manducandam ad salutem dedit; nemo autem illam carnem manducat, nisi prius adoraverit. Oper. Tom. iv. col. 799. Antverp. 1700, Edit. Bened. It is hardly necessary to observe, that no writings of Linus are extant.]

[[6] Supplied from 1563, and Harl. MS.]

[[7] ἆρ' οὐχὶ καὶ σωματικῶς ἐνοικίζουσα τὸν Χριστὸν τῇ μεθέξει καὶ κοινωνίᾳ τῆς ἁγίας αὐτοῦ σαρκός; Cyril. Alexandr. Oper. Tom. iv. p. 862, Lutetiæ, 1638. See also Cranmer, *De præsentia Christi*, &c. p. 71, Park. Soc. Edit. where the bearing of this citation is explained.]

Latimer:—" The solution of this is in my lord of Canterbury's book."

Smith:—" Cyril was no papist, and yet these be his words : ' Christ dwelleth in us corporally :' but you say, he dwelleth in us spiritually."

Latimer:—" I say, both ; that he dwelleth in us both corporally and spiritually, according to his meaning : spiritually by faith, and corporally by taking our flesh upon him. For I remember I have read this in my lord of Canterbury's book[1]."

<small>The immodest behaviour of this Jack Scorner is to be noted.</small>

Weston:—" Because[2] your learning is let out to farm, and shut up in my lord of Canterbury's book, I will recite unto you a place of St Ambrose[3], *De apparatione ad missam,* where he saith : *Videmus principem Sacerdotem ad nos venientem et offerentem sanguinem,* &c. that is, ' We see the chief priest coming unto us, and offering blood,' &c. Likewise both Augustine on Psalm xxxviii[4], and Chrysostom, Concerning the incomprehensible nature of God[5], say, *Non solum homines,* &c."

<small>Chrysos. de incompreh. Dei natura.</small>

Latimer:—" I am not ashamed to acknowledge mine ignorance ; and these testimonies are more than I can bear away."

Weston:—" Then you must leave some behind you, for lack of carriage."

<small>Chrysostom full of figurative speeches and emphatical locutions.</small>

Latimer:—" But for Chrysostom, he hath many figurative speeches and emphatical locutions in many places ; as in that which you have now recited : but he saith not, ' For the quick and the dead ;' he taketh the celebration for the sacrifice."

Weston:—" You shall hear Chrysostom[6] again, upon

[[1] Cranmer, *De præsentia Christi,* &c. pp. 71, 72, and Answer to Gardiner, pp. 54, 55, 93, et seq. Park. Soc. Edit.]

[[2] For because, 1563.]

[[3] The spurious tract, *Precationes ad missam præparantes,* seems to be here intended.]

[[4] Probably for Psal. xxxiii. Ferebatur Christus, &c., that being the passage usually cited by Romanists. August. Oper. Tom. IV. col. 160. Antverp. 1700, Edit. Bened.]

[[5] οὐκ ἄνθρωποι μόνοι βοῶσι τὴν φρικωδεστάτην ἐκείνην βοὴν, ἀλλὰ καὶ ἄγγελοι προσπίπτουσι τῷ δεσπότῃ, καὶ ἀρχάγγελοι δέονται· κ. τ. λ. Chrysos. Oper. Tom. I. p. 470, Paris. 1718. Edit. Bened.]

[[6] τί λέγεις; ἐν χερσὶν ἡ θυσία, καὶ πάντα πρόσκειται ηὐτρεπισμένα. Oper. Tom. IX. p. 176. Paris. 1731. Edit. Bened.]

Acts ix., *Quid dicis? Hostia in manibus sacerdotis*, &c. : He doth not call it a cup of wine."

Latimer :—" Ye have mine answer there with you in a paper : and yet he calleth it not *propitiatorium sacrificium*, that is, a propitiatory sacrifice."

Weston :—" You shall hear it to be so; and I bring another place of Chrysostom out of the same treatise[7], *Non temere ab apostolis est institutum*, &c."

Latimer :—" He is too precious a thing for us to offer; he offereth himself."

Weston :—" Here, in another place of Chrysostom to the people of Antioch, Hom. 69, and also to the Philippians[8], he saith, 'there should be a memory and sacrifice for the dead.'"

Latimer :—" I do say, that the holy communion beareth the name of a sacrifice, because it is a sacrifice memorative."

Weston :—" How say you to the sacrifice for the dead?"

Latimer :—" I say it needeth not, or it booteth not."

Weston :—" Augustine, in his Enchiridion[9], the 110th chapter, saith : *Non est negandum defunctorum animos pietate suorum viventium relevari, quum pro illis sacrificium Mediatoris offertur;* this is, 'We must not deny that the souls of the dead are relieved by the devotion of their friends which are living, when the sacrifice of the Mediator is offered for them.' Where he proveth the verity of Christ's body, and praying for the dead. And it is said, that the same Augustine said mass for his mother."

Latimer :—" But that mass was not like yours; which thing doth manifestly appear in his writings, which are against it in every place. And Augustine is a reasonable man; he requireth to be believed no farther than he bringeth scripture for his proof, and agreeth with God's word.

Weston :—" In the same place he proveth a propitiatory sacrifice, and that upon an altar, and no oyster-board."

Latimer :—" It is the Lord's table and no oyster-board."

[7 A mistake. The passage is that next given from the Homily on the Epistle to the Philippians.]

[8 In Epist. ad Philip. Hom. 3. sub fin. οὐκ εἰκῆ ταῦτα ἐνομοθετήθη ὑπὸ τῶν ἀποστόλων, τὸ ἐπὶ τῶν φρικτῶν μυστηρίων μνήμην γίνεσθαι τῶν ἀπελθόντων. ἴσασιν αὐτοῖς πολὺ κέρδος γενόμενον, πολλὴν τὴν ὠφέλειαν. Chrys. Oper. Tom. XI. p. 217. Paris. 1734. Edit. Bened.]

[9 Oper. Tom. VI. col. 174. Antverp. 1701. Edit. Bened.]

It may be called an altar, and so the doctors call it in many places; but there is no propitiatory sacrifice, but only Christ. The doctors might be deceived in some points, though not in all things. I believe them when they say well."

Doctores legendi sunt cum venia.

Cole:—" Is it not a shame for an old man to lie? You say, you are of the old fathers' faith, where they say well; and yet ye are not."

Latimer:—" I am of their faith when they say well. I refer myself to my lord of Canterbury's[1] book wholly herein."

Smith:—" Then are you not of Chrysostom's faith, nor of St Augustine's faith?"

Latimer:—" I have said, when they say well, and bring scripture for them, I am of their faith; and further Augustine requireth not to be believed."

Weston:—" Origen, Homily thirteen, upon Leviticus."

Latimer:—" I have but one word to say: *panis sacramentalis*, the sacramental bread, is called a propitiation, because it is a sacrament of the propitiation. What is your vocation?"

Weston:—" My vocation is, at this time, to dispute; otherwise I am a priest, and my vocation is to offer[2]."

Latimer:—" Where[3] have you that authority given you to offer?"

"Facere" for "sacrificare" with Dr Weston.

Weston:—" *Hoc facite*, 'Do this;' for *facite*, in that place, is taken for *offerte*, that is, ' offer you.'"

Latimer:—" Is *facere* nothing but *sacrificare*, ' to sacrifice?' Why, then, no man must receive the sacrament but priests only: for there may none other offer but priests. Ergo, there may none receive but priests."

Weston:—" Your argument is to be denied."

Latimer:—" Did Christ then offer himself at his supper?"

Pie:—" Yea, he offered himself for the whole world."

If Christ offered himself at the supper, and the next day upon the cross, then was Christ twice offered.

Latimer:—" Then if this word *facite*, ' do ye,' signify *sacrificate*, ' sacrifice ye,' it followeth, as I said, that none but priests only ought to receive the sacrament, to whom

[1 See Cranmer, *De præsentia Christi*, &c. pp. 96, 97, and Answer to Gardiner, pp. 352, et seq. Park. Soc. Edit.]

[2 otherwise . . . . . to offer: not in 1563, nor Harl. MS.]

[3 Nay: where are you called to offer? 1563; Harl. MS.]

it is only lawful to sacrifice: and where find you that, I pray you?"

Weston:—" Forty years ago whither could you have gone to have found your doctrine?"

Latimer:—" The more cause we have to thank God that hath now sent the light into the world."

Weston:—" The light? Nay, light and lewd preachers: for you could not tell what you might have. Ye altered and changed so often your communions and altars[4], and all for this one end, to spoil and rob the church." *Weston's railing.*

Latimer:—" These things pertain nothing to me. I must not answer for other men's deeds, but only for mine own."

Weston:—" Well, master Latimer, this is our intent, to will you well, and to exhort you to come to yourself, and remember that without Noe's ark there is no health. Remember what they have been that were the beginners of your doctrine; none but a few flying[5] apostates, running out of Germany for fear of the fagot. Remember what they have been, which have set forth the[6] same in this realm. A sort of fling-brains[7] and light heads, which were never constant in any one thing; as it was to be seen in the turning of the table, where, like a sort of apes, they could not tell which way to turn their tails, looking one day west, and another day east, one that way and another this way. They will be like, they say, to the apostles, they will have no churches. A hovel is good enough for them. They come to the communion with no reverence. They get them a tankard, and one saith, I drink, and I am thankful. The more joy of thee, saith another. And in them was it true that Hilary saith, *Annuas et menstruas de Deo fides facimus*[8]; that is, 'We make every year and every month a faith.' A runagate Scot[9] did take away *Dr Weston's apes turn tails.*

[4 your altars, 1563.]   [5 fletyng, 1563.]
[6 this, 1563.]   [7 flying-brains.]
[8 atque ... decernimus. Ad Constant. ii. 5: Opera, col. 1228. Paris. 1693. Edit. Bened.]
[9 The person here alluded to is with reason supposed to have been Alexander Aless, a native of Edinburgh, and who was for some time an exile in Germany on account of his adherence to the doctrines of the reformation. He was employed to translate the first liturgy of king Edward VI. into Latin. See Wordsworth, Eccles. Biogr. Vol. V. pp. 247, note 2; 604, note 3, 3rd edit.]

the adoration or worshipping of Christ in the sacrament; by whose procurement that heresy was put into the last Communion Book; so much prevailed that one man's authority at that time. You never agreed with the Tigurines, or Germans, or with the church, or with yourself. Your stubbornness cometh of a vain glory, which is to no purpose; for it will do you no good when a fagot is in your beard. And we see all by your own confession, how little cause you have to be stubborn, for your learning is in feoffer's hold. The queen's grace is merciful, if ye will turn."

Latimer :—" You shall have no hope in me to turn. I pray for the queen daily, even from the bottom of my heart, that she may turn from this religion."

Weston :—" Here you all see the weakness of heresy against the truth: he denieth all truth, and all the old fathers."

MASTER LATIMER APPEARETH BEFORE THE COMMISSIONERS, [Sept. 30, 1555.]

[Foxe, Acts and Mon. pp. 1365, et seq. Edit. 1563. Vol. III. pp. 421, et seq. Edit. 1684.]

Now, after master Ridley was committed to the mayor[1], then the bishop of Lincoln commanded the bailiffs to bring in the other prisoner, who, eftsoons as he was placed, said to the lords:

Latimer :—" My lords, if I appear again, I pray you not to send for me until you be[2] ready; for I am an old man, and it is great hurt to mine old age to tarry so long gazing upon the cold walls."

Then the bishop of Lincoln[3] :—" Master Latimer, I am sorry you are brought[4] so soon, although it is the bailiff's fault, and not mine; but it shall be amended."

[1 See Ridley's Works, p. 276. Park. Soc. Edit.]
[2 are, 1563.] [3 Lincoln said, 1563.]
[4 were, 1563.]

Then master Latimer bowed his knee down to the ground, holding his hat in his hand, having a kerchief on his head, and upon it a night-cap or two, and a great cap (such as townsmen use, with two broad flaps to button under the chin), wearing an old thread-bare Bristowe frieze-gown girded to his body with a penny leather girdle, at the which hanged by a long string of leather his Testament, and his spectacles without case, depending about his neck upon his breast. After this the bishop of Lincoln began on this manner: *[The order of Latimer's apparel.]*

Lincoln:—" Master Latimer, you shall understand, that I and my lords here have a commission from my lord cardinal Pole's grace, *legate a latere* to this realm of England from our most reverend father in God, the pope's holiness, to examine you upon certain opinions and assertions of yours, which you, as well here openly in disputations in the year of our Lord 1554, as at sundry and at divers other times did affirm, maintain, and obstinately defend. In the which commission be specially two points: the one which we must desire you is, that if you shall now recant, revoke, and disannul these your errors, and, together with all this realm, yea, all the world, confess the truth, we, upon due repentance of your part, shall receive you, reconcile you, acknowledge you no longer a strayed sheep, but adjoin you again to the unity of Christ's church, from the which you in the time of schism fell. So that it is no new place to the which I exhort you; I desire you but to return thither from whence you went. Consider, master Latimer, that without the unity of the church is no salvation, and in the church can be no errors[5]. Therefore what should stay you to confess that which all the realm confesseth, to forsake that which the king and queen their majesties have renounced, and all the realm recanted? It was a common error, and it is now of all confessed: it shall be no more shame to you, than it was to us all. Consider, master Latimer, that within these twenty years this realm also, with all the world, confessed one church, acknowledged in Christ's church an head; and by what means and for what occasion it cut off itself from the rest of Christianity, and renounced that which in all times and ages was *[The oration of Lincoln to Latimer.]*

[5 error, 1563.]

confessed, it is well known, and might be now declared upon what good foundation the see of Rome was forsaken, save that we must spare them that are dead, to whom the rehearsal would be opprobrious: it is no usurped power, as it hath been termed, but founded upon Peter by Christ, a sure foundation, a perfect builder, as by divers places, as well of the ancient fathers, as the express word of God, may be proved."

<small>The pope's authority.</small>

With that master Latimer, which before leaned his head to his hand, began somewhat to remove his cap and kerchief from his ears. The bishop[1] proceeded, saying:

"For Christ spake expressly to Peter, saying, *Pasce oves meas, et rege oves meas:* the which word doth[2] not only declare a certain ruling of Christ's flock, but includeth also a certain pre-eminence and government; and therefore is the king called *rex a regendo;* so that in saying *rege*, Christ declared a power which he gave to Peter, which jurisdiction and power Peter by hand delivered to Clement; and so in all ages hath it remained in the see of Rome. This if you shall confess with us, and acknowledge with all the realm your errors and false assertions, then shall you do that which we most desire, then shall we rest upon the first part of our commission; then shall we receive you, acknowledge you one of the church, and, according to the authority given unto us, minister unto you, upon due repentance, the benefit of absolution; to the which the king and queen their majesties were not ashamed to submit themselves, although they of themselves were unspotted, and therefore needed no reconciliation; yet lest the putrefaction and rottenness of all the body might be noisome, and do damage to the head also, they (as I said) most humbly submitted themselves to my lord cardinal his grace, by him, as legate to the pope's holiness, to be partakers of the reconciliation. But if you shall stubbornly persevere in your blindness; if you will not acknowledge your errors; if you, as you now stand[3] alone, will be singular in your opinions; if by schism and heresy you will divide yourself from your church, then must we proceed to the second part of the commission, which we would be loth to do;

[1 my Lord, 1563.] [2 did, 1563.]
[3 you stand now, 1563.]

that is, not to condemn you, for that we cannot do, (that the temporal sword of the realm, and not we[4], will do,) but to separate you from us[5], acknowledge you to be none of us; to renounce you as no member of the church; to declare that you are *filius perditionis,* a lost child; and, as you are a rotten member of the church, so to cut you off from the church, and so to commit you to the temporal judges, permitting them to proceed against you according to the tenor of their laws. Therefore, master Latimer, for God's love consider your estate: remember you are a learned man; you have taken degrees in the school, borne the office of a bishop; remember you are an old man; spare your body, accelerate not your death; and specially remember your soul's health, quiet of your conscience. Consider, that if you should die in this state, you shall be a stinking sacrifice to God; for it is the cause that maketh the martyr, and not the death: consider, that if you die in this state, you die without grace; for without the church can be no salvation. Let not vain-glory have the upper hand; humiliate yourself; captivate your understanding; subdue your reason; submit yourself to the determination of the church; do not force us to do all that we may do; let us rest in that part which we most heartily desire; and I for my part (then the bishop put off his cap) again with all my heart exhort you." *Reasons to persuade the flesh, but not to satisfy conscience.*

After the bishop had somewhat paused, then master Latimer lifted up his head (for before he leaned on his elbow), and asked whether his lordship had said; and the bishop answered, "Yea."

Latimer:—"Then will your lordship give me leave to speak a word or two?"

Lincoln:—"Yea, master Latimer, so that you use a modest kind of talk, without railing or taunts."

Latimer:—"I beseech your lordship, license me to sit down."

Lincoln:—"At your pleasure, master Latimer, take as much ease as you will."

Latimer:—"Your lordship gently exhorted me in many *His answer to Lincoln.*

[4 "Qui tradiderunt me tibi majus peccatum habent," saith Christ. Foxe.]   [5 us, to acknowledge.]

words to come to the unity of the church. I confess, my lord, a catholic church, spread throughout all the world, in the which no man may err, without the which unity of the church no man can be saved: but I know perfectly by God's word, that this church is in all the world, and hath not his foundation in Rome only, as you say; and methought your lordship brought a place out of the scriptures to confirm the same, that there was a jurisdiction given to Peter, in that Christ bade him *regere*, govern his people[1]. Indeed, my lord, St Peter did well and truly his office, in that he was bid *regere*: but, since, the bishops of Rome have taken a new kind of *regere*. Indeed they ought[2] *regere*, but how, my lord? Not as they will themselves: but this *regere* must be hedged in and ditched[3] in. They must *regere*, but *secundum verbum Dei*; they must rule, but according to the word of God. But the bishops of Rome have turned *regere secundum verbum Dei* into *regere secundum voluntatem suam*; they have turned the rule according to the word of God into the rule according to their own pleasures, and as it pleaseth[4] them best: as there is a book set forth, which hath divers points in it, and, amongst others, this point is one, which your lordship went about to prove by this word *regere*; and the argument which he bringeth forth for the proof of that matter is taken out of Deuteronomy, where it is said, 'If there ariseth[5] any controversy among the people, the priests *Levitici generis*, of the order of Levi[6], shall decide the matter *secundum legem Dei*, according to the law of God, so it must be taken.' Deut. xxi. This book, perceiving this authority to be given to the priests of the old law, taketh occasion to prove the same to be given to the bishops and others the clergy of the new law: but in proving this matter, whereas it was said there, as the priests of the order of Levi[6] should determine the matter 'according to God's law,' that 'according to God's law' is left out, and only is recited, as the priests of the order of Levi[6] shall decide the matter, so it ought to be taken of the people; a large autho-

[1 Argument: Christ bade Peter *regere*, govern his people: Ergo, the pope must play the *rex*, to reign over kings and emperors. Foxe.]
[2 to *regere*, 1563.]   [3 diked, 1563.]
[4 pleasures, as it shall please, 1563.]   [5 riseth, 1563.]
[6 Leviticus, 1563.]

rity, I assure[7] you. What gelding of scripture is this! What clipping of God's coin!" (With the which terms the audience smiled.) "This is much like the *regere* which your lordship talked of. Nay, nay, my lords, we may not give such authority to the clergy, to rule all things as they will. Let them keep themselves within their commission. Now I trust, my lord, I do not rail yet."

Clipping of God's scriptures by the catholics.

Lincoln :—" No, master Latimer, your talk is more like taunts than railing : but in that I have not read the book which you blame so much, nor know not of any such, I can say nothing therein."

Latimer :—" Yes, my lord, the book is open to be read, and is entituled to one which is bishop of Gloucester[8], whom I never knew, neither did at any time see him to my knowledge."

With that the people laughed, because the bishop of Gloucester sat there in commission.

Then the bishop of Gloucester stood up, and said it was his book.

Latimer :—" Was it yours, my lord? Indeed I knew not your lordship, neither ever did I see you before, neither yet see you now through the brightness of the sun shining betwixt you and me."

Then the audience laughed again; and master Latimer spake unto them, saying :—

Latimer :—" Why, my masters, this is no laughing matter. I answer upon life and death. *Væ vobis qui ridetis nunc, quoniam flebitis!*"

The bishop of Lincoln commanded silence, and then said :—

Lincoln :—" Master Latimer, if you had kept yourself within your bounds, if you had not used such scoffs and taunts, this had not been done."

[7 ensure, 1563.]
[8 This was a sermon preached at Paul's Cross, on the 12th Nov. 1553, by Dr Brookes, bishop of Gloucester. That passage of the sermon to which Latimer alludes, is given at length by Dr Wordsworth, Eccl. Biogr. Vol. II. pp. 643, et seq.]

After this the bishop of Gloucester said, in excusing of his book, "Master Latimer, hereby every man may see what learning you have." Then master Latimer interrupted him, saying :—

Latimer :—" Lo, you look¹ for learning at my hands, which have gone so long to the school of oblivion, making the bare walls my library; keeping me so long in prison, without book, or pen and ink; and now you let me loose to come and answer to articles. You deal with me as though two were appointed to fight for life and death, and over night the one, through friends and favour, is cherished, and hath good counsel given him how to encounter with his enemy: the other, for envy or lack of friends, all the whole night is set in the stocks. In the morning, when they shall meet, the one is in strength and lusty, the other is stark of his limbs, and almost dead for feebleness. Think you, that to run through this man with a spear is not a goodly victory?"

But the bishop of Gloucester, interrupting his answer, proceeded, saying :

Gloucester :—" I went not about to recite any place of scripture in that place of my book; for then, if I had not recited it faithfully, you might have had just occasion of reprehension: but I only in that place formed an argument *a majore*, in this sense; that if in the old law the priests had power to decide matters of controversy, much more then ought the authority to be given to the clergy in the new law: and I pray you in this point what availeth their² rehearsal, *secundum legem Dei ?*"

Latimer :—" Yes, my lord, very much. For I acknowledge authority to be given to the spiritualty to decide matter³ of religion; and, as my lord said even now, *regere*⁴: but they must do it *secundum verbum Dei*, and not *secundum voluntatem suam*; according to the word and law of God, and not after their own will, after their own imaginations and fantasies."

The bishop of Gloucester would have spoken more, saving that the bishop of Lincoln said that they came not to dispute

[¹ he looketh, 1563.]   [² the, 1563.]
[³ matters, 1563.]   [⁴ to *regere*, 1563.]

with master Latimer, but to take his determinate answers to their articles; and so began to propose the same articles which were proposed to master Ridley. But master Latimer interrupted him, speaking to the bishop of Gloucester:

Latimer:—" Well, my lord, I could wish more faithful dealing with God's word, and not to leave out a part[5], and to snatch a part here, and another there, but to rehearse the whole faithfully."

But the bishop of Lincoln, not attending to this saying of master Latimer, proceeded in the rehearsing of the articles in form and sense as I declared before in the examination of the articles proposed to master Ridley, and required master Latimer's answer to the first. Then master Latimer, making his protestation, that notwithstanding these his answers, it should not be taken that thereby he would acknowledge any authority of the bishop of Rome, saying that he was the king and queen their majesties' subject, and not the pope's, neither could serve two masters at one time, except he should first renounce one of them[6]; required the notaries so to take his protestation, that whatsoever he should say or do, it should not be taken as though he did thereby agree to any authority that came from the bishop of Rome.

The protestation of Latimer.

The bishop of Lincoln said, that his protestation should be so taken; but he required him to answer briefly, affirmatively or negatively, to the first article[7], and so recited the same again: and master Latimer answered as followeth:

Latimer:—" I do not deny, my lord, that in the sacrament, by spirit and grace, is the very body and blood of Christ; because that every man, by receiving bodily that bread and wine, spiritually receiveth the body and blood of Christ, and is made partaker thereby of the merits of Christ's passion. But I deny that the body and blood of Christ is in such sort in the sacrament, as you would have it."

First article. Latimer against the gross and carnal being of Christ in the sacrament.

Lincoln:—" Then, master Latimer, you answer affirmatively."

[5 a part, and to snatch, 1563.]
[6 and so he required the notaries to, 1563.]
[7 "That the true and natural body of Christ, after the consecration of the priest, is not really present in the sacrament of the altar." See Ridley's Works, p. 271. Park. Soc. Ed.]

Latimer:—" Yea, if you mean of that gross and carnal being, which you do take."

The notaries took his answer to be affirmatively.

Lincoln:—" What say you, master Latimer, to the second article?" and recited the same[1].

Latimer:—" There is, my lord, a change in the bread and wine, and such a change as no power[2] but the omnipotency of God can make, in that that which before was bread should now have the[3] dignity to exhibit Christ's body; and yet the bread is still bread, and the wine still wine. For the change is not in the nature, but in the dignity; because now that which was common bread hath the dignity to exhibit Christ's body: for whereas it was common bread, it is now no more common bread, neither ought it to be so taken, but as holy bread, sanctified by God's word."

With that the bishop of Lincoln smiled, saying:—

Lincoln:—" Lo, master Latimer, see what stedfastness is in your doctrine! That which you abhorred and despised most[4], you now most establish: for whereas you most railed at holy bread, you now[5] make your communion holy bread."

Latimer:—" Tush, a rush for holy bread. I say the bread in the communion is a holy bread indeed."

But the bishop of Lincoln interrupted him and said:

Lincoln:—" Oh, ye make a difference between holy bread and holy bread." (With that the audience laughed.) " Well, master Latimer, is not this your answer, that the substance of bread and wine remaineth after the words of consecration?"

Latimer:—" Yes, verily, it must needs be so. For Christ himself calleth it bread; St Paul calleth it bread; the doctors confess the same; the nature of a sacrament confirmeth the same: and I call it holy bread, not in that I make no difference betwixt your holy bread and this, but for the holy office

[1 " That in the sacrament of the altar remaineth still the substance of bread and wine."]
[2 man, 1563.]   [3 that, 1563.]
[4 greatest, you now establish most, 1563.]   [5 now you, 1563.]

which it beareth, that is, to be a figure of Christ's body; and not only a bare figure, but effectually to represent the same."

So the notaries penned his answer to be affirmatively.

Lincoln :—" What say you to the third question?" and recited the same [6]. Third article.

Latimer :—" No, no, my lord, Christ made one perfect sacrifice for all the whole world; neither can any man offer him again, neither can the priest offer up Christ again for the sins of man, which he took away by offering himself once for all (as St Paul saith) upon the cross; neither is there any propitiation for our sins, saving his cross only."

So the notaries penned his answer to this article also to be affirmatively.

Lincoln :—" What say you to the fourth, master Latimer?" and recited it [7]. After the recital whereof, when master Latimer answered not [8], the bishop asked him, Whether he heard him, or no? Fourth article.

Latimer :—" Yes; but I do not understand what you mean thereby."

Lincoln :—" Marry, only this, that your assertions were condemned by master Dr Weston as heresies. Is it not so, master Latimer?"

Latimer :—" Yes, I think they were condemned. But how unjustly, he that shall be judge of all knoweth."

So the notaries took his answer to this article also to be affirmatively.

Lincoln :—" What say you, master Latimer, to the fifth article?" And recited it [9]. Fifth article.

[6 " That in the mass is no propitiatory sacrifice for the quick and the dead."]

[7 " That these thy foresaid assertions solemnly have been condemned by the scholastical censure of this school, as heretical and contrary to the catholic faith, by the worshipful master Doctor Weston, prolocutor then of the convocation-house, as also by other learned men of both the universities."]

[8 because master Latimer did not answer, 1563.]

[9 " That all and singular the premises be true, notorious, and famous, and openly known by public fame, as well to them near hand, and also to them in distant places far off."]

Latimer:—"I know not what you mean by these terms. I am no lawyer: I would you would propose the matter plainly."

Lincoln:—"In that we proceed according to the law, we must use their terms also. The meaning only is this, That these your assertions are notorious, evil spoken of, and yet common and recent in the mouths of the people."

Latimer:—"I cannot tell how much, nor what men talk of them. I come not so much among them, in that I have been secluded a long time. What men report of them, I know not, nor care not."

This answer taken, the bishop of Lincoln said:

<small>Latimer assigned to appear the next day again.</small> "Master Latimer, we mean not that these your answers shall be prejudicial to you. To-morrow you shall appear before us again, and then it shall be lawful for you to alter and change what you will. We give you respite till to-morrow, trusting that, after you have pondered well all things against to-morrow, you will not be ashamed to confess the truth."

Latimer:—"Now, my lord, I pray you give me licence in three words to declare the causes why I have refused the authority of the pope."

Lincoln:—"Nay, master Latimer, to-morrow you shall have licence to speak forty words."

Latimer:—"Nay, my lords, I beseech you to do with me now as it shall please your lordships: I pray you let not me be troubled to-morrow again."

Lincoln:—"Yes, master Latimer, you must needs appear again to-morrow."

Latimer:—"Truly, my lord, as for my part I require no respite, for I am at a point; you shall give me respite in vain: therefore I pray you let me not[1] trouble you to-morrow."

Lincoln:—"Yes, for we trust God will work with you against to-morrow. There is no remedy: you must needs appear again to-morrow, at eight of the clock, in St Mary's church."

And forthwith the bishop charged the mayor with master Latimer, and dismissed him, and then brake up their session for that day, about one of the clock at afternoon.

[1 let not me, 1563.]

THE LAST APPEARANCE AND EXAMINATION OF MASTER LATIMER BEFORE THE COMMISSIONERS.
[Oct. 1, 1555.]

[Foxe, Acts and Mon. pp. 1372, et seq. edit. 1563. Vol. III. pp. 426, et seq. edit. 1684. The latter edition is here followed.]

THIS sentence[2] being published by the bishop of Lincoln, master Ridley was committed as a prisoner to the mayor, and immediately master Latimer was sent for: but in the mean season the carpet or cloth, which lay upon the table whereat master Ridley stood, was removed, because (as men reported) master Latimer had never the degree of a doctor, as master Ridley had. But eftsoons as master Latimer appeared, as he did the day before, perceiving no cloth upon the table, he laid his hat, which was an old felt, under his elbows, and immediately spake to the commissioners, saying:

Latimer:—" My lords, I beseech your lordships to set a better order here at your entrance: for I am an old man, and have a very evil back, so that the press of the multitude doth me much harm."

Lincoln:—" I am sorry, master Latimer, for your hurt. At your departure we will see to better order."

With that master Latimer thanked his lordship, making a very low courtesy. After this the bishop of Lincoln began on this manner:

Lincoln:—" Master Latimer, although yesterday, after we had taken your answers to those articles which we proposed, we might have justly proceeded to judgment against you, especially in that you required the same; yet we, having a good hope of your returning, desiring not your destruction, but rather that you would recant, revoke your errors, and turn to the catholic church, deferred further process till this day: and now, according to the appointment, we have called you here before us, to hear whether you are content to revoke your heretical assertions and submit yourself to the

The bishop of Lincoln's words to Latimer.

[2 See Ridley's Works, p. 286. Park. Soc. Edit.]

determination of the church, as we most heartily desire, and I for my part, as I did yesterday, most earnestly do exhort you; or[1] to know whether you persevere still the man that you were, for the which we would be sorry."

<small>Latimer short with the commissioners.</small>
It seemed[2] that the bishop would have further proceeded, saving that master Latimer interrupted him, saying:

Latimer:—"Your lordship often doth repeat[3] the catholic church, as though I should deny the same. No, my lord, I confess there is a catholic church, to the determination of which I will stand; but not the church which you call catholic, which sooner might be termed diabolic. And whereas you join together the Romish and catholic church, stay <small>The catholic church, and the Romish church, be two things.</small> there, I pray you. For it is one[4] thing to say Romish church, and another thing to say catholic church. I must use here, in this mine answer, the counsel of Cyprian[5], who at what time he was ascited before certain bishops that gave him leave to take deliberation and counsel, to try and examine <small>Cyprian's counsel: in truth no deliberation to be taken.</small> his opinion, he answered them thus: 'In sticking and persevering in the truth, there must no counsel nor deliberation be taken.' And again, being demanded of them sitting in judgment, which was most like to be of the church of Christ, whether[6] he who was persecuted, or[6] they who did persecute? 'Christ,' said he, 'hath foreshewed[7], that he that doth follow him must take up his cross and follow him. Christ gave knowledge that the disciples should have persecution and trouble.' How think you then, my lords, is it like[8] that the see of Rome, which hath been a continual persecutor, is rather the church, or that small flock which hath continually been persecuted of it, even to death? Also the flock of Christ hath been but few in comparison to the residue, and ever in subjection:" which he proved, beginning at Noah's time even to the apostles.

[[1] either, 1563.]   [[2] seemeth, 1563.]
[[3] inculke, 1563.]   [[4] another, 1563.]
[[5] The sentiments here quoted belong in the main to Cyprian, but the history is not altogether accurate. It was to the Roman proconsul that he said: In re tam justa nulla est consultatio. See Cypriani Vita, and the treatise De Exhortat. Martyrii, c. 11, pp. 13 and 177, edit. Fell. Oxon. 1682.]
[[6] either, 1563.]   [[7] promised, 1563.]   [[8] most like, 1563.]

Lincoln:—"Your cause and St Cyprian's is not one, but clean contrary: for he suffered persecution for Christ's sake and the gospel; but you are in trouble for your errors and false assertions, contrary to the word of God and the received truth of the church."

Master Latimer, interrupting him, said: "Yes, verily, my cause is as good as St Cyprian's: for his was for the word of God, and so is mine[9]."

But Lincoln goeth forth in his talk: "Also at the beginning and foundation of the church, it could not be but that the apostles should suffer great persecution. Further, before Christ's coming, continually, there were very few which truly served God; but after his coming began the time of grace. Then began the church to increase, and was continually augmented, until it[10] came unto this perfection; and now hath justly that jurisdiction which the unchristian princes before by tyranny did resist. There is a diverse consideration of the estate of the church now in the time of grace, and before Christ's coming. But, master Latimer, although we had instructions given us determinately to take your answer to such articles as we should propose, without any reasoning or disputations, yet we, hoping by talk somewhat to prevail with you, appointed you to appear before us yesterday in the divinity school, a place for disputations. And whereas then, notwithstanding you had licence to say your mind, and were answered to every matter, yet you could not be brought from your errors; we, thinking that from that time ye would with good advisement consider your estate, gave you respite from that time yesterday when we dismissed you, until this time; and now have called you again here in this place, by your answers to learn whether you are the same man[11] you were then or no. Therefore we will propose unto you the same articles which we did then, and require of you a determinate answer, without further reasoning;" and eftsoons recited the first article.

Latimer:—"Always my protestation saved, that by these mine answers it should not be thought that I did condescend and agree to your lordships' authority, in that you are

[9 The cause of the martyrs of the primitive time, and of the latter time, is all one. Foxe.]

[10 until that it, 1563.]   [11 man as you, 1563.]

legaced[1] by authority of the pope, so that thereby I might seem[2] to consent to his jurisdiction—to the first article I answer now, as I did yesterday, that in the sacrament the worthy receiver receiveth the very body of Christ, and drinketh his blood by the Spirit[3] and grace: but, after that corporal being which[4] the Romish church prescribeth, Christ's body and blood is not in the sacrament under the forms of bread and wine."

The very body of Christ received in the sacrament by the Spirit and grace.

The notaries took his answer to be affirmatively. For[5] the second article he referred himself to his answers made before. After this the bishop of Lincoln recited the third article, and required a determinate answer.

The second and third articles.

Latimer:—" Christ made one oblation and sacrifice for the sins of the whole world, and that a perfect sacrifice; neither needeth there to be any other, neither can there be any other, propitiatory [sacrifice[6].]"

The notaries took his answer to be affirmatively. In like manner did he answer to the other articles, not varying from his answers made the day before.

After his answers were penned of the notaries, and the bishop of Lincoln had exhorted him in like sort to recant, as he did master Ridley, and revoke his errors and false assertions, and master Latimer had answered that he neither could nor would[7] deny his Master Christ and his verity, the bishop of Lincoln desired master Latimer to hearken to him: and then master Latimer hearkening for some new matter and other talk, the bishop of Lincoln read his condemnation; after the publication of the which, the said three bishops[8] brake up their sessions, and dismissed the audience. But master Latimer required the bishop to perform his promise in saying the day before, that he should have licence briefly to declare the cause[9], why he refused the pope's authority. But the bishop said that now he could not hear him, neither ought to talk with him.

Latimer will not deny his master, Christ.

His condemnation read.

Papists false in their promises.

[1 legasid, 1563.]
[2 be seemed, 1563.]
[3 by spirit, 1563.]
[4 the which, 1563.]
[5 To, 1563.]
[6 sacrifice, not in 1563.]
[7 ne could ne would, 1563.]
[8 lords, 1563.]
[9 causes, 1563.]

Then master Latimer asked him, whether it were not lawful for him to appeal from this his judgment. And the bishop asked him again, To whom he would appeal? "To the next general council," quoth master Latimer, "which shall be truly called in God's name." With that appellation the bishop was content; but, he said, it would be a long season before such a[10] convocation as he meant would be called.

Then the bishop committed master Latimer to the mayor, saying, "Now he is your prisoner, master Mayor."

Because the press of the people was not yet diminished, each man looking for further process, the bishop of Lincoln commanded avoidance, and willed master Latimer to tarry till the press were diminished, lest he should take hurt at his egression, as he did at his entrance.

[[10] such a true, 1563.]

WHAT MASTER LATIMER, BEING BISHOP OF WORCESTER, TAUGHT ALL THEM OF HIS DIOCESE TO SAY TO THE PEOPLE.

[Foxe, Acts and Mon. p. 1348, edit. 1563. Vol. III. p. 384, edit. 1684.]

In giving Holy Water.

Remember, your promise in Baptism,
Christ, his mercy and blood-shedding,
By whose most holy sprinkling
Of all your sins you have free pardoning.

What to say in giving Holy Bread.

Of Christ's body this is a token,
Which on the cross for our sins was broken.
Wherefore of your sins you must be forsakers,
If of Christ's death ye will be partakers.

LETTERS.

LETTER I[1].

LATIMER *to* Dr GREENE[2].

[Parker MSS. in C.C.C. Camb. Cod. cxix. 15.]

Right worshipful Father,

WHEN I last night arrived at Kimbolton on my way to my native place, I readily ascertained from Mr Thorp, and other persons of good credit, (after we had exchanged mutual greetings and compliments,) that nothing could just now occur more agreeable to Mr Wingfield[3] than that he should succeed to Lovell's[4] place among us, and hold whatever office that

[1 The original of this letter, and of the rest which were written in Latin, will be found in the Appendix.]

[2 In all probability, Dr Thomas Greene, who, at the time this letter was written, was master of Catharine Hall, and vice-chancellor of the University of Cambridge.]

[3 Sir Richard Wingfield, of Kimbolton Castle, in Huntingdonshire, Knight of the Garter, the eleventh son of Sir John Wingfield, of Leatheringham, in Suffolk. This gentleman was employed in many services of importance, both by Henry VII. and Henry VIII. In the 14th Henry VIII. he obtained a grant from the crown of the castle and manor of Kimbolton, and of other possessions forfeited by the duke of Buckingham. He was employed in an embassy to the emperor in Spain, and in that service died at Toledo, July 22, 1525, and was there buried with great solemnity, in the church of the Friars Observants of St John de Pois. In the 38th Vol. of the Baker MSS. there is a copy of a joint letter from Tunstall, bishop of London, and Dr Sampson, which contains an interesting account of Sir Richard's last illness and funeral. The register of the University states that he was elected high-steward of that body in 1524, "on the death of Thomas Lovell." The object of Latimer's letter is obviously to further Sir Richard's election. Blore, Hist. of the Co. of Rutland, I. Part. ii. pp. 68 et seq; Leland, Itinerary, Vol. I. p. 2; Magna Britan. Vol. II. p. 1056.]

[4 Sir Thomas Lovell, it is conjectured, is the person here alluded to. He was the youngest of three brothers, all very eminent knights of the age in which they lived, and the sons of Sir Ralph Lovell of West-Hall, or Beauchamp Well, in the county of Norfolk. Sir Thomas was made chancellor of the Exchequer, when only an esquire, was afterwards elected a Knight of the Garter; then made

person held: not that so small a salary is an object to one
of his high rank, and so signally enriched with abundance of
every thing; but in accordance with the ingenuous nobility of
his mind, he has the greatest possible desire to form an intimate
acquaintance with learned men and those who cultivate
polite literature. And this object is so seriously taken up,
and canvassed for, moreover, in so eager or rather so ardent
a spirit, that since we had nothing but a pledge given beforehand
to the honoured More[1] to plead in excuse, More is already
prevailed upon, and that (it is said) by the mediation of the
King, to give way to Wingfield, and to allow us, without any
dishonour, to comply with Wingfield's wishes. And certain it is
that this personage, by his matchless politeness, renders people
here in all directions friendly to the object he has in view,
and by acts of kindness firmly secures those who have been
won over; in short, he does good to every body. Your
discretion, therefore, will take this matter into consideration.
On you alone, more especially, this whole business, and the
advantage, the credit, the splendour of the university depends.
Thorp, the man of all others whom we most esteem, and who
is always very much attached to you, thinks that nothing
would be more for the advantage of our commonwealth than
the granting of this favour. For, that I may say a word or
two respecting Wingfield, who, I ask, in the present day, is
more in the royal confidence, or would be more willing and
ready to speak for his friends to the king, than this very
Wingfield? Or who among the lay nobility has a greater
regard for literature than he? But I shall, perchance, appear
more meddling than discreet in writing thus boldly to your
lordship. Yet Thorp urges me on,—zeal, a sense of duty, a
regard for our literary commonwealth impel me. Make
allowance for him who errs, but means well.

treasurer of the household and a privy councillor to Henry VII.; and
was an executor of the will of that sovereign, as well as of the will of
lady Margaret, the king's mother, and foundress of the colleges of St
John and Christ, in Cambridge. Under Henry VIII. Sir Thomas
Lovell held several important offices, and was employed on many important
occasions. He died on the 25th of May, 1524. Blore, Hist.
of the county of Rutland, Vol. I. Part ii. pp. 46 et seq.; Blomefield
and Park, in Norfolk, Vol. I. p. 218 et seq.; Nichols, Royal Wills,
p. 366.]

[1 Sir Thomas More.]

Farewell, your worship. I write this late at night, after equinoctial rains, and after being well nigh suffocated and out of my wits with the heat of the sun, the fumes of victuals, and the excessive feasting besides.

Kimbolton, 14 Oct. [1524.]

H. LATIMER.

LETTER II.

The sum of Master LATIMER's *answer to* Dr REDMAN[2].

[Foxe, Acts and Mon. p. 1305, edit. 1563. Vol. III. p. 351. edit. 1684.]

REVEREND master Redman, it is even enough for me, that Christ's sheep hear no man's voice but Christ's: and as for you, you have no voice of Christ against me, whereas, for my part, I have a heart that is ready to hearken to any voice of Christ that you can bring me. Thus fare you well, and trouble me no more from the talking with the Lord my God.

LETTER III.

A Letter of Master LATIMER *written to* King HENRY [VIII.] *for restoring again the free liberty of reading the holy scriptures.*

[Foxe, Acts and Mon. pp. 1344, et seq. edit. 1563; Vol. III. pp. 410, et seq. edit. 1684.]

To the most mighty prince, king of England, Henry the Eighth, grace, mercy, and peace from God the Father, by our

[2 This Dr Redman, "being of no little authority in Cambridge," wrote to Latimer, (probably about 1527,) to dissuade him from his "manner of teaching;" taking occasion, also, to charge Latimer with being under the influence of delusion and self-opinion. The letter in the text is a reply to Dr Redman's communication. Respecting Dr Redman himself, who was the first master of Trinity college, Cambridge, and the intimate friend of Roger Ascham, see Wood, Athen. Oxon. Vol. I. pp. 193 et seq. Edit. Bliss.; Strype, Eccl. Mem. Vol. II. i. pp. 527, &c. Oxf.; Mem. of Cranm. pp. 386 et seq. Oxf.]

Lord Jesus Christ. The holy doctor, St Augustine, in an epistle which he wrote to Casulanus[1], saith, that he which for fear of any power hideth the truth, provoketh the wrath of God to come upon him; for he feareth men more than God. And according to the same, the holy man St John Chrysostom saith, that he is not only[2] a traitor to the truth, which openly for truth teacheth a lie; but he also which doth not freely pronounce and shew the truth that he knoweth. These sentences, most redoubted king, when I read now of late, and marked them earnestly in the inward parts of mine heart, they made me sore afraid, troubled, and vexed me grievously in my conscience; and at the last drave me to this strait, that either I must shew forth such things as I have read and learned in scripture, or else be[3] of that sort that provoke the wrath of God upon them, and be traitors unto the truth: the which thing rather than it should happen, I had rather suffer extreme punishment. For what other thing[4] is it to be a traitor unto the truth, than to be a traitor and a Judas unto Christ, which is the very truth, and cause of all truth? The which saith, that whosoever denieth him before men, he will deny him before his Father in heaven. The which denying ought more to be feared and dreaded, than the loss of all temporal goods, honour, promotion, fame, prison, slander, hurts, banishments, and all manner of torments and cruelties, yea, and death itself, be it never so shameful and painful. But, alas! how little do men regard those sharp sayings of these two holy men, and how little do they fear the terrible judgment of Almighty God! And specially they which boast themselves to be guides and captains unto other, and challenging[5] unto themselves the knowledge of holy scripture, yet will neither shew the truth themselves (as they be bound), neither suffer them that would. So that unto them may be said that which our Saviour Christ said to the Pharisees,

Matt. xxiii. "Wo be unto you, scribes and Pharisees, which shut up the

---

[1 Quisquis metu cujuslibet potestatis veritatem occultat, iram Dei super se provocat, quia magis timet hominem quam Deum. Quoted in Decret. Gratian. Decr. Sec. Pars, Caus. xi. Qu. iii. can. 80, as from the Epist. of Augustine to Casulanus, but the passage is not found in the writings of Augustine.]

[2 alonely, 1563.]   [3 to be of the sort, 1563.]
[4 what thing, 1563.]   [5 challenge, 1563]

kingdom of heaven before men, and neither will you enter in yourselves, neither suffer them that would, to enter in[6]!" And they will, as much as in them lieth, debar not only the word of God, which David calleth "a light to direct" and shew every man how to order his affections and lusts, according to the commandments of God, but also by their subtle wiliness they instruct, move, and provoke in a manner all kings in Christendom, to aid, succour, and help them in this their mischief. And especially in this your realm they have so[7] blinded your liege people and subjects with their laws, customs, ceremonies, and Banbury glosses, and punished them with cursings, excommunications, and other corruptions, (corrections I would say.) And now, at the last, when they see that they cannot prevail against the open truth (which the more it is persecuted, the more it increaseth by their tyranny), they have made it treason to your noble grace to have the scripture in English.

The subtle wiliness and practice of the Pharisees.

Here I beseech your grace to pardon me a while, and patiently to hear me a word or two; yea, though it be so that, as concerning your high majesty and regal power whereunto Almighty God hath called your grace, there is as great difference between you[8] and me, as between God and man: for you be here to me and to all your subjects in God's stead, to defend, aid, and succour us in our right; and so I should tremble and quake to speak to your grace. But again, as concerning that you be a mortal man, in danger of sin, having in you the corrupt nature of Adam, in the which all we be both conceived and born; so have you no less need of the merits of Christ's passion for your salvation, than I and other of your subjects have, which be all members of the mystical body of Christ. And though you be a higher member, yet you must not disdain the lesser[9]. For, as St Paul saith, "Those members that be taken to be most vile[10], and had in least reputation, be as necessary as the other, for the preservation and keeping of the body." This, most gracious king, when I considered, and also your favourable[11] and gentle nature, I was bold to write this rude, homely, and simple letter unto your grace, trusting that you will accept my true and faithful mind even as it is.

Kings stand as much in need of Christ's passion, as any inferior subject.

Eph. ii.
Rom. xii.
1 Cor. ii.
Eph. iv.
1 Cor. xii.

[[6] enter, 1563.]
[[7] sore, 1563.]
[[8] your grace, 1563.]
[[9] less, 1563.]
[[10] taken most vilest, 1563.]
[[11] lowly, favourable, 1563.]

First, and before all things, I will exhort your grace to mark the life and process of our Saviour Christ, and his apostles, in preaching and setting forth of the gospel; and to note also the words of our master Christ, which he had to his disciples when he sent them forth to preach his gospel; and to these have ever in[1] your mind the golden rule of our master Christ, "The tree is known by the fruit:" for by the diligent marking of these, your grace shall clearly know and perceive who be the true followers of Christ and teachers of his gospel, and who be not.

Matt. vii. The rule of Christ.

And concerning the first, all scripture sheweth plainly, that our Saviour Jesus Christ's life[2] was very poor. Begin at his birth, and I beseech you, who ever heard of a poorer, and[3] so poor as he was? It were too long to write how poor[4] Joseph and the blessed Virgin Mary took their journey from Nazareth toward Bethleem, in the cold and frosty winter, having nobody to wait upon them, but he both master and man, and she both mistress and maid. How vilely, thinks your grace, were they[5] entreated in the inns and lodgings by the way! And in how vile and abject place was this poor maid, the mother of our Saviour Jesus Christ, brought to bed[6], without company, light, or any other thing necessary for a woman in that plight! Was not here a poor beginning, as concerning this[7] world? Yes, truly. And according to this beginning was the process and end of his life in this world. And yet he might by his godly power have had all the goods and treasures of this world at his pleasure, when and where he would.

The poverty of Christ's life.

But this he did to shew to us, that his followers and vicars should not regard and[8] set by the riches and treasures of this world, but after the saying of David we ought to take them, which saith thus: "If riches, promotions, and dignity happen to a man, let him not set his affiance, pleasure, trust, and[9] heart upon them." So that it is not against the poverty in spirit, which Christ preacheth[10] in the gospel of St Matthew, chapter v., to be rich, to be in dignity and in honour, so that their

The poor condition of Christ's life is an example to us to cast down our pride, not to set by riches.

It is not against the poverty of the spirit, to be rich.

[1 have in, 1563.]   [2 Christ his life, 1563.]   [3 or, 1563.]
[4 poorly, 1563.]   [5 they were, 1563.]
[6 bed in, 1563.]   [7 the, 1563.]
[8 nor, 1563.]   [9 his heart, 1563.]
[10 praiseth, 1563.]

hearts be not fixed and set upon them so much, that they neither care for God nor good men. But they be enemies to this[11] poverty in spirit, have they never so little, that have greedy and desirous minds to the goods of this world, only because they would live after their own pleasure and lusts. And they also be privy enemies (and so much the worse), which have professed, and they say, wilful poverty, and will not be called worldly men; and they have lords' lands, and kings' riches. Yea, rather than they would lose one jot of that which they have, they will set debate between king and king, realm and realm, yea, between the king and his subjects, and cause rebellion against the temporal power, to the which our Saviour Christ himself obeyed, and paid tribute, as the gospel declareth; unto whom the holy apostle St Paul teacheth every christian man to obey: yea, and beside all this, they will curse and ban, as much as in them lieth, even into the deep pit of hell, all that gainsay their appetite, whereby they think their goods, promotions, or dignities should decay.
Privy enemies to spiritual poverty.
Monks, friars, and prelates of the spiritualty.
Matt. xvii.
Subjection to superior powers.

Your grace may see what means and craft the spiritualty (as they will be called) imagine, to break and withstand the acts which were made in your grace's last parliament[12] against their superfluities. Wherefore they that thus do, your grace may know them not to be true[13] followers of Christ. And although I named the spiritualty to be corrupt with this unthristy ambition; yet I mean not all to be faulty therein, for there be some good of them: neither will I that your grace
Ambition of the spiritualty.

[11 his, 1563.]
[12 The acts alluded to were: (1) For regulating the Fees on the Probate of Wills; (2) For limiting Mortuaries; and, (3) For abridging Pluralities of Benefices, and enforcing the residence of the Clergy. (21 Hen. VIII. c. 5, 6, 13.) These acts were passed by the Commons as the result of their communing "of their grefes wherwith the Spiritualtie had before tyme grevously oppressed them." Hall states, that when the bill "concerning probates of Testaments" was sent up to the house of lords, "the Archbishop of Canterburie, in especiall, and all other bishoppes in generall, both frowned and grunted." Dr Fisher, bishop of Rochester, attributed the proceedings of the commons to the "lacke of faith:" whilst the Commons, on their part, resented the fastening on them the stigma of heresy, and thereupon complained to the king. Bishop Fisher explained away the obnoxious part of his speech, and the king mediated, but the Commons were not to be so easily pacified. Hall's Chronicle, by Ellis, pp. 756 et seq. Lond. 1809.]
[13 the true, 1563.]

should take away the goods due to the church, but take away all[1] evil persons from the goods, and set better in their stead.

I name[2] nor appoint no person nor persons, but remit your grace to the rule of our Saviour Christ, as in Matthew, the seventh chapter: "By their fruits you shall know them." As touching the words that our Saviour Christ spake to his disciples when he sent them to preach his gospel, they be read in Matthew, the tenth chapter; where he sheweth, that here they shall be hated and despised of all men worldly, and brought before kings and rulers, and that all evil should be said by them, for their preaching sake. But he exhorteth them to take patiently such persecution by his own example, saying, "It becometh not the servant to be above the master: and seeing they called me Beelzebub, what marvel is it, if they call you devilish persons and heretics?" Read the fourteenth[3] chapter of St Matthew's gospel, and there your grace shall see that he promised to the true preachers no worldly promotions or dignity; but persecution and all kinds of punishment, and that they should be betrayed even by their own brethren and children. In John also he saith, "In the world ye shall have oppression, and the world shall hate you: but in me you shall have peace." John xvi. And in the tenth chapter of St Matthew's gospel saith our Saviour Christ also, "Lo, I send you forth as sheep among wolves." So that the true preachers go like sheep harmless, and be persecuted, and yet they revenge not their wrong, but remit all to God; so far is it off that they will persecute any other but with the word of God only, which is their weapon. And so this is the most evident token that our Saviour Jesus Christ would that his gospel and the preachers of it should be known by, that it should be despised among those[4] worldly wise men, and that they should repute it but foolishness, and deceivable doctrine; and the true preachers should be persecuted and hated, and driven from town to town, yea, and at the last lose both goods and life. And yet they that did this persecution, should think that they did well, and a great pleasure to God. And the apostles, remembering this lesson of our Saviour Christ, were content to suffer such persecutions,

[1 such evil, 1563.]   [2 I mean, 1563.]
[3 A mistake no doubt for the "tenth."]   [4 these, 1563.]

as you may read in the Acts of the Apostles and the Epistles. But we never read that they ever persecuted any man. The holy apostle St Paul saith, that "every man that will live godly in Christ Jesus, should suffer persecution." And also he saith further, in the epistle written to the Philippians, in the first chapter, that "it is not only given to you to believe in the Lord, but also to suffer persecution for his sake."

Wherefore take this for a sure conclusion, that there, where the word of God is truly preached, there is persecution, as well of the hearers, as of the teachers: and where as is quietness and rest in[5] worldly pleasure, there is not the truth. For the world loveth all that are of the world, and hateth all things that are[6] contrary to it. And, to be short, St Paul calleth the gospel the word of the cross, the word of punishment. And the holy scripture doth promise nothing to the favourers and followers of it in this world, but trouble, vexation, and persecution, which these worldly men cannot suffer, nor away withal. *Persecution a sure mark of true preaching.* *The word of the cross.*

Therefore pleaseth it your good grace to return to this golden rule of our Master and Saviour Jesus Christ, which is this, "By their fruits you shall know them." For where you see persecution, there is the gospel, and there is the truth; and they that do persecute, be void and without all truth, not caring for the clear light, which (as our Saviour Jesus Christ saith in the third chapter of St John's gospel) "is come into the world, and which shall utter and shew forth every man's works." And they whose works be naught, dare not come to this light, but go about to stop it and hinder it, letting as much as they may, that the holy scripture should not be read in our mother tongue, saying that it would cause heresy and insurrection: and so they persuade, at the least way they would fain persuade, your grace to keep it back. But here mark their shameless boldness, which be not ashamed, contrary to Christ's doctrine, to gather figs of thorns and grapes of bushes, and to call light darkness, and darkness light, sweet sour, and sour sweet, good evil, and evil good, and to say, that that which teacheth all obedience, should cause dissension and strife. But such is their belly-wisdom, wherewith they judge and measure every thing, to hold and keep still this wicked mammon, the goods of this world, *Crafty pretences of the prelates to stop the scripture.* *Belly-wisdom.*

[5 in the, 1563.]   [6 is, 1563.]

which is their God, and hath so blinded the eyes of their hearts, that they cannot see the clear light of the sacred scripture, though they babble never so much of it.

Persuasion to let the scripture to be read in English.

But as concerning this matter, other men have shewed your grace their minds, how necessary it is to have the scripture in English. The which thing also your grace hath promised by your last proclamation[1]: the which promise I pray God that your gracious highness may shortly perform, even to-day, before to-morrow. Nor let[2] the wickedness of these worldly[3] men detain you from your godly purpose and promise. Remember the subtle worldly wise counsellors of Hammon the son of Nahas, king of the Amonites, which when David had sent his servants to comfort the young king for the death of his father, by crafty imaginations counselled Hammon, not only[4] not to receive them gently, but to entreat them most shamefully and cruelly, saying that "they came not to comfort him, but to espy and search his land; so that afterward they, bringing David word how every thing stood, David might come and conquer it." 1 Sam. x. And they[5] caused the young king to shear their heads, and to cut their coats by the points, and sent them away like fools; whom he ought rather to have made much of, and to have entreated them gently, and have given them great thanks and rewards. O wretched counsellors! But see what followed of this carnal and worldly wisdom. Truly, nothing but destruction of all the whole realm, and also of all them that[6] took their parts.

Sinister counsel about princes.

1 Sam. x.

Wicked policy turned to its own destruction.

Under the pretence of insurrections and heresies, the prelates stop the liberty of Christ's gospel.

Therefore, good king, seeing that the right David, that is to say, our Saviour Christ, hath sent his servants, that is to say, his true[7] preachers, and his own word also, to comfort our weak and sick souls, let not these worldly men make your grace believe that they will cause insurrections and heresies, and such mischiefs as they imagine of their own mad brains, lest that he be avenged upon you and your

[[1] The proclamation alluded to is "against erroneous books and heresies, and against translating the Bible in English, French, or Dutch." Wilkins's Concilia, Vol. III. pp. 740, et seq. Some interesting particulars connected with this document are given by Dr Wordsworth, Eccl. Biog. Vol. III. pp. 470, et seq. 3rd Edit.]

[[2] let not the, 1563.]   [[3] worldly wise, 1563.]
[[4] alonely, 1563.]   [[5] and so they, 1563.]
[[6] which, 1563.]   [[7] say true, 1563.]

realm, as was David upon the Amonites, and as he hath ever been avenged upon them which have[8] obstinately withstood and gainsaid his word. But peradventure they will lay this against me, and say that experience doth shew, how that such men as call themselves followers of the gospel regard[9] not your grace's commandment, neither set by your proclamation: and that[10] was well proved by those persons which of late were punished in London for keeping such books as your grace had prohibited by proclamation[11]; and so, like as they regarded not this, so they will not regard or esteem other your grace's laws, statutes, or ordinances. But this is but a crafty persuasion: for your grace knoweth that there is no man living, specially that loveth worldly promotion, that is so foolish to set forth, promote, or enhance his enemy, whereby he should be let of his worldly pleasures and fleshly desires; but rather he will seek all the ways possible that he can, utterly to confound, destroy, and put him out of the way. And so as concerning your last proclamation, prohibiting such books, the very true cause of it and chief counsellors (as men say, and of likelihood it should be) were they, whose evil living and cloaked hypocrisy these books uttered and disclosed. And howbeit that there were three or four, that would have had the scripture to go forth in English[12], yet it happened there, as it is evermore seen, that the most part overcometh the better. And so it might be that these men did not take this proclamation as yours, but as theirs set forth in your name, as they have done many times more: which hath put this your realm in great hinderance and trouble, and brought it in great penury, and more would have done, if God hath not mercifully provided to bring your grace to knowledge of the falsehood and privy treason, which their head and captain was about[13]; and, be you

Objection prevented and answered.

Cause of the proclamation against scripture books in English.

A practice of prelates to convey their own proclamations under the king's name and authority.

[8 which obstinately withstand and againsay, 1563.]
[9 regardeth, 1563.]   [10 and that that was, 1563.]
[11 "A proclamation for resisting and withstanding of most damnable heresies, sown within this realm by the disciples of Luther, and other heretics, perverters of Christ's religion." This was in 1529. Foxe, Acts and Mon. Vol. II. pp. 236 et seq. Edit. 1684.]

[12 He meaneth of Cranmer, Cromwell, and one or two more, against whom the bishop of Winchester and his faction did prevail. Foxe.]

[13 He meaneth of the pope, which went about to drive king Henry

sure, not without adherents, if the matter be duly searched. For what marvel is it, that they, being so nigh of your counsel and so familiar with your lords, should provoke both your grace and them to prohibit these books, which before by their own authority have forbidden the new Testament, under pain of everlasting damnation? For such is their manner, to send a thousand men to hell, ere they send one to God: and yet the new Testament (and so I think by the other) was meekly offered to every man that would and could, to amend it, if there were any fault.

The cause of insurrections. Moreover, I will ask them the causes of all insurrections, which have[1] been in this realm heretofore; and whence is it, that there be so many extortioners, bribers, murderers, and thieves, which daily do not break only your grace's laws, ordinances, and statutes, but also the laws and commandments of Almighty God? I think they will not say these books, but rather their pardons, which causeth many a man to sin in trust of them. For as for those malefactors which I now rehearsed, you shall not find one amongst a hundred, but that he will cry out both of these books, and also of them that have them; yea, and will be glad to spend the good which he hath wrongfully gotten, upon fagots, to burn both the books, and them that have them.

The greatest enemies to the gospel. And as touching these men, that were lately punished for these books[2], there is no man, I hear say, that can lay any word or deed against them that should sound to the breaking of any of your grace's laws, this only except, if it be yours, and *The froward life of the gospellers not to be laid to the gospel.* not rather theirs. And be it so that there be some that have these books, that be evil, unruly and self-willed persons, not regarding God's laws, nor man's: yet these books be not the cause thereof, no more than was the bodily presence of Christ, and his words, the cause that Judas fell; but their own froward mind and carnal wit, which should be amended by the virtuous example of living of their curates, and by the true exposition of the scripture. If the lay people had such curates that would thus do their office, neither[3] these books,

out of his kingdom, and that not without some adherents near about the king. Foxe.] [1 hath, 1563.]

[2 Probably he alludes to Tewksbury, Freese, &c. Foxe, Acts and Mon. Vol. II. pp. 242 et seq. Edit. 1684. Wordsworth.]

[3 office, these books, nor, 1563.]

nor the devil himself, could hurt them[4], nor make them to go out of frame: so that the lack of good curates is the destruction and cause of all mischief. Neither do I write these things because that I will either excuse these men lately punished, or to affirm all to be true written in these books, which I have not all read; but to shew that there cannot such inconvenience follow of them, and specially of the scripture, as they would make men believe should follow.

Lack of good curates is the cause of all mischief in the realm.

And though it be so that your grace may by other books, and namely by the scripture itself, know and perceive the hypocrite-wolves clad in sheep's clothing, yet I think myself bound in conscience to utter unto your grace such things as God put in my[5] mind to write. And this I do (God so judge me!) not for hate of any person or persons living, nor for that[6] I think the word of God should go forth without persecution, if your grace had commanded that every man within your realm should have it in his mother's tongue. For the gospel must needs have persecution unto the time that it be preached throughout all the world, which is the last sign that Christ shewed to his disciples[7] should come before the day of judgment: so that if your grace had once commanded that the scripture should be put forth, the devil would set forth some wile or other to persecute the truth. But my purpose is, for the love that I have to God principally, and the glory of his name, which is only known by his word, and for the true allegiance that I owe unto your grace, and not to hide in the ground of my heart the talent given me of God, but to chaffer it forth to others, that it may increase to the pleasure of God, to exhort your grace to avoid and beware of these mischievous flatterers, and their abominable ways and counsels.

The gospel will not go forth without persecution, though the reading thereof be free.

The last sign before the judgment-day.

Latimer chaffereth forth his talent.

And take heed whose counsels your grace doth take in this matter: for there be some that, for fear of losing of their worldly worship and honour, will not leave of[8] their opinion, which rashly, and that to please men withal by whom they had great promotion[9], they took upon them to

[4 hurt them to go out of frame, 1684.]
[5 put in mind, 1563.]   [6 that that I think, 1563.]
[7 disciples that should, 1563.]   [8 leave their, 1563.]
[9 He meaneth this belike by Sir Thomas More, who, for the bishops' pleasure, set his pen against the gospel. Foxe.]

defend by writing; so that now they think that all their felicity, which they put in this life, should be marred, and their wisdom not so greatly regarded, if that which they have so slanderously oppressed, should now be put forth and allowed.

Paul a good example for all persecutors to follow.

But, alas! let these men remember St Paul, how fervent he was against the truth (and that of a good zeal) before he was called: he thought no shame to suffer punishment and great persecutions[1] for that which before he despised and called heresy. And I am sure that their living is not more perfect than St Paul's was, as concerning the outward works of the law, before he was converted.

David a good example for all kings, to submit their intents and purposes to God's word.

Also the king and prophet, David, was not ashamed to forsake his good intent in building of the temple, after that the prophet Nathan had shewed him that it was not the pleasure of God that he should build any house for him; and, notwithstanding that Nathan had before allowed and praised the purpose of David, yet he was not ashamed to revoke and eat his words again, when he knew that they were not according to God's will and pleasure.

Wherefore they be sore drowned in worldly wisdom, that think it against their worship to acknowledge their ignorance[2]: whom I pray to God that your grace may espy, and take heed of their worldly wisdom, which is foolishness before God; that you may do that God commandeth, and not that seemeth good in your own sight without the word of God; that your grace may be found acceptable in his sight, and one of the members of his church; and, according to the office that he hath called your grace unto, you may be found a faithful minister of his gifts, and not a defender of his faith: for he will not have it defended by man or man's power, but by his word only, by the which he hath evermore defended it, and that by a way far above man's power or reason, as all the stories of the bible make mention.

Wherefore, gracious king, remember yourself; have pity upon your soul; and think that the day is even at hand,

[1 There is no more of this letter in the edition of 1563. Foxe observes, "More of this letter came not to our hands, gentle reader, and yet we would not defraud thee of that we had, considering the pithiness thereof."]

[2 By Nathan we may learn not to be ashamed to call back our words, when we know God's pleasure to be otherwise. Foxe.]

when you shall give account of your office, and of the blood that hath been shed with your sword. In the which day that your grace may stand stedfastly, and not be ashamed, but be clear and ready in your reckoning, and to have (as they say) your *quietus est* sealed with the blood of our Saviour Christ, which only serveth at that day, is my daily prayer to him that suffered death for our sins, which also prayeth to his Father for grace for us continually: to whom be all honour and praise for ever! Amen. The Spirit of God preserve your grace!—Anno Domini 1530. 1 die Decembris.

LETTER IV.

An Answer to a Letter from Dr SHERWOOD[3].

[Foxe, Acts and Mon. p. 1318, et seq. edit. 1563. Vol. III. pp. 394 and 5, edit. 1684.]

ABUNDANT health! I am neither so churlish, good sir, (so far as I know myself) as to take amiss a christian admoni-

[3 The date of this letter (which is translated from the Latin printed by Foxe) may with great probability be assigned to 1531. It is an answer to a letter written to Latimer by Dr Sherwood, who dates his communication from Derham, or Dirham, a village in Gloucestershire, but so near the borders of Wilts as to be almost the next parish to West Kington. It appears from Dr Sherwood's letter (which is printed in Foxe), that he charged Latimer with rash judgment and uncharitableness. The ground of that charge was an exposition of the 10th chapter of St John, in which Latimer was alleged to have asserted that all bishops, all popes, and all ecclesiastics, were thieves and robbers, for the hanging of whom all the hemp in England would barely suffice: that in the church were more goats than sheep: that it was, accordingly, hard to say where the true church was to be found: yet that whosoever confessed with Peter that Jesus was the Son of the living God, was Peter and of the church: that, consequently, the 16th chapter of St Matthew had as much reference to every christian man upon earth, as to St Peter; and that there was, therefore, less necessity for upholding the primacy of Peter, than for adopting his confession of Christ. Mr Latimer was further charged with having taught the doctrine: "That all Christians are priests, and that persons, when ordained to the ministry of the church, receive no power which they had not before;" and he was, finally, reported to have said, that when our Lord spoke of some precepts being "least," he

tion from a christian man, nor yet so without sensibility and void of common feeling (if I mistake not) as to be always pleased at having been insulted by you more than once, and that over your cups, before I received your admonition: nay, I am not admonished after all, but rather most bitterly chided, yea assailed, I might say, wickedly assailed with calumnies, and what is more, falsely condemned. Should I now reply to this letter of yours as it deserves, and as my natural disposition would lead me—but I check myself, lest whilst I aim at curing your distemper I stir up your bad humour; for (as your letter of itself tells us) you are a man who, without goading, are more wrathful than is seemly. Yea rather, may God grant to us both, what he himself knoweth to be for our advantage: to me such patience, even in the midst of evil report, as becometh a Christian; and to you as much soundness of judgment, in time to come, as you now have fervency of zeal in your own cause! It will be more profitable, methinks, thus to pray, than to prepare an answer to such an attack as yours: besides that I am too much engaged by daily preaching conveniently to answer you; and all your charges are too flagrantly untrue to deserve a confutation at my hands. But to answer, if it may be, many accusations in few words, it will be worth while to bring forward both what I stated, and what you gathered from what I said. You gathered indeed much, as one determined to strike blood out of a flint. Yes: such, I perceive, is your feeling towards me, which from the violence of it you can ill dissemble.

Suppose I said all popes, all bishops, vicars, and rectors, who do not enter by the door, but climb up another way, are thieves and robbers: in saying so I passed a judgment, as Christ also did, on the manner of entering and on the climbing, not on persons or dignities. Hence you, in your wisdom, gather that all popes, all bishops, and all rectors and vicars, are absolutely thieves; at least that I said so. Is this, my brother, a fair conclusion? Does not that saying of Paul to the Romans justly apply to you? "They say that we thus speak; thus they speak evil of us:" but he adds, "whose damnation is just." And yet the adversaries of Paul may

referred to the impieties of the scribes and Pharisees. The object of Dr Sherwood's letter was to refute these allegations; and this called forth the reply from Latimer, which is given in the text.]

seem to have interpreted his words more justly than you did mine.

If the word of God be still the same as it then was, and equally pleasing and acceptable to God, does not the same condemnation await those who speak falsely of the minister of the word, be that minister who he may? It makes a great difference, whether you say, "All who enter not in by the door are thieves," or simply, "All are thieves." But how is it, I pray, that while I say, all who enter not in by the door are thieves, I seem to you to say that all are actually thieves; unless, haply, almost all men seem to you to climb up another way, and not to enter in by the door? If this be your persuasion, at least forbear, if you have wit, (and wit enough you have,) to say what you think; for you must perceive what peril you would bring yourself into by such an assertion. And, unless you thus think, why, I demand, can I not say, that all are thieves who enter not in by the door, but climb up another way, whatever be their glittering titles, without forthwith seeming to you to say, that all are thieves to a man? And then I may rather say, What phrenzy has seized you when you so draw your conclusion, as by it to make there to be more thieves than shepherds? For whether you will or no, what I said is true, namely, that as many as enter not in by the door, but climb up another way, are thieves and robbers, be they popes or be they bishops. To what purpose, then, is it to examine your statements further, when you thus get out of your way at the first off-set.

But come, this pleases you most, that the scribes and Pharisees are so covertly reproved by Christ, and not openly. How totally repugnant then to your feelings must be that most bitter and open impeachment thrown in their face and before the multitude, "Woe unto you, scribes and Pharisees, hypocrites," where they are censured by name! But "Christ," say you, "was God, perceiving the perversity of the heart, while you are a mere man, a looker upon the outside, no searcher of hearts." I am indeed a man, as you say, a fact I had discovered some time since without your assistance: I am, I say, a man not seeing the evil that lies hid in another man's heart, but his manner of life which is open and exposed to the view of all; and so I know those by their fruits, who, as Christ taught us, are thus to be known; and freely condemn the manner of life of some; briefly, that manner of life which I find so often condemned in holy scripture, and by the interpreters of God's word, not troubling myself about what the persons are who live it. While I thus act, nor search further into men's hearts, am I not unjustly reproved by you? You, forsooth, are not a man like myself, but something more than mere man; since you arrogate to yourself to know the particular bent of my heart better than I myself do; inasmuch as it is not enough for you to know what I say, but you know my yet unuttered thoughts; having most thoroughly searched the very depths of my heart, lest it happen that you should not discover that which you have attempted to twist against me. Judge not, say I too, before the time, condemn not; that you may learn how necessary it is for a liar to have a good memory, lest haply his throat be cut with his own sword, and himself fall into the pit that he digged for another. For whilst I pronounce all to be thieves, as many as enter not in by the door, but climb up another way, I seem to you (who not only hear my words, but behold my inmost heart) to pronounce all to be thieves to a man, except myself, of course, and those men no body (you say) knows whom, that are of my own kidney. Yet who made the exception, but you who, knowing the secrets of hearts, say, "Such appeared to have been your thoughts?" But thus I seem to have thought, in your judgment, to whom also I seem to have said what, most manifestly, I said not at all. But it is your privilege to forbid others to look into the heart, that you exclusively may behold whatever is in the heart; and that forsooth with so penetrating an eye, that you can see in the heart what the heart has not yet given birth to!

Such is the case where, as is your custom, you wickedly censure without cause what I rightly stated concerning the church; as if I had made all Christians equal to Peter as regards the use of the keys, when not a word was said or even thought of respecting the power of the keys; nor did I use any expression derogating to the primacy of Peter, as that subject was not mentioned. But with your accustomed candour you so interpret me; whereas I did but put my hearers in mind that the church of Christ hath its foundation on a rock not on the sand; that they should not unduly cling to a dead faith and so perish, being shamefully vanquished by the gates of hell; but shew forth their faith by good works, and thus obtain everlasting life.

What could be farther from the meaning of my words than that all Christians are priests, as I am? But the envious are very keen-sighted in discovering their game. Am I not here, with the best reason, compelled to think there is somewhat of christian charity lacking in your breast, who, because you cannot confute what I really did say, use strange devices to fix upon me something which you may be able to confute? But you know full well what Luther holds respecting the church: and I will not trouble myself to write down what Lyra[1], in accordance with many others, holds on the sixteenth of Matthew; where that father remarks that "the church consists not of men by virtue of ecclesiastical or secular power and dignity, for many princes and supreme pontiffs and others of inferior dignity, saith he, have been found to apostatise from the faith; wherefore, he saith, the church consists of those persons in whom abideth the true knowledge and confession of faith and verity." Hereunto Chrysostom[2] and Jerome[3] also agree; for they speak to this effect. I know not whether their language is approved by you, since you are manifestly of those, who are more ready to uphold the primacy of Peter, even when there is no occasion, than to re-echo the blessed confession of Peter by kindred fruits of holiness. But you refer me to Augustine, and I thank you for the hint. I would have you read, if you please, his third treatise on St John's epistles; for you do not appear particularly well versed in Augustine's writings, when you argue so subtilly concerning justification by faith. Wherefore, not to trouble you to search out more passages either of that father or of other authors, I would fain have you better acquainted with the *collectanea* of Bede, since your own *collectanea* breathe so little the spirit of Augustine.

[1 See Biblia cum Glossis Ordinar. in loc. cit.]

[2 Comm. in Matt. xvi. 18. ἐκκλησία γὰρ οὐ τεῖχος καὶ ὄροφος, ἀλλὰ πίστις καὶ βίος, κ. τ. λ. Hom. de Capto Eutropio, Oper. Tom. III. p. 386. Paris. 1721, Edit. Bened.]

[3 Alluding most probably to that quotation in the Canon Law, which is referred to Jerome, but not found in his writings: "Non est facile &c. ... non sanctorum filii sunt qui tenent loca sanctorum, sed qui exercent opera eorum." Decret. prim. par. Distinct. 40. Can. 2.]

Yet, though much pressed by other business, I cannot omit to notice your assertion that Christ made no allusion to the impiety of the Pharisees, when he spake of certain precepts as the least. So you venture to say, because you have read a different interpretation in Origen[1]. A goodly objection truly, as if one and the same passage of scripture were not quite differently expounded by different men! Origen does not notice the allusion, therefore no one doth. What a conclusion! But, say you, Christ had nothing just then to do with the Pharisees. Well said again; as if Christ did not immediately subjoin mention of the scribes and Pharisees, calling off the people from their righteousness which rested on human (that is, their own) traditions, saying, "Unless your righteousness shall exceed the righteousness of the scribes," &c. But, say you, Christ was at that time with a very few disciples, apart from the multitude. Now this is a most manifest untruth, as the words of Matthew, at the close of the seventh chapter, shew clearer than day-light: so that I may the more easily endure your falsehoods respecting me, seeing that you dare to belie Christ himself and his sayings: "And it came to pass," saith he, "that when Jesus had made an end of these sayings, the multitude were astonished at his doctrine." But lo! if Christ spake apart from the multitude, how were they astonished at the doctrine which, by your account, they never had heard? But St Luke the evangelist, speaking either of the same or of a similar discourse of Christ, testifies that the people heard it. He says, "When Jesus had made an end of these sayings in the audience of the people." See! what becomes of that hasty decision of yours, so wretchedly distorted by spleen? Is it not yourself who are totally wrong? And that the more deservedly, because you must needs fish out and note the errors of others, and call on them to recant. Is it not you who trust to your own understanding? "Physician, heal thyself;" and learn what that means, "Thou hypocrite, why seest thou the mote?" &c. Learn from your own beams to make allowance for your neighbour's motes.

I said nothing, (I call God to witness, that I lie not) which I borrowed from Luther, Œcolampadius, or Melanc-

[1 The passage in Origen, referred to, may be seen in his works, Tom. III. p. 590. Paris, 1740, Edit. Bened.]

thon: yet you hesitate not (such is your charity) to fix this charge upon me. If I have done this thing, may I fall as I deserve, stript bare by mine enemies. But you know not, methinks, what manner of spirit you are of, while you would rather assail a minister of God's word with your most impudent falsehoods, than bear testimony to the truth. What a wickedness this is in the sight of God, you know full well without my teaching; to your greater condemnation, if you repent not.

But do I now blame a man for believing as the church believes? I blame him not; only your malice toward me has so stopped up your ears, that even when hearing you do not hear what is said. But this I find fault with—that a man persuade any private Christian (as many false preachers are wont to persuade) that it is, in all things, enough for him to believe what the church believes; though in the mean time he knows not, what or how the church does believe; and thus keep back the wretched people from seeking after a more perfect knowledge of God!

The last charge you thrust upon me is false, and beside unmannerly beyond expression; nor do you take my words in the sense in which I spoke them; and so (as Jerome[2] observes on Matthew xxvi.) you shall be accounted a false witness before God. Read the passage, and give over bearing false witness. I affirm that a Christian, that is, a person received by baptism into the number of Christians, if he live not according to his profession, but yield himself up to the lusts of the flesh, is no more a Christian, as touching the inheriting of eternal life which is promised to Christ's people, than a Jew or a Turk; yea, rather his condition at that day will be worse than the others', if you allow that Peter spoke truly, "It is better not to know the way of truth than having known it," &c. And to whom saith Christ, "I never knew you?" Is it not to those who prophesied in his name, and performed miracles? Will not Christ deny us, if we deny him before men? We shall not be placed amongst Christ's sheep on the right hand, if, while professing Christ, we have not lived a life worthy of Christ, but disgrace our profession by an evil life. Such men are to be accounted

[2 Falsus testis est, qui non eodem sensu dicta intelligit quo dicuntur. Oper. Tom. IV. col. 132, Paris. 1706, Edit. Bened.]

false Christians rather than Christians, and are called by Augustine[1], and by Christ himself, "antichrists." I do not deny that the obligation remains, but it remains only to greater condemnation, if a man do not fulfil the conditions of the engagement. It is the duty of a preacher to exhort his hearers, that they be Christians after such sort, that suffering here together with Christ, they may reign with him in heaven; teaching them that to be otherwise a Christian is to be no Christian at all. Thus speak the scriptures, thus the interpreters of scripture; though you may deem the words heretical. But the covetous man, the fornicator, the murderer, say you, is a catholic, and a servant of Christ. Yet on this wise, to indulge my humour, I will jest with you. By your account, a fornicator is a servant of Christ; but he is also a servant of sin, and of the devil: then the man can at once serve two masters; of which Christ was not aware. And if dead faith makes a catholic, the very devils belong to the catholic church; for they, according to St James, "believe and tremble." A fornicator, say you, believes in Christ; "hope maketh not ashamed;" "whosoever believeth in Christ shall not perish, but have eternal life." Yet I am aware that Paul wrote to the Galatians, when they erred from the faith, and yet addressed them as the church: so the same apostle, writing to the Corinthians, calls them in the same chapter, in one place, carnal; in another, the temple of God; meaning by both expressions Corinthians, but different individuals. For they who were carnal were not the temple of God: albeit I know also that the church, that is, the body of those who profess Christ, consists partly of good and partly of evil men; forasmuch as the gospel net gathereth of every kind. How does this contradict what I said, whose aim was to make all good and not bad, and so would have my hearers think it no great matter if ecclesiastics be of the number of the wicked? But it did not seem good to you to interpret my preaching piously, as it was meant; yet you think it consistent with piety to repeat, in a bad spirit, what was said with holy purpose. If your discourse be not milder than your writings, I would fain be delivered from both: but may all bitterness and pride and anger and clamour and evil

[1 De Baptismo, iii. 26. Oper. Tom. ix. col. 80. Antverp. 1700. edit. Bened.]

speaking be taken from you, with all malice! Yet neither your words nor your writings will trouble me. You would not wish, I trow, for such hearers as you have shewn yourself to be: then may God make you of a better spirit, or keep you as far away as possible from my preaching!

Farewell.

LETTER V.

LATIMER *to* HUBBARDINE[2].

[Printed in Strype, Eccl. Mem. I. ii. 175 et seq. Oxf. ed.]

THE Spirit of God be with you to seal the truth and follow the same! Amen. I doubt not, master Hubbardine, that you have read the saying of the Spirit by his prophet Isaiah: *Væ qui dicunt*[3] *malum bonum, et bonum malum, ponentes lucem tenebras, et tenebras lucem, &c.*[4] which words, after mine understanding, be this much in English: "Woe," or eternal damnation, "be unto them which say[5] that good is evil and evil is good; calling light darkness, and darkness light, &c." Take heed. Remember yourself well. Ye may mock and deceive us: *Deus non irridetur,* "God will not," for all that, "be mocked." It is not the saying of wise Aristotle, of godly Plato, of holy Thomas[6], no, nor yet of subtile Duns[7], (who for all their wisdom, godliness, holiness and subtilty, deceived, were deceived, and lied,) but it is the eternal and perpetual word of God; who, as he deceiveth no man, so can he be deceived of no man, nor yet make any lie. God it is that saith, "Woe," or eternal damnation, "be unto him that saith that good is evil, &c." It is no threatening of man, but it is the sentence of God: wherefore it is

[2 The following note occurs in the margin of a MS. copy of this letter, (Harl. MSS. 422, Art. 14): "This is in Latimer's hand, if I mistake not, to Hubbardin, that opposed his doctrine *circuitim,* 1531 or 1532." The accounts of the imprisonments, &c. which Foxe gives, of the several persons mentioned at the close of the letter make the earlier of these dates the more probable one.]

[3 dicitis, Harl. MS.]
[4 tenebras lucem, et lucem tenebras, Harl. MS.]
[5 sayeth, Harl. MS.]   [6 Thomas Aquinas.]
[7 Duns Scotus.]

the more to be feared, and undoubtedly to be looked for. For it is only the word of God that lasteth ever, and may sustain no change[1]. Do you marvel[2] wherefore I say this? It is only brotherly love, and my conscience, which compelleth me, as bounden, brotherly to admonish you not only of the grievous blasphemies against the truth which ye uttered here on the Ascension-day, but also to exhort you to desist of your proposed blasphemy and lies against God and his word, which ye have promised to prove in this same place this day. And that ye may know that ye have inexcusably blasphemed and belied the truth, and promised to do the same, partly[3] here I will confute your blasphemies that be past, and partly[3] that be promised.

And so first to begin with that which is past. Ye said, that it was plain that this *new learning* (as ye call it) was not the truth, and so not of God; but contrariwise that it was lies, and so surely of the devil. This your assertion ye proved by two manner of conjectures: the one is, that the professors of it live naughtily; and the other is, that priests be prosecuted of them. Which two persuasions, though they be in very deed lies, as I trust in God to shew them, yet though they were true, did but easily prove your intention. For after the same manner ye may as well openly improve Christ and all his doctrine, as ye do now under a colour, which I will entreat more largely hereafter. But to our purpose: that, as ye say, it is plain that this *new learning* (as ye call it) is not the truth, and so not of God; but contrariwise it is lies, and surely of the devil. Herein are contained three great blasphemies and abominable lies, injurious both to God and his word; and, I fear, sin against the Holy Ghost: for they are even the same words with the example of Christ, declaring the sin against the Holy Ghost. For to begin withal: ye call the scripture the *new learning*, which I am sure is older than any learning which ye wot to be the old. But[4] if ye will say, that it is not the scripture that ye call new, but other books lately put in English: I answer, that the scripture was the first which you and your fautors condemned; besides that those other, for the most, teach nothing but that which is manifest in the scripture, and also

[1 imitation, Harl. MS.]   [2 You marvel, Harl. MS.]
[3 presently, Harl. MS.]   [4 and, Harl. MS.]

plain in the ancient doctors. I speak not of your old doctors, Duns and St Thomas, Halcot[5], Briget[6] and others[7], but of Augustine, Hierome, Chrysostom, Ambrose, Hilary, and such other; which, in like manner, be called new doctors, as the scripture new learning; and as Tully, new Latin; as the text of Aristotle, new philosophy; and likewise of all sciences.

And so in this appeareth your first lie, that ye call the scripture *new doctrine;* except that ye would call it new, either because it makes the receivers of it new men, or else that it was now newly received into the world, for the condemnation of them that reject it, and the salvation of the receivers; of which newness I am sure ye spake not. I pray you, was not the scripture, if ye would contend, before your most ancient doctors, that ye can allege to have written of it? Was it not, afore they wrote upon it, better received, more purely understand, of more mighty working, than it is now, or since they wrote upon it? In St Paul's time, when there was no writers upon the new Testament, but that the plain story was then newly put forth, were there not more converted by (I dare boldly say) two parties, than there be at this hour, I will not say christian men, but that profess the name of Christ? Is it not now the same word as it was then? Is not the same schoolmaster, that taught them to understand it then (which, as St Peter saith, is the Spirit of God) alive, as well as he was then? Doth he not favour us now as well as he did then? Have we him not now, as well as we had then? If we have not the Spirit of Christ, St Paul saith, so be we no christian men. And if we be no christian men, so be you deceivers and false prophets; preaching unto yourself your authority and your constitutions, without the word of God; which is only the rule of faith according to the saying of St Paul, where he saith that "faith is of hearing," and not of all manner hearing, but of

[5 Robert Holcot, a Dominican friar at Northampton, one of the most eminent English schoolmen and a voluminous writer. Tanner, Biblioth. Brit. p. 407.]

[6 In the Harl. MS. Bright: possibly William Brito, or Breton, a Franciscan, the author of a popular biblical lexicon and other theological works, which were had in repute at the time. Tanner, Biblioth. p. 128; Antiq. of the English Franciscans, pp. 163 et seq.]

[7 others, supplied from Harl. MS.]

hearing of the word of God: which faith, also, is the first-fruit of the Spirit of God: which Spirit if we have not, so testify ye against us, that we be no christian men; and against yourself, that ye be no ministers or stewards of Christ, but ministers of antichrist, and shepherds of your own bellies. Which Spirit if we have, so beareth us witness St Paul that we be Christ's men; and St Peter, that we may understand the scripture. Which only is that the lay-people desire; utterly contemning all men's draughts, and all men's writings, how well learned soever they be; only contented with their old and new schoolmaster[1], the Holy Spirit of God, and the minister thereto of him elect, and of him sent.

But you will say, that you condemn not the scripture, but Tyndal's translation. Therein ye shew yourself contrary to your words; for ye have condemned it in all other common tongues, wherein they be approved in other countries. So that it is plain, that it is the scripture, and not the translation, that ye bark against, calling it *new learning*. And this much for the first lie.

And as for the two other, [they] be soon confuted, that it is not the truth, nor of God, but lies and of the devil. O Jesu, mercy! that ever such blasphemy against the Holy Ghost should proceed out of a christian man's mouth! Is it not all one to say, that the doctrine of Christ is lies, and cometh of the devil, and that Christ is a liar, and the devil? What difference, I pray you, is here[2] betwixt this blasphemy, and that which the Pharisees imputed unto Christ, when they said, "We know that thou art a Samaritan, and hast a devil within thee?" when that Christ said, that the blasphemy against the Holy Ghost should never be forgiven. If ye have said this of ignorance, I pray God bring you to knowledge and repentance. If ye spake it against your conscience, of malice against the truth, (as he knoweth *qui scrutator cordium est,*) I fear me lest time of repentance (which God forbid!) shall ever[3] be given you in this life. O Lord God! what a wresting of the scripture was it to interpretate and ... those words of St Paul, "Before the coming of antichrist, there shall be a departure from the pope;" when, as the text

[1 new school after the, Harl. MS.]
[2 there, Harl. MS.]   [3 never, Harl. MS.]

saith plainly, antichrist was come already, and that he then worked secretly, and that there should be a departing from the faith, and that he should be opened unto all men afore the coming of Christ. For shame, nay for conscience, either allege the scriptures aright, without any such wresting, or else abstain out of the pulpit.

But now, to come to your conjectures by which you persuaded your assertions; that is, that the scripture was new learning, Christ a liar and the devil: which are, that the fautors and professors thereof live naughtily, and that they persecute priests. First, besides that it is manifest that your conjectures both be false; for the pureness of life of the favourers of it, (I speak of them that are of my only knowledge[4],) their virtuous living is so well known, that it is but folly for me to labour to confute it. And that they persecute priests, I would gladly hear of one priest so much as once prisoned[5],—I mean not for whoredom, theft, and murders, with such their common practices, but for his faith's sake; except it were such as you yourself persecuted, as ye do us for knowledging the truth. Need ye that I bring forth examples? Remember ye not the honest priest that the last year was martyred by you in Kent? Do you not hold Nicholson, Smyth, Patmore, and Philips[6], with many other[7], in prison yet at this hour?

[The rest is wanting.]

[4 favours, I speak of, that are of my knowledge, Harl. MS.]

[5 imprisoned, Harl. MS.]

[6 Some account of these several persons are given by Foxe, Acts and Mon. Vol. III. pp. 260—264, edit. 1684.]

[7 other men, Harl. MS.]

LETTER VI.

LATIMER *to* SIR EDWARD BAYNTON, Knight[1].

[Foxe, Acts and Mon. pp. 1321, et seq. edit. 1563. Vol. III. pp. 396, et seq. edit. 1684.]

Salutem in Domino[2].

RIGHT worshipful sir, I recommend me unto your mastership with hearty thanks for your so friendly, so charitable, and so mindful remembrance of me, so poor a wretch.

Whereas of late I received your letters by master Bonnam, perceiving therein both who be grieved with me, wherefore, and what behoveth me to do, in case I must needs come up; which your goodness towards me, with all other such like, to recompense, whereas I myself am not able, I shall not cease to pray my Lord God, who both is able, and also doth indeed reward all them that favour the favourers of his truth for his sake; for the truth is a common thing, pertaining to every man, for the which every man shall answer another day. And I desire favour neither of your mastership, neither of any man else; but in truth and for the truth, I take God to witness, which knoweth all.

In very deed master chancellor[3] did shew me, that my

[1] The allusion to the correspondence of the bishop of London with the chancellor of the diocese of Sarum; the mention of "this deep winter;" the purpose expressed by Latimer to "make merry with his parishioners this Christmas,"—all go to fix the date of this letter to the latter end of December, 1531.

Sir Edward Baynton was the head of an ancient and honourable family in Wiltshire, which inherited the property of the Beauchamps, lords St Amand. The seat of the Beauchamps, and afterwards of the Bayntons, was Bromham, situate between Calne and Chippenham, and Devizes. The house was burnt down during the civil wars in 1652, when the family removed to Spye Park, in the immediate neighbourhood of Bromham. Sir Edward Baynton was a near relative of Cardinal Pole, was in great favour with Henry VIII. and was vice-chamberlain to three of his queens. The property of Sir Edward lay within a few miles of Latimer's parish. Wordsworth, Eccles. Biogr. Vol. III. pp. 490, 499, 3rd edit.]

[2] Christo, 1684.]

[3] Dr Richard Hilley. Foxe, Acts and Mon. Vol. III. p. 382, edit. 1684.]

lord bishop of London[4] had sent letters to him for me: and I made answer, that he was mine ordinary; and that both he might and should reform me, as far as I needed reformation, as well and as soon as my lord of London: and I would be very loth, now this deep winter, being so weak and so feeble[5], (not only[6] exercised with my old disease[7] in my head and side, but also with new, both the cholic and the stone), to take such a journey; and though he might so do, yet he needed not, for[8] he was not bound so to do. Notwithstanding, I said, if he, to do my lord of London pleasure, to my great displeasure would needs command me to go, I would obey his commandment, yea, though it should be never so great a grievance and painful to me: with the which answer he was content, saying, he would certify my lord of London thereof, trusting his lordship would be[9] content with the same; but as yet I hear nothing from him. Master chancellor also said, that my lord of London maketh as though he were greatly displeased with me, for that I did contemn his authority at my last being in London.

Forsooth, I preached in Abb-church, not certain then (as I remember) whether in his diocese or no[10], intending nothing less than to contemn his authority: and this I did not of mine own seeing[11] or by mine own procuration, but at the request of honest merchantmen (as they seemed to me), whose names I do not know, for they were not of mine acquaintance before. And I am glad thereof for their sakes, lest, if I knew them, I should be compelled to utter them so, and their godly desire to hear godly preaching should return to their trouble: for they required me very instantly, and, to say the truth, even importunately. Whether they were of that parish or no, I was not certain; but they shewed not only themselves, but also many other, to be very desirous to hear me, pretending great hunger and thirst of the word of God and ghostly doctrine. And upon consideration, and to avoid all inconveniences, I put them off, and refused them twice or

[4 Dr John Stokesly. See Newcourt, Repertorium, Vol. I. p. 11.]
[5 and feeble, 1563.]   [6 alonely, 1563.]
[7 my disease, 1563.]   [8 nor, 1563.]   [9 would to be, 1563.]
[10 Some of the London churches being Peculiars; and some being then attached to monasteries, and exempt from episcopal jurisdiction.]   [11 suing, 1563.]

thrice; till at the last they brought me word that the parson[1] and curate were not only content, but also desired me, notwithstanding that they certified him both of my name plainly, and also that I had not the bishop's seal to shew for me, but only a licence of the university[2]; which curate did receive me, welcomed me, and, when I should go into the pulpit, gave me the common benediction: so that I had not been alone[3] uncharitable, but also churlishly uncharitable, if I should[4] have said nay. Now all this supposed to be truth (as it is), I marvel greatly how my lord of London can allege any contempt of him in me.

First, he did never inhibit me in my life: and if he did inhibit his curate to receive me, what pertaineth that to me, which neither did know thereof, nor yet made any suit to the curate deceitfully? Nor did it[5] appear to me very likely that the curate would so little have regarded my lord's inhibition, which he maintaineth so vigilantly, not knowing my lord's mind before. Therefore I conjectured with myself, that either the curate was of such acquaintance with my lord, that he might admit whom he would; or else, and rather, that it was a train and a trap laid before me, to the intent that my lord himself, or some other pertaining to him, were appointed to have been there, and to have taken me, if they could, in my sermon: which conjecture both occasioned me somewhat to suspect those men which desired me, though they spake never so fair and friendly, and also the rather to go. For I preach nothing, but (if it might be so) I would my lord himself might hear me every sermon I preach. So certain I am that it is truth, that I take in hand to preach. If I had with power of my friends (the curate gainsaying and withstanding) presumed to have gone into the pulpit, there had been something wherefore to pretend a contempt. I preached in Kent also, at the instant request of a curate; yet hear I not that his ordinary layeth any contempt to my charge, or yet doth trouble the curate.

[1 Thomas Clark, M.A. Newcourt, Repert. Vol. I. p. 432.]
[2 The university of Cambridge, which has still the power to license twelve persons to preach in any part of the realm. See Strype, Life of Parker, I. 382, et seq. III. 121, et seq. Oxf. edit. where forms of this Licence are given.]
[3 alonely, 1563.]   [4 would, 1563.]   [5 nor it did not, 1563.]

I marvel not a little how my lord bishop of London, having so broad, wide, and large a diocese committed unto his cure, and so peopled as it is, can have leisure for preaching and teaching the word of God, *opportune, importune, tempestive, intempestive, privatim, publice,* to his own flock, *instando, arguendo, exhortando, monendo, cum omni lenitate et doctrina;* have leisure (I say) either to trouble me, or to trouble himself with me, so poor a wretch, a stranger to him, and nothing pertaining to his cure, but as every man pertaineth to every man's cure; so intermixing and intermeddling himself with another man's cure, as though he had nothing to do in his own. If I would do as some men say my lord doth, gather up my joyse (as we call it) warily and narrowly, and yet neither preach for it in mine own cure, nor yet otherwhere, peradventure he would nothing deny me.

In very deed I did monish judges and ordinaries to use charitable equity in their judgments towards such as be accused, namely of such accusers which be as like to hear and bewray, as other be to say amiss; and to take men's words in the meaning thereof, and not to wrest them in another sense than they were spoken in: for all such accusers and witnesses be false before God, as St Jerome saith upon the twenty-sixth chapter of St Matthew[6]. Nor yet do I[7] account those judges well advised, which wittingly will give sentence after such witnesses; much less those which procure such witnesses against any man: nor no I think[8] judges now-a-days so deeply confirmed in grace, or so impeccable, but that it may behove and become preachers to admonish[9] them to do well, as well as other kinds of men, both great and small. And this I did, occasioned of the epistle which I declared, (Rom. vi.) wherein is this sentence, *Non estis sub lege, sed sub gratia;* "Ye christian men, that believe in Christ, are not under the law."

What a saying is this (quoth I), if it be not rightly understood; that is, as St Paul did understand it? For the words sound as though he would go about to occasion christian men to break law, seeing they be not under the law: and what if [10] the pseudo-apostles, adversaries to St Paul,

[6 See the passage quoted before, p. 315.]
[7 Nor yet I do not, 1563.]   [8 nor I think not judges, 1563.]
[9 monish, 1563.]   [10 and, 1563.]

would have so taken them, and accused St Paul of the same to my lord of London? If my said lord would have heard St Paul declare his own mind of his own words, then he should have escaped, and the false apostles have been put to rebuke: if he would have rigorously followed *utcunque allegata et probata*, and have given sentence after relation of the accusers, then good St Paul must have borne a fagot at Paul's Cross, my lord of London being his judge. Oh! it had been a godly sight, to have seen St Paul with a fagot on his back, even at Paul's Cross, my lord of London, bishop of the same, sitting under the cross. Nay verily, I dare say, my lord should sooner have burned him: for St Paul did not mean that christian men might break law, and do whatsoever they would, because they were not under the law: but he did mean, that christian men might keep the law, and fulfil the law, if they would; because they were not under the law, but under Christ, by whom they were divided from the tyranny of the law, and above the law; that is to say, able to fulfil the law to the pleasure of him that made the law, which they could never do of their own strength, and without Christ: so that to be under the law, after St Paul's meaning, is to be weak to satisfy the law; and what could St Paul do withal, though his adversaries would not so take it?

But my lord would say, peradventure, that men will not take the preacher's words otherwise than they mean therein. *Bona verba:* as though St Paul's words were not otherwise taken; as it appeareth in the third chapter to the Romans, where he saith, *Quod injustitia nostra Dei justitiam commendat;* that is to say, "Our unrighteousness commendeth and maketh more excellent the righteousness of God:" which soundeth to many as though they should be evil, that good should come of it, and by unrighteousness to make the righteousness of God more excellent. So St Paul was reported to mean: yet he did mean nothing so; but shewed the inestimable wisdom of God, which can use our naughtiness to the manifestation of his unspeakable goodness; not that we should do naughtily to that end and purpose. Now my lord will not think, I dare say, that St Paul was to blame that he spake no more circumspectly, more warily, or more plainly, to avoid evil offence of the people; but rather he will blame the people, for that they took no better heed and attendance to Paul's speaking, to the understanding of the same: yea, he will rather pity the people, which had been so long nurseled[1] in the doctrine of the Pharisees, and wallowed so long in darkness of man's traditions, superstitions, and trade of living, that they were unapt to receive the bright lightness of the truth, and wholesome doctrine of God, uttered by St Paul. Nor do I think that my lord will require more circumspection, or more convenience to avoid offence of errors in me, than was in St Paul, when he did not escape malevolous corrections and slanderous reports of them that were of perverse judgments, which reported him to say whatsoever he appeared to them to say, or whatsoever seemed to them to follow of his saying.

But what followeth? *Sic aiunt nos dicere, sic male loquuntur de nobis:* "So they report us to say," saith St. Paul; "so they speak evil of us:" *sed quorum damnatio justa est,* "but such, whose damnation is just," saith he. And I think the damnation of all such that evil report preachers now-a-days, likewise just; for it is untruth now and then. Yea, Christ himself was mis-reported, and falsely accused, both as touching his words, and also as concerning the meaning of his words. First he said, *destruite,* that is to say, "destroy you;" they made it *possum destruere,* that is to say, "I can destroy:" he said, *templum hoc,* "this temple;" they added, *manu factum,* that is to say, "made with hand," to bring it to a contrary sense[2]. So they both inverted his words, and also added unto his words, to alter his sentence: for he did mean of the temple of his body, and they wrested it to Solomon's temple.

Now I report me, whether it be a just fame raised up and dispersed after this manner. Nay verily, for there be three manner of persons which can make no credible information: first, adversaries, enemies; secondly, ignorant and without judgment; thirdly, *susurrones,* that is to say, whisperers and blowers in men's ears, which will spew out in hudder-mudder[3] more than they dare avow openly. The first will not, the second cannot, the third dare not: therefore the relation of such is not credible, and therefore they

[1 noseled, 1563.]   [2 Evil will never saith "well." Foxe.]
[3 Commonly written *hugger-mugger,* "secretly." See Todd's Johnson's Dictionary.]

can make no fame lawful, nor occasion any indifferent judge to make process against any man. And[1] it maketh no little matter what they be themselves that report of any man, whether[2] well or evil: for it is a great commendation to be evil spoken of of them that be naught[3] themselves; and to be commended of the same is, many times, no little reproach. God send us once all grace to wish well one to another, and to speak well one of[4] another!

Meseems it were more comely for my lord (if it were comely for me to say so) to be a preacher himself, having so great a cure as he hath, than to be a disquieter and a troubler of preachers, and to preach nothing at all himself. If it would please his lordship to take so great a labour and pain at any time, as to come to preach in my little bishopric at West-Kington[5], whether I were present or absent myself, I would thank his lordship heartily, and think myself greatly bounden to him, that he of his charitable goodness would go so far to help to discharge me in my cure; or else I were more unnatural than a beast unreasonable: nor yet I would dispute, contend, or demand by what authority, or where he had authority so to do, as long as his predication were fruitful and to the edification of my parishioners.

As for my lord, he may do as it pleaseth his lordship. I pray God he do always as well as I would wish him ever to do: but I am sure St Paul, the true minister of God, and faithful dispenser of God's mysteries, and right exemplar of all true and very bishops, saith in the first chapter to the Philippians, that in his time some preached Christ for envy of him, thinking thereby so to grieve him withal, and as it were to obscure him, and to bring his authority into contempt; some of good will and love, thinking thereby to comfort him: "Notwithstanding," saith he, "by all manner of ways, and after all fashions, whether it be of occasion or of truth (as ye would say, for truth's sake), so that Christ be preached and shewed, I joy and will joy:" so much he regarded more the glory of Christ, and promotion of Christ's doctrine, to the edification of christian souls, than the maintenance of his own authority, reputation, and dignity; con-

[1 nor, 1563.]   [2 neither, 1563.]
[3 naughty, 1563.]   [4 upon, 1563.]
[5 Nay, my lord will none of that. Foxe.]

sidering right well (as he said), that what authority soever he had, it was "to edification, and not to destruction."

Now I think it were no reproach to my lord, but very commendable, rather to joy with St Paul, and be glad that Christ be preached *quovis modo*, yea, though it were for envy, that is to say, in disdain, despite, and contempt of his lordship, (which thing no man well advised will enterprise or attempt,) than when the preaching cannot be proved justly, to demand of the preacher austerely, as the Pharisees did of Christ, *qua auctoritate hæc facis, aut quis dedit tibi istam auctoritatem?* As my authority is good enough, and as good as my lord can give me any, yet I would be glad to have his also, if it would please his lordship to be so good a lord unto me. For the university of Cambridge hath authority apostolic to admit twelve yearly, of the which I am one: and the king's highness (God save his grace!) did decree that all admitted of universities should preach throughout all his realm as long as they preached well, without distrain of any man, my lord of Canterbury[1], my lord of Durham[2], with such other not a few, standing by, and hearing the decree, nothing gainsaying it, but consenting to the same. Now to contemn my lord of London's authority, were no little fault in me: so no less fault might appear in my lord of London to contemn the king's authority and decree, yea, so godly, so fruitful, so commendable a decree, pertaining both to the edification of christian souls, and also to the regard and defence of the[3] popish grace and authority apostolic. To have a book of the king not inhibited is to obey the king; and to inhibit a preacher of the king's admitted, is it not to disobey the king? Is it not one king that doth inhibit and admit, and hath he not as great authority to admit as to inhibit? He that resisteth the power whether admitting or inhibiting, doth he not resist the ordinance of God? We low subjects are bound to obey powers and their ordinances: and are not the highest subjects also, who ought to give us ensample of such obedience? As for my preaching itself, I trust in God, my lord of London cannot rightfully belack it, nor justly reprove it, if it be taken with the circumstance thereof, and as I spake it; or else it is not my preaching, but his

[6 Dr Warham.]   [7 Dr Tonstal.]
[8 of popish, 1563.]

that falsely reporteth it, as the poet Martial[1] said to one that depraved his book:

> Quem recitas meus est, O Fidentine, libellus:
> Sed male cum recitas, incipit esse tuus.

But now I hear say that my lord of London is informed, and upon the said information hath informed the king, that I go about to defend Bilney and his cause against his ordinaries and his judges, which I assure you is not so: for I had nothing to do with Bilney, nor yet with his judges, except his judges did him wrong; for I did nothing else but monish all judges indifferently to do right; nor am I[2] altogether so foolish as to defend the thing which I knew not. It might have become a preacher to say as I said, though Bilney had never been born. I have known Bilney a great while, I think much better than ever did my lord of London; for I have been his ghostly father many a time. And to tell you the truth, what I have thought always in him, I have known hitherto few such, so prompt and ready to do every man good after his power, both friend and foe; noisome wittingly to no man, and towards his enemy so charitable, so seeking to reconcile them as he did, I have known yet not many; and to be short, in sum[3], a very simple good soul, nothing fit or meet for this wretched world, whose blind fashion and miserable state (yea, far from Christ's doctrine) he could as evil bear, and would sorrow, lament, and bewail it, as much as any man that ever I knew: as for his singular learning, as well in holy scripture as in all other good letters, I will not speak of it. Notwithstanding, if he either now of late, or at any time, attempted any thing contrary to the obedience which a christian man doth owe either to his prince or to his bishop, I neither do nor will allow and approve that, neither in him, nor yet in any other man: we be all men, and ready to fall; wherefore he that standeth, let him beware he fall not. How he ordered or misordered himself in judgment, I cannot tell, nor will I[4] meddle withal; God knoweth, whose judgments I will not judge. But I cannot but wonder, if a man living so mercifully, so charitably, so patiently, so continently, so studiously and virtuously, and killing his old

[1] Mart. i. 39.]
[3] in a sum, 1563.]
[2] I am not, 1563.]
[4] I will not, 1563.]

Adam (that is to say, mortifying his evil affections and blind motions of his heart so diligently), should die an evil death, there is no more, but "Let him that standeth, beware that he fall not:" for if such as he shall die evil, what shall become of me, such a wretch as I am?

But let this go, as little to the purpose, and come to the point we must rest upon. Either my lord of London will judge my outward man only, as it is said, *Omnes vident quæ foris sunt;* or else he will be my God, and judge mine inward man, as it is said, *Deus autem intuetur cor.* If he will have to do only with mine outward man, and meddle with mine outward conversation, how that I have ordered myself toward my christian brethren, the king's liege people, I trust I shall please and content both my Lord God, and also my lord of London: for I have preached and teached but according to holy scripture, holy fathers, and ancient interpreters of the same, with the which I think my lord of London will be pacified: for I have done nothing else in my preaching, but with all diligence moved my auditors to faith and charity, to do their duty, and that that is necessary to be done.

As for things of private devotion, mean things, and voluntary things, I have reproved the abuse, the superstition of them, without condemnation of the things themselves, as it becometh preachers to do: which thing if my lord of London will do himself (as I would to God he would do), he should be reported, no doubt, to condemn the use of such things, of covetous men which have damage, and find less in their boxes by condemnation of the abuse; which abuse they had rather should continue still, than their[5] profit should not continue: so thorny be their hearts. If my lord will needs coast and invade my inward man, will I, nill I, and break violently into my heart, I fear me I shall either displease my lord of London, which I would be very loth, or else my Lord God, which I will[6] be more loth; not for any infidelity, but for ignorance, for I believe as a christian man ought to believe. But peradventure my lord knoweth and will know many things certainly, which (perchance) I am ignorant in; with the which ignorance though my lord of London may, if he will, be discontent, yet I trust my Lord God will pardon

[5 your, 1563.]   [6 would, 1563.]

it, as long as I hurt no man withal, and say to him with
diligent study and daily prayer, *Paratum cor meum, Deus,
paratum cor meum;* so studying, preaching, and tarrying the
pleasure and leisure of God; and in the mean season (Acts
xviii.), as Apollo did, when he knew nothing of Christ but
baptismum Johannis, teach and preach mine even christian[1],
that and no further than I know to be true.

There be three Creeds, one in my mass, another in my
matins, the third common to them that neither say mass nor
matins, nor yet know what they say, when they say the
Creed: and I believe all three, with all that God hath left in
holy writ, for me and all other to believe. Yet I am ignorant in things which I trust hereafter to know, as I do now
know things in which I have been ignorant heretofore: ever
to learn, and ever to be learned; to profit with learning, with
ignorance not to annoy[2]. I have thought in times past, that
the pope, Christ's vicar, hath[3] been Lord of all the world, as
Christ is; so that if he should have deprived the king of his
crown, or you of the lordship of Bromeham, it had been
enough; for he could do no wrong. Now I might be hired
to think otherwise; notwithstanding I have both seen and
heard scripture drawn to that purpose. I have thought in
times past, that the pope's dispensations of pluralities of benefices, and absence from the same, had discharged consciences
before God; forasmuch as I have[3] heard, *Ecce vobiscum sum*,
and *Qui vos audit*, bended to corroborate the same. Now I
might be easily entreated to think otherwise, &c. I have
thought in times past, that the pope could have spoiled
purgatory at his pleasure with a word of his mouth: now
learning might persuade me otherwise; or else I would
marvel why he would suffer so much money to be bestowed
that way, which so needful is to be bestowed otherwise, and
to deprive us of so many patrons in heaven, as he might deliver out of purgatory, &c. I have thought in times past,
that[4] if I had been a friar, and in[5] a cowl, I could not have
been damned, nor afraid of death; and by occasion of the
same, I have been minded many times to have been a friar,
namely when I was sore sick and diseased[6]: now I abhor my

[1 christened, 1563.] [2 noy, 1563.]
[3 had, 1563.] [4 that and if, 1563.]
[5 friar in a, 1563.] [6 diseased, &c. 1563.]

superstitious foolishness, &c. I have thought in times past, that divers images of saints could have holpen me, and done me much good, and delivered me of my diseases: now I know that one can help as much as another; and it pitieth mine heart, that my lord, and such as my lord is, can suffer the people to be so craftily deceived. It were too long to tell you what blindness I have been in, and how long it were ere[7] I could forsake such folly, it was so corporate in me: but by continual prayer, continual study of scripture, and oft communing with men of more right judgment, God hath delivered me, &c. Yea, men think that my lord himself hath thought in times past, that by God's law a man might marry his brother's wife[8], which now both dare think and say contrary: and yet this his boldness might have chanced, in pope Julius's[9] days, to stand him either in a fire, or else in a fagot. Which thing deeply considered, and pondered of my lord, might something stir him to charitable equity, and to be something remiss[10] toward men which labour to do good, as their power serveth, with knowledge, and do[11] hurt to no man with their ignorance: for there is no greater distance, than between God's law and not God's law: nor is it so or so, because any man thinketh it so or so; but, because it is so or so indeed, therefore we must think it so or so, when God shall give us knowledge thereof: for if it be indeed either so or not, it is so, or not so, though all the world hath thought otherwise these thousand years, &c.

And finally, as ye say, the matter is weighty, and ought substantially to be looked upon, even as weighty as my life is worth: but how to look substantially upon it, otherwise know not I, than to pray my Lord God day and night, that as he hath emboldened[12] me to preach his truth, so he will strengthen

[7 or, 1563.]

[8 Stokesley was particularly zealous and effective in promoting Henry's view in his great matter of the divorce. To him the king referred Sir Thomas More, lord chancellor, for satisfaction in that very important point, that his marriage with the widow of prince Arthur, being directly against the law of nature, could in no wise by the church be dispensable. Roper's Life of Sir Thomas More, p. 54, edit. 1729. Quoted in Wordsworth, Eccl. Biogr. II. p. 500. See also p. 128 of the volume last mentioned.]

[9 Pope Julius II.]   [10 remissible, 1563.]
[11 doth, 1563.]   [12 boldened, 1563.]

me to suffer for it, to the edification of them which have taken, by the working of him, fruit thereby. And even so I desire you, and all other that favour me for his sake, likewise to pray: for it is not I, without his mighty helping hand, that can abide that brunt; but I have trust that God will help me in time of need; which if I had not, the ocean-sea, I think, should have divided my lord of London and me by this day. For it is a rare thing for a preacher to have favour at his hand, which is no preacher himself, and yet ought to be. I pray God that both he and I may both discharge ourselves, he in his great cure, and I in my little, to God's pleasure and safety of our souls. Amen.

I pray you pardon me, that I write no more distinctly, nor more truly: for my head is[1] out of frame, that it would[2] be too painful for me to write it again; and, if I be not prevented shortly, I intend to make merry with my parishioners this Christmas, for all the sorrow, lest perchance I never return to them again: and I have heard say, that a doe is as good in winter, as a buck in summer.

LETTER VII.

LATIMER *in reply to* SIR EDWARD BAYNTON[3].

[Foxe, Acts and Mon. pp. 1326, et seq. edit. 1563. Vol. III. pp. 399, et seq. edit. 1684.]

RIGHT worshipful sir, and my singular good master, *salutem in Christo Jesu*, with due commendation, and also thanks for your great goodness towards me, &c. And whereas you have communicated my last letters to certain of your friends, which rather desire this or that in me, &c.; what I think therein I will not now say; not for that there could be

[1 is so out, 1563.]   [2 should, 1563.]

[3 The Letter of Sir Edward Baynton, to which this is a reply, is given by Foxe in the pages cited above. The date of this Letter is ascertained within a few days, from the circumstance that, at the close of it, Latimer states that he had just received a "citation" to appear before the bishop of London; that citation being dated Jan. 10, 1531—2. See Foxe, Acts and Mon. Vol. III. p. 382, edit. 1684.]

any peril or danger in the said letters[4], well taken, as far as I can judge; but for that they were rashly and unadvisedly scribbled, as ye might well know both by my excuse, and by themselves also, though none excuse had been made. And besides that, ye know right well, that where as the bee gathereth honey, even there the spinner gathereth venom, not for any diversity of the flower, but for divers natures in them that suck the flower: as in times past, and in the beginning, the very truth, and one thing[5] in itself, was to some offence, to some foolishness; to others, otherwise disposed, the wisdom of God. Such diversity was in the redress of hearers thereof.

But this notwithstanding, there is no more but either my writing is good or bad. If it be good, the communicating thereof to your friends cannot be hurtful to me; if it be otherwise, why should you not communicate it to them which both could and would instruct you in the truth, and reform my error? Let this pass, I will not contend: "had I wist" cometh ever out of season. Truly I were not well advised, if I would not either be glad of your instruction, or yet refuse mine own reformation: but yet it is good for a man to look ere[6] he leap; and God forbid that ye should be addict and sworn to me so wretched a fool, that you should not rather follow the doctrine of your friends in truth, so great learned men as they appear to be, than the opinions of me, having never so christian a breast.

Wherefore do as you will; for as I would not if I could, so I cannot[7] if I would, be noisome unto you: but yet I say, I would my letters had been unwritten, if for none other cause, at least-way inasmuch as they cause me to more writing, an occupation nothing meet for my mad head. And as touching the points which in my foresaid letters mislike your friends, I have now little leisure to make an answer thereto, for the great business that I have in my little cure (I know not what other men have in their great cures), seeing that I am alone without any priest to serve my cure, without any[8] scholar to read unto me, without any book necessary to be looked upon, without learned men to come and counsel withal: all which things other have at hand abundantly. But something must

[4 danger in them, 1563.] [5 truth one thing, 1563.]
[6 or, 1563.] [7 can I not, 1563.]
[8 my, 1563.]

be done, howsoever it be. I pray you take it in good worth, as long as I temper mine own judgment, affirming nothing with prejudice of better.

First ye mislike, that I say I am sure that I preach the truth; saying in reproof of the same, that God knoweth certain truth. Indeed, alone[1] God knoweth all certain truth, and alone[1] God knoweth it as of himself; and none knoweth certain truth but God, and those which be taught of God, as saith St Paul, *Deus enim illis patefecit;* and Christ himself, *Erunt omnes docti a Deo.* And your friends deny not but that certain truth is communicated to us, as our capacity may comprehend it by faith; which if it be truth, as it is, then there ought no more to be required of any man, but according to his capacity. Now certain it is, that every man hath not like capacity, &c. But as to my presumption and arrogancy; either I am certain or uncertain that it is truth that I preach. If it be truth, why may not[2] I say so, to courage my hearers to receive the same more ardently, and ensue it more studiously? If I be uncertain, why dare I be so bold to preach it? And if your friends, in whom ye trust so greatly, be preachers themselves, after their sermon, I pray you, ask them whether they be certain and sure that they taught you the truth or no; and send me word what they say, that I may learn to speak after them. If they say they be sure, ye know what followeth: if they say they be unsure, when shall you be sure, that have so doubtful teachers and unsure? And you yourselves, whether are you certain or uncertain that Christ is your Saviour? And so forth of other articles that ye be bounden to believe. Or whether be ye sure or unsure, that civil ordinances be the good works of God, and that you do God service in doing of them, if ye do them for good intent? If ye be uncertain, take heed he be your sure friend that heareth you say so; and then with what conscience do ye doubt, *cum quicquid non est ex fide, peccatum est?* But contrary say you, alone God knoweth[3] certain truth, and ye have it but *per speculum in ænigmate;* and there have been *qui zelum Dei habuerunt, sed non secundum scientiam.* And to call this or that truth,

[1 alonely, 1563.]   [2 may I not, 1563.]
[3 *peccatum est?* If you be certain and sure. *Contra,* alonely God knoweth, 1563.]

it requireth a deep[4] knowledge, considering that to you unlearned, that you take for truth may be otherwise, not having *sensus exercitatos*, as Paul saith, *ad discernendum bonum et malum;* as ye reason against me, and so you do best to know surely nothing for truth at all, but to wander meekly hither and thither, *omni vento doctrinæ, &c.* Our knowledge here, you say, is but *per speculum in ænigmate.* What then? *ergo,* it is not certain and sure.

I deny your argument, by your leave; yea, if it be by faith, as ye say, it is much sure, *quia certitudo fidei est maxima certitudo;* because the certainty of faith is the most surest certainty, as Duns and other school-doctors say, that there is a great discrepance between certain knowledge and clear knowledge; for that may be of things absent that appear not, this requireth the presence of the object, I mean of the thing known; so that I certainly and surely know the[5] thing which I perfectly believe, though I do not clearly and evidently know it. I know your school subtleties as well as you, which dispute as though enigmatical knowledge, that is to say, dark and obscure knowledge, might not be certain and sure knowledge, because it is not clear, manifest, and evident knowledge: and yet there have[6] been, say they, *Qui zelum Dei habuerunt, sed non secundum scientiam;* "which have had a zeal, but not after knowledge[7]." True it is, there have been such, and yet be too many, to the great hinderance of Christ's glory, which nothing doth more obscure than a hot zeal accompanied with great authority without right judgment. There have been also, *Qui scientiam habuerunt absque zelo Dei, qui, veritatem Dei in injustitia detinentes, plagis vapulabunt multis, dum voluntatem Domini cognoscentes nihil minus quam faciunt;* "which have had knowledge without any zeal of God, who holding the verity of God in unrighteousness, shall be beaten with many stripes, while they, knowing the will of God, do nothing thereafter." I mean not among Turks and Saracens, that be unchristened, but of them that be christened. And there have been also, *Scientiam Dei, id est, spiritualem divini verbi sensum, quem prius habuerunt;* "that have lost the,

[4 deep and profound, 1563.] [5 that, 1563.] [6 hath, 1563.]
[7 It may be stated once for all, that the Edition of 1563 does not usually contain a translation, in each case, of the Latin sentences which occur in this Letter.]

spiritual knowledge of God's word which they had before;" because they have not ensued after it, nor promoted the same; but rather with their mother-wits have impugned the wisdom of the Father, and hindered the knowledge thereof, which therefore hath been taken away from them, *ut justificetur Christus in sermonibus suis, et vincat cum judicatur;* threatening, *Ei vero, qui non habet, etiam quod habet, id est, quod videtur habere, auferetur ab eo; cum abuti habito, vel non bene uti, sit non habere; necnon sit verum illud quoque, non habitaturam videlicet sapientiam in corpore peccatis subdito; qui adhuc etsi carnaliter sapiat plus satis, at stat sententia, nempe carnalem et philosophicam scripturarum intelligentiam non esse sapientiam Dei, quæ a sapientibus absconditur, parvulis revelatur:* "To him that hath not, that also which he hath (that is, that which he seemeth to have) shall be taken from him: because to abuse that which a man hath, or not to use it well, is as not to have it; and also seeing it is true, that God's wisdom will not dwell in a body subject to sin, albeit it abound in carnal wisdom too much; for the mere carnal and philosophical understanding of God's scriptures is not the wisdom of God, which is hid from the wise, and is revealed to little ones." And if to call this or that truth, requireth a deep and profound knowledge, then either every man hath a deep and profound knowledge, or else no man can call this or that truth: and it behoveth every preacher to have so deep and profound knowledge, that he may call this or that truth, which this or that he taketh in hand to preach for the truth: and yet he may be ignorant and uncertain in many things, both this and that, as Apollos was; but which things, whether this or that, he will not attempt to preach for the truth. And as for myself, I trust in God, I may have *sensus exercitatos ad discernendum bonum et malum;* "senses well enough exercised to discern good and evil in those things, which, without deep and profound knowledge in many things, I preach not:" yea, there be many things in scripture in which I cannot certainly discern *bonum et malum*, I mean, *verum et falsum;* not[1] with all the exercise that I have in scripture, nor yet with help of all interpreters that I have, to content myself and others in all scrupulosity that may arise. But in such I am wont to wade

Matt. xiii.

[1 no, not, 1563.]

no further into the stream, than that I may either go over, or else return back again; having ever respect, not to the ostentation of my little wit, but to the edification of them that hear me, as far forth as I can, neither passing mine own nor yet their capacity.

And such manner of argumentations might well serve the devil *contra pusillanimes*, to occasion them to wander and waver in the faith, and to be uncertain in things in which they ought to be certain: or else it may appear to make and serve against such preachers which will define great subtleties and high matters in the pulpit, which no man can be certain and sure of by God's word to be truth, *ne sensus quidem habens ad discernendum bonum et malum exercitatissimos*: as whether, if Adam had not sinned, we should have stockfish out of Iceland: how many larks for a penny, if every star in the elements were a flickering hobby: how many years a man shall lie in purgatory for one sin, if he buy not plenty of the oil that runneth over our lamps to slake the sin withal; and so forget hell, which cannot be slaked, to provide for purgatory.

Such argumentation, I say, might appear to make well against such preachers; not against me, which simply and plainly utter true faith and fruits of the same, which be the good works of God, *quæ præparavit Deus ut in eis ambularemus*, "which he hath prepared for us to walk in;" every man to do the thing that pertaineth to his office and duty in his degree and calling, as the word of God appointeth[2]; which thing a man may do with soberness, having *sensus ad discernendum bonum et malum vel mediocriter exercitatos*. For it is but foolish humility, willingly to continue always *infantulus in Christo et infirmitate*; "an infant still in Christ, and in infirmity:" in reproof of which it was said, *Facti estis opus habentes lacte, non solido cibo*. For St Paul saith not, *estote humiles, ut non capiatis*: for though he would not that we should think arrogantly of ourselves, and above that that it becometh us to think of ourselves, but so to think of ourselves, *ut simus sobrii ac modesti*; yet he biddeth us so to think of ourselves, *ut cuique Deus partitus est mensuram fidei*; "as God hath distributed to every one the measure of faith." For he that may not with meekness

[2 appointeth it, 1563.]

think in himself what God hath done for him, and of himself as God hath done for him, how shall he, or when shall he, give due thanks to God for his gifts? And if your friends will not allow the same, I pray you inquire of them whether they may, *cum sobrietate et modestia,* be sure they preach to you the truth; and whether we may, *cum sobrietate et modestia,* follow St Paul's bidding, where he saith unto us all, *Nolite fieri pueri sensibus, sed malitia infantes estote;* "Be not children in understanding, but in maliciousness be infants." God give us all grace to keep the mean, and to think of ourselves neither too high nor too low; but so that we may restore unto him, *qui peregre profectus est,* his gifts again *cum usura,* that is to say, with good use of the same, so that *ædificemus invicem* with the same, *ad gloriam Dei!* Amen.

For my life, I trust in God that I neither have, neither by God's grace shall I, neither in soberness nor yet in drunkenness, affirm any truth of myself, therewith intending to divide that unity of the congregation of Christ, and the received truth agreed upon by the holy fathers of the church, consonant to the scripture of God, though it be shewed you never so often, that an opinion or manner of teaching, which causeth dissension in a christian congregation, is not of God, by the doctrine of St John in his epistle, where he saith, *Omnis qui confitetur Jesum Christum in carne ex Deo est;* "Every one that confesseth Christ in the flesh is of God." First, not every thing whereupon followeth dissension, causeth dissension[1]; as I would that they that shewed you that, would also shew you, whether this opinion, that a man may not marry his brother's wife, be of God or of men: if it be of men, then, as Gamaliel said, *dissolvetur;* if it be of God, as I think it is, and perchance your friends also, *quis potest dissolvere, nisi qui videbitur Deo repugnare?* "who can dissolve it, but shall seem to repugn against God?" And yet there be many, not heathens[2], but in Christendom, that dissent from the same, which could bear full evil to hear said unto them, *Vos ex patre diabolo estis.* So that such an opinion might seem to some to make a dissension in a

[1 He meaneth the pope and his papists, which could not abide the dissolving of the marriage between king Henry and his brother's wife. Foxe.]   [2 in heathenness. 1563.]

christian congregation; saving that they may say perchance with more liberty than others, that an occasion is sometimes taken and not given, which with their favour I might abuse for my defence, saving that *non omnia omnibus licet in hac temporum iniquitate.*

The Galatians having for preachers and teachers the false apostles, by whose teaching they were degenerate from the sweet liberty of the gospel into the sour bond of ceremonies, thought themselves peradventure a christian congregation, when St Paul did write his epistle unto them, and were in a quiet trade under the dominion of masterly curates: so that the false apostles might have objected to St Paul that his apostleship was not of God, forasmuch as there was dissension in a christian congregation by occasion thereof, while some would renew their opinions by[3] occasion of the epistle; some would *opinari,* as they were wont to do, and follow their great lords and masters, the false apostles, which were not heathen and unchristianed, but christianed, and high prelates of the professors of Christ. For your friends, I know right well what Erasmus hath said in an epistle set before the paraphrases of the first epistle to the Corinthians: which Erasmus hath caused no small dissension with his pen in a christian congregation, inasmuch as many have dissented from him, not alonely in cloisters, (men more than christened men, of high perfection,) but also at Paul's Cross, and St Mary Spital[4]; besides many that with no small zeal have written against him, but not without answer.

And I would fain learn of your friends, whether that St Hierome's writings were of God, which caused dissension in a christian congregation, as it appeareth by his own words in the prologue before the canonical epistles, which be these: *Et tu virgo Christi Eustochium, dum a me impensius scripturæ veritatem inquiris, meam quodammodo senectutem invidorum dentibus vel morsibus corrodendam apponis*[5], *qui me*

[3 the occasion, 1563.]

[4 A priory and hospital which formerly stood within the parish of St Botolph, Bishopsgate, London, and where sermons used to be preached in the church-yard on every Easter Monday, Tuesday and Wednesday, the lord mayor and aldermen being present in their robes. Stowe, Surv. of London, Vol. I. b. ii. p. 98, edit. Strype.]

[5 *exponis.*]

falsarium corruptoremque scripturarum pronunciant[1] : *sed ego in tali opere nec illorum invidentiam pertimesco, nec scripturæ veritatem poscentibus denegabo*[2]. I pray you, what were they, that called St Hierome *falsarium*, and corrupter of scripture, and for envy would have bitten him with their teeth? Unchristian or christian? What had the unchristian to do with christian doctrine? They were worshipful fathers of a christian congregation, men of much more hotter stomachs than right judgment, of a greater authority than good charity: but St Hierome would not cease to do good for the evil speaking of them that were naught, giving in that an ensample to us of the same; and if this dissension were in St Hierome's time, what may be in our time? *De malo in pejus, scilicet.*

And, I pray you, what mean your friends by a christian congregation? All those, trow ye, that have been christianed? But many of those be in worse condition, and shall have greater damnation, than many unchristianed. For it is not enough to a christain congregation that is of God, to have been christened: but it is to be considered what we promise when we be christened, to renounce Satan, his works, his pomps: which thing if we busy not ourselves to do, let us not crack that we profess Christ's name in a christian congregation, *in uno baptismo*, "in one baptism." And whereas they add, *in uno Domino*, "in one Lord," I read in Matt. vii., *Non omnis qui dicit Domine, Domine, &c.;* "Not every one that saith Lord, Lord," &c. And in Luke the Lord[3] himself complaineth, and rebuketh such professors and confessors[4], saying to them, *Cur dicitis, Domine, Domine, et non facitis quæ dico?* "Why call you me Lord, Lord, and do not that I bid you?" Even as though it were enough to a christian man or to a christian congregation to say every day, *Domine, Dominus noster*, and to salute Christ with a double *Domine*. But I would your friends would take the pains to read over Chrysostom, *super Matthæum*, Hom. xlix. cap. 24[5], to learn to know a christian congregation, if it will please them to learn at him. And whereas they add, *In una fide*, "in one faith," St James saith boldly, *Os-*

[1 *pronuntiant scripturarum.*]
[2 Oper. Tom. I. col. 1668 et seq. Paris. 1693—1706, edit. Bened.]
[3 *Dominus* himself, 1563.] [4 *professores* and *confessores*, 1563.]
[5 Oper. Tom. VII. pp. 504 et seq. Paris. 1727, edit. Bened.]

tende mihi fidem ex operibus; " Shew me thy faith by thy works." And St Hierome, *Si tamen credimus, inquit, opere veritatem ostendimus;* " If we believe, we shew the truth in working." And the scripture[6] saith, *Qui credit Deo, attendit mandatis;* " He that believeth God, attendeth to his commandments:" and the devils do believe to their little comfort. I pray God[7] to save you and your friends from that believing congregation, and from that faithful company!

Therefore all this toucheth not them that be unchristened, but them that be christened, and answer not unto their christendom. For St Hierome[8] sheweth how true preachers should order themselves, when evil priests and false preachers, and *populus ab his deceptus,* " the people by them deceived," should be angry with them for preaching the truth, exhorting them to suffer death for the same of the evil priests and false preachers with the people deceived of them; which evil priests and false preachers, with the people deceived, be christened as well as others. And I fear me that St Hierome might appear to some christian congregation, as they will be called, to write seditiously, to divide the unity of a great honest number confessing Christ, *in uno baptismate, uno Domino, una fide,* saying: *Populus qui ante sub magistris consopitus erat, ibit ad montes; non illos quidem qui vel leviter tacti fumigant, sed montes veteris et novi Testamenti, prophetas, apostolos, et evangelistas. Et cum ejusmodi montium lectione versatus, si non invenerit doctores (messis enim multa, operarii autem pauci), tunc et populi studium comprobabitur, quo fugerit ad montes, et magistrorum desidia coarguetur*[9]: " The people which before were brought asleep by their masters, must go up to the mountains; not such mountains which smoke when they are touched, but to the mountains of the old and new Testament, the prophets, apostles, and evangelists. And when they are occupied with reading in these mountains, if they find no instructors (for the harvest is great, and the workmen be few), yet shall the diligent study of the people be approved in fleeing to the mountains, and the slothfulness of the masters shall be rebuked."

[6 and scripture, 1563.]   [7 to God, 1563.]
[8 Comment. in Jerem. xxvi. Oper. Tom. III. col. 655.]
[9 The following is the passage as found in the commentary of St Jerome on Nahum iii. sub fine:—Elevabitur et properabit populus,

I do marvel why our christian congregations be so greatly grieved that lay-people would read scripture, seeing that St Hierome alloweth and approveth the same; which compareth not here the unchristened to the christened, but the lay-people christened to their curates christened, under the which they have been rocked and locked asleep in a subtle trade a great while full soundly, though now of late they have been waked but to their pain; at the leastway to the pain of them that have wakened them with the word of God. And it is properly said of St Hierome, to call them masters and not servants: meaning that servants teach not their own doctrine, but the doctrine of their master Christ, to his glory. Masters teach not Christ's doctrine, but their own, to their own glory; which masterly curates cannot be quiet till they have brought the people asleep again: but Christ, the very true master, saith, *Vigilate, et orate, ne intretis in tentationem. Non cogitationes meæ cogitationes vestræ, neque viæ meæ viæ vestræ, dicit Dominus:* and there have been, *qui cogitaverunt consilia, quæ non potuerunt stabilire;* "which have gone about counsels, which they could not establish." I pray God give our people grace so to wake, *ut studium illorum comprobetur,* and our masters so to sleep, *ut non desidia illorum coarguatur.* For who is so blind that he seeth not how far our christian congregation doth gainsay St Hierome, and speaketh after another fashion?

<blockquote>
God amend that is amiss:
For we be something wide, I wis.
</blockquote>

But now your friends have learned of St John, that *omnis qui confitetur Jesum Christum in carne, ex Deo est;* "Every one that confesseth Jesus Christ in flesh, is of God:" and I have learned of St Paul, that there have been, not among the heathen but among the Christians, *qui ore confitentur, factis autem negant,* "which confess Christ with their

---

qui sub magistris ante fuerat consopitus; et ibit ad montes scripturarum, ibique inveniet montes Moysen et Jesum filium Nave; montes, prophetas; montes novi Testamenti, apostolos et evangelistas: et quum ad tales montes confugerit, et in hujusmodi montium fuerit lectione versatus, si non invenerit qui eum doceat, (*messis enim multa, operarii autem pauci,*) tunc et illius studium comprobabitur, quia confugerit ad montes, et magistrorum desidia coarguetur. Oper. Tom. III. col. 1590, Paris. 1704, edit. Bened.]

mouth, and deny him with their acts:" so that St Paul
should appear to expound St John, saving that I will not
affirm any thing as of myself, but leave it to your friends to
shew you, *utrum qui factis negant Christum et vita, sint ex
Deo necne per solam oris confessionem:* for your friends
know well enough by the same St John, *Qui ex Deo est, non
peccat;* and there both have been and be now too many, *qui
ore tenus confitentur Christum venisse in carne;* "which
with mouth only confess Christ to be come in the flesh;" but
will not effectually hear the word of God, by consenting to
the same, notwithstanding that St John saith, *Qui ex Deo est,
verbum Dei audit; vos non auditis, quia ex Deo non estis.*
And many shall hear, *Nunquam novi vos,* "I never knew
you," which shall not alonely be christened, but also shall
prophetare, and do puissant things, *in nomine Christi*: and
St Paul said there should come *lupi graves qui non parcerent
gregi,* "ravening wolves which will not spare the flock;"
meaning it of them that should *confiteri Christum in carne,*
in their lips, and yet usurp by succession the office, which
Christ calleth *pseudo-prophetas,* "false prophets," and biddeth us beware of them, saying, *in vestimentis ovium;* "they
shall come in sheep's clothing;" and yet they may wear both
satin, silk, and velvet, called afterwards *servi nequam, non
pascentes, sed percutientes conservos, edentes et bibentes cum
ebriis, habituri tandem portionem cum hypocritis:* "naughty
servants, not feeding but smiting their fellow-servants, eating
and drinking with the drunken, which shall have their portion
with hypocrites." They are called *servi,* "servants," I trow,
*quod ore confitentur Christum in carne; nequam vero, quia
factis negant eundem, non dantes cibum in tempore, domi-
nium exercentes in gregem:* "because they confess Christ in
the flesh; and naughty they are called, because they deny
him in their deeds, not giving meat in due season, and exer-
cising mastership over the flock." And yet your friends
reason as though there could none bark and bite at true
preachers, but they that be unchristianed; notwithstanding
that St Augustine, upon the same epistle of John, calleth
such confessors[1] of Christ, *qui ore confitentur, et factis negant,* "*antichristos*[2];" a strange name for a christian congregation. And though St Augustine could defend his saying,

[1 *confessores*, 1563.]   [2 Antichrists, 1563.]

yet his saying might appear not to be of God, to some men's judgment, in that it breaketh the chain of Christ's charity, so to cause men to hate *antichristianismum*, "antichrists," according to the doctrine of St Paul, *Sitis odio persequentes quod malum est*, "hate that is evil;" and so making division, not between christened and unchristened, but between Christians and antichristians, when neither pen nor tongue can divide the antichristians from their blind folly. And I would you would cause your friends to read over St Augustine upon the epistle of St John, and tell you the meaning thereof, if they think it expedient for you to know it. As I remember, it is in his Tractate iii[1]. But I am not sure nor certain of that, because I have not seen it since I was at Cambridge; and here I have not Augustine's works to look for it: but well I wot, that there he teacheth us to know the Christians from the antichristians, which both be christened, and both confess *Jesum esse Christum*, if they be asked the question; and yet the one part denieth it in very deed. But to know whether, *non linguam, sed facta attendamus et vivendi genus, num studeamus officia vocationis præstare an non studeamus: imo persuasi forte sumus non necesse esse ut præstemus, sed omnia in primitivam ecclesiam et tempora præterita referimus, quasi nobis sat sit dominari, et secularibus negotiis nos totos volvere, ac voluptatibus et pompæ inhiare:* "let us not stand upon our talk, but attend to our doings and manner of life, whether we strive to perform the duties of our calling or not: yea, rather, we perhaps persuade ourselves that it is not necessary for us to perform them, referring them all to primitive usage; but that it is enough for us to bear rule and authority, and to bestow ourselves wholly upon secular matters, pleasures, and pomp of this world." And yet we desire to appear *vel soli ex Deo esse; sed longe aliter Christum confitentur, qui confitendo ex Deo esse comprobantur.*

And yet, as long as they minister the word of God or his sacraments, or any thing that God hath ordained to the salvation of mankind, wherewith God hath promised to be present, to work with the ministration of the same to the end of the world, they be to be heard, to be obeyed, to be honoured for God's ordinance sake, which is effectual and

[1 Oper. Tom. III. Pars 2, col. 614 et seq. edit. Bened. Antv. 1700.]

fruitful, whatsoever the minister be, though he be a devil, and neither church nor member of the same, as Origen saith, and Chrysostom; so that it is not all one to honour them, and trust in them, St Hierome saith. But there is required a judgment, to discern when they minister God's word and ordinance of the same, and their own; lest peradventure we take chalk for cheese, which will edge our teeth, and hinder digestion. For, as it is commonly said, "the blind eat[2] many a fly," as they did which were persuaded *a principibus sacerdotum ut peterent Barabbam, Jesum autem crucifigerent;* "of the high priests, to ask Barabbas, and to crucify Jesus:" and ye know that to follow the blind guides, is to come into the pit with the same. "And will you know," saith St Augustine, "how apertly they resist Christ, when men begin to blame them for their misliving and intolerable secularity and negligence? They dare not for shame blaspheme Christ himself, but they will blaspheme the ministers and preachers of whom they be blamed[3]."

Therefore, whereas ye will pray for agreement both in the truth and in uttering of the truth, when shall that be, as long as we will not hear the truth, but disquiet with crafty conveyance the preachers of the truth, because they reprove our evilness with the truth? And, to say the truth, better[4] it were to have a deformity in preaching, so that some would preach the truth of God, and that which is to be preached, without cauponation and adulteration of the word, (as Lyranus saith in his time few did; what they do now-a-days, I report me to them that can judge,) than to have such a uniformity, that the silly people should be thereby occasioned to continue still in their lamentable ignorance, corrupt judgment, superstition, and idolatry, and esteem things, as they do all, preposterously; doing that that they need not for to do, leaving undone[5] that they ought to do, for lack or want of knowing what is to be done; and so shew

[2 blind man eateth, 1563.]

[3 Et vultis nosse quam aperte resistant isti Christo? Aliquando evenit ut aliquid mali faciant, et incipiant corripi : quia Christum non audent blasphemare, ministros ejus blasphemant a quibus corripiuntur. In Epist. Johan. Tract. III. 9. Oper. ubi supr.]

[4 And better it were, 1563.]

[5 leaving that undone, 1563.]

their love to God, not as God biddeth, which saith, *Si diligitis me, præcepta mea servate;* "If ye love me, keep my commandments;" and again, *Qui habet præcepta mea et facit ea, hic est qui diligit me;* "He that knoweth my precepts, and doth them, he it is loveth me:" but as they bid, *qui quærunt, quæ sua sunt, non quæ Jesu Christi;* "which seek their own things, not Christ's;" as though to tithe mint were more than judgment, faith, and mercy.

And what is to live[1] in state of curates, but that he taught, which said, *Petre, amas me? Pasce, pasce, pasce;* "Peter, lovest thou me? Feed, feed, feed:" which is now set aside, as though to love were to do nothing else, but to wear rings, mitres, and rochets, &c. And when they err in right living, how can the people but err in loving, and be all of the new fashion, to his dishonour that suffered his passion, and taught the true kind of loving, which is now turned into piping, playing, and curious singing, which will not be reformed, I trow, *nisi per manum Dei validam?* And I have both St Augustine and St Thomas[2], with divers others, that *lex* is taken not alonely for ceremonies, but also for morals, where it is said, *Non estis sub lege;* though your friends reprove the same. But they can make no division in a christian congregation. And whereas both you and they would have a soberness in our preaching, I pray God send it unto us, whatsoever ye mean by it. For I see well, whosoever will be happy, and busy with *væ vobis,* he shall shortly after come *coram nobis.*

And where your friends think that I made a lie, when I said that I have thought in times past that the pope had been lord of the world, though your friends be much better learned than I, yet am I sure that they know not what either I[3] think, or have thought, better than I; *juxta illud, Nemo novit quæ sunt hominis, etc.:* as though better men than I have not thought so; as Bonifacius (as I remember) Octavus[4], and the great learned man John of the Burnt

[1 love, 1563.]

[2 Oper. Tom. III. Pars 2, col. 661, Antv. 1700. Thom. Aquin. in Epist. ad Rom. cap. vi. Oper. Tom. VI. p. 76, Venet. 1775.]

[3 I either, 1563.]

[4 Allusion is here had, most probably, to the decretal of pope Boniface VIII. in the canon law *de majoritate et obedientia:* "Porro

Tower[5], *presbyter cardinalis,* in his book, where he proveth the pope to be above the council general, and specially where he saith that the pope is *Rex regum* and *Dominus dominantium;* "king of kings, and lord of lords;" and that he is *Verus dominus totius orbis, jure, licet non facto;* "the true lord of the whole world by good right, albeit in fact he be not so;" and that Constantinus[6] did but restore his own unto him, when he gave unto him Rome; so that *in propria venit,* (as St John saith Christ did), *et sui eum non receperunt;* "He came unto his own, and his own received him not:" and yet I hear not that any of our christian congregations have reclaimed against him, until now of late dissension began. Who be your friends, I cannot tell; but I would you would desire them to be my good masters, and if they will do me no good, at the least way do me no harm: and though they can do you no more good than I, yet I am sure I would be as loth to hurt you as they, either with mine opinions, manner of preaching, or writing.

And as for the pope's high dominion over all, there is one Raphael Maruphus in London, an Italian, and in times past a merchant of dispensations[7], which I suppose would die in the quarrel, as God's true knight and true martyr.

subesse Romano Pontifici omni humanæ creaturæ declaramus, dicimus, definimus, et pronunciamus omnino esse de necessitate salutis." Extravag. Commun. Lib. I. tit. 8. c. i.]

[5 Better known by the name of de Turrecremata. He was by birth a Spaniard, and by profession a Dominican, of which order he became general. He was made a cardinal and bishop by pope Eugenius IV. and died an old man in 1468. As a canonist and papal advocate, "John of the Burnt Tower" was among the most eminent men of his day. The "book" here referred to is most probably the *Summa de Ecclesia,* which treats of the papal authority, and in which the pope is made out to be *Rex regum,* &c. and in authority of jurisdiction superior to a general council, (see more particularly, Lib. II. c. lii. liii. cxiii.; Lib. III. c. xliv. fol. 166 et seq. 262 et seq. 324 et seq. Venet. 1561.) An account of de Turrecremata and his writings is given by Antonius, Biblioth. Hispana Vetus, &c. Tom. II. p. 286 et seq. Matrit. 1788, curant. Bayer. and by Freher. Theatrum Viror. p. 20 et seq. Noriburg. 1688.]

[6 Alluding to the well-known forgery which passes under the name of the *Donatio Constantini.* See Decret. Gratian. Pars Prima, Dist. xcvi. cann. 13, 14. and Sec. Pars, Caus. xii. Quæst. I. can. 15.]

[7 A papal agent for selling dispensations and indulgences.]

As touching purgatory, and worshipping of saints, I shewed to you my mind before my ordinary: and yet I marvelled something, that after private communication had with him, ye would (as it were) adjure me to open my mind before him, not giving me warning before, saving I cannot interpret evil your doings towards me; and yet neither mine ordinary, nor you, disallowed the thing that I said. And I looked not to escape better than Dr Crome[1]; but when I have opened my mind never so much, yet I shall be reported to deny my preaching, of them that have belied my preaching, as he was: *Sed opus est magna patientia ad sustinendas calumnias malignantis ecclesiæ;* "I shall have need of great patience to bear the false reports of the malignant church."

Sir, I have had more business in my little cure, since I spake with you, what with sick folks, and what with matrimonies, than I have had since I came to it, or than I would have thought a man should have in a great cure. I wonder how men can go quietly to bed, which have great cures and many, and yet peradventure are in none of them all. But I pray you, tell none of your friends that I said so foolishly, lest I make a dissension in a christian congregation, and divide a sweet and a restful union, or *tot quot,* with *hæc requies mea in seculum seculi.* Sir, I had made an end of this scribbling, and was beginning to write it again more truly and more distinctly, and to correct it; but there came a man of my lord of Farley[2], with a citation to appear before my lord of London[3] in haste, to be punished for such excesses as I committed at my last being there; so that I could not perform my purpose: I doubt whether ye can read it as it is. If ye can, well be it: if not, I pray you send it me again, and that you so do, whether you can read it or not.

[[1] Dr Edward Crome, rector of St Mary Aldermary, who, in March, 1530, was "convented before the bishop of London and other bishops," on suspicion of heresy. In order to free himself from that suspicion he had to make confession of his faith in a series of articles, in most respects similar to those which the bishops afterwards required Latimer to subscribe to. Strype, Eccl. Mem. III. i. pp. 158 et seq.]

[[2] Sir Walter Hungerford, of Farley Hungerford, a place about six miles from Bath. Wordsworth, Eccl. Biog. III. 516, note.]

[[3] Bp. Stokesly.]

Jesu mercy, what a world is this, that I shall be put to so
great labour and pains, besides great costs, above my power,
for preaching of a poor simple sermon! But, I trow, our
Saviour Christ said true, *Oportet pati, et sic intrare: tam
periculosum est in Christo pie vivere velle;* "I must needs
suffer, and so enter: so perilous a thing it is to live virtuously with Christ," yea, in a christian congregation. God
make us all Christians after the right fashion! Amen.

LETTER VIII.

Latimer *to the Archbishop of* Canterbury[4].

[Foxe, Acts and Mon. pp. 1333, et seq. edit. 1563; Vol. III. pp. 382 et seq. edit. 1684.]

I cannot come to your palace, most reverend prelate, by
reason of sickness; not any new indisposition, but one of old
standing, though lately increased by fresh aggravations. As
far as I can see, I say, and conjecture, it will not be in my
power to come to you to-day, without great injury to myself.
And that your lordship may not any longer in vain expect
my arrival, lo! I send you this strange sheet, blotted by my
own hand, which will be a satisfactory evidence to you of the
truth of my excuse. In what I am now about to write, I wish
I might be able (but the pressure of the time, and this pain
in my head, both forbid it) to expostulate with you, in a

[4 Dr William Warham. The date of the letter may be assigned
to the middle of March, 1532. For Latimer excuses himself for
declining to subscribe certain articles, though repeatedly pressed to
subscribe, and thus alludes to what took place in the convocation held
March 11, 1532. As, also, from the tenor of the letter it may be
collected, that Latimer was still under the displeasure of the archbishop and bishops, he must be presumed to have written it before
the 21st of March, when he made his submission to the convocation.
The translation of this letter is supplied, by Dr Wordsworth's kind
permission, from the Ecclesiastical Biography, Vol. II. pp. 517 et seq.
3rd Edit.]

manner that I have great reason to do; for that you so long detain me, against my will, from the care of those souls which are under my charge; and particularly at this season of the year[1], when there is most occasion for pastors to be present with their flocks.

And why should I not expostulate with you? If indeed it may be permitted at all to me, so vile a slave, to plead with you, so great a father. For if Peter thought it was fit, in respect of his office, that he should never cease, so long as he continued in this earthly tabernacle, to teach and admonish the people, and that so much the more urgently, the nearer he approached to death; can it otherwise than appear very unjust, that there are, who neither teach themselves, even at this time of day (to say nothing of their not having taught in former times), nor permit those who wish to teach so to do, except only such persons as are ready to comply with their wishes through and in every thing?

In the first place, then, I had liberty indeed to present myself before your lordship; but to depart, and extricate myself again, seems no longer to be at my own disposal. And seeing that for this long time one object is pretended in the beginning, and another always aimed at in the progress of my cause, I have much reason to doubt of what kind the issue will be. But the truth, as I hope, will in the end deliver me. The Lord, who is the guardian of truth, will deliver me for ever. And therefore may I never forget the words of Saint Jerome[2] in this behalf: "Nothing can give me pain which I shall suffer in defence of truth: for God liveth, and he will take care of me." Secondly, I was summoned to appear only before the bishop of London; and yet the whole process is carried on before you, my lord of Canterbury, occasionally surrounded by many other reverend fathers. My affair had some bounds and limits assigned it by him who sent for me up, but is now protracted by intricate and wily examinations, as if it would never find a

[[1] "From this passage," Dr Wordsworth observes, "we may presume that this letter was written in *Lent*. The year was 1531-2. His first citation was in 'deep winter;' but some time had now elapsed since then."]

[[2] The reference seems to be to Jerome's Com. in Jerem. i. Oper. Tom. III. col. 532. Paris. 1704. edit. Bened.]

period; while sometimes one person, sometimes another, asks me questions, which do or do not relate to me, without measure or end. So, I say, it would seem to be, did not I myself (though perhaps somewhat uncourteously, yet I think not indiscreetly) impose some limit to their interrogatories; fearing, as I do, lest while singly I have to answer to so many, something, as it often happens, should unadvisedly fall from me, to injure a cause in other respects unimpeachable[3].

Let them be contented to profess, to assert, to defend their own propositions; but why should the opinions of others be obtruded upon me, and I be compelled, I know not by what right, to make confession of them? This hardship I think is unexampled; and yet I am accounted untractable, for refusing to comply with what I deem unjust importunities. If any man has any fault to object against my preaching, as being obscure or incautiously uttered, I am ready to explain my doctrine by further discourse: for I have never preached any thing contrary to the truth, nor contrary to the decrees of the fathers, nor, as far as I know, contrary to the catholic faith; all which I can prove to be true by the testimonies of my enemies and calumniators. I have desired, I own, and do desire, a reformation in the judgment of the vulgar. I have desired, and still do, that they should distinguish between duties; and that each should maintain among them its proper value, its place and time, its rank and degree; and so that all men should know, that there is a very great difference between those works which God hath prepared for each of us, zealously discharging the duties of our respective callings, to walk in, and those that are voluntary, which we undertake by our own strength and pleasure. It is lawful, I own, to make use of images; it is lawful to go on pilgrimage; it is lawful to pray to saints; it is lawful to be mindful of souls abiding in purgatory: but these things, which are voluntary, are so to be moderated, that God's commandments of necessary obligation, which bring eternal life to those that keep them, and eternal death to those who neglect them, be not deprived of their just value; lest from a mistaken love of God, and by a foolish devotion, we meet with a return from him, not of love, but rather of hatred. For this is truly to love God,

[3 It is to this period that Latimer seems to have alluded in his sermon at Stamford. See Vol. I. p. 294.]

that we diligently keep his commandments, according to those words of Christ, " He that hath my commandments and doeth them, he it is that loveth me." Let no one then so account of those precepts which respect our calling in God, as to choose rather to wander in his own inventions; seeing that in the end we shall all be judged before the tribunal of Christ according to those, and not these; as Christ says, " The word which I have spoken, it shall judge at the last day." Who can recompense for a single commandment of God by any inventions of his own, however numerous or specious? O that we were as zealous in the things of God, as we are busy and careful about our own fantasies! There are many works which, when done in a simple and honest heart, God does not condemn, yea rather, out of compliance with men's infirmities, does in some degree approve, which, if he were asked before they were done, he would neither command nor counsel; as being things rather to be tolerated, when so done, than to be recommended to be done; lest haply by occasion of that commendation those duties should come to be neglected, which are to be performed on peril of damnation. But what can be more unseemly, than to employ our preaching in that which God would neither command nor counsel, so long at least as those things thereby fall into neglect, which are commanded? I therefore hitherto stand fixed on the side of the commandments of God; so aiming, not at my own gain, but that of Christ; so seeking not my own glory, but that of God: and as long as life shall be permitted to me, I will not cease thus to continue, imitating herein all true preachers of the word, that have hitherto lived in the world.

There are, no doubt, and have long been, some intolerable abuses amongst us. Why then should a preacher be called upon to recommend from the pulpit works, which though they were seldomer performed (not to say never), I do not see that the christian religion would suffer any loss? Unless indeed we be so wretchedly blind as to think, that religion consists in our own unworthy lucre, and not in the true worship of God. It cannot be, I own, that the blameable abuse of these observances can be duly censured, but that straightway the use of them shall become less frequent. And yet I had rather that some things were never done at all, than with that sort of confidence in them, which diminishes the regard to real duties. Some things, we know, are to be done, and others are not to be left undone: others again we are under no obligation of doing, and may leave undone.

But now, is there one that does not see amongst us many manifest abuses? Who is there that sees and does not greatly lament them? Who shall lament and will not endeavour to remove them? And when will they be removed, if the use be ever extolled in preaching, and the abuse passed over in silence? Nay verily, it cannot be, but that the abuse must prevail, and bear the sway. It is one thing to tolerate that which may be permitted on fit occasions, and another to be always extolling it as a necessary matter, and to establish it by a law. "Go ye," says Christ, "and teach all things." All what things? "All," says he, "which I have commanded you." He does not say, all which you yourselves may choose to account necessary for preaching. Well then, for God's sake, let us so exert ourselves, as with one accord to preach the doctrines of God; lest we become as they who corrupt and make a traffic of preaching, rather than true ministers of the word: seeing especially, that men are very slow towards heavenly things, and so swift about their own, as to stand in no need of the spur; being miserably deceived by false judgment, and innate superstition, contracted even from their youth; vices which we shall hardly be able to cure by any preaching, how frequent, how vehement, how pure and sincere so ever. May God therefore provide a remedy, that, in these evil days, they whose duty it is rather to preach themselves (for as Peter says, he gave us commandment to preach) do not hinder those that are willing and able to exhort (contrary to those words, "Hinder not him who can do good"), or else compel those to preach, who make traffic of the word, that they may so detain to their destruction the miserable commonalty in superstitions, and a confidence that cannot but fail them. Rather, O God! do thou have mercy on us, that we may learn thy way in the earth; and not be like those of whom it is said, "Your thoughts are not as my thoughts, nor your ways as my ways, saith the Lord."

For these reasons I dare not, most reverend father, subscribe the bare propositions which you require of me; being unwilling, as far as I may, to be the author of any longer continuance of the superstition of the people; and that I may not be also at the same time the author of my own damnation. Could I but be thought worthy, most venerable father, to offer unto you one piece of counsel! But I restrain myself. It is not hard to conjecture, how depraved and insufferable the heart of man is. But "no man knows the things of a man, save the spirit of man that is in him." It is not any pride that withholds me from that subscription, which has so often been asked of me by your lordship to my great uneasiness. It cannot but be blame-worthy, not to obey the fathers and leaders of the church. But it is their duty meantime to take care what, and to whom, they give commandment, since there are occasions in which we must obey God rather than men. My head is so out of frame, and my whole body so weak, that I am neither able to come to you, nor to write over again and correct this letter. Your lordship however, I hope, will approve, if not the judgment, at least the affection with which it is written.

Farewell.

LETTER IX.

Latimer to Greenwood[1].

[Harleian MSS. 6989, Art. 90.]

MASTER GREENWOOD, *salutem in Christo Jesu.* I pray your goodness be charitable, and *redime nobiscum tempus. In hac dierum malitia non omni credendum est auditui;* but, if all be truth that I hear, *cogor equidem desiderare in te Christianæ caritatis nonnihil: satis est adversariorum, si tu amicus esse pergeres; sat perversi obloquii, si tu etiam sileres: de otioso verbo rationem reddes; quanto magis de*

[1 William Greenwood, B.D. fellow of St John's college, Cambridge, and one of those who openly impugned Latimer's preaching in that university. He was either executed for denying the royal supremacy, or died in prison. This seems to be the letter for which Latimer was called to account by convocation, on the 19th of April, 1532, and may, therefore, be dated in that month. Baily [or Hall], Life of Bp. Fisher, p. 31, London, 1655; Lamb, Collection of Letters, &c. pp. 14, et seq.; Wilkins, Concilia, Vol. III. p. 748.]

perniciosis! Quod ad rem a me prædicatam attinet, vel prædicandi consilium, ut non sum mihi conscius erroris, ita nec errorem sum publice fassus : though, peradventure, more out some time than well advised; not entreating *justum verbum, quod potest salvare animas,* with such reverence, majesty or gravity, as either I ought, or I would have had; nor with due discretion at all times, having respect to the time, and the rudeness and the rashness of the people. And yet, in this behalf, I would I were alone without fellows[2], though more uncomfortable. Report ever as ye would be reported, well and not evil, truth and not otherwise; for else *statim in foribus peccatum erit. Et caritas multitudinem peccatorum operit, falso impingit multum ;* and yet, peradventure, the misbehaviour of the people might as well be imputed to other things as to my preaching : but yet I will not be contentious. As to the people, though I will have more respect to their capacity, yet as to my old preaching, I will not change the verity ; and I will with all diligence, according to my promise in my *scriptis,* do all that is in me to reprove their infirmity. There is no wretch living had more need to say with David than I, *Redime, Domine, a calumniis hominum, ut custodiam mandata tua.* Of this foolish scribbling ye may know my meaning. *Vale. Tuus Latimerus.*

LETTER X.

Latimer *to* Morice[3].

[Printed in Foxe, pp. 1314, et seq. edit. 1563. Vol. III. pp. 390, et seq. edit. 1684.]

Right worshipful and mine own good master Morice, *salutem in Christo Jesu.*—And I thank you for all hearty kindness, not only heretofore shewed unto me, but also that now of late you would vouchsafe to write unto me, so poor

[2 folows, MS.]

[3 The same person who was afterwards secretary to archbishop Cranmer. See above, p. 222. The letter itself, as is apparent, relates to the articles imputed to Mr Latimer by Dr Powell and others. The probable date of it is May or June, 1533.]

a wretch, to my great comfort among all these my troubles. I trust and doubt nothing in it, but God will reward you for me, and supply abundantly mine unability, &c. Master Morice, you would wonder to know how I have been entreated at Bristol, I mean of some of the priests, which first desired me, welcomed me, made me cheer, heard what I said, and allowed my saying in all things whiles I was with them. When I was gone home to my benefice, perceiving that the people favoured me so greatly, and that the mayor had appointed me to preach at Easter, privily they procured an inhibition for all them that had not the bishop's licence, which they knew well enough I had not, and so craftily defeated master mayor's appointment, pretending that they were sorry for it; procuring also certain preachers to blatter against me, as Hubberdin and Powell, with other more[1], whom[2] when I had brought before the mayor and the wise council of the town, to know what they could lay to my charge, wherefore they so declaimed against me, they said they spake of information: howbeit no man could be brought forth that would abide by anything. So that they had place and time to belie me shamefully; but they had no place nor time to lay to my charge, when I was present and ready to make them answer. God amend them, and suage their malice that they have against the truth and me, &c.

Our lady was a sinner[3].

So they did belie me to have said, when I had said

[1 A letter from Richard Brown, priest, to a member of convocation, dated March 18, 1533, states that "The same Latimer is assigned for to preach again at Bristow, the Wednesday in Easter-week, except by your commandment to the dean there he be denied and forbid to preach." And the report of the commissioners who were appointed by Cromwell to inquire into the religious feuds, which had grown up in Bristol in consequence of Mr Latimer's preaching, sets forth, that at the "tyme of Ester [1533] Huberdyn came to Brystow and preached in Sainte Thomas Chyrche, at after none on Ester eve and at Saynte Nycholas Chyrche, before none on Ester day, and there prechyd scharply agenst Latomer's artycules, provenynge them be auctorytes, as well by the Olde as the New Testamentes, sysmatyke and yrronyous." Strype, Eccl. Mem. I. i. 248, Oxf. Edit. Letters relating to the suppression of the Monasteries, p. 9. See also above, p. 325, note 1.]

[2 which, 1563.] [3 See above, p. 225, &c.]

nothing so, but to reprove certain, both priests and beneficed men, which do give so much to our lady, as though she had not been saved by Christ, a whole Saviour both of her, and of all that be and shall be saved. I did reason after this manner: that either she was a sinner, or no sinner. If a sinner, then she was delivered from sin by Christ; so that he saved her, either by delivering or preserving her from sin; so that without him neither she, nor none other, either be, or could be saved. And, to avoid all offence, I shewed how it might be answered, both to certain scriptures which make all generally sinners, and how it might be answered unto Chrysostom and Theophylact[4], which make her namely and specially a sinner. But all would not serve, their malice was[5] so great; notwithstanding that five hundred honest men can and will bear record. When they cannot reprove that thing that I do say, then they will belie me to say that thing that they can reprove; for they will needs appear to be against me.

Saints are not to be worshipped.

So they lied, when I had shewed divers significations of this word "saints" among the vulgar people. First, images of saints are called saints, and so they are not to be worshipped: take worshipping of them for praying to them; for they are neither mediators by way of redemption, nor yet by way of intercession. And yet they may be well used, when they be applied to that use that they were ordained for, to be laymen's books for remembrance of heavenly things, &c.

Take saints for inhabiters of heaven, and worshipping of them for praying to them, I never denied, but that they might be worshipped, and be our mediators, though not by way of redemption (for so Christ alone[6] is a whole mediator, both for them and for us), yet by the way of intercession[7].

Pilgrimage.

And I never denied pilgrimage. And yet I have said

[4 See above, p. 226, note 1. The state of the controversy on this subject is given at large by Chamier, Panstratia Catholica, Tom. III. Lib. v, c. ii. et seq. Genevæ, 1626.]
[5 is, 1563.] [6 alonely, 1563.]
[7 See master Latimer's error in those days. Foxe.]

that much scurf must be pared away[1], ere ever it can be well done; superstition, idolatry, false faith and trust in the image, unjust estimation of the thing, setting aside God's ordinance for doing of the thing: debts must be paid, restitutions made, wife and children be provided for, duty to our poor neighbours discharged. And when it is at the best, before it be vowed, it need not to be done; for it is neither under the bidding of God, nor of man, to be done. And wives must counsel with husbands, and husbands and wives with curates, before it be vowed to be done, &c.

Ave Maria.

As for the *Ave Maria*, who can think that I would deny it? I said it was a heavenly greeting or saluting of our blessed lady, wherein the angel Gabriel, sent from the Father of heaven, did annunciate and shew unto her the good-will of God towards her, what he would with her, and to what he had chosen her. But I said, it was not properly a prayer, as the *Pater noster*, which our Saviour Christ himself made for a proper prayer, and bade us say it for a prayer, not adding that we should say ten or twenty *Ave Marias* withal: and I denied not but that we may well say *Ave Maria* also, but not so that we shall think that the *Pater noster* is not good, a whole and perfect prayer, nor cannot be well said without *Ave Maria*. So that I did not speak against well saying of it, but against superstitious saying of it, and of the *Pater noster* too: and yet I put a difference betwixt that, and that which[2] Christ made to be said for a prayer.

No fire in hell.

Who ever could say[3] or think so? Howbeit good authors do put a difference betwixt a suffering[4] in the fire with bodies, and without bodies. The soul without the body is a spiritual substance, which they say cannot receive a corporal quality; and some make it a spiritual fire, and some a corporal fire. For as it is called a fire, so it is called a worm;

[1 "Pare away the scurf," and clean take away all popery. Foxe.]
[2 betwixt that that Christ made, 1563.]
[3 either say, 1563.]   [4 betwixt suffering, 1563.]

and it is thought of some not to be a material worm, that is a living beast, but it is a metaphor; but that is neither to nor fro: for a fire it is; a worm it is; pain[5] it is; a torment it is; an anguish it is; a grief, a misery, a sorrow; a heaviness inexplicable, intolerable, whose nature and condition in every point who can tell, but he that is of God's privy council, saith St Augustine[6]? God give us grace rather to be diligent to keep us out of it, than to be curious to discuss the property of it: for certain we be, that there is little ease, yea, none at all, but weeping, wailing, and gnashing of teeth; which be two effects of extreme pain, rather certain tokens what pain there is, than what manner of pain there is.

No purgatory.

He that sheweth the state and condition of it, doth not deny it. But I had rather[7] be in it, than in Lollards' Tower, the bishop's prison, for divers skills and causes.

First, In this I might die bodily for lack of meat and drink: in that I could not.

Item, In this I might die ghostly for fear of pain, or lack of good counsel: there I could not.

Item, In this I might be in extreme necessity: in that I could not, if it be peril of perishing.

Item, In this I might lack charity: there I could not.

Item, In this I might lose my patience: in that I could not.

Item, In this I might be in peril and danger of death: in that I could not.

Item, In this I might be without surety of salvation: in that I could not.

Item, In this I might dishonour God: in that I could not.

Item, In this I might murmur and grudge against God: in that I could not.

Item, In this I might displease God: in that I could not.

Item, In this I might be displeased with God: in that I could not.

Item, In this I might be judged to perpetual prison, as they call it: in that I could not.

[5 a pain, 1563.]   [6 See above, p. 236, note 1.]
[7 leaver, 1563.]

Item, In this I might be craftily handled: in that I could not.

Item, In this I might be brought to bear a fagot: in that I could not.

Item, In this I might be discontented with God: in that I could not.

Item, In this I might be separated and dissevered from Christ: in that I could not.

Item, In this I might be a member of the devil: in that I could not.

Item, In this I might be an inheritor in hell: in that I could not.

Item, In this I might pray out of charity, and in vain: in that I could not.

Item, In this my lord and his chaplains might manacle me by night: in that they could not.

Item, In this they might strangle me, and say that I[1] hanged myself: in that they could not.

Item, In this they might have me to the consistory, and judge me after their fashion: from thence they could not.

Ergo, I had rather[2] to be there than here. For though the fire be called never so hot, yet if[3] the bishop's two fingers can shake away a piece, a friar's cowl another part, and *scala cœli* altogether, I will never found abbey, college, nor chantry for that purpose.

For seeing there is no pain that can break my charity, break my patience, cause me to dishonour God, to displease God, to be displeased with God, cause me not to joy in God, nor that can bring me to danger of death or to danger of desperation, or from surety of salvation; that can separate me from Christ, or Christ from me; I care the less for it. John Chrysostom[4] saith, that the greatest pain that damned souls have, is to be separate and cut off from Christ

[1 I had hanged, 1563. The allusion is to the story of Richard Hun, Foxe, Acts and Mon. Vol. II. p. 8 et seq. edit. 1684.]

[2 leiffer, 1563.] [3 yet and if, 1563.]

[4 ὁ γὰρ καιόμενος καὶ τῆς βασιλείας ἐκπίπτει πάντως· αὕτη δὲ ἐκείνης χαλεπωτέρα ἡ τιμωρία· καὶ οἶδα μὲν ὅτι πολλοὶ τὴν γέενναν μόνον πεφρίκασιν, ἐγὼ δὲ τὴν ἔκπτωσιν τῆς δόξης ἐκείνης πολὺ τῆς γεέννης πικροτέραν εἶναί φημι. In Matth. Hom. 23, Oper. Tom. VII. pp. 294, et seq. Paris. 1727. edit. Bened. See also above, p. 236, note 2.]

for ever; which pain, he saith, is greater than many hells: which pain the souls in purgatory neither have[5] nor can have.

Consider, master Morice, whether provision for purgatory hath not brought thousands to hell. Debts have[5] not been paid; restitution of evil-gotten lands and goods hath not been made; christian people (whose necessities we see, to whom whatsoever we do Christ reputeth done to himself, to whom we are bounden under pain of damnation to do for as we would be done for ourself) are neglected and suffered to perish; last wills unfulfilled and broken; God's ordinance set aside; and also for purgatory, foundations have[5] been taken for sufficient satisfaction: so we have trifled away the ordinance of God and restitutions. Thus we have gone to hell with masses, diriges, and ringing of many a bell. And who can pill pilgrimages from idolatry, and purge purgatory from robbery, but he shall be in peril to come in suspicion of heresy with them, so that they may pill with pilgrimage and spoil with purgatory? And verily the abuse of them cannot be taken away, but great lucre and vantage shall fall away from them, which had rather[6] have profit with abuse, than lack the same with use; and that is the wasp that doth sting them, and maketh them to swell. And if purgatory were purged of all that it[7] hath gotten by setting aside restitution and robbing of Christ, it would be but a poor purgatory; so poor, that it should not be able to feed so fat, and trick up so many idle and slothful lubbers.

I take God to witness, I would hurt no[8] man; but it grieveth me to see such abuse continue without remedy: I cannot understand what they mean by the pope's pardoning of purgatory, but by way of suffrage; and as for suffrage, unless he do his duty, and seek not his own but Christ's glory, I had rather[6] have the suffrage of Jack of the scullery, which in his calling doth exercise both faith and charity, but for his mass: and that is as good of another simple priest as of him. For, as for authority of keys, it is to loose from guiltiness of sin, and eternal pain due to the same, according to Christ's word, and not to his own private will. And as for pilgrimage, you would wonder what juggling there is to

[5 hath, 1563.]   [6 leiffer, 1563.]
[7 he, 1563.]   [8 hurt to no, 1563.]

get money withal. I dwell within half a mile of the Fossway[1], and you would wonder to see how they come by flocks out of the west country to many images, but chiefly to the blood of Hales[2]. And they believe verily that it is the very blood that was in Christ's body, shed upon the mount of Calvary for our salvation, and that the sight of it with their bodily eye doth certify them, and putteth them out of doubt, that they be in clean life, and in state of salvation without spot of sin, which doth bolden them to many things. For you would wonder, if you should commune with them both coming and going, what faiths they have: for as for forgiving their enemies, and reconciling their christian brethren, they cannot away withal; for the sight of that blood doth requite them for the time.

I read in scripture of two certifications: one to the Romans, *Justificati ex fide, pacem habemus;* "We, being justified by faith, have peace with God." If I see the blood of Christ with the eye of my soul, that is true faith that his blood was shed for me, &c.

Another in the Epistle of John: *Nos scimus quod translati sumus de morte ad vitam, quoniam diligimus fratres;* "We know that we are translated from death to life, because we love the brethren." But I read not that I have peace with God, or that I am translated from death to life, because I see with my bodily eye the blood of Hales. It is very probable, that all the blood that was in the body of Christ, was united[3] and knit to his divinity; and then no part thereof shall return to his corruption. And I marvel that Christ should have two resurrections. And if it were that they that did violently and injuriously pluck it out of his body, when they scourged him and nailed him to the cross, did see it with their bodily eye, yet they were not in clean life. And we see the selfsame blood in form of wine, when we have consecrated, and may both see it, feel it, and receive it to our damnation, as touching bodily receiving.

[1 The Roman road leading from Bath by Cirencester on to Lincoln. Hoare, Ancient Wiltshire, Vol. II. p. 23.]

[2 The famous relic referred to, Vol. I. p. 231. A more particular account of this object of superstition will be found in the notes to a letter from Latimer to Cromwell, under date of Oct. 28, 1538.]

[3 unite, 1563.]

And many do see it at Hales without confession, as they say. God knoweth all, and the devil in our time is not dead.

Christ hath left a doctrine behind him, wherein we be taught how to believe, and what to believe: he doth suffer the devil to use his crafty fashion for our trial and probation. It were little thankworthy to believe well and rightly, if nothing should move us to false faith, and to believe superstitiously. It was not in vain that Christ, when he had taught truly, by and bye bade beware of false prophets, which would bring in error slily. But we be secure and uncareful, as though false prophets could not meddle[4] with us, and as though the warning of Christ were no more earnest and effectual than is the warning of mothers when they trifle with their children, and bid them beware the bug, &c.

Lo, sir, how I run at riot beyond measure. When I began, I was minded to have written but half a dozen lines; but thus I forget myself ever when I write to a trusty friend, which will take in worth my folly, and keep it from mine enemy, &c.

As for Dr Wilson[5], I wot not what I should say; but I pray God endue him with charity. Neither he, nor any[6] of his countrymen, did ever love me, since I did inveigh against their factions and partiality in Cambridge. Before that, who was more favoured of him than I? That is the bile that may not be touched, &c.

A certain friend shewed me, that Dr Wilson is gone now into his country about Beverley in Holderness; and from thence he will go a progress through Yorkshire, Lancashire, Cheshire, and so from thence to Bristol. What he intended effectual by this progress, God knoweth, and not I. If he come to Bristol, I shall hear tell, &c.

As for Hubberdin, no doubt he is a man of no great learning, nor yet of stable wit. He is here *servus hominum;*

[4 not have meddled, 1563.]

[5 Strype, not without reason, conjectures that this person may have been Dr Nicholas Wilson, parson of St Thomas the Apostle, in London, who was attainted with bishop Fisher and others, in 1534, for refusing the oaths of supremacy and succession. He appears also to have been prebendary of St Paul's, and archdeacon of Oxford. Strype, Eccl. Mem. I. i. 246. Newcourt, Repertorium, Vol. I. p. 164.]

[6 none, 1563.]

for he will preach whatsoever the bishops will bid him preach. Verily, in my mind, they are more to be blamed than he. He doth magnify the pope more than enough. As for our Saviour Christ and christian kings, they are[1] little beholden to him. No doubt he did miss the cushion in many things. Howbeit they that did send him, men think, will defend him: I pray God amend him and them both. They would fain make matter against me, intending so either to deliver him by me, or else to rid us both together, and so they would think him well bestowed, &c.

As touching Dr Powell, how highly he took upon him in Bristol, and how little he regarded the sword, which representeth the king's person, many can tell you. I think there is never an earl in this realm, that knoweth his obedience by Christ's commandment to his prince, and wotteth what the sword doth signify, that would have taken upon him so stoutly. Howbeit master mayor, as he is a profound wise man, did twit[2] him prettily; it were too long to write all. Our pilgrimages are not a little beholden to him; for, to occasion the people to them, he alleged this text[3]: *Omnis qui relinquit patrem, domos, uxorem;* "Whosoever leaveth father, house, wife," &c. By that you may perceive his hot zeal and crooked judgment, &c. Because I am so belied, I could wish that it would please the king's grace to command me to preach before his highness a whole year together every Sunday, that he himself might perceive how they belie me, saying, that I have neither learning, nor utterance worthy thereunto, &c. I pray you pardon me; I cannot make an end.

[[1] kings are little, 1563.]   [[2] twicke, 1563.]
[[3] text for them, 1563.]

LETTER XI.

LATIMER to SECRETARY CROMWELL.

[Orig. State Pap. Off. Crom. Corr. Vol. 49, 1. 475.]

RIGHT honourable sir. *Salutem in Christo Jesu.* And as to the thing that I moved unto your mastership, at my departure yesterday, this bearer is the gentleman of whom I told you of, ready to all things that you shall require of him, and only for lack of calling on hitherto slow; as he himself can tell you. And perchance he can tell you of more as far behindhand as he, if commissioners[4] were always as mindful to further the king's business as they be to advance their own profits about their tenants, &c. But I ween, if you might make progress throughout England, you should find how acts declareth hearts. But you can use all things to the best according to your approved wisdom. And meseemeth it were not amiss that gentlemen of lands and arms should so swear to the king's issue, that their oaths and also names be registered, &c.; for so you should know surely who were sworn and who not. I pray you be good master to this gentleman my prisoner, and pardon me of this my foolish scribbling.

Yours, to his little power,
H. LATIMER.

It may chance that I shall send you more to the same purpose. God preserve you in long life to God's pleasure!

To the right honourable master,
 secretary to the king's grace,
 his singular good master.

[4 The "commissioners" mentioned in this letter were those employed to administer the oath exacted by the act which entailed the crown on the issue of Henry VIII. by Queen Anne Boleyn. That act was passed in 1534 (25 Hen. VIII. c. 22), and confirmed in 1535 (26 Hen. VIII. c. 2); and as this letter appears to have been written before Latimer was raised to the episcopacy, the probable date of it is the summer of 1535. The recommendation of Latimer that the "oaths and names" of parties who had been sworn should be registered, was in accordance with the plan adopted as regarded the members of both houses of parliament. See Holinshed, Chronicle, III. p. 937; Herbert, Life of Hen. VIII. pp. 408, et seq.]

LETTER XII.

LATIMER *to* SECRETARY CROMWELL.

[Orig. State Pap. Off. Crom. Corr. Vol. 49, 1. 476.]

HONOURABLE sir. *Sis salvus in Christo*, and do certify your mastership how we succeed in our matters. We have been here now all this fortnight in vain, obtaining as yet neither confirmation, nor yet of temporalities restitution[1]. For lack of the royal assent with your signification, my lord of Canterbury[2] cannot proceed; and we hear nothing of it, neither of master Gostwyck[3] nor other where. For expedition of these things it had been better for us to have given attendance of your mastership still in the court; and so we would have been glad to have done, if it had been seen to your mastership so to have appointed us. I did speak this day with Mr Polsted[4], which hath no further instructions from your mastership yet, as he saith, but to receive our sureties for the first-fruits: and he is uncertain as yet what they shall be. And as touching my part in that behalf, I trust your mastership hath not forgotten my last suit, for the which I was minded to have gone to the king's grace myself; but the queen's grace[5], calling to remembrance at what

[1 The deed for the restoration of the temporalities of the see of Worcester on the election and consecration of Bishop Latimer is dated Oct. 4, 1535. Rymer, Vol. xiv. p. 533.]

[2 Archbishop Cranmer.]

[3 "Master Gostwyck," or Gostwick, of Willington in Bedfordshire, was one of the commissioners employed by king Hen. VIII. to rate all ecclesiastical preferments. He seems to have been otherwise patronised by that monarch, if his ability to purchase estates be taken as any indication of court favour: for Leland [1538] mentions him as purchasing the lordship of Willington, and "beside Willington v. or vi. Lordshippes mo." By the part he was instigated to take against Cranmer toward the latter end of the reign of Hen. VIII. he incurred the displeasure of the king, who threatened to make him a "poor Gostwick, and otherwise punish him." Fuller, Ch. Hist. Vol. II. p. 92. edit. 1837; Leland, Itinerary, Vol. I. pp. 92, 93; Strype, Mem. of Cran. pp. 176, et seq. Oxf. edit.]

[4 Mr Polsted's name appears as one of the commissioners appointed to visit the religious houses. Letters connected with the Suppress. of Monasteries, p. 89; Strype, Eccl. Mem, I. i., 402, Oxf. edit.]

[5 Queen Anne Boleyn.]

end my lord of Salisbury[6] was at, said I should not need to move the king, but that it should be enough to inform your mastership thereof. It shall be your mastership's pleasure whether I shall tarry your return hither, or whether this bearer shall tarry your leisure to bring further instruction from you. Thus I am bold to interrupt you, and yet not without great lothness, forasmuch as I consider your hourly business in matters of more weightiness than this. God preserve you long in health to God's pleasure, which is my daily prayer. My brother of Rochester[7] commendeth him most heartily unto you.

Yours,

H. LATIMER, Elect.

The 4th day of September, [1535].

To the right honourable Mr Secretary to the king's grace, his singular good master.

[[6] Nicholas Shaxton. He was distinguished in early life for his zeal and sufferings for the doctrines of the reformation; was elected Bishop of Sarum in 1535; and resigned that see at the same time that Latimer retired from the bishoprick of Worcester. After enduring imprisonment and hardships, for opposing the Act of the Six Articles, Shaxton relapsed into popery, wrote in favour of it, and persecuted those who remained faithful to the Reformation. Strype, Eccles. Mem. III. i., 570, et seq. Godwin, de Præsul. p. 353, edit. Richardson.]

[[7] John Hildesley or Hilsey. He was prior of the Dominicans in Bristol, and succeeded Fisher in the bishoprick of Rochester. He seems to have been a person of learning, sound judgment and piety; the friend, also, and coadjutor of Archbishop Cranmer in promoting the Reformation. He is best known, perhaps, as one of the bishops employed in drawing up "The Institution of a Christian man", and as the compiler of a Primer which was published during the reign of Henry VIII. Strype, Mem. of Cranm. p. 53, et seq.; Wood, Athen. Oxon. I. 112, edit. Bliss; Primers put forth in reign of Hen. VIII. Pref. liv.]

LETTER XIII.

LATIMER *to* SECRETARY CROMWELL.

[Orig. State Pap. Off. Crom. Corr. Vol. 49, 1. 479.]

HONOURABLE sir, *salutem in salutis omnium Authore.* I was in a near disposition to an [illness] yesterday, which letted me to come to your mastership for the draft you wot of. And now this day my lord of Westminster[1] hath put unto me to preach there with him, else he should be like to be disappointed. If you would of your goodness send it to me by this bearer, I would apply my little wit to the imitation of the same. And I will write and certify my lord of Canterbury[2] according to your advertisement in all haste.

Yours,

[Oct. 1535.]   HUG. WYGORN.

To the right honourable Mr
*   Secretary, his singular*
*   good master.*

LETTER XIV.

LATIMER *to* SECRETARY CROMWELL.

[Orig. State Pap. Off. Crom. Corr. Vol. 49, 1. 477.]

HONOURABLE sir, *salutem.* And I pray you forgive me for that I have not, according to my duty, delivered unto you the draft before this time, I have been so distract in preparing

[[1] William Benson or Boston, abbot of Westminster, who, with seventeen of the monks, surrendered that abbey into the hands of Henry VIII. 16 Jan. 1539, and was created first Dean of Westminster. By an agreement entered into between Henry VII. and the abbot and convent of Westminster, it was provided that the abbot for the time being should cause a sermon to be preached in his church on "every Good Friday, Monday in Easter week, the Feast of our Lady, and every sunday in the year," except certain sundays which are specified in the agreement above mentioned. Le Neve, Fasti. p. 363; Newcourt, Repertorium, Vol. I. pp. 711, et seq.; Rymer, Fœd. Vol. XIV. p. 459.]

[[2] Archbishop Cranmer.]

homewards, &c. God preserve you long to his pleasure in health and well-doing!

Yours to his little power,
H. WYGORN.

Postridie sanctissimorum sutorum, [26 Oct. 1535.]

If your mastership have the old seal of my office, I would recompense you according to the weight.

Bene sit tibi ut sis longævus super terram.

*To the right honourable master
  Thomas Cromwell, the king's
  principal secretary, and his
  singular good master.*

LETTER XV.

LATIMER *to* SECRETARY CROMWELL[3].

[Orig. State Pap. Off. Crom. Corr. Vol. 49, p. 480.]

AFTER my right hearty commendations to your mastership. Where you write unto me that the king's grace, moved with pity, and having also divers other considerations stirring to the same, is inclined to restore the Prior of Worcester[4] to his room and office again; desiring nevertheless to

[3 As Latimer was not Bishop of Worcester in Jan. 1535, and Cromwell was a peer before Jan. 1537, this letter must have been written after the Epiphany, 1536.]

[4 William Moore, or More, who resigned his office, or was turned out of it, some time in the 27 Hen. VIII. Holbeach was elected prior in March 13, 1536, and Moore is styled the "late prior" in a deed 28 Hen. VIII., by which the then prior and convent of Worcester covenant to allow him one of their manors, with plate, linen, and furniture. A monk also was assigned to wait on him and to say mass: he received also a present of 1000 marks, and had his debts paid. Browne Willis (Hist. of Abbies, Vol. I. p. 311) asserts that Moore lived till the reign of Q. Elizabeth; which is hardly compatible with the notion of "extreme age" at the time Latimer wrote. But it is plain from this letter, that the prior was not personally known to Latimer. Wood says that Moore succeeded Thos. de Mildenham as prior in 1518, and

know my opinion therein in writing to you, or ever his grace do resolve himself thoroughly upon the same: in consideration whereof, I do you to understand, by this letter written with my own hand, that I rejoice not a little to perceive that the king's grace is moved of his gracious goodness to have pity of that simple man. But there is divers degrees in pity, as I think; for if that great crime was not alonely detected, but also proved against him, as you do say it was, then to pardon him of his life is to shew a great pity. To add thereunto a competent living for himself and one to wait upon him, is to shew a greater pity, and so far forth. I wish, and have done always, that the king's highness would extend his pity unto him. And verily I marvel greatly if his heart be so stony, so flinty, that so great pity and compassion as it is cannot reconcile him to the king's highness sufficiently. Marry, to burden him with his busy office again, and to clog him again with his great cure, namely now, he being so debile, so weak, and of so great age as you write him to be, whether it be to pity him or trouble him, I cannot say. But for mine opinion in this behalf, (to say what I think without fiction to my prince,) the king's grace had need after such a sort to be pitiful toward one man, that his grace seem not for pitying of one to be pitiless toward many: I mean the whole house of the country thereabout. For either he is able to discharge that great cure, and can serve God and the king sufficiently therein, or not. If he be able and can, it were well done that the king's grace would extend his pity thereunto: if not, it were great pity to trouble him, and to charge him with that thing now, in his extreme age, which thing (perchance) he was never able to discharge in midst of his youth.

But now, what ability is required to discharging of such an office, no man can tell better than the king's grace himself. Again: what ability this man hath to discharge such an office, no man can tell better than my lord of Canterbury, or than Mr doctor Lee[1], which both did visit there, as know-

"resigned upon a foresight of ruin." Nash, Hist. of Worcester. Vol. I. p. 280; Letters on the Supp. of Monaster. p. 285; Wood, Fasti Oxon. Vol. I. p. 46, edit. Bliss.]

[1 Dr Thomas Legh, a civilian, much employed by Hen. VIII. in the visitation of religious houses.]

eth both what he can do, and what the house needeth to be
done. And I think you yourself is not ignorant therein;
for I have heard you speak your mind both of their house,
and also of him. And this is all that I can say. If I have
one there to help me, I shall do the more good; if not, I
shall boggle[2] myself as well as I can. When I perceived that
there was no hope to speak for this man, I named two other
to the king, of the which two his grace preferred Coton[3];
and I certified you his highness's pleasure thereof, and the
queen's grace hath remembered you since. As God and the
king will have it, so be it, Amen: for if they two be well
served, I am right well pleased; and thus I commit you to
God's preservation. This messenger maketh so great haste,
that I have leisure to write no better.

By yours,

HUGH OF WORCESTER
to command.

Sabbato post Epiphaniam proximo, [8 Jan. 1536].

*To my singular good master,
Thomas Cromwell, high
secretary to the king's
noble grace.*

LETTER XVI.

LATIMER *to* SECRETARY CROMWELL[4].

[Printed by Strype, Eccl. Mem. I. i. 470, et seq. Oxf. ed.]

RIGHT honourable sir. *Salutem plurimam.* And be-

[2 buggell, orig.]

[3 The person appointed to succeed Moore was Henry Holbeach, as above stated.]

[4 Strype guesses the date of this letter to be 1538, but as the writer was bishop of Worcester, and Cromwell (as appears by the indorsement) not yet a peer, the letter must have been written between October 1535 and July 1536. The MS. readings are from the Cotton MS. Cleopat. E. V. fol. 363.]

cause I hear[1] your mastership hath sent for master Coots[2], which preached at Halls, to come to you, therefore I do now send unto you his sermon; not as he spake it, (if he spake it as his hearers reported[3],) but rather as he had[4] modified and tempered it, since he perceived that he should be examined of it. And yet, peradventure, you will not judge it everywhere very well powdered[5]. He seems[6] to be very well studied in master Moor's[7] books, and to have framed him a conscience and a judgment somewhat according to the same. And to avoid all falsities, he appeareth to stick stiffly to unwritten verities. I would fain hear him tell who be those new fellows that would approve no sciences but grammar. *Qui vos audit, &c., obedite præpositis, &c., qui ecclesiam non audivit, &c.*, serveth him gaily, for traditions and laws to be made of the clergy authoritatively; and to be then observed of the laity necessarily, as equal with God's own word; as some, saith he, both thinketh and heareth[8] &c.

As far as I can learn of such as here[9] commoned[10] with him, he is wilfully[11] witted, Dunsly learned, Moorly affected, bold not a little, zealous more than enough: if you could monish him, charm him, and so reform him, &c. Or else, I pray you, inhibit him my diocese. You may send another, and appoint him his stipend; which God grant you do. To whom I now and ever commit you.

Yours,

H. WIGORN.

To the right honourable master T. Cromwell, high secretary to the king's highness, and his singular [good] master.

[1 as I hear, MS.]
[2 Coots was probably one of the monks of Hales.]
[3 do report it, MS.]   [4 hath, MS.]
[5 pondered, MS.]   [6 seemeth, MS.
[7 Sir Thomas More's books against Tyndal and others.]
[8 some saith that he both thinketh and sayeth, &c. MS.]
[9 have, MS.]   [10 communed, MS.]   [11 wilily, MS.]

LETTER XVII.

LATIMER to LORD CROMWELL[12]

[Cotton, MS. Cleop. E. iv. 142.]

RIGHT honourable. *Salutem*. And, sir, this bearer can tell your lordship to what effect he doth expound this prophecy inclosed: howbeit he hath it, I trow, but of hearsay. But your lordship can try the truth, because you love antiquities; therefore I do send it to you by my man that hath heard further than I. Thus fare your good lordship well in God.

H. L.

Wigorn.

19 October, [1536], at Hartl[ebury].

*To the right honourable the lord
  privy seal, his singular good
  lord.*

LETTER XVIII.

LATIMER to LORD CROMWELL[13]

[Orig. State Pap. Off. Crom. Corr. Vol. 49, 1. 499.]

SALUTEM in Christo diutinam et plurimam, with thanks to your lordship for your goodness; though not as duty requireth, yet as power sufficeth. And, sir, according to your

[12 The prophecy to which this letter refers is a mysterious kind of jargon in Latin verse, which will neither scan nor construe. In those times, when persons were made "offenders for a word," prophecyings and visions were the more in vogue; until (33 Hen. VIII. c. 14,) it was found requisite to legislate on the subject. This letter is printed by Nichols, Hist. of Leicestershire, Vol. III. p. 1065.]

[13 The inquiry respecting "letters of instruction," &c. indicates that episcopal "visitations" had been decided upon. This would point to 1536 as the date of this letter, for the visitations took place in 1537. It is known also, that "Silvester Darius" was deprived, on the 11th Nov. 1536, of the rectory of Ripple in Worcestershire, the "benefice" to which Dr Bagard succeeded. Nash. Hist. of Worcestershire, Vol. II. p. 299.]

commandment, I was occupied at Paul's Cross upon Sunday next after your departure from London, not otherwise (I trust) than according to your discreet monition and charitable advertisement, so moving to unity without any special note of any man's folly, that all my lords there present seemed to be content with me, as it appeared by the loving thanks that they gave me. And now, sir, I look for your letters of instructions and further knowledge of your pleasure as touching our visitations. Moreover, I have bestowed the two benefices that Silvester Darius[1] had, the one to doctor Bagard[2], my chancellor, the other to doctor Bradford[3], my chaplain; for the king's grace charged me to bestow them well. But now, after that we have begun, we have a scruple how to proceed and end: if according to form hitherto used, it will not be done without great tract of time. The king's grace said no more to me but "Give'em, give'em." You know my chancellor's

[1 Silvester Dario was one of that army of Italian ecclesiastics who were quartered upon the church of England from time to time. Three Italians had successively held the see of Worcester.]

[2 Thomas Baggard, D.C.L., became Chancellor of Worcester in 1535. He was an Oxford man, and one of the first canons of Cardinal's college there. His name occurs as the successor of Dario in the rectory of Ripple, but the date of his institution to that benefice is not given. If the number and variety of the preferments which Dr Baggard consented to hold be taken as an index, his "scrupulosity" seems to have undergone some modification before he died. Wood, Fasti Oxon. Vol. I. p. 80, edit. Bliss; Nash, Hist. of Worcesters. ubi supr.]

[3 Rodolph Bradford was educated at Eton, and was removed from thence to King's college, Cambridge, in 1519, of which society he afterwards became Fellow. He took so earnest a part in furthering the doctrines of the Reformation, that letters were sent to the vice-chancellor directing that Bradford should be apprehended for circulating Frith's English testament. To avoid the persecution meditated against him, Bradford fled to Ireland, and there openly preached the gospel; but his pursuers followed him, apprehended him, and cast him into prison, where he lay for two years. On being set at liberty he returned to Cambridge, and became a member of Corpus Christi college. He proceeded to the degree of D.D. 1535, and, whilst resident in Cambridge, let no holy day pass without preaching a sermon. That Bradford was regarded as a person of note, may be concluded from his having been one of the divines who were commissioned to draw up "The Institution of a Christian Man," which was published in 1537. Masters, Hist. of Corp. Christi Coll. pp. 244, et seq.; Strype, Eccl. Mem. I. i. pp. 486, et seq. Oxford edit.]

scrupulosity; and I myself, though I am not altogether so scrupulous, yet I would it were done inculpably and duly. If we might know your advice herein, we should be very well ridded and eased. Finally, this bringer, my chaplain, would be a poor suitor to your lordship in a poor man's cause. I know not well the matter; but if you would give him the hearing, &c. I am the bolder, because I think you are set up of God to hear and to help the little ones of God in their distress. God preserve your good lordship in prosperity as long as you promote God's word with all sincerity! *Postridie Stephani sancti,* [27 Dec. 1536.]

Yours,

H. WYGORN.

To the right honourable and his singular good lord, lord privy seal.

LETTER XIX.

LATIMER *to* LORD CROMWELL.

[Orig. State Pap. Off. Crom. Corr. Vol. 49, 1. 522.]

SALUTEM in Christo plurimam. Sir, These two fellows of St John's college, Cambridge, do come to your lordship in the name of the whole college, to the intent to shew to your lordship the tenor of their statute as touching the election of a new master; and I doubt not but with a word or two you may make master Day[4], or any else eligible by their statute, as Mr Nevell, yet fellow of the same college, can commune with your lordship further, as shall please you; for they have great need of your lordship's charitable favour in many suits and traverses appertaining unto them not yet perfectly established.

[[4] George Day was admitted master of St John's college, 27 July, 1537. He was afterwards Provost of King's college, and Bishop of Chichester. His subsequent career did not bespeak him to be a person of any steadiness of character; for after having made a profession of the doctrines of the Reformation, he became a violent persecutor of the reformers. Strype, Mem. of Cranm. pp. 331, et seq. Oxf. edit. Le Neve, Fasti, p. 333; Godwin, de Præsul, p. 512, edit. Richardson.]

I trust also your lordship doth remember poor Clare Hall, that the master[1] neither transgress the statute himself, nor yet bring into his room Mr Swynbourne[2] of the same house, a man, as they say, of perverse judgment, and too factious for such a cure.

Mr Nevell shall deliver to you a bill of the gravaments of two or three of the fellows, most given to good letters.

I pray God preserve you, and send you hither shortly again, that we might end and go home into our diocese, and do some good there.

My lord of York[3] hath done right well at Paul's Cross as touching the supremacy, and as touching condemnation of the rebels; as well as he did before, if not better.

Dr Barnes[4], I hear say, preached in London this day a very good sermon, with great moderation and temperance of himself. I pray God continue with him, for then I know no one man shall do more good.

I send you here a bullock[5] which I did find amongst my

[1 John Crayford was originally of Queens' college, Cambridge, but being from thence ejected, he removed to Oxford, where he was elected Fellow of University college, in 1519. Afterwards, leaving Oxford, he was appointed one of the proctors in Cambridge from 1520 to 1522; but in 1525, he returned to Oxford, having been made one of the canons of Cardinal's college. For the third time he returned to Cambridge, and was elected master of Clare Hall, 1530. He was vice-chancellor in 1535 and 1536, afterwards archdeacon of Berkshire, prebendary of Salisbury, and died master of University college, Oxford. Wood, Fasti Oxon. I. p. 124, edit. Bliss. Parker, Academ. Hist. Cant. p. lii., edit. Drake.]

[2 Rowland Swynbourne, or Swynburn, did succeed Dr Crayford in the mastership of Clare Hall, in 1539. He was "expulsed" from his office by King Edward VI., an. 1549, but was afterwards restored to the mastership in 1553, by the mandate of Bp. Gardiner, the chancellor of England and of the university. Le Neve, Fasti, p. 422; Strype, Life of Park. I. pp. 59, et seq: Eccl. Mem. III. i., p. 80; Lamb, Collect. of Documents, &c. p. 113.]

[3 Dr Edward Lee.]

[4 The well-known Dr Robert Barnes, whose story is related by Foxe, Acts and Mon. Vol. II. p. 435, edit. 1684.]

[5 Most probably one of those secret missives from Rome which had been received by some of Latimer's predecessors in the see of Worcester. Thus respecting the prior of Wych, Richd., suffragan of Dover, writes to Cromwell: "in his cofer I fowne xj bulles of the bischopis of Rome." Letters on the Suppression of the Monasteries, p. 195.]

bulls; that you may see how closely in time past the foreign prelates did practise about their prey. If a man had leisure to try out who was king in those days, and what matters were in hand, perchance a man might guess what manner a thing *illud secretum quod nosti* was; such cloked conveyance they had.

Valeat tua dominatio in salvatore Christo.

H. L. W.

Sub diem Swythineum, [15 July 1537.]

To the right honourable and his singular good lord, the lord privy seal.

LETTER XX.

LATIMER *to* LORD CROMWELL[6].

[Orig. State Pap. Off. Crom. Corr. Vol. 49, l. 520. State Papers, Vol. I. p. 563.]

Salutem in Christo plurimam. This day, sir, which is Saturday, we had finished (I trow) the rest of our book, if my lord of Hereford[7] had not been diseased, to whom surely we owe great thanks for his great diligence in all our proceedings. Upon Monday I think it will be done altogether, and then my lord of Canterbury will send it unto your lordship with all speed; to whom also, if anything be praiseworthy, *bona pars laudis optimo jure debetur.* As for myself, I can nothing else but pray God that when it is done it be well

[6 A letter from Cranmer to Cromwell of precisely similar purport fixes the "Saturday" mentioned here by Latimer to have been July 21, 1537. The "book" alluded to is, *The Godly and Pious Institution of a Christian Man,* printed by Berthelet the king's printer, 1537. See an interesting note by Jenkyns, Remains of Cranmer, Vol. I. pp. 187, et seq.]

[7 Edward Fox: whose letter to Cromwell (*State Papers,* Vol. I. pp. 555, et seq.) throws further light on this of Latimer. Dr Fox was almoner to King Hen. VIII., and much employed by the sovereign in foreign embassages. Among other services of this nature may be mentioned his embassy to the protestant princes at Smalcald in 1535. Godwin, de Præsul. p. 494, edit. Richardson. Strype, Eccl. Mem. I. i., 348, et seq. Tanner, Biblioth. Brit. p. 294.]

and sufficiently done, so that we shall not need to have any more such doings. For verily, for my part, I had lever be poor parson of poor Kinton again, than to continue thus bishop of Worcester; not for anything that I have had to do therein, or can do, but yet forsooth it is a troublous thing to agree upon a doctrine in things of such controversy, with judgments of such diversity, every man (I trust) meaning well, and yet not all meaning one way. But I doubt not but now in the end we shall agree both one with another, and all with the truth, though some will then marvel. And yet, if there be anything either uncertain or unpure, I have good hope that the king's highness will *expurgare quicquid est veteris fermenti;* at leastway give it some note, that it may appear he perceiveth it, though he do tolerate it for a time, so giving place for a season to the frailty and gross capacity of his subjects.

Sir, we be here not without all peril[1]: for beside that two hath died of my keeper's folks, out of my gate-house, three be yet there with raw sores; and even now master Nevell cometh and telleth me that my under cook is fallen sick, and like to be of the plague. *Sed duodecim sunt horæ diei, et termini vitæ sunt ab eo constituti, qui non potest falli; neque verius est tamen, quod nascimur, quam quod sumus morituri.*

As for Dr King's matter, I refer to your knowledge of justice, and to the use of your charity; but as touching *Defensor Fidei,* I think that title due to the king.

As for my lord of Hayles[2], I fear he will be too cocket now with his great authority and promotion: his friends can jest upon such a bishop, that can with complaining promote, and would he should complain more. But I wot what I intended, let them jest at large.

But now, sir, this bringer, Thomas Gybson[3], is a poor suitor to your lordship, that he may by your favour have

[1 Cranmer, also, mentions the prevalence of a fatal sickness at that time in the metropolis and neighbourhood.]

[2 Stephen Whalley, the last abbot of Hales, or Hayles, in Gloucestershire. He surrendered his monastery to the crown, 24 Dec. 1539. Stevens, Hist. of Ancient Abbeys, &c. Vol. II. p. 56.]

[3 The printer of the first Concordance to the English New Testament, 1534.]

the printing of our book. He is an honest, poor man, and will set it forth in a good letter, and sell it good cheap: whereas others do sell too dear, which doth let many to buy. Dr Crom[4] and other my friends obtained of me, not without some importunity, to write unto you for him: but I wot not what I do, saving that I know that you wot both what is to be done, and what may be done; I nothing else but commit him to your charitable goodness.

[July 21, 1537.]   Yours,

HUGO WYGORN,

more hastily than wisely.

To his singular good lord Cromwell,
the lord privy seal.

LETTER XXI.

LATIMER *to* LORD CROMWELL[5].

[Orig. State Pap. Off. Crom. Corr. Vol. 49. 1. 482.]

RIGHT honourable sir, and my singular good lord. *Salutem.* And, sir, as touching all matters in the parts of this master Lucy[6], he himself shall be my letters unto your good lordship. Only I desire you so to use him, as far as may stand with right, that his good-will towards all goodness may be encouraged by communing with you, and promoted by hearing of you. There be too few such gentleman in the king's realm. And he can open to you all together, as to the priest of Hampton's[7] judgment, what proceedings it had. I would wish better judgments to be in some of the king's judges, and

---

[4 Dr Edward Crome. See above, p. 350.]

[5 The reference to "Clare Hall" and "St John's College," Cambridge, would seem to assign this letter to 1537.]

[6 Either sir Thomas Lucy of Charlcote, Warwickshire, or one of that family.]

[7 Probably Hampton-upon-Avon, or Bishop's Hampton, not far from the residence of Mr Lucy.]

more prepense favour towards reformation of things amiss in religion. There be many judgments, and yet few or none be brought to the Ordinary's knowledge, after due form of the king's acts.

But now, sir, as for my brother Prior's matter, my lord of Hereford's[1], and mine of Clare Hall's matter, dependeth only of your opportune and behoofable remembrance.

As for St John's College, I can say no more but that all factions and affections be not yet exiled out of Cambridge: and yet, my good lord, extend your goodness thereunto, forasmuch as you be their chancellor[2], that in your time they be not trodden under foot.

As for master Ponnes, sir, I assure you I am not so light of credence as he pretendeth me to be, as I can affirm unto you with certain and sure arguments, as you shall hereafter know all together *ab origine.*

Postridie Laurentii, at Har[t]lebury.
[Sep. 6, 1537.]

H. LATIMER, bishop.

To the right honourable lord Cromwell, lord privy seal, and his singular good lord.

LETTER XXII.

LATIMER *to* LORD CROMWELL.

[Orig. State Pap. Off. Crom. Corr. Vol. 49, 1. 486.]

SALUTEM *in Christo plurimam.* And, my singular good lord, I doubt nothing but that your good lordship will extend

[1 Dr Edward Fox, the bishop of that see. It ought, however, to be stated that in the original it is "Herforde," which if taken to be "Hertford," the date of this letter must be 1538, for there was no "lord of Hertford" in Sept. 1537. Nicolas, Synopsis of Peerage, Vol. I. p. 320.]

[2 The original has "vice-chancellor," but that is a clerical error. Lord Cromwell succeeded bishop Fisher as chancellor of the university of Cambridge.]

your goodness to that poor priest, sir Large, in my conscience injured and wronged by means of one Mr Clopton[3], which neither did hear him, nor, if he had, could judge his doctrine; but zealously, for lack of right judgment, stirred the people against him, as master Nevell can tell you, whom I do make my letters to you at this time. And thus I commit good master Lucy to your goodness, and his whole cause.

Yours,

H. LATIMER,
Wigorn.

6 October [1537], at Pershore[4] in his visitation.

To the right honourable and his singular good lord, lord privy seal.

LETTER XXIII.

LATIMER *to* LORD CROMWELL.

[Orig. State Pap. Off. Crom. Corr. Vol. 49, 1. 484.]

RIGHT honourable. *Salutem in Christo Jesu.* And, sir, as touching your request concerning your friend, master Barker[5], shall be accomplished and done; it shall not stick on my behalf. He seemeth a man, as your lordship doth

[3 Mr Wm. Clopton of Clopton, not far from Stratford on Avon. He was one of the royal commissioners for ascertaining the value of the free chapel of Fulbrooke, in co. of Warwick, and seems to have been a rigid papist. Dugdale, Hist. of Warwicks. pp. 698, et seq. 2nd edit. Valor Eccles. Vol. III. p. 67.]

[4 In Worcestershire, where was a Benedictine monastery. Willis, Hist. of Abbies, Vol. II. p. 260.]

[5 Anthony Barker, warden of the collegiate church of Stratford on Avon; which office this letter shews he obtained by the resignation of Doctor John Bell, and at the recommendation of Cromwell: that the "poor college was not bounden for the pension," appears from the circumstance, that at the suppression of this college in 37 Hen. VIII.,

say, of honest conversation, and also not without good letters. Let them both commune and conclude; I shall confer the resignation once exhibited unto me, according to your desire. Only I require two things upon your good lordship: the one, that the poor college be not bounden for the pension; and to that master Barker himself is agreeable, for I telled him plainly my mind therein; for it may right well chance that Mr doctor Bell[1] do outlive Mr Barker, and then the succeeder should come in to a warm office, to be charged not alonely with fruits and tenths, but also with pension. The other, that your lordship would persuade master Barker to tarry upon it, keep house in it, preach at it and about it, to the reformation of that blind end of my diocese. For else what are we the better for either his great literature or good conversation, if my diocese shall not taste and have experience thereof? And the houses (I trow) be toward ruin and decay, and the whole town far out of frame for lack of residence. When the head is far off, the body is the worse.

Thus I commit altogether to your customable gentleness and charitable goodness, which is not wont to regard more the wealthy and pleasant living of one body, than the necessary relief of many souls.

As to Sir Large, your commandment shall be done, whose cause, in my mind, your lordship doth judge rightly: malice to be in one part, and simplicity in the other. But God shall reward you, that will not suffer malice to prevail. *Postridie Edwardi* at Warwick, visiting and busily alway.

[Warwick, 14 Oct. 1537.] Yours,

H. LATIMER,

Bishop of Worcester.

To the right honourable the lord privy seal, his singular good lord.

a pension of 22*l*. a year was still paid to Dr Bell out of Mr Barker's own stipend. Anthony Barker seems to have been, at the time of his death, prebendary of Winchester, canon of Windsor, and vicar of East Ham. Dugdale, Warwicks. p. 693, 2nd. edit. Strype, Eccl. Mem. II. ii. 267.]

[1 Dr John Bell, afterwards the successor of Latimer in the see of Worcester. Godwin de Præsul. p. 469, edit. Richardson.]

LETTER XXIV.

LATIMER *to* LORD CROMWELL[2].

[Orig. State Pap. Off. Crom. Corr. Vol. 49, l. 515.]

RIGHT honourable, *salutem in Christo Jesu*. And, sir, here is no less joying and rejoicing in these parts for the birth of our prince[3], whom we hungered so long, than there was, I trow, *inter vicinos*, at the birth of St John Baptist; as this bearer, master Evance, can tell you. God give us all grace to yield due thanks to our Lord God, God of England! for verily he hath shewed himself God of England, or rather an English God, if we consider and ponder well all his proceedings with us from time to time. He hath overcome all our illness with his exceeding goodness; so that we are now more than compelled to serve him, seek his glory, promote his word, if the devil of all devils be not in us. We have now the stop of vain trusts, and the stay of vain expectations: let us all pray for his preservation; and I for my part will wish that his grace always have, and even now from the beginning, governors, instructors, and officers of right judgments, *ne optimum ingenium non optima educatione depravetur.* But what a great fool am I! So, what devotion sheweth many times but little discretion. And thus the God of England be ever with you in all your proceedings!

Yours,

H. LATIMER,

bishop of Worcester.

The 19th of October, now at Hartlebury, [1537].

If you would excite this bearer to be more hearty against the abuse of imagery, and more forward to promote the verity, it might do good; not that it came of me, but of yourself, &c.

To the right honourable lord
   privy seal, his singular
   good lord.

[2 Printed in the State Papers, Vol. I. p. 571.]   [3 Edward VI.]

[LATIMER, II.]

LETTER XXV.

LATIMER *to* LORD CROMWELL[1].

[Cotton, MS. Cleop. E. IV. p. 139.]

RIGHT honourable, *salutem in Christo*. And, sir, when I was with your lordship last, you were desirous to know where you might have good monks. I told you of two with my lord of Westminster; I could not then name them to you, but now I can: the one is called Gorton, the other Clarke[2]; both bachelors of divinity, well learned, of right judgment, of very honest name. The prior of Coventry[3], as I hear say, is dead. The matter is somewhat entered with the king's grace, and like to go forward, if you put thereto your helping hand. I doubt not but my brother abbot of Westminster, as ill as he might spare them, yet will forego them, for such a purpose; but much the rather if he perceive your pleasure therein.

I would have waited upon your lordship myself, as my duty had been; but surely, sir, I do what I can to enable myself to stand in the pulpit upon Tuesday. I am in a faint weariness over all my body, but chiefly in the small of my back: but I have a good nurse, good mistress Statham[4], which, seeing what case I was in, hath fetched me home to her own house, and doth pymper me up with all diligence: for I fear a consumption. But it maketh little matter for me. I pray God preserve your lordship long in health to all such good

[1 This letter is printed in Nichols, Hist. of Leicestershire, Vol. III. p. 1066; and among the Letters connected with the suppression of the monasteries, pp. 147 et seq.]

[2 Probably father Richard Gorton, a Benedictine, who commenced B.D. at Oxford, Feb. 27, 1527, and D.D. in July 1539. A father John Clerke was admitted D.D. at the same time. Wood, Fasti, Vol. I. pp. 77, 109, edit. Bliss.]

[3 Thomas Weford. As his successor, Thomas Camsele or Kampswell, had the temporalities of the monastery restored to him, March 21, 1538, the date of this letter is thus fixed. Stevens, Hist. of Ancient Abbies, &c. Vol. I. p. 233; Rymer, Fœder. XIV. p. 586.]

[4 Archbishop Cranmer, in a letter to lord Cromwell, writes: "I heartily require your lordship to be good lord unto Master Statham and Mistress Statham my lord of Worcester his nurse." Rem. of Cranm. edit. Jenkyns, Vol. I. p. 256.]

purposes as God hath ordained you to! In master Statham's house.

H. LATIMER,

Wigorn.

8th of November, [1537].

LETTER XXVI.

LATIMER *to* LORD CROMWELL.

[Orig. State Pap. Off. Crom. Corr. Vol. 49, l. 495.]

RIGHT honourable, *salutem*. And, sir, I am so malapert, saving that your goodness towards me maketh me bold, I should have remembered your lordship of Gorton and Clarke[5], the two monks of Westminster, as concerning Coventry, but I had forgotten it; and nevertheless I trust it needeth not.

As for master Haynes[6], [he] thinketh to keep the Wednesday himself, so that I shall not need to advertise my brother prior[7] of that; but I would be glad that he had a Sunday, to the intent that the king's grace might taste what he can do, if it were so seen to your good lordship; and then I would know what Sunday.

This bearer, master Acton[8], my godsib and friend, hath something to say to your lordship. He is faithful and hearty in all good causes, no man more ready to serve God and the king, and your lordship's hearty lover to his power. I commit both him and his cause to your accustomable goodness, and you and yours to God's goodness.

[5 See preceding Letter.]

[6 Most probably Simon Haynes, president of Queens' College in Cambridge, canon of Windsor, and afterwards dean of Exeter. Wood, Fasti, Vol. I. p. 71, edit. Bliss; Strype, Eccl. Mem. I. i. pp. 543 et seq. Oxf.; Le Neve, Fasti, pp. 86, 382, 429.]

[7 Prior of Worcester. See above, p. 371.]

[8 Probably Mr Richard Acton, of Sutton Park, in the parish of Tenbury, Worcestershire; for that gentleman was married to a niece of Humphry Monmouth, an alderman of London, and a great friend of Latimer. Strype, Eccl. Mem. I. i. p. 562, ii. p. 371, Oxf.; Nash, Hist. of Worcesters. II. p. 418.]

There is one Anthony Throgmorton[1], servant (as they say) to master Pole, cardinal: if he be the king's true subject, well and taill; if not, I would master Robert Acton[2], the king's true and faithful subject and servant, had his thing at Wynche, for it lieth very commodiously for him; and then, as he is always willing, so he should be more able to do his grace service. Thus I run riot, but presuming of your goodness.

If Frere Ganlyne have suffered condignly for his misbehaviour, I doubt not but, when you see your time, you will extend your charity unto him, with some injunctions to do better.

Your lordship's own,
H. LATIMER,

[1537.] Wigorn.

To the right honourable his singular good lord Cromwell, the lord privy seal.

LETTER XXVII.

Latimer *to* Lord Cromwell.

[Orig. State Pap. Off. Crom. Corr. Vol. 49, 1. 509.]

Salutem in Christo plurimam. Alack, my singular good lord, saving that I have experience of your benign goodness, that you can be *omnia omnibus*, to do all men good, I might be irk of my own importunity. As for this letter inclosed, it shall speak for itself, and be heard as God shall work with your ready goodness. When I moved the king's grace in the cause, his highness did favourably hear me, &c.

[[1] The brother of Michael Throgmorton, who was known to be "Master Pole's" servant; and who having been gained over by the agents of Henry VIII. was employed as a spy upon the cardinal. These persons were sons of Sir Robert Throgmorton, of Coughton, Warwickshire. Dugdale, Warwicks. pp. 750 et seq. 2nd edit.; Nicolas, Testam. Vetust. p. 561; Herbert, Life of Hen. VIII. pp. 488 et seq.]

[[2] Second son of Mr Richard Acton, above-mentioned, afterwards Sir Robert Acton, of Elmley Lovet, Worcestershire. Nash, Hist. of Worcesters. Vol. I. p. 378.]

As for the Coventry matter[3], master Acton and master Nevell's matters, and all other my further suits, I commit to your approved wisdom, high discretion, and charitable goodness.

Mr doctor Barns hath preached here with me at Hartlebury, and at my request at Winchester, and also at Evesham. Surely he is alone in handling a piece of scripture, and in setting forth of Christ he hath no fellow. I would wish that the king's grace might once hear him: but, I pray you, let him tell you how two monks hath preached alate in Evesham[4]: I wist you will hearken to them and look upon them; for though they be exempt from me, yet they be not exempt from your lordship. I pray God amend them, or else I fear they be exempt from the flock of Christ, very true monks; that is to say, pseudo-prophets and false christian men, perverters of scripture; sly, wily, *disobedientiaries* to all good orders; ever starting up, as they dare, to do hurt.

Yours,
H. LATIMER,
W.

This Christmas Day [1537].
To the right honourable lord
  privy seal, his singular
  good lord.

LETTER XXVIII.

Latimer *to* Lord Cromwell.

[Orig. State Pap. Off. Crom. Corr. Vol. 49, 1. 500.]

RIGHT honourable, and my very good lord, *salutem in Domino*. And, sir, this bearer is an honest poor gentleman, whose chance hath been to travel much in Wales and in the borders of the same, as in the diocese of Landaff and other where; and by the reason of the same hath perceived some

[3 The "Coventry matter" being mentioned as still unsettled points to 1537 as the date of this letter.]

[4 A famous monastery of Benedictine monks, in Worcestershire. The monastery was surrendered to the crown in November, 1539. Stevens, Hist. of Ancient Abbies, &c. Vol. I. pp. 459 et seq.]

thing seeming to him not well, which he of a good zeal that he hath, and in discharging of his bounden duty, would be glad to disclose unto your lordship, for reformation of the same, with such expedition as should be thought unto your lordship convenient. He is my servant, though much away from me by occasion of his own business; but now returning to me, required my letters, whereby he might the sooner approach to your lordship's speech. Thus I commit both him and his cause to your lordship's goodness, and your lordship with all yours to the goodness of God.

H. L.
Wigorn.

Postridie natalis Chris. [26 Dec. 1537?]
Hartl[ebury]

To the honourable the lord privy
seal, his singular good lord.

LETTER XXIX.

LATIMER *to* LORD CROMWELL.

[Orig. State Pap. Off. Crom. Corr. Vol. 49. l. 516.]

RIGHT honourable, *salutem.* And, sir, this bearer, Mr Butler[1] of Droitwich, one of the commissioners, hath to certify your lordship of the misbehaviour of a certain priest in the commotion time[2]. *Sed reus ille nunc non comparet:* but yet I would your lordship would allow this man's diligence, both in that and other things more; for though he do but his duty to serve the king's grace truly, yet your allowance of the same cannot be in vain. The man is honestly reputed in his country, and witnessed for one that hath done the king's grace good service in many his grace's affairs, many times. If your good lordship do hear him honestly in his honest suits, I think you shall not bestow your so doing unworthily. He can tell your lordship of that unpriestly priest, whose

[1 The name of Butler occurs among those of the "gentlemen of worth," then residing in Droitwich. Nash, Hist. of Worcesters. Vol. I. p. 303.]

[2 "The Pilgrimage of Grace," so called. See Vol. I. pp. 25, 29.]

damsel was brought to bed alate, not without offence of many; and of another priest also, as lewd as he, of the same town, which hath defiled a young girl alate, of thirteen years of age, and burnt her almost to death. O unholy and also unchaste chastity, which is preferred in a christian realm to chaste and holy matrimony!

I pray you, my good lord, pardon me that I do write unto you so unadvisedly, for I am light-headed for lack of sleep; not that I can sleep and will not, but that I would sleep and cannot; but all as doth please Almighty God, to whom I commit your good lordship: but too I cannot forget my nurse, to bring her to your good remembrance, with all opportunity, *et Nevellus præsens suspirat benignitatem tuam.* [1537?]

H. L.
Wigorn.

To the right honourable lord Cromwell, the lord privy seal, his very good lord.

LETTER XXX.

LATIMER *to* LORD CROMWELL.

[Orig. State Pap. Off. Crom. Corr. Vol. 49, 1. 518.]

SALUTEM in Christo plurimam. And, sir, if it be your pleasure, as it is, that I shall play the fool after my customable manner when Forest[3] shall suffer, I would wish that my

[3 A letter from archbishop Cranmer to lord Cromwell, dated April 6, 1538, intimates that it had just then been resolved upon "to proceed against Forest according to the order of the law;" and this letter shews that the friar was under sentence of death at the time it was written. These circumstances fix the date of the Letter. Respecting Forest himself, a panegyrical account of him is given by Bouchier and by Wood, which is copied by the compiler (Pulton) of the Antiquities of the English Franciscans. But Burnet gives reasons for regarding friar Forest as but an indifferent kind of person, both as respects learning and morals. It is probable, however, that the denial of the royal supremacy by Forest would have been sufficient to have secured his execution, even if he had been that paragon of excellence which his partisans would make him out to have been. Cran-

stage stood near unto Forest; for I would endeavour myself so to content the people that therewith I might also convert Forest, God so helping, or rather altogether working: wherefore I would that he should hear what I shall say[1], *si forte, etc.* Forest, as I hear, is not duly accompanied in Newgate, for his amendment[2], with the White Friars[3] of Doncaster, and monks of the Charter-house[4], in a fit chamber, more like to indurate than to mollify: whether through the fault of the sheriff or of the jailer, or both, no man could sooner discern than your lordship. Some think he is rather comforted in his way than discouraged; some think he is allowed both to hear mass and also to receive the sacrament; which if it be so, it is enough to confirm him in his obstinacy, as though he were to suffer for a just cause: these things would be tried, *ut retegantur ex multis cordibus cogitationes.* It is to be feared that some instilled into him, that though he had persevered in his abjuration, yet he should have suffered after-

mer, Remains, I. 239, edit. by Jenkyns; Bouchier, De Martyrio Fratr. Ordin. Minor. &c. pp. 24 et seq.; Wood, Athen. Oxon. I. 107 et seq.; Burnet, Hist. Refor. Vol. I. p. 647, Oxf. 1816; Antiq. of Engl. Francis. pp. 241 et seq.]

[1 "At his commyng to the place of execution, there was prepared a pulpit, where a right reverend father in God, and a renowned and famous clerk, the bishop of Worcester, called Hugh Latimer, declared to him his errors, and openly and manifestly by the scripture of God confuted them, and with many and godly exhortacions moved him to repentance." Hall, Chronicle, p. 826, edited by Ellis.]

[2 Holinshed observes that Forest, "upon his submission, having more liberty than before he had to talk with whom he would, and others having liberty to talk with him, he was incensed by some such as had conference with him, that when his formal abjuration was sent to him to read and peruse he utterly refused it, and obstinately stood in all his heresies and treasons." III. p. 945.]

[3 The White Friars of Doncaster were divided in their opinions, some favouring the reformation, and some opposing the measures of Henry VIII. Cooke, the last prior of this house, was suspected of being concerned in the Pilgrimage of Grace. He and six of the friars surrendered the monastery, on the 13th Nov. 1538, but Cooke was afterwards executed at Tyburn. Burnet, Hist. of Refor. Vol. I. part ii. p. 226, Oxf. 1816; Hunter, Hist. of South Yorks. Vol. I. pp. 17 et seq.]

[4 The names of ten Carthusians, who were at that time imprisoned in Newgate, are given by Chauncey, Innocentia et Constantia, Victrix, p. 98, Wirceb. 1608.]

ward for treason: and so by that occasion he might have been induced to refuse his abjuration. If he would yet with heart return to his abjuration, I would wish his pardon; such is my foolishness. I thank your good lordship for Gloucester[5], desiring the continuance of your goodness to master Nevell: for I doubt not but that you will of yourself remember my nurse. Thus I can not but be bold with your lordship.

It were good you would sometimes send for masters of colleges in Cambridge and Oxford, with their statutes; and if the statutes be not good and to the furtherance of good letters, change them. If the masters be not good, but honourers of drawlatches, change them.

H. L. Wigorn.

18 Ma[y. 1538.]

To the right honourable lord privy seal, his singular good lord.

LETTER XXXI.

LATIMER *to* LORD CROMWELL[6].

[Orig. State Pap. Off. Crom. Corr. Vol. 49. 1. 513.]

RIGHT honourable, *salutem in eo qui unus salvare potest*. And, sir, I was minded to have been a suitor to your

[5 Possibly referring to the interest Cromwell took in providing for a school at Gloucester. Or it may be to the act, 27 Hen. VIII., which had been passed for rebuilding part of the city of Gloucester, and which had a good effect on the prosperity of the city. Rudder, Hist. of Gloucest. p. 83.]

[6 The suit of which this letter states Mr Nevell made "himself sure" and so "got the widow," was for the lands &c. formerly belonging to the Friary of St Augustine, in Droitwich. This we learn from a letter dated May 23, 1538, (Sir John Russell being mentioned in it as the sheriff of Worcestershire,) and which speaks of Mr Nevell's intended marriage, in case he obtained his suit. The mentioning also of " our great Sibyll " and her " old sister of Walsingham," indicates that those images had not yet been disposed of; though they, with others, were burnt at Chelsea, in the autumn of 1538. The "demesnes of Bordslay" too were evidently on the point of passing out of the

lordship, seeing I cannot attain to the use of my park at
Allchurch, for my preferment to some good part of the demesne of Berslay, for my money, which is even at hand, to
relief of my great need to such things. For I trow no man,
having the name of so many things, hath the use of so few
as I, handled indeed like a ward. But now, hearing that
this bearer, Mr Evance[1], hath begun and entered into the
same suit beforehand with your lordship, and is put in comfort
of the same to be furthered therein, as I perceive by a letter
come to him alate, I leave my purpose to begin for myself,
and wish good success to his beginning; very loth to hinder
or lett any man's suit begun. And surely, sir, I suppose you
shall bestow it right well upon him; for I suppose him to be
a witty and a politic man, both active and expert in things to
be done, and no less prompt and ready than many ways able
to do you service in your affairs. Now, sir, the more you
incline your goodness to further him in this his suit, the more
able he shall be to do you service from time to time, as you
shall call upon him. And though this you know to be true
much better than I, without my relation, yet I trust you will
not mislike nor ill expound, but take in good part, this my
writing; forasmuch as I must needs, being desired, something
write, though never so foolishly, after my accustomed manner.
And you have been so good, and hath shewed your goodness
so largely unto me, that many men doth think that my poor
remembrance with a word or two unto your lordship should
further their causes with you. But yet methink you smile
at one thing, that I, a man of so little policy, so little experience and activity, so little wit and wisdom, would take
upon me to judge another man politic and expert, active,
witty and wise. Well, sir, if I have done but only that made
you to smile, to the refreshing of your mind in the midst of
your matters, I have not done nothing: and the rest I commit

hands of their old possessors, an event which occurred in July 1538.
Letters on the Suppr. of the Monasteries, pp. 194. et seq.; Holinshed,
III. p. 945; Rymer, XIV. p. 608; Nash, Hist. of Worcesters. II. pp. 406
et seq.]

[1 Probably Thomas Evance, one of the royal commissioners for
valuing the first-fruits in that part of the diocese of Hereford, which
belonged to Worcestershire. The demesne of Bordesley was not
granted to him, but to Andrew, lord Windsor. Valor Eccles. III. p.
277; Nash, Hist. of Worcesters. ubi supr.; Tanner, Notitia, p. 622.]

to your accustomable goodness, with the suit of my nurse, which I am certain you will remember with all opportunity. And master Nevell[2], making himself sure of his suit, hath got the widow, trusting surely in your lordship's goodness for the performance of the same, not without pledging of my poor honesty in the same behalf.

I trust your lordship will bestow our great Sibyll[3] to some good purpose, *ut pereat memoria cum sonitu.* She hath been the devil's instrument to bring many (I fear) to eternal fire: now she herself, with her old sister of Walsingham[4], her young sister of Ipswich[5], with their other two sisters of Doncaster and Penrice[6], would make a jolly muster in Smithfield; they would not be all day in burning.

Thus God be with you and perserve you long to such good purposes, that the living God may be duly known in his spirit and verity!

H. L. Wigorn.

13 *Junii,* [1538]. At Hartlebury.

To the right honourable lord
  Cromwell, the lord privy
  seal, and his singular
  good lord.

[2 The following extract from the letter above-mentioned, from Richard, suffragan of Dover, to Cromwell, will explain the allusion to Mr Nevell's success with "the widow:" "Toucheing Wheych... their be iij labur for yt, that ys sir John Russell schreyve of Wisitorschere, he ys cum to London to sewe for yt., Mr Pye; and Mr Newell, servant with my lorde of Wisitor, ffor whom at the desyar of my lorde of Wisitor I spake to your lordscipe, for and excepte he have yt I thinke he schall lese a mariage of xl markys by yere." It would seem however, that Mr Nevell did not "lese" the marriage; albeit he lost the suit, as the next letter but one shews.]

[3 The image of our "lady of Worcester," which, when stripped, turned out to be the statue of some bishop. Herbert's Life of Hen. VIII., p. 496.]

[4 See Vol. I. p. 474.]

[5 A marvellous story respecting the virtue derived from a pilgrimage to this image is related by Sir Thomas More, Works, p. 137.]

[6 Penrice is a village in Glamorganshire, not far from Swansea. Leland speaks of "Penrise village where the pilgrimage was." Itinerary, Vol. IV. p. 23.]

LETTER XXXII.

LATIMER to LORD CROMWELL.

[Orig. State Pap. Off. Crom. Corr. Vol. 49, 1. 506.]

RIGHT honourable, *salutem.* And, sir, by this bill inclosed[1] your lordship can perceive something, how the world doth wag with Warwick college[2]. I advertised master Wattwood[3], speaking with him at London, to hasten himself homeward for sparing of expenses, and to refer their whole suit to your good remembrance; but the man, belike, doth delight to lie at London upon the college cost, caring neither for statutes, nor yet injunctions, bearing him bold (I trow) of some authority from your lordship, not considering that his authority is to see the statutes kept, and not to break them. I pray you, be good lord to the poor college: so poor, that in good sooth I took not my customable procurations of them in my visitation. And whereas I enjoined them a lecture of scripture, I am fain to reward the reader myself, for anything that doth come from them: *verum id curat populus scilicet*[4], Master Wattwood careth greatly for it. And where the treasure-house should have three sundry keys, both by their statutes and also my injunctions,

[1 The bill here mentioned accompanies the original letter. It is dated on the 13th of June, in the 30th year of the reign of king Henry VIII. [1538], and is in the names of John Carbanell, dean, John Fyshcr, canon, and David Vaughan, canon, complaining of Mr Wetwood for doing many acts contrary to their statutes, and in breaking the lord bishop's injunctions.]

[2 The collegiate church of St Mary. Henry de Newburgh, first earl of Warwick, projected the design of making this church collegiate; but he dying, his intention was carried into effect by his son Roger, the second earl, who finished the church in 1123, and established in it a dean and secular canons. At the time of the dissolution of it, there were a dean, five canons, ten priest vicars, and six choristers, who, at the survey in 26 Hen. VIII. had possessions of the yearly value of £334. 2s. 3d. These were all granted, 37 Hen. VIII., by the crown to the burgesses of Warwick. Dugdale, Hist. of Warw. pp. 428 et seq. 2nd edit.]

[3 One of the canons of the collegiate church of St Mary, at Warwick. Dugdale, p. 433.]

[4 Ter. Andr. I. 2, 14.]

to which both they be all sworn, he looketh upon him altogether as pleaseth himself. Sir, seeing the king's grace hath their chief jewel that they had, they being so poor themselves, his highness should do graciously to remember them with some piece of some broken abbey, or else I fear they will grow shortly to nought; for, as I hear, the vicars and other ministers sing and say unwaged. But your approved wisdom can consider better than I what is to be done herein, and so God prosper you with good remembrance of mistress Statham's suit.

H. L. Wigorn.

17 Junii, [1538.]
At Hartlebury, short-winded.

To the right honourable lord Cromwell, the lord privy seal, and his very good lord.

LETTER XXXIII.

LATIMER *to* LORD CROMWELL.

[Orig. State Pap. Off. Crom. Corr. Vol. 49. 1. 504.]

AH! my good lord privy seal, what should I say? *Quum tuo solius verbo laxabam rete, et nunc tandem res rediit in ignominiam meam;* with an honest gentlewoman my poor honesty I pledged, which is now distained, and my poor credence, the greatest treasure that I have, not a little minished: for that in Durtwych and here about the same we be fallen into the dirt, and be all-to dirtied, even up to the ears; we be jeered, mocked and laughed to scorn, *ut qui cœpimus ædificare, neque consummare potuimus*. A wily Py hath wilily gone between us and home, when we thought nothing less, but, as good simple souls, made all cocksure. In good faith I would wish to Mr Py[5] as good a thing as it, and better too; but not so, and after that manner, to the defeating

[[5] The lands belonging to the friary of St Augustine at Droitwich, were granted to Mr John Pye. Tanner's Notitia, p. 626.]

of a suit begun and near hand obtained; which if I had suspected, I could perchance have prevented, saving that I would not shew myself to mistrust your pretence nor to have either in doubt or fear your enterprise. But it is now too late to call yesterday again, and to go about to undo that that is done. For master Py doth say that the king hath given it him. I pray God much good might it do him; for I will no longer anguish myself with a matter that I cannot remedy. But I commit altogether to God and to your high discretion, which I am sure meant rightly, and with the loss of the same (*ut in humanis fit rebus*) sought opportunity.

But I trust you will not forget the common suit of the whole country: for better a sheriff annual than perpetual[1], unless he be good, which is not easy to find; and here is much bearing and bolstering, and malefactors do not lack their supporters; yet by many changings we may chance some time to light upon some one good one, among many ill. And your lordship doth know well enough that if I be ruled of one at home, I am unmeet to rule many from home: for if affection do reign in me, then I will not; if ignorance and unexpertness, then I cannot.

As for the town-clerk of Kethermyster [Kidderminster], after due probation hath confessed his folly: but forasmuch as the commissioners have not authority to punish him accordingly, but it is reserved to the assize, where as men be friended, so (they say) things be ended, I have no great expectation; but I think the commissioners will shortly certify. And as for master Cornwell and his pretty doing, I will write shortly. Thus God preserve you! *Postridie Jo. Bapt.* At Hartlebury.

H. L.

Wigorn.

[25 June, 1538.]

To the right honourable lord
   Cromwell, lord privy seal,
   and his singular good lord.

[1 Sir William Compton had been sheriff of Worcestershire for 19 years successively up to the 27 Hen. VIII. Nash, Hist. of Worcestershire, Vol. I. p. xviii.]

LETTER XXXIV.

LATIMER *to* LORD CROMWELL.

[Orig. State Pap. Off. Crom. Corr. Vol. 49, 1. 493.]

Now, my good lord privy seal, shew your charitable goodness in this matter of Mr Lucy[2]. I have sent unto your lordship his letters. If that Mr William Clapton may be suffered thus to rage, it will be but folly for any true preachers to come into that part of my diocese. I heartily require herein both the use of your authority and also of your counsel; and that you would send for the priest and also that Mr Clapton, and to reduce him into some order; and, according to justice, to end the matter, which is now at length made treason, and so not appertaining to my court. And in what case are they in, that hath veiled treason so long! But I refer all things to your approved wisdom, and singular favour towards the truth of God's word and execution of justice, that good master Lucy be not discouraged in his hearty goodness.

Yours, this St James' day, even now going to horse, when master Lucy's servant came to me, which, if your lordship be at leisure, can tell the whole process.

H. Wigorn.

At Har[tle]bury, [25 July, 1538].

To the right honourable lord
Cromwell, lord privy seal,
his singular good lord.

LETTER XXXV.

LATIMER *to* LORD CROMWELL.

[Orig. State Pap. Off. Crom. Corr. Vol. 49, 1. 510.]

RIGHT honourable, *salutem*. And, sir, as I perceive by this bearer, Mr Evance, I have to thank your good lordship

[2 See Letter XXI. p. 381.]

for the same, for that you were good lord unto him, and that the rather for my sake, as he saith: for the which and all other your singular goodness I most heartily [thank] you, and even so desire you to continue the same; and I shall daily pray for your prosperous estate, according to my bounden duty, &c.

A certain man told me that the bloody abbot[1] should have said alate among his brethren, that his last coming up to London, by my occasion, cost him, besides the charges of his journey up and down, seven score pounds: wherefore he was not able to make provision for household; and therefore required the best mitre, the best cross, and another thing or two, to make chevance[2] withal for provision. But now you say, "What matter maketh that to you?" Truth it is; but yet to tell it you I thought it not amiss, because it may make matter to you; for so may all the jewels of the house be surveyed away and you not knowing, &c.

This letter inclosed came to me yesterday from your lordship's visitor[3]. I send it, *ut videat dominatio tua, quid sit actum.* God forbid but his labour should be well taken! and God forbid that such deceivable hypocrisy should up again and stand at any man's suit! no, though they would give *aureos montes* therefore, &c.

Mr Nevell, your hearty servant to all his power, took a pardoner[4] alate misordering himself, and therefore took his seal from him; and because the pardoner doth not return

[1 As mention is made of the sale of the "best mitre, the best cross," &c. it is probable that the person here (somewhat uncourteously) alluded to, was Clement Lichfield, or Lychfield, the last abbot but one of Evesham, which was a mitred abbey. He refused to surrender his abbey to the crown, but was at length induced to resign his office some time before Oct. 1538. The abbots of this house were continually disputing with the bishops of Worcester, for the time being, respecting questions of privilege and jurisdiction. Wood, Fasti, Vol. I. p. 6, edit. Bliss; Nash, Hist. of Worcests. pp. 400 et seq.]

[2 *Chevantia*, a loan or advance of money upon credit.]

[3 The letter is from Richard Ingworth, suffragan of Dover, giving an account of his proceedings in visiting monasteries, and expressing some anxiety at not having heard from lord Cromwell, whether his proceedings gave satisfaction or not.]

[4 One of those persons who used to carry about the country papal indulgences for sale. See Prologue to Chaucer's Pardoner's Tale.]

again for it, hath sent it to your lordship, trusting that your lordship will pardon him for so doing. Such new things do but maintain the people in their old superstition, as the pardoners doth abuse them and the poor people doth take them.

I trust in your good lordship as touching to have a good neighbour; *unde pendet ut cum fructu ipse prædicem, alioquin totam noctem laboraturus et parum aut nihil capturus.* But I doubt nothing but your lordship hath me in remembrance.

Hereby is an hermitage[5] in a rock by Severn, able to lodge five hundred men, and as ready for thieves or traitors as true men. I would not have hermits masters of such dens, but rather that some faithful man had it. Mr Robert Acton, at his return, shall shew you further.

I pray your good lordship take in worth this foolish farraginary scribbling.

Yours,

H. L. Wigorn.

Postridie Bartho. [25 Aug. 1538.]
At Hartlebury.

To the right honourable and his singular good lord, the lord privy seal.

LETTER XXXVI.

Latimer *to* Lord Cromwell.

[Orig. State Pap. Off. Crom. Corr. Vol. 49, 1. 491.]

Right honourable, *salutem*. And, sir, as touching Mr Wattwood[6], you wot what you have to do; and I doubt not but will do as appertaineth thereunto: whereas he was put up in my visitation for a lecher, a fighter, and a disquieter of his company, I cannot have him to answer thereunto. He beareth him very boldly of your lordship; and how much he

[5 The Hermitage at Redstone Ferry, in the parish of Ashley. Nash, Hist. of Worcesters. Vol. I. p. 40.]
[6 See Letter XXXII. p. 396.]

regardeth my injunctions, your lordship may perceive by the testimony of all his company, whose letter I do send unto your lordship here inclosed. As for master Wattwood, so that he be reformed and I discharged, I care not how little I have to do with him; saving only I pray for him that God would make him a good man. I write nothing of him but I dare avow it, with more. And I write it of no malice that I do bear him, but of good-will that I bear both to him and others. I desire you to be good lord to the college, and set you therein some good order, for it is not without need; for master Wattwood, I ascertain you, is no meet man to do what he listeth. If he inform any thing of me, as I know he can feign and lie to make for his purpose, I dare come to my answer. And thus Almighty God be with you!

Yours,

H. L. Wigorn.

At Hartl[ebury] 2 Oct. [1538.]

To the right honourable the lord privy seal, his good lord.

LETTER XXXVII.

LATIMER *to* LORD CROMWELL[1].

[Orig. State Pap. Off. Crom. Corr. Vol. 49, 1. 531.]

RIGHT honourable, *in Domino salutem*. And, sir, I may marvel greatly that you do not blame me, but will take so patiently this my importunity. Well! to my purpose; for I must go on like myself. As for Bristow, sir, I am sure you will remember *in tempore*, of yourself, without me. Gloucester

[1 The assertion "their Lady... is gone" decides that this letter was written after the removal of the image of "our Lady of Worcester," in September, 1538; and as Latimer ceased to be bishop of that see in July, 1539, the date of the letter is ascertained. The image of "their Lady" at Worcester was in great repute, but on being disrobed, was found to be a tall statue of some bishop. Hall, Chronicle, p. 826, edit. by Ellis; Herbert, Life of Hen. VIII. p. 496.]

you have remembered already[2], by my occasion partly. Now Worcester is behind, an ancient and a poor city, and yet replenished with men of honesty, though not most wealthy; for by reason of their lady they have been given to much idleness; but now that she is gone, they be turned to laboriousness, and so from ladyness to godliness. But, sir, this city is greatly charged with three things: their school, their bridge, and their wall[3]. As for their school, it hath been maintained heretofore by a brotherhood, called a Gyld[4], I trow, not without some guile, popishly pardoning, and therefore now worthily decried; so that I am fain myself, as poor as I am, to retain the school-master there with my livery, meat and drink upon the holiday, and some part of his living beside, because he is honest and bringeth up their youth after the best sort. And as for their bridge[5] and their wall, as they be necessary for the city and the country both, so they be now not without great need of reparation, as I hear say.

Wherefore, these premises considered, if the king's grace of his most gracious goodness, through your lordship's good advertisement, would vouchsafe to bestow the two friaries, Black and Grey[6], with their appurtenance, upon this his poor ancient city, to the maintenance of the foresaid three things, so necessary for so many good purposes, *et illius majestas rem optimo regum dignam proculdubio faceret*, an honourable foundation, a comely commutation; popishness changed into holiness, beggars unbeggared to avoid beggary: *quæ sit mutatio dextræ*

[2 See above, p. 393. An act was passed 32 Hen. VIII. c. 18, to rebuild Worcester.]

[3 A school was founded in 1542, by king Hen. VIII. for forty poor scholars.]

[4 The Guild of the Holy Trinity in Worcester. Nash, Hist. of Worcestershire, Vol. II. Append. cxxxviii.]

[5 From this account of the bridge at Worcester, compared with Leland's statement, that "The bridge is a royal piece of worke, high and stronge, and hath six great arches of stone" (Itinerary, p. 84.), it may be presumed, that between the date of this letter and that of Leland's visit to Worcester, a bridge of stone had been substituted for the wooden-bridge which formerly existed over the Severn. Nash, Hist. of Worcesters. Vol. II. Append. cxv.]

[6 These two friaries were accordingly granted to the bailiff and citizens of Worcester, in the following year. Tanner, Notitia, pp. 626 et seq. Lond. 1744.]

Excelsi[1], when lip-labouring of a few lewd friars should be turned into right praying of the whole city and town for the king's majesty and all his grace's posterity!

Thus we commit our whole matter to your goodness, and you yourself to the goodness of God, long to continue to such good purposes. Amen.

H. L.

Wigorn.

At Hartl[ebury]. 6 October [1538].

And your lordship would have thanked the king's grace's highness for my stag, in my name, I had been much bounden to you. I have made many merry in these parts, for I eat not all myself. God save the king!

To the right honorable lord Cromwell, the lord privy seal, his singular good lord.

LETTER XXXVIII.

LATIMER *to* LORD CROMWELL.

[Orig. State Pap. Off. Crom. Corr. Vol. 49, 1. 536.]

RIGHT honourable, *in Domino dominorum salutem plurimam.* And, sir, as touching John Scurfeld, the prisoner of Bristol, we have sent for him and examined him according to the tenor of your lordship's letters, and in process, after much ado with him, we perceive neither malice nor yet subtlety in him, but rather much simplicity and innocency, though his letters were written, as they seemed, very suspiciously. His delight was to have them punished, which were bruited to deny the sacrament; and of that he had somewhat heard already, trusting to hear more, and so after his affection enlarged his pen at liberty, and so brought himself into suspicion for lack of discretion, he being not yet nineteen years of age: but he hath been hampered therefore meetly well already, and is now re-carried again to Bristol, there to put in sureties, lacking such here, for his forthcoming whensoever upon any

[1] Psal. lxxvii. 10, according to the Vulgate.

occasion any of the king's grace's council shall call for him. And after such sort, much grating of him, and yet finding no other thing in him, we thought best to dispatch him, and to remit him. And so we now commit your good lordship most heartily to God.

Yours,

H. L. Wigorn.

18th Oct. [1538?] at Hartl[ebury].

Your orator, John Russell.

This bearer can tell your lordship how your lordship's letters might perfect the commonwealth about Tewksbury.

The same hath to thank your lordship, and I also for his sake, for your goodness toward him. *Valeat in Christo Dominatio tua.*

> *To the right honourable their lord privy seal, their very good lord.*

LETTER XXXIX.

LATIMER *to* LORD CROMWELL.

[Orig. State Pap. Off. Crom. Corr. Vol. 49, 1. 497.]

RIGHT honourable, *salutem.* And, sir, this bearer, Mr Acton[2], is altogether yours, under the king's grace, to be where as your lordship shall think his service most necessary; but when he is above, then we much lack him here beneath. He can tell you what proceedings be in our sessions, and how men be inclined either to justice or from. I can no more; but I pray God send the king's grace many such trusty servants in all parts of his grace's realm. And God continue your life to the performance of all your good purposes!

H. L. Wigorn.

19th Oct. [1538.]   At Hartl[ebury].

[2 See Letter XXVI. p. 387.]

Sir, the prior of the Black Friars in Worcester, called Richard Edwards, when he surrendered up his house[1], was promised his capacity freely, both for himself and all his brethren. He is honest, as Mr Acton can tell. I tolerate him in my diocese, trusting that you will extend your charity to him, &c.

*To the right honourable the lord
privy seal, his singular good
lord.*

LETTER XL.

LATIMER *to* LORD CROMWELL.

[Orig. State Pap. Off. Crom. Corr. Vol. 49. 1. 487.]

RIGHT honourable, *salutem multo plurimam in omnium Salvatore.* And, sir, as to master Wattwood[2], I have done according to the tenor of your lordship's letters; and at my next speaking with your lordship I will purge myself of his false accusation, as he himself hath confessed that he made untrue relation upon me in one thing, &c.

Ad hæc: a certain man did write unto me alate these words, "Frere Bartlow doth much hurt in Cornwall and in Devonshire, both with open preaching, and also with private communication, &c."

If this be true, he hath some comfort from Rome, I fear me, and, I divine, much of doctor Nicolas[3]; a man with whom my fantasy never wrought withal, &c.

Now, sir, this bearer, the abbot of Evesham[4], required me to make some mention of him, and to thank your good lordship for him; which I am bounden to do most heartily.

[1 In August, 1538. This letter may, therefore, with great probability be assigned to the same year. Letter on the Suppres. of the Monast. p. 203.]

[2 See above, p. 401.]

[3 Nicholas de Burgo, an Italian by birth. He is mentioned as very forward in taking the part of Henry VIII, when the subject of that monarch's divorce was in agitation at Oxford. Wood, Fasti Oxon. p. 62, edit. Bliss. Wordsworth, Eccl. Biogr. Vol. II. p. 124. 3rd edit.]

[4 Philip Hawford or Ballard; see above, p. 389.]

And, sir, among many that your lordship hath done for, I think you shall find but few that will better remember, to his power, your beneficialness, than he will. Verily, he seemeth to me a very civil and honest man; and one that putteth all his trust in your good lordship, that of your goodness, as you have begun with him and made him, so you will continue good lord unto him, to the maintaining of him in his right of such things which he hath obtained by your only goodness. Thus God continue you among us to do many men good!

Yours,

H. L.

Wigorn.

Sir, we have been bolting and sifting the blood of Hailes[5] all this forenoon. It was wonderously closely and

[5. The popular belief respecting this relic is related by Latimer himself, (see above, p. 364), and his account accords with that usually given of the matter by the historians. This letter now supplies accurate information, respecting what the relic really was. The following is a copy (the orthography being modernized) of the official report made to lord Cromwell by the commissioners appointed to examine the relic:

"Pleaseth your lordship to be advertised, that, according to the king's grace's commission to us directed, bearing date the fourth day of October, [1538] in the xxxth year of his reign, we, Hugh, bishop of Worcester, Henry, prior of the monastery of Worcester, Stephen, abbot of the monastery of Hales, and Richard Tracy, esquire, the xxviiith day of October, in the year abovesaid, have repaired to the said monastery of Hales, and there, according to the tenor of the said commission, have viewed a certain supposed relic, called the blood of Hales, which was inclosed within a round berall, garnished and bound on every side with silver, which we caused to be opened in the presence of a great multitude of people. And the said supposed relic we caused to be taken out of the said berall, and have viewed the same, being within a little glass; and also tried the same according to our powers, wits, and discretions by all means. And by force of the view, and other trials thereof, we think, deem, and judge the substance and matter of the said supposed relic to be an unctious gum coloured; which, being in the glass, appeared to be a glistering red, resembling partly the colour of blood. And after we did take out part of the said substance and matter out of the glass, then it was apparent glistering yellow colour, like amber, or base gold, and doth cleave to as gum or bird-lime. Which matter, craftily inclosed and stopped up, for taking of care. And it cleaveth fast to the bottom of the little glass that it is in. And, verily, it seemeth to be an unctious gum and compound of many things. It hath a certain unctious moistness, and though it seem somewhat like blood when it is in the glass, yet when any parcel of the same is taken out, it turneth to a yellowness, and is cleaving like glue. But we have not yet examined all the monks; and therefore this my brother abbot shall tell your lordship what he hath seen and heard in this matter. And in the end your lordship shall know altogether. But we perceive not, by your commission, whether we shall send it up or leave it here, or certify thereof as we know.

H. L.
Wigorn,
At Hailes.

28 Oct. [1538.]

and feigned relic, with the glass containing the same, we the said commissioners, have inclosed in red wax, and consigned it with our seals. And also, we have locked it in a coffer [*with two locks] remaining by deed indented, with the said abbot of Hales. The key whereof [*the one] is committed to the custody of [*said Abbot, and the other] to the said Richard Tracy. Wherefore we desire your lordship, that we may know further the king's gracious pleasure herein to be done, which we, according to our most bounden duty, shall accomplish, with all our endeavour and diligence."

Now, inasmuch as Hilsey, bishop of Rochester, preached at Paul's Cross on the 24th Nov. 1538, and there publicly exhibited the blood of Hales, " affirming the same to be no blood, but honey clarified, and coloured with saffron," it is difficult to understand how William Thomas, lord Herbert, Burnet, and many others after them, should have asserted that the "blood of Hales" was found on examination to be nothing but "the blood of a duck, which was renewed every week." Nor does there seem to be any ground for the usual description given of the glass in which the relic was contained; viz., that it was a " crystal vessel which was very thick on one side, but thin and transparent on the other," so that the opaque side might be kept toward the unshriven and stingy votary, and the transparent side presented to him when the amount of his offerings induced the monks of Hales to let him have a sight of the relic. Hearne, Benedicti, &c. Abbatis, Tom. II. pp. 75, et seq.; Holinshed, III. p. 946; Pegge, Life of Grosseteste, p. 161, note.]

---

* Obliterated in the original.

LETTER XLI.

LATIMER to LORD CROMWELL.

[Orig. State Pap. Off. Crom. Corr. Vol. 49, 1. 489.]

RIGHT honourable. If it be your pleasure to know with what kind of relics the blood of Hailes is accompanied, read this letter inclosed, and then do as shall be seen unto your approved wisdom. The letter must return again to me to satisfy the writer's mind, &c.

If master Nevell shall remove St Kenelm[1], then he shall find his shoe full for a relic, &c.

I would have waited upon your lordship myself, but that I must preach to-morrow for master Manworth at Barking. I doubt not but your good lordship of your accustomed goodness doth remember Gloucester. Lady abbess of Malling[2] hath instantly desired me to thank your good lordship for your goodness towards her.

Yours,

H. L.

Wigorn.

[16 Nov. 1538.]

To the right honourable, and his singular good lord, the lord privy seal.

[1 A chapel connected with the manor of Hales. Among the goods belonging to St Kenelm, in the year 1503, were "a lytyll shryne with odour relique therein. A hede of seynt Kenelme sylver and gyld." Nash, Hist. of Worcesters. Vol. I. p. 520. Append. pp. x. et seq.]

[2 Elizabeth Rede. Valor Eccles. Vol. I. p. 106.]

LETTER XLII.

LATIMER *to* LORD CROMWELL[1].

[Cotton, MS. Cleop. E. IV. p. 264, et seq.]

RIGHT honourable, *salutem in Salvatore*. And, sir, I have to thank your good lordship for many things; and now alate for your singular goodness shewed, as I understand, to master Lucy, a very[2] good gentleman; and also towards master Acton, another of the same sort: but of this my duty more at more leisure. And yet thus much now I will say, and not say it alone, but with many, that your lordship (one man) have promoted many more honest men, since God promoted you, than hath many men done before your time, though in like authority with you: *tamquam non tibi natus soli, sed multorum commodo. Efficiat, qui omnia facit, et in eundem finem diutissime vivat dominatio tua, ut sic inter nobiles nobilissimus evadas. Quod quidem nihil esse possit nobilius quam bonos viros evehere, malos autem reprimere. Id quod tibi hactenus usu venit, plus omnibus facere.*

But now, sir, another thing that, by your favour, I might be a motioner unto you, at the request of an honest man, the prior of Great Malvern[3], in my diocese, though not of my diocese[4]; referring the success of the whole matter to your only approved wisdom and benign goodness, in any[5] case: for I know that I do play the fool, but yet with my foolishness I somewhat quiet an unquiet man, and mitigate his heaviness: which I am bold to do with you, for that I know, by experience, your goodness, that you will bear with fools in their frailness. This man both heareth and feareth (as he saith) the suppression of his house, which, though he will be

[1 This letter is printed by Nichols, Hist. of Leicestershire, Vol. III. p. 1065, and partly by Strype, Eccl. Mem. I. i. p. 562, Oxf. edit.]

[2 right, Nichols.]

[3 Richard Whitborne, or Bedyll, the last prior of that house. Willis, Hist. of Abbies, Vol. II. p. 260. Nash. Hist. of Worcesters. Vol. II. p. 124.]

[4 The priory of Malvern was subject to the jurisdiction of the abbots of Westminster, by a compact dated as far back as the reign of king Edward I. Nash, *ubi sup*.]

[5 every, Nichols.]

conformable in all points to the king's highness' pleasure, and yours once known, as both I advertised him, and also his bounden duty is to be; yet nevertheless, if he thought his enterprise would not be mistaken, nor turn to any displeasure, he would be an humble suitor to your lordship, and, by the same, to the king's good grace, for the upstanding of his foresaid house, and continuance of the same to many good purposes: not in monkery, he meaneth not so; God forbid! but any other ways as should be thought and seem good to the king's majesty: as to maintain teaching, preaching, study, with praying, and (to the which he is much given) good housekeeping; for to the virtue of hospitality he hath been greatly inclined from his beginning, and is very much commended in these parts for the same. So, if five hundred marks to the king's highness, with two hundred marks to yourself, for your good will, might occasion the promotion of his intent, at least way for the time of his life, he doubteth not to make his friends for the same, if so little could bring so much to pass. The man is old, a good housekeeper, feedeth many, and that daily; for the country is poor, and full of penury. And alas! my good lord, shall we not see two or three in every shire changed to such remedy? Thus, too, this honest man's importunity hath brought me beyond my duty; saving for the confidence and trust that I have always in your benignity. As he hath knowledge from you, so he will prepare for you, ever obedient to your advertisement. Sir William Kingston[6] can make report of the man.

God prosper you to the uttering of all hollow hearts! Blessed be the God of England, that worketh all, whose instrument you be! I heard you say once, after you had seen that furious invective of cardinal Pole, that you would make him to eat his own heart, which you have now, I trow, brought to pass; for he must now eat his own heart, and be as heartless as he is graceless.

H. L.

13 December [1538].   Wigorn.
Hartl[ebury].

[6 Constable, or lieutenant of the Tower.]

LETTER XLIII.

LATIMER to LORD CROMWELL.

[Orig. State Pap. Off. Crom. Corr. Vol. 49, 1. 524.]

RIGHT honourable and my singular good lord, *salutem plurimam in Christo*. And, sir, to be short with you and not to trouble you, thus is now my state, and in this condition I am. All manner of my receipts, since I was bishop, amounts to four thousand pounds and upward. My first-fruits, reparations and solutions of my debts, amounts to seventeen hundred pounds: there remaineth in ready money now at my last audit, ending upon Christmas even's even, nine score pounds; of the which, five score pound and five is payable forth withal, for my tenths of this year, other twenty goeth to my new year's gift, and so have I left to myself, to keep my Christmas withal, and to come up withal, three score pounds. All the rest is spent: if well, that is my duty; if otherwise, that is my folly. As any man can complain, I must make answer; else, God knoweth all. It is spent, I say, saving that I have provision for household, in wheat, malt, beeves, and muttons, as much as would sustain my house this half year and more, if I should not go forth of my diocese: and in this standeth much the stay of my house; for I am more inclined to feed many grossly and necessarily, than a few deliciously and voluptuously. As for plate and hangings, hath not cost me twenty shillings. In plate, my new year's gifts doth my need with glass and byrral; and I delight more to feed hungry bellies, than to clothe dead walls. Thus it is, my lord, therefore you may me credit; and as you have been always my good lord, so I desire you to continue, and to take this rude signification of my condition for a new year's gift, and a poor token of my good will toward you, for this time. Another year, and I live, it shall be better; for, I thank my Lord God, I am within forty pounds out of debt, which doth lighten my heart not a little. And shortly cometh on my half-year's rent; and then I shall be afloat again, and come clean out of debt.

Sir, my brother suffragan, the prior of Worcester[1], is

[[1] Henry Holbeach, last prior of Worcester, was consecrated suffragan to the bishop of Worcester (by the title of bishop of Bristol)

your orator and beadsman, if it be your pleasure that he shall preach before the king's highness, this Lent coming, his day once appointed, he will be at your commandment; but now it were time to know his day.

H. L. W.

Sub natalem Christi, [24 Dec. 1538.]

Hartl[ebury.]

To the right honourable the lord privy seal, his singular good lord.

LETTER XLIV.

LATIMER *to* LORD CROMWELL.

[Orig. State Pap. Off. Crom. Corr. Vol. 49, 1. 526.]

RIGHT honourable, *salutem*. And, sir, I doubt not, but the king's highness, of his gracious and accustomable goodness, will remember his poor subjects now in Lent as touching white meat, of the which I now motion unto your lordship, to the intent it may come betime among them; for heretofore it hath been Midlent as ever it hath come to the borders of the realm, &c.

Sir, this master Lucy shall be now a great piece of my letters unto you. I trust you will give to him the hearing as you may have leisure.

Sir, I like not these honey-mouthed men, when I do see no acts nor deeds according to their words. Master Anthony Barker[2] had never had the wardenship of Stratford at my hands, saving at contemplation of your lordship's letter. I am sure your lordship can bolt out what should be meant by such instructions as master Anthony Barker gave to his parish priest, whose voluntary confession without any provocation of me, I do send unto your lordship, written with his

at Lambeth, March 24, 1538. The date of this letter must therefore be assigned to that year, because Latimer ceased to be bishop of Worcester before Christmas, 1539. Willis, Hist. of Abbies, Vol. I. p. 311; Strype, Mem. of Cranm. p. 90, Oxf.]

[2 See above, p. 383.]

own hand, his own name subscribed; Mr Lucy with all my house being at the publishing of the same.

Sir, I ascertain you before God, that I never presented any matter unto you, of any malice or ill will to any person, but only of good zeal to the truth and discharging of my duty.

And as for the Arches[1], I could have had fewer matters there with more money in my purse, by not a little, if I would have followed the old trade in selling of sin and not doing of my duty.

I do send unto your lordship also a copy of master Anthony Barker's parish priest's recantation or revocation, which shall be done upon Sunday next, at Stratford, one of my chaplains being there to preach, and he the same.

Sir, our master sheriff[2] hath kept such a sessions at Worcester, as hath not been seen here these many years.

Sir, to be master of the game in the forest of Fecknam[3] is to be leader of many men. It were meet that he that should be leader of many men, should [have] a true faithful heart to his sovereign Lord. In that point you know our sheriff; he dwelleth within with four miles of Fecknam.

Dixi,

H. L. W.

17 Jan. [1539], Hartl[ebury].

To the right honourable the lord
privy seal, his singular good
lord.

[1] The Court of Arches, which is a court of appeal, among other things.]

[2] The sheriff of Worcestershire, of whom it might about that time be most correctly said that "he dwelleth within four miles of Feckenham," was Sir Gilbert Talbot, of Grafton Park, in Bromsgrove. But then he was not sheriff until 31 Hen. VIII. or Nov. 1539. Nash, Hist. of Worcesters. Vol. I. p. xviii.]

[3] The forest of Feckenham, Worcestershire, was then a royal demesne. Nash, Hist. Worcesters. Vol. I. pp. 439 et seq.]

LETTER XLV.

LATIMER to LORD CROMWELL[4].

[Orig. State Pap. Off. Crom. Corr. Vol. 49, 1. 502.]

RIGHT honourable, *salutem*. And, sir, I pray you give this bearer, my fellow Moore, the king's servant, the hearing of a matter which I have charged him to open to your lordship, even as he did open it to me. Your lordship shall perceive what conveyance there is by night. It were meet to know to what purpose. If your lordship return my fellow, with your letters of commission to master sheriff and me, to examine the parties, we shall lack no good will to do our best. Some words, meseemeth, soundeth not well toward the king. I refer all to your high wisdom.

This bearer, Moore, seemeth to me an honest man: one word of your lordship's mouth might occasion master captain[5] to be his good master; and something better than he is, as this man doth say.

God forbid that this poor man should forego his right! my counsel hath seen his writings, and they think that he is debarred of right. Your good lordship may ease all with one word. It hangeth betwixt sir John Ashley and him.

Sir, Mr Tracy[6], your lordship doth know what manner of man he is; I would wish there were many of that sort. He had a lease of the demesnes of Winchcombe, as other more had. The others have theirs renewed without a condition; if you would of your goodness write to the Abbot and Convent, that he might have his renewed again, without

[4 This letter is indorsed "A° xxx°." intimating seemingly that it was written in the 30th year of Hen. VIII. The circumstance, too, that the "demesnes" belonging to the abbot and convent of Winchcombe were still under the control of that body, when the letter was written, would agree with the date mentioned.]

[5 Most probably Sir Anthony Wingfield, captain of the king's guard, with whose family Latimer was acquainted. Holinshed, III. p. 949.]

[6 Henry Tracy, of Todington, in co. of Gloucester, who held lands on lease under the convent of Winchcombe. Rudder, Hist. of Gloucester, p. 828; Stevens, Hist. of Ancient Abbies, &c. I. pp. 275 et seq.]

a condition, your lordship should do an act not unworthy yourself. He is given to good hospitality, and hath need of such things for the maintenance of the same; and he is always ready to serve the king in commissions and other ways, with most hearty fashion, according to his duty, letting for no costs nor charge at any time.

Sir, I know that I am a bold fool; but till you rebuke me for the same, I must needs be malapert with you for such honest men. God be with you, and I pray God preserve you *ad promotionem bonorum, vindictam malorum!*

Yours altogether,
H. L. Wigorn.

18 Jan. [1539], Hartl[ebury.]

To the right honourable the lord privy seal, his singular good lord.

LETTER XLVI.

LATIMER *to* LORD CROMWELL.

[Orig. State Pap. Off. Crom. Corr. Vol. 49, 1. 533.]

RIGHT honourable, *salutem in Domino.* And, sir, you be indeed *scius artifex,* and hath a good hand to renew old bottles, and to polish them and make them apt to receive new wine. I pray you, keep your hand in ure; and to the intent your lordship may perceive what a work you have wrought upon this man, Mr Wattwood, I do send unto you Mr Benett's letter, my chaplain, testifying what good change and renovation he perceiveth in him, of the which I am very glad. And so, I am sure, your good lordship will be also, and the rather for that he is your own workmanship, under God, to whom be all honour and glory. Amen.

Yours,
H. L. Wigorn.

2 April [1539], at Sutton[1].

[[1] Sutton in Tenbury, the seat of the family of Acton.]

LETTER XLVII.

LATIMER *to* LORD CROMWELL.

[Orig. State Pap. Off. Crom. Corr. Vol. 49, l. 494.]

Sir,—As touching you wot what, I have written again, guessing at your advice; I trust, not far wide. But yet pity it is to see God so dishonoured, and no remedy provided, at leastway that God hath provided; not free to be used, but the vengeance of God more and more to be provoked; *when comperites*[2] *doth shew what fedities*[3] *doth grow.*

Now, sir, if you be listy to hear of Furnes fools, this simple priest can tell you the state of those parts: he hath come far to shew you his grief; a world to know how pardoners doth prate in the borders of the realm. If you help not that men of both learning and judgment be resident there, they shall perish in their ignorance.

God send you well again to us[4], for without you we shall make no end.

Postridie Benedicti, at Strownd[5].

H. WIGORNIEN.

[15 April, 1539.]

LETTER XLVIII.

LATIMER *to* LORD CROMWELL.

[Orig. State Pap. Off. Crom. Corr. Vol. 49, l. 528.]

Right honourable, *salutem*. And, sir, I have to thank your good lordship for many things; but I will not now trouble your better businesses therewith, but shall pray to

[2 More frequently *compertes*, things found out by means of judicial inquiry. See Letters on the Suppr. of Monaster. pp. 50, 66, 85.]

[3 Base practices. See Wordsworth, Eccl. Biogr. Vol. II. p. 235. 3rd Edit.]

[4 The date of this obscure letter is probably April 1539, at which time lord Cromwell was ill of a tertian ague. See his letter to Henry VIII. State Papers, Vol. I. p. 613. *Note by Mr Lemon.*]

[5 Probably Stroudend, in Painswick, Gloucestershire, where lord Cromwell had the manor. Rudder, Hist. of Gloucestersh. p. 595.]

God to reward you for all together. And now, sir, your good lordship hath begun right graciously with the school of Gloucester[1]: if of your goodness you would now make an end, your perseverance cannot be unrewarded. If the king's highness doth use to sell of such lands as hath been belonging to monasteries, lady Cooke, foundress of the school, would give after twenty years' purchase for a parcel which lieth near unto the town, and was belonging to Llanthony[2]. This bill inclosed doth specify the value, and I did send this bearer, Mr Garrett[3], my chaplain, to speak with lady Cooke, and to know further of the same, and to advertise your lordship of the same. But I refer all to your known both wisdom and goodness; and upon your pleasure known herein lady Cooke shall make ready thereunto.

As to my nurse, I say no more; but if your good lordship do remember her friendly, she both will and shall remember your good lordship again accordingly. But I will go no further, neither in this suit, nor yet in no other, but as I shall perceive your lordship agreeable to hear the same. Thus God preserve you in long life to the finishing of many things well begun, and to the performance of many things yet unperfect!

[1539?] H. L.
Wigorn.

To the right honourable and his very good lord, the lord privy seal.

[[1] The school here referred to is the free grammar school of St Mary de Crypt, in the city of Gloucester. The lady Cooke here mentioned purchased of the Crown (31 Hen. VIII.) lands that formerly belonged to the abbey of Gloucester, as well as some that belonged to Llanthony, and endowed the school in compliance with the will of her late husband, John Cooke, alderman of Gloucester. She is said, in an old book, "to have taken the ring and mantle after her husband's death, and therefore became a lady." The probable date of this letter is the spring of 1539. Rudder, Hist. of Gloucestersh. pp. 440, 490; Carlisle, Endowed Gram. Schools, Vol. I. p. 452.]

[[2] See Stevens, Hist. of Ancient Abbies, &c. Vol. II. p. 130.]

[[3] Possibly Thomas Garret, or Gerrard, who was martyred in Smithfield with Dr Barnes, in 1541. Foxe, Acts and Mon. II. pp. 438 et seq. Edit. 1684; Wood, Fasti Oxon. I. p. 45, Edit. Bliss.]

LETTER XLIX[4].

LATIMER to a CERTAIN GENTLEMAN[5].

[Foxe, Acts and Mon. pp. 1349, et seq. edit. 1563; Vol. III. pp. 413 et seq. 1684.]

RIGHT worshipful, *salutem in Domino*. And now, sir, I understand that you be in great admirations at me, and take very grievously my manner of writing to you, adding thereunto that "you will not bear it at my hand, no, not and I were the best bishop in England," etc.

Ah, sir! I see well I may say as the common saying is, "Well I have[6] fished and caught a frog;" brought little to pass with much ado. "You will not bear it with me," you say. Why, sir, what will ye do with me? You will not fight with me, I trow. It might seem unseemly for a justice of peace to be a breaker of peace: I am glad the doting time of my foolish youth is gone and past. What will you then do with me, in that you say you will not bear it at my hand? What hath my hand offended you? Perchance you will convent me before some judge, and call me into some court. *Deus bene vertat. Equidem non recuso judicium ullum. Accusemus invicem, ut emendemus alius alium in nomine Domini. Fiat justitia in judicio:* "God turn it to good. I refuse no judgment. Let us accuse one another, that one of us may amend another in the name of the Lord. Let justice proceed in judgment[7];" and then and there, do best, have best, for club half-penny. Or peradventure ye will set pen to paper, and all-to rattle me[8] in a letter, wherein, confuting me, you will defend yourself and your brother against me. Now that would I see, quoth long Robin, *ut*

[4 This letter having been written from Baxterly, it may be presumed that the writer was then living in the house of Mr John Glover; but that house was not built until the reign of king Edward VI. As, moreover, "Sergeant Hales" is named in the letter, it may be concluded that the date of it is 1547 or 1548; for the "Sergeant" became "Justice" Hales on the 20th May, 1549. Dugdale, Hist. of Warwicks. p. 1054, 2nd edit.: Origines Juridic. Chronic. Series, pp. 87, et seq. 3rd edit. 1680.]

[5 A fruitful letter of Master Latimer to a certain gentleman. Foxe.]

[6 well have I, 1563.]

[7 The translations of the Latin quotations were for the most part given in the margin of 1563.]

[8 rattle me up, 1563.]

dicitur vulgariter. Non potero sane non vehementer probare ejusmodi industriam: "I cannot choose but must allow such diligence;" for so should both your integrities and innocencies best appear, if you be able to defend both your own proceedings, and your brother's doings, in this matter to be upright. *Et ego tum justis rationibus victus, libenter cedam, culpam humiliter confessurus:* "And then will I gladly give place, confessing my fault humbly, as one conquered with just reasons." But I think it will not be.

But now, first of all, let me know what it is that ye will not bear at my hand. What have I done with my hand? What hath my hand trespassed you? Forsooth, that can I tell; no man better: for I have charitably monished you in a secret letter of your slipper-dealing[1], and such like misbehaviour. *O quam grave piaculum:* "What a sore matter is this!" And will ye not bear so much with me? Will ye not take such a shew of my good will towards you, and toward the saving of your soul at my hand? O Lord God, who would have thought that master N.[2] had been so impudent, that he would not bear a godly monition for the wealth of his soul! I have in use to commit such trespass many times in a year with your betters by two or three degrees, both lords and ladies, and the best of the realm[3]; and yet hitherto I have not heard that any of them have said in their displeasure, that they will not bear it at my hand. Are you yet to be taught what is the office, liberty, and privilege of a preacher? What is it else, but even *arguere mundum de peccato,* "to rebuke the world of sin," without respect of persons? *Quod quidem ipsum est ipsius Spiritus Sancti peculiare in ecclesia munus et officium, sed non nisi per prædicatores legitimos exsequendum:* "Which thing undoubtedly is the peculiar office of the Holy Ghost in the church of God, so that it be practised by lawful preachers." You could but ill bear (belike) to hear your fault openly reproved in the pulpit, which cannot bear the same in a secret sealed up letter, written both friendly, charitably, and truly. *Nisi forte acriter reprehendere peccata sit jam omni caritate, amicitia, veritate carere:* "Unless perhaps to rebuke sin sharply be now to lack all charity, friendship, and truth." But,

[1 supper-dealing, 1684.]   [2 M. 1563.]

[3 As may well appear by his letter sent to the king before. Foxe.]

master N., if you will give me leave to be plain with you, I fear me you be so plunged in worldly purchasings, and so drowned in the manifold dregs of this deceivable world, that I ween you have forgotten your catechism. Read therefore again the opening of the first commandment, and then tell me whether you of me, or I of you, have just cause to complain, etc.

Item, sir, you said[4] further, "that I am wonderfully abused by my neighbour," &c. How so, good master N.? Wherein? Or how will you prove it to be true, and when? So you said, that he had abused you, and given you wrong information; but the contrary is found true by good testimony of master Chamber, which heard as well as you what my neighbour said, and hath testified the same, both to you, and against you, full like himself. Master N., to forge and feign (which argueth an ill cause), that is one thing; but to prove what a man doth say, that is another thing: as though you were privileged to outface poor men, and bear them in hand what you list, as may seem to make some maintenance for your naughty cause. Trust me, master N., I was but a very little acquainted with my neighbour, when this matter began; but now I have found him so conformable to honesty, upright in his dealings, and so true in his talk, that I esteem him better than I do some others whom I have perceived and found otherways. For I will flatter no man, nor yet claw his back in his folly; but esteem all men as I find them, allowing what is good, and disallowing what is bad. *In omnibus hominibus, sive amicis sive inimicis, juxta præceptum Paulinum, a filiis hujus seculi in pretio non habitum, Sitis odio, inquit, prosequentes quod malum est, adhærentes autem ei quod bonum est: neque bonum malum, nec malum bonum in gratiam hominum affirmemus unquam, id quod filii hujus seculi vulgo faciunt, ut est videre ubique:* " Among all men, either friends or enemies, according to Paul's precept, not esteemed of the children of this world, hate you, saith he, that which is evil, and cleave to that which is good. And let us not any time, for the favour of men, call good evil, and evil good, as the children of this world are commonly wont to do, as it is everywhere to be seen." And now what manner of man do you make me, master N., when you note me

[4 say, 1563.]

to be so much abused by so ignorant a man, so simple, so plain, and so far without all wrinkles? Have I lived so long in this tottering world, and have I been so many ways turmoiled and tossed up and down, and so much as it were seasoned with the powder of so many experiences to and fro, to be now so far bewitched and alienated from my wits, as though I could not discern cheese from chalk, truth from falsehood; but that every silly soul and base-witted man might easily abuse me to that[1] enterprise he listed at his pleasure? Well, I say not nay, but I may be abused. But why do you not tell me how your brother abused me, promising before me and many more, that he would stand to your awardship, and now doth deny it? Why do you not tell me how those two false, faithless wretches abuse me, promising also to abide your award, and do[2] it not? Yea, why do you not tell me how you yourself have abused me, promising me to redress the injury and wrong that your brother hath done to my neighbour, and have[3] not fulfilled your promise? These notable abuses be nothing with you, but only you must needs burden me with my neighbour's abusing[4] me, which is none at all, as far forth as ever I could perceive, so God help me at my need! For if he had abused me as you and others[5] have done, I should be soon at a point with him, for anything further doing for him, &c.

Item, sir, you said further, that I shall never be able to prove that either your brother or the two tenants agreed to stand to your award, etc. No sir, master N., you say belike as you would have it to be, or as your brother with his adherents have persuaded you to think it to be; so inducing you to do their request to your own shame and rebuke, if you persevere in the same, beside the peril of your soul, for consenting, at least way, to the maintenance by falsehood of your brother's iniquity. For in that you would your awardship should take none effect, you show yourself nothing inclinable to the redress of your brother's unright dealing with an honest poor man, which hath been ready at your request to do you pleasure with his things, or else he had never come into this wrangle for his own goods with your brother[6].

[1 what, 1563.]   [2 doth, 1563.]   [3 hath, 1563.]
[4 abusing of, 1563.]   [5 the other, 1563.]
[6 Brother ought not to bear with brother, to bear down right and truth, especially being a justice. Foxe.]

Ah, master N., what manner of man do you shew yourself to be? Or what manner of conscience do you shew yourself to have? For first, as touching your brother, you know right well that sir Thomas Coking[7], with a letter of his own handwriting, hath witnessed unto your brother's agreement; which letter he sent to me unsealed, and I shewed the same to my neighbour and other more, or I sealed it, and perchance have a copy of the same yet to shew. With what conscience then can you say that I shall never be able to prove it? Shall not three men upon their oaths make a sufficient proof, trow you? *Vel ipso dicente Domino, In ore duorum vel trium,* &c. : "the Lord himself saying, In the mouth of two or three," &c. Yea, you think it true, I dare say, in your conscience, if you have any conscience, though I were in my grave, and so unable to prove any thing. And as for the two tenants, they be as they be, and I trust to see them handled according as they be; for there be three men yet alive that dare swear upon a book that they both did agree. But what should we look for at such men's hands, when you yourself play the part you do? *Verum vivit adhuc Deus, qui videt omnia, et judicat juste,* &c. "But God is yet alive, which seeth all, and judgeth justly."

Item, sir, you said yet further, that the justices of peace in the country think you very unnatural, in taking part with me before your brother[8], &c. Ah, master N., what a sentence is this to come out of your mouth! For partaking is one thing, and ministering of justice is another thing; and a worthy minister of justice will be no partaker, but one indifferent between party and party. And did I require you to take my part, I pray you? No, I required you to minister justice between your brother and my neighbour, without any partaking with either other. But what manner of justices be they, I pray you, which would so fain have you to take part naturally with your brother, when you ought and should reform and amend your brother as you yourself know, no man better? What! justices? No, jugglers you might more

[7 Cokin, 1563. Probably Sir Thomas Cokain, of Pooley, in the parish of Polesworth, Warwickshire. Dugdale, Hist. of Warwicksh. pp. 1120 et seq. 2nd edit.]

[8 Were not here good sort of justice, trow you? Foxe.]

worthily call[1] such as they be, than justices. Be they those justices which call you unnatural for that you will not take your brother's part against all right and conscience, whom you had picked out and appointed to have the final hearing and determining of my neighbour's cause, after your substantial and final award-making? Verily, I think no less. Forsooth he is much beholding to you, and I also for his sake. Is that the wholesome counsel that you have to give your poor neighbours in their need? Indeed you shew yourself a worthy juggler. Oh! I would have said a justices[2] among other of your juggling and partaking justices. *Deum bonum,* " O good God!" what is in the world? Marry, sir, my neighbour had spun a fair thread, if your partaking justices, through your good counsel, had had his matter in ordering and finishing. I pray God save me and all my friends, with all God's [3]flock, from the whole fellowship of your so natural and partaking[4] justices. Amen.

Lord God! who would have thought that there had been so many partaking justices, that is to say, unjust justices in Warwickshire, if master N. himself, one of the same order (but altogether out of order), and therefore knoweth it best, had not told us the tale? But these call you, you say, very unnatural, &c. And why not rather, I pray, too much natural? For we read *de natura duplici, integra et corrupta. Illa erat justitiæ plena; hæc nisi reparata, semper manet injusta, injustitiæ fructus alios post alios paritura:* " of a double nature, sound, and corrupt. That was full of justice; this, unless it be restored, abideth always unjust, bringing forth the fruits of wickedness one after another :" so that he that will not help his brother, having a just cause, in his need, may be justly called unnatural, as not doing *juxta instinctum naturæ, sive integræ, sive reparatæ;* " according to the instinct of nature, either as it was at the beginning, or as it was restored." But he that will take his brother's part against right, as to ratify his brother's wrong deceiving, he is too much natural; *tanquam sequens ingenium sive inclinationem naturæ corruptæ, contra voluntatem Dei;* " as one following the disposition and inclination of corrupt nature

[1 all such, 1563.] [2 justicier, 1563.]
[3 little flock, 1563.] [4 parttaking, 1563.]

against the will of God :" and so to be natural may[5] seem to be cater-cousin, or cousin-germain with to be diabolical.

I fear me, we have too many justices that be too much natural, to their own perishment both body and soul. For worthy justices, having ever the fear and dread of God before their eyes, (*quales sunt pauciores apud nos quam vellem,* "of which sort we have a fewer amongst us than I would") will have no respect at all in their judgments and proceedings *ad propinquitatem sanguinis,* "to vicinity of blood;" but altogether *ad dignitatem et æquitatem causæ, ut quod justum est semper judicent intuitu Dei, non quod injustum est intuitu hominum;* of which number I pray God make you one. Amen. *Justus est qui facit justitiam.* At *qui facit peccatum* (*id quod facit, quisquis injuste facit in gratiam et favorem ullius hominis*) *ex diabolo est:* " He is just," saith St John, " that doth justice : but he that sinneth (as they all do which do unjustly for favour and pleasure of men) is of the devil," saith he; of which sort all our partaking and natural justices be, with all their partiality and naturality. *Quare dignum et justum est,* that as many as be such justices, *juste priventur munere, et amplius quoque plectantur pro sui quique[6] facinoris quantitate, ut vel sic tandem abscindantur, tanquam nati in incommodum reipublicæ nostræ, qui nos conturbant, cum adjuvare debeant;* " be justly deprived of their offices, and further also be punished, according to the quantity or quality of their crime; so that by that means they may be cut off, as men born and bred to the hurt and detriment of the commonwealth, which trouble us, when they ought to help us." Amen. *Quare seponite justitiam, et sequimini naturam,* as your naturals and diabolicals would have you to do; that is, even as just as Germain's lips, which came not together by nine mile, *ut vulgo dicunt,* &c.

Item, sir, finally and last of all, you added these words following : " Well," quoth you, " let master Latimer take heed how he meddleth with my brother; for he is like to find as crabbed and as froward a piece of him as ever he found in his life," &c. Ah, sir! and is your brother such an one as you speak of indeed ? Merciful God! what a commendation is this for one brother to give another! *Estne ejus-*

[5 well seem, 1563.]   [6 *quisque,* 1563.]

modi gloriatio tua, mi amice? "Is this your glorying, my friend?" And were it not possible, trow you, to make him better? It is written, *Vexatio dat intellectum;* "Vexation giveth understanding." And again, *Bonum mihi, Domine, quod humiliasti me;* "It is good, O Lord, that thou hast humbled me." At least way, I may pray to God for him, as David did for such like, *ad hunc modum: Chamo et fræno maxillas eorum constringe, qui non approximant ad te;* "After this sort: Bind fast asses with bridle and snaffle, that they approach not near unto thee." In the mean season, I would I had never known either[1] of you both; for so should I have been without this inward sorrow of my heart, to see such untowardliness of you both to godliness; for I cannot be but heavy hearted to see such men so wickedly minded.

Well, let us ponder a little better your words, where you say, "I shall find him[2] as crabbed and as froward a piece," &c. Mark well your own words. For by the tenor of the same it plainly appeareth that you confess your brother's cause, wherein he so stiffly standeth, to be unjust and very naught. For he that standeth so stiffly in a good quarrel and a just cause, as many good men have done, is called a fast man, a constant, a trusty man. But he that is so obstinate and untractable in wickedness and wrong doing, is[3] commonly called a crabbed and froward piece, as you name your brother to be. Wherefore, knowing so well your brother's cause to be so naughty, why have you not endeavoured yourself, as a worthy justice, to reform him accordingly, as I required you, and you promised me to do, now almost twelve months ago, if not altogether? *Summa summarum,* master N., if you will not come off shortly, and apply yourself thereunto more effectually hereafter, than you have heretofore, be you well assured thereof, I shall detect you to all the friends that I have in England, both high and low, as well his crabbedness and frowardness, as your colourable supportation of the same; that I trust I shall be able thereby either to bring you both to some goodness, or at least way I shall so warn my friends and all honest hearts to beware of your illness, that they shall take either no hurt at all, or at least way less harm by you through mine advertisement; in that

[1 neither, 1563.]
[2 where, "I shall find him," you say, as, 1563.]   [3 he is, 1563.]

knowing you perfectly, they may the better avoid and shun your company.

You shall not stay me, master N.; no, though you would give me all the lands and goods you have, as rich as you are noted to be. *Ego nolo tam justam causam derelinquere, ego nolo peccatis alienis in hac parte communicare;* "I will not forsake such a just cause, neither will I communicate with other men's sins." For whether it be, *per detestabilem superbiam,* by detestable pride; whether *per abominabilem avaritiam,* by abominable avarice; or by both two linked together, it is no small iniquity to keep any[4] poor man so long from his right and duty so stiff-neckedly and obstinately, or, whether ye will, crabbedly and frowardly. And what is it then any manner of ways to consent to the same? You know, I trow, master N., *furtum quid sit, nempe, quovis modo auferre vel retinere alienam rem invito domino, ut quidam definiunt. Si fur sit qui sic palam facit, quis erit qui facientem probat, tutatur, propugnat, vel quibuscunque ambagibus suffulcit?* "What theft is; that is, to take or detain by any manner of way another man's good against his will that is the owner, as some define it. If he be a thief that so doth openly, what shall he be that approveth him which is the doer, defendeth, maintaineth, and supporteth him by any manner of colour?" Consider with yourself, good master N., *quid sit opprimere et fraudare in negotio fratrem;* "what it is to oppress and to defraud your brother in his business, and what followeth thereof." It is truly said, *non tollitur peccatum, nisi restituatur ablatum;* "the sin is not forgiven, except the thing be restored again that is taken away." No restitution, no salvation: which is as well to be understood *de rebus per fraudes, technas, et dolos, ut de rebus per manifestum furtum et latrocinium partis;* "of things gotten by fraud, guile, and deceit, as of things gotten by open theft and robbery." Wherefore let not your brother, master N., by cavillation continue in the devil's possession. 'I will do the best I can, and wrestle[5] with the devil, *omnibus viribus,* to deliver you both from him. I will leave no one stone unmoved to have both you and your brother saved. There is neither archbishop nor bishop, nor yet any learned man neither[6] in universities or elsewhere, that I am acquainted withal, that

[4 any one poor, 1563.]   [5 travell, 1563.]
[6 either, 1563.]

shall not write unto you, and in their writing by their learning confute you. There is no godly man of law in this realm that I am acquainted withal, [as master Goodrick, master Gosnal, master Chamber, and, as I should say first, sergeant Hales, and such like[1],] but they shall write unto you, and confute you by the law. There is neither lord nor lady, nor yet any noble personage in this realm, that I am acquainted withal, but they shall write unto you, and godly threaten you with their authority.

I will do all this; yea, and kneel upon both my knees before the king's majesty, and all his honourable council, with most humble petition for your reformation, rather than the devil shall possess you still to your final damnation: so that I do not despair, but verily trust, one way or other, to pluck both you and also your crabbed brother (as crabbed as you say he is) out of the devil's claws, maugre the devil's heart. These premises well considered, look upon it, good master N., that we have no further ado. God's plague is presently upon us; therefore let us now diligently look about us, and in no wise defend, but willingly reknowledge and amend, whatsoever hath been amiss.

These were the capital points of your talk, as I was informed, after you had perused that my nipping and unpleasant letter; and I thought good to make you some answer to them, if perchance I might so move you the rather to call yourself to some better remembrance, and so more earnestly apply yourself to accomplish and perform what you have begun and promised to do, namely, the thing itself; being of such sort as apparently tendeth both to your worship, and also to God's high pleasure.

Thus, lo! with a mad head, but yet a good will, after

[[1] Inserted from 1563. "Master Goodrick," doubtless, Richard Goodrich, an eminent lawyer, who was many times in commission under king Edw. VI. and queen Elizabeth.

"Master Gosnal," most probably John Gosnol, who was solicitor-general 1552, and who exerted himself in favour of John Rogers, when that martyr was unjustly imprisoned in the reign of queen Mary.

"Sergeant Hales," the same person who is mentioned by archbishop Cranmer as one of his "counsel," and whose "lamentable history" is related at large by Foxe.

Dugdale, Origin. Juridic. ubi supr. Foxe, Acts and Mon. III. p. 101, 152, et seq. edit. 1684. Jenkyns, Remains of Cranmer, I. 280.]

long scribbling, I wot not well what (but I know you can read it, and comprehend it well enough), I bid you most heartily well to fare in the Lord, with good health and long life to God's pleasure. Amen.—From Baxterley, the 15th of June.

Yours to do you good to his power,
HUGH LATIMER.

LETTER L.

LATIMER *to* ONE IN PRISON FOR THE PROFESSION OF THE GOSPEL[2].

[Strype, Eccl. Mem. Vol. III. ii. pp. 296, et seq.]

THE eternal consolation of the Spirit of God comfort and stablish your faithful heart in this your glorious cross of the gospel, until the day of reward in our Lord Jesus Christ! Amen.

Blessed be God, dear brother after our common faith, that hath given you hitherto a will with patience to suffer for his gospel sake! I trust that he, which hath begun this good work in you, shall perform the same to the end. But I understand by your letters, that he which tempteth and envieth you this glory, ceaseth not to lay stumblingblocks before you, to bereave you of that crown of immortality which is now ready to be put on your head: persuading that you may for money be redeemed out of a glorious captivity into a servile liberty; which you by your godly wisdom and spirit do perceive well enough, and that he which hath put his hand to the plough and looketh back, is not meet for the kingdom of God; and that none which is a good soldier to Christ entangleth himself with worldly markets. Christ saith, that "foxes have their holes, and the birds of the air have their nests, but the Son of man hath not where to hide his head." The wise men of the world can find shifts to avoid the cross; and the unstable in faith can set themselves to rest with the world: but the simple servant of ^{Luke ix.} ^{Matt. viii.}

[2 Old Father Latimer to one in prison for the profession of the Gospel; giving his judgment whether it be lawful to buy off the cross. Strype.]

Christ doth look for no other but oppression in the world. And then is it their most glory, when they be under the cross of their master Christ; which he did bear, not only for our redemption, but also for an example to us, that we should follow his steps in suffering, that we might be partakers of his glorious resurrection.

I do therefore allow highly your judgment in this behalf, who think it not lawful for money to redeem yourself out of the cross; unless you would go about to exchange glory for shame, and to sell your inheritance for a mess of pottage, as Esau did, who afterwards found it no more; and to think the good gifts of God to be procured with money, as Simon Magus, or else to sell Christ for thirty pence, as Judas did. Good authority you may have out of the scriptures to confirm your judgment against all gainsayers.

Gen. xxv.

Acts viii.

The first is that our Saviour Christ saith, "There is none worthy of him except he daily take up his cross and follow him." If we must daily take up our cross, how may we then shift that cross, which Christ hath put upon us, by our own procurement, and give money to be discharged of that we are called unto? If that in taking up the cross we must also follow Christ, then we may not cast the same off, until we have carried it with him unto death.

St Paul to the Philippians saith, that "It is not only given to us to believe, but also to suffer for his name." If it be the gift of God to suffer for Christ's sake; if it be the gift of God, with what conscience may a man sell the gift of God, and to give money to be rid thereof? God giveth this grace but to a few, as we see at this day. Therefore we ought to shew ourselves both faithful and thankful for the same.

Phil. i.

Moreover St Paul saith, "That every man must abide in that vocation he is called." But we are called to suffer.

1 Cor. vii.

St Peter doth manifestly declare, saying, "If when you do well, and yet be evil handled, ye do abide it, this is a grace of God. For ye are called to this; because Christ was afflicted, leaving us an example, that we should follow his steps." Since then this is our calling, how may we, without the displeasure of God, go about to redeem us with money out of the same?

1 Pet. ii.

St Paul affirmeth the same to the Romans, saying, "For we are all day long delivered unto death, and accounted as

Rom. viii.

sheep appointed to the slaughter." Also he saith in the same chapter, "that we are predestinate to be like and conformable to the image of his Son;" that as they persecuted him, so shall they persecute us; and as they slew him, so shall they slay us.

And Christ saith in St John, that "they shall excommu- John xvi. nicate you and kill you, and think to do God worship thereby. And this they shall do unto you: and this have I spoken unto you, that when the time cometh you shall not be offended in me."

I cannot see how we might go about to deliver ourselves from the death we are called unto for money. St Peter sheweth what we must do that be under the cross, saying, "Let them that suffer according to the will of God, commit 1 Pet. iv. their souls to him, as unto a faithful Creator." And, "Let him not be ashamed that suffereth as a christian man, but rather glorify God in this condition." St Paul also to the Hebrews sheweth that we may not faint under the cross, neither by any means fly aside, saying, "Let us lay away all that press- Heb. xii. eth down, and the sin that hangeth so fast on, and let us run with patience unto the battle that is set before us; looking unto Jesus, the author and finisher of our faith; which for the joy set before him abode the cross and despised the shame, and is set down on the right hand of the throne of God. Consider therefore that he endured such speaking against him of sinners, lest we should be weary and faint in our mind. For we have not yet resisted unto blood-shedding, striving against sin; and have forgotten the consolation, which speaketh unto us as unto children: My son, despise not the chastening of the Lord, neither faint when thou art rebuked of him. For whom the Lord loveth, him he chasteneth, yea, he scourgeth every son whom he receiveth. If we endure chastening, God offereth himself unto us as unto sons." And blessed be they that continue unto the end.

In the Apocalypse the church of God is commanded not Rev. ii. to fear those things which she shall suffer. "For, behold! the devil shall cast some of you into prison, that ye may be tempted, and ye shall have ten days affliction. Be faithful unto the death, and I will give thee the crown of life. He that hath ears to hear, let him hear what the Spirit speaketh to the congregations. He that hath overcome shall not be hurt by the second death."

Be these undoubted scriptures? We may be sufficiently taught that here is no means for us to fly, that are caught under the cross, to any such worldly means as the flesh can devise. Again, we were created to set forth God's glory all the days of our life; which we, as unthankful sinners, have forgotten to do, as we ought, all our days hitherto. And now God by affliction doth offer us good occasion to perform, one day of our life, our duty. And shall we go about to chop away this good occasion, which God offereth us for our honour and eternal rest? And in so doing we shall declare, that we have no zeal to God's glory; neither to the truth, which is so shamefully oppressed; neither to our weak brethren and sisters, who have need of strong witnesses to confirm them. Therefore we should now be glad with St Paul in our afflictions for our weak brethren's sake, and "go about to supply that which wanteth of the afflictions of Christ in our flesh, in his body, which is the church." Not that the afflictions of Christ were not sufficient for our salvation; but that we which be professors of Christ must be contented to be afflicted, and to drink of the cup of his passion, which he hath drank: and so shall we be assured to sit at his right hand, or at his left, in the kingdom of his Father.

Col. i.

Christ saith in John, "Except ye eat the flesh of the Son of man, and drink his blood, ye shall have no life in you." Which, in the interpretation of most ancient and godly doctors, is, to be partakers, both in faith and deed, of the passion of Christ. The which if we refuse, what do we but, as the Capernaites did, go from everlasting life? And here we are with Christ, who hath the words of eternal life. Whither shall we go, or what may we give, to be separated from him?

John vi.

But perchance the worldly-wise man, or carnal gospeller, will confess, and object this to be true, and that he intendeth not to deny the truth, although he buy himself out of the yoke of the cross; minding hereafter, if he be driven thereto, to die therein. But to him I answer, with Solomon, "Defer not to do well to-morrow, but do it out of hand, if thou have liberty." So I say, that little we know whether God will give us such grace, as he doth now offer us, at another time, to suffer for his sake: and it is not in us to choose it when we will. Therefore let us offer the counsel of St Paul: "Serve the time," which we are in, of affliction, and be glad to be afflicted with the people of God, which is the recognizance of the children of God; and rather to redeem the time with our death for the testimony of the truth, to the which we are born, than to purchase a miserable life for the concupiscence of the world, and to the great danger of falling from God. For as long as we are in the body, we are strangers to God, and far from our native country, which is in heaven, where our everlasting day is. We are now more near to God than ever we were, yea, we are at the gate of heaven; and we are a joyful spectacle become, in this our captivity, to God, to the angels, and to all his saints, who look that we should end our course with glory. We have found the precious stone of the gospel; for the which we ought to sell all that we have in the world. And shall we exchange or lay to gage the precious treasure which we have in our hands for a few days to lament in the world, contrary to our vocation? God forbid it! But let us, as Christ willeth us in St Luke, "look up, and lift up our heads, for our redemption is at hand." *Eph. v.*

Matt. xiii.

A man that hath long travelled, and hath his journey's end before him, what madness were it for him to set further compass about, and put himself in more trouble and labour than needeth! If we live by hope, let us desire the end and fruition of our hope. "No man is crowned, but he that lawfully striveth: none obtaineth the goal, but he that runneth out." Run, therefore, so as ye may be sure to obtain. You have run hitherto right well, good christian brethren. God be praised therefore! But now what letteth you but a persuasion, "that is not sprung of him that calleth you," as it is written? *2 Tim. ii. 1 Cor. ix.*

Gal. v.

Example hereof we have, first our Saviour Jesus Christ, who being advised by Peter to provide better for himself than to go to Jerusalem to be crucified, received the reproach, "Go behind me, Satan; thou knowest not the things of God. Shall I not drink of the cup which my Father giveth me?" If Christ would not, at his friend's counsel, provide to shun the cross, no more ought we, whose disciples we are, being called thereto at our friends' flattering notions. "For the *John xv.*

[LATIMER, II.]

28

disciple is not greater than his master. For if they have persecuted me," saith he, "they will persecute you." St Paul, being in prison for the gospel, was ofttimes brought before Felix the judge, who looked for some piece of money for his deliverance; but I cannot read that Paul went about at all to offer him any. John and Peter, being imprisoned for the testimony of the word, did with all boldness confess the same, and sought no other means of redemption than by faithful confession. Paul and Silas, being of God miraculously delivered from their chains and bands of death, having all the doors open of their prison to depart if they would, yet departed they not out of prison, but abode still the good pleasure of God, and his lawful deliverance. God in time past was angry with his people of Israel for sending into Egypt for help in their necessity; saying by the prophet Esay, "Wo be unto you runagate children, who go about to take advice, and not of me, and begin a work, and not of my Spirit." "Cursed is he," by the prophet Jeremy, "that maketh flesh to be his strength." Moses choosed rather to be afflicted with the people of God than to be counted the son of king Pharaoh's daughter. The martyrs in the old time were racked, as St Paul testifieth, and would not be delivered, that they might have a better resurrection.

Let us follow them, and leave the pope's market, who buyeth and selleth the bodies and souls of men, to Balaam and his false prophets, "who love the reward of iniquity."

If any man perceive his faith [not] to abide the fire, let such an one with weeping buy his liberty, until he hath obtained more strength; lest the gospel by him sustain an offence of some shameful recantation. Let the dead bury the dead. Let us that be of the lively faith follow the Lamb wheresoever he goeth, and say to them that be thus curious and wise, Dispute us in this matter with St Paul, "Stretch forth the hands that were let down, and the weak knees, and see that you have straight steps to your feet, lest any halting turn you out of the way: yea, rather let it be healed."

Embrace Christ's cross, and Christ shall embrace you. The peace of God be with you for ever, and with all them that live in captivity with you in Christ!

Written by Mr Latimer, being in captivity. [1553-1555.]

LETTER LI.

An epistle sent by Mr LATIMER *to all the unfeigned lovers of God's truth, out of a prison in Oxford, called Bocardo, where the said* LATIMER *was imprisoned for the testimony of Christ, the* 15th *of May,* 1555.

[Printed by Strype, Eccl. Mem. III. ii. pp. 302, et seq. Oxf. edit.[1]]

THE same peace that our Saviour Christ left with his people, which is not without war with the world, Almighty God make plentiful in your hearts now and ever! Amen. Brethren, the time is[2] come when[3] the Lord's ground will be known: I mean, it will now[4] appear who hath received God's word[5] in their hearts in deed, to the taking of good root Luke viii. therein. For such will not shrink for a little heat or sunburning weather; but stoutly stand and grow, even maugre the malice of all burning showers[6] and tempests. For he that hath played the wise builder, and laid his foundation on a rock, will not be afraid that every drizzling rain or mist shall hurt his buildings, but will stand, although a great tempest do come, and drops of rain as big as fir-fagots. But they that have builded upon a sand will be afraid, though they see but a cloud arise a little black, and no rain or wind doth once touch them; no, not so much as to lie one week in prison, to trust God with their lives which gave them. For they have forgot what St Paul saith, "If we die we are the Rom. xiv. Lord's, and if we live we are the Lord's: so that whether we live or die, we are the Lord's." Yet we will not put him in trust with his own[7].

And forasmuch, my dearly beloved brethren and sisters[8] in the Lord, as I am persuaded of you that you be in the number of the wise builders, which have made their founda-

[1 The readings given in the margin are those of a MS. in the library of Emmanuel College, Cambridge.]

[2 is, I perceive, come.] [3 wherein.]
[4 now shortly.] [5 gospel.] [6 sun.]
[7 The paragraph, "For he that hath . . . . . with his own," does not occur in the Emm. MS.]
[8 my beloved in the Lord, as I am persuaded of you, that ye be indeed God's good ground, which groweth and will grow on still, by God's grace, bringing forth fruit to God's glory.]

tion sure by faith upon the infallible word of God's truth, and will now bring forth the fruits to God's glory after your vocation, as occasion shall be offered, although the sun burn never so hot, nor the weather be never so foul[1] : wherefore I cannot but signify unto every of you to go forward accordingly[2] after your master Christ; not sticking at the foul way and stormy weather, which you are come unto, or are like to come[3] : of this being most[4] certain, that the end of your sorrow[5] shall be pleasant and joyful, in such a perpetual rest and blissfulness as cannot but swallow up the storms which both you and they[6] now feel, and are like to feel, at the hands of those sacrificing prelates[7]. But set often before your eyes St Paul's counsel to the Corinthians, and remember it as a restorative to refresh you withal, lest you faint in the way, where he saith: "Though our outward man perish, yet is our inward man renewed day by day; for our exceeding tribulation (which is momentary and light) he hath prepared for us an exceeding weight of glory: whilst we look not on things that are seen, but on things that are not seen. For things that are seen are temporal, but the things that are not seen are eternal." And again he saith: "If this body were destroyed, we shall have another, which shall not be subject to corruption nor to persecution[8]." Besides this, set before you also[9], though the weather be stormy and foul, yet strive to go apace, for you go not alone[10]; many other of your brethren and sisters pass by the same path, as St Peter saith and telleth us, that company might[11] cause you to be the more courageous and cheerful: but if you had no company at all

Cor. iv.

1 Pet. iv.

[1 "nor the . . . . foul," not in Emm. MS.]
[2 signify unto you, and heartily pray you, every one of you, accordingly to go on forward.]
[3 do.]   [4 sure and certain.]
[5 journey.]   [6 storms which you now feel.]
[7 Prelates, if ye often set it before your eyes, after St Paul's counsel in the latter end of the fourth and beginning of the fifth of the second epistle to the Corinthians. Read it, I pray you, and remember it often as.]
[8 "where he saith . . . . to persecution," not in Emm. MS.]
[9 that though.]
[10 weather be foul and storms grow on apace, yet go not ye alone, but many.]
[11 should.]

to go presently with you, stick not to go still forward[12]. I pray you, tell me, if any from the beginning, yea, the best of God's friends, have found any fairer way or weather to the place whither we are going (I mean to heaven) than we now find and are like to find. Except ye will with the worldlings, which have their part and portion[13] in this life, tarry still by the way till the storms be overpast; and then either night will approach[14], that ye[15] cannot travel, or else the doors will be shut up[16], that ye[15] cannot go in, and so without ye[15] shall have wonderful evil lodgings[17]; I mean, in a bed of fire and brimstone, where the worm dieth not, and the fire goeth not out[18]. John xii.

Matt. xv.

Read from the first of Genesis to the Apocalypse: begin at Abel[19], and so to Noah, Abraham, Isaac, Jacob, the patriarchs; Moses, David[20], and the saints in the old testament; and tell me whether any of them find any fairer ways[21] than we now find. If the old[22] will not serve, I pray you come to the new, and begin with Mary and Joseph, and come from thence to Zechariah, Elizabeth, John the Baptist, Stephen, James, Peter, and Paul[23], and every one of the apostles and evangelists: and see[24] whether any of them all found any other way unto the city whereunto we travel than by many tribulations. Besides this, if you should[25] call to remembrance the primitive church, (Lord God!) we should see many that have given cheerfully[26] their bodies to most grievous torments rather than they would be stopped in their journey[27]. There was no day scarce in the year but I dare say a thousand was the fewest that with joy left their houses and lives here[28]; but in the city that they went unto they found another manner of dwellings than many minds be[29] able to conceive. But if Acts xiv.

[12 do not you stick to go forward still.]   [13 have their portion in.]
[14 so approach.]
[15 Strype reads "he," but to the manifest injury of the sense.]
[16 sparred up before ye come, that.]
[17 shall lodge without in wonderful.]
[18 "I mean . . . . not out," not in Emm. MS.]
[19 beginning at Abel, and come from him down, and so.]
[20 David, Samuel, and.]
[21 if any of them found any fairer weather than you now find.]
[22 Old Testament.]   [23 John Baptist and every one.]
[24 search.]   [25 shall.]
[26 ye shall see the same giving cheerfully.]
[27 that there.]   [28 lost their homes here.]
[29 other manner of homes than man's mind is able to conceive.]

none of these[1] were, if you had no company to[2] go with you, yet have you me[3] your poorest brother and bondman in[4] the Lord, with many other, I trust in God. But if[5] ye had none of the fathers, patriarchs, good kings, prophets, apostles, evangelists, martyrs, holy saints, and children of God, which in their journey to heaven found that you are like to find[6], (if you go on forwards, as I trust you will,) yet you have your general captain and master, Christ Jesus[7], the dear darling and only-begotten and beloved Son of God, in whom was all the Father's[8] joy and delectation; ye have him to go before you: no fairer was his way than ours[9], but much worse and fouler, towards his city of the heavenly Jerusalem. Let us remember[10] what manner of way Christ[11] found: begin at his birth, and go forth until ye come at his burial; and you shall find that every[12] step of his journey was a thousand times worse than yours is. For he had laid upon him at one time the devil, death, and sin; and with one sacrifice, never again to be done, he overcame them all[13].

Wherefore, my dear beloved[14], be not so dainty to look to have at the Lord's hands, your dear Father, that which the patriarchs, prophets, and evangelists, martyrs, and saints, yea, and his own Son Jesus Christ, did not find.

Hitherto ye have found fairer[15] weather and fairer way too, I trow; but because we have loitered by the way, and not made the speed that we should have done, our loving Father and heavenly Lord[16] hath overcast the weather, and hath stirred up storms and tempests, that we might[17] the more speedily run out the[18] race before night come, and before the

Heb. xiii.

Heb. ix.

[1 all these.]   [2 now to.]
[3 as you have in your poorest.]   [4 of.]
[5 God, if you had.]   [6 you now find, &c.]
[7 yet the same master and captain, Jesus Christ.]
[8 pleasure, joy.]
[9 no fairer way than yours, but much fouler.]
[10 and consider.]   [11 He.]
[12 foot and step of his journey was no better, but much worse than yours now is.]
[13 "For he .... them all," not in Emm. MS.]
[14 dearly beloved in the Lord.]
[15 fair weather, I trow, and fair way also; now because.]
[16 have made, our loving Lord and sweet Father.]
[17 should.]   [18 run on our.]

doors be barred[19] up. Now the devil and his ostlers and tapsters stand in every inn-door in city and country of this world, crying unto us, " Come in and lodge here; for here is Christ, and there is Christ; therefore tarry with us[20] until the storm be overpast." Not that they would not have us wet to the skin, but that the time might be overpast[21], to our utter destruction. Therefore beware of his enticements, and cast not your eyes upon things that be present, how this man doth or that man doth, (for you may not follow a multitude to do evil[22];) but cast your eyes on the wager or mark that you run at, or else you will lose the game. You know, he that runneth at the mark doth not look on other that stands[23] by, or of them that offer[24] to go this way or that way, but looketh altogether on the glove[25] or mark, and on them that run with[26] him, that those that are behind overtake him not, and that he may overtake them that are before. Even so should we do, and leave looking at those that will not run the way or race[27] to heaven's bliss by suffering persecution[28]. And we should cast our eyes on the end of the race, and on them that go before us, that we may overtake them, and that we may provoke others[29] to come the faster after us. He that shooteth will not cast his eyes in his shooting on them that stand[30] or ride by the way, I trow not[31]; but rather on the mark that he shooteth at, or else he were like to win the wrong way. Even so, my dear beloved, let our[32] eyes be set on the mark that we[33] shoot at, even Jesus Christ, "who for the joy that was set before him abode the cross, and despised the shame[34];" therefore he now sitteth on the right hand of God, all power and rule subdued unto him[35]. Let us therefore

Matt. xxiv.

Heb. xii.

[19 sparred up.]
[20 The devil now standeth in every inn-door of this his city and country of this world, crying unto us for to have us to tarry or lodge in this place till.]   [21 overpass us.]
[22 "for you may . . . . evil," not in Emm. MS.]
[23 upon others that stand.]   [24 that come after.]
[25 goal.]   [26 before.]   [27 onward.]
[28 by the path of persecution with us.]
[29 overtake them, and upon them that run after us, that we may provoke them to come.]   [30 stand by.]
[31 I trow.]   [32 your.]   [33 you.]
[34 joyfully carry his cross, contemning the shame thereof.]
[35 "all power . . . . him," not in Emm. MS.]

follow him: for thus did he, that we should not be faint-hearted; for we may be most sure, that "if we suffer with him, we shall also¹ reign with him. But if we deny him, he will surely² deny us." "For he that is ashamed of me," saith Christ, "and of my gospel, before³ this faithless generation, I will be ashamed of him before my Father and his angels in heavens⁴." Oh! how heavy a sentence is this to all those that know the mass to be an abominable idol, full of idolatry, blasphemy, sacrilege against God and the dear sacrifice of⁵ his Christ, as undoubtedly it is; and that you have well seen, both by disputing of noble clerks, and also by willing shedding of their bloods against that heinous sacrilege⁶. And yet for fear or favour of men, for the loss of life and goods, (which is none of theirs, but lent them of God, as David saith, "it is the Lord that maketh rich and poor;" and as St Paul saith, "if we live we are the Lord's, and if we die we are the Lord's;" therefore let us give him his own⁷;) yea, some for advantage and gain will honour⁸ with their presence this pernicious blasphemy against the death of our Redeemer⁹; and so dissemble¹⁰ both with God and man, as their own hearts and conscience¹¹ do accuse them. Oh! vain men, do you not remember that God is greater than your conscience¹²? It had been good that such men had never known the truth, nor that the gospel had never been taught amongst them, that thus wittingly and for¹³ fear of men (who are but dust, and their breath is in their nostrils) do dissemble, or rather in deed utterly deny Christ and his sacrifice, the price of their redemption; and so bring on them the blood of us, and all other that have sincerely taught the gospel,

Margin notes: 2 Tim. ii.; Mark viii.; Rom. xiv.; Luke xi.

[¹ undoubtedly.]
[² But surely if we deny Him, he will.]   [³ in.]
[⁴ before the angels of God in heaven.]
[⁵ God and his Christ.]
[⁶ "and that . . . . sacrilege," not in Emm. MS.]
[⁷ "which is none of . . . . his own," not in Emm. MS.]
[⁸ honour it.]
[⁹ "this pernicious . . . . Redeemer," not in Emm. MS.]
[¹⁰ dissembling.]   [¹¹ hearts do accuse.]
[¹² "Oh! vain . . . . conscience," not in Emm. MS.]
[¹³ Better it had been for such men if they never had known the truth, than thus wittingly, for favour or fear of men, (who breath is in their nostrils).]

with the adorning and honouring of that false idol with their bodies, being the temples of God[14]. The end of such men is like to be worse than the beginnings. Such men had need to take heed of[15] their dissemblings and cloakings; for it will once be espied; I mean, when our Christ shall come in his glory, which I trust will be shortly. But if he tarry, the time of all flesh is but short, and fadeth away like a flower. I would wish such men to read the terrible place of St Paul to the Hebrews, in the sixth chapter, where he saith: "It cannot be that they which were once lighted, and have tasted of the heavenly gift, and were become partakers of the Holy Ghost, and have tasted of the good word of God, and the power of the world to come; if they fall away, and as concerning themselves crucify the Son of God afresh, making a mock of him." And read the tenth chapter, lest ye fall into the danger of them. *Heb. vi.*

And let men beware that they play not wilily, beguiling themselves, as I fear me they do[16] that go to mass. And because they worship not, nor kneel not down[17], as others do, but sit still in their pews[18], therefore they think rather to[19] do good to others than hurt. But, alas! if such men would look on their own consciences, there they[20] shall see if they be very dissimulers; and seeking to deceive others, they deceive themselves. For by this means the magistrates think them to be of their sort. They think that at the elevation time all men's eyes are set on them, to mark how they do; they think that other, hearing of such men's going to mass, do see or inquire of their behaviour there; and thus they play wilily, beguiling themselves. But if there were in these men either love to God or to their brethren, then would they, for one or for both, take God's part, admonishing the people of their idolatry. But "they fear men more than God, that hath authority to cast both body and soul into hell-fire." They halt on both sides[21]; they "serve two masters." God have mercy on such *Matt. x.* *Matt. vi.*

[14 "and his sacrifice .... of God," not in Emm. MS.]
[15 Such men had need to heed of the terrible place of St Paul to the Hebrews, in the sixth chapter. Avoid them, lest ye fall into the danger of them. And let men beware.]

[16 as some (I fear me) that.] [17 neither bemark not as.]
[18 seats.] [19 they rather do.]
[20 should they.] [21 parts.]

men, and anoint their eyes with salve¹, that they may see, that they which take not part with God are against him, and they that gather not with Christ scatter abroad²! The counsel given to the church of Laodicea is good counsel for such men.

But now, dearly beloved, to come again³, be not ashamed of the gospel of God; "for it is the power of God unto salvation to⁴ them that believe it." Be⁵ therefore partakers of the afflictions of Christ, as God shall make you able⁶ to bear; and think that⁷ no small grace of God, to suffer persecution for God's truth's sake; "for the Spirit of glory and the Spirit of God doth rest upon you. Therefore if any man suffer as a christian man, let him not be ashamed, but glorify God on that behalf:" for "whosoever," saith Christ, "shall lose his life for my sake and for the gospel, the same shall save it." Yea, happy are you if that come so⁸ to pass, as you shall find one day, when "the fire shall try every man's work what it is⁹." And as the fire hurteth not the gold, but maketh it finer¹⁰, so shall ye be more pure in¹¹ suffering with Christ. The flail or the wind hurteth not the wheat, but cleanseth it from the chaff. And ye, dearly beloved, are God's wheat: fear not the fanning wind, fear not the millstone; for all these things¹² make you the meeter for God's¹³ tooth. Soap, though it be black, soileth not the cloth¹⁴, but maketh it¹⁴ clean: so doth the black cross of Christ¹⁵ help us to more whiteness, if God strike with the battledoor. Because you be God's sheep, prepare yourselves to the slaughter¹⁶, always knowing, that in the sight of God¹⁷ our death is precious. The souls under the altar look for us

Luke xi.

Rom. i.

1 Pet. iv.

Mark viii.

1 Cor. iii.

John x.
Psal. cxvi.
Rev. vi.

[¹ eye-salve.]
[² O that they would read what Saint John saith shall be done to the unfaithful! The counsel given.]
[³ But yet [to] come again, dearly beloved. Be not ashamed of God's gospel; it is.]
[⁴ to all them.]   [⁵ Be ye.]
[⁶ able, knowing for certain that he will not tempt you further than he will make you able to bear.]   [⁷ it.]
[⁸ if it so come.]
[⁹ Read the second of the first to the Corinthians. And as.]
[¹⁰ fairer and finer.]   [¹¹ by.]
[¹² all these make.]   [¹³ the Lord's.]
[¹⁴ clothes: them.]   [¹⁵ black cross help.]
[¹⁶ slaughter-house.]   [¹⁷ the Lord your.]

to fulfil their number. Happy are we if God have so appointed it[18].

Dearly beloved, cast yourselves wholly upon the Lord, with whom all the hairs of your head be numbered; so that not one of them shall perish without his knowledge. "It is appointed unto all men that they shall once die." Therefore, will we nill we, we must drink of the Lord's cup which he hath appointed for us. Drink[19] willingly therefore, and at the first, whilst it is full; lest peradventure, if we[20] linger, we[20] shall drink at the last of the dregs with the ungodly, if we[20] at the beginning drink not with the children[21]; for with them his judgment beginneth. And when he hath wrought his will upon mount Sion, then will he visit the nations round about. "Submit yourselves therefore under the mighty hand of God." No man shall once touch you without his knowledge; and when they touch you[22], it is for your profit: God[23] will work thereby to make you like unto Christ[24], here or elsewhere. That ye may be, therefore, like unto him, acknowledge your unthankfulness and sin, and bless God which correcteth us in the world, because he would not have us condemned with the world. Otherwise might he correct us than to make us suffer for righteousness' sake: but this he doth because he loveth us. Call upon God through Christ for the joy[25] and gladness of his salvation. Believe that he is our merciful Father, and will hear us and help us; as the Psalmist saith, "I am with him in trouble, and will deliver him." Know that the Lord hath appointed bounds, over the which the devil and all the world shall not pass. If all things seem to be against you, yet say with Job, "Though he kill me, yet will I hope in him."

Read the tenth Psalm[26]; and pray for me your poor brother and fellow-sufferer for God's sake: his name therefore be praised! And let us pray to God that he of his

<small>Matt. x.</small>
<small>Heb. ix.</small>
<small>1 Pet. iv.</small>
<small>Heb. xii.</small>

[18 if God hath appointed it, howsoever it be.]
[19 drink of it willingly therefore, when it.]
[20 ye, you.]   [21 righteous.]
[22 then know ye that it is for your wealth.]
[23 God thereby will.]
[24 that both here and elsewhere you make be like unto him. Acknowledge your.]
[25 wine and gladness of.]
[26 and let us pray to God that he of his mercy would vouchsafe.]

mercy will vouchsafe to make both you and me meet to suffer with good consciences for his name's sake. Die once we must; how and where, we know not. Happy are they whom God giveth[1] to pay nature's debt (I mean to die) for his sake. Here is not our home; let us therefore accordingly consider things, having always before our eyes that heavenly Jerusalem, and the way thereto in persecution. And let us consider all the dear friends of God, how they have gone after the example of our Saviour Jesus Christ; whose footsteps let us also follow, even to the gallows, (if God's will be so,) not doubting, but as he rose[2] again the third day, even so shall we do at the time appointed of God, that is, when the trump[3] shall blow, and the angel shall shout, and the Son of man shall appear in the clouds, with innumerable saints and angels, in his majesty and great glory, and the dead shall arise, and we shall be caught up into the clouds, to meet the Lord, and to be always with him. Comfort yourselves with these words, and pray for me, for the Lord's sake, and God be merciful unto us[4] all! So be it.   HUGH L.

<small>Heb. xiii.</small>

<small>1 Thess. iv.</small>

[From Bocardo in Oxford, the xvth day of May, An. 1555. Emm. MS.]

LETTER LII.

LATIMER *to* Mrs WILKINSON, *of London, widow*[5].

[Foxe's Acts and Mon. p. 1356, edit. 1563; Vol. iii. p. 415, edit. 1684.]

IF the gift of a pot of water[6] shall not be in oblivion with God, how can God forget your manifold and bountiful gifts, when he shall say unto you, "I was in prison, and you visited me?" God grant us all to do and suffer while we be here as may be his will and pleasure! Amen.

Yours in Bocardo,

HUGH LATIMER.

[1 hath given.]   [2 awoke.]   [3 trumpet.]
[4 unto us. Amen.
[5 A letter sent to Mistress Wilkinson, of Soper Lane, London, (widow), she being at the manor of English in Oxfordshire, from master Hugh Latimer, out of Bocardo, in Oxford, where he was a prisoner for the testimony of Christ, An. 1555. Edit. 1563.]
[6 cold water, 1563.]

APPENDIX.

		PAGE
1.	Concio habita in conventu Spiritualium, Jun. 9, 1537 447	
2.	Articuli ab Episcopis Latimero ut subscriberet propositi . . 466	
3.	Epistolæ:	
	1. Ad Doctorem Greene 467	
	2 Ad Doctorem Redmannum 468	
	3. Ad Doctorem Sherwood . . . . ibid.	
	4. Ad Archiepiscopum Cantuariensem 474	
4.	Disputatio habita Oxoniæ 18 Aprilis, 1554, inter D. Hugonem Latimerum, etc. 479	

Concio quam habuit

Reverendus in Christo Pater

Hugo Latimerus, Episcopus

Worcestriæ, in Conventu

spiritualium, nono Junii

ante inchoationem Parliamenti

celebrati Anno 28

Invictissimi Regis

Henrici

Octavi.

1537.

CONCIO HABITA IN CONVENTU SPIRITUALIUM,

Jun. 9, 1537.

FILII HVIVS SECVLI, &c.[1]

CONVENISTIS hodie, fratres, de rebus maximis (quod sciam) audituri. Convenistis et de rebus ad Reip. utilitatem in primis spectantibus deliberaturi. Proinde et a me, qui coram nobis jubeor præfari, quamlibet indoctus et indignus, talia (scio) exspectatis, propter quæ convenistis. Ego igitur non solum primatis jussioni parere, verum etiam vestræ omnium exspectationi satisfacere, si modo possim, perquam cupiens, ecce, jam de rebus, et vestra congregatione et meo in hac parte officio dignissimis, paucis et quam lucidissime possim, aggredior dicere.

Id quod quo facerem commodius, en! decerpsi mihi tractandum ex evangelio eulogium illud, in quo Dominus hujus seculi filios prudentiores filiis lucis esse in generatione sua non veritus est pronunciare. Neque ego illius auspiciis fretus eandem sententiam, tanquam basim et fundamentum eorum omnium, quæ dicturus sum, verebor usurpare. Jam non potest (opinor) vestram eruditionem latere, quo consilio hoc Dominus dixerit, ut mea in hac parte industria nihil opus habeatis. Atqui ego tamen (si vultis veniam dare) hoc, quicquid est, paulo altius repetam, et rem omnem fere a prima origine pandam; quia mirum sane dictu videri poterat, si perpendatis et quid dicatur, et quis dixerit. Definitote mihi prudentiam, seculum, lucem, et horum filios, quid sint in scripturis; et miror si filios seculi filiis lucis prudentiores illico omnes affirmaveritis. Verum, ut ad rem proprius accedam, sic demum auspicatur Dominus:

Homo quidam (inquit) erat dives, qui habebat dispensatorem; et hic delatus est apud illum, ut qui dissiparet bona

[1 Vid. Vol. I. p. 33.]

ipsius; et vocavit illum, et ait illi, 'Quid hoc audio de te? Redde rationem dispensationis tuæ; non enim poteris posthac dispensare.'

Hæc, fratres, quoniam sic per parabolam dicuntur, et sic involucris quibusdam teguntur, ut tamen in speciem rei gestæ aut historiæ faciem habere videantur; non inutile igitur fuerit in his aliquandiu immorari. Quæ quidem omnia ut fortasse vera fuisse credere sustineamus et patiamur; at ad nos hæc CHRISTI verba pertinere, et nos nostri officii commonefacere, id quidem credere ambiguum non sustineamus, inque nos ipsos descendentes, quam nobis hæc dicta quadrent, videamus; utpote qui sic agimus et sic vivimus plerique omnes, perinde ac si CHRISTUS, cum loqueretur, suo duntaxat instituto pro temporis ratione disseruisset, neque successura tempora curasset, non nobis et rebus nostris prospexisset: quemadmodum olim philosophati sunt, Deum circa cardines cœli ambulare, neque considerare nostra.

At ne sic erretis vos, fratres mei: nolite sic vos cogitationibus vestris inniti. Nam si penitius introspiciatis, si diligenter omnia evolvatis et explicetis; videbitis hæc mysteria etiam nostram ætatem attingere: intelligetis Dominum hoc exemplo nostros nasos pervellere, nostras aures vellicare; et apertissime, quid nos fugere, quid nos sequi debeamus, perspicietis Dominum hac similitudine nobis ob oculos proponere. Hæc enim perhibet Lucas Dominum discipulis suis dixisse. Proinde et ad nos dixisse sit omnibus indubitatum, qui discipulorum successores ac vicarii, ut haberi ac dici volumus, ita et sumus, si qui modo boni sumus, et officium præstamus ejusdem.

Hæc ille partim ad nos dixit, qui et eadem partim de seipso dixit. Ipse est enim homo ille dives, qui non solum habebat, sed etiam habet, adeoque semper habiturus est, non dico dispensatorem, sed dispensatores suos, usque ad consummationem seculi.

Homo est, cum Deus sit et homo. Dives est, non solum in misericordia, sed in omni opum genere. Ipse est enim, qui nobis præbet omnia abunde; de cujus manu et vitam et omnia ad vitam tuendam necessaria accepimus; de cujus plenitudine, quid (quæso) quis habet, quod non accepit? Ipse est denique, qui aperit manum suam, et implet omne animal benedictione: nedum nos benedictione sua semper prosequitur amplissime. Neque thesauri illius exhauriri queant: quantumvis effuderit ille, quantumvis hauserimus nos, manet tamen thesaurus ejus inexhaustus.

Postremo ipse est paterfamilias: tota ecclesia est ejus familia, puro illius verbo et sacramentis quam officiosissime pascenda. Et hæc sunt bona illius longe pretiosissima, quorum dispensationem et administrationem voluit episcopos et pastores habere; neque solum habere, sed et exercere eandem, ut Dei ministri. Id quod nec divus Paulus formidat affirmare, prima ad Corinthios quarto: Sic nos existimet homo (inquiens) ut ministros CHRISTI, et dispensatores mysteriorum Dei. Ceterum in dispensatore quid (quæso) requiritur? Illud sane requiritur, ut fidus quis reperiatur; qui fideliter dispenset bona domini, quique det cibum in tempore. Non vendat, sed det: non venenum, sed cibum. Illud intoxicat; hic alit ac nutrit. Non proroget denique, quod facere debeat; sed in tempore officium faciat: ut sit, quem constituat dominus, non qui præsumpserit ipse, et sibi ipsi honorem assumpserit.

Quid autem requiritur? Si hoc ipsum, quod dixi, requiratur, facilius fuerit (opinor) tale quiddam in dispensatore ubique requirere, quam talem aliquem dispensatorem alicubi invenire. Sed quis (inquam) fidus dispensator? Quis (inquam) fidus? Fidus vero quispiam fuerit, si non novam ipse pecuniam excuderit, sed excusam a patrefamilias acceperit, nec adulteret aut diminuat acceptam. Verum ipsissimam dominicam pecuniam ad præscriptum Domini, non in suum quæstum expendat, nec in morem servi nequissimi in terra defodiat, et abscondat denique. Hoc, fratres, si fidus dispensator facere debeat, paulisper (quæso) mecum perpendite, ecquid episcopi nostri et abbates, ecquid nostri prælati et pastores, fideles hactenus fuerint dispensatores, aut nunc sint plerique, necne?

Agite jam, et bona fide mihi dicite, (ut de multimodis aliis sit silentium:) nonne fuere aliqui, qui pecuniam Domini ceu adulterinam contemnentes, vel novam excuderunt, vel aliis noviter excusam pro pecunia dominica publicarunt, nunc adulterantes, aut etiam cauponantes verbum; nunc loco divini verbi humana somnia ebuccinantes?—dum sic vulgo prædicarunt e suggestu, nimirum redemptionem CHRISTI pro veteri duntaxat Testamento valere, abinde pecuniariam et humanam vigere, minime Christianam; (neque deesse poterat exemplum uxoris cujuspiam splendidissimum, quæ maritum, innumerato jam pretio, ex fornace illa multo maxime meritoria et quæstuaria

[LATIMER, II.]

jure optimo redemerit; et redemptum tanquam jure jam sibi debitum a Domino requisiverit:)—dum sic vulgo prædicarunt e suggestu, nimirum mortuarias imagines, in initio nonnisi ad repræsentandum (opinor) erectas, tam ab omnibus Christi fidelibus, in misera etiamnum hac omnium rerum penuria et caritate, non solum auro obducendas, sed et sericis vestibus, et his quidem pretiosissimis donariis onustis, excolendas; insuper et lucernis cereis, tum intra templum, tum extra, vel in media luce illuminandas: quasi hic nullus sumptus, quamlibet magnus, poterat esse nimius; cum interim ipsos Christi fideles, imagines (inquam) vivas, nec minoris quam pretiosissimo sanguine CHRISTI redemptas, (proh dolor!) esurire, sitire, algere, in tenebris vel ad mortem usque squalescere denique, misere ubique videamus:—dum sic vulgo prædicarunt e suggestu, nimirum hæc voluntaria opera minus quidem necessaria esse, quam opera misericordiæ et præcepta Dei; at magis tamen principalia, magis excellentia esse, hoc est (ut horum sensum teneatis) Deo Optimo Maximo magis placitura: quasi nunc Deo magis placere possent humana quam divina, et aliena quam sua:—dum sic vulgo prædicarunt e suggestu, nimirum plus frugis ac devotionis ex momentanea quadam imaginis mortuæ contemplatione ortum iri, quam si quis in sacra lectione vel universum septennium contemplando versaretur:—dum sic denique vulgo prædicarunt e suggestu, nimirum purgatorianas illas animas et multo maxime egere ope nostra, nec quicquam auxilii nisi a nobis in hoc seculo habere posse; quorum alterum si non est falsum, est certe ad minus anceps, dubium et incertum; ideoque temere, arroganter, et asseveranter coram populo e suggestu assertum: alterum est omnium calculis quam manifestissime falsum. Ut prætermittam alia hujus monetæ quam plurima, per totas tres horas et amplius interdum a quibusdam ebuccinata et exhalata. Scilicet hæc sunt mysteria divina et Christiana, et non potius somnolentitia et humana? Scilicet hi sunt dispensatores mysteriorum Dei fideles, et non potius dissipatores infidissimi? Quos constituit, non Dominus, sed dæmon verius, super famulitium miserum, super famulitium miserabiliter habitum et tractatum. Bene fuerit populo, ubi tales concionantur perraro.

Et tamen mirum est videri prudentiores esse tales in generatione sua, quam fideles dispensatores sunt in sua; dum illi humana prudentius stabilire satagunt, quam hi divina. Hinc opera quæstuaria, spontanea et humana regnare; Christiana vero, necessaria et frugifera, jacere passim videmus. Sic malitia a malis, quam bonitas a bonis, promovetur efficacius: cum mali sint prudentiores, quam boni, in generatione sua. Et hi sunt dispensatores illi perfidi, quos fidi omnes non sine altis suspiriis apud divitem illum patremfamilias quotidie deferunt, quod dissipent bona ipsius: quos et ille aliquando vocaturus est, et eadem voce compellaturus, qua œconomum compellavit, dicens, Quid hoc audio de te, &c.

Hic Dominus nostram ingratitudinem et perfidiam partim admiratur, partim objurgat nos ob illam, et admirabundus simul et objurgabundus velut interrogat nos, dicens, Quid hoc audio de vobis? Quasi diceret Dominus nobis: Omnes ubique pii queruntur de vobis, et vestram avaritiam, vestram tyrannidem incusant apud me: diligentiam et sinceritatem jam diu in vobis desiderant.

Ego præcepi ut cum omni diligentia et labore pasceretis oves meas: vos sedulo pascitis vosmetipsos, in deliciis et otio de die in diem diffluentes. Ego in mandatis dedi, ut doceretis mea, non vestra; ut meam gloriam, meum lucrum quæreretis: vos docetis vestra; vestram gloriam, vestrum lucrum quæritis. Vos prædicatis quidem perraro; et quando prædicatis, nil aliud quam veros prædicatores, quantum in vobis est, impeditis: ut multo præstiterit, omnino tales a prædicando abstinere, quam tam perniciose prædicare. Deum bonum! quid ego audio de vobis?

Vos qui deberetis esse mei prædicatores, quid aliud quam meos prædicatores in invidiam, in ignominiam, in contemptum ducere; imo in pericula, in carceres, in mortes denique, quantum vestræ suppetunt vires, pertrahere satagitis? Breviter: Ego volui ut omnes Christiani audirent, et quotquot vellent per otium legerent quoque, doctrinam meam: vos nec curatis ut omnes audiant, et obnixe curatis ne laici legant; scilicet, ne legendo intelligant, et intelligendo forte vestram ignaviam merito condemnare discant.

Hæc est generatio vestra; hæc est dispensatio vestra: hæc est vestra prudentia. In hac generatione, in hac dispensatione vos estis prudentissimi. Et hæc demum sunt, quæ ego audio de vobis, qui optabam audire meliora. Siccine me decepistis? an vosmetipsos potius decepistis? Ego, cum unicam tantum haberem familiam, nempe ecclesiam, et eam a me tam unice dilectam, ut memetipsum pro ea exponerem, et sanguinem meum pro ea effunderem ; hanc hinc ego ascensurus vestræ curæ commisi, eam vobis tradidi pascendam, alendam, fovendam. Vos in meum locum succedere volui ; vos consimilem amorem et affectum vere paternum induere jussi. Vos vicarios meos etiam in rebus maximis constitui : sic enim palam docui, ut qui vos audiret, me audiret ; qui vos sperneret, et me sperneret. Dedi vobis et claves, non terrestres, sed cœlestes ; et bona mea, quæ semper in summo pretio mihi sunt habita, nempe verbum et sacramenta, vobis dispensanda reliqui. Hæc beneficia ego in vos contuli ; et nunc hanc gratiam mihi retulistis. Siccine abuti benignitate mea sustinuistis ? Siccine me fefellistis ? Quanquam non me sane, sed vos ipsos fefellistis ; quia dona et beneficia mea cedent vobis in majorem cumulum damnationis. Et quia clementiam patrisfamilias contempsistis, severitatem judicis sentire meruistis. Agite ergo : reddite rationem dispensationis vestræ. O vocem horribilem ! Non enim potestis posthac dispensare. O flebilem ac tremebundam vocem !

Videte, fratres, videte, quid mali malos dispensatores maneat. Operæ pretium igitur fuerit cavere, ne tam acerbam sententiam tandem audire vobis contingat. Imo nobis omnibus cavendum, ne hæc in nos aliquando quadrare reperiantur.

Sed ego jam, ne vos longitudine sermonis enecem, quod reliquum est parabolæ relinquam, et ad colophonem ac finem parabolæ me accingam ; enarraturus videlicet, quomodo filii hujus seculi prudentiores sunt filiis lucis in generatione sua. Quam quidem sententiam utinam esset facultatis meæ tanta verborum luce explicare, ut ego non tam dixisse, quam pinxisse dicerer ; vos vero non tam audiisse, quam spectasse videremini ! Verum hoc longe supra vires meas esse positum ingenue fateor. Proinde (quod unum est reliquum) opto, quod non habeo ; et adesse velim, quod abesse doleo, nempe facultatem sic tractandi id quod in manibus habeo, ut in gloriam Dei, salutem vestram, corporis CHRISTI ædificationem cedat, quicquid id est, quod inter dicendum dixero.

Quare rogatos vos velim, fratres, ut communibus precibus Deum mecum interpelletis : atque in hoc interpelletis, ut mihi nunc os ad loquendum recte, vobis vero aures ad audiendum cum fruge, dignetur præstare. Quod ut fiat, orabitis eum, quem præceptor noster JESUS CHRISTUS orandum docuit, Patrem nostrum; dicturi orationem eam, quam idem præceptor dicendam instituit.

Oraturi pro invictissimo Domino Rege, summo ac supremo ecclesiæ Anglicanæ capite sub CHRISTO, et pro omnibus suis, sive ex clero, sive ex reliquo ordine, sive ex nobilibus, sive ex subditis: memores interim omnium qui sunt hac ærumnosa vita defuncti, et jam dormiunt in somno pacis, et requiescunt a laboribus suis in requie et somno pacis; fideliter, amanter, et patienter exspectantes quod sunt clare et conspicue (quando visum est Deo) visuri: dicturi, inquam, pro his omnibus, et pro gratia nobis perutili ac necessaria, ad Dominum orationem dominicam, *Pater noster.*

Filii hujus seculi, etc. Lucas, xvi.

CHRISTUS hac clausula socordiam suorum taxavit; non aliorum fraudulentiam probavit. Neque rem ita habere lætabatur, sed conquerebatur potius: ut multa pronunciantur a multis, non quia ita esse debeant, sed quia ita esse soleant. Hoc male CHRISTUM habebat, quod filii hujus seculi filiis lucis prudentia præstabant. Quod quidem ipsum verum fuit tamen ætate CHRISTI, et idem est nostra ætate non nisi verissimum. Quis tam cæcutit ut hoc non clare videat, nisi si quis sit, qui inter filios seculi et filios lucis non probe discernat? Filii seculi prudentius concipiunt et generant, concepta et generata prudentius nutriunt et servant, quam filii lucis. Quod tam miserum est dictu, quam absurdum auditu.

Verum cum filios seculi auditis, seculum pro patre intelligite. Est enim seculum velut pater multorum liberorum, non prima quidem creatione et opere, sed imitatione et amore. At neque pater est solum, sed et alterius patris filius. Quod si patrem illius noris, illico noris ejusdem et liberos. Non enim potest non habere liberos diabolicos, quod parentis loco ipsissimum habet diabolum.

Diabolus enim non modo parens, sed et princeps seculi hujus, hoc est, hominum secularium jam olim esse perhibetur: ut vel idem sit, vel non longe diversum, vel filios seculi vel filios diaboli pronunciare, juxta illud CHRISTI ad Judæos, Vos ex patre diabolo estis; cum et filios seculi CHRISTUS dubio procul alloqueretur. Jam vero diabolus cum sit et auctor et rector tenebrarum harum, in quibus obambulant vel oberrant potius hujus seculi filii, hi lucem et filios ejus odio inexplicabili necesse est prosequantur. Et hinc est, quod filii lucis nunquam aut perraro hic in hoc seculo persequutione careant a filiis hujus seculi, hoc est, diaboli, illis intentata. Et prudentiores esse hos ad lædendum, quam illos ad defendendum, nemo non clarissime perspicit.

Colligite igitur, fratres, ingenium et studium liberorum ex ingenio et studio parentum. Cognoscitis proverbium esse, et idem celeberrimum: Mali corvi malum ovum. Quare non possunt filii seculi non esse mali, qui tam malum patrem, nempe seculum, tam malum avum, nempe diabolum, dignoscuntur habere. Habent enim generis sui primarium auctorem serpentem illum callidissimum diabolum, monstrum omnium monstrorum monstrosissimum; nescio quid, sed quasi quiddam totum ex odio Dei, ex diffidentia in Deum, ex mendaciis, dolis, perjuriis, discordiis, homicidiis, atque (ut uno verbo dicam) ex omni nequitiarum genere concretum, coalitum diabolum. Quid ego diaboli ingenium sigillatim describere conor? Cum id nulla ratio, nulla vis mentis humanæ complecti possit. Hoc tantum crasse et in summa dicere possum, quod nos omnes cum nostro magno malo experimur esse verum, nempe diabolum omnium vitiorum sentinam fœtidissimam esse, omnium malorum cloacam sordidissimam esse; neque dissimile quiddam esse hoc seculum, tali patre dignissimum filium.

Hic igitur diabolus cum ejusmodi fuerit (ut nunquam poterit esse sui dissimilis), en! ex Invidia, carissima amica, veluti hoc seculum suscepit. Susceptum Discordiæ alendum tradidit. Quod quidem seculum cum in virilem ætatem adolevisset, velut ex variis concubinis prolem aggeneravit longe numerosissimam. Et adeo fœcundus pater evaserat, et tot ex Superbia, Gula, Avaritia, Luxuria, Astutia filios procreaverat, ut jam fere nullum sit videre hujus orbis angulum, nec ullum sit reperire vitæ genus, in quo liberos illius non reperias quam plurimos: in aula, in cuculla, in claustro, in rocheto denique quamlibet candido, et ubi non? quamquam non illico filii hujus seculi sunt omnes, qui seculares et laici vulgo consuevere dici; neque protinus filii lucis sunt omnes, qui spirituales et ex clero obtinuere appellari. Sed ut inter laicos est invenire filios lucis, ita et ex clero est reperire filios hujus seculi: quantumvis sacrosanctum illud nobis ipsis arrogamus, et nobis solis dici contendimus, Vos estis lux mundi, peculium CHRISTI, regale sacerdotium, gens sancta, et ejusmodi quid non? quia nusquam suos liberos non generat seculum. Inter laicos non cessat seculum efficere, ut qui seculares dicuntur, seculares etiam sint, et secularibus desideriis præcipites rapiantur; ut sic mores cum nomine a patre contrahere videantur.

In clero etiam movit seculum ex spiritualibus seculares componere, et ibi quoque, ibi filios hujus seculi bene multos efformare, ubi nomen seculi mira sanctitatis specie, et artificioso religionis fuco, multo maxime nituntur tegere et dissimulare: quasi vero sui parentis liberos jam pudeat, qui patrem tamen suum, hoc est, seculum et verbis et signis externis execrari et abominari videantur. At corde et opere amplectuntur, et exosculantur egregie, et tota pene vita agnoscunt verissime: adeo ut ipsos (quos vocant) seculares omni jam secularitatis genere longe superent et vincant. Tam officiose et per omnia patrem sequitur, adjuvante quidem avo, sua proles.

Hi sunt demum sanctuli nostri, qui seculo se mortuos profitentur; cum nulli uspiam magis vivant seculo, quam illorum aliqui, ne dicam multi. Sed sint hi quantumvis volunt professione et nomenclatura ab hoc seculo longissimi et alienissimi, ut nihil commercii, nihil cognationis aut affinitatis, nihil commune cum illo videantur habere: at vita et factis tamen palam faciunt, et sese produnt, non spurios, sed cum primis germanos esse hujus seculi filios; quippe quos seculum ex carissima sua velut uxore hypocrisi olim suscepit, susceptos educavit, educatos jam multiplicavit plus satis: plus satis, etiam si per divos omnes et divas dejerent, se neutrum parentem, nec seculum nec hypocrisim, novisse; ut omnia simulare et dissimulare optime norunt, id quod a parentibus suis commodissime addiscere poterant.

Verum hæc ego non de omnibus loquor religiosis, sed de his, quos hoc seculum vel in media religione habet sibi religatissimos et devotissimos: hoc est, de multis, et plus satis multis; nam in omni hominum ordine vereor ne bona pars sint inordinati et filii hujus seculi. Et istiusmodi filii quibusdam ingrati poterant videri, quod parentes suos verbis et reliquo prætextu non melius agnoscunt et recognoscunt, sed renuntiant potius et rejiciunt, quasi cane pejus et angue eos odissent. Sed sic sunt demum parentibus gratissimi, utpote illis ipsis quam simillimi; ita vultu et moribus eos referentes, ut jam reflorescere in his illi videantur: cum aliud in lingua editum, aliud in pectore clausum habeant: cum *Curios simulent, et Bacchanalia vivant*[1]: cum parentes sic imitentur denique, ut odisse nihilominus videantur. Sic morigeri liberi instituta parentum imbibere. Neque hi demum sunt solitarii, quantumvis religiosi, quantumvis monachi. Sed dixeris, Monachum esse idem est quod solitarium esse. Demus. Isti tamen sic sunt monachi, quod non solitarii, sed frequenti fraternitate undique stipati et associati. Et miror ego, si fratres non habeant inter eos, qui episcopi et prælati dicuntur, ut non paucos, ita longe germanissimos. Sed quoniam de singulis disserere non suppetet tempus, dum prælatos dicimus, episcopos, abbates, priores, archidiaconos, decanos, et id genus alios intelligimus: qui huc in præsentiarum convocantur (uti video), ut non nisi de rebus publicis ad gloriam Christi et populi Anglicani commodum spectantibus consultent et confabulentur. Quod utinam tam sedulo faciant, quam facere merito debeant! Ceterum periculum est, ne ex horum numero, ut lux suis liberis non careat, ita et seculum suos habeat: inter quos (ego scio) haudquaquam conveniet, quantumlibet in uno et eodem congregentur loco. Attamen inter filios seculi et filios lucis haudquaquam conveniet (quod scio), dum animos habent tam dissimiles, et studia tam contraria, judicia denique penitus diversa. Quod si filii hujus seculi vel plures sint futuri, vel prudentiores in hac congregatione, quam filii lucis; quorsum tum (quæso) attinebat convenisse? An non satius fuerat minime convocatos fuisse? Nam filii hujus seculi, ut sunt mali, ita generant male; et tamen fere fit, ut sint vel plures ubique, vel certe prudentiores, quam filii lucis in generatione sua. Et nunc loquor de generatione qua generant, non de generatione qua generantur: quandoquidem, quomodo filii lucis per ostium, filii vero hujus seculi aliunde generantur et intrant, perlongum fuerit pertractare.

Quanquam non omnes (opinor) vos univoca generatione estis generati, nec una ratione in tam illustri loco estis constituti. Hoc unum faxit Deus, ne seculariter generati seculariter generetis! Et nunc ego nihil moror, quomodocunque sitis generati, quacunque ratione sitis promoti; modo pium sit ac commodum, quicquid in hac consultatione vestra sitis facturi et generaturi.

[[1] Juv. ii. 3.]

Quicquid id sit futurum, exitus convocationis vestræ probabit, fructus et finis generationis vestræ declarabit. Nam hactenus per totos jam septem annos, et amplius, quid (quæso) generastis? Quid produxistis? Quid peperistis? Quid edidistis in hac celebri congregatione vestra? Quid, inquam, quo aut populus Anglicanus fuerit vel pilo melior, aut vos ipsi vel erga Deum aliquo modo acceptiores, vel erga populum vobis concreditum exoneratiores? Nam quod populus plus solito eruditior et doctior interim evaserit, utri tribuendum? vestræ industriæ, an providentiæ potius divinæ et regiæ? vobis, an regi potius tribuendum? Utrum prius vos regem, an rex vos potius ad frequentiores conciones habendas literis excitavit? An obscurum jam sit, quanta violentia et vos et parochi vestri huc adducti sitis, ut libri non a vobis, sed a profanis et laicis hominibus elucubrati passim venderentur, et legerentur in commodum populi? Audacior sum, sed Latine loquor, non Anglice; clero, non populo; præsentibus, non absentibus; benevolo animo loquor quicquid loquor, testor Deum qui novit cor meum et me loqui compellit. Quid ergo (per immortalem Deum) vos tanti patres, tam multi, tam longo tempore, tam sæpe in uno loco congregati, emachinati estis, si tuleritis duo facinora? Alterum, quo hominem mortuum, quod audivi, combussistis; alterum quo hominem vivum, quod sensi, comburere voluistis: illum, nescio quomodo, vestris commodis in suo testamento, quod audivi, contrarium; hominem, ut audio, bonæ vitæ, et dum viveret bonorum operum plenissimum, utpote clero juxta ac populo beneficum: hunc vero, de vobis sane nunquam male meritum, tantummodo quia articulis quibusdam, quorum aliqui contra supremitatem regiam erant concinnati, nolebat subscribere. Tollite hæc præclara facinora; et mihi sit hactenus incognitum, quid tam diu enixi et emoliti estis: nisi quod jam occurrit memoriæ, contra dominum Erasmum aliquid attentatum, etsi in lucem non editum.

Sæpe antehac a vobis consultum: sed quid tandem actum? Sæpe deliberatum; sed quid editum, quo Christus gloriosior, populus Christi sanctior sit redditus? Appello conscientias vestras. Cur sic? Cur sic? An quia non fuere inter vos filii lucis, hoc est filii Dei, qui, contempto seculo, Deo studerent, et quod Dei gloriam referret in lucem ederent, et ita se filios lucis esse commonstrarent? Non opinor, non equidem opinor. Absit hoc a vobis, ut omnes prætextu lucis congregati filii fueritis seculi! Cur tum demum? Cur tum? Forsitan, quia filii hujus seculi vel plures erant (ut fit) in hoc concilio vestro, vel certe prudentiores quam filii lucis in generatione sua. Quo fieri poterat, ut illi ad generandum male, quam hi ad generandum bene, evaderent potentiores.

Siquidem filii lucis prudentiam quidem habent, sed serpentinam, et cum simplicitate columbina conjunctam, non nisi simpliciter, fideliter, ac plane generantes et agentes omnia; eoque faciliores impeditu in generatione sua, et injuriis capessendis opportuniores. At filii hujus seculi secularem prudentiam, vulpinam astutiam, leoninam ferociam, et potentiam nocendi denique plusquam aspideam aut basiliscariam habent, fraudulenter et insidianter generant et agunt universa: qui tanquam Nembrothi quidam, ac venatores coram Domino robustissimi, cum sint omni simulatione et dissimulatione plenissimi, filiis lucis imponunt et impedimento sunt quam facillime. Qui enim venantur, non palam incedunt, sed clanculum agunt, ac insidiis (ut nostis) utuntur, et crebra frequentique venatione indies callidiores efficiuntur. Sunt enim filii hujus seculi veluti venatores insidiarii. Hi immerito filii lucis dici volunt, cum tantopere lucem oderint, et opera tenebrarum tanta sedulitate generare studuerint: qui si filii lucis essent, tenebras utique non amarent. Neque mirum est, quod alios in tam densis tenebris detinere satagunt, cum sint ipsi toti tam tenebricosi, et caligine tantum non tartarea undique circumfusi.

Quocirca pulcherrimum fuerit in omni hominum ordine, maxime in prælatorum ordine, inter filios lucis et filios seculi discriminare; quia ingens impostura suboritur, quando alteri pro alteris indiscriminatim capi permittuntur. Ingens (inquam) impostura passim grassatur, quando qui lux mundi vulgo habentur, solem et lucem e mundo tollere nituntur. Sed horum diversitatem ex diversitate cum animorum, tum armorum dignoscere licet: cum filii lucis sic sint animis affecti, ut adversariorum salutem, vel cum sui commodi jactura, interdum et vitæ discrimine quærant; filii hujus seculi contra tales mentes deprehenduntur habere, ut sanguinem benefactorum prius sitiant, quam ullius rei secularis jacturam faciant.

Arma filiorum lucis sunt, primum, verbum Dei, quod nunquam non promovent, et divulgant quantum possunt, ut fructum ferat: deinde, patientia et oratio, quibus in omnibus angustiis nixi confortantur a Domino. Cetera Deo committunt, cui et omnem vindictam relinquunt. Arma vero filiorum hujus seculi sunt, nunc fraudes et doli, nunc mendacia et nummi. Illis sua commenta aggenerant: his generata, quamlibet absurda, stabiliunt et confirmant. Quod si qui resistant, hos iisdem armis et instrumentis trucidandos procurant. Sic CHRISTUM, lucem ipsam, emerunt ad mortem, et post mortem obscurarunt redivivum. Sic filios lucis emunt et obscurant quotidie, et obscurabunt continue usque ad consummationem seculi; ut nunquam non sit verum, quod olim dicebat CHRISTUS, nempe, filios hujus seculi, etc.

Filii seculi vividam fidem in CHRISTUM extenuant, alienam et suam erigunt: filii lucis contra. Filii seculi opera a Deo præparata faciunt minimi; traditionaria vero opera et sua faciunt maximi: filii lucis contra. Filii seculi, si quando quæstum in rebus vident, quamlibet frivolis, si non etiam interdum perniciosis, illas prædicant, si quando prædicant: illas dentibus et unguibus defensant, illarum abusum quantumvis intolerabilem ægre improbant, ne improbando abusum quæstum amittant. Filii lucis contra. Res omnes suo ordine digerunt: necessarias, Christianas, et a Deo præceptas erigunt et extollunt: voluntarias, humanas, et commentitias dejiciunt, et in suum locum redigunt. Abusus rerum omnium vehementer redarguunt. Et tamen sic ista fiunt utrinque, et sic isti generant utrique ut filii hujus seculi, etc., ut fraudes et doli, mendacia et nummi videantur prævalere: ut nunc nihil dicam, quomodo opima convivia sunt filiis hujus seculi ad sua negotia peragenda instrumenta cum primis efficacia.

Neque solum filii hujus seculi sunt filiis lucis prudentiores, sed et inter hujus seculi filiis fuere alii aliis prudentiores in generatione sua: quia etsi eadem fuerit (quod ad finem attinet) omnium hujus seculi filiorum generatio, tamen in hac ipsa generatione alii aliis prudentius generavere.

Nam Romæ quid a centesimo quoque anno in centesimum quemque annum a filiis hujus seculi generatum est, et quam prudenter generatum, apud suggestum Paulinum in exordio ultimi parliamenti poteratis audire; quomodo alii canonizationes, alii exspectationes, alii pluralitates et uniones, alii totas quotas et dispensationes, alii indulgentias, et has mira varietate splendidas, nunc stationarias, nunc jubilarias, nunc pocularias, nunc manuarias, pedarias, et oscularias;

alii alias denique hoc genus fœturas generarunt, et prudenter quidem per omnia omnes : adeo sane prudenter, ut sua prudentia totum pene mundum stultificare valerent.

Ceterum qui purgatorium illud nostrum antiquum et lucrosum generarunt ; illud a Franciscana cuculla mortuo cadaveri circumjecta quoad quartam partem mitigandum ; illud non nisi a prudentissimo domino papa, vel quoties libuerit, in totum spoliandum ; illud more solito satisfactorium, missaticum, et scalarium : qui hoc (inquam) purgatorium tam prudenter generarunt, fuere illi, mea quidem opinione, in generatione sua longe omnium prudentissimi : quibus, sive filii lucis, sive reliqui hujus seculi filii, comparati non nisi stultissimi in generando poterant videri. Lepidissimum sane commentum, et a prima illius generatione commentatoribus ejusdem tam quæstuarium, ut parum absit quin ausim affirmare, nullum hactenus fuisse in toto terrarum orbe imperatorem, qui uberiorem ex vivorum vectigalibus proventum collegerit unquam, quam illi verissimi hujus seculi filii ex mortuorum tributis et donariis hoc commento sibi corrasere.

Quod si jam in Anglia adhuc sunt reliqui hujus seculi filii, qui hoc seculi suavium, nempe purgatorium, non minus prudenter continuare, quam olim Roma generare noverint ; quis tuum insimulaverit Christum falsitatis, quin, ut hactenus fuerit verum, ita semper futurum, quod filii hujus seculi sint non solum ad generandum, sed etiam ad fulciendum et continuandum generatum, quam filii lucis longe prudentiores ?

Nescio quid sit, sed aliquid sibi vult, quod tam ægre vident aliqui hujus monstri abusum quamlibet horrendum ; quasi nullus sit, vel esse poterit illius abusus : et rem antiquam videri volunt vehementer amare, qui nomen antiquum tam ardenter satagunt instaurare. Non pili faciunt nomen, nisi ob rem. Non enim ignorant (ut sunt callidi) rem commode et opportune sequuturam suum nomen.

Hinc jactant aliqui inventum ab illis purgatorium, vel invitis omnibus. Ego nescio quid sit inventum. Ut pro mortuis oretur non est inventum, quia non erat amissum. Quomodo potest esse inventum quod non est perditum ? O acutissimos rerum inventores, qui rem nondum perditam (si diis placet) inveniunt ! Nam liberationem illam suam cucullariam, solutionem illam suam scalariam, et spoliationem illam suam papariam, et reliqua sua figmentaria, non possunt invenire. Hæc sic sunt perdita (quod et illi fatentur) ut, quantumvis anxie quæsita, at nunquam erunt inventa: nisi forte hæc omnia cum suo nomine reditura bene sperant ut nummos colligant, et denuo decipiant; et ita in omni regno suum quoddam regnum consolident. Ceterum quo hoc jurgii inter filios seculi et filios lucis evadet, hoc ille novit, qui et filios lucis et filios seculi aliquando judicabit.

Et jam, ut multis aliis prætermissis ad finem acceleremus: Vos agite, quæso, fratres et patres, per Deum immortalem, agite, et posteaquam convenimus, aliquid congregati nunc agamus, quo filios lucis esse nos commonstremus; ne qui filii hujus seculi hactenus fuimus visi, filii hujus seculi pergamus perpetuo videri. Omnes prælatos nos vocant: ergo ita nos geramus, posteaquam convenimus, ut qui prælati sumus honore et dignitate, prælati etiam simus sanctimonia, benevolentia, diligentia, sinceritate. Omnes huc convenisse nos cognoscunt, et fructum conventus nostri quam avidissime anhelant et exspectant. Qualis est futura nostra generatio, talis est futura et nostra ab illis nominatio: ut jam sit penes nos, vel filios lucis vel filios seculi ab illis perpetuo appellari.

Igitur levate capita vestra, fratres, et oculis collustrate ac dispicite, et quid sit demum in ecclesia Anglicana reformandum considerate. An vobis difficile fuerit quam plurimos rerum abusus in clero, et item in populo videre? Quid in Arcubus conspicitis? Nihilne corrigendum? Quid ibidem faciunt? Expediuntne negotia populi, an impediunt? Peccatane semper corrigunt, an alibi correcta interdum defendunt? Quot ibi judicia, citra munera, opportune et in tempore (ut ferunt) clausa? Aut si omnia ibidem recte, quid in consistoriis pontificiis? Punitionesne legitimas, an redemptiones pecuniarias est sæpius videre? Quid de ceremoniis Anglicanis sentitis? sæpe cum non mediocri offendiculo contemptis, sæpius tanta superstitione vitiatis, depravatis, et veluti obductis, ut fere dubites an eas aliquas sic perdurare an penitus e medio tolli utilius fuerit. Nonne de nummo, de superstitione, de æstimatione conquesti sunt antehac majores vestri?

Ecquid in feriis nostris et diebus festis conspicamini? Quorum nisi pauci primitus pietatis gratia instituti erant: exinde in quibusdam locis neque finis neque modus instituendi: quasi hoc unum fuerit Deum colere, nimirum ut ab operibus vacaretur. Et tamen quid populus in his? Pietati an impietati potius vacant? Ecquid vos videtis, fratres? At videt Deus, si vos non videtis. Deus videt totos pene dies in ebrietate, comessatione, contentione, æmulatione, chorea, alea, otio, gula, miserabiliter consumptos esse. Hæc videt ille et minatur, qui nec fallitur videndo, nec fallit minando. At sic diabolo servitur, non Deo; etsi prætexitur Deus. Imo plus uno die festo quam profestis multis servitur diabolo. Ut nihil sint hæc: at quem non piget videre, et valde piget videre, in tam multis diebus proceres et divites in deliciis defluere, et tam variis deliciis diffluere; operarios vero et pauperes victum uxoribus et liberis perquam necessarium nec paratum interim habere, nec per festivitatem dierum nostrorum posse parare; nisi citari velint, et ab officialibus nostris compellari? Nonne bonorum prælatorum fuerit de his consultare, et consultando his morbis mederi? Vos videritis, fratres mei, vos tandem aliquando videritis.

Quid tandem de imaginibus istis, in tanta celebritate præter ceteras habitis, et tanta corporum nostrorum lassitudine aditis ac frequentatis; tam sumptuose denique et fiducialiter inquisitis ac visitatis; de famosis istis, nobilibus, et notoriis imaginibus, quarum extant undique in Anglia multæ et diversæ, quid opinamini? Sic dispescere et discriminare imagines, pro usu an pro abusu imaginum habetis?

Imo cur tu sic interrogas, et interrogando bonæ devotioni bonæ plebis male obstas? An non bene fiunt omnia, quæ bona intentione sunt facta, modo nobis commoda et lucrosa? Sane sic et sentit et loquitur avaritia.

An non dignius fuerit, fratres, aliquid ejusmodi lucri (si non etiam universum) nobis decidere, quam ad tantam impietatem pro lucro connivere, et tamdiu connivere; si modo impietas est, et impietas vobis visa est? Aliud est meras imagines tam sæpe adire, tam anxie quærere; aliud sanctorum reliquias interdum visere. Et tamen, ut ibi multum impietatis, ita hic aliquid superstitionis potest latere, dummodo ossa porcorum forsan pro reliquiis sanctorum aliquoties visantur, pene dixerim, in Anglia.

Ergo cæcitas est nimis quam crassa, et tenebræ sunt plus quam palpabiles, dum hæc sic prædicantur a quibusdam, et sic prædicantur fieri ; quasi non poterant male fieri, quæ nihilominus sunt ejusmodi ut nec a Deo nec ab hominibus præcipiantur fieri. Imo ab hominibus præcipiuntur potius, vel prorsus non fieri, vel certe segnius et rarius fieri, cum sic a majoribus nostris sit constitutum, videlicet :

"Præcipimus ut sacerdotes sæpe moveant populum, maxime mulieres, ne faciant vota, nisi cum deliberatione, de consensu virorum, de consilio sacerdotum denique."

Sic olim constituit ecclesia Anglicana. Quid (quæso) videbant, qui sic constituebant ? Intolerabilem imaginum abusum videbant: periculosam ad imagines peregrinationem videbant : superstitiosam imaginum discriminationem videbant. Certe aliquid videbant. Et talis est constitutio quæ tales peregrinationes fere aboleat ; utpote quæ sic abusum tollat, ut usum vel nullum vel perrarum relinquat.

Nam qui vota ad peregrinandum restringunt, etiam et ipsam peregrinationem restringunt ; cum fere sit ut non peregrinentur nisi votarii, et qui voto se astringunt ad peregrinandum. Et quando (quæso) peregrinaretur uxor, si non nisi seipsa secum bene deliberante, prudenti viro consentiente, perdocto sacerdote consulente denique peregrinaretur ; hoc est, ad famosam aliquam imaginem peregre profisciseretur ? Nam hoc est fere apud Anglicanum vulgus peregrinari, nimirum ad mortuam aliquam et notoriam imaginem peregre, hoc est procul e domo, proficisci. Jam si sic majores vestri constituere, nec aliquid constituendo sunt assequuti ; sed abusus, ut videri licet, non obstante constitutione, indies magis ac magis accrevere : quid restat vobis agendum, fratres et patres, si modo certum est vobis aliquid agere, nisi vel fallaces illas et præstigiosas imagines e medio tollere ; vel si aliunde noveritis abusum amovere, illam rationem indicare ; si modo visum est abusum amovere ?

Et jucundum fuerit, serium majorum vestrorum animum et desiderium in constitutione sua animadvertere, quando " præcipimus" inquiunt ; non consulimus, sed præcipimus. Quomodo nos ad tam salutiferum ecclesiæ Anglicanæ præceptum tam diu friguimus, cum quædam lucrosa interim nec præcepta nec consulta tantopere coluerimus ; quasi abusum rerum perseverare, quam lucrum cum abusu amittere mallemus ?

Ut nihil nunc de nocturnis illis bacchanalibus disseram ; ut nihil de præscriptis ac præstitutis miraculis, tam festiviter in occidente celebratis nunc dicam; audivistis, opinor, de Blesiano corde apud Malborne, et Algarianis ossibus alibi, quomodo et quamdiu lusum et delusum fuerit; vereor ne in multarum animarum dispendium: ut facillimum fuerit hinc conjicere, ejusmodi præstigiosis imposturis hoc regnum passim scatere. Neque tamen aliquid remedii est tam longo tempore a vobis excogitatum et constitutum. Sed misellus populus falsaria miracula pro veris continuo suscipere, et omnigena superstitione securus jacere permittitur. Deus misereatur nostri, &c.

Postremo, de matrimonio quid? Omnia bene? De baptismo quid? Semper Latine, an Anglice potius (ut populus quid geratur intelligat) ministrandum? Quid tum de missalibus sacerdotibus, et missis ipsis? Quid dicitis? An sic omnia vacant abusu, ut nihil in his castigandum videatis? At majores vestri videbant, qui contra venalitatem missarum sub pœna suspensionis constituebant, ne tricennalia aut annalia (sic enim vocant) more solito forent pro pretio celebrata. Quid videbant, qui sic constituebant? Quales sacerdotes, quales missationes videbant? Sed quorsum tandem evasit constitutio? Deus misereatur nostri!

Si nihil est emendandum in communi, saltem emendemus nos ipsos singuli. Quod si videmur nec in communi nec singuli emendatione egere; euge, domini mei, euge! saltem de nummis congerendis aliquandiu disseramus, et suaviter inter nos invicem conferamus, et postea quales huc accessimus tales domum redeamus: hoc est, filii hujus seculi et undequaque mundani. Et dum sumus in mundo, vivamus corde jucundo; quia post hanc vitam nihil jucunditatis est nobis sperandum, si nihil est nunc in nobis emendandum. Sed dicamus, non cum divo Petro, quod "rerum omnium finis appropinquat;" hoc triste: sed cum servo malo, quod " cunctatur dominus meus venire;" illud suave: " percutiamus conservos, cum ebriis edamus et bibamus." Siquidem quoties abusus rerum non auferimus, toties conservos percutimus. Quoties populo verum pabulum non adhibemus, toties conservos percutimus. Quoties in superstitione perire sinimus, toties conservos percutimus. Breviter, quoties cæci cæcos ducimus, toties conservos percutimus, et magna percussione percutimus. Quando vero deliciose ac otiose vivimus, tunc cum ebriis edamus et bibimus.

Sed veniet Dominus, veniet, et non tardabit. In die quo non exspectamus veniet; et hora qua ignoramus veniet, et nos dissecabit: partem nostram cum hypocritis ponet. Ibi nos collocabit denique, ubi fletus erit, fratres mei; ubi stridor dentium erit, fratres mei. Et hic esto (si vultis) hujus nostræ tragœdiæ finis. Hæ sunt deliciæ deliciosis hujus seculi filiis præparatæ: hæ sunt placentæ secularibus prælatis destinatæ —fletus et stridor dentium! Ecquid illic jucunditatis, ubi fletus, stridor dentium commixtus? Hic ridemus, ibi flebimus. Hic dentibus deliciamur, et lautitias rodimus; ibi dentibus dilacerabimur et stridebimus. Quorsum nunc prudentia excelluimus? Quid tandem generavimus?

Videtis supplicium, si pertinetis ad seculum. Si non vultis tam graviter affligi, cavete ne sitis filii hujus seculi. Si non vultis esse filii hujus seculi, nolite rebus secularibus affici; nolite secularibus rebus inniti. Summa summarum: Si non vultis æternaliter perire, nolite seculariter vivere.

Sed agite, fratres mei, agite, et iterum atque iterum dico, agite. Quæstus vestri studium amittite; gloriæ et lucro CHRISTI studete. In consultationibus vestris quæ CHRISTI sunt quærite; et quod Christo complaceat, aliquid tandem generate. Christi gregem diligenter pascite; divinum verbum sinceriter prædicate: lucem amate; in luce ambulate; et sic filii lucis estote in hoc seculo, ut in futuro fulgeatis lucidi ut sol, cum Patre et Filio et Spiritu Sancto. Cui honor et gloria! Amen.

Impressum in suburbio Londinensi, vulgo dicto
Southvvarke, per me Jacobum Nicolai.
Pro Johanne Gough, bibliopola.
Cum privelegio Regali.

HUGO LATIMERUS IN SACRA THEOLOGIA BACC. IN UNIVERSITATE CANTAB. CORAM CANT. ARCHIEPISCOPO, JOHAN. LOND. EPISCOPO, RELIQUAQUE CONCIONE APUD WESTMONAST. VOCATUS, CONFESSUS EST, ET RECOGNOVIT FIDEM SUAM, SIC SENTIENDO, UT SEQUITUR IN HIS ARTICULIS 21 DIE MARTII. ANNO 1531.

[Foxe, Acts and Mon. p. 1334, edit. 1563[1].]

1. SENTIO purgatorium esse pro animabus defunctorum purgandis post hanc vitam.

Animarum in purgatorio residentium memores esse licet.

2. Sentio quod animæ in purgatorio juvantur missis, orationibus et eleemosynis superstitum.

3. Sentio quod sancti apostoli et martyres Christi, a corporibus exuti, sint in cœlis.

Sanctos invocare licet.

4. Sentio quod iidem sancti in cœlis tanquam mediatores orant pro nobis.

5. Sentio quod iidem sancti in cœlis a nobis honorandi sunt.

6. Sentio quod conducit Christianis sanctos invocare, ut ipsi pro nobis ut mediatores Deum deprecentur.

Peregrinare licet.

7. Sentio quod peregrinationes et oblationes possunt pie et meritorie fieri apud sepulcra et reliquias sanctorum.

8. Sentio quod qui voverunt castitatem perpetuam, non possunt ducere uxores, nec votum solvere, sine dispensatione pontificis summi.

9. Sentio quod claves ligandi et solvendi traditæ Petro perseverant in successoribus ejus pontificibus, etiamsi male vivant, nec ullo modo nec unquam laicis commissæ sunt.

10. Sentio quod homines per jejunia, orationes, et alia pietatis opera mereri possunt a Deo.

11. Sentio quod prohibiti ab episcopis tanquam suspecti cessare debent a prædicatione, donec se apud eosdem vel superiorem legitime purgaverint, fueritque restituti.

12. Sentio quod jejunium quadragesimale et alia jejunia a canonibus indicta, et Christianorum moribus recepta, sunt (nisi necessitas exigat) servanda.

13. Sentio quod Deus in quolibet septem sacramentorum, meritis passionis Christi, confert gratiam rite recipienti.

[[1] Vid. supra, p. 218.]

14. Sentio quod consecrationes, sanctificationes, benedictiones, usu Christianorum in ecclesia receptæ, laudabiles sunt et utiles.

15. Sentio quod laudabile est et utile, ut venerabiles imagines crucifixi et sanctorum statuantur in ecclesiis, in memoriam, honorem, et venerationem Jesu Christi et sanctorum ejus. *Imaginibus uti licet.*

16. Sentio quod laudabile est et utile easdem imagines ornare, et coram eisdem lucernas ardentes statuere in honore eorundem sanctorum.

EPISTOLA I.

H. LATIMERUS *ad* Doctorem GREENE.

QUANDO hesterno vesperi Kymboltoniam inde in patriam discessurus veneram, amplissime Pater, ex M. Thropo et aliis haud vulgari fide hominibus, post mutuas salutationes et gratulationes, facile didici nihil posse hoc tempore M. Wynfyldo evenire jucundius quam in Luffvelli locum apud nos succedere, et quicquid ille habuerat muneris obtinere: non quod tantillo salario sit opus tam honorifico viro et rerum omnium affluentia tam insigniter locupletato, sed pro liberali sui animi generositate quam maxime cupit cum literatis viris et Musarum cultoribus familiaritatem contrahere. Et hæc res tam serio agitur, et tam grato atque adeo tam ardenti petitur animo, ut quum nihil præter fidem antea venerando Moro datam causari supererat nobis, exoratur jam Morus, sed regia id quidem (ut fertur) intercessione, ut Wynfyldo cedat, liceatque nobis citra omnem ignominiæ notam Wynfyldi votis obsecundare. Certumque est eum heic quoquoversum amicos singulari humanitate conciliare, et conciliatos beneficiis devincire, denique omnibus benefacere. Tua ergo prudentia viderit. Ex te uno vel maxime pendet totius rei summa, et Academiæ commodum, decus, ornamentum. Thropus nobis unus admiratissimus, et amantissimus semper tui, hanc concessionem nostræ reipublicæ tam commodum fore existimat ut nihil magis. Nam, ut de Wynfyldo perstringam, cui (quæso) vel major his diebus apud regem fides, vel promptior alloquendi eundem pro suis voluntas, quam uni Wynfyldo? Aut quis ex profanis proceribus literarum observantior? At ego videbor fortasse officiosior quam prudentior, quod tam audacter ad tuam dominationem scribo. Sed Thropus impulit, studium, pietas, observantia in nostram rempublicam impulit. Parce erranti et bene volenti.

Valeat tua dignitas. Has scripsi intempesta nocte, post pluvios equatorios, et cum eram ardore solis in ciborum fumis et reliqua ingurgitatione veluti suffocatus, et mentis impos.

Ex Kymboltonia postridie Edvardi.

H. LATIMERUS.

Reverendo Doctori Greene, Gymnasiarchæ.

EPISTOLA II.

Summa literarum LATIMERI REDMANNO.

[E Foxii Act. et Mon. p. 1308, edit. 1563.]

SUFFICIT mihi, venerande Redmanne, quod oves Christi non nisi vocem Christi audiunt; et vos non habetis adversum me ullam vocem Christi, et ego habeo cor cuivis voci Christi parere paratum. Valeto, et nolito me tuis literis amplius a colloquio Dei mei turbare.

EPISTOLA III.

HUGO LATIMERUS *ad* Doctorem SHERWOOD.

[Fox. Act. et Mon. p. 1318, edit. 1563.]

SALUTEM plurimam.—Non equidem sum ego vel adeo ferox (quod sciam), vir item eximie, ut ab homine christiano christiane admoneri moleste feram; vel adeo insensatus et a communi sensu alienus (ni fallor), ut me prius suggillatum fuisse abs te, et inter pocula, neque semel suggillatum, quam admonitum, imo nec admonitum tandem, sed acerrime potius redargutum, sed convitiis et mendaciis male habitum potius, sed calumniis inique affectum potius, sed falso condemnatum potius, constanter probem. Quod si tuis hisce literis pro illarum jure et mei animi ductu ego jam responderem,—Sed cohibeo me, ne dum conor tuo morbo mederi, bilem tibi moveam, homini vel citra stimulum, ut præ se ferunt literæ, plus quam oportet bilioso. Imo det utrique Deus, quod ipse utrique norit commodo fore, et mihi videlicet vel in mediis calumniis patientiam christiano homine dignam, et tibi judicium aliquando tam rectum, quam nunc habes zelum tuopte marte bene fervidum. Conducibilius, opinor, fuerit sic orare, quam ejusmodi criminationi apologiam parare, quum et ego jam negotiosior sum pro concione mihi perendie dicenda, quam ut commode possim respondere, et mendaciora sint tua omnia, quam ut jure debeam ea confutare. Sed ut paucis tamen multis, si fieri possit, satisfaciam, primum operæ pretium fuerit in medium statuere et quid ego dixi, et quid tu ex dictis collegisti. Collegisti quidem multa, veluti sanguinem e silice collidendo excussurus. Sed sic est affectus, uti video, erga me tuus, quem ob rabiem ejusdem ægre nosti dissimulare.

Esto, dixerim ego omnes papas, omnes episcopos, vicarios, rectoresque omnes, per ostium non intrantes, sed ascendentes aliunde, fures et latrones esse. Dum sic dixi, ex introitu et ascensu, non ex personis et titulis, cum Christo sum rem metitus. Hinc tu tua Minerva colligis, omnes papas, omnes episcopos, vicarios rectoresque omnes, simpliciter fures esse, saltem sic me dixisse. Num justa hæc, mi frater, collectio? An non juste in te quadret illud Pauli ad Romanos? Sic aiunt nos dicere, sic male loquuntur de nobis, sed quorum damnatio justa est (inquit): et tamen justius videri possunt ex Paulo collegisse adversarii, quam tu ex me.

Jam si idem Dei verbum nunc quod prius, neque minus Deo gratum acceptumque, quisquis interim minister verbi fuerit, nonne et eadem damnatio calumniatores ministri nunc manet quæ olim? Longe interest, dicas, omnes per ostium non intrantes fures esse, et omnes simpliciter fures esse. Sed unde (quæso), dum ego dico omnes per ostium non intrantes fures esse, videor tibi dicere omnes simpliciter fures esse? nisi forte plerique omnes videntur tibi aliunde ascendere, et non per ostium intrare? Quod si senseris, at nolito dicere, si sapis (sapis autem plurimum), quod sentis. Cum quanto enim id dixeris tuo periculo, ipse videris. Et nisi id senseris, cur, per Deum immortalem, ego non possum dicere omnes esse fures, qui per ostium non intrantes ascendunt aliunde, quibuscunque interim titulis splendescant, nisi videar tibi dicere statim omnes ad unum fures esse? Et tum quæ te potius cepit dementia, dum sic colligis, ut plures fures quam pastores colligendo esse feceris? Nam, velis nolis, verum est quod ego dixi, nempe quotquot per ostium non intrant, sed aliunde ascendunt, fures et latrones esse, seu papæ seu episcopi fuerint. Quare dum sic in ipso exorbitas limine, quorsum attinet reliqua examinare?

Sed age, hoc tibi arridet plurimum, quod Pharisæi sunt tam tecte a Christo reprehensi, et non palam : quomodo tum non displicebit e regione tibi acerbissima illa simul et apertissima criminatio in os et coram turba illis objecta, 'Væ vobis Scribæ et Pharisæi hypocritæ,' ubi nominati taxantur? Sed Christus, inquis, Deus erat, pervicaciam cordis conspicatus: tu vero homo, patentium intuitor, non mentium rimator. Sum sane homo (uti dicis), id quod citra tuam operam jam olim habeo exploratum : homo (inquam) sum, non labem in alieno corde delitescentem, sed vitam omnibus patentem et expositam intuitus, adeoque ex fructibus cognoscens quos Christus admonuit ex fructibus cognoscendos, ipsum quorundam vivendi genus libenter damnans : denique, quod in sacris literis sacrisque interpretibus damnatum toties comperio, nihil id quidem moratus, quæcunque ipsum amplectuntur personæ. Quod dum ego facio, neque cordium latebras ulterius penetro, nonne immerito abs te reprehendor? qui non homo mecum, sed plusquam homo es, dum mei animi emphasim melius nosti per arrogantiam, quam egomet novi ; utpote qui non sat habes quæ dico novisse, sed quæ sentio nondum dicta noveris, abditissima cordis mei penitissime rimatus, ne non scire in te ipsum competeret, quod in me torquere molitus es. Nimirum "noli ante tempus judicare, noli condemnare," ut discas quam oportet mendacem non esse immemorem, ne proprio forsan gladio juguletur, et in foveam incidat ipse, quam struxerat alteri. Nam dum ego pronuntio fures esse, quotquot per ostium non intrantes ascendunt aliunde; tibi, non verba solum audienti sed et corculum meum contemplanti, omnes ad unum fures esse pronuntio, excepto meipso videlicet et aliis meæ farinæ hominibus, nescio (inquis) quos. Sed quis illam fecit exceptionem nisi tu, qui, cognoscens occulta cordium, sic (inquis) sensisse videris? Sed tibi sic sensisse videor, cui et dixisse videor, quod (ut liquidissime constat) neutiquam dixi. Sed tibi peculiare est alios a cordis intuitu prohibere, ut ipse intuearis solus, quicquid est in corde, acie videlicet tam perspicaci, ut videas in corde quod in corde nondum est natum.

Id quod ibi facis quoque, dum quod ego de ecclesia recte dixi, tu tuo more calumniaris inique, quasi ego, quod ad usum clavium attinet, æquassem omnes cum Petro, cum ne unum quidem verbum de clavium potestate sit dictum, imo ne cogitatum quidem; neque Petri primatui derogatum, ut cujus nulla sit facta mentio. Sed tu, pro tuo candore, sic colligis, dum ego nil aliud quam admonui auditores ecclesiam Christi super petram, non super arenam fundatam; ne mortua fide plus satis hæreant, tum perituri et portis inferorum fœdissime cessuri, sed fidem operibus ostendant, tum demum vitam æternam habituri.

Quid ego minus quam omnes Christianos, ut ego sum, sacerdotes dixerim esse? Sed oculatissimi sunt invidi ad colligendum quod venantur. Nonne hic optimo jure cogor nonnihil christianæ caritatis in tuo pectore desiderare, qui dum nescis confutare quod dico, miris modis mihi impingis quod possis confutare? Tu vero optime nosti quid sentit Lutherus de ecclesia. Et ego non gravabor subscribere quid sentit, post multos alios, Lyranus super xvi. Matthæi; ex quo "patet," inquit, "quod ecclesia non consistit in hominibus, ratione potestatis vel dignitatis ecclesiasticæ seu secularis, quia multi principes et summi pontifices, [et alii inferiores]," inquit, "inventi sunt apostatasse a fide: propter quod ecclesia consistit," inquit, "in illis personis, in quibus est notitia vera et confessio fidei et veritatis." Hic consensit et cum Hieronymo Chrysostomus: sic enim dicunt (nescio an applaudatur tibi quod dicunt, quippe qui in illis te prodis esse:) Qui promptiores sunt ad primatum Petri defensandum, etiam cum nihil sit opus, quam ad beatificam Petri confessionem germanis fructibus referendam. Sed tu mittis me ad Augustinum: bene liberalis consultor. Ego optem te eundem legere, si libeat, in Epist. Johannis tractatu tertio: videris enim in Augustinianis operibus non adeo exercitatus, cum de fidei justificatione tam argute philosopharis. Quocirca cuperem te in collectaneis Bedæ exercitatiorem fore, cum tua ipsius collectanea Augustinum non spirent; ut jam non pluribus neque illius neque aliorum auctorum locis quærendis te gravem.

Sed illud non omittam tamen, etsi alio etiam me avocent negotia, "non allusisse videlicet Christum Pharisæorum impietati, cum præcepta vocaret minima." Sic enim tu audes dicere, quia aliam in Origene interpretationem legisti. Pulchre admodum objectum, quasi unus et idem scripturæ locus non sit ab aliis aliter fere expositus! Origenes de allusione non meminit, igitur nemo: qualis consecutio! Sed nihil, inquis, ibi Christo cum Pharisæis. Et id quoque non minus pulchre abs te dictum; quasi non statim post subderet Christus de Scribis et Pharisæis mentionem, populum ab illorum justitia humanis, i.e. suis ipsorum, traditionibus stabilita revocans, "Nisi abundaverit justitia vestra," inquiens, "plus quam Scribarum, etc." At versabatur tum, inquis, Christus cum pauculis discipulis seorsum a turba: imo hoc apertissimum mendacium est, id quod verba Matthæi caput septimum claudentia luce clarius commonstrant; ut tolerabiliora sint mihi de me mendacia tua, qui audes de ipso Christo et ejus sermone mentiri. "Et factum est," inquit, "ut cum finisset Jesus sermones hos, obstupuerunt turba super doctrina ejus." Ecce autem, si Christus seorsum a turba sit locutus, quomodo obstupuerunt super doctrina, quam (per te) non audiverant? Sed Lucas evangelista, sive de eodem sive de consimili Christi sermone locutus, testatur turbam audiisse, capite septimo: "Cum consummasset Jesus sermones hos" (inquit) "audienti populo." En, quo prolabitur præceps judicium tuum invidia male deformatum! Scilicet tu ipse hic non toto erras cœlo? Dignius videlicet, quia aliorum errores expisceris et notes, et ad palinodiam revoces. Tu tuo sensui hic non fidis? Medice, cura teipsum, et disce quid sit illud, "Hypocrita, cur vides festucam, etc." Disce ex tuis[1] trabibus alienis festucis parcere.

Ego nihil dixi (testor Deum, non mentior), quod vel Œcolampadio, vel Luthero, vel Melancthoni acceptum referre debeam; et tamen tu, quæ est tua caritas, non vereris id meo assuere capiti. Ego si feci istud, decidam merito ab inimicis meis inanis. Sed nescis tu quidem, opinor, cujus spiritus sis, dum mavis ministrum verbi impudentissimis mendaciis lacessere quam testimonium veritati perhibere: quod quantum sit piaculum in conspectu Dei, tu absque doctore non ignoras; in cumulum damnationis tuæ, nisi resipiscas.

Jam vero num ego vitupero, ut quis credat quemadmodum ecclesia credit? Non sane vitupero, nisi quod malevolentia erga me tua tam surdas reddidit aures tuas, ut ne audiens quidem audias quæ dicuntur. Sed hoc vitupero, ut quis cui Christianorum suadeat (quemadmodum suadere solent pseudo-prædicatores non pauci), sat per omnia esse credere quemadmodum ecclesia credit, et nescire interim quid aut quomodo

[1 suis, 1563.]

credit ecclesia; et sic miserum populum ab ampliori Dei agnitione quærenda dehortetur.

Quod postremo mihi obtrudis, mendacium est, et illud plus quam dici possit inhumanum: neque eo mea verba sensu accipis, sensu quo sint a me dicta; ideoque (Hieronymo super xxvi. Matthæi teste) falsus testis corum Deo futurus. Lege locum, et relinque falsum testimonium. Ego dico Christianum, id est, baptismo in Christianorum numerum receptum, si professioni non respondeat, sed carnis desideriis sese dedat, non magis Christianum esse, quod ad consecutionem æternæ vitæ spectat quæ promittitur Christianis, quam Judæum aut Turcam: imo illius quam[2] hujus conditionem in illo die deteriorem fore, si verum tibi dixit, "Melius esse viam veritatis non agnoscere quam post agnitam, etc." Et quibus dicit Christus, "Nunquam novi vos?" Nonne his qui, per nomen ejus prophetantes, virtutes non præstiterint[3]? Nonne[4] negabit Christus nos illum prænegantes coram hominibus? Non statuemur inter oves Christi a dextris, si non vitam Christo dignam retulerimus, professi Christum, sed professionem mala vita contaminantes. Sunt verius pseudo-Christiani quam Christiani habendi: et ab Augustino et Christo vocantur Antichristi. Non nego quin obligatio manet; sed in majorem damnationem manet, si non satisfacit[5] obligationi. Officium concionatoris est hortari auditores ut sic sint Christiani, ut, compatientes hic cum Christo, cum Christo conregnent in cœlo, ut aliter Christianum esse non sit illis Christianum esse. Sic scripturæ, sic interpretes scripturæ loquuntur, ut verbis hæretica tibi videatur locutio. Sed avarus, fornicator, homicida, inquis, catholicus est et Christi servus. Tamen sic (animi gratia) tecum ludam. Fornicator per te est Christi servus, sed idem est peccati et diaboli servus; ergo idem potest duobus dominis servire, quod Christum latuit. Et si fides mortua efficit catholicum, et dæmones pertinent ad ecclesiam catholicam, utpote qui juxta Jacobum credunt et contremiscunt. Fornicator (inquis) fidit Christo: spes non pudefacit; qui fidit Christo non peribit, sed habebit vitam æternam. Neque me latet ad Galatas scripsisse Paulum fide aberrantes, ecclesiam tamen vocasse: sic idem ad Corinthios scribens eos in eodem capite nunc carnales appellat, nunc Dei templum; Corinthios nimirum in-

[2 inquam, hujus, 1684.]   [3 virtutes præstiterint, 1684.]
[4 et, nonne, 1563.]   [5 satisfit, 1563.]

telligens, sed alios atque alios. Neque enim templum Dei erant qui carnales erant; quanquam nec me latet ecclesiam, i.e. multitudinem profitentium Christum, partim ex bonis, partim ex malis conflatam esse, nempe rete evangelicum ex omni genere congregari. Quid hoc adversum ea quæ ego dixi, qui conabar omnes bonos, non malos, efficere, et ideo laborabam ut auditores mei non putarent magnum esse si in malis ecclesiastici invenirentur? Sed non visum est tibi piam prædicationem pie interpretari, dum existimas ad pietatem pertinere si pie dicta impie revocarentur. Si colloquia tua non sunt quam scripta clementiora, [1]neutra ego optem mihi contingere: sed omnis amarulentia, tumor, ira, vociferatio, maledicentia tollatur a te cum omni malitia! Et tamen neque colloquiis neque scriptis me gravabis. Tu non optares (opinor) tales auditores qualem te præstiteris: sed Deus te reddat benigniorem, vel a meis concionibus quam longissime ableget. Vale.

EPISTOLA IV.

Hugo Latimerus ad Archiepiscopum Cantuariensem.

[Fox. Act. et Mon. p. 1333, edit. 1563.]

Non licet, reverendissime præsul, per supervenientem ægrotationem ad tuum palatium venire; non novam quidem illam, sed inveteratam, etsi novis occasionibus nuper exasperatam. Certe quantum videre videor, et quantum conjecturis ducor, hodie non licebit, citra meum (inquam) magnum malum non licebit. Et ne meum exspectaret adventum diutius tua dominatio frustra, en! hanc qualemcunque schedulam mea manu oblitam ad tuam amplitudinem mitto, velut excusationis nostræ certissimum indicem. In qua utinam vel per temporis importunitatem, vel per capitis gravedinem, justam aliquam expostulationem liceret tecum facere, qui me, curam animarum habentem, ab earundem curatione debita tamdiu detines invitum, et hac quidem tempestate detines, qua pastores cum gregibus adesse oportet vel maxime! Quidni enim expostulem, si modo tam vili mancipio cum tanto patre expostulare sit licitum? Nam si Petrus arbitrabatur justum esse ratione officii sui, quamdiu in hoc foret tabernaculo, ut populum ad-

[1 neque neutra, 1563.]

monere et docere neutiquam cessaret, et quo propius morti hoc instantius; ergo non potest non videri injustum, si qui hodie neque docent ipsi (ut jam nihil mirer si non ante docuerunt) neque cupientes docere permittunt, nisi quos habuerunt votis per omnia et in omnibus obsecundantes.

Primum, liberum erat meipsum amplitudini vestræ præsentare et offerre; sed inde meipsum eripere et extricare, parum nunc quidem videtur mihi liberum esse. Et dum aliud in principio prætenditur, aliud in progressu tam longo temporis tractu agitur, nostri negotii quis aut qualis sit futurus exitus non immerito dubitatur; sed veritas tandem liberabit, uti spero. Dominus qui custodit veritatem in seculum liberabit, super quo quid scribit Hieronymus utinam nunquam e memoria excideret! "Non poterat me molestare, quicquid essem pro veritate passurus; sed vivit Deus, et ipsi cura est de nobis." Tum modo ad Londinensem missus sum; ceterum coram Cantuariensi, interdum multis formidandis patribus stipato, geruntur omnia. Res velut cancellos quosdam et limites habet, ab eo qui me misit præstitutos: verum sic tractatur causa et ambagibus ducitur, quasi in infinitum abitura, nullo tandem claudenda termino; dum sine modo et fine alia post alia, ad me sive pertinentia sive impertinentia, nunc ab hoc nunc ab illo interrogantur, si non egomet modo, etsi forte inciviliter, at non imprudenter tamen (ni fallor), modum imponerem; veritus ne inter multa, dum multis respondet unus, unum aliquod (ut fit) ex inconsulto erumperet, quod causam læderet (alioqui justissimam), et me malum ostendat oportet, nemini volentem male moliri, si quid in conscientia est erroris: et meminisse omnino illud oportet, nempe "ad gehennam ædificare, contra conscientiam facere."

His sat fuerit sua profiteri, sua asserere, sua defensare: mihi vero assertiones alienæ obtruduntur, nescio quo jure asserendæ. Sine exemplo, opinor, hoc fit mihi, qui tamen intractabilis fere videor, dum nihil aliud quam iniquis efflagitationibus (quod ego judico) acquiescere detrecto. Adversus prædicationes meas si quis quid intentare conabitur, tanquam vel obscuriores, vel parum caute pronunciatas, paratus sum prædicationes prædicationibus illustrare, qui nihil adversus veritatem, nihil adversus decreta patrum, nil non catholice (quod sciam) prædicavi unquam: id quod per adversariorum et obloquentium testimonia commonstrare poteram esse verum. Optavi et opto judicium vulgi reparari. Optavi et opto discrimen rerum deprehendi, et sua dignitate, suo loco et tempore, suo gradu et ordine, unamquamque rem pollere, gaudere; ut ingenue sciant omnes, permultum interesse inter ea quæ præparavit Deus, ut in eis ambularemus, quisque vocationis opera sedulo facturi, postquam quæ omnibus sunt communia pari sedulitate sunt facta, et inter ea quæ spontanea sunt, ut in quibus non nisi nostropte marte obambulamus. Imaginibus uti licet, peregrinari licet, sanctos invocare licet, animarum in purgatorio residentium memores esse licet: sed sic temperanda sunt quæ voluntaria sunt, ut præcepta Dei factu necessaria (quæ facientibus vitam æternam, non facientibus æternam mortem, afferunt) justa æstimatione non priventur; ne præpostere diligentes Deum, stulte devoti, Deum contra experiamur non redamantem nos, sed odio potius prosequentem; cum hoc est Deum vere diligere, nimirum præcepta Dei diligenter servare, juxta illud Christi, " Qui habet præcepta mea et facit ea, hic est qui diligit me." Ne quis tam vilia reputet præcepta Dei vocationem concernentia, in suis potius adinventionibus aberraturus, cum in fine ante tribunal Christi secundum illa, non secundum has omnes ad unum judicabimur, juxta illud Christi, " Sermo quem locutus sum, ipse judicabit in novissimo die." Et quis potest unum præceptum Dei ullis addititiis inventis, quamlibet aut multis aut speciosis, compensare? O si essemus ad ea quæ Deo sunt peragenda tam propensi, quam sumus ad nostra excogitamenta exercenda seduli et devoti! Multa sunt quæ simplici fide facta non improbat Deus, sed probat utcunque saltem quorundam infirmitati indulgens, quæ tamen, antequam fierent interrogatus, nec præciperet nec consuleret fieri, utpote quæ justius toleranda sunt, dum sic fiant, quam prædicanda ut fiant; ne occasione prædicationis (ut fit) omittantur, quæ periculo damnationis fieri debeant. Et quid magis indecorum, quam ad id prædicationem convertere, quod Deus ipse nec præciperet nec consuleret fieri, saltem quamdiu negligenter fiunt quæ præcipiuntur facienda? Proinde ego ex parte mandatorum Dei sto hactenus immobilis, sic non meum sed Christi lucrum, non meam sed Dei gloriam quæritans; et, donec respirare licebit, stare non desinam, sic germanos verbi præcones, quotquot hactenus fuere, imitaturus.

Intolerabiles sane sunt, et diu fuere, quarundam rerum abusus; ut nemo christianæ gloriæ studiosus potest, nisi abusibus rerum multo etiam magis improbatis, res ipsas e suggestu probare: quæ si rarius fierent (ut ne dicam nunquam), modo hac occasione quæ mandantur a Deo fieri fierent officiosius, quid (quæso) pateretur jacturæ religio christiana? nisi forte sic cæcutimus miseri, ut illa turpi quæstu nostro, non cultu Dei vero, putentur consistere. Jam non potest (opinor) fieri, ut damnabilis ejusmodi rerum abusus juste reprobetur, nisi protinus infrequentior earundem usus sequatur. Quanquam præstiterit quædam nunquam fieri, quam tam fiducialiter fieri, ut minus curentur quæ oportuit fieri; cum alia oportet facere, alia oportet non omittere, alia nec oportet facere, et omittere licet.

Et quis manifestum multarum rerum abusum non videt? Quis videt, et non vehementer dolet? Quis dolet denique, et non laborat amovere? Et quando amovebitur, si usus prædicatione celebrabitur, tacebitur abusus? Imo non potest non regnare et dominari abusus. Aliud est, res quæ possunt in loco fieri tolerare, aliud easdem pro rebus quæ debent fieri aut passim prædicare, aut legibus prædicandas constituere. "Euntes docete (inquit) omnia." Quænam omnia? "Omnia quæ ego præcepi vobis," inquit; non dicit omnia quæ vobis ipsis videntur prædicanda. Agite igitur per immortalem Deum. Sic nervos intendamus nostros, ut quæ Dei sunt prædicemus ad unum omnes, ne adulteri[1] et caupones prædicationis verius, quam veri prædicatores evadamus; maxime, dum homines ad divina sunt pigerrimi, ad sua velocissimi, ut nihil sit opus calcaribus; injusta rerum æstimatione et innata superstitione (certe ab ineunte ætate a majoribus contracta) miserabiliter decepti: quibus rebus mederi vix ullis prædicationibus, quamlibet frequentibus, quamlibet vehementibus, quamlibet sinceris[2] et puris, quimus. Quare prohibeat Deus: sed in hac dierum malitia qui debent ipsi potius prædicare (præcepit enim nobis, inquit Petrus, prædicare) vel volentes et potentes prædicare præpediunt, contra illud, "Noli prohibere eum benefacere qui potest," vel cauponantes prædicare compellunt; sic miseram plebeculam in superstitione et fallaci fiducia damnabiliter detinentes. Quin Deus potius misereatur nostri, ut cognoscamus in terra viam tuam, ne videamur in quos illud quadret digne, "Non cogitationes meæ cogitationes vestræ, neque viæ meæ viæ vestræ, dicit Dominus."

His ego nudis sententiis subscribere non audeo, domine cum primis observande, quia popularis superstitionis diutius

[1 adulterarii, 1684.] [2 frequentibus, quamlibet sinceris, 1684.]

duraturæ, quoad possum, auctorculus esse nolo, ne mei ipsius damnationis simul sim auctor. Quod si dignus essem qui tibi consilium darem, colendissime pater,—sed cohibeo me; quam sit pravum et intolerabile hominis cor, detur vel conjectare. Neque sane quisquam novit quæ sunt hominis, nisi spiritus hominis qui est in eo. Non me superbia detinet ulla ab illa subscriptione, toties a tua dominatione cum maxima mei animi molestia rogata. Non potest non esse impium patribus et proceribus ecclesiæ non obtemperare: sed videndum interim illis, et quid et quibus imperent; cum, in loco, Deo quam hominibus obedire oportet magis. Sic dolet mihi caput, et reliquum corpus languet, ut nec venire, nec hæc rescribere licet et emendare. Sed tua dominatio, si non judicium meum, certe studium (spero) probabit. Valeat dominatio tua.

DISPUTATIO HABITA OXONIÆ[1],

18 APRILIS, 1554,

INTER DOMINUM HUGONEM LATIMERUM RESPONDENTEM, ET MAGISTRUM SMITH ET DOCTOREM CARTWRIGHT, OPPONENTES.

[Harl. MS. 422, Art. 16.]

DOCTOR WESTON, *Prolocutor.*

VIRI fratres, convenimus hodie, divini numinis auxilio, profligaturi argumentorum vim et dispersas adversariorum opiniones contra veritatem realis præsentiæ corporis et sanguinis Domini in eucharistia. Et tu, pater, si quid habes quod respondeas, admoneo ut responsis succinctis et concisis utaris.

Latimer :—" I pray you, good master Prolocutor, do not exact that of me which is not in me. I have not these twenty years used any Latin tongue."

Prolocutor :—" Take your ease."

Latimer :—" I thank you, sir, I am well. Let me here protest my faith, for I am not able to dispute it; and afterwards do your pleasure with me. The conclusions whereunto I must answer are these:

1. *In sacramento altaris virtute verbi divini a sacerdote prolati, etc.*
2. *Post consecrationem non remanet substantia panis, etc.*
3. *In missa est vivificum ecclesiæ sacrificium, etc. Ut supra.*

Quod ad primam sententiam attinet, videtur mihi illa fact[iciis] quibusdam verbis assectata quandam obscuritatem continere, neque secundum modum sacrarum scripturarum eloqui. Sed quantum assequor, sic respondeo, bona fide, etsi non sine periculo: nimirum ad cænam Domini rite celebrandam non nisi spiritualem Christi præsentiam requiri, et eam sufficere homini christiano, ut per quam in Christo maneamus, et Christum in nobis manentem habeamus, ad consequutionem usque [eternæ vitæ,] si permanserimus. Et hæc ipsa præsentia realis dici potest

[1 Vid. p. 250, seqq.]

commodissime, utpote quæ non ficta est, sed vera et frugifera. Idque ego nunc dico, ne nasutulus [quispiam] existimet me non nisi nudum et vacuum signum sacramentum facere, Anabaptistarum more. Quicquid autem de corporali illa præsentia [fingitur,] illud non nisi pro commento papistico habendum esse puto, et ideo omnino rejiciendum.

Secundam sententiam dicere ausim non [inniti] verbo Dei, sed humanitus adinventam esse, ideoque commentitiam et falsam, quam pene dixerim reliquorum errorum veluti matricem esse. Et quomodo transubstantiatores non videbuntur conspirare cum Nestorianis, viderint ipsi.

Tertia conclusio, quatenus eam intelligo, videtur inimicitias insidiose struere adversus oblationem ab ispsomet Christo factam pro nobis in persona propria, juxta emphaticam illam loquutionem ad Hebræos, "Per semetipsum purgatione facta peccatorum nostrorum;" et paulo post, "ut misericors esset et fidelis pontifex in his quæ apud Deum forent agenda ad expiandum peccatum;" ut videatur nostrorum peccatorum [expiatio] magis ex hoc pendere, quod Christus erat pontifex offerens, quam quod erat oblatus; nisi quatenus a seipso oblatus est, ut non sit necesse eum ab aliis offerri: ut ne dicam mirum præsumptuosum id abs quopiam tentari citra vocationem apertam, maxime cum tendat, si non in totum, certe in partem, ad evacuandam crucem Christi. Neque enim est humile quiddam offerre Christum; ut merito dici possit dominis oblatoribus, "Qua auctoritate sic facitis, et quis dedit vobis istam auctoritatem, ubi et quando?" "Non potest homo accipere quicquam," inquit Baptista, "nisi fuerit ei datum e cœlo;" ut honorem præsumere videatur priusquam ad illum vocetur.

Item, "Si quis peccaverit," inquit Johannes, non statim subdit, sacrificum habeat domi conductum, qui sacrificet pro eo in missa; sed, "Advocatum," inquit, "habemus in Jesum Christum," qui semel se ipsum obtulit jam olim, cujus unius oblationis efficacia et durabilis est in sempiternum, ut nullis jam sit opus ejusmodi oblatoribus. Quid sibi Paulus dicendo, "Qui altari deserviunt cum altari participant?" et subjiciendo, "Sic et Dominus ordinavit, ut qui evangelium prædicant ex evangelio vivant?" Imo cur [non] subdidit, "Sic et Dominus ordinavit, ut qui sacrificant in missa de sacrificando vivant?" Ut esset victus nostratis sacri-

ficatoribus destinatus æque atque veteribus? Imo non habent quod pro suo victu allegent, ut prædicatores habent. Ut videri possit sacrificatorium sacerdotium ordinatione Dei in prædicatorium et concionatorium mutatum esse, et cessasse prorsus oblatorium, nisi [quatenus sumus omnes Christiani sacerdotes sacrificatorii.]

Cœna Domini instituebatur ad excitandam gratiarum actionem pro oblatione dominica verius quam oblatores ibi agant res suas. " Pascite quantum in vobis est gregem Christi," inquit Petrus. Imo, Sacrificate nunc potius quantum in vobis est pro grege Christi, si ita res habeat ut prætenditur. Et mirum est Petrum tanti muneris oblitum esse, cum hodie tanti habeatur sacrificare, pascere pene nihil apud multos. Quis es si desinas pascere? Bene catholicus. Et quis es, inquam, si desinas sacrificare et missare? Ut minimum hæreticus. Unde hæc papistica judicia, nisi forte existimant se sacrificando pascere? Et tamen quid opus est erudito pastore, cum nemo sit tam stolidus quin facile didicerit sacrificare et missare?

Thus, lo! I have taken the more pain to write, because I refused to dispute in consideration of mine unability thereunto, *ut omnibus notum esse possit me merito et optimo jure id fecisse.* I beseech your mastership to take it in good part, as I have done it with great pain, having not my man to help me, as I have never before been debarred to have. O sir, ye may chance to live until ye come *ad hanc ætatem et debilitatem.* I have spoken in my time before two kings, more than one, or two, or three hours together, without interruption; *verum sit cum pace* [*et venia*] *tua dictum,* I could not be suffered to declare my mind before you, no, not to have a quarter of an hour, without snatches, revilings, checks, taunts, rebukes, such as I have not felt the like in such an audience all my life long. *Oportuit grave esse periculum. Quid commerueram, quid tandem hoc erat?* Forsooth, I had spoke of the four marrowbones of the mass; *neque nunquam legeram sic in Spiritum sanctum peccatum esse.* I could not be allowed to tell what I meant by the metaphor: but now, sir, by your favour, I will tell your mastership what I meant. The first is the popish consecration, which hath been called God's bodymaking. The second is transubstantiation. The third is the missal oblation. The fourth the adoration. Meaning by marrow-bones the chief and principal portion, parts, points, belonging or incident to the mass, and most esteemed or had in respect in the same: which indeed you may by violence, might, and power, thrust and intruse into sound of words of some places of scripture, with racking, and tramping, injuring and wronging the same; but else they be all indeed clean out of the scripture, as I am thoroughly persuaded, although in disputation I could nothing do to persuade the same to other, being both unapt to study in such reading as should be requisite to the same. I have heard much talking of[1] master doctor Weston, to and fro, in my time; but I never knew your person, to my knowledge, till I came before you as the queen's majesty's commissioner. I pray God send you as right a judgment as I perceive you have a great wit, great learning, with many other qualities. God give you ever grace well to use them, and ever to have in remembrance, *quod qui in altis habitat, humilia respicit;* and also, *quod non est consilium adversus Dominum;* and also that this world hath been and is a tottering world; and yet again, *quod tametsi obediendum sit principibus,* yet that hath his limitation, *nempe, in Domino, non contra Dominum:* for whosoever doth obey them *contra Dominum,* they be most pernicious to them, and the greatest adversaries they have; for they do to the procurement of God's vengeance upon them, *si Deus modo sit solus pater. Sunt quidam sic mente corrupti ut quibus adempta sit veritas, existimantes quæstum esse pietatem;* great learned men, *et tamen nihil scientes, sed insanientes circa quæstiones et disputationum pugnas; nihil scientes, inquam, quod non noverint Christum, ut oportuit, quantumquantum præterea noverint. Id quod solet dici, Id est nescire, sine Christo plurima scire: Christum si bene scis, satis est si cetera nescis. In quem sensum Paulus apud Corinthios fatebatur, se nihil scire præter Jesum Christum, et eum crucifixum. Multi multa blaterant de Christo, qui Christum tamen nesciunt; sed prætexentes Christum ejus gloriam dolose obscurant. Sejungere ab his, qui ejusmodi sunt,* saith St Paul to Timothy. *Pulchrum fuerit meminisse quod Augustinus dixerit, etiamsi locus non occurrit, nisi contra litteras Petiliani habeatur:*

[1 "of" interpolated by a later hand.]

Quisquis tradit necessario credendum quod non sit legalibus vel evangelicis litteris contentum, anathema sit. Cavete vobis ab hoc anathemate, si sapitis. *Et multum fallor si non simile quiddam habeat Basilius in hunc modum: Quicquid extra divinam scripturam est, si tradatur ut necessario credatur, peccatum est.* Cavete vobis ab hoc peccati genere. Sunt qui dicunt, multa falsa multis veris probabiliora et verisimiliora. Therefore Paul giveth a watchword: *Ne quis vobis imponat, inquit, probabilitate sermonis. Sed quorsum hæc, inquis, mihi? Sed est ut sinas senem interdum suaviter ineptire et veluti puellum quendam denuo agere. O Deum immortalem!* You have changed *sacratissimam communionem in privatam actionem;* and you deny to the laity the Lord's cup, *contra præceptum Domini;* and you do blemish the annunciation of the Lord's death till he come: for you have changed the common prayer, called divine service, with the ministration of Christ's sacraments, from the vulgar and known language *in peregrinam linguam,* contrary to the will of the Lord revealed in his word. *Deus aperiat tibi ostium cordis tui ad videndum quæ videnda sunt in hac parte.* I would as fain obey my sovereign as any subject in this realm; but in these things I can never do it with an upright conscience. *Deus misereatur nostri!*

Prolocutor:—"Then refuse you to dispute? Will you then subscribe?"

Latimer:—"No, good master: I pray you be good to an old man; you may, if it please God, be once old, as I am. Ye may come *ad hanc ætatem, atque etiam ad hanc debilitatem.*"

Prolocutor:—"Ye said upon Saturday last, that ye could not find the mass nor the marrow-bones thereof in your book; but we will find a mass in that book."

Latimer:—"No, good master doctor, ye cannot."

Prolocutor:—"What find ye then there?"

Latimer:—"Forsooth, a communion I find there."

Prolocutor:—"Which communion; the first, or the last?"

Latimer:—"I find no great diversity in them; they are one supper of the Lord. But I like the last very well."

Prolocutor:—"Then the first was naught, belike?"

Latimer:—"I do not remember wherein they differ."

Prolocutor :—" Then cake-bread and loaf-bread are all one with you. Ye call it the supper of the Lord; but ye are deceived in that, for they had done their supper before. And therefore the scripture saith, *Postquam cœnatum est;* for ye know St Paul findeth fault with the Corinthians, for that some of them were drunken at this supper : and ye know none can be drunken at your communion."

Latimer :—" The first was called *Cœna Judaica,* when they did eat the paschal lamb together. The other was called *Cœna Dominica.*"

Prolocutor :—" That is false; for Chrysostom denieth that: and St Ambrose saith, that *mysterium eucharistiæ inter cœnandum datum non est Cœna Dominica, in cap. x. 1ª. ad Corinth.:* and Gregorius Nazianzenus affirmeth the same: *Rursus paschæ sacra cum discipulis in cœnaculo, ac post cœnam, dieque unica ante passionem celebrat; nos vero ea in orationis domibus, et ante cœnam, et post resurrectionem peregimus.* And that first supper was called *Agape :* can you tell what that is ?"

Latimer :—" *Ego non calleo Græce :* I understand no Greek ; yet I think it meaneth charity."

Prolocutor :—" Will you have all things done that Christ did then ? Why, then must the priest be hanged on the morrow. And where find ye, I pray you, that a woman should receive the sacrament ?"

Latimer :—" Will you give me leave to turn my book? I find it in the eleventh chapter of the first to the Corinthians. I trow, these be his words : *Probet seipsum homo.* I pray you, good master, *cujus generis homo ?* Marry, the common gender."

Cole :—" It is in the Greek ὁ ἄνθρωπος."

Harding :—" It is ἀνήρ, that is, *vir.*"

Latimer :—" It is in my book of Erasmus' translation, *Probet seipsum homo.*"

Fecknam :—" It is *probet seipsum,* indeed, and therefore it importeth the masculine gender."

Latimer —" What then ? I know when the woman touched Christ, he said, *Quis tetigit me? Et scio quod aliquis tetigit me.*"

Prolocutor :—" I will be at host with you anon. When Christ was in his supper, none were with him but his apostles; *ergo*, he meant no woman, if he will have his institution kept."

Latimer :—" In the twelve apostles was represented the whole church, in the which ye will grant both men and women to be."

Prolocutor :—" So through the whole heretically translated bible ye never make mention of priest, till ye come to the putting of Christ to death. Where find you then that a priest or minister—a minstrel I may call him—should do it of necessity?"

Latimer :—" A minister is a more fit name for that office; for the name of a priest importeth a sacrifice."

Prolocutor :—" Well! Remember that you cannot find that a woman should receive, by scripture. *Domine opponens, age.*"

Smith :—" *Quoniam video mihi impositam hanc disputandi tecum provinciam, ut id ratione et methodo fiat, proponam quæstiones tres eo ordine quo mihi proponerentur. Et primo id quæro quod minime vocari debet in quæstionem: sed ea est ecclesiæ conditio, ut semper agitetur ab hominibus perfidis. Rogo, num Christi corpus sit realiter in eucharistia?*"

Latimer :—" I trust I have obtained of my good master Prolocutor, that no man shall exact that thing of me which is not in me; and I am sorry that this worshipful audience shall be deceived of their expectation for my sake. I have given up my mind in writing to Mr Prolocutor."

Smith :—" *Quicquid exhibueris referetur in acta.*"

Latimer :—" Disputation requireth a good memory. *Ast abolita est mihi memoria:* my memory is gone clean and marvellously decayed, and never the better, I wis, for the prison."

Prolocutor :—" How long have you been in prison?"

Latimer :—" This three quarters of this year."

Prolocutor:—"And I have been in prison these six years."

Latimer :—" The more pity, master."

Prolocutor:—" How long have you been of this opinion?"

Latimer :—" It is not long, sir, since I have been of this opinion."

Prolocutor :—" Ye have said mass at Greenwich full devoutly."

Latimer:—"Yea; I cry God mercy heartily for it."

Here they hiss and clap their [hands] at him.

Prolocutor:—"Where learned you this new-fangledness?"

Latimer:—"I have long sought for the truth in this matter of the sacrament; and have now been of this mind past seven years; and my lord of Canterbury's book hath specially confirmed [my] judgment herein. If I could remember all therein contained, I would not fear to answer any in this matter."

Tresham:—"There are in that book six hundred errors."

Prolocutor:—"You were once a Lutheran."

Latimer:—"No; I was a papist; for I never could perceive how Luther could defend his opinion without transubstantiation. The Tigurines wrote a book against Luther; and I oft desired God that he might [live] so long to make them an answer."

Prolocutor:—"Luther, in his book *de Privata Missa*, saith that the devil reasoned with him and persuaded him the mass was not good, fol. 14, *Contingit me, etc.*: whereof it may appear that Luther said mass, and that the devil dissuaded him from it."

Latimer:—"I do not take in hand here to defend Luther's sayings or doings; if he were here, he would defend himself, I trow: I told you before, I am not meet for disputation. I pray you read mine answer, wherein I have declared my faith."

Prolocutor:—"Do ye believe this as ye have written?"

Latimer:—"Yea, sir."

Prolocutor:—"Then ye have no faith."

Latimer:—"Then would I be sorry, sir."

Tresham:—"*Joh.* 6 *scribitur, Nisi manducaveritis carnem Filii hominis, et biberitis ejus sanguinem, non habebitis vitam in vobis. Quod cum audissent Capernaitæ multique ex discipulis Christi, dixerunt, Durus est hic sermo, etc. Ut ergo veritas ipsa magis sit dilucida, hic abs te quæro, an Christus hæc dicens intellexit de carne sua ore manducanda, an de spirituali manducatione ejusdem?*"

Latimer:—"*Ut Augustinus sensit, ego respondeo: Christum intellexisse de carne sua spiritualiter manducanda.*"

Tresham:—"*De qua carne intelligebat Christum, vera necne?*"

Latimer :—" *De sua vera carne spiritualiter manducanda per fidem, non sacramentaliter in cœna.*"

Tresham :—" *De qua carne intelligebant Capernaitœ ?*"

Latimer :—" *De vera quoque carne, sed ore sumenda.*"

Tresham :—"*Illi, ut fateris, de vera carne ore sumenda sentiebant, et Christus, ut probabo etiam, de carne sua ore sumenda loquebatur. Utrique ergo de unius* [*rei*] *manducatione, quœ corporis ore perficitur, intelligebant.*"

Latimer :—" *Non de ore corporeo intellexit Christus, sed de ore spiritus, animi, et cordis.*"

Tresham :—" *Contra probo quod Christus intelligit de manducatione quœ ore corporeo fit. Nam consuetudo cum sit optima rerum magistra et interpres, cumque acta prœstita a Christo certo declarent, quœ sœpius dixerat, factum Christi in cœna sua, ubi tradidit corpus ore sumendum, una cum consuetudine ex eo tempore de manducatione quœ ore fit recepta, evidenter infert Christum de oris manducatione intellexisse verba Johannis* 6, *hic a me citata.*"

Latimer :—" *Non tradidit corpus suum ore sumendum, sed sacramentum corporis tradebat ori, corpus autem menti.*"

Tresham :—" *At ratio mea concludit Christum sua verba protulisse de carne sua ore corporeo sumenda : nam alioqui* (*quod absit !*) *is fuisset impostor, et scandalisasset Capernaitas et discipulos suos, si non intellexissent sicut illum in hoc intellexisse sentiebant. Si vero ut tu comminisceris, sensisset ille, facillime eis dicere potuisset, Non comedetis carnem meum ore, sed sacramentum carnis meœ, non rem ipsam, sed ipsius rei figuram ore sumetis; et satisfecisset eis. At sic non dixit, sed prœstitit in veritate verborum suorum prout sonabant. Id ipsum ergo intelligebat Christus quod et Capernaitœ, quoad rem ipsam ore sumendam; nempe quod ejus vera caro vere est ore manducanda. Ad hœc, quoniam per corpus Christi sacramentum corporis Christi interpretaris, atque hinc non nisi spiritualem sive mentalem unionem inter nos et Christum consequi putas; te multum in hac re hallucinari, et a patrum sententiis exorbitare palam est. Nam illi nos Christo corporaliter et realiter, carnaliter conjungi disertis verbis asseverant. Hilarii quidem verba hœc sunt : Si vere igitur carnem corporis nostri Christus assumpsit, et vere homo ille, qui ex Maria natus fuit, Christus est, nos quoque sub mysterio carnem corporis Christi sumimus, et per hæc unum erimus, quia Pater in illo est et ille in nobis: quomodo voluntatis unitas asseritur, cum naturalis per sacramentum proprietas perfecte sacramentum sit unitatis. Hac ille. En, vides quam manifeste hæc verba assertionem tuam confundunt. Denique, ego ipse audivi te coram rege Henrico octavo Grenewychii concionantem, ubi de vera et reali præsentia corporis [dominici] in sacramento nulli Christiano dubitandum esse palam docebas, propterea quod verbum scripturæ habebat [nempe], Hoc est corpus meum, [quo confirmetur]; et nunc ea veritas idem scripturæ verbum habet quod tum habuit: quid ergo modo negas, de quo prius te docente dubitare non licuit?"*

Latimer:—" Will ye give me leave to speak?"

Tresham:—" Latine, quæso, loquaris. Potes enim, si vis, sat prompte loqui Latine."

Latimer:—" I cannot speak Latin so long and so large: my good master hath given me leave to speak English. And as for the words of Hilary, I think they make not so much for you. But he that shall answer the doctors had no need to be in my case; but should have them in a readiness, and know their purpose. Melancthon saith, if the doctors had foreseen that they should have been so taken in this controversy, they would have written more plainly."

Smith:—" Ego reducam verba Hilarii in flexum dialecticum: Qualis est unitas carnis nostræ cum Christi carne, talis est, imo major, unitas Christi cum Patre: sed unitas carnis Christi cum nostra est vera et substantialis; ergo unitas Christi cum Patre vera est et substantialis."

Latimer:—" Ego non intelligo."

Seton:—" Ego novi eruditionem tuam, et quam sis versipellis. Paucis tecum agam, idque ex Cypriano, de Cœna Domini: Vetus Testamentum prohibet haustum sanguinis: novum præcipit haustum et gustum sanguinis. Sed ubi præcipit haustum sanguinis novum Testamentum?"

Latimer:—" His verbis, Bibite ex hoc omnes."

Seton:—" Ergo verum sanguinem gustamus."

Latimer:—" Gustamus verum sanguinem, sed spiritualiter."

Seton:—" Imo novum et vetus Testamentum in hoc

dissentiunt; nam alterum jubet, alterum vetat sanguinem bibere."

Latimer :—" Verum est quoad rem, non quoad modum rei."

Seton :—" Jam nulla est contrarietas inter haustum sanguinis in novo Testamento cum veteri. Nam et illi bibebant spiritualiter."

Latimer :—" Et nos spiritualiter; sed nos pretiosiorem sanguinem bibimus."

Prolocutor :—" Augustinus in Psal. xlv. *Secure bibite sanguinem quem fudistis: ergo sanguinem bibimus."*

Latimer :—" I never denied it; nor never will go from it, but that we drink the very blood of Christ indeed, but spiritually. For the same St Augustine saith, *Crede, et manducasti."*

Prolocutor :—" Nay, credere non est edere nec bibere: you will not say, 'I pledge you,' when I say, 'I believe in God.' Is not *manducare* in your learning put for *credere?"*

Latimer :—" Yes, sir."

Prolocutor :—" I remember my lord chancellor demanded Mr Hooper of these questions, whether *edere* were *credere;* and *altare, Christus,* in all scripture; and he answered, 'Yea.' 'Then,' said my lord chancellor, ' why then *habemus altare de quo non licet edere,* is as much to say as, *habemus Christum in quem non licet credere.*'"

Tresham :—" Crede, et manducasti, dicitur de spirituali manducatione."

Latimer :—" Verum est: probo quod dicis, ego enim sic sentio."

Prolocutor :—" We are commanded to drink blood in the new law; *ergo,* it is very blood."

Latimer :—" We drink blood so as appertains to us to drink to our comfort, in sacramental uses, *sacramentaliter :* he gave us to drink it spiritually; he went about to shew that, as certainly as we drink wine, so certainly we drink his blood spiritually."

Prolocutor :—" Where find you that *sacramentaliter* in God's book ?"

Latimer :—" It is necessarily gathered upon scripture. I was in a thing, and I have forgotten it."

Prolocutor :—" But *vetus Testamentum prohibet gustum sanguinis, novum autem præcipit.*"

Latimer :—" *Verum est, non quoad rem, sed quoad modum.*"

Prolocutor :—" Hear, ye people, this the argument. That which was forbidden in the old Testament is commanded in the new. To drink blood was forbidden in the old Testament, and it is commanded in the new; *ergo*, it is very blood that we drink in the new."

Latimer :—" It is commanded to be drunken spiritually: I grant it is blood that is drunken in the new Testament; but we receive spiritually."

Pius :—" It was not forbidden spiritually to be drunken in the old law."

Latimer :—" *Substantia sanguinis bibitur; sed non eodem modo.*"

Pius :—" *Non requirit eundem modum bibendi.*"

Latimer :—" It is the same thing, not the same manner. I have no more to say."

Prolocutor :—" *Adfero locum e Chrysostomo, De proditione Judæ : O Judæ dementia! Ille cum Judæis paciscebatur ut triginta denariis Christum venderet; et Christus ei sanguinem, quem vendidit, offerebat.*"

Latimer :—" *Fateor, offerebat Judæ sanguinem suum, quem ille vendiderat; sed in sacramento.*"

Prolocutor :—" Because ye cannot defend your doctors no better; ye shall see what worshipful men ye hang upon, and one that hath been of your mind shall dispute with you. Master Cartwright, pray you dispute."

Cartwright :—" *Reverendissime pater, quoniam mihi datum est in mandatis ut tecum disputem, faciam libens; sed hoc primum scias, me in eodem tecum errore fuisse. Sed pœnitet me; fateor me errasse; confiteor peccatum meum, et opto rogoque Deum, ut tu pariter resipiscas.*"

Latimer :—" Will ye give me to tell what hath caused master doctor to recant here? It is *causa legis*, the pains of the law, which hath brought you back and converted you and many more, the which letteth many to confess God; *et hoc magnum est argumentum.* There are but few here but can dissolve it."

Cartwright :—" That is not my cause; but I will make you this short argument, by which I was converted from my errors. *Si verum corpus Christi non sit realiter in eucharistia, ecclesia erravit integra et tota ab apostolorum temporibus: sed Christus noluit ecclesiam suam errare; ergo, est vere corpus Christi.*"

Latimer :—"*Ecclesia papistica erravit et errat.* I think, for the space of six or seven hundred year, there was no mention made of any eating but spiritually; for these five hundred years the church did ever confess a spiritual manducation. But *ecclesia Romana peperit errorem transubstantiationis.* My lord of Canterbury's book handleth that matter very well, and by him I could assure you, if I had time."

Cartwright :—"*Linus et reliqui omnes fatentur corpus Christi esse in sacramento, et Augustinus quoque fatetur esse adorandum in Psal.* xcviii."

Latimer :—"*Ego non dico doctores errasse. Adoramus eum in cœlo, et adoramus itidem Christum in eucharistia. Missalica adoratio non est adhibenda.*"

Smith :—"*Putas Cyrillum fuisse ex veterum ecclesia?*"

Latimer :—"*Ita.*"

Smith :—"*Is ait Christum habitare in nobis corporaliter.*"

Latimer :—"*Illud corporaliter habet aliam significationem quam vos crasse putatis.*"

Smith :—"*Per communionem corporis Christi Christus habitat in nobis corporaliter.*"

Latimer :—" The solution hereof is [in] my lord of Canterbury's book."

Smith :—" Cyril was no papist, and yet these be his words: *Christus habitat in nobis corporaliter. Sed tu dicis habitare in nobis spiritualiter.*"

Latimer :—"*Ego utrumque dico. Habitat et corporaliter in nobis, et spiritualiter, secundum ejus intelligentiam; spiritualiter per fidem, et corporaliter per assumptionem nostræ carnis.* For I remember I have read this in my lord of Canterbury's book."

Prolocutor :—" For because your learning is let to farm, and shut up in my lord of Canterbury's book, I will recite unto you St Ambrose, *De Apparatione ad Missam. Vidi-*

mus principem sacerdotem ad nos venientem et offerentem sanguinem, etc. *Et Augustinum in Psalm.* xxxiii.; *et Chrysostomus De Incomprehensibili Dei Natura, homilia tertia, Non solum homines*, etc."

Latimer :—" I am not ashamed to acknowledge mine ignorance, and these testimonies are more than I can bear away."

Prolocutor :—" Then you must leave some of them behind you for lack of carriage."

Latimer :—" But as concerning Chrysostom, he hath many figurative speeches and emphatical locutions in many places, as in that ye have now recited; but he saith not, for the live and the dead; he taketh the celebration for the sacrifice."

Prolocutor :—" *Audies Chrysostomum iterum, in nonum caput Actorum : Quid dicis? Hostia in manibus sacerdotis.* He doth not call it a cup of wine."

Latimer :—" You have mine answer in a paper with you; and yet he calleth it not *propitiatorium sacrificium.*"

Prolocutor :—" You shall hear it to be so. *Et adduco alium locum eodem loco ex Chrysostomo : Non temere est ab apostolis institutum,* etc."

Latimer :—" He is too precious a thing for us to offer. He offereth himself."

Prolocutor :—" There is another place of Chrysostom, *Ad populum Antiochenum, Hom.* 69, *et ad Philippenses.* He saith there should be a memory and sacrifice for the dead."

Latimer :—" I say it needeth, or it booteth, not."

Prolocutor :—" St Augustine, *in Enchiridio*, cap. 110: *Non est negandum defunctorum animas pietate suorum viventium relevari, cum pro illis sacrificium mediatoris offertur.* Where he proveth the verity of Christ's body, and praying for the dead."

Latimer :—" Augustine is a reasonable man; he requireth to be believed no farther than he bringeth scripture for his proof and agreeth with God's word."

Prolocutor :—" In the same place he proveth a propitiatory sacrifice, and that upon an altar, and no oyster-board."

Latimer :—" It is my Lord's table, and it may be called an altar, and so the d[octors call] it in many places. But there is no propitiatory sacrifice, only Christ. The doctors might be dec[eived] in some points, and not in all things. I believe them w[hen] they say well."

Cole :—" Is it not a shame for an old man to lie ? You say you are of those fathers' faith where they say well, &c."

Latimer :—" I am of their faith when they say well. I refer my f[aith] to my lord of Canterbury wholly herein."

Smith :—" Then you are not of Chrysostom's faith; nor of St Augustine's faith."

Latimer :—" I have said, when they say well and bring scripture for [proof], I am of their faith, and further Augustine requireth not to be believed."

Prolocutor :—" Origen, Hom. 13. *in Leviticum*."

Latimer :—" I have one word to say. *Panis sacramentalis* is called a propitiation, because it is a sacrament of propitiation. Where is your vocation ?"

Prolocutor :—" My vocation now is to dispute."

Latimer :—" Nay, where are ye called to offer ?"

Prolocutor :—" *Hoc facite;* for *facite* in that place is taken for *offerte*."

Latimer :—" Is *facere* nothing but *sacrificare?* Why, then no man must receive the sacrament but priests only: for there may no man offer but priests; *ergo*, there may none receive but priests."

Prolocutor :—" *Negandum argumentum*."

Latimer :—" For whom did Christ offer at his supper ?"

Pius :—" For all the world."

Prolocutor :—" Augustine, li. 9, *Confess*. ca. 9."

Prolocutor :—" Ten years ago whither could ye have gone to have found your doctrine ?"

Latimer :—" The more cause we have to thank God, that he has now sent the light into the world."

Prolocutor :—" Light ! Light and lewd preachers. For ye could not tell what ye might have: ye altered and changed so often your communion and your orders, and all for this one intent, to spoil and rob the church."

Latimer :—" These things pertain nothing to me. I must not answer for other men's deeds, but only for mine own."

Prolocutor :—" Well, master Latimer, this is our intent, to will you well, and to exhort you to *redire ad cor*, and to remember that *extra navem Noæ non est salus*. Remember what they have been that were the beginners of your doctrine; none but a few fleeting apostates running out of Germany for fear of the fagot. Remember what they have been that have set forth the same in this realm, a sort of fling-brains and light-heads, which were never constant in any thing, as it was to be seen in turning of the table, where, like a sort of apes, they could not tell which way to turn their tail; looking one day east, another west, another day south, another north. They will be like, they say, to the apostles. They will have no churches; a hovel is good enough for them. They came to the communion with no reverence. They get them a tankard, and one saith, 'I drink, and I am thankful.' 'The more joy of thee,' saith another. And in that was it truth that Hilary saith : *Annuas et menstruas de Deo fides facimus.* A renegade Scot made such an heresy that Christ was not God, and patched it in the last communion book, so well was that accepted. You never agreed with the Tigurines or Germans, or with the church, or with yourselves. Your stubbornness cometh of vain glory, which is to no purpose; for it will do you no good when the fagot is at your beard: and we see all, by your own confession, how little cause you have to be stubborn, for your learning is in feoffers' hold. The queen's grace is merciful [if] you will turn."

Latimer :—" You shall have no hope in me to turn. I pray for the queen daily from the bottom of my heart, that she may turn from this religion."

Prolocutor :—" Here you see the w[ic]k[ed]ness of here[sy] against the truth. He denieth all truth and all the old fathers."

Latimer :—" I will not believe in the sacrament and sacrifice."

INDEX.

A.

ABBEYS ordained for the poor, i. 93; enormities of, abominable, 123; people buy livings in, 392; were enriched by massmongers, 522.
Abbots made bishops, i. 123; compared to Pharisees, 297.
Absolution, a general, at Pentecost, i. 135, ii. 13; words of, at Paul's Cross, i. 140; authorized form of, 424; none but in Christ, ii. 13.
Abundance does not make us blessed; an example thereof, i. 277.
Act of blood, the law of Six Articles, xi.
Acton, Mr Richard, recommended to Cromwell by Latimer, ii. 387.
——— Sir Robert, his son, ii. 388—401.
Adonias' (Adonijah's) ambition, i. 113; the effects of it, 116.
Adoption, we are children of God by, ii. 99, 136.
Adoration, one of the marrow-bones of the mass, ii. 257.
Adrian changes the name of Jerusalem, ii. 48.
Adultery, open, common in England, i. 244; among priests, ii. 390.
Ælia, the name of Jerusalem changed to, by Adrian, ii. 48.
Afflictions necessary preparation for heaven, i. 464; are better than prosperity, 466; example of David, 467; merit not reward, 490.
Agur's prayer, i. 442.
Ajax, his blasphemy (in Sophocles), i. 491.
Alasco, John, i. 141.
Aldermen are become colliers, i. 279.
Aless, Alex., translates Liturgy of Edward VI. ii. 277; took away adoration in the sacrament, 278.
Alexander, Pope, VI. i. 185.
Alexandrines, by Pope Alexander III. i. 212.
Algar, St, bones, i. 55.

Alms, no man poorer for giving, i. 303, 411, 414.
Alum, the pope's merchandise, i. 181.
Amaral, Andrew d', his ambition and death, ii. 83.
Ambition, the ruin of many; ii. 33.
Ambrose, St, converts St Augustine, i. 201; story of, 435, 483; asserts that the mystery of the sacrament is not the Lord's supper, ii. 263; on the bodily presence in our Lord's supper, 274; referred to, 319.
Anabaptists' opinions pernicious, i. 106; heretics, popish emissaries, allow no judges on earth, 151, 273; were burned, 160; infer the unlawfulness of war and shedding of blood, 495, 496; segregate themselves from society, ii. 197; affirm that they only have the true word of God, 209; make the sacrament a bare sign, 252.
Ananias and Sapphira, their crime and its punishment, i. 407, 502.
Ancient Laws and Institutes of England, i. 54.
Angels always ready to execute God's commands, i. 386; are diligent, ii. 85; are appointed to defend us, 86; not to be prayed to, 87; rejoice in our salvation, 123.
Anthony, St, and the cobbler, i. 392, ii. 94.
Antichrist judgeth at his own pleasure, i. 149.
Antonius, Bibliothec. Hispan. ii. 349.
Apollo taught and preached that he knew to be true, ii. 332.
Apostles, why they had things in common, i. 406; were called more than once, ii. 26; had not much faith, yet wakened Christ, 186; the twelve represented the whole church, 264.
Apparel, laws relating to, i. 372.
Apples, a dainty dish of, i. 186.
Aquinas, Thomas, referred to, i. 384, ii. 226, 235, 317, 319, 348.

Appropriations want reformation, i. 100.
Arches and Consistory courts require reformation, i. 52.
Arians, their opinion of Christ's humanity, ii. 98.
Aristotle's works preserved by the ethnicks, i. 105; not referred to, but God's word, ii. 317.
Armour of war, of righteousness, i. 499.
────── godly, what it is, and its use, i. 26.
Articles, the Six, i. xi., 487.
Ascham, Roger, his account of Cambridge, i. 178, 179; friend of Dr Redman, ii. 297.
Aske, Robert, i. 25.
Astyages and Harpagus, history of, i. 457.
Athanasius, ii. 235.
Attalus and Blandina, the history of, ii. 80.
Augmentation court, office of, i. 261.
Augustine thinks every man should be be a bishop in his own house, i. 14; doubteth whether oblations avail or no till thy neighbour be reconciled, 19; when a Manichee, converted by hearing St Ambrose, 201; says, sin must be wilful, 195; God's mercy is greater than our iniquity, 267; the intention of a question is to be considered, 272; observes, that if Stephen had not prayed, Paul had not been converted, 338; calls the blood of Christians as the seed of the fruit of the gospel, 361; calls the virgin Mary vain-glorious, 383, ii. 163, 164, and arrogant, i. 515; submits himself to the will of God, 387; declares robbery (without restitution) cannot be forgiven, 405; states the opinions on sin against the Holy Ghost, 463; writeth terribly of lying, 503; telleth of one who lay in a trance seven days, 539; says a proud man is a son of the devil, ii. 170; is certain that there is a fire in hell, but what manner of, or where, no man can tell, 236; says if God hides sins, &c. he will not punish them, 246; omits all mention of purgatory, 246, 247; admits we may think contrary to the fathers, 248; declares that an angel teaching any thing contrary to scripture is accursed, 261; understandeth that Christ meant the spiritual eating of Christ's body, 266; is said to grant that it is to be worshipped, 273; believes in the efficacy of masses, 275; says, he who for the fear of man hideth the truth, provoketh the wrath of God, 298; calleth Christians who confess Christ but obey him not, antichrists, 316, 345; teacheth how to know Christians from antichristians, 346; says evil ministers blaspheme such as blame them, i. 347; says *lex* is used for morals as well as for ceremonies, ii. 348.
Augustine referred to, ii. 119, 246, 269, 274, 313, 319, 361.
Auricular confession, the use of, ii. 13; the abuse of, 179.
Authority shews what a man is, i. 177.
Avarice condemned, i. 400.
Ave Maria, a salutation, not a prayer, ii. 229; the abuse of it, 230.

B.

Bagard, Dr, succeeds Silvester Darius in the rectory of Ripple, ii. 376.
Bainham, James, in Newgate visited by Latimer and others, ii. 221; their communication, 222; was burned, 224.
Baily, (or Hall) Life of Bp. Fisher, ii. 356.
Bakehouse (or Pardon) Bowl, i. 75.
Banbury glosses, corruptions of the truth, ii. 299.
Bankside, Southwark, i. 196.
Banqueting and drunkenness condemned, i. 254.
Baptism, entering into, i. 7; is a thing of great weight, ii. 127; to be baptized, and not to keep God's commandment, is worse than heathenism, i. 346.
Barnes, Dr Robert, commended, ii. 378, 389.
Barker, Anthony, warden of collegiate church of Stratford-on-Avon, ii. 383; Latimer complains of him, 413.
Bartlow, Frere, does hurt in Cornwall, ii. 406.
Basil says, if it is taught that any thing is necessary (for salvation) besides the holy scriptures, it is a sin, ii. 261.

INDEX.

Baker MSS., ii. 295.
Bayn, M., an opponent of Latimer, i. iv.
Baynton, sir Edward, i. vii.; letters from Latimer to him, ii. 322, 334.
Bead-telling to be regulated by the king's ordinance, ii. 243.
Beaufort, cardinal, story of, i. 118.
Becket, Thomas, house he was born in, i. 201.
Beckman, Hist. of Inventions, i. 181.
Becon, his account of Latimer's sermons, i. iii.; early writings, 30, 50, 56, 71, 75, 97, 170.
Bede, Collectanea, ii. 313.
Believers in Christ shall be justified, ii. 125, 154.
Bell, Dr John, resigns collegiate church of Stratford-on-Avon, ii. 383; successor of Latimer in the see of Worcester, 384.
Bells, evil spirits put to flight by ringing of holy, i. 498.
Benefices, fee-farming and selling of, i. 203, 317.
Benett, Mr, Latimer's chaplain, ii. 416.
Benson, Wm. See *Boston*.
Bernard, St, story of, i. 519.
Bernher, Augustine, servant to Latimer, i. xvi.; his account of Latimer, 319; his reasons for publishing Latimer's sermons, 324, 477, 455; his dedication to duchess of Suffolk, 312.
Berthelet, king's printer, ii. 379.
Bertie, Richard, husband of duchess of Suffolk, i. 81.
Bexterly, sermons preached at, ii. 84.
Bible must not be forgotten in time of pastimes, i. 121; ordered to be set up in every parish-church, ii. 240, 241.
Bilney, Thomas, acquainted with Latimer, i. i. 222, 334; in great fear of death, but died a martyr, 222; his confession the cause of Latimer's conversion, 334; book against him by sir T. More, 251; he visits the prisoners at Cambridge, 335; is in despair, ii. 51; Latimer's commendation of him, 330.
Bingham, Antiquities, i. 237.
Bishops of Rome have been the devil's great guns, some in England and elsewhere his serpentines, i. 27; must teach and preach, 63; cannot discharge their office and be lords presidents also, 70, 176; the most diligent in England, 70; appoint deputies, 77; and suffragans, 175; devil teacheth them diligence, 77; if negligent, may be turned out, and laymen called to the office, 122; upbraid the people with ignorance where they are the cause of it, 137; ought not to receive unworthy men to the cure of souls, 152; a bishop angry with Latimer, 154; rung into towns, one finds fault with a bell, 207; bishops complain to parliament of increase of immorality, 258; granted licences to midwives, ii. 114; their duty, 120; may use no violence to compel people to goodness, 195; bishops, popes, and all others, who enter not in by the door, are thieves and robbers, 311; ought rather to preach for others than trouble them, 328; two fingers of a bishop can shake off part of fire of purgatory, 362.
Blackstone, Commentaries, i. 52, 100, 175.
Blaise, St, or Blesis, his heart, i. 55.
Blanchers, in all times, stop word of God, i. 76; patch truth with popery, 290.
Blandina and Attalus, the history of, ii. 80.
Blessing, what it is, i. 302; who is blessed, 303, 418.
Blomefield and Park, referred to, ii. 296.
Blood-letting of horses customary on St Stephen's day, ii. 100.
Blore, History of county of Rutland, ii. 295, 296.
Bocardo, or Little Ease, i. 250, 293, 323.
Bochart, Hierozoicon, ii. 89.
Boniface VIII. instituted first jubilee, i. 49; asserts supremacy of pope, ii. 348.
Bonner, Dr, opposes reformation, i. 118.
Bonnam, master, ii. 322.
Book of Oaths, ii. 114.
Boston, or Benson, William, abbot and dean of Westminster, ii. 370.
Bouchier de Martyrio, 392.

Bradford, John, said to have repaid conscience-money, i. 262; sent to the Tower, ii. 258.
Bradford, Rodolph, account of him, ii. 376.
Brand, on Popular Antiq. (Ellis' ed.) i. 71, 175, 207, 208, 498, ii. 100.
Bread, daily, the meaning of, i. 389.
Breviary, Roman, ii. 231.
Brooks, Dr, bishop of Gloucester, claims supremacy of clergy, ii. 283.
Brown, Richard, complains against Latimer, i. viii.
Bribery, a kind of thieving, i. 139; a secret fault, 188; a rich murderer escapes by, 189; of a jury in a case of murder, 190; in a case of infanticide, 191.
Bribers as guilty as office or benefice-sellers, i. 186; believe not in hell or heaven, 187; advice to, 260; the reward of, 404; Zaccheus an example to, 405, 414.
Bribes, have a new name, i. 139; are steps of the *scala inferni*, 178; are like pitch, 188.
Briget, Bright, Brito, or Breton, referred to, ii. 319.
Bryganden, Mr, an opponent of Latimer, i. iv.
Bull, bishop, Works, i. xiv.
Burgesses are become regraters, i. 279.
Burgh, John de, i. 4, 14.
Burgo, Nicholas de, Latimer suspects him, ii. 404.
Burials, communion celebrated at, i. 237; ought not to take place too soon, 539; minstrels attended, 546; were and ought to be without the city, ii. 66; in a pious cowl or coat, superstitiously thought to be a passport to heaven, 200, 332.
Burnet, bishop, Hist. of Reformation, i. 321, ii. 240, 391.
Bury St Edmund's, monastery of, i. 75.
Butcher, or Bouchier, Joan, of Kent, her heresy, ii. 114.
Butler, Mr, of Droitwich, carries letter from Latimer to Cromwell, ii. 390.
Butts, Dr, solicits benefice for Latimer, i. vi.

C.

Cæsar, give that that is Cæsar's to, sermon on, i. 282, 296; what that is, 295, 503, 511, ii. 169.
Calais, in possession of English, i. 5.
Calvin, his commentary, i. 338; Instit. 478.
Cambridge, state of divinity in, i. 178; has power to license twelve preachers, ii. 324; yearly, 329; Cromwell succeeds Fisher as chancellor of, 382.
Cambyses flays a bribing judge, i. 146.
Camden, Britannia, i. 474.
Camel, cable of a ship, not the beast, ii. 202.
Camsele, or Kampswell, Thomas, prior of Coventry, ii. 386.
Canonizations, i. 49.
Canterbury tales, i. 107.
——— archbishop of. See *Warham, Cranmer*.
Capernaites, believed that the corporal body of Christ is eaten, i. 459, ii. 266, 432.
Carbanell, John, dean of Warwick college, ii. 396.
Cardwell, Documentary Annals, i. 122.
Careless, John, gives information to Latimer, i. 321; dies in prison, *ib. n.*
Carlisle endowed grammar-schools, ii. 418.
Carrion, where it is, eagles will gather together, i. 200.
Carte, Hist. of England, i. 25, 29, 99, 101, 102, 118, 119, 151, 163, 181, 183, 247, 263, 271.
Carthusian friars, confined in Newgate, ii. 392.
Cartwright, Nicholas, B.D., disputes with Latimer at Oxford, ii. 250, 272.
Casulanus, Augustine's letter to, quoted, ii. 298.
Catherine, queen, used daily prayer, i. 228.
Celsus, i. 385; his objection to Christianity, 315.
Ceremonies, book of, drawn up by Gardiner and others, i. 132.
Chamber, M. bears witness in favour of Latimer, ii. 421.
Chambers, abbot, made bishop of Peterborough, i. 123.
Chambering and wantonness to be avoided, ii. 18.
Chamier, *Panstratia Catholica*, ii. 359.

Chantry priests made beneficed clergymen, i. 123.
Chaplain, at-hand or elbow-chaplain, i. 264, 380; some will not do their duty, 381.
Charity, indispensable, i. 448, (see *Love*); must be agreeable to the sincerity of the faith, ii. 80.
Charles V., orders the 'Interim' to be drawn up, i. 305; at war with France, 390.
Chaucer, Pardoner, ii. 400.
Chauncey, Innocen. et Constant, ii. 392.
Chemnitz, Examen Concil. Triden. ii. 226.
Cheke, Mrs, mother of sir John Cheke, god-mother to a child in prison, i. 335.
Chichester, Dr Sampson, bishop of, i. xi.
Children of light, seldom lack persecution, i. 42; their armour, 48; clergy not all children of light, 43.
———— of the world, are crafty hunters, i. 47; their armour, 48.
———— to be corrected with stripes, i. 501; the obedience they owe their parents, ii. 158.
Christ, John's testimony of, i. 297; was revealed before he came, ii. 3; his birth witnessed by angels, 82; and announced to shepherds, 119; came to take our sins upon him, 97, 204; his extreme poverty, 300; laboured in his vocation, i. 214, 318, ii. 158; Lord of water as well as land, i. 212; Lord over death, ii. 67; refused not to consort with sinners, i. 15; abhorreth covetousness and cruelty, 285; was followed by common people more than by scribes, 199; teaches both, i. 475, ii. 314; prefers Peter's boat, Rhemists' explanation thereof, 205; shews infirmity of his manhood, 205; was tormented in his manhood, 223; suffers affliction, 219; prays, 218; again, and yet again, 231; came not to deliver from civil burdens, 283; nor as a judge 275, 299; but to call sinners to repentance, 273; preached the kingdom of God, 199; against the leaven of the Pharisees, 257; an example to preachers, 199; his example in ordaining preachers, 292; is the preacher of all preachers, yet his preaching not all fruitful, 155; his last sermon, 447; his commandment, 453; when given, 454; receives no human comfort at his death, 228; is comforted by an angel, and why, 232; his humanity, ii. 85, 110, 115, 136—183; the Arians' opinion on it, 98; descended into hell, i. 233; descent denied by some, Latimer's opinion, 234; suffered for us, i. 21, 331, ii. 113, 287; not for the angels, ii. 123; his sacrifice a continual one, i. 73, ii. 259; a bloody, not a dry one, i. 74; a perfect sacrifice and a free offering, ii. 253, 287, 292, 432, 433; his death killed our death, i. 550, ii. 145; destroyed power of the devil, i. 360; his passion blasphemed by us, 231; his marriage to the church, 456; the church is his household, has many stewards, 35; his church appeared to approach ruin in England, 105; his kingdom not of this world, i. 360, ii. 91; is our advocate, i. 330, ii. 254, 359; our high priest, i. 331; our helper in time of need, i. 233, ii. 187; and comforter, ii. 67, 179; giveth the Holy Ghost, ii. 204; our redeemer, ii. 85, 125, 149, 430; the only purgation from sin, i. 223, 232, 343, 417, 420, 422, 457, ii. 102, 103, 172, 194, 287, 309; no condemnation to such as are in him, if they agree not unto sin, i. 367; merited heaven for us, i. 488, ii. 74, 147; his doctrine was sufficiently sealed, i. 272; crosses call us to him, i. 465; he draweth all men to salvation who trust in him, 74; calls all, i. 544, ii. 144, 205; his promises are general, i. 463; is no respecter of persons, 545; in him all are equal, i. 249, ii. 199; hath ransomed us, i. 330, ii. 106; had [no sin, ii. 5, 113, 182; took our sins on him, 5, 113; what manner of a Saviour he is, ii. 124, 144, 168; his love to us, 168; is the Saviour of both soul and body, *ib.*; is the book of life, ii. 206; in his doctrine is consolation for the afflicted, i. 200; is whole Christ that worketh our salvation, 235; his words spoken to the

500   INDEX.

Pharisees, a doctrine to us, 283; as many as believe in him are children of God, i. 329, ii. 144; giveth wisdom to his elect to avoid snares and subtleties, i. 293; example of, 294; his body and blood eaten spiritually, i. 458, ii. 127, 252, 259, 266, 292; alone merited remission and justification, i. 521, ii. 139; all his merits are ours, i. 461, ii. 138, 140, 149, 193, 194; is with the faithful always, i. 495; is here already by his Spirit and power, 530; is found among the poor, ii. 127; is very God, i. 548, ii. 99; and very man, ii. 101; unity of his Godhead and manhood, ii. 103; overcame the devil with the word, i. 505; performed miracles by his own power, i. 550, ii. 67—75; he, and not his garment, cured the sick woman, i. 542; the badge of his servants, what, 448; his death profitable only to believers, ii. 3; was revealed more clearly by his bodily presence than in the promises, 4; why he called fishers to be apostles, 24; his first and second coming, 44, 54, 59, 98; his knowledge is infinite, 45; his witnesses are his works, &c. 73, 100; his deeds were perfect, 137, 147, 193; proclaimed himself to be the Son of God, 75; why he was circumcised, 135; how we may apply his benefits, 139; what the offerings of the wise men to him signified, 132, 154; why he worked miracles, 160, 165; there is none but may be saved through him, 208; his preaching was plain and simple, 210; the merits of his passion as indispensable to kings as subjects, 299; his golden rule, 300, 303; will deny us if we deny him, 315; misreported in his words, 327; we ought not always to continue infants in him, 339; commands his precepts to be taught, not man's inventions, 355; his blood believed to be at Hales, 364; his human blood was in all probability united to his divinity, 364; looking carnally on his blood will not obtain justification, 364; his doctrine teacheth us what to believe, 365; bore the cross as an example to us, 430; will embrace those who embrace his cross, 434; will deny those who deny him, 440.

Christians must labour for their living, i. 211; their blood is the seed of the fruit of the gospel, 361; their pilgrimage, 474; sum of their lives, 475; what Christ requireth of, 15; may they seek vengeance? 145; rulers harass christian preachers, ii. 66; may be both rich and honourable, 214; if after baptism they live not according to their profession, are no more Christians than Jews are, 315, 342; Christians may not break the law although under Christ, 326; who confess Christ, yet do not obey him, are anti-christian, 346.

Chrysostom, referred to, ii. 271, 274, 319, 359; marvels if any ruler can be saved, i. 98, 158, 178; says Christ was heard in silence, 204; his opinion on prayer, 338; on childbirth, 252; infers that the virgin Mary was a little vainglorious, 383; and arrogant, 515; his conception of hell, 236; condemns purgatory, 248; denieth the *Cœna Dominica* to be the Lord's supper, 263; saith the body of Christ resides in us corporally, 273; asserts a memory and sacrifice for the dead, 275; teaches that he is a traitor to the truth who hideth the truth, or for it teacheth a lie, 298; declares the church consists of those in whom knowledge and confession of the faith abides, 313; describes a christian congregation, 342; says the greatest pain of the damned is to be separate and cut off from Christ for ever, 362.

Church, the supreme head of, is a chargeable dignity, i. 152; appeared near ruin in England, 105; is Christ's household, 35; marriage of to Christ, 456; what doctrine should be taught in, 59; constitution of the Church of England by archbishop of Canterbury, in 1236, 54; those in the church shall be saved, those without damned, ii. 182, 281; infallibility of the church of Rome, 279; of Rome governs not according to God's will, but its own, 282; mutilates the holy scriptures,

283; the church has authority in matters of religion to govern according to the word of God, 284; the catholic church and Romish church are different, 290; before and after Christ compared, 291; to believe as the church believes is not enough, 315.

Church of the virgin at Rome, i. 97.

Churchwardens are great officers, i. 534.

Circumcision, its signification, &c. ii. 132; its pain, 136.

Clare hall, Cambridge, regarding the master of, ii. 378, 381, 382.

Clark, Thomas, desires Latimer to preach in Abchurch, London, ii. 324.

Clarke, John, D.D., recommended by Latimer to Cromwell, ii. 386.

Clement I. received by hand from Peter the supremacy of the church, ii. 280.

Clement V., pope, remitted part of sins of those who were buried in clerical dress, i. 50, ii. 200; his Clementines, i. 212.

Clement VI. i. 49.

Clergy, worldling, ashamed of their father, i. 43; what have they brought forth, 46; had too much, have too little, 100; if good, are entitled to double honour, 153; their duty, i. 350, ii. 28, 38, 120; ought not to wear delicate apparel, ii. 82; their dress, 83; may be absent from their flock a short time, 121; careless clergymen allow the devil to sow his seed among their people, 189; may not use violence, 195; must use the sword of the Spirit, 196; ought to have bibles of their own, 241, 243; cannot be learned being ignorant of Christ, 258; their absence the cause of much evil, 384.

Clopton, M., a royal commissioner, injures a poor priest, ii. 383.

Clothmakers, cunning of, i. 138.

Coals of fire, the meaning of, i. 439.

Cœna Judaica and *Cœna Dominica*, when they were eaten, ii. 263.

Coin, debased, ii. 41.

Coke's Institutes, i. 69, 175.

Colet, Dr John, dean of St Paul's, i. 58, 440.

Collier, Eccles. Hist. i. 46, 258.

Cologne, the wise men came not to, ii. 132; came to Jerusalem, 143.

Comestor, Peter, Hist. Evangel. ii. 116.

Commendation of the evil is often a reproach, ii. 328.

Commissioners were employed to administer oaths of succession, ii. 367.

Communion. See *Lord's supper*.

——— of saints in prayer, i. 338.

Community of goods, not insisted on, i. 406.

Compton, sir William, sheriff of Worcester for 19 years, ii. 398.

Conscience-money restored to king's use, i. 262.

Consecration, one of the marrow-bones of the mass, ii. 257.

Consistory courts need reformation, i. 52.

Constable, sir Robert, in the Tower, i. 163.

Constantine's pretended gift to the pope, i. 349.

Contarini, cardinal, i. 58.

Contentment is riches, i. 215; we may learn to be content when scorned, 546.

Cooke, lady, purchases lands, ii. 418.

Coots, who preached at Hales, summoned before Cromwell, ii. 373; Latimer's account of him, 374.

Cornwell, master, ii. 398.

Coton preferred by the king, ii. 373.

Cottonian MSS. ii. 245, 246, 373, 375, 386, 410.

Court of wards, i. 69.

Coverdale, Miles, bishop of Exeter, a bishop indeed, i. 272.

Covetous, the end of the, i. 256; believe not the promises, i. 270, ii. 155; are too covetous, i. 270; become more covetous, 278; mock God when they pray, i. 403; a lesson to the, ii. 90; will hear nothing against covetousness, 213; and greedy prelates, 303.

Covetousness the root of all evil, i. 109, 184, 246, 280; a great sin, 239; the sin of Nineveh, 241; of London, 242; of the giants, 245; the cause of rebellion, must be cut down, 247; many suffered for Achan's, 144; is still prevalent, ii. 107, 155.

Cranmer, archbishop of Canterbury, ii. 368; referred to, 372; patronises

502 INDEX.

Latimer, i. ix.; Crewkehorne, x.; attempt to send him to the Tower, ii. 258; wishes the scriptures to be read in English, 305; his book *De præsentia Christi,* referred to, ii. 276, 380; letter to Cromwell, 379; recommends Mr and Mrs Statham to Cromwell, 386.

Cranmer, Remains, (Jenkyns' ed.) i. ix. xii., ii. 240; (Park. Soc. ed.) ii. 265, 267, 272, 273, 274, 276.

Crayford, master of Clare hall, account of him, ii. 378.

Creeds, the three, Latimer believes, ii. 332.

Creeping to the cross, recognised by Henry VIII., i. 132.

Cressy, Church Hist., i. 55.

Crome, Dr Edward, counselled and devised with Latimer, i. xii.; made confession of his faith, ii. 350; solicits Latimer to write to Cromwell in favour of Thomas Gibson, ii. 381.

Cromwell, lord, i. vi. x. xi. 244; obtained licence for the scriptures to be read in English, ii. 240, 305; letters to, from Latimer, 367, 368, 370; regarding late prior of Worcester, 371; Coots', of Hales, sermon, 374; with a prophecy, 375; respecting Silvester Davis, 376; regarding St John's college and Clare hall, Cambridge, 377; concerning the institution of a christian man, 379; about master Lucy, &c. 381; chancellor of Cambridge, 382; about a poor priest, sir Large, 383; on the birth of the prince, 385; recommending Gorton and Clarke, 386, 387; about the monks of Evesham, and recommending Dr Barns, 389; introducing an honest poor gentleman, 389; regarding the misbehaviour of certain priests, 390; concerning friar Forest's execution, 391; regarding M. Nevell's suit for the lands of the Augustine friary of Droitwich, 393; respecting the collegiate church of St Mary, Warwick, 396; M. Pye and the lands of Droitwich, 397; Mr Lucy and Clapton, 399; regarding the bloody abbot, 400; concerning M. Wattwood and Warwick college, 401, 406; on behalf of the city of Worcester, 403; regarding John Scurfield, 404; recommending M. Acton, 405; and Richard Edwards, 406; and the abbot of Evesham, 406; exposing the imposition of the blood of Hales, 407, 409; concerning Whitborne or Bedgel, prior of Malvern, 410; with an account of his income, 412; suspects Anthony Barker, 413; recommends the sheriff to be master of the game of the forest of Feckenham, 414; respecting master Moore, sir John Ashley, and Mr Tracy, 415; Furnes fools, 417; about grammar-school at Gloucester, 418; recounts various suits, 418.

Cross, salutation of the, not praying to it, ii. 231; neither Christ nor the early martyrs would purchase freedom from the cross, 434.

Curates, are not to be hastily made, i. 152; for prisons, are desirable, 180; may be complained against, 304; an admonition to, 416; their duty, ii. 88; the lack of good ones is the cause of all mischief, 307; some preach their own doctrine, and endeavour to set the people to sleep, 344; what the love of consists in, 348; in great cures may find sufficient work, 350.

Curius Dentatus, i. 44.

Cursing very prevalent, i. 380.

Cusa, cardinal Nicholas de, his opinion on the article " descended into hell," i. 234.

Cyril (of Alexandria) saith that Christ dwelleth corporally in us, not in the bread, ii. 273.

Cyrus, prophecy concerning, i. 457.

Cyprian, mentions no middle state, ii. 247; asserts bodily presence in Lord's supper, 269; says no deliberation is required in sticking to the truth, 290.

D.

Darcy, sir Arthur, i. 93.

Darcy, lord, in prison, i. 163.

Darius, Silvester, deprived of the rectory of Ripple, ii. 375.

Daughters of men and sons of God, who they were, i. 212.

David, his example held up to us, i. 89; account of, 113; his presumption, punishment, and penitence, 386.

Day, George, master of St John's college, Cambridge, and bishop of Chichester, account of him, ii. 377.

Day, John, printer, i. 477.

Dearth, cause of, i. 99; great, 527.

Death and hell, what are, i. 220; the sight of, a terror—one of the bitterest parts of Christ's passion, *ib.*; what is to be done when the hour of it cometh, 224, 227; fear of, is a punishment for our sins, 227; meeting death is receiving a delivery from trouble, 347; why the time of it is hidden, 416; is fearful to children in God and to customable sinners, 549.

Deceits and falsehood exposed, i. 401; the reward of, i. 402, ii. 190.

Decretals, i. 212.

Decret. Gratiani, ii. 349.

Denmark, Christian III., the king of, sitteth openly in judgment, i. 274.

Devil, what he is, i. 42; his nature, 493; the most diligent preacher in England, 70; the author of all superstition, 71, 72; attempts to evacuate Christ's death, 72; when he has the upper hand, reigns quietly, 130, 151, 234; an enemy to preaching, i. 202, ii. 210; invented fee-farming of benefices, &c., i. 203; always ready to tempt, 284, 497; his arts to hinder prayer, 329, 342, 360; a liar, &c.— his servants, i. 375, ii. 191; is a crafty and experienced enemy, i. 429, 438, 493; maketh weapons of everything, 432; has no power against us but by permission, 438, 442; must be overcome, i. 439, ii. 11; by resistance, i. 442, ii. 149; livery of his servants, i. 448; laboureth to make sauce for us, 467; devils were angels, 493; tremble when Christ is with us, 394; have not their full torments till the last day, 494; the devil was ruined through pride, ii. 170; our only weapon against him, i. 505, ii. 149; he shall be loosed in the last days, i. 317; taketh upon him to be lord over all, ii. 42; the nature of his fall, 123; strange tale of him, 149; picketh up the seed that falleth on stony ground, 212; he, his hostlers, and tapsters, stand in every inn-door crying to us, 439.

Devonshire rebels, considered not the petition, "Thy will be done," i. 371; the faithful in Devonshire suffered, 376.

Dionysius Carthusianus, his testimony against unwritten verities, i. 210; respecting the state of lost souls, ii. 235.

Diriges, what they are, i. 292.

Dishonour of a king, i. 94.

Dispensations, i. 49.

Dissensions are few when the devil ruleth, i. 130.

Dives, a warning to us, i. 365.

Divinity, state of, in Cambridge, i. 178; English, i. 179.

Doctors, the old, ii. 319.

Doctrine, what should be taught in Christ's church, i. 59; those educated in false doctrine may be preserved from perishing, 526, 527; of the Lord's supper set forth by Paul, i. 195.

Dodipole, Dr, or Dodepole, the representative of folly, i. 245, 304.

Doeg, the Edomite, a peace-breaker, i. 486.

Doers, not hearers of the word, shall be saved, ii. 93.

Domitian, a gainsayer, i. 129.

Donatists, what they were, went to death boldly, i. 160.

Dorset, Thomas, i. x.

Drink to be taken in moderation, i. 169, ii. 15, 61, 81.

Drunkenness and banqueting condemned by inference, i. 254.

Dugdale, Hist. of St Paul's Cath. i. 49.
——— Origines Jurid. ii. 419, 428.
——— Hist. of Warwicksh. i. 272, ii. 84, 383, 384, 388, 396, 419, 423.

Duns Scotus, referred to, ii. 317, 319; says the certainty of faith is the surest certainty, 337.

Dunstable way, as plain as, i. 113.

Duty, performing our, shorteneth not life, ii. 35; our special duty must be followed, 37.

E.

Eating and drinking, what is allowed, i. 169, ii. 14, 61, 81; laws relating to, i. 372, ii. 15.

Education, the force of, i. 116; of children to be attended to, 391.

Edward VI. succeeds to the crown, i. xii.

Edwards, Richard, prior of Black Friars, Worcester, ii. 406.

Elect, fallibility of the, ii. 175, 193, 204, 252; shall be judges, not judged, at the last day, 191; the joys of the elect, 193, 195.

Election, God's, tokens of, i. 263, ii. 175, 205, 206.

Elijah and Elisha raised the dead, but were not gods, ii. 68.

Eli and Samuel compared, i. 188.

Ely, bishop of, forbids Latimer to preach, i. iii.

Emmanuel coll. Camb. MS. ii. 435.

Emperors, kings, and magistrates, are bound to obey God's word, i. 85.

Enemy, the use and benefit of one, i. 427; ought to be overcome with well-doing, 440.

Envy, a child of the devil, i. 450, ii. 18.

Erasmus, i. 46; quoted, ii. 341.

Estius, Commen. in Sentent. i. 384.

Ethnicks, wrought by natural motions and anticipations, i. 105.

Eugenius, IV. pope, determines the question of the Lord's supper, i. 209.

Eusebius Pamphilius, Hist. Ecc. i. 129, ii. 80; relates stories of the impotency of the devil, ii. 149.

Euthymius. See *Zigabenus.*

Eve repented and took hold of the promise, i. 243; her unmeasurable talk was the cause of the fall of man, ii. 92.

Evance, Thomas, royal commissioner, makes suit for the lands of Bordesley, ii. 394.

Evesham, the monks of, ii. 389; the abbot of, 406.

Examination, three rules for self-examination, ii. 176.

Executions at Oxford, i. 163; Newgate and the Marshalsea, 164.

Exeter, the bishop of, (Coverdale,) a bishop indeed, i. 272.

Expectations, i. 49.

Extravagantes Commun. i. 212, ii. 349.

F.

Fabricius, *Lux Evangelii,* ii. 49.

Facts do not vary with men's opinions of them, ii. 333.

Faith, true, hard to be found, i. 168; its forerunner and train, 168, 237; cometh by hearing, i. 200, ii. 174, 320; the cause of justification, i. 235, ii. 147; what faith will serve, i. 237, 421, ii. 138; is the marriage-garment, i. 286; faith with repentance procures forgiveness of sin, 370, 379; of the saints before Christ, i. 378, ii. 171; repentance is by faith which cometh of hearing, i. 418; tokens of true faith, i. 420, 421, ii. 194; Paul underrates not justifying faith, i. 449; faith and love have different offices, faith is the mother of love, 454; purifieth the heart, 485; what is required of us in the fight of faith, 491; is our buckler, 504; alone makes us partakers of Christ's passion, i. 521, ii. 138, 140, 163, 313; maketh us not afraid, i. 535, ii. 152; giveth us the victory over death, ii. 148, 194; availeth not without the word, i. 544; must be special as well as general, ii. 10, 124; no success without faith, 31, 32; the nature of, 88; is the hand by which we receive the benefits of God, 170; the disciples had not much faith, 186; how we may ascertain the presence of faith, 194; faith, not works, esteemed of God, 201; stubbornness and want of faith is the cause of our damnation, 206; faith and the feeling of it are different, 207; God will not have his faith defended by man, 308; dead faith is useless, 316; the certainty of faith is the surest certainty, 337; faith may be perfect, although knowledge is not clear, 337.

Faithful, congregation of the, in Edward's days, i. 313; in Mary's time, *ib.*; their sins cannot hinder their prayers, i. 330; all faithful men have made but short prayers, 352; God will provide for their immediate wants, ii. 154; their reward, 155, 195;

they shall have trouble in this world, examples of it, 183, 321, 430.
Falsehood and false practices exposed, i. 400; the reward of, 401, 404; fearfully punished, 407; prevalent, 451.
Familists, their belief on election, i. 229, 233.
Fathers, their doctrines not to be implicitly and blindly followed, i. 218.
Fardingales and such like gear invented by the devil, ii. 108.
Farley, my lord of. See *Sir W. Hungerford*.
Feckenham, royal forest, ii. 414.
Ficino, commends shooting as an exercise, i. 197.
Fisher, Dr, bishop of Rochester, stigmatizes the commons with heresy, ii. 301; was attainted, 365.
Flacius, Math. Clavis Sac. Scrip. i. 385.
Flagellants, who they were, i. 465.
Flesh, resisteth the Spirit, i. 228.
Flower, the same yields honey or venom according to the spirit of the gatherer, ii. 335.
Folkes, Table of English silver Coins, i. 95, 137.
Forefathers, we must seek not what they did, but what they should have done, i. 97.
Forest, friar John, his execution and sayings, i. xi. 266; an account of him, ii. 391; is accompanied in Newgate by White friars and Carthusians, 392.
Forgiveness of our debtors must precede our petition for pardon, i. 422, 428; the doctrine of reciprocal forgiveness, 424. See also *Sin*.
Foss-way, Roman road, Latimer lives near, ii. 364.
Fox, Dr, writes to the vice-chancellor of Cambridge, i. iv.; his letter to Cromwell, ii. 379.
Foxe, John, his Acts and Monuments, referred to, i. i. ii. iii. v. vi.—xiv. 46, 81, 222, 250, 321, 322, 440; ii. 219, 221, 229, 250, 262, 265, 270, 278, 282, 289, 291, 297, 305—309, 317, 321, 322, 327, 328, 334, 360, 378, 418—420, 422, 423, 428, 444.
Franciscans. See *Grey friars*.

Freese, punished for selling scriptures, ii. 306.
Freher, Theatrum Viror. ii. 349.
Friars' coat, is a feigned armour, i. 29; sold their coats and cowls for people to be buried in, ii. 200, 332; cowl said to take away part of purgatory, 362.
Friars, the White, of Doncaster, confined in Newgate, the prior executed, ii. 392.
Friday sermons, the, gathered by T. Some, i. 82.
Friendship, once broken will never be well made whole again, i. 19; friends when most needed are asleep, 228.
Fuller, Worthies of England, i. 113; Church History, ii. 368.
Fysher, John, canon of St Mary's, Warwick, ii. 396.

G.

Game of Triumph, i. 9.
Gaming, laws relating to, i. 372.
Ganlyne, Frere, ii. 388.
Garden, meditations for a, i. 225, 236.
Gardiner, Stephen, bishop, deprived, and committed to the Tower, i. 321, ii. 270.
Garret or Gerrard, Thomas, martyred in Smithfield, ii. 418.
Gaufridus, Fr. de Bello-Loco, i. 95.
George, David, his followers, i. 229, 233.
Gentiles, who are, ii. 46.
German protestants and papists, compromise between, i. 147.
Gervayes, abbey of, i. 93.
Giving is gaining, if we give as we should, i. 409.
Gloucester, provided with a school, &c. by Cromwell, ii. 393, 418.
Gloucester, duke of, quarrel with cardinal Beaufort, i. 118; death of, 119.
Glover, Robert, the martyr, and his brother John, ii. 84, 419.
Gnathos and parasites, smell-feasts, are not to be followed, i. 124.
God, his word is our light, i. 90; will recompense his forbearance with grievous punishments, 106; in our deeds too many of us deny him, 106; is against private authority, 115;

his book has been preserved by miracle, 120; how to come to him in adversity, i. 142, ii. 141; is the father of widows and orphans, i. 146; visits by preaching and vengeance, 147; blessing cometh of keeping his word, 170, 193; is not to be tempted, 205; punishes our sin by not hearing our prayers, 230; giveth time for repentance after his threatenings, 242, 245, 541; sons of, who they were, i. 242, ii. 99; his proverb, i. 259; his providence is over all, i. 263, ii. 30; is Lord over all, i. 374; is omniscient and omnipotent, ii. 30, 173, 336; defends those that cleave to him, i. 264, ii. 153; his mercy greater than our iniquity, i. 267; his promises are not believed, 269; giveth men riches sufficient for exercise of faith and charity, 280; his host is always victorious, i. 285, ii. 133; he must open the heart of sinners, i. 285; granteth as much to two or three gathered in his name as to thousands, 288; giveth wisdom to his elect to escape snares, i. 293, ii. 153; example of, i. 294, ii. 153; give to him what are his, i. 295, ii. 169; what things are his, i. 303; is the only judge of kings, 300; his kingdom to be first sought, and all other things will be added, 302, 337, 359; is not honoured with tapers and candles; his true service, i. 305, ii. 94; his love towards us, i. 333, ii. 86, 126, 205; hath no respect to persons, i. 337, 391, ii. 93, 201; is Father of and to all, i. 337; what is meant by his name, 345; by whom it was and is hallowed, 347; his will is to be submitted to, i. 348, ii. 185; and done, i. 384; created, ruleth, and assisteth all things, 355; setteth up and pulleth down kings, i. 356; hears the cry of the oppressed, i. 357, ii. 141; his judgments are just, i. 364; his will is in part unsearchable, in part revealed in the new and old testaments, i. 369; came not to send peace but a sword, the meaning of, 337; despisers of his word, 385; nothing disobeyeth him but man, 387; his liberality, 397; before him all are beggars, 397; his storehouse, 399; he is to be trusted both for soul and body, i. 402, ii. 153, 154, 203, 443; outward appearances shew not who are in his favour, i. 403; forgiveth man *et a culpa et a pœna* of his sins, 426; tempteth us for our profit, 435; suffereth us not to be tempted beyond what we can bear, i. 436, ii. 141; accepteth us and our works through Christ, i. 167, 330, 420, 453, ii. 85, 140, 151; sends us temptations, i. 466; why he does so, ii. 184; we see him by faith, i. 485; his word better than peace, 487; the armour of, 492; hath delivered us from gross ignorance, 498; his word is our spiritual sword, 505; he loveth a cheerful obeyer, i. 513, ii. 112; he, and not saints, to be followed in our vocation, i. 517, ii. 88, 153, 186, 234; the dishonour of him ought to grieve man, i. 518; can preserve from perishing those educated in false doctrine, 526; hearing of his word is not for that reason to be slighted, 528; his word shall lead us to salvation, 531; we became his children through Christ, i. 535, ii. 99; his love greater than a parent's, i. 535, 537; is always able and ready to help us, 536, ii. 141, 153, 334; his love expressed, i. 536; his general will is expressed in decalogue, 537; his special will, 537, 538; is a God of amity and concord, 540; why he answers not our prayers immediately, 547; his gifts not to be abused, ii. 2; to mistrust his promises is to make him a liar, 36; spared not his only Son for us, 103, 205; all that fear and love him and repent are accepted, 122; his wisdom not according to our wisdom, 126; dwelleth in the faithful spiritually, 134; his promises cannot be stolen from us, 155; at his own time confounds the devil, 185; we must call upon him in all afflictions, 185, 213, 234; but conditionally, 185; he will send a Comforter, 213; we are justified by his free gift, not by our merits, 74, 194;

respecteth not diversity of works, but of faith, 201; looketh not to the gift, but to the spirit of the giver, 202; hateth not riches, but the abuse of them, 202; if he send riches, refuse them not, 214; he hath always a church, 215; our infidelity causeth him to appear to neglect us, 224; his commands must take precedence of our imaginings, 238, 354; is able to defend his faith without man's assistance, 308; must be trusted, 435; happiness of those who die for his sake, 444.

God's people, may be governed by kings, i. 172. See *Faithful.*

Godwin, de *Præsulibus,* i. 123, 272, 321, 369, 377, 379, 384.

Goodrick, Richard, an eminent lawyer, ii. 428.

Goodryche, master, preaches against Latimer, ii. 225.

Good Friday, sermon on, i. 216.

Gorrham, or de Gorrain, Nicholas, his commentaries, i. 199.

Gorton, Richard, D.D., recommended by Latimer to Cromwell, ii. 386.

Gosnal, John, solicitor-general, ii. 428.

Gospel, the, comforteth, i. 61; some are professors of for the bread's sake, 502; a brief sum of the, 284; not palatable to the worldly, 313; was preached in paradise, ii. 3; was revealed unto Abraham, 4; the preaching of it is universal, 205; called the word of the cross, 203; must meet with persecution, 303.

Gospellers, mock, i. 67; worse than papists, 256; divers sorts of, 286, 360; talkers, not walkers, are not true gospellers, ii. 92.

Gostwyck, master, commissioner to rate ecclesiastical preferments, ii. 368.

Gratiæ expectativæ, i. 49.

Greene, Dr, letter from Latimer to, ii. 295.

Gregory I. appoints stations, i. 49; a worthy saying of, 161.

Gregory Nazianzen distinguishes the *Cœna Judaica* and *Cœna Dominica,* ii. 263.

Grenewode, Mr, i. iv.; impugns Latimer's preaching; letter to him from Latimer, ii. 356.

Grey friars, receive no bribes themselves, but have others to receive for them, i. 189; divided into conventuals and observants; beware of them, they are spies, 287; story of a limitour, 524.

Grimsthorpe, sermons at, i. 447, ii. 96, 111, 129.

Gybson, Thomas, printer of first concordance to English new testament, a suitor to Cromwell, ii. 380.

H.

Haberdyne, master. See *Hubberdin.*

Halcot, or Holcot, Robert, referred to, ii. 319.

Hales, Mr, i. 99, 101; sergeant Hales, ii. 419, 428.

Hales, the blood of, i. xi.; what it was 231; report of the commissioners appointed to examine it, ii. 407; the superstition of refuted by argument, 364; the secretary Cromwell sends for Coots, who preached at Hales, 374; the abbot of, 380; the relics of, 409.

Hall, Chronicle, ii. 33, 301, 392, 402.

Hampson, Medii Ævi Kalend. ii. 100.

Hampton, the priest of, ii. 381.

Hanged, an innocent man for a guilty, i. 191.

Harleian MSS. ii. 218, 221, 265, 317, 319—321.

Harman, or John Voysey, bishop of Exeter, i. 272.

Harpagus and Astyages, the story of, i. 457.

Hasted, Hist. of Kent, ii. 221.

Haynes, Simon, president of Queens' college, Cambridge, ii. 387.

Hearne, Ben. Abbat, i. xi. 231, ii. 408.

Heart is inscrutable to us, i. 149, ii. 80; example thereof at Oxford, i. 149; Jeremiah describeth the heart of man, 159.

Heathen rulers more merciful than some christian, ii. 65.

Heavens, two, spiritual, i. 385; corporal, 387; the way to, 488; the joys of pass all men's thoughts, 531; where it is, ii. 86.

Hell, what it is, i. 220, ii. 191; degrees of punishment in, i. 11, 224; to say that Christ suffered in it derogates nothing from his death, 236; two dishes in, 238; the nature of the fire in, ii. 235, 360.

Helvidius, his heresy on the brethren of Christ, &c., ii. 105.

Henry VII., anecdote of, ii. 150.

Henry VIII., i. vi.; licenses reading of the Bible in English, ii. 240; his answers to Latimer's arguments against purgatory, 245; letter to him from Latimer for restoring liberty to read the scripture, 297; allows all admitted by the universities to preach without control of any, 329; refers sir Thomas More to bishop Stokesley, 333.

Henry II. of France, at war with Charles V., i. 390.

Herbert, ii. 367; Life of Hen. VIII., i. 395, 402.

Hereford, bishop of, ii. 379, 382. See *Dr Edward Fox.*

Herod, what he was, i, 289, ii. 130, 152; his cunning, ii. 131, 152.

Herolt, John, or Discip. Prompt. Exempl. i. 497.

Hilary, referred to, ii. 277; his meaning of peace, i. 487; mentions no middle state, ii. 247; asserts the bodily presence in the sacrament, 267.

Hill, Dr Adam, his controversy with Dr Richard Humes, i. 233.

——————, Defence of the article of Creed, "Descent into hell," i. 233.

Hilley, Dr Richard, ii. 322.

Hilsey, Dr John, preaches against Latimer, ii. 225; bishop of Rochester, 369.

Hilsey, Primers, ii. 369.

Hist. Eccles. Anton. Sabellicus, i. 129.

Hoare, Ancient Wilts, ii. 364.

Holbeach, Henry, succeeds More as prior of Worcester, ii. 371, 373; solicits to preach before the king, 412.

Holcot. See *Halcot.*

Holidays, abuse of, i. 52; right use of, i. 471, ii. 39.

Holinshed, i. xi. 81, 266, ii. 367, 392, 394, 408, 415.

Holsten, Codex Regularum, i. 189.

Holy beads, bells, &c. See *Superstitions.*

Holy Ghost, the sin against, i. 266,

462, ii. 441; will support us against adversaries of the truth, i. 268.

Homilies, called homelies, i. 121.

Homily against adultery, i. 244.

Honour, although a gift of God, is used as a snare by the devil, i. 430.

Hooper, (Park. Soc. ed.) i. 474.

Horace, de Art. Poet. i. 92; Epist. 431.

Hospinian, de Orig. Monach. i. 189, ii. 196; Hist. Sac. 265.

Hubberdin or Heberdynne, Haberdyne or Hyberden, i. viii. ii. 365; preaches against Latimer, ii. 225, 358; account of him, 229—232, 234; a man of little learning and unstable wit, a lickspittle, 365.

Hugo de Vienna says death is more cause of rejoicing than of weeping, ii. 245.

Humbled,' some that have been, are to be exalted, i. 544.

Humes, Alexander, controversy on creed, i. 233.

Hun, Richard, the story of alluded to, ii. 362.

Hungerford, sir Walter, sends to Latimer with a citation to appear before bishop of London, ii. 350.

Hunter, Hist. of South Yorksh. ii. 292.

Hussey, lord, in the Tower, i. 163.

Hutchinson's Works, (Park. Soc. ed.) ii. 114.

Hypocrites, shall reign over us if we repent not, i. 91; their salutation and conduct, 289; cannot be known in this world, ii. 62; known only to God, 130; assert they have works of supererogation, i. 482, 521.

I.

Idolatry, to be guarded against, ii. 234; the reward of, 259.

Ignorance, wilful, is no excuse, i. 385; is a sin, ii. 211.

Images, the abuse of, i. 52; prevented by the Church of England, 54; deceitful and juggling images to be taken away, *ib.*; of saints, not to be prayed unto, ii. 233, 333; the right use of, 233; of our lady of Worcester (statue of some bishop), of Walsingham, of Ipswich, and of Doncaster, and Penrice, would make a jolly muster in Smithfield, 395.

INDEX.

Impropriations, i. 100.
Ingworth, Richard, visitor of monasteries, ii. 400.
Interim, the, drawn up by Romish and popish divines, i. 305.
Ippiswitch, (Ipswich,) our lady of, i. 53.
Isaac, Edward, visits Bainham in Newgate, ii. 221.
Isaiah meddles with the coin of the mint; with vintners, i. 137.
Islip, Simon, archbishop of Canterbury, i. 55.

J.

Jairus and his daughter, i. 533 ; a believer, 534; an example in his fleeing to Christ and in his paternal affection, 535, 537; in the constancy of his faith, 546.
Jerome, referred to, i. 173, ii. 119, 198, 319, 344, 352; ever thought he heard the last trumpet, i. 530, ii. 60; will not believe that a great winedrinker is chaste, ii. 63; his treatise against Helvidius, 105; mentions no purgatory, 247; says that any assertion beyond scripture may be rejected with the same facility as admitted, 249 ; declares the church to consist of those in whom knowledge and confession of faith resides, 313 ; declares one who wrests the meaning of any expression bears false witness, 315, 325; accused of corrupting the scripture, 342; says we shew our faith by our works, 343; shews how true preachers under persecution should conduct themselves, *ib.*; calls the prophets, apostles, and evangelists, the mountains of the old and new testament, *ib.*; approves of laymen reading scripture, 344; declares that honouring and trusting in ministers is different, 347.
Jerusalem, the destruction of, ii. 46 ; the name of changed by Adrian, 48 ; the rebuilding of by Julian, *ib.*
Jervaulx, or Jorvalles, abbey of, i. 93.
Jewel of Joy, Becon's, i. iii.
Jews, and Englishmen compared, i. 111, 118, 139, 177; offence of, in asking a king, 187, 192; sold at thirty a-penny, ii. 46; cause of their destruction, 47, 49; look for a worldly powerful saviour, 124 ; why they met three times a-year at Jerusalem, 156; taught commonly by parables, 210.
Jenkyns' Remains of Cranmer, ii. 379, 386—392, 428.
Joan Butcher, or Bouchier, of Kent, her heresy, ii. 114.
John de Turrecremata, bishop and cardinal, account of him, ii. 349.
John's disciples esteemed him greater than Christ, ii. 69 ; his question to Christ, 70.
Johnson, Collect. of all Ecclesiastical Laws, i. 56.
John's, St, college, Cambridge, concerning master of, ii. 378, 381, 382.
John-Ten-Commands, friar, story of, i. 524.
John XXII., pope, the decretals of, i. 212.
Jortin, Life of Erasmus, i. 46.
Josephus referred to, ii. 89, 146.
Journals of House of Commons, i. xii.
Jovius Paulus, Descrip. Britan. i. 197.
Joye, Geo., Conjecture of end of world, i. 365.
Jubilaries, i. 49.
Jubilee, first, instituted, i. 49.
Judges, will not hear poor men's causes, i. 128; follow gifts, 140; the common manner of a wicked judge, 145 ; are afraid to hear the poor, 145; a bribing judge flayed alive, 146; acts of to be judged of charitably, 148, 160 ; must minister justice speedily, 155; in ancient times could be easily approached, 156 ; if just, are to be honoured, 157 ; unjust, the place of punishment of, 158; why wicked judges confess their faults, 159; the sign of the judge's skin, 181, 260; bribing judges have been long suffered, 193 ; exhorted to avoid bribes and delays, 171 ; bribed in a case of infanticide, 191 ; required to judge justly, 501 ; the elect shall be judges, not judged, at the day of judgment, ii. 191 ; judges are not impeccable, 325.
Judgment, rash, condemned, i. 382 ; the day of, ii. 45, 55, 59 ; not known even to the angels, 45 ; preparation for it, 60 ; form and manner of judg-

ment on the last day, 191; private judgment to be exercised, 347.
Julian, the apostate, attempts to rebuild Jerusalem, ii. 48.
Julius II., pope, his oppressions and persecutions, i. 181, ii. 333.
Jurors, advice to, i. 379.
Jury, bribed with twelve crowns, i. 190, 380.
Just man may not be deposed from his office, i. 193.
Justice is to be done by all to all, i. 503.

K.

Katherine, queen, her confessor, i. 266.
Kempe, Hist. Notices of the Church of St Martin-le-Grand, i. 196.
Kenelm, the shrine of, ii. 400.
Kennet, Case of Impropriations, i. 100.
Kent, maid of, i. xi.
Ketherminster, (Kidderminster), townclerk of, confessed his folly, ii. 398.
Keys, the authority of, is to loose from guilt of sin, according to Christ's word, ii. 363.
Kill, thou shalt not, applied by the Jews to the use of material weapons, i. 10; may be done in two ways, 13.
King, Dr, referred to, ii. 380.
Kings, emperors, and magistrates, are bound to obey the scriptures, i. 85, 86, 250; the king may correct the preacher, 86; the election of, appointed by God, 87, 89, 193; the dishonour of, 94; the wife he ought to choose, 94; may impose taxes, 97, 299; his treasure should be ready, 299; may require too much, i. 98, ii. 260; his honour, what it is, i. 99; although children, are still kings, 117; the office of a king, 119; the example of proud kings is not to be followed, 124, 132; a king has clawbacks and pickmotes, 133; our duty towards him, his laws and authority, i. 148, 373, ii. 260; kings must not look at faults through their fingers, i. 152; should be learned, 184; title of king is lawful, 193; a great and chargeable office, 193; is the high vicar of God, 204; the deputy of God, 444; a king's labour, 215; abuse of his officers, 261; must be obeyed even in unjust demands, i. 300, ii. 260; his dues ought to be paid, i. 307; paying them makes no man poorer, 301; monition to, 355; lesson to, 386; to be prayed for, 391; fighting against the king's enemies is in God's service, 416, 496; kings reign through God, 444; the king entreated to remedy corruption in judges, 191; required to look to his office himself, 273; and take example by David, ii. 308; by the king of Denmark, i. 274; who are the queen's enemies, ii. 260; God to be obeyed in preference to kings, 260, 298; they stand in need of the merits of Christ's passion as much as their subjects, 298; king's authority used by prelates as a cloke to persecution, 305.
Kingdom of God, what it is, i. 357; beginneth in this world, 358; to be first sought, 359; is double, of grace and of glory, 361; of heaven, who shall enter into it, 384; sermon on the parable of, 455.
Kingston, sir Wm., constable of the Tower, ii. 411.
Knight's Life of Colet, i. 58.
Know thyself, i. 368; vexation and trouble make us know ourselves, 480.
Knowledge maketh proud, i. 230; precedeth belief, ii. 74; certain and clear knowledge are different, 337; knowledge without zeal shall be punished, *ib.*

L.

Labour is ours, the increase God's, i. 213, 404, 408, ii. 39; all labour is not godly, i. 376; nor to be condemned because sometimes useless, 540; the reward of, ii. 39.
Lactantius, i. 106.
Lady, our, how may be likened to a saffron-bag, i. 60.
Lamb, Dr, Collect. of Letters, i. v., ii. 356, 378.
Lambarde, Dict. Angl. i. 476.
Lambert, martyr, i. x.
Lanfrank, bishop, claims supremacy for Peter, i. 209.
Landlords obtain acts of parliament to

inclose their lands, i. 248; are become graziers, 279.
Large, sir, a poor priest, ii. 383, 384.
Latimer, his parentage, i. 101; birth, sent to Cambridge, i.; chosen fellow of Clare hall, M.A., is a zealous papist, his acquaintance with Bilney, i. ii., ii. 52; forsakes the school-doctors, i., ii. 335; account of his sermons; bishop of Ely forbids his preaching, preaches in Austin Friars, papists complain to cardinal Wolsey, iii.; vice-chancellor calls parties before him, iv.; appointed to determine lawfulness of king's marriage, is favourable to the divorce, v., ii. 340; selected to meet Oxford divines, i. v.; B.D. ii. 218; is appointed a royal chaplain, retires to West Kington, vi.; is cited to appear before bishop of London, i. vii., ii. 219, 323, 334; writes to the primate, ii. 219; appeals to his own ordinary, is excommunicated and imprisoned, i. vii.; appeals, is inhibited from diocese of London, complaint to convocation against him, Hubberdin opposes him, viii., ii. 225; articles imputed to him by Dr Powell of Salisbury, ii. 225; Cranmer empowers him to withdraw licences of preachers, is elected and consecrated bishop of Worcester, i. ix.; takes cognisance of Crewkehorne and Lambert, x.; preaches at the execution of friar Forrest, xi., ii. 392; resigns his bishoprick, is placed in ward, i. xi.; is committed to the Tower, xii., ii. 258; declines restoration to the see of Worcester, resides with Cranmer, xii.; is summoned to London, and committed to the Tower, sent to Oxford, xiii.; disputes there with Smith, Cartwright, and Harpsfield, ii. 250; excommunicated, committed to gaol, is condemned, i. xiii. 323, ii. 292; and martyred along with Ridley; his last words, i. xiii. 323; list of his works, xiv.; editions consulted, xv.; his sermons gathered by Augustine Bernher, xvi.; is troubled with poor men's suits, 127; called a seditious fellow, and accused to Henry VIII. as such, 134; his answer, 135; ground of the charge, is noted for singularity, 136; was very scrupulous in the time of his blindness, i. 138, ii. 332; a bishop angry with him, i. 154; expects execution, 164; his remarks on a case of murder not well taken, 194; his father taught him to shoot, 197; gives place to Robin Hood's men, 208; his opinion on Christ's descent into hell, 234; seeks no blind believer in his words, 236; advice to king about marriage, takes his last farewell, 243, 252, 257; craves the king to restore the discipline to the church, 258; his answer on transubstantiation at his examination, 276; his first wish to his enemy, 278; pleads for a maintenance to schools, &c. 291; in his examination before bishops is questioned subtlely, 294; Bernher's account of him, 319; foretells the troubles that occurred, 320; Careless informs him of coming danger, his conduct, and behaviour before the council, 321; an example to bishops, 322; is godfather to a child while in prison, 355; his manner of teaching, 341; a story of him at Cambridge, 499; articles to which he was required to subscribe, ii. 218; visits Bainham in Newgate, 222; preaches at Bristol, 225; answers the articles brought against him by Dr Powell, 225, 358; his injunctions to the prior and convent of St Mary's, Worcester, 240; injunctions to the clergy of his diocese, 242; his arguments against purgatory, 245; against transubstantiation, 252; and the mass, 253; complains of his treatment, 256; studies the testament with Cranmer, Ridley, and Bradford, 259; disputes with Dr Weston, 262; his opinions were confirmed by Cranmer's book, 265; was no Lutheran, 265; his faith, 276; is examined before the commissioners, 278; his dress, 279; is urged by bishop of Lincoln to recant, 279; his protestation against the authority of the pope, 285; denieth the carnal presence of Christ in the sacrament, 285; his last appearance before the commissioners, the bishop of Lincoln again addresses

him, 289; charged by Dr Sherwood with rash judgment, &c., his answer, 309; his letter to Hubberdin, 317; defends his preaching in Abchurch, London, 324; his commendation of Bilney, 330; asserts the performance of his duty, 331; the three creeds which he believes, 332; formerly believed supremacy of the pope, dispensations of pluralities, purgatory and the pope's power therein, that a friar could not be afraid of death, and when sick, wished many times to be a friar, 332; believed in assistance of images of saints, 333; letters to sir E. Baynton, 322, 334; maintains the statements in his former letter to sir E. Baynton, 336; letter to archbishop of Canterbury expostulating with him, 351; himself limits his questioners, 353; allows the lawfulness of the use of images, pilgrimages, praying to saints, to be mindful of souls in purgatory, 353; declines to subscribe the propositions required of him, 355; letter to Greenwood, 356; professes his intention of persevering in his preaching, 357; letter to Morice, 357; LETTERS to secretary Cromwell, 367—418; regarding the late prior of Worcester, 371; with M. Coot's sermon, 374; with a prophecy, 375; respecting Silvester Dario's benefices, 376; regarding St John's college and Clare hall, Cambridge, 377; concerning the 'Institution of a Christian Man,' 379; is in peril of great sickness, 380; letter to Cromwell concerning master Lucy, &c. 381; regarding sir Large, 382; on birth of prince, 385; recommending Gorton and Clarke, 386; fears consumption, 386; about the monks of Evesham and recommending Dr Barns, 389; introducing an honest poor gentleman, 389; regarding the misbehaviour of certain priests, 390; concerning friar Forest, 391; about the lands of Droitwich, 393; regarding Warwick college, 396; Mr Pye and Droitwich, 397; about Mr Lucy, 399, 410; and Mr Clapton, 399; respecting the bloody abbot, 400; regarding master Wattwood, a lecher, fighter, and disquieter of his company, 401, 406, 416; on behalf of the city of Worcester, 403; regarding John Scurfield, 404; recommending Mr Acton, 405; and Richard Edwards, 406; and the abbot of Evesham, 406; exposing the imposition of the blood of Hales, 407, 409; concerning Whitborne or Bedyll, prior of Great Malvern, 410; with an account of his income, 412; suspects Antony Barker, 413; recommends the sheriff to be master of the game of the forest of Feckenham, 414; respecting master Moore, sir John Ashley, and Mr Tracy, 415; Furnes fools, 417; about grammar-school at Gloucester, 418; recounts various suits, 418; letter to a certain gentleman, 419; to one in prison for the faith, 429; from Bocardo to the unfeigned lovers of truth, 434; letter of thanks to Mr Wilkinson out of Bocardo, 444.

Law of God, feareth, i. 61; is a looking-glass, ii. 6.

―――― is badly administered, i. 128; may be used as an ordinary help against adversaries, 151; the reason of it is the soul of it, the end, that no man be injured, 182; how a Christian may go to law, 481; must be obeyed, i. 512, ii. 179; laws general and special, ii. 6.

Lawyers, have too much, i. 98; are very diligent about their own profit, 110; are like Switzers, 127; their covetousness hath almost devoured England, 318; some are false and greedy, 344; they shall be judged, ii. 56.

Laymen, not all children of the devil, i. 43; some are able and willing to fill the place of bishops, 122; swallow up spiritual livings, 317; not to be discouraged from reading good books, ii. 244; entreated to leave forged sacrifices, 259.

Learned, least need expositions, i. 34; are not learned if without Christ, ii. 258, 260.

Learning, the new, proved to be old, ii. 318.

INDEX.

Leaven of the Pharisees, what it is, i. 257, 258.
Lechery, the sin of Sodom and Gomorrah, prevalent in England, i. 244, 257; Moses' law against it ought to be restored, 258; the king requested to punish it, 276.
Lee, Dr Edward, archbishop of York, ii. 378.
Legenda Sanctorum, ii. 132.
Legh, Dr, testifies to prevalence of open adultery, &c., i. 244; Latimer refers the king to him, ii. 372.
Leland, Itinerary, ii. 295, 368, 395, 402.
Le Neve, ii. 370, 377, 378, 387.
Letters on Suppression of Monasteries, i. x. 93, 244, 474, ii. 225, 372, 378, 386, 394, 406, 417.
Lewis IX. of France, story of, i. 95.
Liars, their inheritance and numbers, i. 500; why they are not punished now as they were in the days of Ananias, 503.
Liber Festivalis, ii. 132.
Liberty, must be subject to charity, ii. 80.
Licence, especial, examples of, i. 516.
Lichfield, or Lychfield, abbot of Evesham, pawns the jewels, ii. 400.
Life is not to be thrown away for trifles, ii. 223; life eternal is the free gift of God, ii. 74.
Limitour, a friar, story of one, i. 524.
Lincoln, bishop of, address to Latimer before the commissioners, ii. 279.
Lingard, Dr, animadverts upon Latimer, i. 161.
Linus referred to, ii. 273.
Liturgies of Edw. VI., (Parker Soc. edit.) i. 460.
Live within measure, i. 107.
Lives of the Fathers, ii. 73.
Livius, Titus, ii. 146.
Loins girded, Paul's meaning of, i. 28.
Lombard, Peter, writes that Lucifer has his being in *aëre caliginoso*, i. 27.
London, full of pride, &c. i. 63; warning to London to repent, 64; as it was, and as it is, 64; full of whoredom; a privileged place in it for whoredom, 196; mayor and aldermen attend St Mary, Bishopsgate, in their robes at Easter, ii. 341.

London, bishop of. See *Dr Stokesley*.
Lord protector should himself hear poor men's suits, i. 127.
Lords lieutenant introduced, i. 175.
Lord's supper, celebration of, hath been long abused, i. 236, 459; primitive practice of, who eats it worthily, 237; why ordained, 459; holy loaves for, how furnished, 460; the benefits to partakers of, i. 460, 461, ii. 127; papistical doctrine of, confuted, ii. 251; what instituted for, 255; partaken of by women, 263.
Lord's Prayer, is the sum of all prayers, i. 327, 341, 443; few can truly say "Our Father," 339; sermons, on first petition, 341; on second petition, 354; on third petition, 368; on fourth petition, 389; on fifth petition, 413; on sixth and seventh petitions, 428; on the conclusion, 444.
Love, and not a pennyworth of ale, will remove thy neighbour's malice, i. 20, ii. 2; of self, the root of all mischief, i. 434.
Love one another, sermon on, i. 447; Christians known by love, 448; daughter of faith; is eternal, 449; seeketh reformation, not destruction, 451; the reward of, 452; the consummation of the law, 452; is the livery of Christ, ii. 1; one another, 88.
Lovell, sir Thomas, high steward of the University of Cambridge, account of him, ii. 296.
Lucifer has his being in *aëre caliginoso*, i. 27.
Lucy, sir Thomas, commended of Latimer, ii. 381.
Ludovicus, S. i. 96.
Luther, referred to, ii. 313, 314; *de Privata Missa*, 265; was called on by his enemies to work miracles, i. 212; was in agony of the spirit, ii. 52; the devil endeavoured to bring him to desperation for saying mass, 265; proclamation issued by instigation of prelates against the works of, 305.
Lyndewode, i. 54, 56.
Lyra referred to, ii. 313; declares that the opinions of the fathers may be rejected in things not determined by scripture, 248.

[LATIMER, II.]

M.

Magdalenes, all be, in falling into, but not in forsaking, our sins, i. 16.

Magistrates, wherefore ordained, i. 67, 350; are bound to obey God's word, 85, 86; some follow gifts, 140; some are painful and good, 142; deeds of, to be judged of charitably, 148; the office of, is grounded on God's word, 298; must see the people instructed, 316; and the wicked punished, ii. 196; are God's ordinary ministers, i. 373; how they may become esteemed, 381; necessary, 390; must be obeyed, ii. 135.

Magna Britan. ii. 295.

Maid of Kent, Joan Butcher, her heresy, ii. 114.

Major, John, Mag. Spec. Exemp., i. 426.

Malvern, priory of, ii. 410.

Man, is born for man, i. 81; requires recreation, 196; arraigned, must answer for himself, no lawyer allowed, 182; dieth not before his time, 265; has plenty of riches for the exercise of faith and charity, 280; no man is poorer for giving king's dues, alms, &c., 301, 408, 513; his duty to his wife, 343, 352; must labour in his calling, 359, 402, 412, 442, 508, 530, 537, ii. 94; his greatest promotion in this world, i. 361; men are God's lieutenants, or deputies, 375; ruined by the devil, *ib.*; he may serve the devil by prayer, 377; of his own power he is able to do nothing, 388, 432; all are beggars before God, 398; no man may do what he listeth with his goods, 398, 407, 414; rich, ought to succour poor, is God's treasurer, 399; can do nothing but sin, i. 429, ii. 113; shall always have trouble in this world, i. 436; man's example cannot make evil good, 516; cannot merit heaven, 521; should settle his affairs in this life by testament, 540; man's necessity is God's time, 543; is born in iniquity, ii. 101; Christ hath delivered him, 102; must submit to the will of Christ, 113; and not murmur, 115, 185; if so, he shall lack nothing, 116; may sometimes make merry, 162; is the cause of his own damnation, 192.

Manichees and Manes, account of, i. 201.

Manuaries, consecrated gloves, i. 50.

Marcionites, their opinion of Christ's humanity, ii. 98.

Marriage, spoken against, why, i. 169; is ungodly without parents' consent, 170; advice to king about, 243; state and abuse of in England, 243, 244; of priests, is lawful, i. 293, ii. 162; when lawful, when unlawful, i. 366; is honourable, i. 393, ii. 160, 162; single life is preferable, if without sin, i. 394; a comfortable lesson for the married, ii. 161, 165; privy contracts of marriage to be prevented, i. 244.

Marriage of Christ to his church, i. 456; when made, 467; the marriage-feast, the sauces, the sweetmeats, 467; who are the callers to it, their reward, 468.

Martial, quoted, ii. 330.

Martyr, Peter, in England, i. 141.

Martyrologe after the use of the church of Salisbury, ii. 80.

Martyrs, from their ashes thousands were stirred up, i. 105; their blood is as the seed of the fruit of the gospel, 361; the cause, not the death, makes the martyr, ii. 281.

Maruphus, Raphael, seller of dispensations and indulgences in London, ii. 349.

Mary, (king's sister), i. 91; (queen), submits herself to the pope's authority and reconciliation, ii. 280.

Mary, St, hospital, Bishopsgate, London, ii. 341.

Mary, virgin, not without sin, i. 383, ii. 117, 157, 228, 358; was vainglorious, i. 383, ii. 117, 163, 164; doctors call her arrogant, i. 384, 515; her psalter, 425; her faith increased with temptation, ii. 93; her obedience to the magistrates, 96; whether she had any more children than Christ, 105; her poverty, 108, 300; suffered as other mothers, 115; was saved by her faith, 116, 227, 230; not by her maternity, 227; is not to be worshipped, 153; in her necessity applied to Christ,

163; was saved by him, 226; her relation to him, 227; her true honour, 228; "Ave Maria" is a salutation, not a prayer, 229, 360.

Masses, forbidden to be sold, i. 55; sacrifice of the mass a horrible blasphemy, 445, ii. 440; a foul abomination, i. 237, ii. 440; an useless foolery, ii. 58, 60, 192; a daring presumption, 253; ought now to cease, 225; the four marrow-bones of, 257; no sacrifice for sin, 259.

Massmongers, usurp Christ's office, i. 275; mislead the people, i. 314, ii. 441; deny Christ, are enemies to the cross, i. 522.

Masters, their duty to servants, i. 351, 394, 538; and to their cattle, 395.

Masters' Hist. of Corp. Christi Coll., Cambridge, ii. 376.

Maxentius, a gainsayer, i. 129.

Maximus, Valerius, i. 146.

Means, are not to be despised, i. 528; but used, 543,

Meek, who they are, i. 480; their reward, 482.

Melancthon, referred to, ii. 315; coming to England, i. 141; his opinion of the old doctors, ii. 268.

Melchior Canus, ii. 226.

Merciful, who they are, i. 484.

Mercy preferred to oblation, i. 23.

Merit-mongers, are murmurers against God, ii. 200; monks and friars were, *ib.*

Midwives, are superstitious, ii. 114; were licensed by the archbishop or bishop, *ib.*

Mildenham, Thomas de, prior of Worcester, ii. 371.

Ministers, the office of, and requisites for, i. 35; will be called to account, 38; are God's vicars, 39; ought not to be comptrollers of the mint, 67; a more proper name than priests, ii. 264; are to be obeyed so long as they minister the word of God, 346. See also *Clergy.*

Ministration of the word is effectual, whatsoever the minister be, ii. 347.

Miracles, supposed to be performed in West of England, i. 55; performed by Christ to confirm his doctrines, ii. 160, 165.

Missal oblation, one of the marrowbones of the mass, ii. 257.

Monasteries, (monk's houses,) widows buy livings in, i. 392; ignorance in, is intolerable, ii. 240; dissolved by act of parliament, 245.

Money will purchase no mercy on the day of judgment, i. 107; but may witness against us, 108; the fall of, caused great loss, ii. 112; will not procure freedom from the cross in this life, 430.

Monk, of Cambridge, the merry, i. 153, 170; monks and friars sold their coats and cowls for people to be buried in, ii. 260; are hypocrites and stir up rebellion, 301.

Monmouth, Humfrey, alderman of London, anecdote of, i. 440; an example to others, i. 441, ii. 387.

Moore, or More, William, late prior of Worcester, account of him, ii. 371.

More, sir Thomas, asserts that Bilney died a Roman catholic, i. 222; his testimony to prevalence of open adultery, 244; inquires about the cause of Goodwin sands, 251; gives place to sir R. Wingfield, ii. 296; writes against the gospel, 307; referred by Henry VIII. to bishop Stokesley, 333; his book against Tyndal referred to, 374; his works referred to, i. 52, 222, 244, 251, ii. 100, 239, 395.

Moreri, Dict. i. 426.

Morice, Wm., attached to the household of the lady Margaret, countess of Richmond, with his brother Ralph, secretary to archbishop Cranmer, visits Bainham in Newgate, ii. 222; letter from Latimer to him, 357.

Moses gave laws, but not the spirit to fulfil them, i. 453.

Mosheim, Inst. of Eccles. Hist. i. 160, 274, 425, 465; Comment. ii. 98.

Mourning, what sort maketh blessed, i. 479.

Mule, the gentleman's, i. 140.

Mumpsimus, he keeps his, origin of the saying, ii. 17, 211.

Murder cannot be purged without bloodshedding, i. 190.

N.

Nabuchadonoser sent by God to punish the Jews, i. 285.
Nash, Hist. of Worcestersh., ii. 372, 375, 376, 387, 389, 394, 398, 400—402, 409, 410, 414.
Neander, Hist. of Chris. Relig. and Church, by Rose, i. 201.
Neighbour, our conduct to, ii. 186.
Nero, i. 27; a gainsayer, 129; a persecutor, ii. 66.
Nestorians, deny a natural body to Christ, ii. 253.
Nevell, Mr, fellow of St John's college, Cambridge, goes to lord Cromwell, ii. 377; makes suit for friars' lands and a widow, 393.
Newburgh, Henry de, made St Mary's church, Warwick, collegiate, ii. 396.
Newcourt, Repertorium, ii. 323, 324, 365, 370.
New-fangled men, i. 90.
Nicene council, their minds changed by one old man, i. 288.
Nichols, Royal Wills, ii. 296.
Nichols, Hist. of Leicestershire, ii. 375, 410.
Nicholas I., pope, claims supremacy for Peter, i. 209.
Nicholas, Privy Purse Expenses, i. v.
——— Synopsis of Peerage, ii. 382, 386; Testam. Vetust. 388.
Nicholson, in prison for the truth, ii. 321.
Noblemen, most, are not sufficiently educated to be lords president, i. 69; their sons are unpreaching prelates, 102; the chief point of their calling, ii. 37.
Norfolk rebels, considered not the petition, "Thy will be done," i. 371; those who remained faithful suffered miserably, 376.
Northumbria, dissensions of, i. 271.
Novatians, deny the remission of sin, i. 425.

O.

Obedience, passive, to all laws, except to those against God, enforced, i. 371; what true obedience is, ii. 111; God suffereth not the obedient to perish, 112.

Oblations, what they are, i. 17; how to be made, 18; must be our own property, not another man's, 22; the oblation we ought to offer unto God, 74.
Octavius, his proclamation and taxation, ii. 96.
Œcolampadius, ii. 314.
Offences, be of two kinds, *acceptum* and *datum*, ii. 77; rash offences to be avoided, 81.
Offering-days, i. 23; offerings of the wise men to Christ, what they signified, ii. 132, 154.
Officers, king's, give and take bribes, i. 261; what officers ought to be, ii. 27.
Offices, are bought, i. 185, ii. 26; it is bribery, ought to be given to meet men, 185; ought not to be sought, ii. 30; nor accepted unless called thereto, ii. 31; if diligently fulfilled, God will aid us, 35.
Offices of faith and of love are different, example of, i. 449.
Officium Beatæ Virginis, i. 426.
Origen, referred to, ii. 276, 314; declares the ministration effectual, whatsoever the minister may be, 347.
Ovid, i. 415.

P.

Papacy, a poisoned and blasphemous doctrine, i. 313, ii. 147; fruits of, i. 47.
Paphnutius, i. 288.
Papists, are crafty disposers of God's mysteries, i. 37; wise in their generation, 38; deceive not God, but themselves, 39; doctrine of a daily expiatory sacrifice, i. 73, ii. 251; supremacy of the pope visible only to them, i. 206; abuse the name of the Lord, 288; similar to Pharisees, 287, 289; their vain inventions, 292; are ashamed to repent, 314; their doctrine of sacrifice for the dead, 515; of purgatory, i. 57, ii. 245; are enemies of the cross of Christ, i. 520, ii. 147; their doctrine of works satisfactory, i. 520; and of supererogation, 521; impute holiness to Christ's garments, 543; make Christ half a Saviour, ii. 124, 125, 146; make him

a judge, not a Redeemer, 146; their doctrine on marriage of priests abominable and false, 162; articles which Latimer was required to subscribe 218; opinions of the, 239; on transubstantiation, 251; papists use feigned sacrifices to get money, 259; have changed the holy communion into a private act, 261; and the prayers into a strange tongue, 261; condemn all translations of the scripture into common tongues, 320; wrest the scripture, i. 60, ii. 283, 320; some articles of their faith, ii. 332.

Pains of mind greater than those of body, i. 219, 233.

Parable, the meaning of, ii. 188; every one hath a certain scope, 199; Jews taught commonly by parables, 210.

Pardon-bowl, i. 50, 75; pardons, 49; a pardoner taken and deprived of his seal, ii. 400.

Parental affection less than God's for us, i. 535.

Parents sometimes unnatural, i. 536; Jairus is an example to follow, 537; ought not to be too careful or too careless of their children, ii. 158; parental authority, how far to be obeyed, 164, 202.

Parker, Acad. Hist. Cant. ii. 378.

Parliament may err, how its doings are to be interpreted, i. 182; one parliament will reform and put in order all things, 363.

Partakers of other men's sins, how, i. 134.

Patience is part of the livery of God, i. 450; a Christian must suffer patiently, ii. 185.

Patmore, in prison for the truth, ii. 321.

Patrons, the office of, tale of one, i. 186; sell their benefices, 290; what they strive together for, 290; many believe not in the immortality of the soul, 187.

Paul should be followed in preference to doctors, i. 121; would have been burned by the bishop of London, ii. 326; misreported in his words, 327.

Paul's Cross, i. 49.

Paul II., pope, i. 49.

Peace-makers, who are, i. 485.

Peculiars, some London churches were, ii. 323.

Pedaries, consecrated sandals, i. 50.

Pegge, Life of Bishop Grosseteste, i. 56, 122, 203, ii. 408.

Pen, made of the aiglet of a point, i. 162.

Penance and repentance is a salve for all sin, ii. 9; what penance consists of, *ib.*

Pentecostal, what it is, i. 135.

Perjury, common, i. 380.

Persecution, blessed are they who suffer for righteousness' sake, i. 487; shews forth who are reeds, ii. 82, 213; is the appointed treatment of true preachers, 303; a sure mark of true preaching, 303.

Persecutors should follow St Paul, ii. 308.

Petilianus, the epistle of, referred to, ii. 261.

Phicinus Marcelius. See *Ficino.*

Philips, in prison for the truth, ii. 321.

Philosophers held that God thought not of our affairs, i. 34.

Philpot's Works, (Park. Soc. ed.) ii. 250.

Phineas kills Jambri and Cozbe, i. 516.

Physicians have too much, i. 98; are to be honoured for need's sake, 540; seek their own profit, not to be too much trusted in, 541; example in king Asa, 541.

Pilate, Mistress, took a nap in the morning, ii. 123.

Pilgrimage, the Christian's, i. 474.

"Pilgrimage of Grace," i. 25, ii. 390.

Pilgrimages done away with by Church of England, i. 54; are not to be required, ii. 233; are lawful, 359; when and how they ought to be done, 360; juggling to get money from, 364; going a pilgrimage cannot procure justification, *ib.*

Plato, i. 105, ii. 317.

Platonist, Ammonius Saccas, i. 202.

Ploughman, and prince equal in Christ, i. 249, 343; what food, &c. he requires, 249.

Pluralities, how originated, i. 49; an enormity, 122; pope's power of dispensation of, ii. 332.

Pocularies, i. 49.

Pole, cardinal, i. 58, 173; legate from the pope, ii. 279; his argument against kings answered, i. 174; his book, 198; his commission to bishop of Lincoln and others, ii. 279; *Pro Ecclesias. Unitatis Defensione*, i. 173, 174.

Polsted, Mr, a commissioner to visit religious houses, ii. 368.

Poor, our duty to them, i. 406; no man is poorer for giving to the poor, 408, 414; are more frequently oppressed than relieved, 409; to be poor is no blessing in our eyes, 476; are most diligent in hearing the gospel, 477, ii. 72; what sort of poverty is blessed, 127, 478; poverty joined with simplicity is laudable, ii. 109; wilful poverty is hypocritical, 127; have equal privileges in Christ as the rich, 201; poor man does God service by living uprightly in his vocation, 215.

Pope Alex. Breviar. Roman. i. 75.

Pope, is the devil's chaplain, i. 74; his supremacy, ii. 332, 348; visible only to papists, i. 206; determines the Lord's supper, claims pre-eminence through Peter, i. 209, ii. 280; popery now extirpated, i. 418.

Popish priests and massmongers mislead the people, i. 314; their perjuries in Henry, Edward, and Mary's reigns, 315; a priest turns midwife, 336; keep alehouses, 383; draw riches to themselves, and their believers to the devil, 74.

Pope's pardon to those in purgatory, ii. 239, 362; legate from, 279; attempted to drive Henry VIII. out of his kingdom, 306; popish pardons the cause of sin, 306; popes, bishops, or others, who come not in by the door, are thieves and robbers, 311.

Poverty. See *Poor*.

Powell, Dr, prebendary of Salisbury, preaches against Latimer, and imputes various articles to him, ii. 225, 230, 358; on the Ave Maria, 232; upholds pilgrimages in his sermons at Bristol, 366.

Prayer, our Lord's. See *Lord's Prayer*.

Prayers, departed saints may be remembered in, i. 40, 217, 284; may be interrupted by wickedness, to be resorted to in trouble, i. 165, ii. 163, 177; not to be made to saints, i. 225, 337, ii. 172; to be made to God alone, i. 88, 166, 225, ii. 172; are acceptable only through Christ, i. 167, 330, ii. 164; are a sacrifice free to all, i. 168; Christ prayed, 218; the order of prayer used by Moses as an instrument in adversity, 143; the example of Joshua and Josaphat, 144; prayer with tears is of great efficacy, acceptable only through faith, i. 172, 354, 389, 419, ii. 176; will be heard, i. 383, 387, ii. 104, 172, 173, 176; if not heard, must be repeated, i. 144, 229, 337, 346, 547, ii. 164; to be made for grace, i. 284; our order of prayer, 302; those who do not pray deny God, 311; three parts of, 312; three things move us to pray, ii. 177; sermon on, i. 326; the Lord's Prayer the sum and abridgement of all other prayers, 327; of the faithful are not hindered by sin, 330; Stephen's prayer the cause of Paul's conversion, 338; the peculiar property of, 338, 355; must be made with understanding and with fervour, 344, 507; to be made to God to assist us to overcome temptation, 433; a good prayer, i. 442, ii. 172, 174; faithful men have all made short prayers, i. 352; the meaning of "deliver us from evil," 443; through prayer we receive the Holy Ghost, 444; to be made at all times, 445, 509; is the Christian's special weapon against the devil, 506; our only refuge, 508; is the *ars artium*, ii. 180; the Paternoster is made to God, Ave Maria no prayer, 229.

Preachers, who are to be in Christ's Church, i. 59; have a busy work, 61; admonition to, 65, 286; may correct the king, 86; and admonish judges, ii. 325; let them never fear, i. 87; preaching evil doctrines is to be eschewed, 87; must have respect unto their audience, i. 87, 173, 241, ii. 210; the reward of true preachers, ii. 302; the preacher hath two offices, to teach and to confute, i. 129; ought to be a mouth-stopper, 121; if negligent, his office is not honourable; the drift of negligent preachers, 153; what negligent preachers are worthy of, 154; preachers are God's instruments, 155; Christ's vicars, 349; Christ is the preacher of all preachers, 155; ought to be called of God, ii. 38; hearing of vice, ought to speak, i. 195, ii. 40; good preachers slandered in England, i. 240; must strike at covetousness, the root of all evil, 247; number of, diminished, 269; their livings ought not to be given to secular men, 269; can do no more but call sinners to repentance, 285; the properties of true preachers, i. 290, 292, ii. 210; how to stop their mouths, i. 374; the hunger they ought to have, 382; must rebuke all estates, 468, 506, 509; are to be followed only so far as they follow Christ, 514, 523; their punishment if unfaithful, 524, 529; false preachers are enemies of the cross, 529; shall not rule, but be ruled by the word of God, ii. 117; the angels of God were the first preachers, 118; have no other sword but the sword of the Spirit, 196; only the active and earnest preachers of the word are persecuted, 325, 345, 352; ought to be sure of the truth of their preaching, 336; and have knowledge thereof, 338; some preachers forget hell in providing for purgatory, 339; office of a preacher, 420.

Preaching-place at Westminster, i. 79, 239; noise in during sermon, 204.

Preaching of the gospel is the power of God, i. 202; through preaching we are regenerate, 202; the lack of preaching is the cause of ignorance and rebellion, 273; likened to a fisher's net, 285; is the only appointed mean to salvation, 291, 349, 358, 418; the office of, decayeth, 291, 306; the office of, not to be despised, 470; must be maintained, 504; is no rebellion, 249; the preaching of Christ himself brought forth little fruit, ii. 209; preaching better than massing, 255.

Predestination, false opinion on, ii. 175, 204.

Prelates, who are right, i. 51; likened to a ploughman, 61; admonition to, 65; why prelates have been so idle, 65; how unpreaching prelates are occupied, 67, ii. 24; their place of punishment, 158; should not be lords president, 68, 176; nor clerks of kitchens, ii. 120; what they should be, 24; have been long suffered, i. 193; unpreaching ones are made by the devil, 202; an unpreaching one finds fault with a bell without a clapper, 207; are to be blamed for the king's belief in the blood of Hales, 232; are the cause of commotions and rebellions, 275; Christ an example to, 475; have not Paul's zeal, 520; their crafty pretences to stop the reading of the scriptures, ii. 303; stop the gospel on pretence of insurrections, 304; issue their own proclamations under the king's name and authority, 305.

President, two lords appointed, i. 175.

Presumption blameable, i. 551, ii. 182, 232, 254.

Pride and its effects are abominable, ii. 109; ruined the devil, 170.

Priests, chantry, to teach children to read English, ii. 244; make their offerings for gain, 254.

Primogeniture, the law of, i. 271.

Prior of St James' preaches against Latimer, ii. 225.

Proctor, M. of the "Blak Frears," i. iv.

Professors are many, true ministers few, i. 31.

Promises, all are not to be kept, i. 116; the promises pertain only to the faithful, 340; cannot be stolen from us, ii. 155.

Promoters (informers) are much wanted, i. 279.

Promotion, the highest in this life is to suffer for the truth, i. 294.

Provincials, what they are, i. 296.

Proverb, God's, i. 259; a true proverb, 277; an old one, 280, 502, 506; a naughty one, 431; common ones, i. 113, 357, 363, 410, 437, 482, ii. 150.

Psalter, or rosary, our lady's, what it was, i. 425.

Pulpits, advisable, but not necessary, i. 207; a pulpit without a clapper, ib.

Pulton, Antiq. of Eng. Franciscans, i. 287, ii. 319, 391.

Punishments of the worldly, i. 57; different degrees of in hell, 11, 224, 324; delayed, maketh it greater, ii. 50.

Purgatory, a pickpurse, i. 36, 50; papists' doctrine of, i. 37, ii. 332; more profitable than taxes, i. 50; no middle state, i. 305, ii. 56, 58, 191, 246, 249; a falsehood, i. 426, 550; state of souls in, ii. 237; preferable to prison, 237, 361; or to earth, 362; needy brethren in this world to be provided for in preference to purgatory, 238; abuses of, 238; Augustine, Jerome, Hilary, Cyprian, and Chrysostom, quoted against it, 248; preparation for it hath caused many great sins on earth, 363; cannot be taken away without great loss to those who feed by it, ib.

Purification, superstitious observance of, i. 336, 343.

Pusillanimes, ii. 339.

Pye, Mr John, gets the lands of Droitwich, ii. 397.

Q.

Quarter-service proscribed by Latimer in diocese of Worcester, ii. 243.

Queen (Mary), who are her enemies, ii. 260.

R.

Rainbow, what it teacheth, i. 270.

Rebellion caused by ignorance, i. 371; is the devil's service, 496; will receive punishment, 538; caused by covetousness, 247.

Rebels in Devonshire and Norfolk considered not the petition, "Thy will be done," i. 371.

Reconciliation must precede petition for forgiveness of sin, i. 423.

Rectories, pensions granted out of, i. 203.

Rede, Elizabeth, abbess of Malling, ii. 409.

Redemption is by faith, which cometh by hearing, i. 418; is nearer than it was, ii. 55, 433; is by the blood of Christ, not of martyrs, 234.

Redman, Dr, letter to, from Latimer, ii. 297.

Redstone Ferry Hermitage, able to lodge 500 men, ii. 401.

Reflections on the Devotions of the Roman Church, ii. 132, 200.

Reformation in Denmark settled, i. 274.

Regeneration cometh by hearing and believing, i. 471.

Relics of saints, in visiting them we may visit pig's bones, i. 52; blood of Hales, 231; garments, 544; St Algar's bones, St Blaise's heart, &c. 55.

Religion, true, in what it consists, i. 392, ii. 354; not to be condemned for the faults of some of its professors, ii. 306.

Religious houses, true, what they are, i. 392.

Remission of sin indispensable to salvation, i. 417; is in Christ alone, i. 419, ii. 139.

Repentance, this is the place for, i. 195; this life the time for, 162, 246, 549; follows preaching, i. 240, ii. 196; with faith obtains remission of sin, i. 405, ii. 207; useless without restitution, i. 405; this a certain doctrine asserted by all, 414; sick-bed repentance, what it is, i. 443, ii. 58; and penance a salve for all sin, ii. 9; what constitutes repentance, 10, 50.

Restitution must be made, i. 414, ii. 41, 63, 238; secretly and openly, i. 262, 452; examples of secret restitution, 262; of open restitution, 263; the penalty of non-restitution, i. 404, 405, ii. 13.

Resurrection of the body, i. 531, ii. 192; of the good, of the wicked, i. 548, ii. 192; the manner of, ii. 53, 444.

Revenge, must be left to God, i. 465; may be lawful or unlawful, 481; private or public, 495.

Rhodes in possession of Turks, i. 13, ii. 33.

Rich murderer escapes punishment by bribery, i. 189; riches make no man's life happy, but rather troublous, 277, 280, 303, 442; are a drawback from heaven, ii. 214; worldly and godly riches, i. 280; riches ill-bestowed on images, &c. 292; are God's gift, 398, 430; the rich man is God's treasurer, 411, 477; riches neither to be condemned nor worshipped, i. 430, 470, ii. 20; a blessing in our eyes, i. 476; are dangerous, 477, 214; not riches, but the abuse of them, evil spoken of in scripture, i. 545, ii. 202; rich men contemn the gospel, ii. 72, 91; riches are not to be greedily sought, 214, 300; are uncertain, 214.

Richard III., cause of his usurpation, i. 271.

Ridley, bishop of London, i. xiii.; sent to the Tower, ii. 258.

Ridley's Works, (Park. Soc. ed.) i. 49, 250, 278, 285, 289, 446, ii. 268.

Righteousness, the armour of, what it is and how used, i. 491; ours consists in our unrighteousness being forgiven, ii. 140, 193, 194.

Robertson, Charles V., i. 305.

Robin Hood, i. 107; on his day he is preferred to God's minister, 208.

Rochester, bishop of. See *Hilsey*.

Roper, Life of Sir T. More, ii. 333.

Roses, the wars of the, what the cause of them was, i. 271.

Rudder, Hist. of Gloucester, ii. 393, 415, 417, 418.

Rugg, or Reppes, bishop of Norwich, i. 123.

Russell, sir John, sheriff of Worcester, ii. 393; makes suit for Friary lands, 395.

Rymer, ii. 363, 370, 386, 394.

S.

Sabbath-breakers will be punished, i. 472.

Sabellicus, Anton. i. 129.

Saccas, Ammonius, a Platonist, his system, i. 102.

Sacrament. See *Baptism, Lord's Supper*.

Sacrifice, used by patriarchs in faith, i. 236; papistical doctrine of a daily expiatory one, 73; Christ once offered is sufficient for the whole world, 522; sacrifice-cattle and first-born of beasts due to God, 303; a propitiatory sacrifice denied, ii. 275, 292.

Sadler, sir R., i. 164.

Sadolet, cardinal, i. 58.

Saints to be honoured, ii. 232, 234; not to be prayed to, i. 225, 337, ii. 88, 99, 172, 186, 231, 333; see not down from heaven, i. 332; communion of, 338; before Christ, used the prayer "Thy will be done," 377; they were justified by faith, ii. 171; who are saints, i. 507; the right worship of saints, ii. 99, 163, 234, 359; have been sinners, 163; we make them equals to God if we pray to them, 172, 186; images of saints, the proper use of, 233, 359; are not redeeming mediators, 234; need no spur to induce them to pray for us, 234; prayer to be made rather to him which can make us saints, than to saints, 235; praying to God as he commands is not dishonouring saints, 235.

St Martin-le-grand in London, a sanctuary, i. 196.

Salcot, bishop of Salisbury, i. 123.

Salisbury, bishop of. See *Shaxton*.

———— Missal, i. 138.

Salvation is not refused to any one, ii. 208; is the free gift of God, 74; none without preaching, i. 200; none without a special faith, ii. 10; none without restitution, i. 452, ii. 13; the free gift of Christ, i. 402; is our helmet, 505; is not to him that beginneth, but to him that continueth, 361; is not to be doubted of, ii. 174; none without the church, 281; things necessary for salvation are clear, 339.

Sampson, Dr, bishop of Chichester, has the wardship of Latimer, i. xi.; himself in ward, 164; his account of sir R. Wingfield's death, ii. 295.

Samuel, and Eli compared, his sons bribers and perverters of judgment, i. 188; would not be partaker of his sons' offences, 189; purgeth himself of bribery, 192.

Sandys, archbp., (Park. Soc. ed.) i. 530.

Saxo, Ludolph, *de vita Christi*, ii. 109.

Sayer, Gregory, *Clavis Regia*, ii. 63.

Scala Cœli, i. 97, 178, ii. 239, 362; the true one, i. 123, 200, 419, 470; *scala inferni*, 178, 179.

Scalary loosings, i. 51.
Scarcity and enhanced prices, i. 99.
Scheltco, translated by Rogers, 'Of the end of this world,' ii. 51.
Scholars, supplication for, i. 179; have not exhibition, 291; must be maintained, 307, 358, 418, 504.
Schools not maintained, i. 291, 349, 478.
Scripture, wrested by the papists, i. 60, ii. 283, 320; the peculiar phrase of is to be noted, i. 235, 236, 282, ii. 105; can people be governed without scripture? i.121; is great and eternal, 85; all kings, &c. are bound to obey it, 85, 86; the order of names in, proves no preference of the persons, ii. 91; things temporal set forth in scripture to be applied spiritually, 171; divers expositions of allowable, ii. 198; licence granted to read the scriptures in English, 240; prelates try to prevent the reading of them, 305; meekly offered to all, 306; condemned as new learning, 318, 320; the scriptures only to be received, 320.
Scurfield, John, of Bristol, examined by Latimer, ii. 404.
Seaton, Dr, argues with Latimer on transubstantiation, ii. 269.
Sermon, a short but pithy one, i. 239; Jonas' sermon compared with those of present day, 240.
Serpent, brasen, a figure of Christ, i. 73.
Servants, if faithful, do their masters' commands with a good mind, i. 19, 350; a slothful one asks "when?" "which way?" 20; advice to, i. 350, ii. 6, 87, 90; in serving with a good mind they serve Christ; God to be obeyed rather than man, i. 351; must be overseen, 394, 395; evil ones shall be condemned, 394; not always to be trusted, 395; Eleazar and Jacob examples to, i. 396, ii. 119; their duty, i. 538, ii. 85, 87, 90; chief point of their office, ii. 37; follow evil examples more readily than good ones, 79.
Seymour, Lord, lord high admiral, character and death of, i. 161; cause of his execution, 271; his pen, 162; a wanton blames him, 164; believed not in the immortality of the soul, 165; was covetous and a contemner of prayer, 228.
Shaw, Dr, preaches on the bastardy of the sons of Edward IV., i. 183.
Shaxton, Nicholas, bishop of Sarum, reformer and papist, ii. 369.
Shepherds of Bethlehem, their faith, charity, an example to us, ii. 87; their faith proved, 91.
Sherrington, sir William, makes open restitution of conscience-money, i. 263.
Sherwood, Dr, letter to, from Latimer in reply to one intended to refute Latimer's assertions, ii. 309.
Shilling, a pretty little one, i. 95.
Shooting commendable for exercise, i. 196; is a gift of God, method of teaching, 197.
Shrouds, the, at St Paul's, i. 59.
Sick, to be visited, i. 479; may use physic, but not trust in it, example, 542.
Silence in a woman is a great virtue, ii. 92.
Singer, Researches into Hist. of Playing Cards, i. 8.
Sins, provoke God's wrath, i. 91; all have sinned, the remedy of, 216; one sin waits on another, 245; our own two burdens of, are sufficient without other people's, 191; what sin is, ii. 5; two sorts of, deadly and venial, 7; what they are, 8; will not escape unpunished, 171; is wilful, else it cannot be called sin, i. 195; is punished by God's not hearing our prayers, 230; is horrible, 232, 461; nothing can remedy it but Christ's blood, i. 232, 343, ii. 145; must be rebuked, i. 241; secret sin shall be revealed, 259; what sin against the Holy Ghost is, 266, 425, 462; some sins called irremissible; no sin is too great to be forgiven, 267, 425, 462; sin is the heaviest burden that can be, 298; punishments for sins, i. 300, ii. 171; sins (if we believe) cannot hinder our prayers, i. 330, 342; forgiveness of to be prayed for, 415; our goodness consists in God's forgiveness of our

INDEX.   523

sins, i. 415, ii. 140; forgiven through Christ's blood, ii. 139; how they may be hidden, i. 417; a minister may absolve in such way as he is commanded, 423; sin forgiven both in pain and guilt, 426; return to obliterates former forgiveness, 429; a general proclamation of forgiveness of, unto all believers, 461; remained in the best saints, 537; is heinous in God's sight, ii. 104.

Sinners, what sinners Christ suffered for, i. 331; accustomed sinners are not much tempted, 441.

Sir John, a term of contempt applied to the more illiterate clergy, i. 317.

Slander, all telling of faults is not slandering; what slander is, i. 518; example of, 519.

Sleep, spiritual, ii. 2, 13; natural sleep must not be exceeded in, 5.

Sleidan's Hist. of Reformation, translated by Bohun, i. 147, 305, 425.

Smith, sir Thomas, the plurality of his offices an enormity, i. 122.

Smith, master, disputes with Latimer at Oxford, ii. 250, 264.

—— in prison for the truth, ii. 321.

Socrates, i. 105.

Solomon proclaimed king, i. 114; his prayer a precedent for kings', 125; his wise judgment, 126; prayed for wisdom, heard the complaints and causes of his people, 132.

Some, Thomas, his dedication of "The seven sermons" to duchess of Suffolk, i. 81.

Sons are not always to walk in their father's ways, i. 176.

Sorcerers and witches are consulted, i. 345, 534; dishonour the name of God, 349.

Soul must be fed as well as body, i. 66, 412; where was the soul of Jairus' daughter after her death? i. 550.

Spira, Francis, his sin and death, i. 425.

Spirit, may be lost after having received it, i. 229; how to use the sword of, 439; teacheth the word, ii. 319, 320.

Spiritual livings swallowed up by laymen, i. 317.

Stafford, Mr George, lady Margaret's preacher, i. 440.

Stamford, sermon preached at, i. 282; recapitulated, 511.

Standish, Dr, i. 46.

State Papers, i. xi. xiii., 164, 276, ii. 367, 368, 370, 375, 377, 379, 382, 383, 385, 387—389, 390, 393, 396, 397, 399, 401, 402, 404—406, 409, 412, 413, 415—417.

Statham, Mistress, Latimer's nurse, ii. 386, 397.

Stations, stationaries, i. 49.

Statutes touching commons and inclosers, i. 101; of mortmain, the effect of, 522.

Staveley, *Romish Horseleech*, i. 50.

Stevens' Hist. of Ancient Abbeys, ii. 380, 386, 389, 415, 418.

Stewards, faithful, are not counterfeiters of coin, i. 36.

Stews, suppressed, i. 133.

Stokesley, bishop of London, inhibits Latimer, i. viii.; sends letters to Dr Hilley for him, ii. 322; changes his opinion respecting the law of matrimony, 333; sir Thomas More referred to him on that subject by Henry VIII., *ib.*; would have burned St Paul, 326; cites Latimer to appear before him, 350.

Stowe, Survey of London, i. 59, 223, ii. 341.

Strange things seen in the element, ii. 51.

Strawberry preachers, i. 62.

Strype, Eccles. Mem. i. ii. iv. viii. ix. xi. 23, 90, 99, 102, 118, 122, 132, 141, 142, 178, 179, 201, 223, 262, 272, ii. 98, 114, 221, 229, 240, 245, 246, 250, 297, 324, 365, 368, 369, 373, 376, 377, 378, 379, 384, 387, 410, 413, 429, 435.

Study and prayer must go together, i. 125.

Subjects may not resist any magistrate, i. 163.

Suffolk, &c., duchess of, i. 81; dedications to her, by T. Some, *ib.*; by Augustine Bernher, i. 311; commendation of, 324; Latimer's sermons before her, 326; delivered at Grimsthorpe, 416.

Suffragans chosen by Samuel; authorised by Henry VIII., i. 175.

Suicide, cursed in the sight of God, i. 435.

Superstitions, ii. 60; in monasteries, 240; holy bread, i. 498, ii. 286, 294; holy garments, i. 544; holy water, i. 75, 132, 342, 498, ii. 294; hallowed beads, i. 75; holy bells, 498; blood of Hales, i. xi. 231, ii. 364, 407; blood-letting on St Stephen's day, ii. 100; repetition of Ave Maria, 231.
Supper, Lord's. See *Lord's Supper.*
Swearing and lying go together, ii. 64.
Swords, the temporal and the spiritual, i. 85.
Swynbourne, or Swynburn, Rowland, master of Clare hall, Cambridge, account of him, ii. 378.

T.

Talbot, sir Gilbert, sheriff of Worcestershire, ii. 414.
Tale, a merry and wise one, i. 89, ii. 109.
Tanner, Bp. Bibliothec. i. xiv., ii. 319, 379; Notitia, 394, 397, 403.
Taxes ought to be paid, i. 299, 512; if to a heathen, much more to a christian king, 306; payment of, impoverishes no man, 301, 408, 513.
Teachers, who are to be, in Christ's Church, i. 59.
Temptation, never ceases, i. 226; is a good and necessary thing, 433; temptations are declarations of God's favour, 434; sent for our profit, 435; shall be rather a furtherance than a hinderance to eternal life, 437; two manners of temptation, 437; are appointed by God, 466.
Tenants are so hardly dealt with, that they cry daily to God for vengeance, i. 317.
Tenterden steeple, said to be the cause of Goodwin sands, i. 251.
Terence, i. 124, 287.
Tertullian adv. Marcion. ii. 98.
Testament, every man ought to make one, i. 540.
Tewksbury punished for selling scriptures, ii. 306.
Theatrum Crudel. Hæret. i. 250.
Theodore, Penitentiale, i. 54.
Theodoret, Hist. Eccles. ii. 49.
Theophylact calls Mary not faultless, ii. 226, 359.

Thieving, two sorts of, i. 139; realm full of, 512; thieves ought to expose their confederates, 519; what it is, ii. 427.
Thorp, Mr, ii. 295.
Throgmorton, Anthony and Michael, servants of cardinal Pole, sons of sir Robert Throgmorton, ii. 388.
Tigurines, the, write a book against Luther, ii. 265; Latimer agrees not with the Tigurines, or Germans, 278.
Tithes are due to God, i. 303; for what purpose appointed, *ib.*; payment of, may not be withheld, 304.
Titus, i. 147; sent of God to punish the Jews, 285.
Tonstal, bishop of London and Durham, consents to king's licence to university preachers, ii. 329; writes an account of sir Richard Wingfield's death, 295.
Tot quots, i. 49.
Tracy, Henry, of Todington, ii. 415.
Tracy, Richard, a commissioner appointed to examine the blood of Hales, ii. 407.
Tracy, William, his body burned, i. 46.
Traditions followed by the Jews, ii. 51.
Transubstantiation denied, i. 275, ii. 286; the Capernaites believed in, i. 459; papists assert it, ii. 251; converted, 253; is one of the marrowbones of the mass, 257; against scripture, 258; disputation on, 264.
Traitor hanged at Oxford, revived, i. 149.
Tresham, Dr, disputes with Latimer on Transubstantiation, ii. 266.
Trespasses, forgive us our, i. 415.
Tricennials or trentals, i. 56; stopped by Latimer, ii. 243.
Trinity, doctrine of the, i. 456.
Truth preferable to peace, i. 487, ii. 347; must not be left unspoken because some take offence, ii. 75; to be spoken always, 90.
Turner, *Triacle against the poison of Pelagius,* i. iii.
Tyndale, Works, i. 68, 175; his translation of the Bible condemned by the papists, ii. 320.
Tytler, England under Edward and Mary, i. 161.

U.

Universal History, i. 13, 274.
Universities decay, i. 102 ; and schools diminished in number of students, 269; masters of colleges in them to be visited and reformed, ii. 393.
University Register, i. iii., ii. 195.
Usurers in England take 40 per cent, i. 279 ; have their gains of the devil, ii. 42.
Usury allowed by law in England, acts repealed, i. 410; of one sort, may be committed, 411.

V.

Valor Eccles., ii. 383, 394, 409.
Vaughan, David, canon of St Mary's, Warwick, ii. 396.
Vergil, Polydore, i. 49.
Vespasian, i. 147; sent by God to punish the Jews, 285.
Victory, is always God's, i. 285.
Visiting prisons is a commendable thing, i. 180.
Visitors, can best tell who feed their flocks, i. 62 ; should be sent after bishops, 122.
Vocation, man must labour in his, i. 359, 402, 412, 442, 508, 530, 537, ii. 94, 111, 154, 159, 214, 330, 430.
Voluntary sufferings are not the cross of Christ, i. 465.
Voragine, Jacobus de, *Sermones Aurei de Sanct.* ii. 132.
Vyllers, Philippe de, chosen grand master of Rhodes, ii. 33.

W.

Wadding, *Annales Minorum*, i. 50.
Wakeman, bishop of Gloucester, i. 123.
Walsingham, our lady of, i. 53.
Waltham abbey, bakehouse or pardon bowl, i. 75.
War, in the king's service allowable, i. 416.
Warburton's Julian, ii. 49.
Warham, Dr, archbishop of Canterbury, admits the right of the universities to license preachers, ii. 329 ; letter to him from Latimer, 351.
Wards, stealing of, i. 170.

Warwick college recommended to the patronage of Cromwell, ii. 396.
Watkins, i. 62.
Wattwood reprimanded by Latimer, ii. 396 ; cares neither for statutes nor injunctions, 397, 401, 406.
Weeping and sorrow commanded, but not as they that have no hope, i. 547.
Weford, prior of Coventry, dies, ii. 386.
Weston, Dr, his preface to the disputation with Latimer at Oxford, ii. 250; Latimer's address to, 257, 269 ; rails against the reformers, 277.
Whalley, Stephen, the last abbot of Hales, ii. 380.
Whitborne, Richard, prior of Great Malvern, ii. 410.
Wicelius, *Via Regia*, i. 58.
Wicked cursed by God, yet enjoy blessings in this world, why ? i. 363, 466 ; shall be punished temporally and eternally, i. 531, ii. 55; must be rooted out by the civil power with the temporal sword, by the ecclesiastical power with the sword of the Spirit, ii. 196 ; we may not desert the place where they dwell, 196 ; their wickedness must be rebuked, not consented to, 197 ; hate the word of God, 211 ; advice turns to the destruction of the givers and followers of it, 304.
Widows, the poor, may do the wicked judge much hurt, i. 157 ; a rich widow condemned and converted, 180 ; bribes the judge, 181; gave up housekeeping and went to religious houses to live, 392.
Wife, the, a king may choose, i. 94.
Wilkins' Concilia, i. v. vii. viii. 33, 45, 54, 56, 60, 132, ii. 240, 304, 356.
Willis, Browne, Hist. of Abbeys, ii. 371, 383, 410, 413.
Wilson, Dr Nicholas, mislikes Latimer, ii. 365.
Windsor, lord, gets the lands of Bordesley, ii. 594.
Wingfield, sir Richard, high steward of the university of Cambridge, account of him, ii. 295.
─────── sir Anthony, captain of the king's guard, alluded to, ii. 415.
Witches and sorcerers are consulted, i. 345, 534.

Witchcraft should be removed, i. 349.
Wolf, *Lectiones Memorab.* i. 50, ii. 51, 149.
Wolsey discharges Latimer, i. iv.; causes great perjury, 301.
Woman and man were equal till she believed the serpent, i. 252, ii. 161; women who will rule their husbands, break God's injunction in so doing, i. 252; are underlings, why their heads are covered, are not immediately under God, their dress, i. 253, ii. 108; their tussocks, tufts, and curls, &c. condemned, i. 254, ii. 108; some are unnatural, i. 334; a woman's duty to her husband, 352; may soon bring man into evil, 95; Paul's advice to them to be followed, ii. 108.
Wood, *Athenæ Oxon.* ii. 225, 229, 297, 369, 371, 392; *Fasti*, ii. 250, 372, 376, 378, 386, 387, 400, 406, 418.
Worcester, injunctions to the prior and convent of, i. x.; act to rebuild Worcester, ii. 403; guild of Holy Trinity at, bridge of, 403.
Word of the Lord endureth for ever, 281; is the instrument of all good, 354; its despisers, 385; it availeth not without faith, 544; is of great power, ii. 167; our duty is to search for the meaning of it, 189; refusers of the word shall be condemned, 206; it bringeth forth much fruit on a good ground, 210; woe to those who refuse it, 211; the hearer is better than the refuser, 213; the true hearer keeps it and yields much fruit, 215; it is a light to direct, 299; is to some foolishness, to others wisdom, 335.
Wordsworth's Eccles. Biog. i. ii. viii. 317, 440, ii. 272, 277, 283, 304, 306, 322, 333, 351, 406, 417.
Works, what voluntary, necessary, and works of mercy are; voluntary are useless without those of necessity and mercy, i. 23, ii. 243, 353; will-works not so necessary as those of mercy or the precepts of God, i. 37, 353; are no derogation from faith, 235; are of themselves useless, 368; merit nothing, i. 419, 488, ii. 74, 148, 193, 200; they condemn us, ii. 137, 151; works and prayer must go together, i. 403; will be rewarded in, but cannot purchase heaven, i. 420, 427, 488, ii. 140; our works are accepted by God through Christ as perfect, i. 420, 453, ii. 57, 140, 148; hypocrites say they have works of supererogation, i. 482, 521, ii. 200; papists' opinion of satisfactory works, i. 520; we must do good works, but not trust in them, i. 521, ii. 141, 148, 194, 200; must lose no opportunity to do good works, i. 545; why and how they are to be done, ii. 141, 151, 200; we are justified by the free gift of God through Christ, not through our works, 194; some works which when done are not condemned, God would neither command nor counsel, 354; not acceptable without love, 1; the works of Christ are his witnesses, 73; faith, not works, justifieth, 147, 151, 201; must be done without respect to reward, 203.
Worldly-minded, are enemies of the cross, i. 529; care not for religion, ii. 131, 214; cannot agree with Christians, 184; worldly men have foolish minds, 215; worldly wisdom is foolishness in the sight of God, 308, 338.
World, the, approaches its end, i. 172, 364, ii. 20, 53; signs thereof, i. 365; may be divided into faithful and unfaithful, 531; is ruled by two swords, 85; is crafty and deceitful, 176.
Worshipping of images, i. 36.
Writings of learned Christians, our prelates have defaced; those of learned heathen were preserved, i. 105.
Wych, the prior of, ii. 378.

Y.

Yeomen's sons have chiefly maintained the faith of Christ, i. 102.
York, archbishop of. See *Dr Edward Lee.*

Z.

Zaccheus, an example to bribers, i. 405—414.
Zigabenus, Euthymius, calls the virgin Mary not faultless, ii. 226; and Theophylact on John, *ib.*
Zoroaster, i. 201.

www.ingramcontent.com/pod-product-compliance
Lightning Source LLC
Chambersburg PA
CBHW071133300426
44113CB00009B/958